2016 SBBI Yearbook

Stocks, Bonds, Bills, and Inflation

U.S. Capital Markets Performance by Asset Class 1926–2015

Duff & Phelps

WILEY

About the Data

The information and data presented in the *2016 Stocks, Bonds, Bills, and Inflation*® *(SBBI*®*)* *Yearbook ("2016 SBBI Yearbook")* has been obtained with the greatest of care from sources believed to be reliable, but is not guaranteed to be complete, accurate, or timely. Duff & Phelps, LLC (www.duffandphelps.com) and/or its data providers expressly disclaim any liability, including incidental or consequential damages, arising from the use of the *2016 SBBI Yearbook* or any errors or omissions that may be contained in the *2016 SBBI Yearbook,* or any other product (existing or to be developed) based upon the methodology and/or data published herein. One of the primary sources of raw data used to produce the derived data and information herein is Morningstar, Inc. Use of raw data from Morningstar, Inc. to produce the information herein does not necessarily constitute agreement by Morningstar, Inc. of any investment philosophy or strategy presented in this publication. "Stocks, Bonds, Bills, and Inflation" and "SBBI" are registered trademarks of Morningstar, Inc. All rights reserved. Used with permission.

About Duff & Phelps

Duff & Phelps is the premier global valuation and corporate finance advisor with expertise in complex valuation, dispute and legal management consulting, M&A, restructuring, and compliance and regulatory consulting. The firm's more than 2,000 employees serve a diverse range of clients from offices around the world. For more information, visit www.duffandphelps.com.

M&A advisory, capital raising, and secondary market advisory services in the United States are provided by Duff & Phelps Securities, LLC. Member FINRA/SIPC. Pagemill Partners is a Division of Duff & Phelps Securities, LLC. M&A advisory and capital raising advisory services are provided in a number of European countries through Duff & Phelps Securities Ltd, UK, which includes branches in Ireland and Germany. Duff & Phelps Securities Ltd, UK, is regulated by the Financial Conduct Authority.

Additional Resources

To learn more about the latest theory and practice in cost of capital estimation, see *Cost of Capital: Applications and Examples* 5th edition, by Shannon P. Pratt and Roger J. Grabowski (John Wiley & Sons, Inc., 2014).

The *Cost of Capital: Applications and Examples* 5th edition is a one-stop shop for background and current thinking on the development and uses of rates of return on capital. This book contains expanded materials on estimating the basic building blocks of the cost of equity capital, the risk-free rate, and equity risk premium, plus in-depth discussion of the volatility created by the 2008 financial crisis, the subsequent recession and uncertain recovery, and how those events have fundamentally changed how we need to interpret the inputs to the models we use to develop these estimates.

The *Cost of Capital: Applications and Examples* 5th edition includes case studies providing comprehensive discussion of cost of capital estimates for valuing a business and damages calculations for small and medium-sized businesses, cross-referenced to the chapters covering the theory and data. This book puts an emphasis on practical application. To that end, this updated edition provides readers with exclusive access to a companion website filled with supplementary materials, allowing you to continue to learn in a hands-on fashion long after closing the book.

The *Cost of Capital: Applications and Examples* has been published since 1998, and is updated every three to four years. The 6th edition of this book is scheduled to be available in spring 2017.

> *"Shannon Pratt and Roger Grabowski have produced a remarkably comprehensive review of the subject...it is a work that valuation practitioners, CFOs, and others will find an invaluable reference."*
>
> **— Professor Richard Brealey**, London Business School (from the Foreword)

> *"Estimating the cost of capital is critical in determining the valuation of assets, in evaluating the capital structure of corporations, and in estimating the long-run expected return of investments. Shannon Pratt and Roger Grabowski have the most thorough text on the subject, not only providing various estimation methods, but also numerous ways to use the cost of capital."*
>
> **— Professor Roger G. Ibbotson**, Professor Emeritus of Finance at the Yale School of Management, former chairman and founder of Ibbotson Associates, chairman, founder, and CIO of Zebra Capital

Other Duff & Phelps Valuation Data Resources Published by John Wiley & Sons

In addition to the *2016 Stocks, Bonds, Bills, and Inflation (SBBI) Yearbook* (this book) and the *Cost of Capital: Applications and Examples* 5th edition, other Duff & Phelps valuation data resources published by John Wiley & Sons are as follows:

Valuation Handbook – Guide to Cost of Capital: This annual book includes the data previously published in the Morningstar/Ibbotson® *Stocks, Bonds, Bills, and Inflation*® (*SBBI*®) *Valuation Yearbook* and the Duff & Phelps *Risk Premium Report*. The *Valuation Handbook – Guide to Cost of Capital* can be used to develop cost of equity capital estimates for an individual business, business ownership interest, security, or intangible asset.

The *Valuation Handbook – Guide to Cost of Capital* has been published since 2014 (2014, 2015, and 2016 editions are available with data through December 31, 2013, December 31, 2014, and December 31, 2015, respectively). This book includes three optional quarterly updates (March, June, and September).

Valuation Handbook – Industry Cost of Capital: The *Valuation Handbook – Industry Cost of Capital* provides cost of capital estimates (i.e., equity capital, debt capital, and WACC) for approximately 180 U.S. industries and size groupings (i.e., Large-, Mid-, Low-, and Micro-capitalization companies), plus a host of detailed statistics that can be used for benchmarking purposes (over 300 critical industry-level data points calculated for each industry, depending on data availability).

The *Valuation Handbook – Industry Cost of Capital* has been published since 2014 (2014 and 2015 editions are available with data through March 31, 2014 and March 31, 2015, respectively; the 2016 edition, with data through March 31, 2016, is now available). This book includes three optional quarterly updates (June, September, and December).

International Valuation Handbook – Guide to Cost of Capital: This annual book provides country-level equity risk premia (ERPs), relative volatility (RV) factors, and country risk premia (CRPs) which can be used to estimate country-level cost of equity capital globally, for up to 188 countries, from the perspective of investors based in any one of up to 56 countries (depending on data availability).

The *International Valuation Handbook – Guide to Cost of Capital* has been published since 2014 (2014 and 2015 editions are available with data through (i) December 31, 2013 and March 31, 2014, and (ii) December 31, 2014 and March 31, 2015, respectively; the 2016 edition, with data through December 31, 2015 and March 31, 2016, will be available in August 2016). This book includes an optional Semi-annual Update, with data through June and September.

International Valuation Handbook – Industry Cost of Capital: This annual book provides the same type of rigorous industry-level analysis published in the U.S.-centric *Valuation Handbook – Industry Cost of Capital*, on a global scale.

The inaugural *2015 International Valuation Handbook – Industry Cost of Capital* includes industry-level analyses for four global economic areas: (i) the "World," (ii) the European Union, (iii) the Eurozone, and (iv) the United Kingdom.[i.1] Industries in the book are identified by their Global Industry Classification Standard (GICS) code. Each of the four global economic area's industry analyses are presented in three currencies: (i) the euro (€ or EUR), (ii) the British pound (£ or GBP), and (iii) the U.S. dollar ($ or USD).

The *2015 International Valuation Handbook – Industry Cost of Capital* provides industry-level cost of capital estimates (cost of equity, cost of debt, and weighted average cost of capital, or WACC), plus detailed industry-level statistics for sales, market capitalization, capital structure, various levered and unlevered beta estimates (e.g., ordinary-least squares (OLS) beta, sum beta, peer group beta, downside beta, etc.), valuation (trading) multiples, financial and profitability ratios, equity returns, aggregate forward-looking earnings-per share (EPS) growth rates, and more.

The *2015 International Valuation Handbook – Industry Cost of Capital* is published with data through March 31, 2015, and includes one optional intra-year Semi-annual Update (data through September 30, 2015). The inaugural 2015 version of the *International Valuation Handbook – Industry Cost of Capital* is now available.

The inaugural 2015 version of this book was on a delayed publication schedule because of the extensive work involved in gathering the data, establishing the needed data permissions, developing new procedures and methodologies to appropriately deal with international financial data in multiple currencies, and producing the inaugural 2015 book from scratch. The 2016 version of the hardcover book will be published with data through March 31, 2016, and will ship in late July/early August 2016, followed by the Semi-annual Update (with data through September 30, 2016) in PDF format, delivered in late October/early November 2016.

To learn more about cost of capital issues, and to ensure that you are using the most recent Duff & Phelps Recommended ERP, visit www.duffandphelps.com/CostofCapital.

To order additional copies of the *2016 Stocks, Bonds, Bills, and Inflation (SBBI) Yearbook* (this book), or other Duff & Phelps valuation data resources published by John Wiley & Sons, please visit: www.wiley.com/go/ValuationHandbooks.

[i.1] In the *2015 International Valuation Handbook – Industry Cost of Capital*, "World" companies are defined as companies that (i) are components of the MSCI ACWI IMI, and (ii) satisfy the rigorous screening requirements that are employed to define the company sets used therein.

Table of Contents

Acknowledgements   **xi**

Introduction   **xiii**

Chapter 1: Results of U.S. Capital Markets in 2015 and in the Past Decade   **1-1**
A Graphic View of the Decade   1-2
The Decade in Perspective   1-3
Market Results for 2006—2015   1-6

Chapter 2: The Long-Run Perspective   **2-1**
Stocks, Bonds, Bills, and Inflation: Historical Returns   2-1
Logarithmic Scale Used on the Index Graphs   2-2
Large-Cap Stocks   2-4
Small-Cap Stocks   2-4
Long-term Corporate Bonds   2-4
Long-term Government Bonds   2-4
Intermediate-term Government Bonds   2-4
Treasury Bills   2-4
Inflation   2-5
Summary Statistics of Total Returns   2-5
Appreciation, Income, and Reinvestment Returns   2-7
Annual Total Returns   2-10
Rolling-Period Returns   2-10
Real Estate Investment Trusts (REITs)   2-26
Historical Returns on Equity REITs   2-28
Income Returns on Equity REITs   2-29
Correlation of U.S. REITs Compared to Other U.S. Asset Classes   2-30
Summary Statistics for Equity REITs and Basic Series   2-31

Chapter 3: Description of the Basic Series   **3-1**
Large-Cap Stocks   3-1
Small-Cap Stocks   3-2
Long-term Corporate Bonds   3-4
Long-term Government Bonds   3-4
Intermediate-term Government Bonds   3-9
U.S. Treasury Bills   3-11
Inflation   3-13
Bond Capital Appreciation Despite Rising Yields   3-13

Chapter 4: Description of the Derived Series   **4-1**
Derived Series Calculated Using Geometric Differences   4-1
Definitions of the Derived Series   4-1
Equity Risk Premium   4-2
Small-Stock Premium   4-3
Bond Default Premium   4-3
Bond Horizon Premium   4-4
Large-Cap Stock Real Returns   4-5
Small-Cap Stock Real Returns   4-7

Long-term Corporate Bond Returns   4-8
Long-term Government Bond Real Returns   4-9
Intermediate-term Government Bond Real Returns   4-11
Real Riskless Rates of Return (U.S. T-Bill Real Returns)   4-12

Chapter 5: Annual Returns and Indexes   **5-1**
Annual and Monthly Returns   5-2
Calculation of Returns From Index Values   5-3
Calculation of Annual Income Returns   5-4
Index Values   5-5
Inflation-Adjusted Returns and Indexes   5-7

Chapter 6: Statistical Analysis of Returns   **6-1**
Calculating Arithmetic Mean Return   6-1
Calculating Geometric Mean Return   6-1
Geometric Mean Versus Arithmetic Mean   6-2
Calculating Standard Deviation   6-3
Limitations of Standard Deviation   6-4
Semivariance and Semistandard Deviation   6-5
Issues Regarding Semivariance   6-6
Volatility of the Markets   6-7
Changes in the Risk of Assets Over Time   6-9
Correlation Coefficients: Serial and Cross-Correlations   6-13
Is Serial Correlation in the Derived Series Random?   6-16
Basic Series Summary Statistics   6-17
Inflation-Adjusted Series Summary Statistics   6-18
Rolling-Period Standard Deviations   6-18
Rolling-Period Correlations   6-20
The True Impact of Asset Allocation on Return   6-21

Chapter 7: Company Size and Return   **7-1**
Construction of the CRSP Size Decile Portfolios   7-2
Presentation of the Decile Data   7-5
Aspects of the Company Size Effect   7-12
The Size Effect: Empirical Evidence   7-12
Long-term Returns in Excess of Systematic Risk   7-15
Serial Correlation in Small-Cap Stock Returns   7-17
Seasonality   7-21

Chapter 8: Growth and Value Investing   **8-1**
Fama-French Growth and Value Series   8-1
Historical Returns of the Fama-French Series   8-3
Summary Statistics for the Fama-French Series   8-4
Presentation of Annual Fama-French Returns   8-5
Conclusion   8-5

Chapter 9: Liquidity Investing   **9-1**
What Is Liquidity?   9-1
Valuation as Present Value of Cash Flows   9-1
The Liquidity Premium   9-2
Liquidity and Stock Returns   9-3
Liquidity as an Investment Style   9-4

Conclusion   9-7

What's Next?   9-7

Chapter 10: Using Historical Data in Wealth Forecasting and Portfolio Optimization   **10-1**

Probabilistic Forecasts   10-1

Mean-Variance Optimization   10-4

Estimating Returns, Risks, and Correlations   10-5

Using Inputs to Form Other Portfolios   10-9

Enhancements to Mean-Variance Optimization   10-11

Markowitz 1.0   10-13

Markowitz 2.0   10-14

Approaches to Calculating the Equity Risk Premium   10-19

The Historical Equity Risk Premium   10-20

The Supply-Side Model   10-27

Chapter 11: Stock Market Returns From 1815–2015   **11-1**

1815–1925 Data Series Sources and Collection Methods   11-1

Price Index Estimation   11-3

144 Years of Stock Market Drawdowns   11-9

Reaching Back Beyond 1926   11-13

The Origin of Market Bubbles   11-13

Chapter 12: International Equity Investing   **12-1**

Construction of the International Indexes   12-1

Benefits of Investing Internationally   12-2

Risks Typically Associated With International Investment   12-8

International and Domestic Series Summary Data   12-14

Conclusion   12-16

Appendix A – Monthly and Annual Returns of Basic Series

Appendix B – Cumulative Wealth Indexes of Basic Series

Appendix C – Rates of Return for All Yearly Holding Periods 1926–2015

Acknowledgements

Author

Roger G. Ibbotson

Professor Emeritus of Finance at the Yale School of Management, Former chairman and founder of Ibbotson Associates, Chairman, founder, and CIO of Zebra Capital.

Roger G. Ibbotson and Rex A. Sinquefield, formerly a director of Dimensional Fund Advisors LP, Austin, Texas, (i) wrote the two journal articles and four books upon which the *Stocks Bonds, Bills, and Inflation (SBBI) Yearbook* is based, and (ii) formulated much of the philosophy and methodology.

Duff & Phelps Contributors

Roger J. Grabowski, FASA
Managing Director, Duff & Phelps

James P. Harrington
Director, Duff & Phelps

Carla Nunes, CFA
Managing Director, Duff & Phelps

Thank you

We thank others who contributed to this book. Rolf W. Banz provided the small stock returns for 1926–1981. Thomas S. Coleman (Executive Director, Center for Economic Policy, Harris School of Public Policy at the University of Chicago), the late Professor Lawrence Fisher (Rutgers University, The State University of New Jersey), and Roger Ibbotson constructed the model used to generate the intermediate-term government bond series for 1926–1933. The pioneering work of professors Fisher and James H. Lorie of the University of Chicago inspired the original monograph. We also wish to acknowledge the invaluable role of Dr. Stan V. Smith, President of Smith Economics Group, Ltd. and former managing director of Ibbotson Associates, who originated the idea of the *Stocks, Bonds, Bills, and Inflation (SBBI) Yearbook*.

The Center for Research in Security Prices (CRSP®) at the University Of Chicago Booth School Of Business contributed the data and methodology for the returns on the NYSE/NYSE MKT/NASDAQ by capitalization decile used in Chapter 7, "Company Size and Return."

Ken French (Roth Family Distinguished Professor of Finance at the Tuck School of Business at Dartmouth College) and Eugene Fama (2013 Nobel laureate in economic sciences, and the Robert R. McCormick Distinguished Service Professor of Finance at the University of Chicago), contributed the data and methodology for the returns on the growth and value portfolios. Chapter 9, Liquidity Investing, was written by Roger Ibbotson, and Daniel Y.-J. Kim, Research Director of Zebra Capital Management, and Michael Holmgren, of Integrated Time Series Analytics, helped develop the empirical results. William N. Goetzmann (Edwin J. Beinecke Professor of Finance and Management Studies & Director of the International Center for Finance, Yale School of Management), Roger Ibbotson, and Liang Peng (Associate Professor of Risk Management at Penn State University), assembled the NYSE database for the period prior to 1926, while James Licato converted the research into Chapter 11, "Stock Market Returns from 1815–1925." Licato also created Chapter 12, "International Equity Investing"; and contributed to other chapters. Paul D. Kaplan, Ph.D., CFA (director of research for Morningstar Canada), was the main contributor to Chapter 10, "Using Historical Data in Forecasting and Optimization," and more recently created a set of monthly real stock market total returns going back a full 131 years in Chapter 11. Also, in Chapter 10, Kaplan and Sam Savage (a consulting professor of management science and engineering at Stanford University), present research and methodology that they have aptly dubbed "Markowitz 2.0," which promises to take traditional portfolio optimization into a new age. Kaplan and Thomas Idzorek, CPA, CFA (Head of Investment Methodology and Economic Research, Morningstar, Inc.), all continue to provide valuable insights and analysis for the *SBBI Yearbook*. We also want to thank Laurence B. Siegel (Siegel is the Gary P. Brinson director of research at the CFA Institute Research Foundation, senior advisor to OCP Capital LLC; former director director of research at the Ford Foundation (1994 to 2009) and prior to that at Ibbotson Associates).

We also thank Michael Barad (presently Head of Product Capabilities at Morningstar, Inc., and previously Head of Financial Communications at Ibbotson Associates, and then Morningstar, Inc.), and James P. Harrington (presently a Director at Duff & Phelps, co-author of the Duff & Phelps "Valuation Handbook" series, and previously director of valuation research in Morningstar's Financial Communications Business at Morningstar, Inc.) for their many contributions to the *SBBI Yearbook*.

The authors give special thanks to Analyst Kevin Madden, and Interns Aaron Russo and Andrew Vey of Duff & Phelps for their assistance in assembling the exhibits presented herein, analysis, editing, and quality control. We thank Executive Assistant Michelle Phillips for production assistance, and Director Kelly Hunter (both of Duff & Phelps) for securing data permissions. We also thank Drew Carter, former *SBBI Yearbook* senior editor at Morningstar Investment Management LLC, who helped transfer publishing rights and production of the yearbook to Duff & Phelps, starting with the 2016 edition.

Introduction

Morningstar, Inc. announced in February 2016 that it will no longer publish the *Ibbotson® Stocks, Bonds, Bills, and Inflation®* *(SBBI®) Classic Yearbook*[i.2, i.3] Last year's *2015 Ibbotson Stocks, Bonds, Bills, and Inflation (SBBI) Classic Yearbook* (with data through December 31, 2014) was Morningstar's last *SBBI Classic Yearbook*. Morningstar did not publish a 2016 version (with data through December 31, 2015).

Starting with the 2016 edition, the *Ibbotson Stocks, Bonds, Bills, and Inflation (SBBI) Classic Yearbook* is now produced by Duff & Phelps, and published by John Wiley & Sons (Hoboken, NJ). The book will have a slightly different name: the *Stocks, Bonds, Bills, and Inflation (SBBI) Yearbook* (or simply, *"SBBI Yearbook"*).[i.4] The *2016 SBBI Yearbook* (with data through December 31, 2015) (this book) is the first edition of the former *SBBI "Classic" Yearbook* produced by Duff & Phelps and published by John Wiley & Sons.

The Difference Between the *2016 SBBI Yearbook* (this book) and Other Duff & Phelps Data Resources Published by John Wiley & Sons

The *2016 SBBI Yearbook* (this book) provides historical "performance" data of U.S. asset classes, while the other Duff & Phelps data resources published by John Wiley & Sons provide "valuation" data.

Specifically, the other Duff & Phelps data resources published by John Wiley & Sons focus on U.S. and international valuation data and risk premia (e.g., equity risk premia, risk-free rates, size premia, industry risk premia, betas, industry multiples and other statistics, etc.) for use in valuation models, while the *2016 SBBI Yearbook* (this book) is (i) a history of the returns of the capital markets in the U.S. (thus the name, "Stocks, Bonds, Bills, and Inflation," or "SBBI") from 1926 to the present, and (ii) an analysis of the relative performance of U.S. asset classes. The *SBBI Yearbook* has been published for over 30 years. The *SBBI Yearbook* does not provide extensive valuation data or methodology.[i.5]

[i.2]   "Stocks, Bonds, Bills, and Inflation" and "SBBI" are registered trademarks of Morningstar, Inc. All rights reserved. Used with permission.

[i.3]   The *Ibbotson Stocks Bonds, Bills, and Inflation (SBBI) Classic Yearbook* (as it was previously named when published by Morningstar from 2006 to 2015, and Ibbotson Associates in prior years) has been published for over 30 years.

[i.4]   Starting with the *2016 SBBI Yearbook* (this book), the word "Classic" has been removed from the name.

[i.5]   To learn more, see the previous section herein entitled "Other Duff & Phelps Valuation Data Resources Published by John Wiley & Sons," or visit www.wiley.com/go/ValuationHandbooks.

About the *2016 SBBI Yearbook*

A Definitive History of U.S. Asset Returns

The *2016 SBBI Yearbook* is the definitive annual resource for historical U.S. capital markets data. The *SBBI Yearbook* includes total returns, index values, and statistical analyses of U.S. large company stocks, small company stocks, long-term corporate bonds, long-term government bonds, intermediate-term government bonds, U.S. Treasury bills, and inflation from January 1926 through December 2015 (monthly).

The *SBBI Yearbook* also provides historical returns for the U.S. equity risk premium, the small stock premium, the default premium, and the horizon premium from 1926 through 2015.

Updated Annually

The *2016 SBBI Yearbook* (this book), like the other Duff & Phelps data resources published by John Wiley & Sons, is updated annually. In the *2016 SBBI Yearbook* the historical data are updated through December 31, 2015.

The Motivations for Writing (and Updating) the *SBBI Yearbook*

The motivations for writing (and updating) the *SBBI Yearbook* are straightforward:

- To document this history of security market returns.

- To uncover the relationships between the various asset class returns as revealed by the derived series: inflation, real interest rates, risk premiums, and other premiums.

- To encourage deeper understanding of the underlying economic history through the graphic presentation of data.

- To help answer frequently asked questions.

The asset classes analyzed in the *2016 SBBI Yearbook* highlight the differences between targeted segments of the financial markets in the United States. Our intent is to show historical trade-offs between risk and return.

In this book, the equity markets are segmented between (i) large-cap and (ii) small cap stocks. Fixed-income markets are segmented on two dimensions:

"Riskless" U.S. government securities are differentiated by maturity or investment horizon: (i) U.S. Treasury bills with approximately 30 days to maturity are used to describe the short end of the horizon, (ii) U.S. Treasury securities with approximately five years to maturity are used to describe the middle horizon segment, and (iii) U.S. Treasury securities with approximately 20 years to maturity are used to describe the long maturity end of the market.

A corporate bond series with a long maturity is used to describe fixed-income securities that contain risk of default.

Some indexes of the stock and bond markets are broad, capturing most or all of the capitalization of the market. Our indexes are intentionally narrower. The large-cap stock series captures the largest issues (those in the Standard & Poor's 500 Composite Index), while the small-cap stock series is composed of the smallest issues. By studying these polar cases, we identify the small-stock premium (small minus large stock returns) and the premium of large stocks over bonds and bills. Neither series is intended to be representative of the entire stock market.

Likewise, our long-term U.S. government bond and U.S. Treasury bill indexes show the returns for the longest and shortest ends of the yield curve, rather than the return for the entire Treasury float. Readers and investors should understand that our bond indices are not intended to (and do not) describe the experience of the typical bond investor who is diversified *across* maturities; rather, we present returns on carefully focused segments of the market for U.S. Treasury securities.

Same Primary Data Sources

The same data sources used to produce the data in previous versions of the *SBBI Yearbook* are used to produce the *2016 SBBI Yearbook*:

- The primary data source used herein is the Stocks, Bonds, Bills, and Inflation (SBBI) Series from Morningstar's *Direct* database. To learn more about Morningstar's *Direct* database, visit www.corporate.morningstar.com.

- The Center for Research in Security Prices (CRSP) market-cap-based NYSE/NYSE MKT/ NASDAQ indices. To learn more about the Center for Research in Security Prices at the University of Chicago Booth School of Business, visit www.crsp.com.

The *2016 SBBI Yearbook* Is on a Delayed Production Schedule

The *SBBI Yearbook* is traditionally published with data through the *previous* year (specifically December 31), and printed and shipped in late March of the *present* year (e.g., the 2014 book was published with data through December 31, 2013, and printed and shipped in late March 2014; last year's 2015 book was published with data through December 31, 2014, and printed and shipped in late March 2015).

The *2016 SBBI Yearbook*, however, is on a delayed publication schedule because of the extensive work involved in gathering the data and establishing the necessary data permissions needed to produce the book. As usual, the *2016 SBBI Yearbook* is "data through" the previous year (December 31, 2015), but will not be printed and shipped until late July/early August 2016. Next year's *2017 SBBI Yearbook* will be back on a "regular" schedule of shipping in March 2017.

History of the *SBBI Yearbook*

The Journal of Business published Roger G. Ibbotson and Rex A. Sinquefield's two companion papers on security returns in January 1976 and July 1976. In the first paper, the authors collected historical data on the returns from stocks, government and corporate bonds, U.S. Treasury bills, and consumer goods (inflation). To uncover the risk/return and the real/nominal relationship in the historical data, they presented a framework in which the return on an asset class is the sum of two or more elemental parts. These elements, such as real returns (returns in excess of inflation) and risk premiums (for example, the net return from investing in large-capitalization stocks rather than bills), are referred to throughout the book as "derived series."[i.6]

In the second paper, the authors analyzed the time-series behavior of the derived series and the information contained in the U.S. government bond yield curve to obtain inputs for a simulation model of future security price behavior. Using the methods developed in the two papers, they forecast security returns through the year 2000:[i.7]

> *"In May 1974, in the depths of the worst bear market since the 1930s, two young men at a University of Chicago conference made a brash prediction: The Dow Jones industrial average, floundering in the 800s at the time, would hit 9,218 at the end of 1998 and get to 10,000 by November 1999.*
>
> *You probably have a good idea how things turned out: At the end of 1998, the Dow was at 9,181, just 37 points off the forecast. It hit 10,000 in March 1999, seven months early. Those two young men in Chicago in 1974 had made one of the most spectacular market calls in history."*[i.8]

The response to these works showed that historical data are fascinating in their own right. Both total and component historical returns have a wide range of applications in investment management, corporate finance, academic research, and industry regulation. Subsequent work (the 1977, 1979, and 1982 Institute of Chartered Financial Analysts monographs; the 1989 Dow Jones-Irwin Business and Investment Almanac; and the 1983 through 2016 *Ibbotson Stocks, Bonds, Bills, and Inflation Classic Yearbooks*) updated and further developed the historical data and forecasts.[i.9]

In 1981, Ibbotson and Sinquefield began tracking a new asset class: small-cap stocks. This class consists of issues listed on the New York Stock Exchange that rank in the ninth and 10th (lowest) deciles when sorted by capitalization (price times number of shares outstanding), plus non-NYSE issues of comparable capitalization. This asset class has been of interest to researchers and

---

[i.6] For a detailed discussion, see Chapter 3, "Description of the Derived Series" herein.

[i.7] Roger G. Ibbotson, Rex A. Sinquefield, *Stocks, Bonds, Bills and Inflation: The Post (1926–1976) and the Future (1977–2000)*, The *Journal of Finance* Vol. 35, No. 1 (Mar., 1980), pp. 205–209.

[i.8] Justin Fox, "9% Forever?," *Fortune* magazine "Investor's Guide 2006," December 26, 2005.
http://archive.fortune.com/magazines/fortune/fortune_archive/2005/12/26/8364640/index.htm

[i.9] All references to previous works used in the development of *SBBI Yearbook* data appear at the end of this introduction in the section entitled "References."

investors because of its high long-term returns. Intermediate-term (five years to maturity) government bonds were added in 1988. Monthly and annual total returns, income returns, capital appreciation returns, and yields are presented.

Who Should Use the *SBBI Yearbook*

The *SBBI Yearbook* is a history of the returns on the capital markets in the United States from 1926 to the present. It is useful to a wide variety of readers. Foremost, anyone serious about investments or investing needs an appreciation of capital market history. Such an appreciation, which can be gained from this book, is equally valuable to the individual and institutional investor. For students at both the graduate and undergraduate levels, this book is both a source of ideas and a reference. Other intended readers include teachers of these students; practitioners and scholars in finance, economics, and business; portfolio strategists; and security analysts.

Chief financial officers and, in some cases, CEOs of corporations will find this book useful. More generally, persons concerned with history may find it valuable to study the detail of economic history as revealed in more than eight decades of capital market returns.

To these diverse readers, we provide two resources. One is the data. The other is a thinking person's guide to using historical data to understand the financial markets and make decisions. This historical record raises many questions. This book represents our way of appreciating the past only one of the many possible ways but one grounded in real theory. We provide a means for the reader to think about the past and the future of financial markets.

Recent Changes and Additions to the *SBBI Yearbook*

The *Stocks, Bonds, Bills, and Inflation (SBBI) Yearbook* has been published for over 30 years, originally by Ibbotson Associates, and most recently by Morningstar, Inc.[i.10]

The most significant change in 2016 is that the *SBBI Yearbook* is now produced by Duff & Phelps, and published by John Wiley & Sons.

U.S. SBBI Long-term Government Bond Series Data Revision

Morningstar reported a data revision in January 2016 to the "SBBI Long-term Government Bond" series and the "SBBI Intermediate-term Government Bond" series. The data revisions affected data from June 2011 to December 2015, and were reflected in the Morningstar *Direct* database as of December 31, 2015. These revisions were small with nominal changes, for example, to annualized returns and annualized indexes for 2011, 2012, 2013, and 2014, as reported in last year's *2015 SBBI Yearbook* when compared to this year's *2016 SBBI Yearbook*. As such, some values reported in last year's *2015 SBBI Yearbook* have necessarily been revised herein.

[i.10] Morningstar acquired Ibbotson Associates in 2006. Morningstar published the *SBBI Yearbook* under the name *SBBI "Classic" Yearbook* from 2007–2015.

Some Chapters and Sections Previously Reported Have Been Discontinued

Our goal in 2016 is to produce the *2016 SBBI Yearbook* with as much of the critical data and information reported in previous editions of the book as possible. However, we have had to balance that goal with another very important factor: "timeliness."

As previously discussed, the *2016 SBBI Yearbook* (this book) is on a delayed production schedule because of the extensive work involved in gathering the data and establishing the necessary data permissions needed to produce the book.[i.11] In order to get the 2016 book's critical data and information out to users in a more *timely* fashion, certain chapters presented in last year's *2015 SBBI Yearbook* are *not* included in the *2016 SBBI Yearbook* (e.g., Chapters 12 and 15 from the 2015 book entitled "Wealth Forecasting With Monte Carlo Simulation" and "Lifecycle Investing," respectively).

Also, some sections previously included in Chapter 1 are not presented herein (e.g., likely the most visible of these are the sections previously reported in Chapter 1 that included a summary of U.S. and Global news stories). Having said that, Chapter 1 in the *2016 SBBI Yearbook* does include the critical summary asset class performance information traditionally reported in that chapter (e.g., "Results of 2015 Capital Markets," "Graphic View of the Decade," "The Decade in Perspective," and "Table of Market Results for 2006–2015").[i.12]

Another difference (albeit less important) is found in Chapter 7, "Company Size and Return." On October 1, 2008, NYSE Euronext acquired the American Stock Exchange (AMEX). The "NYSE MKT" is the former American Stock Exchange, or AMEX. The CRSP standard market-cap-based NYSE/AMEX/NASDAQ indices are therefore called the NYSE/NYSE MKT/ NASDAQ indices herein.

We welcome reader comments, questions, and suggestions. Your feedback is an important source of information for helping us to improve the *SBBI Yearbook* and our related data resources.

To order additional copies of the *2016 Stocks, Bonds, Bills, and Inflation (SBBI) Yearbook*, or other Duff & Phelps data resources published by John Wiley & Sons, please go to: www.wiley.com/go/ValuationHandbooks.

[i.11] See previous section entitled, "The *2016 SBBI Yearbook* Is on a Delayed Production Schedule."

[i.12] In last year's *2015 SBBI Yearbook*, Chapter 1 was entitled "Highlights of the 2014 Markets and the Past Decade." In the *2016 SBBI Yearbook* (this book), Chapter 1 has been renamed "Results of the U.S. Capital Markets in 2015 and in the Past Decade."

Chapter 1
Results of U.S. Capital Markets in 2015 and in the Past Decade

Large-Cap Stocks

The market for U.S. large-capitalization stocks is represented herein by the S&P 500 Total Return Index ("total return" includes the reinvestment of dividends).

U.S. Large-cap stocks posted a total return of 1.38% in 2015, down from 13.69% in 2014. Six months of 2015 produced positive returns; October delivered the highest return at 8.44%, while August's -6.03% was the lowest. An index of large-cap stock total returns, started at $1.00 on December 31, 1925, increased to $5,390.43 by the end of 2015, up from $5,316.85 at the end of 2014.

Small-Cap Stocks

U.S. small-cap stocks posted a total return of -3.60% in 2015, down from 2.92% in 2014. Six months of 2015 produced positive returns; October and February delivered the highest returns at 6.03% (each), while January and December's -4.90% (each) was the lowest. An index of small-cap stocks total returns, started at $1.00 on December 31, 1925, increased to $26,433.35 by the end of 2015, down from $27,419.32 at the end of 2014.

Long-term Corporate Bonds

U.S. long-term corporate bonds posted a total return of -1.02% in 2015, down from 17.28% in 2014. Seven months of 2015 produced positive returns; January delivered the highest return at 5.99%, while February's -3.20% was the lowest. An index of long-term corporate bonds total returns, started at $1.00 on December 31, 1925, increased to $187.82 by the end of 2015, down from $189.76 at the end of 2014.

The bond default premium, or net return from investing in long-term corporate bonds rather than investing in long-term government bonds of equal maturity, was -0.37% in 2015, compared with -5.95% in 2014.

Long-term Government Bonds

U.S. long-term government bonds posted a total return of -0.65% in 2015, down from 24.71% in 2014. Five months of 2015 produced positive returns; January delivered the highest return at 7.09%, while February's -5.23% was the lowest. An index of long-term government bonds total returns, started at $1.00 on December 31, 1925, increased to $132.03 by the end of 2015, down from $132.90 at the end of 2014.

Intermediate-term Government Bonds

U.S. intermediate-term government bonds posted a total return of 1.79% in 2015, down from 3.00% in 2014. Six months of 2015 produced positive returns; January delivered the highest return at 2.41%, while February's -1.23% was the lowest. An index of intermediate-term government bonds total returns, started at $1.00 on December 31, 1925, increased to $93.97 by the end of 2015, up from $92.32 at the end of 2014.

Treasury Bills

U.S. Treasury bills posted a total return of 0.02% in 2015, equal to the 0.02% posted in 2014. Eight months of 2015 produced positive returns; December delivered the highest return at 0.01016%, while October's -0.00193% was the lowest. An index of Treasury Bills total returns, started at $1.00 on December 31, 1925, increased to $20.59 by the end of 2015, up from $20.58 at the end of 2014.

Inflation

Inflation increased to 1.18% in 2015, compared to 0.76% in 2014. The result is lower than the long-term historical annual average (1926–2015) of 3.0%. Inflation has remained below 5% for 33 of the last 34 years (the exception was the 6.11% rate in 1990). A cumulative inflation index, beginning at $1.00 at year-end 1925, finished 2015 at $13.25, up from $13.10 at year-end 2014. That is, a "basket" of consumer goods and services that cost $1.00 in 1925 would cost $13.25 today. The two baskets are not identical, but are intended to be comparable.

A Graphic View of the Decade

Exhibit 1.1 shows the market results for the past decade illustrating the growth of $1.00 invested on December 31, 2005, in stocks, bonds, and bills, along with an index of inflation. A review of the major themes of the past decade, as revealed in the capital markets, follows.

Exhibit 1.1: Wealth Indexes of Investments in U.S. Stocks, Bonds, Bills, and Inflation Index Over the Most Recent Decade (2006–2015) (Year-end 2005 = $1.00)

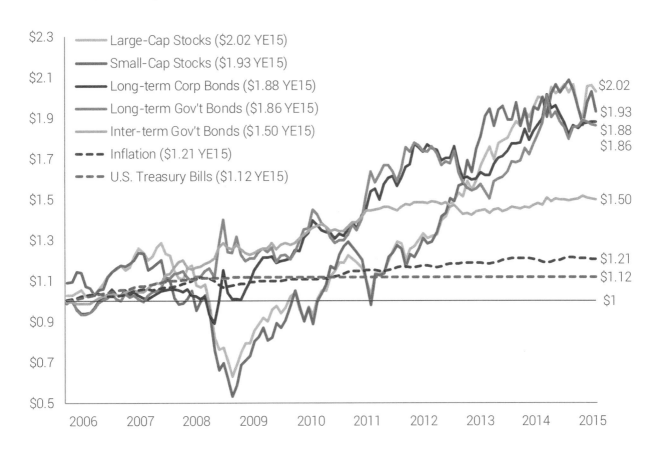

The Decade in Perspective

The great stock and bond market rise of the 1980s and 1990s was one of the most unusual in the history of the capital markets. In terms of the magnitude of the rise, these decades most closely resembled the 1920s and 1950s. These four decades accounted for a majority of the market's cumulative total return over the past 90 years. While the importance of a long-term view of investing is noted consistently in this book and elsewhere, the counterpart to this observation is this: to achieve high investment returns, one needs to participate only in the few periods of truly outstanding returns. The bull markets of 1922 to mid-1929, 1949–1961 (roughly speaking, the 1950s), mid-1982 to mid-1987, and 1991–1999 were such periods. More recently, in the 7-year period ending December 2015, an investor in large and small stocks would have realized annual compound returns of approximately 15% and 16%, respectively.[1.1]

[1.1] An investment of $1.00 (each) at the end of December 2008 in large stocks and small stocks would have grown to $2.63 and $2.77, respectively, by the end of December 2015. This represents a compound annual return of 14.8% for large stocks, and 15.7% for small stocks over this 7-year (84-month) period.

The average annual compound rate of return of the basic SBBI series over the longer 1926–2015 period (90 years) is compared to the average annual compound rate of return of the SBBI series over the most recent 10-year period (2006–2015) in Exhibit 1.2, with the highest return for each time horizon highlighted in red.

Exhibit 1.2: Comparison of the Average Annual Compound Rate of Return of the Basic SBBI Series as Measured Over (i) the 1926–2015 Period (90 years) and (ii) the 2006–2015 Period (most recent 10 years)

SBBI Series	1926–2015	2006–2015
Large-Cap Stocks	10.0%	7.3%
Small-Cap Stocks	12.0%	6.8%
Long-term Corp Bonds	6.0%	6.5%
Long-term Gov't Bonds	5.6%	6.4%
Inter-term Gov't Bonds	5.2%	4.1%
U.S. Treasury Bills	3.4%	1.1%
Inflation	2.9%	1.9%

Looking to Exhibit 1.2, large-cap stocks, small-cap stocks, intermediate-term government bonds, and U.S. Treasury bills posted *lower* returns over the most recent 10-year period (2006–2015) than they did over the 1926–2015 period (90-year). Long-term corporate bonds and long-term government bonds, alternatively, posted *higher* returns in the 2006–2015 period than they did in the 1926–2015 period.

The annual rate of U.S. inflation over the 2006–2015 period was also lower than the rate experienced over the longer-term 1926–2015 period.

Exhibit 1.3: Compound Annual Rates of Return by Decade

SBBI Series	1920s[*]	1930s	1940s	1950s	1960s	1970s	1980s	1990s	2000s	2010s[**]
Large-Cap Stocks	19.2%	-0.1%	9.2%	19.4%	7.8%	5.9%	17.6%	18.2%	-0.9%	13.0%
Small-Cap Stocks	-4.5%	1.4%	20.7%	16.9%	15.5%	11.5%	15.8%	15.1%	6.3%	13.7%
Long-term Corp Bonds	5.2%	6.9%	2.7%	1.0%	1.7%	6.2%	13.0%	8.4%	7.6%	8.0%
Long-term Gov't Bonds	5.0%	4.9%	3.2%	-0.1%	1.4%	5.5%	12.6%	8.8%	7.7%	7.7%
Inter-term Gov't Bonds	4.2%	4.6%	1.8%	1.3%	3.5%	7.0%	11.9%	7.2%	6.2%	3.0%
U.S. Treasury Bills	3.7%	0.6%	0.4%	1.9%	3.9%	6.3%	8.9%	4.9%	2.8%	0.0%
Inflation	-1.1%	-2.0%	5.4%	2.2%	2.5%	7.4%	5.1%	2.9%	2.5%	1.6%

[*] Based on the period 1926–1929. [**] Based on the period 2010–2015

It is interesting to place the decades of superior performance in historical context. The 1920s were preceded by mediocre returns and high inflation and were followed by the most devastating stock market crash and economic depression in U.S. history. This sequence of events mitigated the impact of the 1920s bull market on investor wealth. Nevertheless, the stock market became a liquid secondary market that decade, rendering it important for reasons other than return. In contrast, the 1950s were preceded and followed by decades with roughly average equity returns. The 1980s were preceded by a decade of "stagflation," where modest stock price gains were seriously eroded by inflation and were followed by a period of stability in the 1990s.

The bond market performance of the 1980s and 1990s has no precedent. Bond yields, which had risen consistently since the 1940s, reached unprecedented levels in 1980–1981. (Other countries experiencing massive inflation have had correspondingly high interest rates.) Never before having had so far to fall, bond yields dropped further and faster than at any other time, producing what is indisputably the greatest bond bull market in history. Unfortunately, the boom came to an end in 1994. After falling to 21-year lows one year earlier, bond yields rose in 1994 to their highest level in over three years. Both long-term and intermediate-term government bond yields have generally fallen since 2000.

The historical themes of the past decade, as they relate to the capital markets, can be summarized in three observations. First, the 17.5-year period starting in mid-1982 and ending in 1999 was a rare span of time in which investors quickly accumulated wealth.

Second, the postwar aberration of ever-higher inflation rates ended with a dramatic disinflation in the early 1980s. In the 1990s, inflation was a relatively low 2.9% compound annual rate compared to the long-term compound annual rate as of the end of that decade (1926–1999), which was 3.1%. The trend of relatively low inflation continued in the 2000s, and in more recent periods. For example, the long-term compound annual rate of inflation over the 1926–2015 period (90 years) was 2.9%, but the compound annual rate over the 2000–2009 period, the most recent 10-year period (2006–2015), and the 2010–2015 period were all significantly lower at 2.5%, 1.9%, and 1.6%, respectively.

Finally, participation in the returns of the capital markets since 1982 reached levels not approached in the 1920s, the 1950s, or even in the atypical boom period of 1967–1972. The growth since 1982 in the importance of pension funds and defined contribution pension plans, like the 401(k), as well as the rapidly increasing popularity of stock and bond mutual funds and exchange-traded products as basic savings vehicles, have enabled more individuals to experience the returns of the capital markets than ever before.

Market Results for 2006–2015

Exhibit 1.4 (next page) presents (i) annual total returns for 2006–2015, (ii) quarterly and monthly total returns on the six basic asset classes and inflation for 2015, and (iii) cumulative indexes of the returns based on a starting value of $1.00 invested on December 31, 1925.

Exhibit 1.4 provides the Reader with a plethora of information about the more recent performance of the basic SBBI series which can be used to analyze recent trends. For example, large-cap stocks performed reasonably well in the most recent 10-year period (2006–2015), with 2013 providing the greatest annual return of 32.39%. The only negative return was -37.00% in 2008. Small-cap stocks did not perform as well as large-cap stocks did over the most recent decade, and had more years of negative returns than large-cap stocks, with 2007, 2008, 2011, and 2015 providing -5.22%, -36.72%, -3.26%, and -3.60%, respectively. In 2013 small-cap stocks posted their largest annual returns of the decade, 45.07%, which did eclipse the 32.39% posted by large-cap stocks that year.

Exhibit 1.4: Returns and Indices of Returns on Stocks, Bonds, Bills, and Inflation; Annual, Quarterly, and Monthly Market Results, in Percent (%)

2006–2015 Annual Returns

Period	Large-Cap Stocks	Small-Cap Stocks	Long-term Corp Bonds	Long-term Gov't Bonds	Inter-term Gov't Bonds	U.S. Treasury Bills	Inflation
2006	15.79	16.17	3.24	1.19	3.14	4.80	2.54
2007	5.49	-5.22	2.60	9.88	10.05	4.66	4.08
2008	-37.00	-36.72	8.78	25.87	13.11	1.60	0.09
2009	26.46	28.09	3.02	-14.90	-2.40	0.10	2.72
2010	15.06	31.26	12.44	10.14	7.12	0.12	1.50
2011	2.11	-3.26	17.95	27.10	8.81	0.04	2.96
2012	16.00	18.24	10.68	3.43	1.66	0.06	1.74
2013	32.39	45.07	-7.07	-12.78	-3.68	0.02	1.51
2014	13.69	2.92	17.28	24.71	3.00	0.02	0.76
2015	1.38	-3.60	-1.02	-0.65	1.79	0.02	1.18

2015 Quarterly Returns

	Large-Cap Stocks	Small-Cap Stocks	Long-term Corp Bonds	Long-term Gov't Bonds	Inter-term Gov't Bonds	U.S. Treasury Bills	Inflation
I-15	0.95	3.14	3.19	2.87	1.91	0.00	0.56
II-15	0.28	1.02	-7.28	-6.92	-0.62	0.00	1.07
III-15	-6.44	-10.78	3.05	5.22	1.62	0.00	-0.29
IV-15	7.04	3.70	0.39	-1.39	-1.09	0.01	-0.15

2015 Monthly Returns

	Large-Cap Stocks	Small-Cap Stocks	Long-term Corp Bonds	Long-term Gov't Bonds	Inter-term Gov't Bonds	U.S. Treasury Bills	Inflation
Dec-14	-0.25	3.37	1.83	2.90	-0.60	0.00	-0.57
Jan-15	-3.00	-4.90	5.99	7.09	2.41	0.00	-0.47
Feb-15	5.75	6.03	-3.20	-5.23	-1.23	0.00	0.43
Mar-15	-1.58	2.29	0.58	1.37	0.74	0.00	0.60
Apr-15	0.96	-1.95	-2.23	-2.50	-0.14	0.00	0.20
May-15	1.29	1.38	-2.04	-1.59	0.05	0.00	0.51
Jun-15	-1.94	1.63	-3.20	-2.98	-0.53	0.00	0.35
Jul-15	2.10	-2.44	2.39	3.29	0.51	0.00	0.01
Aug-15	-6.03	-4.43	-0.67	0.12	0.11	0.00	-0.14
Sep-15	-2.47	-4.31	1.33	1.74	0.99	0.00	-0.16
Oct-15	8.44	6.03	0.20	-0.53	-0.52	0.00	-0.04
Nov-15	0.30	2.84	0.20	-0.65	-0.40	0.00	-0.21
Dec-15	-1.58	-4.90	0.00	-0.22	-0.17	0.01	0.11

2006–2015 Annual Indicies

	Large-Cap Stocks	Small-Cap Stocks	Long-term Corp Bonds	Long-term Gov't Bonds	Inter-term Gov't Bonds	U.S. Treasury Bills	Inflation
2006	3,083.564	15,922.427	103.178	71.694	64.643	19.287	11.257
2007	3,252.974	15,091.094	105.858	78.779	71.142	20.186	11.717
2008	2,049.444	9,548.943	115.154	99.161	80.466	20.509	11.728
2009	2,591.819	12,230.866	118.628	84.383	78.532	20.529	12.047
2010	2,982.234	16,054.698	133.384	92.942	84.121	20.553	12.227
2011	3,045.212	15,532.068	157.324	118.130	91.533	20.562	12.589
2012	3,532.552	18,364.597	174.120	122.180	93.054	20.574	12.808
2013	4,676.681	26,641.173	161.802	106.571	89.630	20.579	13.001
2014	5,316.849	27,419.318	189.762	132.900	92.316	20.583	13.100
2015	5,390.425	26,433.349	187.822	132.032	93.970	20.586	13.254

2015 Monthly Indicies

	Large-Cap Stocks	Small-Cap Stocks	Long-term Corp Bonds	Long-term Gov't Bonds	Inter-term Gov't Bonds	U.S. Treasury Bills	Inflation
Dec-14	5,316.849	27,419.318	189.762	132.900	92.316	20.583	13.100
Jan-15	5,157.241	26,075.771	201.120	142.323	94.542	20.583	13.038
Feb-15	5,453.636	27,648.140	194.678	134.875	93.381	20.583	13.095
Mar-15	5,367.389	28,281.283	195.807	136.717	94.076	20.583	13.173
Apr-15	5,418.879	27,729.798	191.443	133.295	93.945	20.584	13.199
May-15	5,488.562	28,112.469	187.541	131.172	93.989	20.584	13.267
Jun-15	5,382.314	28,570.702	181.545	127.260	93.493	20.584	13.313
Jul-15	5,495.080	27,873.577	185.882	131.448	93.967	20.583	13.314
Aug-15	5,163.541	26,638.777	184.631	131.603	94.072	20.584	13.295
Sep-15	5,035.777	25,490.646	187.084	133.898	95.005	20.584	13.274
Oct-15	5,460.566	27,027.732	187.455	133.183	94.513	20.584	13.268
Nov-15	5,476.805	27,795.320	187.821	132.321	94.132	20.584	13.240
Dec-15	5,390.425	26,433.349	187.822	132.032	93.970	20.586	13.254

Chapter 2
The Long-Run Perspective

A long view of capital market history, illustrated by the 90-year period (1926–2015) examined here, uncovers the basic relationships between risk and return among the different asset classes and between nominal and real (inflation adjusted) returns. The goal of this study of asset returns is to provide a period long enough to include most or all of the major types of events that investors have experienced and may experience in the future. Such events include war and peace, growth and decline, bull and bear markets, inflation and deflation, and other less dramatic events that affect asset returns.

By studying the past, one can make inferences about the future. While the actual events that occurred during 1926–2015 will not be repeated, the event-types of that period can be expected to recur. It is sometimes said that only a few periods had unusual events, such as the stock market crash of 1929–1932 and World War II. This logic is suspicious because events that are deemed unusual happen with a certain regularity.[2.1] Some of the most unusual events of the century – the market crash of 1987, the equally remarkable inflation of the 1970s and early 1980s, the more recent events of September 11, 2001, and most recently, the 2008–2009 financial crisis – took place over the last three decades or so. To the degree that historical event-types tend to repeat themselves, the examination of past capital market returns is likely informative about what may be expected in the future.

Stocks, Bonds, Bills, and Inflation: Historical Returns

Exhibit 2.1 depicts the growth of $1.00 invested in large-cap stocks, small-cap stocks, long-term government bonds, Treasury bills, and a hypothetical asset returning the inflation rate over the period from the end of 1925 to the end of 2015. All results assume reinvestment of dividends on stocks, or coupons on bonds, and no taxes. Transaction costs are not included, except in the small stock index starting in 1982.

Each of the cumulative index values is initialized at $1.00 at year-end 1925. The graph vividly illustrates that small-cap stocks and large-cap stocks were the big winners over the entire 90-year period: investments of $1.00 in these assets would have grown to $26,433.35 and $5,390.43, respectively, by year-end 2015. This phenomenal growth was earned by taking substantial risk. In contrast, long-term government bonds (with an approximate 20-year maturity), which exposed the holder to much less risk, grew to only $132.03.

[2.1] In 2010, Laurence B. Siegel, research director at the Research Foundation of the CFA Institute at the time, famously referred to these events as "black turkeys." The reference was to "black swans," the term author Nassim Nicholas Taleb gave to unfortunate events that aren't easily foreseeable. Siegel explained in a paper, "Black Swan or Black Turkey?" that market events like the global financial crisis are "everywhere in the data—(they) happen all the time" but investors are "willfully blind" to them. See: Laurence B. Siegel, "Black Swan or Black Turkey? The State of Economic Knowledge and the Crash of 2007–2009," *Financial Analysts Journal*, July/August 2010, Volume 66 Issue 4.

The lowest-risk strategy over the past 90 years (for those with short-term time horizons) was to buy U.S. Treasury bills. Because Treasury bills tended to track inflation, the resulting real (i.e., inflation-adjusted) returns were just above zero for the entire 1926–2015 period.

Exhibit 2.1: Wealth Indexes of Investments in the U.S. Capital Markets Index 1926–2015

(Year-end 1925 = $1.00)

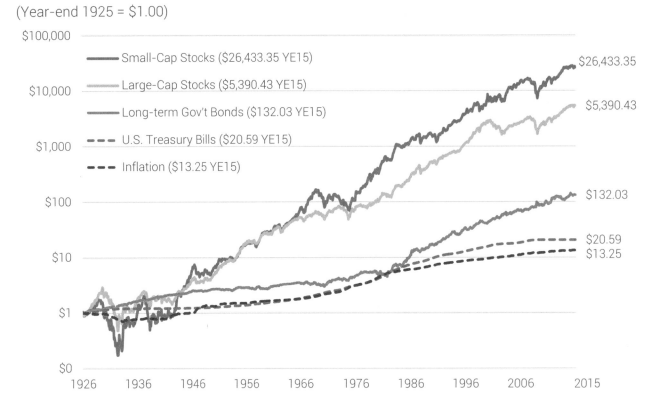

Logarithmic Scale Used on the Index Graphs

A logarithmic scale is used on the vertical axis of the index graphs presented in this book.

A logarithmic scale (see Exhibit 2.2a) allows for the direct comparison of the series' behavior at different points in time. Specifically, the use of a logarithmic scale allows the following interpretation of the data: the same vertical distance, no matter where it is measured on the graph, represents the *same* percentage change in the series. For example, on a logarithmic scale, a 50% gain from $10 to $15 occupies the same vertical distance as a 50% gain from $1,000 to $1,500. On a linear scale, the same percentage gains look different (see Exhibit 2.2b).

A logarithmic scale allows the viewer to compare investment performance across different periods; thus the viewer can concentrate on rates of return, without worrying about the number of dollars invested at any given time.

An additional (and practical) benefit of a logarithmic scale is the way the scale spreads the action out over time. It makes the graph easier to see, and makes it easier to more carefully examine the fluctuations of the individual time series in different periods.

Exhibit 2.2a: Logarithmic Scale

Exhibit 2.2b: Linear Scale

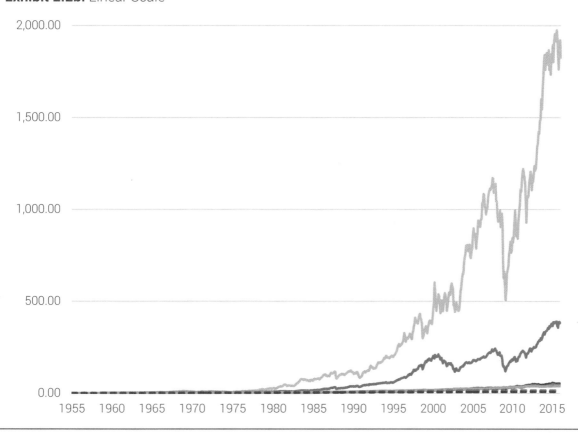

Large-Cap Stocks

As noted above, an index of S&P 500 total returns initialized on December 31, 1925 at $1.00, closed 2015 at $5,390.43, a compound annual growth rate of 10.0%. The inflation-adjusted S&P 500 total return index closed 2015 at a level of $406.69.

Small-Cap Stocks

Over the long run, small-capitalization stock returns surpassed the S&P 500, with the small-cap stock total return index ending 2015 at a level of $26,433.35. This represents a compound annual growth rate of 12.0%, the highest rate among the asset classes studied here.

Long-term Corporate Bonds

Long-term corporate bonds outperformed both types of government bonds over the 1926–2015 period with a compound annual growth rate of 6.0%. This higher return reflected the risk premium that investors require for investing in corporate bonds, which are subject to the risk of default. One dollar invested in the long-term corporate bond index at year-end 1925 was worth $187.82 by the end of 2015.

Long-term Government Bonds

The long-term government bond total return index, constructed with an approximate 20-year maturity, closed 2015 at a level of $132.03 (based on year-end 1925 equaling $1.00). Looking at capital appreciation component alone, the $1.00 index closed at $1.37, a 0.4% capital gain over the 90-year period. This indicates that the majority of the positive historical returns on long-term government bonds was due to income returns. The compound annual total return for long-term government bonds was 5.6%.

Intermediate-term Government Bonds

One dollar invested in intermediate-term bonds at the end of 1925 rose to $93.97 by year-end 2015, compared to $92.32 at year-end 2014. The compound annual total return for intermediate-term government bonds over the 1926–2015 period was 5.2%. Capital appreciation caused $1.00 to increase to $1.67 over the 90-year period, representing a compound annual growth rate of 0.6%.

Treasury Bills

One dollar invested in Treasury bills at the end of 1925 was worth $20.59 by year-end 2015, with a compound annual growth rate of 3.4%. Treasury bill returns followed distinct patterns, described in the next subsection. Moreover, Treasury bills tended to track inflation, so the average annual inflation-adjusted return on Treasury bills (or real riskless rate of return) was only 0.5% over the 90-year period.

Patterns in Treasury Bill Returns

During the late 1920s and early 1930s, Treasury bill returns were just above zero. (These returns were observed during a largely deflationary period.) Beginning in late 1941, the government kept Treasury bill yields low despite high inflation rates. Treasury bills closely tracked inflation after March 1951, when Treasury bill yields were deregulated in the U.S. Treasury/Federal Reserve Accord. This tracking relationship has weakened since 1973. From 1974 to 1980, Treasury bill returns were generally lower than inflation rates. From 1981 to 2008, real returns on Treasury bills have been positive, with the exception of 2002–2005. Real Treasury bill returns were also negative from 2009 to 2015.

Federal Reserve Operating Procedure Changes

The disparity between performance and volatility for the periods prior to and after October 1979 can be attributed to the Federal Reserve's new operating procedures. Prior to this date, the Fed used the federal funds rate as an operating target. Subsequently, the Fed de-emphasized this rate as an operating target and, instead, began to focus on the manipulation of the money supply (through non-borrowed reserves). As a result, the federal funds rate underwent much greater volatility, thereby bringing about greater volatility in Treasury returns. In the fall of 1982, however, the Federal Reserve again changed the policy procedures regarding its monetary policy. The Fed abandoned its new monetary controls and returned to a strategy of preventing excessive volatility in interest rates. Volatility in Treasury bill returns from the fall of 1979 through the fall of 1982 was significantly greater than that which has occurred since.

Inflation

The compound annual inflation rate over 1926–2015 was 2.9%. The inflation index, initiated at $1.00 at year end 1925, grew to $13.25 by year-end 2015. It is interesting to note that the entire increase occurred during the postwar period (specifically, after April 1945).

The years 1926–1933 were generally *deflationary* in nature, and consumer prices did not rise back to their 1926 levels until April 1945. After a brief postwar spurt of inflation (in 1946 and 1947, inflation was 18.2% and 9.0%, respectively), prices rose slowly over most of the 1950s and 1960s. Then, in the 1970s, inflation reached a pace unprecedented in peacetime, peaking at 13.3% in 1979. The 1980s saw a reversion to more moderate, though still substantial, inflation rates averaging about 5% annually. Inflation rates continued to decline in the 1990s with a compound annual rate of 2.9%. Since 2000, inflation has been even milder, with a compound average rate of about 2.2%.

Summary Statistics of Total Returns

Exhibit 2.3 presents summary statistics of the annual total returns on each asset class over the entire 90-year period of 1926–2015. The data presented in these exhibits are described in detail in Chapters 3 and 6.

Exhibit 2.3: Basic Series, Summary Statistics of Annual Total Returns (%)
1926–2015

Series	Geometric Mean (%)	Arithmetic Mean (%)	Standard Deviation (%)	Distribution (%)
Large-Cap Stocks	10.0	12.0	20.0	
Small-Cap Stocks*	12.0	16.5	32.0	
Long-term Corp Bonds	6.0	6.3	8.4	
Long-term Gov't Bonds	5.6	6.0	10.0	
Inter-term Gov't Bonds	5.2	5.3	5.7	
U.S. Treasury Bills	3.4	3.5	3.1	
Inflation	2.9	3.0	4.1	

*The 1933 small-cap stocks total return was 142.9%, and is not shown here.

-90   0   90

Note that in Exhibit 2.3, the arithmetic mean returns are higher than the geometric mean returns. The difference between these two means is related to the standard deviation, or variability, of the series (see Chapter 6).

The "skylines," or histograms, in Exhibit 2.3 show the frequency distribution of returns for each asset class. The height of the skylines shows the number of years in the 1926–2015 period that had a return in that range. The histograms are shown in 5% increments (from -90% to 90%) to fully display the spectrum of returns as seen over the last 90 years, especially in stocks.

Riskier assets, such as large- and small-cap stocks, have spread-out skylines, reflecting the broad distribution of returns from very poor to very good. Less-risky assets, such as bonds, have narrow skylines that resemble a single tall building, indicating the tightness of the distribution around the mean of the series. The histogram for Treasury bills is one-sided, lying almost entirely to the right of the vertical line representing a zero return; that is, Treasury bills almost never experienced negative returns on a yearly basis over the 1926–2015 period (the only negative year was 1938). The inflation skyline shows both positive and negative annual rates. Although a few deflationary months and quarters have occurred recently, the last negative annual inflation rate occurred in 1954.

Appreciation, Income, and Reinvestment Returns

Exhibit 2.4 provides further detail on the returns of large-cap stocks, long-term government bonds, and intermediate-term government bonds. Total annual returns are shown as the sum of three components: capital appreciation returns, income returns, and reinvestment returns. The capital appreciation and income components are explained in Chapter 3. The third component, reinvestment return, reflects monthly income reinvested in the total return index in subsequent months in the year. Thus, for a single month the reinvestment return is zero, but over a longer period of time it is nonzero. Because the returns in Exhibit 2.4 are annual, reinvestment return is relevant.

The annual total return formed by compounding the monthly total returns does not equal the sum of the annual capital appreciation and income components; the difference is reinvestment return. A simple example illustrates this point. In 1995, an "up" year on a total return basis, the total annual return on large-cap stocks was 37.58%. The annual capital appreciation was 34.11% and the annual income return was 3.04%, totaling 37.15%. The remaining 0.43% (37.58% minus 37.15%) of the 1995 total return came from the reinvestment of dividends in the market. For more information on calculating annual total and income returns, see Chapter 5.

Monthly income and capital appreciation returns for large-cap stocks are presented at the back of this book in Appendix A-2 and Appendix A-3, respectively. Monthly income and capital appreciation returns are presented for long-term government bonds in Appendix A-7 and Appendix A-8; and for intermediate-term government bonds in Appendix A-11 and Appendix A-12.

Exhibit 2.4: Large-Cap Stocks, Long-term Government Bonds, and Intermediate-term Government Bonds: Annual Total, Income, Capital Appreciation, and Reinvestment Returns (%)

Year	Large-Cap Stocks				Long-term Gov't Bonds					Intermediate-term Gov't Bonds				
	Capital Appreciation Return	Income Return	Reinvestment Return	Total Return	Capital Appreciation Return	Income Return	Reinvestment Return	Total Return	Year-end Yield	Capital Appreciation Return	Income Return	Reinvestment Return	Total Return	Year-end Yield
1926	5.72	5.41	0.50	11.62	3.91	3.73	0.13	7.77	3.54	1.51	3.78	0.10	5.38	3.61
1927	30.91	5.71	0.87	37.49	5.40	3.41	0.12	8.93	3.17	0.96	3.49	0.07	4.52	3.40
1928	37.88	4.81	0.91	43.61	-3.12	3.22	0.01	0.10	3.40	-2.73	3.64	0.01	0.92	4.01
1929	-11.91	3.98	-0.49	-8.42	-0.20	3.47	0.15	3.42	3.40	1.77	4.07	0.18	6.01	3.62
1930	-28.48	4.57	-0.98	-24.90	1.28	3.32	0.05	4.66	3.30	3.30	3.30	0.11	6.72	2.91
1931	-47.07	5.35	-1.62	-43.34	-8.46	3.33	-0.17	-5.31	4.07	-5.40	3.16	-0.08	-2.32	4.12
1932	-15.15	6.16	0.80	-8.19	12.94	3.69	0.22	16.84	3.15	5.02	3.63	0.16	8.81	3.04
1933	46.59	6.39	1.01	53.99	-3.14	3.12	-0.05	-0.07	3.36	-0.99	2.83	-0.02	1.83	3.25
1934	-5.94	4.46	0.04	-1.44	6.76	3.18	0.09	10.03	2.93	5.97	2.93	0.09	9.00	2.49
1935	41.37	4.95	1.35	47.67	2.14	2.81	0.03	4.98	2.76	4.94	2.02	0.05	7.01	1.63
1936	27.92	5.36	0.64	33.92	4.64	2.77	0.10	7.52	2.55	1.60	1.44	0.02	3.06	1.29
1937	-38.59	4.66	-1.09	-35.03	-2.48	2.66	0.05	0.23	2.73	0.05	1.48	0.03	1.56	1.14
1938	25.21	4.83	1.07	31.12	2.83	2.64	0.06	5.53	2.52	4.37	1.82	0.04	6.23	1.52
1939	-5.45	4.69	0.35	-0.41	3.48	2.40	0.06	5.94	2.26	3.18	1.31	0.03	4.52	0.98
1940	-15.29	5.36	0.14	-9.78	3.77	2.23	0.09	6.09	1.94	2.04	0.90	0.02	2.96	0.57
1941	-17.86	6.71	-0.44	-11.59	-1.01	1.94	0.00	0.93	2.04	-0.17	0.67	0.00	0.50	0.82
1942	12.43	6.79	1.12	20.34	0.74	2.46	0.02	3.22	2.46	1.17	0.76	0.00	1.94	0.72
1943	19.45	6.24	0.21	25.90	-0.37	2.44	0.02	2.08	2.48	1.23	1.56	0.02	2.81	1.45
1944	13.80	5.48	0.47	19.75	0.32	2.46	0.03	2.81	2.46	0.35	1.44	0.01	1.80	1.40
1945	30.72	4.97	0.74	36.44	8.27	2.34	0.12	10.73	1.99	1.02	1.19	0.01	2.22	1.03
1946	-11.87	4.09	-0.29	-8.07	-2.15	2.04	0.01	-0.10	2.12	-0.08	1.08	0.00	1.00	1.12
1947	0.00	5.49	0.22	5.71	-4.70	2.13	-0.06	-2.62	2.43	-0.30	1.21	0.00	0.91	1.34
1948	-0.65	6.08	0.08	5.50	0.96	2.40	0.04	3.40	2.37	0.27	1.56	0.01	1.85	1.51
1949	10.26	7.50	1.03	18.79	4.15	2.25	0.06	6.45	2.09	0.95	1.36	0.01	2.32	1.23
1950	21.78	8.77	1.16	31.71	-2.06	2.12	0.00	0.06	2.24	-0.69	1.39	0.00	0.70	1.62
1951	16.46	6.91	0.65	24.02	-6.27	2.38	-0.04	-3.93	2.69	-1.63	1.98	0.01	0.36	2.17
1952	11.78	5.93	0.66	18.37	-1.48	2.66	-0.02	1.16	2.79	-0.57	2.19	0.01	1.63	2.35
1953	-6.62	5.46	0.18	-0.99	0.67	2.84	0.12	3.64	2.74	0.61	2.55	0.07	3.23	2.18
1954	45.02	6.21	1.39	52.62	4.35	2.79	0.05	7.19	2.72	1.08	1.60	0.01	2.68	1.72
1955	26.40	4.56	0.60	31.56	-4.07	2.75	0.03	-1.29	2.95	-3.10	2.45	0.00	-0.65	2.80
1956	2.62	3.83	0.11	6.56	-8.46	2.99	-0.12	-5.59	3.45	-3.45	3.05	-0.02	-0.42	3.63
1957	-14.31	3.84	-0.30	-10.78	3.82	3.44	0.20	7.46	3.23	4.05	3.59	0.20	7.84	2.84
1958	38.06	4.38	0.93	43.36	-9.23	3.27	-0.14	-6.09	3.82	-4.17	2.93	-0.05	-1.29	3.81
1959	8.48	3.31	0.16	11.96	-6.20	4.01	-0.07	-2.26	4.47	-4.56	4.18	-0.01	-0.39	4.98
1960	-2.97	3.26	0.19	0.47	9.29	4.26	0.23	13.78	3.80	7.42	4.15	0.19	11.76	3.31
1961	23.13	3.48	0.28	26.89	-2.86	3.83	0.00	0.97	4.15	-1.72	3.54	0.03	1.85	3.84
1962	-11.81	2.98	0.10	-8.73	2.78	4.00	0.11	6.89	3.95	1.73	3.73	0.10	5.56	3.50
1963	18.89	3.61	0.30	22.80	-2.70	3.89	0.02	1.21	4.17	-2.10	3.71	0.03	1.64	4.04
1964	12.97	3.33	0.18	16.48	-0.72	4.15	0.07	3.51	4.23	-0.03	4.00	0.07	4.04	4.03
1965	9.06	3.21	0.18	12.45	-3.45	4.19	-0.04	0.71	4.50	-3.10	4.15	-0.03	1.02	4.90
1966	-13.09	3.11	-0.08	-10.06	-1.06	4.49	0.22	3.65	4.55	-0.41	4.93	0.17	4.69	4.79
1967	20.09	3.64	0.25	23.98	-13.55	4.59	-0.23	-9.18	5.56	-3.85	4.88	-0.02	1.01	5.77
1968	7.66	3.18	0.22	11.06	-5.51	5.50	-0.25	-0.26	5.98	-0.99	5.49	0.03	4.54	5.96
1969	-11.36	2.98	-0.13	-8.50	-10.83	5.95	-0.19	-5.07	6.87	-7.27	6.65	-0.11	-0.74	8.29
1970	0.10	3.33	0.43	3.86	4.84	6.74	0.52	12.11	6.48	8.71	7.49	0.66	16.86	5.90

Exhibit 2.4: Large-Cap Stocks, Long-term Government Bonds, and Intermediate-term Government Bonds; Annual Total, Income, Capital Appreciation, and Reinvestment Returns (%)

Year	Large-Cap Stocks Capital Appreciation Return	Income Return	Reinvestment Return	Total Return	Long-term Gov't Bonds Capital Appreciation Return	Income Return	Reinvestment Return	Total Return	Year-end Yield	Intermediate-term Gov't Bonds Capital Appreciation Return	Income Return	Reinvestment Return	Total Return	Year-end Yield
1971	10.63	3.49	0.18	14.30	6.61	6.32	0.31	13.23	5.97	2.72	5.75	0.25	8.72	5.25
1972	15.79	2.95	0.25	18.99	-0.35	5.87	0.17	5.69	5.99	-0.75	5.75	0.16	5.16	5.85
1973	-17.37	2.86	-0.19	-14.69	-7.70	6.51	0.08	-1.11	7.26	-2.19	6.58	0.22	4.61	6.79
1974	-29.72	3.69	-0.44	-26.47	-3.45	7.27	0.54	4.35	7.60	-1.99	7.24	0.44	5.69	7.12
1975	31.55	5.37	0.31	37.23	0.73	7.99	0.47	9.20	8.05	0.12	7.35	0.36	7.83	7.19
1976	19.15	4.49	0.29	23.93	8.07	7.89	0.80	16.75	7.21	5.25	7.10	0.51	12.87	6.00
1977	-11.50	4.35	0.00	-7.16	-7.86	7.14	0.04	-0.69	8.03	-5.15	6.49	0.06	1.41	7.51
1978	1.06	5.33	0.18	6.57	-9.05	7.90	-0.03	-1.18	8.98	-4.49	7.83	0.14	3.49	8.83
1979	12.31	5.89	0.41	18.61	-9.84	8.86	-0.25	-1.23	10.12	-5.07	9.04	0.12	4.09	10.33
1980	25.77	5.74	0.99	32.50	-14.00	9.97	0.08	-3.95	11.99	-6.81	10.55	0.17	3.91	12.45
1981	-9.73	4.88	-0.08	-4.92	-10.33	11.55	0.64	1.86	13.34	-4.55	12.97	1.03	9.45	13.96
1982	14.76	5.61	1.18	21.55	23.95	13.50	2.91	40.36	10.95	14.23	12.81	2.06	29.10	9.90
1983	17.27	5.04	0.24	22.56	-9.82	10.38	0.09	0.65	11.97	-3.30	10.35	0.35	7.41	11.41
1984	1.40	4.57	0.31	6.27	2.32	11.74	1.42	15.48	11.70	1.22	11.68	1.12	14.02	11.04
1985	26.33	4.72	0.67	31.73	17.84	11.25	1.88	30.97	9.56	9.01	10.29	1.04	20.33	8.55
1986	14.62	3.92	0.13	18.67	14.99	8.98	0.56	24.53	7.89	6.99	7.72	0.43	15.14	6.85
1987	2.03	3.64	-0.41	5.25	-10.69	7.92	0.06	-2.71	9.20	-4.75	7.47	0.19	2.90	8.32
1988	12.40	3.99	0.22	16.61	0.36	8.97	0.34	9.67	9.19	-2.26	8.24	0.13	6.10	9.17
1989	27.25	4.03	0.40	31.69	8.62	8.81	0.68	18.11	8.16	4.34	8.46	0.49	13.29	7.94
1990	-6.56	3.43	0.03	-3.10	-2.61	8.19	0.61	6.18	8.44	1.02	8.15	0.56	9.73	7.70
1991	26.31	3.76	0.40	30.47	10.10	8.22	0.98	19.30	7.30	7.36	7.43	0.67	15.46	5.97
1992	4.46	2.98	0.17	7.62	0.34	7.26	0.45	8.05	7.26	0.64	6.27	0.28	7.19	6.11
1993	7.06	2.91	0.12	10.08	10.71	7.17	0.35	18.24	6.54	5.56	5.53	0.15	11.24	5.22
1994	-1.54	2.83	0.03	1.32	-14.29	6.59	-0.08	-7.77	7.99	-11.14	6.07	-0.08	-5.14	7.80
1995	34.11	3.04	0.43	37.58	23.04	7.60	1.03	31.67	6.03	9.66	6.69	0.45	16.80	5.38
1996	20.26	2.43	0.26	22.96	-7.37	6.18	0.26	-0.93	6.73	-3.90	5.82	0.18	2.10	6.16
1997	31.01	2.10	0.25	33.36	8.51	6.64	0.71	15.85	6.02	1.95	6.14	0.30	8.38	5.73
1998	26.67	1.67	0.24	28.58	6.89	5.83	0.34	13.06	5.42	4.66	5.29	0.25	10.21	4.68
1999	19.53	1.36	0.15	21.04	-14.35	5.57	-0.19	-8.96	6.82	-7.06	5.30	-0.01	-1.77	6.45
2000	-10.14	1.11	-0.07	-9.10	14.36	6.50	0.62	21.48	5.58	5.94	6.19	0.46	12.59	5.07
2001	-13.04	1.18	-0.03	-11.89	-1.89	5.53	0.06	3.70	5.75	3.23	4.27	0.12	7.62	4.42
2002	-23.37	1.39	-0.13	-22.10	11.69	5.59	0.56	17.84	4.84	8.65	3.98	0.30	12.93	2.61
2003	26.38	1.99	0.31	28.68	-3.36	4.80	0.01	1.45	5.11	-0.48	2.85	0.03	2.40	2.97
2004	8.99	1.76	0.13	10.88	3.26	5.02	0.23	8.51	4.84	-1.07	3.28	0.04	2.25	3.47
2005	3.00	1.84	0.07	4.91	3.02	4.69	0.10	7.81	4.61	-2.58	3.92	0.03	1.36	4.34
2006	13.62	2.01	0.17	15.79	-3.64	4.68	0.15	1.19	4.91	-1.51	4.54	0.11	3.14	4.65
2007	3.53	1.96	0.00	5.49	4.69	4.86	0.33	9.88	4.50	5.33	4.44	0.28	10.05	3.28
2008	-38.49	1.92	-0.43	-37.00	20.50	4.45	0.93	25.87	3.03	9.92	2.96	0.23	13.11	1.26
2009	23.45	2.48	0.53	26.46	-18.25	3.47	-0.12	-14.90	4.58	-4.42	2.01	0.00	-2.40	2.42
2010	12.78	2.02	0.26	15.06	5.89	4.25	0.00	10.14	4.14	5.16	1.92	0.04	7.12	1.70
2011	0.00	2.13	-0.01	2.11	22.62	3.82	0.66	27.10	2.55	7.09	1.64	0.08	8.81	0.74
2012	13.41	2.50	0.10	16.00	0.95	2.46	0.03	3.43	2.46	0.93	0.73	0.01	1.66	0.61
2013	29.60	2.48	0.31	32.39	-15.70	2.88	0.04	-12.78	3.78	-4.68	1.02	-0.01	-3.68	1.49
2014	11.39	2.16	0.14	13.69	20.93	3.41	0.37	24.71	2.46	1.35	1.63	0.02	3.00	1.55
2015	-0.73	2.10	0.01	1.38	-3.11	2.47	-0.02	-0.65	2.68	0.29	1.51	0.00	1.79	1.69

Annual Total Returns

Exhibit 2.5 shows annual total returns for the six basic asset classes and inflation for the full 90-year period. This exhibit can be used to compare the performance of each asset class for the same year. Monthly total returns for large-cap stocks, small-cap stocks, long-term corporate bonds, long-term government bonds, intermediate-term government bonds, Treasury bills, and inflation rates are presented in Appendices A-1, A-4, A-5, A-6, A-10, A-14, and A-15, respectively.

Rolling-Period Returns

Exhibits 2.6, 2.7, and 2.8 show the compound annual total returns of the six basic classes and inflation for five-, 10-, and 20-year holding periods. Often, these calculations are referred to as rolling period returns because they are obtained by rolling a data window of fixed length along each time series. They are useful for examining the behavior of returns for holding periods similar to those actually experienced by investors and show the effects of time diversification. Holding assets for long periods of time has the effect of lowering the risk of experiencing a loss in asset value.

The highest and lowest returns on the SBBI basic series, expressed as annual rates, are shown for one-, five-, 10-, and 20-year holding periods in Exhibit 2.9. This exhibit also shows the number of times that an asset had a positive return, and the number of times that an asset's return was the highest among all those studied. The number of times positive (or times highest) is compared to the total number of observations – that is, 90 annual, 86 overlapping five-year, 81 overlapping 10-year, and 71 overlapping 20-year holding periods.

Portfolio Performance

A portfolio is a group of assets, such as stocks and bonds that are held by an investor. Because stocks, bonds, and cash generally do not react identically to the same economic or market stimulus, combining these assets can often produce a better risk-adjusted return. There were plenty of years in which stock returns were up at times when bond returns were down, and vice versa, according to the data in Exhibit 2.4. These offsetting movements can assist in reducing portfolio volatility. Some recent examples include the years 2000 through 2002: Large-cap stocks posted returns of -9.10%, -11.89%, and -22.10%, respectively, while long-term government bonds posted positive returns of 21.48%, 3.70%, and 17.84%, respectively. This illustrates the low correlation of stocks and bonds; that is, they tend to move independently of each other. (See Chapter 6 for a more detailed discussion of correlation.)

While bond prices tend to fluctuate less than stock prices, they are still subject to price movement. Investing in a mix of asset classes, such as stocks, bonds, and Treasury bills (cash), may protect a portfolio from major downswings in a single asset class. One of the main advantages of diversification is that it makes investors less dependent on the performance of any single asset class.

Rolling Period Portfolio Returns

While Exhibit 2.9 displays the performance of single asset classes over various rolling periods, Exhibits 2.10 through 2.14 show the performance of different portfolio allocations over various periods. Once again, Exhibit 2.10 outlines the number of times that each portfolio has a positive return, and the number of times that each portfolio's return was the highest among all those studied. Maximum and minimum returns are also shown. The portfolios presented throughout the analysis are rebalanced so that the allocations remain the same. The exception is Exhibit 2.12, which contains portfolios that were never rebalanced; this is for comparison purposes. The data assumes reinvestment of all income and does not account for taxes or transaction costs.

The one-year holding period results in Exhibit 2.10 make it clear that 1933 was a great year for large-cap stocks, while long-term government bonds shined in 1982. The 30% stock and 70% bond portfolio posted positive returns during all but one-year for five-year holding periods, while the 70% stock and 30% bond portfolio was the highest returning portfolio for one-year during the five-year holding periods. The 10-year holding period analysis shows that the 100% stock and the 100% bond portfolios were the only ones that posted negative 10-year holding period returns. For the 20-year period, there were no negative holding period returns. The effects of time diversification are clearly evident. When portfolios, as well as individual asset classes, are held for longer periods of time, the possibility of losing portfolio value is lowered.

Exhibit 2.5: Basic Series
Annual Total Returns (%)

Year	Large-Cap Stocks	Small-Cap Stocks	Long-term Corp Bonds	Long-term Gov't Bonds	Inter-term Gov't Bonds	U.S. Treasury Bills	Inflation
1926	11.62	0.28	7.37	7.77	5.38	3.27	-1.49
1927	37.49	22.10	7.44	8.93	4.52	3.12	-2.08
1928	43.61	39.69	2.84	0.10	0.92	3.56	-0.97
1929	-8.42	-51.36	3.27	3.42	6.01	4.75	0.20
1930	-24.90	-38.15	7.98	4.66	6.72	2.41	-6.03
1931	-43.34	-49.75	-1.85	-5.31	-2.32	1.07	-9.52
1932	-8.19	-5.39	10.82	16.84	8.81	0.96	-10.30
1933	53.99	142.87	10.38	-0.07	1.83	0.30	0.51
1934	-1.44	24.22	13.84	10.03	9.00	0.16	2.03
1935	47.67	40.19	9.61	4.98	7.01	0.17	2.99
1936	33.92	64.80	6.74	7.52	3.06	0.18	1.21
1937	-35.03	-58.01	2.75	0.23	1.56	0.31	3.10
1938	31.12	32.80	6.13	5.53	6.23	-0.02	-2.78
1939	-0.41	0.35	3.97	5.94	4.52	0.02	-0.48
1940	-9.78	-5.16	3.39	6.09	2.96	0.00	0.96
1941	-11.59	-9.00	2.73	0.93	0.50	0.06	9.72
1942	20.34	44.51	2.60	3.22	1.94	0.27	9.29
1943	25.90	88.37	2.83	2.08	2.81	0.35	3.16
1944	19.75	53.72	4.73	2.81	1.80	0.33	2.11
1945	36.44	73.61	4.08	10.73	2.22	0.33	2.25
1946	-8.07	-11.63	1.72	-0.10	1.00	0.35	18.16
1947	5.71	0.92	-2.34	-2.62	0.91	0.50	9.01
1948	5.50	-2.11	4.14	3.40	1.85	0.81	2.71
1949	18.79	19.75	3.31	6.45	2.32	1.10	-1.80
1950	31.71	38.75	2.12	0.06	0.70	1.20	5.79
1951	24.02	7.80	-2.69	-3.93	0.36	1.49	5.87
1952	18.37	3.03	3.52	1.16	1.63	1.66	0.88
1953	-0.99	-6.49	3.41	3.64	3.23	1.82	0.62
1954	52.62	60.58	5.39	7.19	2.68	0.86	-0.50
1955	31.56	20.44	0.48	-1.29	-0.65	1.57	0.37
1956	6.56	4.28	-6.81	-5.59	-0.42	2.46	2.86
1957	-10.78	-14.57	8.71	7.46	7.84	3.14	3.02
1958	43.36	64.89	-2.22	-6.09	-1.29	1.54	1.76
1959	11.96	16.40	-0.97	-2.26	-0.39	2.95	1.50
1960	0.47	-3.29	9.07	13.78	11.76	2.66	1.48
1961	26.89	32.09	4.82	0.97	1.85	2.13	0.67
1962	-8.73	-11.90	7.95	6.89	5.56	2.73	1.22
1963	22.80	23.57	2.19	1.21	1.64	3.12	1.65
1964	16.48	23.52	4.77	3.51	4.04	3.54	1.19
1965	12.45	41.75	-0.46	0.71	1.02	3.93	1.92
1966	-10.06	-7.01	0.20	3.65	4.69	4.76	3.35
1967	23.98	83.57	-4.95	-9.18	1.01	4.21	3.04
1968	11.06	35.97	2.57	-0.26	4.54	5.21	4.72
1969	-8.50	-25.05	-8.09	-5.07	-0.74	6.58	6.11
1970	3.86	-17.43	18.37	12.11	16.86	6.52	5.49
1971	14.30	16.50	11.01	13.23	8.72	4.39	3.36
1972	18.99	4.43	7.26	5.69	5.16	3.84	3.41
1973	-14.69	-30.90	1.14	-1.11	4.61	6.93	8.80
1974	-26.47	-19.95	-3.06	4.35	5.69	8.00	12.20

Exhibit 2.5: Basic Series
Annual Total Returns (%)

Year	Large-Cap Stocks	Small-Cap Stocks	Long-term Corp Bonds	Long-term Gov't Bonds	Inter-term Gov't Bonds	U.S. Treasury Bills	Inflation
1975	37.23	52.82	14.64	9.20	7.83	5.80	7.01
1976	23.93	57.38	18.65	16.75	12.87	5.08	4.81
1977	-7.16	25.38	1.71	-0.69	1.41	5.12	6.77
1978	6.57	23.46	-0.07	-1.18	3.49	7.18	9.03
1979	18.61	43.46	-4.18	-1.23	4.09	10.38	13.31
1980	32.50	39.88	-2.76	-3.95	3.91	11.24	12.40
1981	-4.92	13.88	-1.24	1.86	9.45	14.71	8.94
1982	21.55	28.01	42.56	40.36	29.10	10.54	3.87
1983	22.56	39.67	6.26	0.65	7.41	8.80	3.80
1984	6.27	-6.67	16.86	15.48	14.02	9.85	3.95
1985	31.73	24.66	30.09	30.97	20.33	7.72	3.77
1986	18.67	6.85	19.85	24.53	15.14	6.16	1.13
1987	5.25	-9.30	-0.27	-2.71	2.90	5.47	4.41
1988	16.61	22.87	10.70	9.67	6.10	6.35	4.42
1989	31.69	10.18	16.23	18.11	13.29	8.37	4.65
1990	-3.10	-21.56	6.78	6.18	9.73	7.81	6.11
1991	30.47	44.63	19.89	19.30	15.46	5.60	3.06
1992	7.62	23.35	9.39	8.05	7.19	3.51	2.90
1993	10.08	20.98	13.19	18.24	11.24	2.90	2.75
1994	1.32	3.11	-5.76	-7.77	-5.14	3.90	2.67
1995	37.58	34.46	27.20	31.67	16.80	5.60	2.54
1996	22.96	17.62	1.40	-0.93	2.10	5.21	3.32
1997	33.36	22.78	12.95	15.85	8.38	5.26	1.70
1998	28.58	-7.31	10.76	13.06	10.21	4.86	1.61
1999	21.04	29.79	-7.45	-8.96	-1.77	4.68	2.68
2000	-9.10	-3.59	12.87	21.48	12.59	5.89	3.39
2001	-11.89	22.77	10.65	3.70	7.62	3.83	1.55
2002	-22.10	-13.28	16.33	17.84	12.93	1.65	2.38
2003	28.68	60.70	5.27	1.45	2.40	1.02	1.88
2004	10.88	18.39	8.72	8.51	2.25	1.20	3.26
2005	4.91	5.69	5.87	7.81	1.36	2.98	3.42
2006	15.79	16.17	3.24	1.19	3.14	4.80	2.54
2007	5.49	-5.22	2.60	9.88	10.05	4.66	4.08
2008	-37.00	-36.72	8.78	25.87	13.11	1.60	0.09
2009	26.46	28.09	3.02	-14.90	-2.40	0.10	2.72
2010	15.06	31.26	12.44	10.14	7.12	0.12	1.50
2011	2.11	-3.26	17.95	27.10	8.81	0.04	2.96
2012	16.00	18.24	10.68	3.43	1.66	0.06	1.74
2013	32.39	45.07	-7.07	-12.78	-3.68	0.02	1.51
2014	13.69	2.92	17.28	24.71	3.00	0.02	0.76
2015	1.38	-3.60	-1.02	-0.65	1.79	0.02	1.18

Exhibit 2.6: Basic Series
Compound Annual Returns for 5-Year Holding Periods (% per annum)

5-Year Period	Large-Cap Stocks	Small-Cap Stocks	Long-term Corp Bonds	Long-term Gov't Bonds	Inter-term Gov't Bonds	U.S. Treasury Bills	Inflation
1926–1930	8.68	-12.44	5.76	4.93	4.69	3.42	-2.10
1927–1931	-5.10	-23.74	3.87	2.25	3.11	2.98	-3.75
1928–1932	-12.47	-27.54	4.52	3.69	3.95	2.54	-5.42
1929–1933	-11.24	-19.06	6.01	3.66	4.13	1.89	-5.14
1930–1934	-9.93	-2.37	8.09	4.95	4.71	0.98	-4.80
1931–1935	3.12	14.99	8.42	5.01	4.77	0.53	-3.04
1932–1936	22.47	45.83	10.26	7.71	5.90	0.35	-0.84
1933–1937	14.29	23.96	8.60	4.46	4.45	0.22	1.96
1934–1938	10.67	9.86	7.75	5.61	5.33	0.16	1.29
1935–1939	10.91	5.27	5.81	4.81	4.46	0.13	0.78
1936–1940	0.50	-2.64	4.59	5.03	3.65	0.10	0.38
1937–1941	-7.51	-13.55	3.79	3.71	3.13	0.08	2.02
1938–1942	4.62	10.70	3.76	4.32	3.21	0.07	3.21
1939–1943	3.77	18.71	3.10	3.63	2.54	0.14	4.44
1940–1944	7.67	29.28	3.25	3.01	2.00	0.20	4.98
1941–1945	16.96	45.90	3.39	3.90	1.85	0.27	5.25
1942–1946	17.87	45.05	3.19	3.69	1.95	0.33	6.82
1943–1947	14.86	35.00	2.17	2.49	1.75	0.37	6.77
1944–1948	10.87	18.43	2.43	2.75	1.55	0.47	6.67
1945–1949	10.69	12.66	2.15	3.46	1.66	0.62	5.84
1946–1950	9.91	7.72	1.76	1.39	1.36	0.79	6.57
1947–1951	16.70	12.09	0.87	0.60	1.23	1.02	4.25
1948–1952	19.37	12.55	2.05	1.37	1.37	1.25	2.65
1949–1953	17.86	11.53	1.91	1.41	1.64	1.45	2.23
1950–1954	23.92	18.27	2.31	1.55	1.72	1.41	2.50
1951–1955	23.89	14.97	1.98	1.28	1.44	1.48	1.43
1952–1956	20.18	14.21	1.10	0.93	1.28	1.67	0.84
1953–1957	13.58	10.01	2.10	2.15	2.49	1.97	1.27
1954–1958	22.31	23.22	0.96	0.16	1.58	1.91	1.49
1955–1959	14.96	15.54	-0.29	-1.67	0.96	2.33	1.90
1956–1960	8.92	10.58	1.36	1.16	3.37	2.55	2.12
1957–1961	12.79	15.93	3.77	2.53	3.83	2.48	1.68
1958–1962	13.31	16.65	3.63	2.42	3.39	2.40	1.33
1959–1963	9.85	10.11	4.55	3.97	4.00	2.72	1.30
1960–1964	10.73	11.43	5.73	5.17	4.91	2.83	1.24
1961–1965	13.25	20.28	3.82	2.63	2.81	3.09	1.33
1962–1966	5.72	12.13	2.88	3.17	3.38	3.61	1.86
1963–1967	12.39	29.86	0.30	-0.14	2.47	3.91	2.23
1964–1968	10.16	32.37	0.37	-0.43	3.04	4.33	2.84
1965–1969	4.96	19.78	-2.22	-2.14	2.08	4.93	3.82
1966–1970	3.31	7.51	1.23	-0.02	5.10	5.45	4.54
1967–1971	8.38	12.47	3.32	1.77	5.90	5.38	4.54
1968–1972	7.50	0.47	5.85	4.90	6.75	5.30	4.61
1969–1973	1.97	-12.25	5.55	4.72	6.77	5.65	5.41
1970–1974	-2.39	-11.09	6.68	6.72	8.11	5.93	6.60
1971–1975	3.21	0.56	6.00	6.16	6.39	5.78	6.90
1972–1976	4.89	6.80	7.42	6.82	7.19	5.92	7.20
1973–1977	-0.19	10.77	6.29	5.50	6.41	6.18	7.89
1974–1978	4.35	24.41	6.03	5.48	6.18	6.23	7.94
1975–1979	14.82	39.80	5.78	4.33	5.86	6.69	8.15
1976–1980	14.02	37.35	2.36	1.68	5.08	7.77	9.21
1977–1981	8.13	28.75	-1.33	-1.05	4.44	9.67	10.06
1978–1982	14.12	29.28	5.57	6.03	9.60	10.78	9.46

Exhibit 2.6: Basic Series
Compound Annual Returns for 5-Year Holding Periods (% per annum)

5-Year Period	Large-Cap Stocks	Small-Cap Stocks	Long-term Corp Bonds	Long-term Gov't Bonds	Inter-term Gov't Bonds	U.S. Treasury Bills	Inflation
1979–1983	17.35	32.51	6.87	6.42	10.42	11.12	8.39
1980–1984	14.80	21.59	11.20	9.80	12.45	11.01	6.53
1981–1985	14.67	18.82	17.86	16.83	15.80	10.30	4.85
1982–1986	19.87	17.32	22.51	21.62	16.98	8.60	3.30
1983–1987	16.47	9.51	14.06	13.02	11.79	7.59	3.41
1984–1988	15.31	6.74	15.00	14.98	11.52	7.10	3.53
1985–1989	20.36	10.34	14.88	15.50	11.38	6.81	3.67
1986–1990	13.19	0.58	10.43	10.75	9.34	6.83	4.13
1987–1991	15.36	6.86	10.44	9.81	9.40	6.71	4.52
1988–1992	15.88	13.63	12.50	12.14	10.30	6.31	4.22
1989–1993	14.55	13.28	13.00	13.84	11.35	5.61	3.89
1990–1994	8.70	11.79	8.36	8.34	7.46	4.73	3.49
1991–1995	16.59	24.51	12.22	13.10	8.81	4.29	2.79
1992–1996	15.22	19.47	8.52	8.98	6.17	4.22	2.84
1993–1997	20.27	19.35	9.22	10.51	6.40	4.57	2.60
1994–1998	24.06	13.16	8.74	9.52	6.20	4.96	2.37
1995–1999	28.56	18.49	8.35	9.24	6.95	5.12	2.37
1996–2000	18.33	10.87	5.79	7.49	6.17	5.18	2.54
1997–2001	10.70	11.82	7.66	8.48	7.29	4.90	2.18
1998–2002	-0.59	4.31	8.29	8.85	8.18	4.17	2.32
1999–2003	-0.57	16.44	7.20	6.51	6.60	3.40	2.37
2000–2004	-2.30	14.32	10.70	10.32	7.46	2.70	2.49
2001–2005	0.54	16.44	9.30	7.72	5.22	2.13	2.49
2002–2006	6.19	15.16	7.79	7.19	4.33	2.32	2.69
2003–2007	12.83	17.23	5.12	5.70	3.79	2.92	3.03
2004–2008	-2.19	-2.71	5.81	10.36	5.88	3.04	2.67
2005–2009	0.42	-1.16	4.68	5.13	4.90	2.81	2.56
2006–2010	2.29	3.21	5.94	5.58	6.06	2.23	2.18
2007–2011	-0.25	-0.50	8.80	10.50	7.20	1.29	2.26
2008–2012	1.66	4.00	10.47	9.17	5.52	0.38	1.80
2009–2013	17.94	22.78	7.04	1.45	2.18	0.07	2.08
2010–2014	15.45	17.52	9.85	9.51	3.29	0.05	1.69
2011–2015	12.57	10.49	7.08	7.27	2.24	0.03	1.63

Exhibit 2.7: Basic Series
Compound Annual Returns for 10-Year Holding Periods (% per annum)

10-Year Period	Large-Cap Stocks	Small-Cap Stocks	Long-term Corp Bonds	Long-term Gov't Bonds	Inter-term Gov't Bonds	U.S. Treasury Bills	Inflation
1926–1935	5.86	0.34	7.08	4.97	4.73	1.97	-2.57
1927–1936	7.81	5.45	7.02	4.95	4.50	1.66	-2.30
1928–1937	0.02	-5.22	6.54	4.08	4.20	1.37	-1.80
1929–1938	-0.89	-5.70	6.88	4.63	4.73	1.02	-1.98
1930–1939	-0.05	1.38	6.95	4.88	4.58	0.55	-2.05
1931–1940	1.80	5.81	6.49	5.02	4.21	0.32	-1.34
1932–1941	6.43	12.28	6.97	5.69	4.51	0.21	0.58
1933–1942	9.35	17.14	6.15	4.39	3.83	0.15	2.59
1934–1943	7.17	14.20	5.40	4.62	3.93	0.15	2.85
1935–1944	9.28	16.66	4.53	3.91	3.22	0.17	2.86
1936–1945	8.42	19.18	3.99	4.46	2.75	0.18	2.79
1937–1946	4.41	11.98	3.49	3.70	2.54	0.20	4.39
1938–1947	9.62	22.24	2.96	3.40	2.48	0.22	4.97
1939–1948	7.26	18.57	2.77	3.19	2.04	0.30	5.55
1940–1949	9.17	20.69	2.70	3.24	1.83	0.41	5.41
1941–1950	13.38	25.37	2.57	2.64	1.60	0.53	5.91
1942–1951	17.28	27.51	2.02	2.13	1.59	0.67	5.53
1943–1952	17.09	23.27	2.11	1.93	1.56	0.81	4.69
1944–1953	14.31	14.93	2.17	2.08	1.60	0.96	4.43
1945–1954	17.12	15.43	2.23	2.51	1.69	1.01	4.16
1946–1955	16.69	11.29	1.87	1.33	1.40	1.14	3.96
1947–1956	18.43	13.14	0.98	0.76	1.25	1.35	2.53
1948–1957	16.44	11.27	2.07	1.76	1.93	1.61	1.96
1949–1958	20.06	17.23	1.43	0.79	1.61	1.68	1.86
1950–1959	19.35	16.90	1.00	-0.07	1.34	1.87	2.20
1951–1960	16.16	12.75	1.67	1.22	2.40	2.01	1.77
1952–1961	16.43	15.07	2.43	1.73	2.55	2.08	1.26
1953–1962	13.44	13.28	2.86	2.29	2.94	2.19	1.30
1954–1963	15.91	16.48	2.74	2.05	2.78	2.31	1.40
1955–1964	12.82	13.47	2.68	1.69	2.92	2.58	1.57
1956–1965	11.06	15.33	2.58	1.89	3.09	2.82	1.73
1957–1966	9.20	14.02	3.33	2.85	3.60	3.05	1.77
1958–1967	12.85	23.08	1.95	1.13	2.93	3.15	1.78
1959–1968	10.00	20.73	2.44	1.75	3.52	3.52	2.07
1960–1969	7.81	15.53	1.68	1.45	3.48	3.88	2.52
1961–1970	8.16	13.72	2.51	1.30	3.95	4.26	2.92
1962–1971	7.04	12.30	3.10	2.47	4.63	4.49	3.19
1963–1972	9.92	14.22	3.04	2.35	4.59	4.60	3.41
1964–1973	5.99	7.77	2.93	2.11	4.89	4.98	4.12
1965–1974	1.22	3.20	2.13	2.20	5.05	5.43	5.20
1966–1975	3.26	3.98	3.59	3.03	5.74	5.62	5.71
1967–1976	6.62	9.60	5.35	4.26	6.54	5.65	5.86
1968–1977	3.58	5.50	6.07	5.20	6.58	5.74	6.24
1969–1978	3.15	4.48	5.79	5.10	6.47	5.94	6.67
1970–1979	5.87	11.49	6.23	5.52	6.98	6.31	7.37
1971–1980	8.48	17.53	4.16	3.90	5.73	6.77	8.05
1972–1981	6.50	17.26	2.95	2.81	5.80	7.78	8.62
1973–1982	6.72	19.67	5.93	5.76	8.00	8.46	8.67
1974–1983	10.66	28.40	6.45	5.95	8.28	8.65	8.16
1975–1984	14.81	30.38	8.46	7.03	9.11	8.83	7.34
1976–1985	14.34	27.75	9.84	8.99	10.31	9.03	7.01
1977–1986	13.85	22.90	9.95	9.70	10.53	9.14	6.63
1978–1987	15.29	18.99	9.73	9.47	10.69	9.17	6.39

Exhibit 2.7: Basic Series
Compound Annual Returns for 10-Year Holding Periods (% per annum)

10-Year Period	Large-Cap Stocks	Small-Cap Stocks	Long-term Corp Bonds	Long-term Gov't Bonds	Inter-term Gov't Bonds	U.S. Treasury Bills	Inflation
1979–1988	16.33	18.93	10.86	10.62	10.97	9.09	5.93
1980–1989	17.55	15.83	13.02	12.62	11.91	8.89	5.09
1981–1990	13.93	9.32	14.09	13.75	12.52	8.55	4.49
1982–1991	17.59	11.97	16.32	15.56	13.13	7.65	3.91
1983–1992	16.17	11.55	13.28	12.58	11.04	6.95	3.81
1984–1993	14.93	9.96	14.00	14.41	11.43	6.35	3.71
1985–1994	14.38	11.06	11.57	11.86	9.40	5.76	3.58
1986–1995	14.88	11.90	11.32	11.92	9.08	5.55	3.46
1987–1996	15.29	12.98	9.48	9.39	7.77	5.46	3.68
1988–1997	18.05	16.46	10.85	11.32	8.33	5.44	3.41
1989–1998	19.21	13.22	10.85	11.66	8.74	5.29	3.12
1990–1999	18.21	15.09	8.36	8.79	7.20	4.92	2.93
1991–2000	17.46	17.49	8.96	10.26	7.48	4.74	2.66
1992–2001	12.94	15.58	8.09	8.73	6.73	4.56	2.51
1993–2002	9.34	11.58	8.75	9.67	7.29	4.37	2.46
1994–2003	11.07	14.79	7.97	8.01	6.40	4.18	2.37
1995–2004	12.07	16.39	9.52	9.78	7.20	3.90	2.43
1996–2005	9.07	13.62	7.53	7.60	5.69	3.64	2.52
1997–2006	8.42	13.48	7.72	7.83	5.80	3.60	2.44
1998–2007	5.91	10.58	6.69	7.26	5.96	3.54	2.68
1999–2008	-1.38	6.44	6.50	8.42	6.24	3.22	2.52
2000–2009	-0.95	6.30	7.65	7.69	6.17	2.76	2.52
2001–2010	1.41	9.63	7.61	6.64	5.64	2.18	2.34
2002–2011	2.92	7.05	8.30	8.83	5.76	1.80	2.48
2003–2012	7.10	10.42	7.76	7.42	4.65	1.64	2.41
2004–2013	7.41	9.29	6.42	5.81	4.01	1.54	2.38
2005–2014	7.67	7.77	7.23	7.30	4.09	1.42	2.12
2006–2015	7.31	6.79	6.51	6.42	4.13	1.13	1.90

Exhibit 2.8: Basic Series
Compound Annual Returns for 20-Year Holding Periods (% per annum)

20-Year Period	Large-Cap Stocks	Small-Cap Stocks	Long-term Corp Bonds	Long-term Gov't Bonds	Inter-term Gov't Bonds	U.S. Treasury Bills	Inflation
1926–1945	7.13	9.36	5.52	4.72	3.73	1.07	0.07
1927–1946	6.10	8.67	5.24	4.32	3.51	0.93	0.99
1928–1947	4.71	7.64	4.74	3.74	3.33	0.80	1.53
1929–1948	3.11	5.74	4.80	3.91	3.38	0.66	1.72
1930–1949	4.46	10.61	4.80	4.06	3.20	0.48	1.61
1931–1950	7.43	15.17	4.51	3.82	2.90	0.42	2.22
1932–1951	11.72	19.65	4.47	3.90	3.04	0.44	3.02
1933–1952	13.15	20.16	4.11	3.15	2.69	0.48	3.63
1934–1953	10.68	14.56	3.77	3.34	2.76	0.55	3.64
1935–1954	13.13	16.04	3.37	3.20	2.45	0.59	3.51
1936–1955	12.48	15.17	2.92	2.89	2.07	0.66	3.37
1937–1956	11.20	12.56	2.23	2.22	1.90	0.77	3.46
1938–1957	12.98	16.63	2.52	2.58	2.20	0.91	3.45
1939–1958	13.48	17.90	2.10	1.98	1.83	0.99	3.69
1940–1959	14.15	18.78	1.85	1.57	1.58	1.14	3.79
1941–1960	14.76	18.89	2.12	1.93	2.00	1.27	3.82
1942–1961	16.86	21.13	2.22	1.93	2.07	1.37	3.37
1943–1962	15.25	18.17	2.48	2.11	2.25	1.50	2.98
1944–1963	15.11	15.70	2.45	2.06	2.19	1.63	2.90
1945–1964	14.95	14.44	2.45	2.10	2.30	1.79	2.86
1946–1965	13.84	13.29	2.23	1.61	2.24	1.97	2.84
1947–1966	13.72	13.58	2.15	1.80	2.42	2.19	2.15
1948–1967	14.63	17.03	2.01	1.45	2.43	2.38	1.87
1949–1968	14.92	18.97	1.93	1.26	2.56	2.60	1.96
1950–1969	13.43	16.21	1.34	0.69	2.41	2.87	2.36
1951–1970	12.09	13.23	2.09	1.26	3.17	3.13	2.35
1952–1971	11.64	13.67	2.77	2.10	3.58	3.28	2.22
1953–1972	11.67	13.75	2.95	2.32	3.76	3.39	2.35
1954–1973	10.84	12.04	2.83	2.08	3.83	3.64	2.75
1955–1974	6.86	8.21	2.41	1.94	3.98	4.00	3.37
1956–1975	7.09	9.51	3.08	2.46	4.41	4.21	3.70
1957–1976	7.90	11.78	4.34	3.55	5.06	4.34	3.80
1958–1977	8.12	13.95	3.99	3.15	4.74	4.44	3.98
1959–1978	6.52	12.31	4.10	3.41	4.99	4.72	4.34
1960–1979	6.83	13.49	3.93	3.46	5.22	5.09	4.92
1961–1980	8.32	15.61	3.34	2.59	4.84	5.51	5.46
1962–1981	6.77	14.75	3.03	2.64	5.21	6.12	5.87
1963–1982	8.31	16.92	4.47	4.04	6.28	6.51	6.01
1964–1983	8.30	17.63	4.68	4.01	6.57	6.80	6.12
1965–1984	7.80	16.00	5.25	4.58	7.06	7.12	6.26
1966–1985	8.66	15.25	6.67	5.97	8.00	7.31	6.36
1967–1986	10.18	16.06	7.63	6.94	8.52	7.38	6.24
1968–1987	9.28	12.04	7.88	7.31	8.62	7.44	6.31
1969–1988	9.54	11.47	8.30	7.82	8.70	7.50	6.30
1970–1989	11.56	13.64	9.58	9.01	9.42	7.59	6.22
1971–1990	11.17	13.35	9.01	8.71	9.08	7.66	6.26
1972–1991	11.91	14.58	9.43	9.00	9.40	7.72	6.24
1973–1992	11.35	15.54	9.54	9.12	9.51	7.70	6.21
1974–1993	12.78	18.82	10.16	10.10	9.85	7.49	5.91
1975–1994	14.60	20.33	10.00	9.42	9.25	7.29	5.44
1976–1995	14.61	19.57	10.58	10.45	9.69	7.28	5.22
1977–1996	14.57	17.84	9.71	9.54	9.14	7.28	5.14

Exhibit 2.8: Basic Series

Compound Annual Returns for 20-Year Holding Periods (% per annum)

20-Year Period	Large-Cap Stocks	Small-Cap Stocks	Long-term Corp Bonds	Long-term Gov't Bonds	Inter-term Gov't Bonds	U.S. Treasury Bills	Inflation
1978–1997	16.66	17.71	10.29	10.39	9.51	7.29	4.89
1979–1998	17.76	16.04	10.86	11.14	9.85	7.17	4.52
1980–1999	17.88	15.46	10.66	10.69	9.53	6.89	4.00
1981–2000	15.68	13.33	11.49	11.99	9.97	6.62	3.57
1982–2001	15.24	13.76	12.13	12.09	9.88	6.09	3.21
1983–2002	12.71	11.57	10.99	11.12	9.15	5.65	3.13
1984–2003	12.98	12.35	10.94	11.16	8.89	5.26	3.04
1985–2004	13.22	13.69	10.54	10.82	8.30	4.83	3.00
1986–2005	11.94	12.76	9.41	9.74	7.37	4.59	2.98
1987–2006	11.80	13.23	8.60	8.61	6.78	4.53	3.06
1988–2007	11.82	13.48	8.75	9.27	7.14	4.49	3.04
1989–2008	8.43	9.78	8.65	10.03	7.48	4.25	2.82
1990–2009	8.21	10.61	8.00	8.24	6.69	3.83	2.73
1991–2010	9.14	13.49	8.28	8.44	6.56	3.45	2.50
1992–2011	7.81	11.23	8.19	8.78	6.24	3.17	2.49
1993–2012	8.22	11.00	8.25	8.54	5.96	3.00	2.44
1994–2013	9.22	12.01	7.19	6.90	5.20	2.85	2.37
1995–2014	9.85	12.00	8.37	8.53	5.63	2.66	2.28
1996–2015	8.19	10.15	7.02	7.01	4.91	2.38	2.21

Exhibit 2.9: Basic Series

Maximum and Minimum Values of Compound Returns (% per annum) for 1-, 5-, 10-, and 20-Year Holding Periods Using Data From 1926–2015

Annual Returns

Series	Maximum Return	Year	Minimum Return	Year	Times Positive (Out of 90 Years)	Times Highest Returning Asset
Large-Cap Stocks	53.99	1933	-43.34	1931	66	16
Small-Cap Stocks	142.87	1933	-58.01	1937	62	40
Long-term Corp Bonds	42.56	1982	-8.09	1969	71	6
Long-term Gov't Bonds	40.36	1982	-14.90	2009	66	12
Inter-term Gov't Bonds	29.10	1982	-5.14	1994	80	4
U.S. Treasury Bills	14.71	1981	-0.02	1938	89	6
Inflation	18.16	1946	-10.30	1932	80	6

5-Year Rolling Period Returns

Series	Maximum Return	5-year Period Ending	Minimum Return	5-year Period Ending	Times Positive (Out of 86 Periods)	Times Highest Returning Asset
Large-Cap Stocks	28.56	1999	-12.47	1932	74	24
Small-Cap Stocks	45.90	1945	-27.54	1932	74	45
Long-term Corp Bonds	22.51	1986	-2.22	1969	83	8
Long-term Gov't Bonds	21.62	1986	-2.14	1969	80	5
Inter-term Gov't Bonds	16.98	1986	0.96	1959	86	3
U.S. Treasury Bills	11.12	1983	0.03	2015	86	0
Inflation	10.06	1981	-5.42	1932	79	1

10-Year Rolling Period Returns

Series	Maximum Return	10-year Period Ending	Minimum Return	10-year Period Ending	Times Positive (Out of 81 Periods)	Times Highest Returning Asset
Large-Cap Stocks	20.06	1958	-1.38	2008	77	21
Small-Cap Stocks	30.38	1984	-5.70	1938	79	47
Long-term Corp Bonds	16.32	1991	0.98	1956	81	6
Long-term Gov't Bonds	15.56	1991	-0.07	1959	80	3
Inter-term Gov't Bonds	13.13	1991	1.25	1956	81	2
U.S. Treasury Bills	9.17	1987	0.15	1942	81	1
Inflation	8.67	1982	-2.57	1935	75	1

20-Year Rolling Period Returns

Series	Maximum Return	20-year Period Ending	Minimum Return	20-year Period Ending	Times Positive (Out of 71 Periods)	Times Highest Returning Asset
Large-Cap Stocks	17.88	1999	3.11	1948	71	9
Small-Cap Stocks	21.13	1961	5.74	1948	71	61
Long-term Corp Bonds	12.13	2001	1.34	1969	71	0
Long-term Gov't Bonds	12.09	2001	0.69	1969	71	1
Inter-term Gov't Bonds	9.97	2000	1.58	1959	71	0
U.S. Treasury Bills	7.72	1991	0.42	1950	71	0
Inflation	6.36	1985	0.07	1945	71	0

Exhibit 2.10: Portfolios

Maximum and Minimum Values of Compound Returns (% per annum) for 1-, 5-, 10-, and 20-Year Holding Periods Using Data From 1926–2015

Annual Returns

Annual Return	Maximum Return	Year	Minimum Return	Year	Arithmetic Annualized Mean	Times Positive (Out of 90 years)	% Positive in 90 years	Times Highest Returning Portfolio
100% Large Stocks	53.99	1933	-43.34	1931	11.95	66	73	55
90% Stocks/10%	49.03	1933	-39.73	1931	11.32	67	74	0
70% Stocks/30%	38.68	1933	-32.31	1931	10.09	69	77	0
50% Stocks/50%	34.71	1995	-24.70	1931	8.89	71	79	0
30% Stocks/70%	34.72	1982	-16.96	1931	7.72	72	80	0
10% Stocks/90%	38.48	1982	-11.23	2009	6.58	69	77	0
100% LT Gov't Bonds*	40.36	1982	-14.90	2009	6.02	66	73	35

5-Year Rolling Period Returns

Annual Return	Maximum Return	5-year Period Ending	Minimum Return	5-year Period Ending	Arithmetic Annualized Mean	Times Positive (Out of 86 Periods)	% Positive in 86 Periods	Times Highest Returning Portfolio
100% Large Stocks	28.56	1999	-12.47	1932	10.03	74	86	57
90% Stocks/10%	26.62	1999	-10.31	1932	9.75	78	91	1
70% Stocks/30%	22.75	1999	-6.31	1932	9.08	81	94	0
50% Stocks/50%	20.99	1986	-2.77	1932	8.27	81	94	3
30% Stocks/70%	21.30	1986	0.12	1969	7.34	86	100	2
10% Stocks/90%	21.53	1986	-1.38	1969	6.27	83	97	1
100% LT Gov't Bonds	21.62	1986	-2.14	1969	5.69	80	93	22

10-Year Rolling Period Returns

Annual Return	Maximum Return	10-year Period Ending	Minimum Return	10-year Period Ending	Arithmetic Annualized Mean	Times Positive (Out of 81 Periods)	% Positive in 81 Periods	Times Highest Returning Portfolio
100% Large Stocks	20.06	1958	-1.38	2008	10.39	77	95	52
90% Stocks/10%	18.52	1998	-0.25	2008	10.07	80	99	4
70% Stocks/30%	17.31	1991	1.74	1974	9.32	81	100	6
50% Stocks/50%	16.96	1991	1.98	1974	8.44	81	100	7
30% Stocks/70%	16.49	1991	2.13	1974	7.43	81	100	1
10% Stocks/90%	15.90	1991	1.81	1959	6.28	81	100	5
100% LT Gov't Bonds	15.56	1991	-0.07	1959	5.66	80	99	6

20-Year Rolling Period Returns

Annual Return	Maximum Return	20-year Period Ending	Minimum Return	20-year Period Ending	Arithmetic Annualized Mean	Times Positive (out of 71 Periods)	% Positive in 71 Periods	Times Highest Returning Portfolio
100% Large Stocks	17.88	1999	3.11	1948	11.12	71	100	59
90% Stocks/10%	17.28	1999	3.58	1948	10.70	71	100	1
70% Stocks/30%	16.04	1998	4.27	1948	9.77	71	100	5
50% Stocks/50%	14.75	1998	4.60	1948	8.72	71	100	4
30% Stocks/70%	13.38	1998	3.62	1974	7.55	71	100	1
10% Stocks/90%	12.53	2001	1.98	1969	6.27	71	100	0
100% LT Gov't Bonds	12.09	2001	0.69	1969	5.59	71	100	1

*LT = Long-term

Summary Statistics of Portfolio Total Returns

Exhibit 2.11 presents summary statistics of the annual total returns on each portfolio over the 1926–2015 period. The summary statistics presented are geometric mean, arithmetic mean, and standard deviation. As more fixed-income is added to the portfolio, the returns – as well as the standard deviation – tend to decrease. Moving from a 100% stock portfolio to a 70% stock and 30% bond portfolio decreases the geometric mean by 0.8% (10.0% – 9.2%), but also decreases the standard deviation by 5.7% (20.0% – 14.3%). This corresponds to the risk/return trade-off: large-cap stocks have a higher level of risk than long-term government bonds, and are rewarded accordingly.

A seemingly counter-intuitive result in Exhibit 2.11 to the risk/return trade-off is when the return and standard deviation of the 100% bond portfolio is compared to the return and standard deviation of (i) the 10% stock/90% bond portfolio, and (ii) the 30% stock/70% bond portfolio. In these cases, *adding* stocks both *increases* return and *decreases* standard deviation, when compared to a portfolio of 100% bonds. This obviously defies the risk/return trade-off, but highlights the benefits of *diversification*.

A portfolio's asset mix can change from its original percentages as a result of differing returns among the various asset classes held in the portfolio. Thus, asset allocation percentages can *change over time without the investor's input*. For example, if a hypothetical investor invests $1.00 in stocks and $1.00 in bonds, the portfolio that he holds is initially 50% stocks and 50% bonds. If the returns of stocks and bonds over the next year are 20% and 5%, respectively, the "stock" portion of his portfolio has now increased to $1.20, and the "bond" portion of his portfolio has now increased to $1.05. The investor's portfolio mix has also changed: it is now approximately 53.3% stocks ($1.20/($1.20 + $1.05)), and 46.7% bonds ($1.05/($1.20 + $1.05)).

Exhibits 2.11, 2.12, 2.13, and 2.14: Portfolios: Summary Statistics of Annual Returns Always Rebalanced, Never Rebalanced, by Decade, and in the most recent 10-year period (% per annum) (1926–2015)

Exhibit 2.11: Portfolio Summary Statistics of Annual Returns (Always Rebalanced) (% per annum)

Portfolio (Always Rebalanced)	Geometric Mean	Arithmetic Mean	Standard Deviation
100% Large Stocks	10.0	12.0	20.0
90% Stocks/10% Bonds	9.8	11.3	18.0
70% Stocks/30% Bonds	9.1	10.1	14.3
50% Stocks/50% Bonds	8.3	8.9	11.2
30% Stocks/70% Bonds	7.3	7.7	9.3
10% Stocks/90% Bonds	6.2	6.6	9.2
100% Long-term Gov't Bonds	5.6	6.0	10.0

Exhibit 2.12: Portfolio Summary Statistics of Annual Returns (Never Rebalanced) (% per annum)

Portfolio (Never Rebalanced)	Ending Portfolio Large-Cap Stocks (% of Portfolio 12/31/2015)	Ending Portfolio Bonds (% of Portfolio 12/31/2015)	Geometric Mean	Arithmetic Mean	Standard Deviation
100% Large Stocks	100.0	0.0	10.0	12.0	20.0
90% Stocks/10% Bonds	99.7	0.3	9.9	11.6	19.0
70% Stocks/30% Bonds	99.0	1.0	9.6	11.0	17.3
50% Stocks/50% Bonds	97.6	2.4	9.2	10.4	15.6
30% Stocks/70% Bonds	94.6	5.4	8.6	9.5	13.8
10% Stocks/90% Bonds	81.9	18.1	7.5	8.0	11.0
100% Long-term Gov't Bonds	0.0	100.0	5.6	6.0	10.0

Exhibit 2.13: Portfolio Summary Statistics of Annual Returns by Decade (Always Rebalanced) (% per annum)

Portfolio (Always Rebalanced)	1920s[*]	1930s	1940s	1950s	1960s	1970s	1980s	1990s	2000s	2010s[**]
100% Large Stocks	19.2	-0.1	9.2	19.4	7.8	5.9	17.6	18.2	-0.9	13.0
90% Stocks/10% Bonds	18.0	1.0	8.7	17.4	7.2	5.9	17.2	17.3	0.1	12.7
70% Stocks/30% Bonds	15.3	2.8	7.6	13.4	6.1	6.0	16.5	15.5	2.1	11.9
50% Stocks/50% Bonds	12.5	4.1	6.5	9.5	4.8	6.0	15.5	13.6	3.9	10.9
30% Stocks/70% Bonds	9.6	4.8	5.2	5.6	3.5	5.9	14.5	11.7	5.5	9.8
10% Stocks/90% Bonds	6.6	5.0	3.9	1.8	2.1	5.7	13.3	9.8	7.0	8.5
100% Long-term Gov't Bonds	5.0	4.9	3.2	-0.1	1.4	5.5	12.6	8.8	7.7	7.7

[*] Based on the period 1926–1929   [**] Based on the period 2010–2015

Exhibit 2.14: Portfolio Summary Statistics of Annual Returns 2006–2015 (Most Recent Decade) (% per annum)

Portfolio (Always Rebalanced)	2006–2015
100% Large Stocks	7.3
90% Stocks/10% Bonds	7.4
70% Stocks/30% Bonds	7.6
50% Stocks/50% Bonds	7.5
30% Stocks/70% Bonds	7.2
10% Stocks/90% Bonds	6.7
100% Long-term Gov't Bonds	6.4

Exhibit 2.15: Portfolio Annual Total Returns (%)
1926–2015

Year	100% Large Stocks	90/10	70/30	50/50	30/70	10/90	100% Long-term Gov't Bonds
1926	11.62	11.30	10.61	9.87	9.07	8.22	7.77
1927	37.49	34.45	28.49	22.69	17.06	11.60	8.93
1928	43.61	38.74	29.35	20.44	11.98	3.95	0.10
1929	-8.42	-6.76	-3.77	-1.19	0.97	2.71	3.42
1930	-24.90	-22.08	-16.33	-10.46	-4.48	1.59	4.66
1931	-43.34	-39.73	-32.31	-24.70	-16.96	-9.19	-5.31
1932	-8.19	-4.45	2.43	8.28	12.85	15.93	16.84
1933	53.99	49.03	38.68	27.89	16.80	5.56	-0.07
1934	-1.44	-0.13	2.38	4.76	6.99	9.05	10.03
1935	47.67	42.94	33.80	25.06	16.73	8.80	4.98
1936	33.92	31.15	25.69	20.35	15.12	10.02	7.52
1937	-35.03	-31.93	-25.44	-18.58	-11.34	-3.72	0.23
1938	31.12	29.24	24.93	19.99	14.51	8.61	5.53
1939	-0.41	0.65	2.51	4.00	5.09	5.77	5.94
1940	-9.78	-8.04	-4.65	-1.40	1.70	4.66	6.09
1941	-11.59	-10.33	-7.81	-5.30	-2.80	-0.31	0.93
1942	20.34	18.62	15.18	11.75	8.32	4.91	3.22
1943	25.90	23.43	18.54	13.73	9.00	4.37	2.08
1944	19.75	17.98	14.49	11.06	7.71	4.43	2.81
1945	36.44	33.72	28.39	23.18	18.11	13.16	10.73
1946	-8.07	-7.17	-5.42	-3.78	-2.23	-0.78	-0.10
1947	5.71	4.89	3.24	1.58	-0.10	-1.78	-2.62
1948	5.50	5.46	5.26	4.91	4.41	3.77	3.40
1949	18.79	17.55	15.07	12.60	10.13	7.68	6.45
1950	31.71	28.24	21.50	15.04	8.85	2.93	0.06
1951	24.02	20.97	15.05	9.36	3.88	-1.38	-3.93
1952	18.37	16.60	13.10	9.64	6.22	2.83	1.16
1953	-0.99	-0.50	0.47	1.41	2.32	3.21	3.64
1954	52.62	47.50	37.65	28.33	19.51	11.18	7.19
1955	31.56	27.98	21.02	14.32	7.89	1.70	-1.29
1956	6.56	5.42	3.08	0.68	-1.79	-4.31	-5.59
1957	-10.78	-8.99	-5.39	-1.75	1.92	5.61	7.46
1958	43.36	37.57	26.60	16.38	6.89	-1.93	-6.09
1959	11.96	10.49	7.59	4.72	1.90	-0.88	-2.26
1960	0.47	1.83	4.53	7.21	9.86	12.48	13.78
1961	26.89	24.10	18.65	13.38	8.29	3.37	0.97
1962	-8.73	-7.11	-3.90	-0.74	2.37	5.40	6.89
1963	22.80	20.52	16.03	11.66	7.40	3.25	1.21
1964	16.48	15.13	12.46	9.84	7.27	4.75	3.51
1965	12.45	11.26	8.89	6.53	4.19	1.86	0.71
1966	-10.06	-8.72	-6.02	-3.29	-0.53	2.25	3.65
1967	23.98	20.28	13.14	6.36	-0.10	-6.23	-9.18
1968	11.06	9.98	7.79	5.54	3.25	0.92	-0.26
1969	-8.50	-8.08	-7.28	-6.56	-5.91	-5.33	-5.07
1970	3.86	4.78	6.57	8.27	9.87	11.39	12.11
1971	14.30	14.29	14.21	14.04	13.78	13.44	13.23
1972	18.99	17.62	14.90	12.22	9.57	6.97	5.69
1973	-14.69	-13.31	-10.57	-7.84	-5.12	-2.44	-1.11
1974	-26.47	-23.66	-17.87	-11.82	-5.53	1.00	4.35
1975	37.23	34.30	28.51	22.84	17.29	11.86	9.20

Exhibit 2.15: Portfolio Annual Total Returns (%)
1926–2015

Year	100% Large Stocks	90/10	70/30	50/50	30/70	10/90	100% Long-term Gov't Bonds
1976	23.93	23.28	21.93	20.52	19.06	17.54	16.75
1977	-7.16	-6.50	-5.20	-3.90	-2.61	-1.33	-0.69
1978	6.57	5.86	4.40	2.88	1.30	-0.34	-1.18
1979	18.61	16.52	12.40	8.39	4.47	0.64	-1.23
1980	32.50	28.71	21.19	13.80	6.57	-0.49	-3.95
1981	-4.92	-4.16	-2.69	-1.30	0.02	1.27	1.86
1982	21.55	23.42	27.19	30.95	34.72	38.48	40.36
1983	22.56	20.24	15.68	11.25	6.92	2.71	0.65
1984	6.27	7.26	9.18	11.05	12.87	14.62	15.48
1985	31.73	31.72	31.65	31.53	31.35	31.11	30.97
1986	18.67	19.34	20.64	21.86	23.00	24.04	24.53
1987	5.25	5.07	4.24	2.83	0.93	-1.40	-2.71
1988	16.61	15.92	14.55	13.16	11.77	10.37	9.67
1989	31.69	30.37	27.70	25.00	22.26	19.50	18.11
1990	-3.10	-2.15	-0.26	1.61	3.46	5.28	6.18
1991	30.47	29.41	27.24	25.03	22.77	20.47	19.30
1992	7.62	7.69	7.81	7.91	7.98	8.04	8.05
1993	10.08	10.90	12.53	14.16	15.80	17.43	18.24
1994	1.32	0.40	-1.42	-3.25	-5.06	-6.87	-7.77
1995	37.58	37.02	35.88	34.71	33.51	32.29	31.67
1996	22.96	20.41	15.41	10.56	5.85	1.29	-0.93
1997	33.36	31.59	28.06	24.55	21.05	17.58	15.85
1998	28.58	27.33	24.60	21.59	18.33	14.86	13.06
1999	21.04	17.75	11.36	5.23	-0.63	-6.25	-8.96
2000	-9.10	-6.30	-0.53	5.46	11.70	18.16	21.48
2001	-11.89	-10.18	-6.85	-3.64	-0.58	2.32	3.70
2002	-22.10	-18.45	-10.90	-3.04	5.12	13.54	17.84
2003	28.68	25.86	20.27	14.77	9.36	4.06	1.45
2004	10.88	10.70	10.29	9.84	9.34	8.80	8.51
2005	4.91	5.28	5.96	6.58	7.12	7.60	7.81
2006	15.79	14.30	11.33	8.40	5.49	2.61	1.19
2007	5.49	6.03	7.03	7.95	8.79	9.54	9.88
2008	-37.00	-32.14	-21.55	-9.72	3.43	18.02	25.87
2009	26.46	21.86	12.97	4.49	-3.58	-11.23	-14.90
2010	15.06	14.97	14.52	13.70	12.53	11.02	10.14
2011	2.11	4.69	9.81	14.88	19.85	24.72	27.10
2012	16.00	14.86	12.48	10.00	7.43	4.78	3.43
2013	32.39	27.14	17.16	7.85	-0.84	-8.94	-12.78
2014	13.69	14.80	17.03	19.24	21.44	23.62	24.71
2015	1.38	1.35	1.18	0.84	0.36	-0.28	-0.65

Real Estate Investment Trusts (REITs)[2.2]

Real estate properties can be *directly* owned by individuals (i.e., sole proprietorship), partnerships, corporations (either subchapter C or subchapter S), limited liability company (LLCs) or trusts. An equity investment in real estate can also be made *indirectly* by purchasing shares of an entity holding real property interests. Real estate entities exist substantially for the purpose of holding, directly or indirectly, title to or beneficial interest in real property. The value of a real estate entity includes many components, such as land, buildings, furniture, fixtures and equipment, intangible assets, and often the business operation.

A REIT "is a company dedicated to owning, and in most cases, operating income-producing real estate, such as apartments, shopping centers, offices and warehouses. Some REITs also engage in financing real estate."[2.3] REITs can be classified in three broad categories, (i) equity REITs, (ii) mortgage REITs, and (iii) hybrid REITs.[2.4]

Equity REITs mostly own and operate income-producing real estate. They increasingly have become real estate operating companies engaged in a wide range of real estate activities, including leasing, maintenance and development of real property, and tenant services. One major distinction between equity REITs and other real estate companies is that a REIT must acquire and develop its properties primarily to operate them as part of its own portfolio rather than to resell them once they are developed.

Mortgage REITs mostly lend money directly to real estate owners and operators or extend credit indirectly through the acquisition of loans or mortgage-backed securities. Today's mortgage REITs generally extend mortgage credit only on existing properties. Many mortgage REITs also manage their interest rate and credit risks using securitized mortgage investments, dynamic hedging techniques, and other accepted derivative strategies.

Hybrid REITs generally are companies that use the investment strategies of both equity REITs and mortgage REITs.

[2.2]   Data presented throughout this section come from the National Association of Real Estate Investment Trusts® (NAREIT) Equity Index. NAREIT®, the National Association of Real Estate Investment Trusts, is the worldwide representative voice for REITs and publicly traded real estate companies with an interest in U.S. real estate and capital markets. NAREIT's members are REITs and other businesses throughout the world that own, operate, and finance income-producing real estate, as well as those firms and individuals who advise, study, and service those businesses. To learn more, visit: www.reit.com/nareit.

[2.3]   Glossary of REIT Terms, National Association of Real Estate Investment Trusts (NAREIT), available at: https://www.reit.com/investing/reit-basics/reit-faqs/glossary-reit-terms. NAREIT is the worldwide representative voice for REITs and publicly traded real estate companies with an interest in U.S. real estate and capital markets.

[2.4]   Sources: The National Association of Real Estate Investment Trusts® (NAREIT®) website at www.reit.com/nareit; SEC Office of Investor Education and Advocacy "Investor Bulletin: Real Estate Investment Trusts (REITs)," December 2011, available at: http://www.sec.gov/investor/alerts/reits.pdf.

The number of REITs in the U.S. grew dramatically in the last several decades, to 233 at the end of 2015 from 34 in 1971. This growth enabled a broader group of investors to add real estate to their portfolios and enjoy greater liquidity than they would otherwise be able. Exhibit 2.16 below displays the growth in market cap of U.S. REITs between 1971 and 2015.

Exhibit 2.16: All REITs Market Cap ($ Billions)
1971–2015

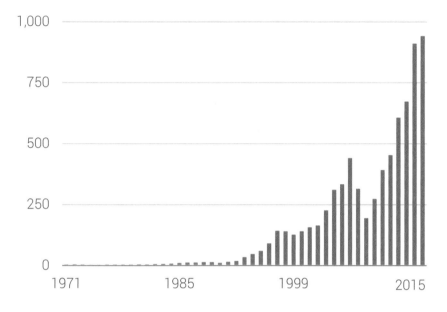

Historical Returns on Equity REITs

Exhibit 2.17 depicts the growth of $1.00 invested in equity REITs as well as in U.S. small- and large-cap stocks, long-term government bonds, Treasury bills, and a hypothetical asset returning the inflation rate over the period from the end of 1971 to the end of 2015. Of the asset classes shown, small-cap stocks accumulated the highest ending wealth. An investment of $1.00 in small-cap stocks at year-end 1971 would have grown to $217.70 by year-end 2015, a compound return of 13.0%. Notice, however, that the same investment in equity REITs would have returned $146.51, a compound return of 12.0%. Equity REITs outperformed all of the remaining asset classes and inflation during the period.

Exhibit 2.17: Wealth Indices of Investments in Equity REITs and Basic Series
Index (Year-end 1971 = $1.00)
1972–2015

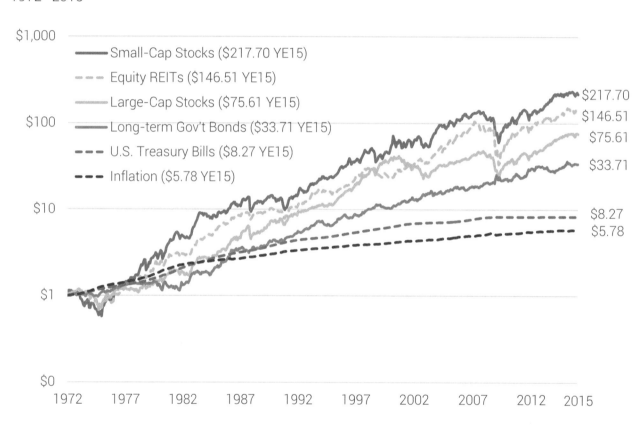

Income Returns on Equity REITs

REITs must pay to shareholders at least 90% of their taxable income each year. As a result, income generated from REITs has proven to be steady and reasonably predictable.

Exhibit 2.18 shows both the income return and capital appreciation return of REITs annually from 1972 to 2015. REITs, similar to equity, can be quite volatile but offer the potential for price appreciation. However, price appreciation is by no means guaranteed (note the large negative price returns of 2007 and 2008). On the other hand, the income produced by REITs has been relatively stable since 1972. Equity REITs posted an average annual income return during that period of 7.4%. The highest annual income return was 21.2% in 1980, while the lowest was 3.6% in 2012.

Exhibit 2.18: Annual Returns on Equity REITs (%)
1972–2015

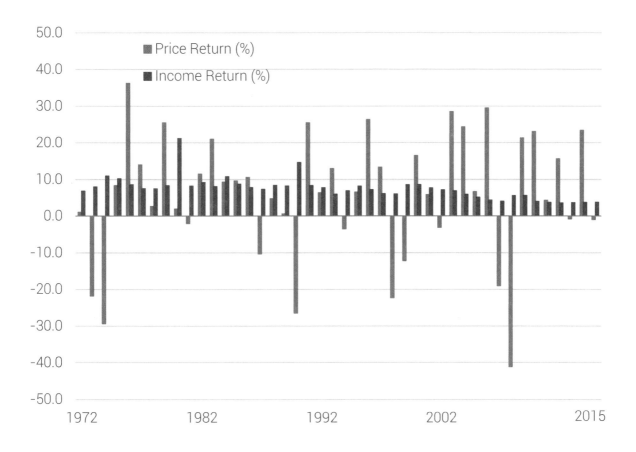

Correlation of U.S. REITs Compared to Other U.S. Asset Classes

Diversification is "spreading a portfolio over many investments to avoid excessive exposure to any one source of risk."[2.5] Put simply, diversification is "not putting all your eggs in one basket." Diversification offers the potential of higher returns for the same level of risk, or lower risk for the same level of return.

REITs have been an attractive investment vehicle to investors because they have traditionally had a relatively low and declining correlation to stocks and bonds. Though the reasons are not quite clear, this relationship changed in the early 2000s, when REITs became increasingly correlated with both stocks and bonds, though correlation levels remain fairly low. A low correlation between assets in a portfolio allows for the possibility of an increase in returns without a corresponding increase in risk, or alternatively, a reduction in risk without a corresponding decrease in return. For example, from 1972 to 2015, a portfolio (rebalanced annually) with a mix of 60% stocks and 40% bonds returned 10.1% annually with a standard deviation of 11.8%. Adding a 13% allocation to REITs to the portfolio increases returns to 10.5% annually, and at the same time decreases standard deviation to 11.6%.

In Exhibit 2.19, the correlation of U.S. REITs and (i) U.S. large company stocks and (ii) long-term U.S. government bonds is shown. Correlation is a measure of the how alternative investments "move" relative to each other, and is thus a measure of potential diversification benefit. The *higher* the correlation (the more investments "move" together), the *less* potential diversification benefit, whereas the *lower* the correlation (the less investments "move" together), the *greater* the potential diversification benefit. The thinking is that by holding a portfolio of assets that do not have high correlation with each other, as some investments decrease in value, others will increase (and vice versa), and thus potentially mitigate overall portfolio losses.

The correlation of U.S. REITs with both stocks and bonds declined during the 1990s, thus increasing the potential diversification benefit. In the immediate years leading up to and following the 2008–2009 financial crisis, the correlation of U.S. REITs with stocks increased significantly, decreasing the potential diversification benefit between these two asset classes. The correlation of U.S. REITs with long-term U.S. government bonds also increased in the immediate years leading up to the 2008–2009 financial crisis, but this trend reversed in the immediate years following the financial crisis.

In the most recent periods (2014 and 2015), both of these trends seem to have reversed, with the correlation of U.S. REITs with stocks decreasing, and the correlation of U.S. REITs with long-term U.S. government bonds increasing. Whether this is a short-term change or the beginning of a longer-term trend remains to be seen.

[2.5] Cara Griffith, "Practical Tax Considerations for Working with REITs," State Tax Notes (October 31, 2011): 315–320, quoting Jennifer Weiss: 316. In 2009, the IRS issued guidance that indicates that the distributions may be in the form of cash or stock in certain instances.

Exhibit 2.19: Rolling 60-Month Correlations of Equity REITs
1972–1976 through 2011–2015

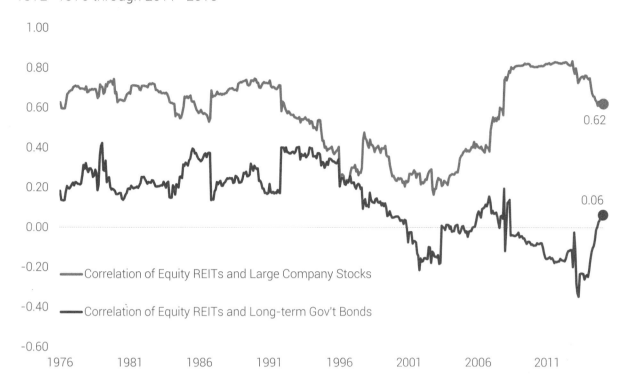

Summary Statistics for Equity REITs and Basic Series

Exhibit 2.20 shows summary statistics of annual total returns for REITs and the SBBI basic series from 1972 to 2015. The summary statistics presented are geometric mean, arithmetic mean, and standard deviation.

While small-cap stocks posted the highest geometric mean over the period analyzed, they also had the highest amount of risk. Equity REITs produced a higher return than large-cap stocks with only slightly higher risk.

Exhibit 2.20: Summary Statistics of Annual Returns (%)
1972–2015

	Geometric Average	Arithmetic Average	Standard Deviation
Equity REITs	12.0	13.6	18.1
Large-Cap Stocks	10.3	11.9	17.7
Small-Cap Stocks	13.0	15.4	22.9
Long-term Corp Bonds	8.4	8.9	10.3
Long-term Gov't Bonds	8.3	9.0	12.4
Inter-term Gov't Bonds	7.1	7.3	6.6
U.S. Treasury Bills	4.9	5.0	3.5
Inflation	4.1	4.1	3.1

Exhibit 2.21 presents annual serial correlations and cross-correlations from 1972 to 2015 for equity REITs and the six basic SBBI asset classes plus inflation. The serial correlation, or the extent to which the return in one period is related to the return in the next period (discussed in greater detail in Chapter 6) of equity REITs suggests no strong pattern; it can best be interpreted as mostly random or unpredictable.

Exhibit 2.21: Serial and Cross-Correlations of Annual Returns
1972–2015

	Equity REITs	Large-Cap Stocks	Small-Cap Stocks	Long-term Corp Bonds	Long-term Gov't Bonds	Inter-term Gov't Bonds	U.S. Treasury Bills	Inflation
Equity REITs	1.00							
Large-Cap Stocks	0.55	1.00						
Small-Cap Stocks	0.74	0.73	1.00					
Long-term Corp Bonds	0.27	0.24	0.10	1.00				
Long-term Gov't Bonds	0.05	0.02	-0.14	0.90	1.00			
Inter-term Gov't Bonds	0.02	0.05	-0.06	0.85	0.87	1.00		
U.S. Treasury Bills	0.00	0.06	0.05	0.05	0.07	0.40	1.00	
Inflation	-0.04	-0.11	0.06	-0.34	-0.28	-0.07	0.68	1.00
Serial Correlation	0.10	0.00	0.01	-0.10	-0.31	0.05	0.88	0.75

In conclusion, equity REITs have historically offered an attractive risk/return trade-off for investors. They have provided a current income stream along with the potential for long-term capital appreciation. The recent increase in correlation of REIT returns with other investments may lead to a decrease in the overall diversification benefit to investors, but they remain an attractive option.

Chapter 3
Description of the Basic Series

This chapter presents the returns for the seven basic SBBI asset classes and describes the construction of these returns. More detail on the construction of some series can be found in the January 1976 *Journal of Business* article, referenced in the Introduction. Annual total returns and capital appreciation returns for each asset class are formed by compounding the monthly returns that appear in Appendix A at the back of this book. Annual income returns are formed by summing the monthly income payments and dividing this sum by the beginning-of-year price. Returns are formed assuming no taxes or transaction costs, except for returns on small capitalization stocks that show the performance of an actual, tax-exempt investment fund including transaction and management costs, starting in 1982.

Large-Cap Stocks

One dollar invested in large-capitalization stocks at year-end 1925, with dividends reinvested, grew to $5,390.43 by year-end 2015; this represents a compound annual growth rate of 10.0% (see Exhibit 3.1). Capital appreciation alone caused $1.00 to grow to $160.18 over the 90-year period, a compound annual growth rate of 5.8%. Annual total returns ranged from a high of 54.0% in 1933 to a low of -43.3% in 1931. The 90-year average annual dividend yield was 4.0%.

Total Returns

From February 1970 to the present, the large-cap stock total return is provided by S&P Dow Jones Indices, which calculates the total return based on the daily reinvestment of dividends on the ex-dividend date. S&P uses closing pricing from stock exchanges in its calculation. Prior to February 1970, the total return for a given month was calculated by summing the capital appreciation return and the income return as described below.

The large-cap stock total return index is based upon the S&P Composite Index. This index is a readily available, carefully constructed, market-capitalization-weighted benchmark of large-cap stock performance. Market-capitalization-weighted means that the weight of each stock in the index, for a given month, is proportionate to its market capitalization (price times the number of shares outstanding) at the beginning of that month. Currently, the S&P Composite includes 500 of the largest stocks (in terms of stock market value) in the U.S.; prior to March 1957 it consisted of 90 of the largest stocks.

Capital Appreciation Return

The capital appreciation component of the large-cap stock total return is the change in the S&P 500 index as reported by S&P Dow Jones Indices from March 1928 to December 2015, and in Standard & Poor's *Trade and Securities Statistics* from January 1926 to February 1928.

Income Return

From February 1970 to December 2015, the income return was calculated as the difference between the total return and the capital appreciation return. From January 1926 to January 1970, quarterly dividends were extracted from rolling yearly dividends reported quarterly in S&P's *Trade and Securities Statistics*, then allocated to months within each quarter using proportions taken from the 1974 actual distribution of monthly dividends within quarters.

Exhibit 3.1: Large Cap Stocks: Total Return and Capital Appreciation Indexes
1926–2015
Index (Year-End 1925 = $1.00)

Small-Cap Stocks

One dollar invested in small-cap stocks at year-end 1925 grew to $26,433.35 by year-end 2015. This represents a compound annual growth rate of 12.0% over the past 90 years. Total annual returns ranged from a high of 142.9% in 1933 to a low of -58.0% in 1937.

DFA U.S. Micro Cap Portfolio (April 2001–December 2015)

For April 2001 to December 2015, the small-cap stock return series is the total return achieved by the DFA U.S. Micro Cap Portfolio net of fees and expenses. In April 2001, Dimensional Fund Advisors renamed the DFA U.S. 9–10 Small Company Portfolio (see below) the DFA U.S. Micro Cap Portfolio and changed some of the criteria. The fund is designed to capture the returns and diversification benefits of a broad cross-section of U.S. small companies on a market-cap weighted basis. The fund's target buy range includes those companies whose market cap falls in the lowest 5% of the market universe defined as the aggregate of the NYSE, NYSE AMEX, and NASDAQ National Market System or companies smaller than the 1,500th largest U.S. company in the same market universe, whichever results in a higher market cap break.

The market universe is examined on a dynamic basis to determine which stocks are eligible for purchase or sale based on market capitalization. To minimize turnover, a hold or buffer range is created for stocks that migrate above the buy range. The upper bound of the hold range is the fifth percentile of the market universe. Stocks that grow above the hold range are eligible for sale and proceeds are reinvested into the portfolio.

At year-end 2015, the DFA U.S. Micro Cap Portfolio contained 1,629 stocks, with a weighted average market cap of $1.008 billion and a median market cap of $355 million.

DFA U.S. 9–10 Small Company Portfolio (January 1982–March 2001)

For January 1982 to March 2001, the small-cap stock return series was the total return achieved by the DFA U.S. Small Company 9–10 (for ninth and 10th deciles) Portfolio. The fund's target buy range was a market-cap-weighted universe of the ninth and 10th deciles of the New York Stock Exchange, plus stocks listed on the NYSE Amex (now the NYSE MKT) and NASDAQ National Market with the same or less capitalization as the upper bound of the NYSE ninth decile. Because the lower bound of the 10th decile is near zero, stocks were not purchased if they were smaller than $10 million in market cap (although they were held if they fell below that level).

NYSE Fifth Quintile Returns (1926–1981)

The equities of smaller companies from 1926 to 1980 are represented by the historical series developed by Professor Rolf W. Banz (see References). This is composed of stocks making up the fifth quintile (i.e., the ninth and 10th deciles) of the New York Stock Exchange (NYSE); the stocks on the NYSE are ranked by capitalization, and each decile contains an equal number of stocks at the beginning of each formation period. The ninth and 10th decile portfolio was first ranked and formed as of December 31, 1925. This portfolio was "held" for five years, with value weighted portfolio returns computed monthly. Every five years the portfolio was rebalanced (i.e., all of the stocks on the NYSE were re-ranked, and a new portfolio of those falling in the ninth and 10th deciles was formed) as of December 31, 1930, and every five years thereafter through December 31, 1980. This method avoided survivorship bias by including the return after the delisting or failure of a stock in constructing the portfolio returns. (Survivorship bias is caused by studying only stocks that have survived events such as bankruptcy and acquisition.)

For 1981, Dimensional Fund Advisors updated the returns using Professor Banz's methods. The data for 1981 are significant to only three decimal places (in decimal form) or one decimal place when returns are expressed in percent.

Long-term Corporate Bonds

One dollar invested in long-term high-grade corporate bonds at the end of 1925 was worth $187.82 by year-end 2015. The compound annual growth rate over the 90-year period was 6.0%. Total annual returns ranged from a high of 42.6% in 1982 to a low of -8.1% in 1969.

Total Returns

For 1969 to 2015, corporate bond total returns are represented by the Citigroup Long-Term High-Grade Corporate Bond Index (formerly Salomon Brothers). Because most large corporate bond transactions take place over the counter, a major dealer is the natural source of these data. The index includes nearly all Aaa- and Aa-rated bonds. If a bond is downgraded during a particular month, its return for the month is included in the index before removing the bond from future portfolios.

For 1926 to 1968, total returns were calculated by summing the capital appreciation returns and the income returns. For the period 1946 to 1968, Ibbotson and Sinquefield (1976) backdated the Salomon Brothers index, using Salomon Brothers' monthly yield data; a methodology similar to that used by Salomon was used for 1969 to 2015. Capital appreciation returns were calculated from yields assuming (at the beginning of each monthly holding period) a 20-year maturity, a bond price equal to par, and a coupon equal to the beginning-of-period yield.

For the period 1926 to 1945, Standard & Poor's monthly High Grade Corporate Composite yield data were used, assuming a 4% coupon and a 20-year maturity. The conventional present-value formula for bond price was used for the beginning and end-of-month prices.[3.1] The monthly income return was assumed to be one-twelfth the coupon.

Long-term Government Bonds

One dollar invested in long-term government bonds at year-end 1925, with coupons reinvested, grew to $132.03 by year end 2015; this represents a compound annual growth rate of 5.6%. Total annual returns ranged from a high of 40.4% in 1982 to a low of -14.9% in 2009 (see Exhibit 3.2). Returns from the capital appreciation component alone caused $1.00 to grow to $1.37 over the 90-year period, representing a compound annual growth rate of 0.4%.

[3.1]   This formula is presented in Ross, S. A., & Westerfield, R.W. 1988. "Level-Coupon Bonds." P. 97 in *Corporate Finance* (St. Louis: Times Mirror/Mosby).

Exhibit 3.2: Long-term Government Bonds: Total Return and Capital Appreciation Indexes 1926–2015

Index (Year-end 1925 = $1.00)

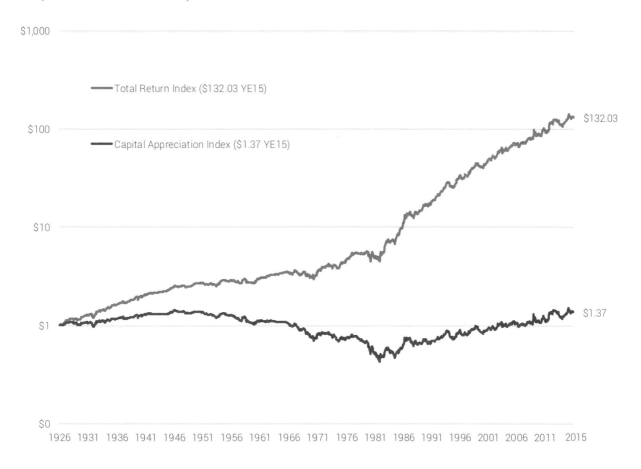

Total Returns

The total returns on long-term government bonds from 1977 to 2015 are constructed with data from *The Wall Street Journal*. The bond used in 2015 is the 4.5% issue that matures on Feb. 15, 2036. The data for 1926 to 1976 is obtained from the Government Bond File at the Center for Research in Security Prices at the University of Chicago Booth School of Business. The bonds used to construct the index from 1926–2015 are shown in Exhibit 3.4. To the greatest extent possible, a one-bond portfolio with a term of approximately 20 years and a reasonably current coupon – whose returns did not reflect potential tax benefits, impaired negotiability, or special redemption or call privileges – was used each year. Where "flower" bonds (tenderable to the Treasury at par in payment of estate taxes) had to be used, we chose the bond with the smallest potential tax benefit. Where callable bonds had to be used, the term of the bond was assumed to be a simple average of the maturity and first call dates minus the current date. The bond was "held" for the calendar year and returns were computed. The annual total returns for the long-term government bond series from 1926–2015 is illustrated in Exhibit 3.3.

Exhibit 3.3: Long-term Government Bonds Annual Total Returns (%)
1926–2015

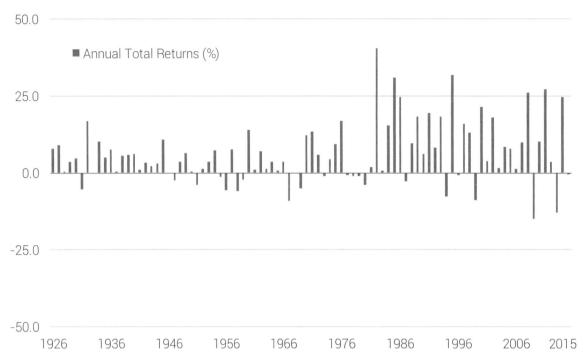

In October 2001, the U.S. Treasury announced that it would no longer issue 30-year Treasury bonds and the 10-year bond became the longest-term Treasury security offered. This decision was reversed in 2005 and the U.S. Treasury resumed issuing 30 year Treasury bonds in February 2006. The lack of trading long-horizon government bonds in this period may influence yields recorded for 2011 through 2015, for which Ibbotson chooses the Treasury bond with the closest term to 20 years.

Total returns for 1977 to 2015 are calculated as the change in the flat (or and-interest) price.[3.2] The flat price is the average of the bond's bid and ask prices, plus the accrued coupon.[3.3] The accrued coupon is equal to zero on the day a coupon is paid, and increases over time until the next coupon payment according to the formula below.

$$A = fC$$

Where:

A	= Accrued coupon
C	= Semiannual coupon rate
f	= (number of days since last coupon payment)/(number of days from last coupon payment to next coupon payment)

[3.2] "Flat price" is used here to mean the unmodified economic value of the bond, i.e., the and-interest price, or quoted price plus accrued interest. In contrast, some sources use flat price to mean the quoted price.

[3.3] For the purpose of calculating the return in months when a coupon payment is made, the change in the flat price includes the coupon.

Income Return

For 1977 to 2015, the income return for the long-term government bond series is calculated as the change in flat price plus any coupon actually paid from one period to the next, holding the yield constant over the period. As in the total return series, the exact number of days composing the period is used. For 1926 to 1976, the income return for a given month is calculated as the total return minus the capital appreciation return.

Capital Appreciation or Return in Excess of Yield

For 1977 to 2015, capital appreciation is taken as the total return minus the income return for each month. For 1926 to 1976, the capital appreciation return (also known as the return in excess of yield) is obtained from the CRSP Government Bond File.

A bond's capital appreciation is defined as the total return minus the income return; that is, the return in excess of yield. This definition omits the capital gain or loss that comes from the movement of a bond's price toward par (in the absence of an interest-rate change) as it matures. Capital appreciation, as defined here, captures changes in bond prices caused by changes in the interest rate.

Yields

The yield on the long-term government bond series is defined as the internal rate of return that equates the bond's price (the average of bid and ask, plus the accrued coupon) with the stream of cash flows (coupons and principal) promised to the bondholder. The yields reported for 1977 to 2015 were calculated from *The Wall Street Journal* prices for the bonds listed in Exhibit 3.4. For non-callable bonds, the maturity date is shown. For callable bonds, the first call date and the maturity dates are shown as in the following example: 10/15/47–52 refers to a bond that is first callable on Oct. 15, 1947, and matures on Oct. 15, 1952. Dates from 47–99 refer to 1947 to 1999; 00–16 refers to 2000 to 2016. For callable bonds trading below par, the yield to maturity is used; above par, the yield to call is used. The yields for 1926 to 1976 were obtained from the CRSP Government Bond File.

Exhibit 3.4: Long-term and Intermediate-term Government Bond Issues

Long-term Gov't Bonds

Period Bond Is Held In Index	Coupon (%)	Call/Maturity Date
1926–1931	4.25	10/15/47–52
1932–1935	3.00	9/15/51–55
1936–1941	2.88	3/15/55–60
1942–1953	2.50	9/15/67–72
1954–1958	3.25	6/15/78–83
1959–1960	4.00	2/15/1980
1961–1965	4.25	5/15/75–85
1966–1972	4.25	8/15/87–92
1973–1974	6.75	2/15/1993
1975–1976	8.50	5/15/94–99
1977–1980	7.88	2/15/95–00
1981	8.00	8/15/96–01
1982	13.38	8/15/2001
1983	10.75	2/15/2003
1984	11.88	11/15/2003
1985	11.75	2/15/05–10
1986–1989	10.00	5/15/05–10
1990–1992	10.38	11/15/07–12
1993–1996	7.25	5/15/2016
1997–1998	8.13	8/15/2019
1999–2001	8.13	8/15/2021
2002	6.25	8/15/2023
2003–2004	7.50	11/15/2024
2005	6.88	8/15/2025
2006	6.75	8/15/2026
2007	6.38	8/15/2027
2008	5.50	8/15/2028
2009	5.25	2/15/2029
2010–2012	5.38	2/15/2031
2013	4.50	2/15/2036
2014	4.50	2/15/2036
2015	4.50	2/15/2036

Intermediate-term Gov't Bonds

Period Bond Is Held In Index	Coupon (%)	Call/Maturity Date
1934–1936	3.25	8/1/1941
1937	3.38	3/15/1943
1938–1940	2.50	12/15/1945
1941	3.00	1/1/1946
1942	3.00	1/1/1947
1943	1.75	6/15/1948
1944–1945	2.00	3/15/1950
1946	2.00	6/15/1951
1947	2.00	3/15/1952
1948	2.00	9/15/1953
1949	2.50	3/15/1954
1950	2.25	6/15/1955
1951–1952	2.50	3/15/1958
1953	2.38	6/15/1958
1954	2.38	3/15/1959
1955	2.13	11/15/1960
1956	2.75	9/15/1961
1957–1958	2.50	8/15/1963
1959	3.00	2/15/1964
1960	2.63	2/15/1965
1961	3.75	5/15/1966
1962	3.63	11/15/1967
1963	3.88	5/15/1968
1964	4.00	2/15/1969
1965	4.00	8/15/1970
1966	4.00	8/15/1971
1967	4.00	2/15/1972
1968	4.00	8/15/1973
1969	5.63	8/15/1974
1970	5.75	2/15/1975
1971	6.25	2/15/1976
1972	1.50	10/1/1976
1973	6.25	2/15/1978
1974	6.25	8/15/1979
1975	6.88	5/15/1980
1976	7.00	2/15/1981
1977	6.38	2/15/1982

Intermediate-term Gov't Bonds (cont.)

Period Bond Is Held In Index	Coupon (%)	Call/Maturity Date
1978	8.00	2/15/1983
1979	7.25	2/15/1984
1980	8.00	2/15/1985
1981	13.50	2/15/1986
1982	9.00	2/15/1987
1983	12.38	1/1/1988
1984	14.63	1/15/1989
1985	10.50	1/15/1990
1986	11.75	1/15/1991
1987	11.63	1/15/1992
1988	8.75	1/15/1993
1989	9.00	2/15/1994
1990	8.63	10/15/1995
1991–1992	7.88	7/15/1996
1993	6.38	1/15/1999
1994	5.50	4/15/2000
1995	8.50	2/15/2000
1996	7.75	2/15/2001
1997	6.38	8/15/2002
1998	5.75	8/15/2003
1999	7.25	8/15/2004
2000	6.50	8/15/2005
2001	6.50	10/15/2006
2002	6.13	8/15/2007
2003	5.63	5/15/2008
2004	5.50	5/15/2009
2005	5.75	8/15/2010
2006	5.00	8/15/2011
2007	4.88	2/15/2012
2008	3.63	5/15/2013
2009	4.25	8/15/2014
2010	4.13	5/15/2015
2011	3.25	7/31/2016
2012	2.75	5/31/2017
2013	2.38	5/31/2018
2014	3.13	5/15/2019
2015	3.50	5/15/2020

Intermediate-term Government Bonds

One dollar invested in intermediate-term government bonds at year end 1925, with coupons reinvested, grew to $93.97 by year-end 2015. This represents a 90-year compound annual growth rate of 5.2%. Total annual returns ranged from a high of 29.1% in 1982 to a low of -5.1% in 1994.

Capital appreciation caused $1.00 to increase to $1.67 over the 90-year period, representing a compound annual growth rate of 0.6%. This increase was unexpected: Because yields rose on average over the period, capital appreciation on a hypothetical intermediate-term government bond portfolio with a constant five-year maturity should have been negative. An explanation of the positive average return is given at the end of this chapter.

Exhibit 3.5: Intermediate-term Government Bonds: Total Return and Capital Appreciation Indexes 1926–2015
Index (Year-end 1925 = $1.00)

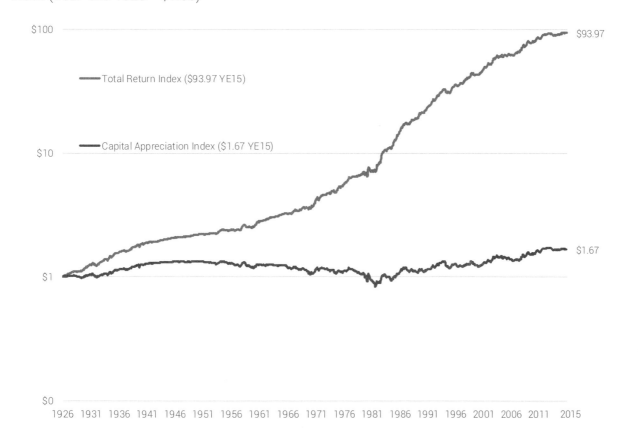

Total Returns

Total returns of the intermediate-term government bonds for 1987 to 2015 are calculated from *The Wall Street Journal* prices, using the coupon accrual method described above for long-term government bonds (see equation in previous section). The bond used in 2015 is the 3.5% issue maturing on May 15, 2020. Returns for 1934 to 1986 are obtained from the CRSP Government Bond File. The bonds used to construct the index for 1934 to 2015 are shown in Exhibit 3.4.

As with long-term government bonds, one-bond portfolios are used to construct the intermediate-term government bond index. The bond chosen each year is the shortest non-callable bond with a maturity not less than five years, and it is "held" for the calendar year. Monthly returns are computed. (Bonds with impaired negotiability or special redemption privileges are omitted, as are partially or fully tax-exempt bonds starting with 1943.)

For 1934 to 1942, almost all bonds with maturities near five years were partially or fully tax-exempt and selected using the rules described above. Personal tax rates were generally low in that period, so that yields on tax-exempt bonds were similar to yields on taxable bonds.

For 1926 to 1933, there are few bonds suitable for construction of a series with a five year maturity. For this period, five-year bond yield estimates are used. These estimates are obtained from Thomas S. Coleman, Lawrence Fisher, and Roger G. Ibbotson, *Historical U.S. Treasury Yield Curves*: 1926 1992 with 1995 update (Ibbotson Associates, Chicago, 1995). The estimates reflect what a "pure play" five-year Treasury bond, selling at par and with no special redemption or call provisions, would have yielded had one existed. Estimates are for partially tax-exempt bonds for 1926 to 1932 and for fully tax-exempt bonds for 1933. Monthly yields are converted to monthly total returns by calculating the beginning and end-of-month flat prices for the hypothetical bonds. The bond is "bought" at the beginning of the month at par (i.e., the coupon equals the previous month-end yield), assuming a maturity of five years. It is "sold" at the end of the month, with the flat price calculated by discounting the coupons and principal at the end-of-month yield, assuming a maturity of four years and 11 months. The flat price is the price of the bond including coupon accruals, so that the change in flat price represents total return. Monthly income returns are assumed to be equal to the previous end-of month yield, stated in monthly terms. Monthly capital appreciation returns are formed as total returns minus income returns.

Income Return and Capital Appreciation

For 1987 to 2015, the income return is calculated according to the methodology stated under "Long-term Government Bonds." Monthly capital appreciation (return in excess of yield) over this same period is the difference between total return and income return.

For 1934 to 1986, capital appreciation (return in excess of yield) is taken directly from the CRSP Government Bond File. The income return is calculated as the total return minus the capital appreciation return. Prior to 1934, the income and capital appreciation components of total return are generated from yield estimates as described earlier for total returns.

Yields

The yield on an intermediate-term government bond is the internal rate of return that equates the bond's price with the stream of cash flows (coupons and principal) promised to the bondholder. The yields reported for 1987 to 2015 are calculated from *The Wall Street Journal* bond prices listed in Exhibit 3.4. For 1934 to 1986, yields were obtained from the CRSP Government Bond File. Yields for 1926 to 1933 are estimates from Coleman, Fisher, and Ibbotson, *Historical U.S. Treasury Yield Curves*: 1926–1992 with 1995 update.

U.S. Treasury Bills

One dollar invested in U.S. Treasury bills at year-end 1925 grew to $20.59 by year-end 2015; this represents a compound annual growth rate of 3.4%. Total annual returns ranged from a high of 14.7% in 1981 to lows close to zero percent in the years shown in Exhibit 3.6. In Exhibit 3.6, all years in which the annual total return of U.S. Treasury bills was less than 0.5% are shown. The years in which Treasury bills had less than 0.5% annual total return primarily occurred during three periods: (i) the Great Depression (the 1930s), (ii) World War II (the 1940s), and (iii) in the period after the 2008 financial crisis (2009–2015).

Exhibit 3.6: Years in which Annual Total Returns of U.S. Treasury Bills Were Less than 0.5% 1926–2015

Year	Total Return	Year	Total Return
1933	0.3%	2009	0.1%
1934	0.2%	2010	0.1%
1935	0.2%	2011	0.0%
1936	0.2%	2012	0.1%
1937	0.3%	2013	0.0%
1938	0.0%	2014	0.0%
1939	0.0%	2015	0.0%
1940	0.0%		
1941	0.1%		
1942	0.3%		
1943	0.3%		
1944	0.3%		
1945	0.3%		
1946	0.4%		

Total Returns

For the U.S. Treasury bill index, data from *The Wall Street Journal* are used for 1977 to 2015; the CRSP U.S. Government Bond File is the source until 1976. Each month a one-bill portfolio containing the shortest-term bill having not less than one month to maturity is constructed. (The bill's original term to maturity is not relevant.) To measure holding-period returns for the one-bill portfolio, the bill is priced as of the last trading day of the previous month end and as of the last trading day of the current month. The price of the bill (*P*) at each time (*t*) is given as:

$$P_t = \left[1 - \frac{rd}{360} \right]$$

Where:

P_t =   Price of the bill at time *t*

r =   decimal yield (the average of bid and ask quotes) on the bill at time *t*

d =   number of days to maturity as of time *t*

The total return on the bill is the month-end price divided by the previous month-end price, minus one.

Negative Returns on Treasury Bills

Monthly Treasury bill returns (as reported in Appendix A-14) were negative in February 1933, and in 12 months during the 1938 to 1941 period. More recently, since July 2011 monthly Treasury bill returns have been negative in 8 months. Annual total returns have been negative only once, in 1938. Since negative Treasury bill returns contradict logic, an explanation is in order.

Negative yields observed in the data do not imply that investors purchased Treasury bills with a guaranteed negative return. Rather, Treasury bills of that era were exempt from personal property taxes in some states, while cash was not. Further, for a bank to hold U.S. government deposits, Treasury securities were required as collateral. These circumstances created excessive demand for the security, and thus bills were sold at a premium. Given the low interest rates during the period, owners of the bills experienced negative returns.

In 2008, yields on U.S. Treasury bills fell from a little over 3.0% at the beginning of the year to approximately zero percent by the end of the year, but the dynamics were different from those for 1938 to 1941. In the wake of the 2008 financial crisis, investors' behavior could be described as an extreme flight to safety; investors were willing to accept little (if anything) in return for the assurance that they would get their principal back. In other words, the return *of* capital took precedence over the return *on* capital.

From 2009 to 2015, U.S. Treasury bill yields remained near historical lows near zero percent. These low yields can be partially explained by the Federal Funds target rate, which was actually a *range* of zero percent to 0.25% from December 16, 2008 to December 17, 2015. On December 17, 2015, the target "range" was increased to 0.25% to 0.50%.

Inflation

A basket of consumer goods purchased for $1.00 at year-end 1925 cost $13.25 by year-end 2015. Of course, the contents of the basket have changed over time. This increase represents a compound annual rate of inflation of 2.9% over the past 90 years. Inflation rates ranged from a high of 18.2% in 1946 to a low of -10.3% in 1932.

Inflation

The Consumer Price Index for All Urban Consumers, or CPI-U, not seasonally adjusted, is used to measure inflation, which is the rate of change of consumer goods prices. Unfortunately, the CPI is not measured over the same period as the other asset returns. All of the security returns are measured from one month-end to the next month-end. CPI commodity prices are collected during the month. Thus, measured inflation rates lag the other series by about one-half month. Prior to January 1978, the CPI (rather than the CPI-U) was used. For 1978 to 1987, the index uses the year 1967 in determining the items composing the basket of goods. After 1987, a three-year period, 1982 to 1984, was used to determine the items making up the basket of goods. All inflation measures are constructed by the U.S. Department of Labor, Bureau of Labor Statistics, Washington.

Bond Capital Appreciation Despite Rising Yields

The capital appreciation component of intermediate-term government bond returns caused $1.00 invested at year-end 1925 to grow to $1.67 by the end of 2015, representing a compound annual growth rate of 0.6%. This is surprising because yields, on average, rose over the period.

An investor in a hypothetical five-year constant maturity portfolio, with continuous rebalancing, suffered a capital loss (that is, excluding coupon income) over 1926 to 2015. An investor who rebalanced yearly, choosing bonds according to the method set forth above, fared better. This investor would have earned the 0.6% annualized capital gain recorded here.

This performance relates to the construction of the intermediate-term bond series. For 1926 to 1933, the one-bond portfolio was rebalanced monthly to maintain a constant maturity of five years. For 1934 to 2015, one bond (the shortest bond not less than five years to maturity) was chosen at the beginning of each year and priced monthly. New bonds were not picked each month to maintain a constant maturity intra-year.

There are several possible reasons for the positive capital appreciation return. Chief among these reasons are convexity of the bond portfolio and the substitution of one bond for another at each year-end.

Convexity

Each year, we "bought" a bond with approximately five years to maturity and held it for one year. During this period, the market yield on the bond fluctuates. Because the duration of the bond shortens (the bond becomes less interest-rate sensitive) as yields rise and the duration lengthens as yields fall, more is gained from a fall in yield than is lost from a rise in yield. This characteristic of a bond is known as convexity.

For example, suppose an 8% coupon bond is bought at par at the beginning of a year; the yield fluctuates (but the portfolio is not rebalanced) during the year; and the bond is sold at par at the end of the year. The price of the bond at both the beginning and end of the year is $100; the change in bond price is zero. However, the fluctuations will have caused the gains during periods of falling yields to exceed the losses during periods of rising yields. Thus the total return for the year exceeds 8%. Because our measure of capital appreciation is the return in excess of yield, rather than the change in bond price, capital appreciation for this bond (as measured) will be greater than zero.

In 1992, the yield for intermediate-term government bonds started the year at 5.97%, rose, fell, and finally rose again to end at 6.11%, slightly higher than the starting point. In the absence of convexity, the capital appreciation return for 1992 would be negative. Because of the fluctuation of yields during the year, however, the capital appreciation return on the intermediate-term government bond index was positive 0.64%.

It should be noted that the return in excess of yield, or capital gain, from convexity is caused by holding, over the year, a bond whose yield at purchase is different from the current market yield. If the portfolio were rebalanced each time the data were sampled (in this case, monthly), by selling the old bond and buying a new five-year bond selling at par, the portfolio would have no convexity. That is, over a period where yields ended where they started, the measured capital appreciation would be zero. However, this is neither a practical way to construct an index of actual bonds nor to manage a bond portfolio.

Bond Substitution

Another reason the intermediate term government bond series displays positive capital appreciation even though yields rose is the way in which bonds were removed from the portfolio and replaced with other bonds. In general, it was not possible to replace a bond "sold" by buying one with exactly the same yield. This produces a spurious change in the yield of the series – one that should not be associated with a capital gain or loss.

For example: Suppose a five-year bond yielding 8% is bought at par at the beginning of the year; at that time, four-year bonds yield 7%. Over the year, the yield curve rises in parallel by 1 percentage point so that when it comes time to sell the bond at year-end, it yields 8% and has four years to maturity. Therefore, at both the beginning and end of the year, the price of the bond is $100.

The proceeds from the sale are used to buy a new five-year bond yielding 9%. While the bond price change was zero over the year, the yield of the series has risen from 8% to 9%. Thus it is possible, because of the process of substituting one bond for another, for the yield series to contain a spurious rise that is not, and should not be expected to be, associated with a decline in the price of any particular bond. This phenomenon is likely to be the source of some of the positive capital appreciation in our intermediate-term government bond series.

Other Issues

Although convexity and bond substitution may explain the anomaly of positive capital appreciation in a bond series with rising yields, there are other incomplete-market problems that may also help explain the capital gain. For example, intermediate-term government bonds were scarce in the 1930s and 1940s. As a result, the bonds chosen for this series occasionally had maturities longer than five years, ranging as high as eight years when bought. The 1930s and the first half of the 1940s were bullish for the bond market. Longer bonds included in this series had higher yields and substantially higher capital gain returns than bonds with exactly five years to maturity might have had if any existed. This upward bias is particularly noticeable in 1934, 1937, and 1938.

In addition, callable and fully or partially tax-exempt bonds were used when necessary to obtain a bond for some years. The conversion of the Treasury bond market from tax-exempt to taxable status produced a one-time upward jump in stated yields, but not a capital loss on any given bond. Therefore, part of the increase in stated yields over 1926 to 2015 was a tax effect that did not cause a capital loss on the intermediate-term bond index. Further, the callable bonds used in the early part of the period may have commanded a return premium for taking this extra risk.

Chapter 4
Description of the Derived Series

Historical data suggests that investors are rewarded for taking risks and that returns are related to inflation rates. The risk/return and the real/nominal relationships in the historical data are revealed by looking at the risk-premium and inflation-adjusted series derived from the basic asset series. Annual total returns for the four risk premiums and six inflation-adjusted series are presented in Exhibit 4.9 of this chapter.

Derived Series Calculated Using Geometric Differences

Derived series are calculated as the geometric differences between two basic asset classes. Returns on basic series A and B and derived series C are related as follows:

$$(1+C) = \left[\frac{1+A}{1+B}\right]$$

where the series returns for A, B, and C are in decimal form (e.g., 5% is indicated by 0.05). Thus C is given by:

$$C = \left[\frac{1+A}{1+B}\right] - 1 \approx A - B$$

As an example, suppose return A equals 15%, or 0.15; and return B is 5%, or 0.05; then C equals (1.15 / 1.05) − 1 = 0.0952, or 9.52%. This result, while slightly different from the simple arithmetic difference of 10%, is conceptually the same.

Definitions of the Derived Series

From the seven basic asset classes (large-cap stocks, small-cap stocks, long-term corporate bonds, long-term government bonds, intermediate-term government bonds, U.S. Treasury bills, and consumer goods (inflation)), 10 additional series are derived that represent the component or elemental parts of the asset returns.

Two Categories of Derived Series

The 10 derived series are categorized as (i) risk premiums, or payoffs for taking various types of risk, and (ii) as inflation-adjusted asset returns. The risk premiums are the bond horizon premium, the bond default premium, the equity risk premium, and the small-stock premium. The inflation-adjusted asset return series are constructed by geometrically subtracting inflation from each of the six asset total return series. The 10 derived series are summarized in Exhibit 4.1 (next page).

Exhibit 4.1: The Derived Series

Risk Premia Series	Derivation
Equity Risk Premium	$\dfrac{(1 + \textit{Large Stock TR})}{(1 + \textit{Treasury Bill TR})} - 1$
Small-Stock Premium	$\dfrac{(1 + \textit{Small Stock TR})}{(1 + \textit{Large Stock TR})} - 1$
Bond Default Premium	$\dfrac{(1 + \textit{LT Corp Bond TR})}{(1 + \textit{LT Govt Bond})} - 1$
Bond Horizon Premium	$\dfrac{(1 + \textit{LT Govt Bond TR})}{(1 + \textit{Treasury Bill TR})} - 1$

Inflation–Adjusted Series	Derivation
Large-Cap Stock Returns	$\dfrac{(1 + \textit{Large Stock TR})}{(1 + \textit{Inflation})} - 1$
Small-Cap Stock Returns	$\dfrac{(1 + \textit{Small Stock TR})}{(1 + \textit{Inflation})} - 1$
Corporate Bond Returns	$\dfrac{(1 + \textit{LT Corp Bond TR})}{(1 + \textit{Inflation})} - 1$
Long-term Government Bond Returns	$\dfrac{(1 + \textit{LT Govt Bond TR})}{(1 + \textit{Inflation})} - 1$
Intermediate-term Government Bond Returns	$\dfrac{(1 + \textit{IT Govt Bond TR})}{(1 + \textit{Inflation})} - 1$
Treasury Bill Returns (Real Riskless Rate of Returns)	$\dfrac{(1 + \textit{Treasury Bill TR})}{(1 + \textit{Inflation})} - 1$

Equity Risk Premium

Large-cap stock returns are composed of inflation, the real riskless rate, and the equity risk premium. The equity risk premium is the geometric difference between large cap stock total returns and U.S. Treasury bill total returns.

Because large-cap stocks are not strictly comparable with bonds, horizon and default premiums are not used to analyze the components of equity returns (large-cap stocks have characteristics that are analogous to horizon and default risk, but they are not equivalent).

The monthly equity risk premium is given by:

$$\frac{(1+Large\,Stock\,TR)}{(1+Treasury\,Bill\,TR)}-1$$

Small-Stock Premium

The small-stock premium is the geometric difference between small-cap stock total returns and large-cap stock total returns. The monthly small-stock premium is given by:

$$\frac{(1+Small\,Stock\,TR)}{(1+Large\,Stock\,TR)}-1$$

Bond Default Premium

The bond default premium is defined as the net return from investing in long-term corporate bonds rather than long-term government bonds of equal maturity. Because there is a possibility of default on a corporate bond, bondholders receive a premium that reflects this possibility, in addition to inflation, the real riskless rate, and the horizon premium.

The monthly bond default premium is given by:

$$\frac{(1+LT\,Corp\,Bond\,TR)}{(1+LT\,Govt\,Bond\,TR)}-1$$

Components of the Default Premium

Bonds susceptible to default have higher returns (when they do not default) than those of riskless bonds. Default on a bond may be a small loss, such as a late or skipped interest payment, or it may be a larger loss, such as the loss of any or all principal as well as interest. In any case, part of the default premium on a portfolio of bonds is consumed by the losses on those bonds that do default.

The remainder of the default premium (the portion not consumed by defaults) is a pure risk premium, which the investor demands and, over the long run, receives for taking on the risk of default. The expected return on a corporate bond, or portfolio of corporate bonds, is less than the bond's or portfolio's yield. The portion of the yield that is expected to be consumed by defaults must be subtracted. The expected return on a corporate bond is equal to the expected return on a government bond of like maturity, plus the pure risk premium portion of the bond default premium.

Callability Risk Is Captured in the Default Premium

Callability risk is the risk that a bond will be redeemed (at or near par) by its issuer before maturity, at a time when market interest rates are lower than the bond's coupon rate. The possibility of redemption is risky because it would prevent the bondholder of the redeemed issue from reinvesting the proceeds at the original (higher) interest rate. The bond default premium, as measured here, also inadvertently captures any premium investors may demand or receive for this risk.

Bond Horizon Premium

Long-term government bonds behave differently from short-term bills in that their prices (and hence returns) are more sensitive to interest-rate fluctuations. The bond horizon premium is the extra return investors demand for holding long-term bonds instead of U.S. Treasury bills.

The monthly bond horizon premium is given by:

$$\frac{(1 + LT\,Govt\,Bond\,TR)}{(1 + Treasury\,Bill\,TR)} - 1$$

Long-term rather than intermediate-term government bonds are used to derive the bond horizon premium so as to capture a "full unit" of price fluctuation risk. Intermediate-term government bonds may display a partial horizon premium, which is smaller than the difference between long-term bonds and short-term bills.

Determining the Bond Premium: Maturity vs. Duration

Duration is the present-value-weighted average time to receipt of cash flows (coupons and principal) from holding a bond, and can be calculated from the bond's yield, coupon rate, and term to maturity. The duration of a given bond determines the amount of return premium arising from differences in bond life. The bond horizon premium is also referred to as the "maturity premium," based on the observation that bonds with longer maturities command a return premium over shorter-maturity bonds. Duration, not term to maturity, however, is the bond characteristic that determines this return premium.

Why a "Horizon" Premium?

Investors often strive to match the duration of their bond holdings (cash inflows) with the estimated duration of their obligations (cash outflows). Consequently, investors with short time horizons regard long-duration bonds as risky (due to price fluctuation risk), and short-term bills as riskless. Conversely, investors with long time horizons regard short-term bills as risky (due to the uncertainty about the yield at which bills can be reinvested), and long-duration bonds as riskless or less risky.

Empirically, long-duration bonds bear higher yields and greater returns than short-term bills; that is, the yield curve slopes upward on average over time. This indicates that investors are more averse to the price fluctuation risk of long-duration bonds than to the reinvestment risk of bills.

Bond duration risk is thus in the eye of the beholder, or bondholder. Therefore, rather than identifying the premium as a payoff for long-bond risk (which implies a judgment that short-horizon investors are "right" in their risk perceptions), it is better to go directly to the source of the return differential (the differing time horizons of investors) and use the label "horizon premium."

Large-Cap Stock Real Returns

Large-cap stock total returns were 10.0% compounded annually over the period 1926 to 2015 in nominal terms. In real (inflation-adjusted) terms, stocks provided a 6.9% compound annual return. Thus, a large-cap stock investor would have experienced a substantial increase in real wealth, or purchasing power, over the 90-year period (i.e., even after adjusting for inflation, large stock investors' wealth increased over the 1926–2015 period).

Construction

The inflation-adjusted return is a geometric difference and is approximately equal to the arithmetic difference between the large-cap stock total return and the inflation rate. The monthly inflation adjusted large-cap stock return is given by:

$$\frac{(1 + Large\, Stock\, TR)}{(1 + Inflation)} - 1$$

The inflation-adjusted large-cap stock return may also be expressed as the geometric sum of the real riskless rate and the equity risk premium:

$$\left[(1 + Real\, Riskless\, Rate) \times (1 + Equity\, Risk\, Premium)\right] - 1$$

Exhibit 4.2 depicts (i) what $1.00 invested at the end of December 1925 in large-cap stocks would have grown to by the end of 2015, and (ii) what $1.00 invested at the end of December 1925 in large-cap stocks would have grown to by the end of 2015 if large-cap stock returns were adjusted for inflation.

Exhibit 4.2: Large-cap Stocks: Real and Nominal Return Indexes
1926–2015
Index (Year-end 1925 = $1.00)

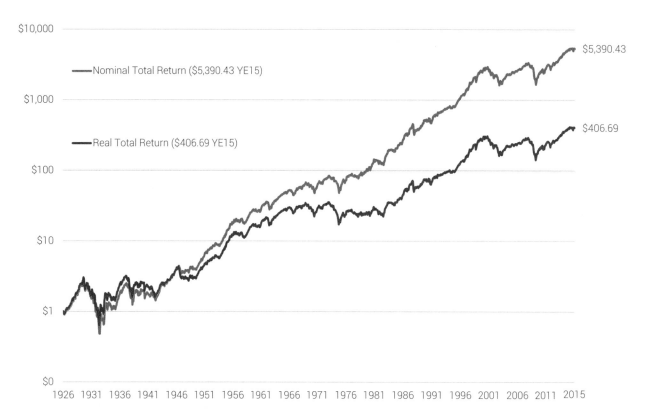

Chapter 4: Description of the Derived Series

Small-Cap Stock Real Returns

Small-cap stock total returns were 12.0% compounded annually over the period 1926–2015 in nominal terms. In real terms, small-cap stocks provided a 8.8% compound annual return. Thus, long term a small-cap stock investor would have experienced a substantial increase in real wealth, or purchasing power, over the 90-year period.

Construction

The inflation-adjusted return is a geometric difference and is approximately equal to the arithmetic difference between the small-cap stock total return and the inflation rate. The monthly inflation-adjusted small-cap stock return is given by:

$$\frac{(1+Small\,Stock\,TR)}{(1+Inflation)}-1$$

Exhibit 4.3 depicts (i) what $1.00 invested at the end of December 1925 in small-cap stocks would have grown to by the end of 2015, and (ii) what $1.00 invested at the end of December 1925 in small-cap stocks would have grown to by the end of 2015 if small-cap stock returns were adjusted for inflation.

Exhibit 4.3: Small-cap Stocks Real and Nominal Return Indexes
1926–2015
Index (Year-end 1925 = $1.00)

Long-term Corporate Bond Real Returns

Corporate bonds returned 6.0% compounded annually over the period 1926–2015 in nominal terms, and a 3.0% compound annual return in real (inflation-adjusted) terms. Thus, corporate bonds have outpaced inflation over the past 90 years.

Construction

The inflation-adjusted return is a geometric difference and is approximately equal to the arithmetic difference between the long-term corporate bond total return and the inflation rate. The monthly inflation-adjusted corporate bond total return is given by:

$$\frac{\left(1 + Corp\,Bond\,TR\right)}{\left(1 + Inflation\right)} - 1$$

Exhibit 4.4 depicts (i) what $1.00 invested at the end of December 1925 in long-term corporate bonds would have grown to by the end of 2015, and (ii) what $1.00 invested at the end of December 1925 in long-term corporate bonds would have grown to by the end of 2015 if long-term corporate bond returns were adjusted for inflation.

Exhibit 4.4: Long-term Corporate Bonds: Real and Nominal Return Indices
1926–2015
Index (Year-end 1925 = $1.00)

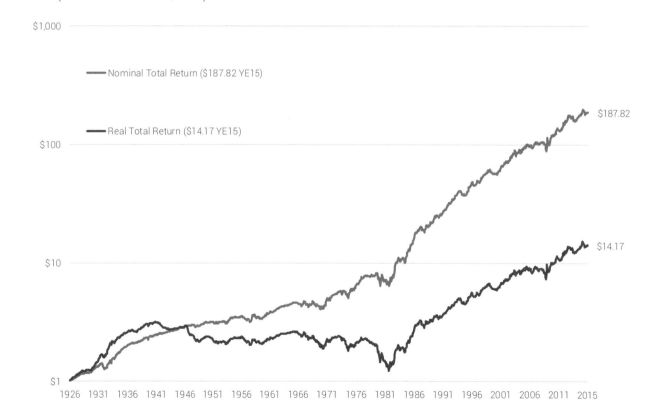

Long-term Government Bond Real Returns

Long-term government bonds returned 5.6% compounded annually over the period 1926–2015 in nominal terms, and a 2.6% compound annual return in real (inflation-adjusted) terms. Thus, long-term government bonds have outpaced inflation over the past 90 years despite falling bond prices over most of the period.

Construction

The inflation-adjusted return is a geometric difference and is approximately equal to the arithmetic difference between the long-term government bond total return and the inflation rate. The monthly inflation-adjusted long-term government bond total return is given by:

$$\frac{(1 + LT\,Govt\,Bond\,TR)}{(1 + Inflation)} - 1$$

Because government bond returns are composed of inflation, the real riskless rate, and the horizon premium, the inflation-adjusted government bond returns may also be expressed as:

[(1+*Real Riskless Rate*) x (1+*Horizon Premium*)] − 1

Exhibit 4.5 depicts (i) what $1.00 invested at the end of December 1925 in long-term government bonds would have grown to by the end of 2015, and (ii) what $1.00 invested at the end of December 1925 in long-term government bonds would have grown to by the end of 2015 if long-term government bond returns were adjusted for inflation.

Exhibit 4.5: Long-term Government Bonds: Real and Nominal Return Indices
1926–2015
Index (Year-end 1925 = $1.00)

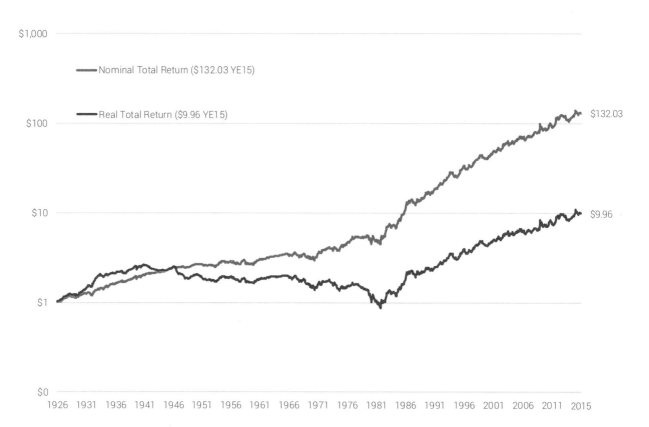

Chapter 4: Description of the Derived Series

Intermediate-term Government Bond Real Returns

Intermediate-term government bonds returned 5.2% compounded annually over the period 1926–2015 in nominal terms, and 2.2% in real (inflation-adjusted) terms.

Construction

The inflation adjusted return is a geometric difference and is approximately equal to the arithmetic difference between the intermediate-term government bond total return and the inflation rate. The monthly inflation-adjusted intermediate-term government bond return is given by:

$$\frac{\left(1 + IT\,Govt\,Bond\,TR\right)}{\left(1 + Inflation\right)} - 1$$

Exhibit 4.6 depicts (i) what $1.00 invested at the end of December 1925 in intermediate-term government bonds would have grown to by the end of 2015, and (ii) what $1.00 invested at the end of December 1925 in intermediate-term government bonds would have grown to by the end of 2015 if intermediate-term government bond returns were adjusted for inflation.

Exhibit 4.6: Intermediate-term Government Bonds: Real and Nominal Return Indices
1926–2015
Index (Year-end 1925 = $1.00)

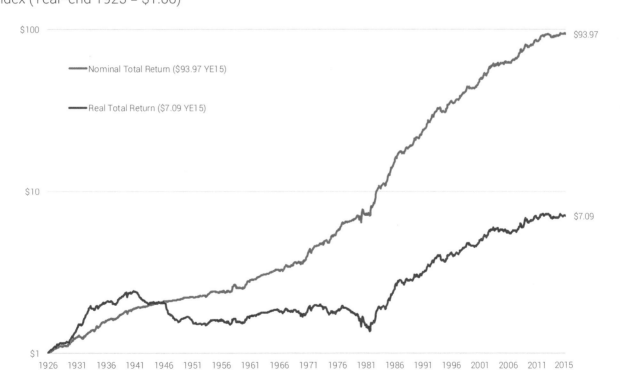

Real Riskless Rates of Return (U.S. T-Bill Real Returns)

Treasury bills returned 3.4% compounded annually over the 1926–2015 period, in nominal terms, but only a 0.5% compound annual return in real (inflation-adjusted) terms. Thus, an investor in Treasury bills would have barely beaten inflation (or retained purchasing power) over the 90-year period.

Construction

The real riskless rate of return is the difference in returns between U.S. Treasury bills and inflation. This is given by:

$$\frac{\left(1+Treasury\,Bill\,TR\right)}{\left(1+Inflation\right)}-1$$

Exhibit 4.7 depicts (i) what $1.00 invested at the end of December 1925 in U.S. Treasury bills would have grown to by the end of 2015, and (ii) what $1.00 invested at the end of December 1925 in U.S. Treasury bills would have grown to by the end of 2015 if U.S. Treasury bill returns were adjusted for inflation.

Exhibit 4.7: U.S. Treasury Bills: Real and Nominal Return Indices
1926–2015
Index (Year-end 1925 = $1.00)

Exhibit 4.8 shows the levels, volatility, and patterns of real interest rates over the last 90 years.

Exhibit 4.8: Annual Real Risk-free rates of return (%)
1926–2015

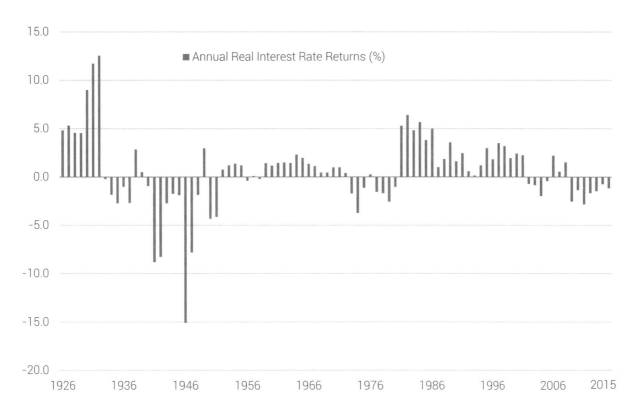

Returns on the Derived Series

Annual returns for the 10 derived series are calculated from monthly returns in the same manner as the annual basic series. Exhibit 4.9 presents annual returns for each of the 10 derived series. Four of the derived series are risk premiums and six are inflation-adjusted total returns on asset classes.

Exhibit 4.9: Annual Return of Derived Series (%)
1926–2015

					Inflation-Adjusted					
Year	Equity Risk Premium	Small Stock Premium	Bond Default Premium	Bond Horizon Premium	Large-Cap Stocks	Small-Cap Stocks	Long-term Corp Bonds	Long-term Gov't Bonds	Inter-term Gov't Bonds	U.S. Treasury Bills
Dec-26	8.09	-10.17	-0.37	4.36	13.31	1.79	9.00	9.40	6.97	4.83
Dec-27	33.32	-11.19	-1.36	5.63	40.41	24.69	9.73	11.24	6.74	5.31
Dec-28	38.67	-2.73	2.73	-3.34	45.01	41.06	3.84	1.08	1.90	4.57
Dec-29	-12.57	-46.89	-0.14	-1.27	-8.59	-51.45	3.07	3.22	5.81	4.54
Dec-30	-26.66	-17.64	3.17	2.20	-20.08	-34.18	14.90	11.38	13.56	8.98
Dec-31	-43.94	-11.33	3.65	-6.31	-37.37	-44.46	8.48	4.66	7.96	11.71
Dec-32	-9.07	3.05	-5.15	15.73	2.35	5.47	23.54	30.26	21.30	12.55
Dec-33	53.53	57.72	10.46	-0.37	53.21	141.63	9.82	-0.58	1.31	-0.21
Dec-34	-1.60	26.04	3.47	9.85	-3.40	21.75	11.58	7.84	6.83	-1.83
Dec-35	47.42	-5.06	4.41	4.81	43.39	36.13	6.44	1.94	3.91	-2.73
Dec-36	33.68	23.06	-0.72	7.32	32.32	62.83	5.47	6.23	1.83	-1.02
Dec-37	-35.23	-35.37	2.51	-0.08	-36.98	-59.27	-0.35	-2.78	-1.50	-2.71
Dec-38	31.14	1.28	0.57	5.55	34.87	36.59	9.16	8.55	9.27	2.84
Dec-39	-0.43	0.76	-1.86	5.92	0.07	0.83	4.46	6.45	5.02	0.50
Dec-40	-9.79	5.13	-2.54	6.08	-10.64	-6.05	2.41	5.08	1.99	-0.94
Dec-41	-11.64	2.93	1.78	0.87	-19.42	-17.06	-6.37	-8.01	-8.40	-8.80
Dec-42	20.02	20.08	-0.60	2.94	10.11	32.23	-6.12	-5.55	-6.73	-8.25
Dec-43	25.46	49.62	0.73	1.73	22.04	82.60	-0.32	-1.04	-0.34	-2.73
Dec-44	19.36	28.37	1.87	2.48	17.28	50.55	2.57	0.69	-0.31	-1.74
Dec-45	35.99	27.25	-6.01	10.37	33.43	69.79	1.78	8.30	-0.03	-1.88
Dec-46	-8.39	-3.87	1.83	-0.45	-22.20	-25.21	-13.91	-15.46	-14.52	-15.07
Dec-47	5.18	-4.53	0.29	-3.11	-3.03	-7.42	-10.41	-10.67	-7.43	-7.80
Dec-48	4.65	-7.22	0.71	2.57	2.72	-4.69	1.39	0.67	-0.84	-1.85
Dec-49	17.50	0.80	-2.95	5.29	20.97	21.95	5.21	8.40	4.20	2.96
Dec-50	30.16	5.34	2.05	-1.12	24.50	31.15	-3.47	-5.42	-4.81	-4.34
Dec-51	22.19	-13.07	1.29	-5.34	17.14	1.82	-8.09	-9.26	-5.21	-4.14
Dec-52	16.44	-12.96	2.33	-0.49	17.33	2.13	2.62	0.27	0.74	0.77
Dec-53	-2.76	-5.55	-0.22	1.78	-1.60	-7.07	2.77	2.99	2.59	1.19
Dec-54	51.32	5.21	-1.68	6.27	53.39	61.38	5.91	7.72	3.20	1.37
Dec-55	29.52	-8.45	1.80	-2.82	31.07	19.99	0.10	-1.66	-1.02	1.19
Dec-56	4.00	-2.13	-1.30	-7.85	3.59	1.38	-9.41	-8.21	-3.19	-0.39
Dec-57	-13.50	-4.25	1.17	4.19	-13.40	-17.08	5.52	4.31	4.67	0.11
Dec-58	41.19	15.01	4.13	-7.52	40.88	62.03	-3.91	-7.72	-3.00	-0.22
Dec-59	8.75	3.97	1.32	-5.06	10.30	14.68	-2.43	-3.70	-1.86	1.43
Dec-60	-2.14	-3.74	-4.14	10.83	-0.99	-4.70	7.48	12.12	10.13	1.17
Dec-61	24.25	4.10	3.81	-1.13	26.04	31.21	4.12	0.30	1.17	1.44
Dec-62	-11.16	-3.48	0.99	4.04	-9.83	-12.97	6.64	5.59	4.29	1.49
Dec-63	19.09	0.62	0.97	-1.85	20.81	21.56	0.54	-0.43	-0.01	1.44
Dec-64	12.50	6.04	1.22	-0.03	15.11	22.07	3.54	2.29	2.82	2.32
Dec-65	8.20	26.06	-1.16	-3.10	10.33	39.08	-2.33	-1.19	-0.89	1.97
Dec-66	-14.15	3.39	-3.33	-1.06	-12.98	-10.03	-3.06	0.29	1.29	1.36
Dec-67	18.97	48.07	4.66	-12.85	20.32	78.15	-7.76	-11.86	-1.97	1.13
Dec-68	5.57	22.43	2.84	-5.20	6.05	29.84	-2.05	-4.76	-0.18	0.46
Dec-69	-14.16	-18.09	-3.18	-10.94	-13.77	-29.37	-13.38	-10.54	-6.45	0.45
Dec-70	-2.50	-20.50	5.59	5.24	-1.55	-21.73	12.21	6.27	10.78	0.98

Exhibit 4.9: Annual Return of Derived Series (%)
1926–2015

Year	Equity Risk Premium	Small Stock Premium	Bond Default Premium	Bond Horizon Premium	Inflation-Adjusted					
					Large-Cap Stocks	Small-Cap Stocks	Long-term Corp Bonds	Long-term Gov't Bonds	Inter-term Gov't Bonds	U.S. Treasury Bills
Dec-71	9.50	1.92	-1.96	8.47	10.59	12.71	7.41	9.55	5.19	0.99
Dec-72	14.59	-12.24	1.49	1.78	15.07	0.99	3.72	2.20	1.69	0.41
Dec-73	-20.22	-19.01	2.27	-7.52	-21.59	-36.49	-7.04	-9.10	-3.85	-1.72
Dec-74	-31.92	8.87	-7.11	-3.38	-34.46	-28.65	-13.60	-6.99	-5.80	-3.74
Dec-75	29.70	11.36	4.99	3.21	28.23	42.80	7.13	2.04	0.76	-1.13
Dec-76	17.93	26.99	1.62	11.11	18.24	50.15	13.20	11.40	7.69	0.26
Dec-77	-11.68	35.04	2.41	-5.53	-13.04	17.43	-4.74	-6.99	-5.02	-1.55
Dec-78	-0.57	15.85	1.12	-7.80	-2.25	13.24	-8.34	-9.36	-5.08	-1.69
Dec-79	7.46	20.96	-2.98	-10.52	4.68	26.62	-15.43	-12.83	-8.13	-2.59
Dec-80	19.12	5.56	1.24	-13.65	17.89	24.45	-13.48	-14.54	-7.55	-1.03
Dec-81	-17.11	19.78	-3.04	-11.20	-12.73	4.53	-9.34	-6.50	0.47	5.30
Dec-82	9.95	5.31	1.57	26.97	17.02	23.23	37.25	35.13	24.28	6.42
Dec-83	12.64	13.96	5.57	-7.49	18.07	34.56	2.37	-3.03	3.48	4.82
Dec-84	-3.26	-12.18	1.20	5.12	2.23	-10.22	12.42	11.08	9.68	5.67
Dec-85	22.28	-5.36	-0.67	21.58	26.94	20.13	25.36	26.21	15.96	3.81
Dec-86	11.78	-9.96	-3.76	17.30	17.34	5.66	18.51	23.14	13.85	4.98
Dec-87	-0.20	-13.82	2.51	-7.76	0.81	-13.13	-4.48	-6.82	-1.44	1.01
Dec-88	9.65	5.37	0.94	3.13	11.67	17.67	6.02	5.03	1.61	1.85
Dec-89	21.51	-16.33	-1.59	8.99	25.84	5.29	11.07	12.87	8.26	3.56
Dec-90	-10.13	-19.05	0.57	-1.51	-8.68	-26.08	0.64	0.07	3.42	1.61
Dec-91	23.55	10.86	0.49	12.98	26.59	40.33	16.32	15.75	12.03	2.46
Dec-92	3.97	14.62	1.24	4.39	4.59	19.87	6.31	5.01	4.17	0.59
Dec-93	6.98	9.90	-4.28	14.91	7.13	17.74	10.16	15.08	8.26	0.14
Dec-94	-2.49	1.76	2.18	-11.24	-1.32	0.42	-8.22	-10.17	-7.62	1.20
Dec-95	30.29	-2.27	-3.39	24.69	34.17	31.13	24.06	28.41	13.91	2.98
Dec-96	16.87	-4.34	2.35	-5.83	19.01	13.84	-1.86	-4.12	-1.18	1.82
Dec-97	26.70	-7.94	-2.51	10.07	31.13	20.72	11.06	13.91	6.57	3.49
Dec-98	22.62	-27.91	-2.04	7.83	26.54	-8.78	9.00	11.27	8.46	3.19
Dec-99	15.63	7.23	1.67	-13.04	17.88	26.39	-9.87	-11.34	-4.34	1.95
Dec-00	-14.16	6.06	-7.09	14.72	-12.08	-6.75	9.17	17.50	8.90	2.42
Dec-01	-15.13	39.33	6.70	-0.13	-13.23	20.89	8.96	2.11	5.97	2.24
Dec-02	-23.36	11.33	-1.28	15.93	-23.91	-15.29	13.63	15.10	10.31	-0.71
Dec-03	27.38	24.88	3.76	0.42	26.31	57.74	3.32	-0.42	0.51	-0.84
Dec-04	9.56	6.77	0.19	7.22	7.39	14.66	5.29	5.09	-0.97	-1.99
Dec-05	1.88	0.74	-1.80	4.69	1.45	2.20	2.37	4.25	-1.99	-0.42
Dec-06	10.49	0.32	2.03	-3.45	12.93	13.29	0.69	-1.32	0.59	2.20
Dec-07	0.79	-10.16	-6.63	4.99	1.36	-8.94	-1.43	5.57	5.74	0.56
Dec-08	-37.99	0.43	-13.58	23.89	-37.06	-36.78	8.68	25.76	13.00	1.51
Dec-09	26.34	1.28	21.06	-14.99	23.11	24.69	0.29	-17.16	-4.99	-2.56
Dec-10	14.92	14.08	2.08	10.01	13.37	29.33	10.78	8.52	5.54	-1.35
Dec-11	2.07	-5.26	-7.20	27.05	-0.83	-6.04	14.55	23.44	5.68	-2.84
Dec-12	15.93	1.93	7.01	3.37	14.02	16.21	8.78	1.66	-0.08	-1.65
Dec-13	32.36	9.58	6.54	-12.80	30.42	42.91	-8.45	-14.07	-5.11	-1.46
Dec-14	13.67	-9.47	-5.95	24.69	12.83	2.15	16.40	23.77	2.22	-0.73
Dec-15	1.36	-4.91	-0.37	-0.67	0.20	-4.72	-2.18	-1.81	0.60	-1.15

Chapter 5
Annual Returns and Indexes

Returns and benchmark indexes are used to measure the rewards investors earn for holding an asset class. Indexes represent levels of wealth or prices, while returns represent changes in levels of wealth. Total returns for specific asset classes can be divided into two primary components: income and capital appreciation. The income return measures the cash stream earned by holding the security, such as coupon interest for bonds or dividend payments for stocks. In contrast, the capital appreciation return results from a change in the price of the security. The method for computing a return varies with the nature of the payment (income or capital appreciation) and the period of measure (monthly or annual). Indexes are computed by establishing a base period and base value and increasing that value by the returns in successive periods. Indexes are used to illustrate the cumulative growth of wealth from holding an asset class. This chapter describes the computation of the annual returns and indexes.

The first generation of stock indexes was created to assess the market's general direction. One of the oldest and most recognizable market indexes is the Dow Jones Industrial Average, or DJIA, first published on May 26, 1896. When Charles Dow initially calculated the DJIA, which originally consisted of only 12 stocks, the process was simple: Add up the share prices of the stocks in the index and then divide by the number of stocks in the index.[5.1] In this type of index, known as a price-weighted index, higher-priced stocks have a greater influence than lower-priced stocks.

Most modern indexes, however, are market-capitalization weighted, meaning companies with greater overall market capitalization (share price times number of shares outstanding) have a larger influence than companies with lesser market capitalization. Market-cap weighting has a strong theoretical motivation because the capital asset pricing model, or CAPM, implies in its simplest form that every investor should hold every security in proportion to its market capitalization. In contrast, price weighting lacks any theoretical motivation so it is rarely used outside of the Dow Jones Averages (S&P Dow Jones Indices uses market-cap weighting for most of its other indexes).

Market-cap weighting is widely considered to be the central organizing principle of good index construction. Its practical advantage is that the weights adjust automatically as share prices fluctuate, eliminating the need for the frequent and expensive rebalancing that can occur with other weighting schemes. So-called strategic beta or smart beta, or other alternative weighting schemes, seek to outperform market-cap weighted indexes, but deviate from CAPM and are not macroconsistent.

[5.1] Of the original 12 companies listed in the DJIA, General Electric is the only company that remains a component of the average. The total number of companies listed in the DJIA has not changed since 1928, when the number of companies in the index was increased to 30. For more information on the historical makeup of the DJIA, please visit the S&P Dow Jones Indices website at http://www.djaverages.com.

Market-cap weighting is usually implemented with a "float" adjustment that subtracts the number of closely-held and illiquid shares from the number of shares outstanding. A float-adjusted market-cap weighted portfolio is macroconsistent, meaning that if all investors held such a portfolio, all available shares of its constituent stocks would be held, with none left over. Accepting this is an extension of Roll's critique, which states in part that no portfolio can capture shares of all assets (e.g., jewelry, fine wine, automobile collections, etc.) and instruments with market value, so indexes can only approximate a true diversified CAPM portfolio.[5.2] With all other weighting schemes, it is mathematically impossible for all investors to hold the index portfolio.

While there is wide agreement on the general principles of equity index construction, index providers differ in their methodologies that determine which stocks are selected for inclusion, the number of stocks to include, and other details. Exhibit 5.3 summarizes the construction methodologies of the major broad indexes of the U.S. equity market.

Annual and Monthly Returns

Returns on the Basic Asset Classes

Summary statistics of annual total returns of the seven basic SBBI asset classes are presented in Exhibit 2.3 in Chapter 2. The monthly total returns on the asset classes and inflation appear in Appendices A-1, A-4, A-5, A-6, A-10, A-14, and A-15.

Calculating Annual Returns

Annual returns are formed by compounding the 12 monthly returns. Compounding, or linking, monthly returns is multiplying together the return relatives, or one plus the return, then subtracting one from the result. The equation is denoted as the geometric sum as follows:

$$r_{year} = \left[(1 + r_{Jan}) \times (1 + r_{Feb}) ... \times (1 + r_{Dec}) \right] - 1$$

Where:

r_{year} = The compound total return for the year

$r_{Jan}, r_{Feb}, ..., r_{Dec}$ = The returns for the 12 months of the year

---

[5.2] See Roll, R. 1977. "A critique of the asset pricing theory's tests Part I: On past and potential testability of the theory." *Journal of Financial Economics*, Vol. 4, No. 2, P. 129.

The compound return reflects the growth of funds invested in an asset. The following example illustrates the compounding method for a hypothetical year:

Month	Return (%)	Return (Decimal)	Return Relative
January	1	0.01	1.01
February	6	0.06	1.06
March	2	0.02	1.02
April	1	0.01	1.01
May	-3	-0.03	0.97
June	2	0.02	1.02
July	-4	-0.04	0.96
August	-2	-0.02	0.98
September	3	0.03	1.03
October	-3	-0.03	0.97
November	2	0.02	1.02
December	1	0.01	1.01

The return for this hypothetical year is the geometric sum:

(1.01 x 1.06 x 1.02 x 1.01 x 0.97 x 1.02 x 0.96 x 0.98 x 1.03 x 0.97 x 1.02 x 1.01) − 1 = 1.0567 − 1 = 0.0567

or a gain of 5.67%. One dollar invested in this hypothetical asset at the beginning of the year would have grown to slightly less than $1.06. Note that this is different from the simple addition result, (1 + 6 + 2 + 1 − 3 + 2 − 4 − 2 + 3 − 3 + 2 + 1) = 6%

Calculation of Returns From Index Values

Equivalently, annual returns, r_t, can be formed by dividing index values according to:

$$r_t = \left[\frac{V_t}{V_{t-1}} \right] - 1$$

Where:

r_t = The annual return in period t

V_t = The index value as of year-end t

V_{t-1} = The index value as of the pervious year-end, t-1

The construction of index values is discussed later in this chapter in the section entitled "Calculation of Index Values."

Calculation of Annual Income Returns

The conversion of monthly income returns to annual income returns is calculated by adding all the cash flows (income payments) for the period, then dividing the sum by the beginning period price:

$$r_I = \frac{(I_{Jan} + I_{Feb} \ldots + I_{Dec})}{P_0}$$

Where:

r_I	=	The income return for the year
$(I_{Jan}, I_{Feb} \ldots, I_{Dec})$	=	The income payments for the 12 months of the year
P_0	=	The price of the security at the beginning of the year

The following example illustrates the method for a hypothetical year:

Month	Beginning of Month Price ($)	Income Return (Decimal)	Income Payment ($)
January	100	0.006	0.60
February	102	0.004	0.41
March	105	0.002	0.21
April	101	0.001	0.10
May	99	0.005	0.50
June	103	0.004	0.41
July	105	0.003	0.32
August	103	0.002	0.21
September	105	0.003	0.32
October	103	0.004	0.41
November	106	0.001	0.11
December	105	0.002	0.21

Sum the income payments (not the returns), and divide by the price at the beginning of the year:

(0.60 + 0.41 + 0.21 + 0.10 + 0.50 + 0.41 + 0.32 + 0.21 + 0.32 + 0.41 + 0.11 + 0.21) / 100 = 0.0381

or an annual income return of 3.81%.

Annual income and capital appreciation returns do not sum to the annual total return. The difference may be viewed as a reinvestment return, which is the return from investing income from a given month into the same asset class in subsequent months within the year.

Index Values

Index values represent the *cumulative* (i.e., compound) effect of investment returns. For example: In 1926 the total return (i.e., with dividends reinvested) of large-cap stocks was approximately 11.6%. A hypothetical investor investing $1.00 as of December 31, 1925, in large-cap stocks would have seen her investment grow to approximately $1.12 ($1.00 x (1+ 0.116)) by the end of 1926. During the following year (1927), the total return of large-cap stocks was approximately 37.5%. The $1.12 our hypothetical investor began 1927 with would have grown to approximately $1.53 ($1.12 x (1 + 0.375)) by the end of 1927. This can also be calculated as:

$1.53 = $1 x (1+ 0.116) x (1 + 0.375)

Of course, the cumulative effect over the entire 1926–2015 period can also be calculated as follows:

$1.00 x (1+ r_{1926}) x (1 + r_{1927})... x (1 + r_{2015})

Where "r_{year}" is the total return in a given year.

Following this methodology, the $1.00 invested in large-cap stocks at year-end 1925 by our hypothetical investor would have grown to $5,390.43 by the end of 2015. Such growth reveals the power of compounding (reinvesting) one's investment returns.

Year-end index levels (based upon $1.00 invested at the end of 1925) for all six SBBI asset classes plus inflation are displayed in Exhibit 5.1 for the most recent 10 years (2006–2015). Exhibit 5.1 also includes year-end index levels for the capital appreciation ("Capital App") component of total return for large-cap stocks, long-term government bonds, and intermediate-term government bonds.[5.3]

Note that the capital appreciation component of total return is generally a small contributor to total return over the longer term. For example, $1.00 invested at the end of 1925 in large cap stocks would have grown to $5,390.43 by the end of 2015, but capital appreciation contributed only $160.18 to total return, or about 3.0% ($160.18 ÷ $5,390.43). This implies that the other two components of total return (dividend return and reinvestment return) contributed approximately 97% to the total return of large-cap stocks over the 1926–2015 period.

[5.3]   See Appendix B, "Cumulative Wealth Indices of Basic Series," for the full 90-year history (January 1926–December 2015, monthly) of the information found in Exhibit 5.1.

Exhibit 5.1: Basic Series

Indexes of the Year-end Cumulative Wealth over Past 10 Years (Year-end 1925 = $1.00)

Year	Large-Cap Stocks Total Returns	Large-Cap Stocks Capital App	Small-Cap Stocks Total Returns	Long-term Corp Bonds Total Returns	Long-term Gov't Bonds Total Returns	Long-term Gov't Bonds Capital App	Inter-term Gov't Bonds Total Returns	Inter-term Gov't Bonds Capital App	U.S. Treasury Bills Total Returns	Inflation
2006	3,083.56	111.15	15,922.43	103.18	71.69	1.03	64.64	1.37	19.29	11.26
2007	3,252.97	115.08	15,091.09	105.86	78.78	1.08	71.14	1.45	20.19	11.72
2008	2,049.44	70.79	9,548.94	115.15	99.16	1.30	80.47	1.59	20.51	11.73
2009	2,591.82	87.39	12,230.87	118.63	84.38	1.06	78.53	1.52	20.53	12.05
2010	2,982.23	98.56	16,054.70	133.38	92.94	1.12	84.12	1.60	20.55	12.23
2011	3,045.21	98.56	15,532.07	157.32	118.13	1.38	91.53	1.71	20.56	12.59
2012	3,532.55	111.77	18,364.60	174.12	122.18	1.39	93.05	1.73	20.57	12.81
2013	4,676.68	144.85	26,641.17	161.80	106.57	1.17	89.63	1.65	20.58	13.00
2014	5,316.85	161.35	27,419.32	189.76	132.90	1.42	92.32	1.67	20.58	13.10
2015	5,390.43	160.18	26,433.35	187.82	132.03	1.37	93.97	1.67	20.59	13.25

Calculation of Index Values

It is possible to mathematically describe the nature of the indexes in Exhibit 5-1 precisely. These indexes are initialized as of December 31, 1925, at $1.00 (represented by V_0 in the equation below). At the end of each month, a cumulative wealth index (V_n) for each of the monthly return series is formed. This index is formed for month n by taking the product of one plus the returns each period, in the following manner:

$$V_n = V_0 \left[\prod_{t=1}^{n} (1 + r_t) \right]$$

Where:

V_n = The index value at end of period n

V_0 = The initial index calue at time 0

r_t = The return in period t

Using Index Values for Performance Measurement

Index values can be used to determine whether an investment portfolio accumulated more wealth over a period than another portfolio would have done, or whether the investment performed as well as an industry benchmark. In the following example, which produced more wealth: the "investor portfolio" or a hypothetical S&P 500 index fund returning exactly the S&P total return?[5.4]

	Investor Portfolio (%)	S&P 500 (%)
January 1990	-5.35	-6.71
February 1990	0.65	1.29
March 1990	0.23	2.65
Accumulated Wealth of $1.00	$0.955	$0.970

Taking December 1989 as the base period (i.e., $1.00 invested at the end of 1989) and using the computation method described above, the S&P 500 outperformed the investor portfolio.

Computing Returns for Non-Calendar Periods

Index values are also useful for computing returns for non-calendar-year periods. For example, using the index values in Appendix B-6 at the back of this book, the capital appreciation return for long-term government bonds from the end of June 1987 through the end of June 1988 can be calculated by dividing the index value in June 1988 (0.661), by the index value in June 1987 (0.683), and subtracting 1.

This yields:

(0.661 / 0.683) − 1 = -0.0322, or -3.22%

Inflation-Adjusted Returns and Indexes

Exhibit 5.2 presents the inflation-adjusted year-end index values of the six basic SBBI asset classes over the 1926–2015 period.

Note that the inflation-adjusted year-end index values in Exhibit 5.2 demonstrate that investors in large-cap stocks and small-cap stocks multiplied their real wealth (i.e., purchasing power), over the 1926–2015 period by a factor of 406.69 and 1,994.30, respectively.

[5.4] In this example, each index measures total return and assumes monthly reinvestment of dividends.

Exhibit 5.2: Inflation-Adjusted Series
Indexes of Year-end Cummulative Wealth 1926–2015
(Year-end 1925 = $1.00)

Inflation-Adjusted

Year	Large-Cap Stocks	Small-Cap Stocks	Long-term Corp Bonds	Long-term Gov't Bonds	Inter-term Gov't Bonds	U.S. Treasury Bills
Dec-26	1.133	1.018	1.090	1.094	1.070	1.048
Dec-27	1.591	1.269	1.196	1.217	1.142	1.104
Dec-28	2.307	1.790	1.242	1.230	1.164	1.154
Dec-29	2.109	0.869	1.280	1.270	1.231	1.207
Dec-30	1.685	0.572	1.471	1.414	1.398	1.315
Dec-31	1.056	0.318	1.596	1.480	1.509	1.469
Dec-32	1.080	0.335	1.971	1.928	1.831	1.654
Dec-33	1.655	0.810	2.165	1.917	1.855	1.650
Dec-34	1.599	0.986	2.415	2.067	1.982	1.620
Dec-35	2.292	1.342	2.571	2.107	2.059	1.576
Dec-36	3.033	2.185	2.712	2.238	2.097	1.560
Dec-37	1.912	0.890	2.702	2.176	2.065	1.517
Dec-38	2.578	1.216	2.950	2.362	2.257	1.561
Dec-39	2.580	1.226	3.082	2.514	2.370	1.568
Dec-40	2.305	1.152	3.156	2.642	2.417	1.554
Dec-41	1.858	0.955	2.955	2.430	2.214	1.417
Dec-42	2.046	1.263	2.774	2.295	2.065	1.300
Dec-43	2.496	2.306	2.765	2.271	2.058	1.264
Dec-44	2.928	3.472	2.836	2.287	2.052	1.242
Dec-45	3.907	5.895	2.887	2.477	2.051	1.219
Dec-46	3.039	4.409	2.485	2.094	1.753	1.035
Dec-47	2.947	4.081	2.227	1.871	1.623	0.955
Dec-48	3.027	3.890	2.258	1.883	1.609	0.937
Dec-49	3.662	4.744	2.375	2.042	1.677	0.965
Dec-50	4.560	6.221	2.293	1.931	1.596	0.923
Dec-51	5.341	6.335	2.107	1.752	1.513	0.885
Dec-52	6.267	6.469	2.162	1.757	1.524	0.891
Dec-53	6.166	6.012	2.222	1.809	1.564	0.902
Dec-54	9.458	9.703	2.354	1.949	1.614	0.914
Dec-55	12.397	11.642	2.356	1.917	1.597	0.925
Dec-56	12.843	11.803	2.134	1.759	1.547	0.922
Dec-57	11.122	9.788	2.252	1.835	1.619	0.923
Dec-58	15.669	15.859	2.164	1.694	1.570	0.921
Dec-59	17.283	18.187	2.112	1.631	1.541	0.934
Dec-60	17.111	17.333	2.270	1.829	1.697	0.945
Dec-61	21.567	22.741	2.363	1.834	1.717	0.958
Dec-62	19.447	19.792	2.520	1.937	1.791	0.973
Dec-63	23.494	24.060	2.534	1.928	1.790	0.987
Dec-64	27.044	29.370	2.623	1.972	1.841	1.010
Dec-65	29.838	40.848	2.562	1.949	1.825	1.029
Dec-66	25.964	36.751	2.484	1.955	1.848	1.043
Dec-67	31.239	65.471	2.291	1.723	1.812	1.055
Dec-68	33.129	85.005	2.244	1.641	1.808	1.060
Dec-69	28.567	60.042	1.944	1.468	1.692	1.065
Dec-70	28.124	46.993	2.181	1.560	1.874	1.075
Dec-71	31.101	52.968	2.343	1.709	1.971	1.086
Dec-72	35.788	53.492	2.430	1.746	2.005	1.091
Dec-73	28.062	33.971	2.259	1.587	1.927	1.072
Dec-74	18.391	24.238	1.951	1.476	1.815	1.032
Dec-75	23.583	34.612	2.091	1.506	1.829	1.020
Dec-76	27.884	51.971	2.366	1.678	1.970	1.023

Exhibit 5.2: Inflation-Adjusted Series
Indexes of Year-end Cummulative Wealth 1926–2015
(Year-end 1925 = $1.00)

Inflation-Adjusted

Year	Large-Cap Stocks	Small-Cap Stocks	Long-term Corp Bonds	Long-term Gov't Bonds	Inter-term Gov't Bonds	U.S. Treasury Bills
Dec-77	24.247	61.029	2.254	1.561	1.871	1.007
Dec-78	23.701	69.108	2.066	1.415	1.776	0.990
Dec-79	24.810	87.502	1.747	1.233	1.632	0.964
Dec-80	29.248	108.894	1.512	1.054	1.508	0.954
Dec-81	25.526	113.831	1.371	0.985	1.515	1.005
Dec-82	29.870	140.278	1.881	1.332	1.884	1.069
Dec-83	35.268	188.759	1.926	1.291	1.949	1.121
Dec-84	36.055	169.470	2.165	1.434	2.138	1.184
Dec-85	45.768	203.588	2.714	1.810	2.479	1.230
Dec-86	53.704	215.106	3.216	2.229	2.822	1.291
Dec-87	54.137	186.866	3.072	2.077	2.782	1.304
Dec-88	60.456	219.893	3.257	2.182	2.826	1.328
Dec-89	76.077	231.516	3.617	2.462	3.060	1.375
Dec-90	69.473	171.148	3.641	2.464	3.164	1.397
Dec-91	87.944	240.179	4.235	2.852	3.545	1.431
Dec-92	91.977	287.908	4.502	2.995	3.693	1.440
Dec-93	98.539	338.990	4.959	3.447	3.998	1.442
Dec-94	97.239	340.412	4.552	3.096	3.693	1.459
Dec-95	130.467	446.387	5.647	3.976	4.207	1.503
Dec-96	155.264	508.167	5.542	3.812	4.157	1.530
Dec-97	203.599	613.460	6.155	4.342	4.430	1.584
Dec-98	257.633	559.616	6.709	4.832	4.805	1.634
Dec-99	303.690	707.325	6.047	4.284	4.597	1.666
Dec-00	266.998	659.577	6.601	5.033	5.006	1.706
Dec-01	231.668	797.393	7.193	5.140	5.305	1.745
Dec-02	176.278	675.462	8.173	5.916	5.852	1.732
Dec-03	222.658	1065.440	8.445	5.891	5.882	1.718
Dec-04	239.104	1221.614	8.892	6.191	5.824	1.683
Dec-05	242.563	1248.459	9.103	6.454	5.709	1.676
Dec-06	273.915	1414.399	9.165	6.369	5.742	1.713
Dec-07	277.633	1287.985	9.035	6.724	6.072	1.723
Dec-08	174.755	814.233	9.819	8.455	6.861	1.749
Dec-09	215.148	1015.290	9.847	7.005	6.519	1.704
Dec-10	243.908	1313.068	10.909	7.601	6.880	1.681
Dec-11	241.893	1233.774	12.497	9.384	7.271	1.633
Dec-12	275.803	1433.810	13.594	9.539	7.265	1.606
Dec-13	359.708	2049.115	12.445	8.197	6.894	1.583
Dec-14	405.877	2093.132	14.486	10.145	7.047	1.571
Dec-15	406.687	1994.297	14.170	9.961	7.090	1.553

Exhibit 5.3: Major Broad Market U.S. Equity Indexes[*]

Broad Market Index	Index Family Morningstar	MSCI	Russell	S&P Dow Jones
Broad Market Index	Morningstar U.S. Market Index	MSCI Investable Market	Russell 3000	S&P Composite 1500[**]
Percent U.S. Market Cap Coverage	97%	>99%	98%	95%
Total Number of Stocks	1,700+	2500	3000	1500
Transparent, Rules-Based Methodology	Yes	Yes	Yes	No
Eligibility	Stocks of companies domiciled in the U.S. listed on the NYSE, NYSE MKT, or NASDAQ	Stocks of companies domiciled in the U.S. listed on the NYSE, NYSE MKT, or NASDAQ	Stocks of the largest 3000 companies domiciled in the U.S. listed on a U.S. exchange	Stocks of companies domiciled in the U.S. listed on the NYSE, NYSE MKT, or NASDAQ chosen for market size, liquidity, and industry group representation by the S&P Index Committee
Exclusion Criteria	ADRs Limited Partnerships, Investment Trusts (except REITs), Tracking Stocks and Holding Companies	ADRs Limited Partnerships, Investment Trusts (except REITs), Mutual Funds, Equity Derivatives, and Royalty Trusts and LLCs	ADRs Limited Partnerships, Closed-end Mutual Funds, Price < $1, and Royalty Trusts and LLCs	ADRs Limited Partnerships, Investment Trusts (except REITs), Tracking Stocks and Holding Companies, and Royalty Trusts and LLCs
Market Cap Cutoff Method	Market Cap Percent	Fixed Number of Stocks	Fixed Number of Stocks	Fixed Number of Stocks
Unique Cap Cutoff Method	Yes	Yes	Yes	Yes
Unique Style Classification	Yes	No, stocks may be included in more than one style index	No, stocks may be included in more than one style index	No, stocks may be included in more than one style index
Core Style Index	Yes	No	No	No
Reconstitution Frequency	Semiannual	Semiannual	Annual	Ad hoc

[*]The broad market indices shown in Exhibit 5.3 can be disaggregated into capitalization and style indices. For example, the S&P Composite 1500 can be disaggregated into the S&P 500 (large-cap stocks), S&P 400 (mid-cap stocks), and the S&P 600 (small-cap stocks).

[**]The market for U.S. large-cap stocks is represented by the S&P 500 throughout the Ibbotson® SBBI® Yearbook series.

Chapter 6
Statistical Analysis of Returns

Statistical analysis of historical asset returns can reveal the growth rate of wealth invested in an asset or portfolio, the riskiness or volatility of asset classes, the comovement of assets, and the random or cyclical behavior of asset returns. This chapter focuses on arithmetic and geometric mean returns, standard deviations, and serial and cross-correlation coefficients, and discusses the use of each statistic to characterize the various asset classes by growth rate, variability, and safety.

Calculating Arithmetic Mean Return

The arithmetic mean of a series is the simple average of the elements in the series. The arithmetic mean return equation is:

$$r_A = \frac{1}{n} \sum_{t=1}^{n} r_t$$

Where:

r_A	=	The arithmetic mean return
r_t	=	The series return in period t, that is, from time t - 1 to time t
n	=	The inclusive number of periods

Calculating Geometric Mean Return

The geometric mean of a return series over a period is the compound rate of return over the period. The geometric mean return equation is:

$$r_G = \left[\prod_{t=1}^{n} (1 + r_t) \right]^{\frac{1}{n}} - 1$$

Where:

r_G	=	The geometric mean return
r_t	=	The series return in period t
n	=	The inclusive number of periods

The geometric mean return can be restated using beginning and ending period index values. The equation is:

$$r_G = \left[\frac{V_n}{V_0}\right]^{\frac{1}{n}} - 1$$

Where:

r_G	=	The geometric mean return
V_n	=	The ending period index value at time n
V_0	=	The initial index value at time 0
n	=	The inclusive number of periods

The annualized geometric mean return over any period of months can also be computed by expressing n as a fraction. For example: starting at the beginning of 2015 to the end of May 2015 is equivalent to five twelfths of a year, or 0.4167. V_n would be the index value at the end of May 2015; V_0 would be the index value at the beginning of 2014; and n would be 0.4167.

Geometric Mean Versus Arithmetic Mean

A simple example illustrates the difference between geometric and arithmetic means. Suppose $1.00 was invested in a large-cap stock portfolio that experiences successive annual returns of 50% and negative 50%. At the end of the first year, the portfolio is worth $1.50 and at the end of the second year, it is worth $0.75. The annual arithmetic mean is 0.0%, whereas the annual geometric mean is -13.4%. Both are calculated as follows:

$$r_A = \frac{1}{2}(0.50 - 0.50) = 0.00$$

$$r_G = \left[\frac{0.75}{1.00}\right]^{\frac{1}{2}} - 1 = -0.134$$

The geometric mean is backward-looking, measuring the change in wealth over more than one period. On the other hand, the arithmetic mean better represents a typical performance over single periods.

In general, the geometric mean for any period is less than or equal to the arithmetic mean. The two means are equal only for a return series that is constant (i.e., the same return in every period). For a non-constant series, the difference between the two is positively related to the variability or standard deviation of the returns. For example, in Exhibit 6.9, the difference between the arithmetic and geometric mean is much larger for risky large-cap stocks than it is for nearly riskless Treasury bills. This is because the "variability" (as measured by standard deviation) of large-cap stock returns (20.0%) is much greater than the standard deviation of Treasury bill returns (3.1%).

Calculating Standard Deviation

The standard deviation of a series is a measure of the extent to which observations in the series differ from the arithmetic mean of the series. For a series of asset returns, the standard deviation is a measure of the volatility, or risk, of the asset.

In a normally distributed series, about two thirds of the observations lie within one standard deviation of the arithmetic mean; about 95% of the observations lie within two standard deviations; and more than 99% lie within three standard deviations.

For example, the standard deviation for large-cap stock returns from 1926 to 2015 was 20.0% with an annual arithmetic mean of 12.0%. Therefore, roughly two-thirds of the observations have annual returns between -8.0% and 32.0% (12.0% plus or minus 20.0%); approximately 95% of the observations are between -28.0% and 52.0% (12.0% plus or minus 40.0%).

The equation for the standard deviation of a series of returns (σ_r) is:

$$\sigma_r = \sqrt{\frac{1}{n-1}\sum_{t=1}^{n}(r_t - r_A)^2}$$

Where:

r_t	=	The return in period t
r_A	=	The arithmetic mean of the return series r
n	=	the number of periods

The scaling of the standard deviation depends on the frequency of the data; therefore, a series of monthly returns produces a monthly standard deviation. For example, using the monthly returns for the hypothetical year on page 5-3, a monthly standard deviation of 2.94% calculated as follows:

$$0.0294 = \frac{1}{12-1} \times \begin{bmatrix} (0.01-0.005)^2 + (0.06-0.005)^2 + (0.02-0.005)^2 + \\ (0.01-0.005)^2 + (-0.03-0.005)^2 + (0.02-0.005)^2 + \\ (-0.04-0.005)^2 + (-0.02-0.005)^2 + (0.03-0.005)^2 + \\ (-0.03-0.005)^2 + (0.02-0.005)^2 + (0.01-0.005)^2 \end{bmatrix}^{\frac{1}{2}}$$

It is sometimes useful to express the standard deviation of the series in another time scale. To calculate *annualized* monthly standard deviations (σ_n), one uses the following equation.[6.1]

$$\sigma_n = \sqrt{\left[\sigma_1^2 + (1+\mu_1)^2\right]^n - (1+\mu_1)^{2n}}$$

Where:

n	=	The number of periods per year, e.g., 12 for monthly, 4 for quarterly, etc.
σ_1	=	The monthly standard deviation
μ_1	=	The months arithmetic mean

Applying this formula to the prior monthly standard deviation of 2.94% results in an annualized monthly standard deviation of 10.78%. The *annualized* monthly standard deviation is calculated as follows:

$$\sqrt{\left[0.0294^2 + (1+0.005)^2\right]^{12} - (1+0.005)^{2(12)}}$$

This equation is the *exact* form of the common *approximation*:

$$\sigma_n \approx \sqrt{n}\sigma_1$$

The "approximation" treats an annual return as if it were the sum of 12 *independent* monthly returns, whereas the "exact form" treats an annual return as the *compound* return of 12 independent monthly returns. While the approximation can be used for "back of the envelope" calculations, the exact formula should be used in applications of quantitative analysis. Forming inputs for mean-variance optimization is one such example. Note that both the exact formula and the approximation assume that there is no monthly autocorrelation.

Limitations of Standard Deviation[6.2]

Using the statistical measure of standard deviation of returns is clearly the easiest and most elegant way to mathematically express the concept of risk. However, practitioners and academics alike have noted that standard deviation misses important and essential qualities of risk from the standpoint of an investor of capital.

One limitation of standard deviation as a measure of risk is the tacit assumption that returns can be described by a measure that assumes a normal distribution of returns, while it is empirically acknowledged that many financial market returns exhibit excess kurtosis relative to the normal

---

[6.1] The equation appears in Levy, H. & Gunthorpe, D. 1993. "Optimal Investment Proportions in Senior Securities and Equities Under Alternative Holding Periods." *Journal of Portfolio Management*, Vol. 19, No. 4, P. 33.

[6.2] The Limitations of Standard Deviation, the Semi-Variance and Semi-Standard Deviation, and the Issues Regarding Semi-Variance sections were written by Erik Kobayashi-Solomon and Philip Guziec.

(Gaussian) distribution. This characteristic is referred to as a leptokurtic, or "fat-tailed," return distribution. Fat-tailed outcomes reflect market movements far larger than one would reasonably expect from a normal distribution of returns. One of the most extreme examples of a fat-tailed return profile occurred on Oct. 19, 1987, when the Dow Jones Industrial Average declined by 22.68%, or more than 20 standard deviations. The magnitude of the deviation from normal returns can be understood when considering that a normal distribution would predict such a move once in more than 4.5 billion years. More recently, 2008 had 11 days with declines greater than 4 standard deviations, and on May 6, 2010, the Dow Jones Industrial Average declined by 9% in a matter of minutes on an intraday basis, a move that on a daily basis would have been among the top 10 declines in recorded history. Clearly, an awareness of the nature of statistical descriptions of market moves beyond standard deviation is helpful in developing a representative profile of market risk.

Semivariance and Semistandard Deviation

Given academic and practitioner concerns about variance, various approaches have been suggested to more appropriately measure risk. We take a moment here to briefly discuss investor perception of risk and to review another measure semivariance.

One criticism of variance and standard deviation is that an investor is less worried about bidirectional variation in value (the essence of the standard deviation measure) than about an ultimately unrecoverable shortfall in investment capital. In considering risk from this point of view, two cases stand out as the most salient: (i) suffering a realized or mark-to-market loss of capital that prevents fulfillment of a goal or mandate over an investment time frame; and (ii) allocating capital in investments that appreciate too little to fulfill a goal or mandate over the investment time frame. The former case involves an excess of variation in an unacceptable direction; the latter case involves a paucity of variation to an acceptable magnitude.

Of these two cases, most academic work has focused on developing a framework to accurately measure and analyze directionally-specific variance. Foremost in this attempt has been the concept of semivariance.

Semivariance characterizes the downside risk of a distribution and focuses on the portion of risk that is below (to the left of) the mean or a specific target. For example, for a 4% target return, the semivariance describes the variance of the data points below (to the left of) the return of 4%. The semivariance below the mean uses the mean return as the target return. The semistandard deviation is simply the square-root of the semivariance. The semivariance (semistandard deviation) is always lower than the total variance (standard deviation) of the distribution.

$$SV_m = \frac{1}{n} \times \sum_{r_t < r_A}^{n} (r_A - r_t)^2$$

$$SV_t = \frac{1}{n} \times \sum_{r_t < r_T}^{n} (r_T - r_t)^2$$

$$SSTD_m = \sqrt{SV_m}$$

$$SSTD_t = \sqrt{SV_t}$$

Where:

SV_m	=	The semi-variance below mean
SV_t	=	The semi-variance below target
r_A	=	The arithmetic mean return
r_t	=	The series return in period t
r_T	=	The target selection return
n	=	The inclusive number of periods
$SSTD_m$	=	The semi-standard deviation below mean
$SSTD_t$	=	The semi-standard deviation below target

Issues Regarding Semivariance

While semivariance seems to intuitively address issues regarding directionality, it does have empirical, theoretical, and practical shortcomings. Empirically, when returns are measured over relatively short time frames, distributions tend to be symmetric. As such, using semivariance for short time frames effectively gives no extra explanatory power (because semivariance simply equates to one half of the variance) and, in fact, limits the data available for analysis (because the calculation of semivariance discards any positive return observations). When returns are measured over relatively longer time frames (on the order of a year or more), asset returns tend to follow a distribution that is positively skewed. As such, for investors with longer time horizons, semivariance has less explanatory power because the data set is limited to the less germane case, while the richer part of the data set is discarded.

From a theoretical standpoint, the assumption implicit in the calculation of semivariance – that investors do not care about positive variance – has repercussions regarding investor utility functions. Namely, ignoring positive variation implies that an investor is indifferent when presented with the choice between making an uncertain but positive return bet and making a bet that is certain to generate the expected payoff. For example, investors would, under the assumptions of semivariance, be agnostic between a 50-50 bet of generating either 5% or 10% and a sure bet paying 7.5%.

Practically speaking, ignoring upside variation means that we ignore the second aspect of risk mentioned above — a paucity of magnitude. In other words, if one attempts to minimize semivariance, without regard to the degree to which an asset or allocation has upside potential, one runs the risk of generating returns which, while low in downside variance, are also low in upside variance. In this case, one has protected oneself from one class of risk by taking on yet another. Given these issues, semivariance has met with limited acceptance among academics and practitioners alike.

Volatility of the Markets

The volatility of stocks and long-term government bonds is shown by the bar graphs of monthly returns in Exhibit 6.1. The stock market was tremendously volatile in the first few years studied; this period was marked by the 1920s boom, the crash of 1929–1932, and the Great Depression years. The market seemingly settled after World War II and provided more stable returns in the postwar period. In the 1970s and 1980s, stock market volatility increased, but not to the extreme levels of the 1920s and 1930s. In the 1990s and 2000s, volatility was relatively moderate.

Bonds present a mirror image. Long-term government bonds were extremely stable in the 1920s and remained so through the crisis years of the 1930s, providing shelter from the storms of the stock markets. Starting in the late 1960s and early 1970s, however, bond volatility soared; in the 1973–1974 stock market decline, bonds did not provide the shelter they once did. Bond pessimism (i.e., high yields) peaked in 1981 and subsequent returns were sharply positive. While the astronomical interest rates of the 1979–1981 period have passed, the volatility of the bond market remains higher.

Exhibit 6.1: Month-by-Month Returns on Stocks and Bonds (%)
1926–2015

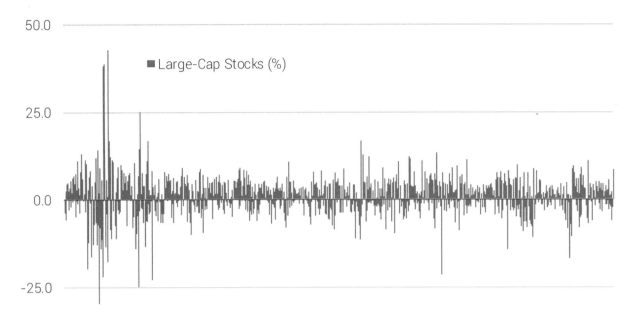

Changes in the Risk of Assets Over Time

Another time series property of great interest is change in volatility or riskiness over time. Such change is indicated by the standard deviation of the series over different subperiods. Exhibit 6.2 shows the annualized monthly standard deviations of the basic data series by decade beginning in 1926 and illustrates differences and changes in return volatility. In this exhibit, the 1920s cover the period 1926–1929 and the 2010s cover the period 2010–2015 (the most recent 10-year period, 2006–2015, is provided in Exhibit 6.3). Equity returns have been the most volatile of the basic series, with volatility peaking in the 1930s due to the instability of the market following the 1929 market crash. The significant bond yield fluctuations of the 1980s caused the fixed-income series' volatility to soar compared to prior decades. Small-cap stocks were the *most* volatile SBBI asset class in all time periods shown in Exhibit 6.2 and 6.3. Treasury bills were the *least* volatile SBBI asset class in all time periods shown in Exhibit 6.2 and 6.3.

Exhibit 6.4 displays the *annualized* standard deviation of the *monthly* returns on each of the basic and derived series from January 1926 to December 2015. The estimates in Exhibit 6.2 and in Exhibit 6.4 are not strictly comparable to Exhibits 2.3, 6.9, and 6.10, where the 90-year period standard deviation of *annual* returns around the 90-year annual arithmetic mean is reported. The arithmetic mean drifts for a series that does not follow a random pattern. A series with a drifting mean will have much higher deviations around its long-term mean than it has around the mean during a particular calendar year.

Exhibit 6.2: Annualized Monthly Standard Deviations by Decade (%)

	1920s*	1930s	1940s	1950s	1960s	1970s	1980s	1990s	2000s	2010s**
Large-Cap Stocks	23.9	41.6	17.5	14.1	13.1	17.2	19.4	15.9	16.3	14.8
Small-Cap Stocks	24.7	78.6	34.5	14.4	21.5	30.8	22.5	20.2	26.1	20.3
Long-term Corp Bonds	1.8	5.3	1.8	4.4	4.9	8.7	14.1	6.9	11.7	9.3
Long-term Gov't Bonds	4.1	5.3	2.8	4.6	6.0	8.7	16.0	8.9	12.4	11.5
Inter-term Gov't Bonds	1.7	3.3	1.2	2.9	3.3	5.2	8.8	4.6	5.2	3.3
U.S. Treasury Bills	0.3	0.2	0.1	0.2	0.4	0.6	0.9	0.4	0.6	0.0
Inflation	2.0	2.5	3.1	1.2	0.7	1.2	1.3	0.7	1.6	1.1

*Based on the period 1926–1929   **Based on the period 2010–2015

Exhibit 6.3: Annualized Monthly Standard Deviations in the Most Recent 10-year Period (2006–2015) (%)

	2006–2015
Large-Cap Stocks	16.3
Small-Cap Stocks	22.2
Long-term Corp Bonds	11.7
Long-term Gov't Bonds	12.7
Inter-term Gov't Bonds	4.1
U.S. Treasury Bills	0.5
Inflation	1.5

As shown in Exhibit 6.4, large-cap stocks and equity risk premiums have virtually the same annualized monthly standard deviations because there is very little deviation in the U.S. Treasury bill series. The series with drifting means (U.S. Treasury bills, inflation rates, and inflation-adjusted U.S. Treasury bills) all tend to have very low annualized monthly standard deviations, since these series are quite predictable from month to month. As seen in exhibits 6.9 and 6.10, however, there is much less predictability for these series over the long term. Because it is difficult to forecast the direction and magnitude of the drift in the long term mean, these series have higher standard deviations over the long term in comparison to their annualized monthly standard deviations.

While equity investors may have the impression that the 2008–2009 global financial crisis was mainly one of the equity markets, a careful look at Exhibit 6.4 will show the much greater effect the crisis had on the price fluctuation of bonds in general and long-term corporate bonds in particular. The annualized standard deviation of long-term corporate bonds recorded a historic high value of 25.5% in 2008, a year that saw the collapse of storied investment banks Lehman Brothers and Bear Sterns. The previous record annualized standard deviation for long-term bonds of 20.2% − measured during 1981 − is more than one fifth lower than the 2008 value, and more than twice the Depression era record of 11.7%, recorded in 1933. In contrast, the peak in large-cap stocks clearly falls early in the series (99.8% in 1933), dwarfing 2009's recorded value of 28.5%. Despite the large number of record-breaking daily index point movements during 2009, this year only represents the eighth-most volatile year in our series. Even removing Depression-era records, 2009 only turns up as the second-most volatile year on record, behind 1987 (34.2%) and just ahead of 1998 (27.9%). Another mark of the severity of bond price fluctuations can be seen by noting that the annualized standard deviations for long-term corporate bonds in 2008 were only three percentage points shy of the annualized standard deviations for the S&P 500 in 2009.

Exhibit 6.4: Basic and Derived Series
Annualized Monthly Standard Deviations (%)

	Basic Series							Derived Series				
Year	Large-Cap Stocks	Small-Cap Stocks	Long-term Corp Bonds	Long-term Gov't Bonds	Inter-term Gov't Bonds	U.S. Treasury Bills	Inflation	Equity Risk Premium	Small Stock Premium	Bond Default Premium	Bond Horizon Premium	U.S. Treasury Bills
1926	13.10	16.89	0.96	1.88	1.02	0.32	2.03	12.73	9.74	1.63	1.68	2.06
1927	17.90	21.19	1.49	2.88	1.05	0.11	2.78	17.35	11.13	2.90	2.76	3.03
1928	24.62	28.68	1.87	3.21	1.27	0.32	1.72	23.65	14.48	2.74	3.06	1.84
1929	30.55	18.35	2.42	6.56	2.82	0.21	1.62	29.16	7.76	6.79	6.20	1.62
1930	21.19	25.55	2.38	2.34	2.43	0.30	2.03	20.65	11.68	2.45	2.12	2.31
1931	30.04	45.35	5.91	5.24	3.72	0.16	1.35	29.72	27.44	5.25	5.18	1.75
1932	83.36	147.23	7.71	9.50	2.94	0.29	1.74	82.72	41.92	12.69	9.35	2.40
1933	99.82	286.56	11.74	5.11	3.70	0.10	4.24	99.27	72.06	7.67	5.06	4.15
1934	22.64	73.85	3.10	4.50	4.07	0.04	2.03	22.59	42.03	2.52	4.46	1.94
1935	23.73	36.09	2.53	2.88	2.78	0.01	2.18	23.69	15.08	1.36	2.88	2.05
1936	19.06	66.23	1.18	2.25	1.27	0.02	1.55	19.02	37.72	1.78	2.25	1.51
1937	16.33	21.81	1.99	5.04	2.44	0.05	1.74	16.28	16.46	3.93	5.01	1.63
1938	58.87	114.31	2.38	2.35	2.48	0.07	1.78	58.85	30.94	1.89	2.31	1.89
1939	31.09	95.06	5.36	8.59	5.06	0.02	2.26	31.07	43.55	8.40	8.59	2.24
1940	25.56	46.88	2.02	5.20	3.25	0.02	1.09	25.55	25.68	3.92	5.19	1.07
1941	12.95	29.10	1.67	3.71	1.50	0.03	2.30	12.92	20.75	3.59	3.70	1.90
1942	17.67	37.55	0.73	1.42	0.79	0.03	1.39	17.60	25.78	1.16	1.42	1.17
1943	19.59	71.56	0.90	0.65	0.51	0.01	2.35	19.53	33.94	0.58	0.65	2.21
1944	9.30	28.75	1.34	0.37	0.29	0.01	0.97	9.27	15.14	1.11	0.37	0.94
1945	17.64	37.50	1.42	2.97	0.50	0.01	1.32	17.59	16.92	1.92	2.96	1.26
1946	17.72	27.25	2.15	2.73	0.94	0.00	6.65	17.65	12.20	1.74	2.72	4.66
1947	10.15	18.24	2.13	2.86	0.52	0.07	3.34	10.09	10.58	3.26	2.90	2.79
1948	21.49	24.11	2.20	1.95	0.59	0.07	2.90	21.30	6.44	1.92	1.96	2.73
1949	12.02	18.75	2.17	1.83	0.47	0.02	1.63	11.89	6.72	2.44	1.80	1.71
1950	13.99	20.58	1.07	1.45	0.34	0.03	1.81	13.83	8.82	1.35	1.44	1.62
1951	15.04	16.02	3.92	3.03	1.91	0.05	1.79	14.80	6.12	2.67	2.95	1.63
1952	13.32	9.66	2.85	3.24	1.32	0.08	1.15	13.11	3.78	3.82	3.23	1.14
1953	9.32	10.90	5.53	5.16	3.26	0.11	1.01	9.21	8.74	3.50	5.07	0.95
1954	19.27	20.02	2.35	3.47	1.93	0.06	0.74	19.08	10.08	2.32	3.42	0.77
1955	16.11	7.70	2.17	3.60	1.65	0.14	0.67	15.91	8.83	2.36	3.47	0.71
1956	15.86	8.39	3.00	4.28	2.64	0.10	1.08	15.50	7.87	2.60	4.15	1.00
1957	11.48	10.42	9.40	8.26	5.57	0.07	0.66	11.13	9.98	5.48	8.00	0.65
1958	8.74	15.44	4.56	6.29	4.50	0.27	0.90	8.47	7.99	3.73	6.16	0.88
1959	8.91	10.34	3.91	3.25	2.72	0.18	0.65	8.67	7.31	3.35	3.18	0.59
1960	13.63	13.37	3.93	6.45	4.99	0.27	0.71	13.36	7.07	3.85	6.22	0.80
1961	11.16	19.02	3.63	3.55	1.57	0.07	0.51	10.94	7.72	3.93	3.51	0.50
1962	18.97	21.58	2.27	3.70	2.15	0.08	0.67	18.46	8.38	2.17	3.63	0.70
1963	11.91	13.47	1.25	0.72	0.60	0.08	0.55	11.54	7.26	1.28	0.72	0.55
1964	4.63	7.05	1.46	0.91	0.78	0.06	0.41	4.47	3.78	1.84	0.87	0.38
1965	9.56	20.55	1.96	1.51	1.83	0.08	0.67	9.26	11.19	1.09	1.47	0.64
1966	9.96	17.80	4.80	8.08	4.13	0.11	0.71	9.50	13.76	5.39	7.66	0.73
1967	14.89	36.96	7.33	6.58	3.81	0.16	0.44	14.24	17.30	5.14	6.27	0.54
1968	14.49	28.29	7.39	7.93	3.50	0.09	0.42	13.76	16.40	3.57	7.52	0.40
1969	12.10	18.71	6.93	9.95	5.54	0.22	0.62	11.35	9.73	7.39	9.34	0.63
1970	21.43	27.68	11.28	15.07	7.05	0.22	0.44	20.17	13.26	9.22	14.11	0.47
1971	15.74	29.73	11.12	10.67	6.98	0.19	0.57	15.07	14.50	6.12	10.15	0.63
1972	7.28	16.60	3.21	5.85	1.97	0.17	0.41	7.00	11.36	3.97	5.61	0.42
1973	12.53	21.94	7.57	8.38	4.99	0.37	1.53	11.62	13.88	5.12	7.71	1.34
1974	18.93	20.15	11.45	8.64	5.73	0.36	0.91	17.69	21.83	5.76	8.05	0.89
1975	24.35	46.28	11.49	9.13	5.68	0.21	0.78	22.96	19.59	4.43	8.55	0.77
1976	17.34	50.83	5.21	5.43	4.24	0.13	0.48	16.42	27.60	1.55	5.15	0.45
1977	8.85	17.05	4.57	5.69	2.73	0.19	0.77	8.38	13.50	1.56	5.41	0.85

Exhibit 6.4: Basic and Derived Series
Annualized Monthly Standard Deviations (%)

	Basic Series							Derived Series				
Year	Large-Cap Stocks	Small-Cap Stocks	Long-term Corp Bonds	Long-term Gov't Bonds	Inter-term Gov't Bonds	U.S. Treasury Bills	Inflation	Equity Risk Premium	Small Stock Premium	Bond Default Premium	Bond Horizon Premium	U.S. Treasury Bills
1978	17.92	42.56	4.45	4.45	2.07	0.36	0.67	16.73	27.21	1.66	4.21	0.78
1979	16.00	34.71	10.43	10.81	7.31	0.29	0.53	14.48	15.59	2.16	9.77	0.60
1980	23.94	39.80	20.12	21.16	16.77	0.98	1.45	22.02	14.48	4.57	18.60	1.18
1981	12.33	21.37	20.21	23.25	11.84	0.51	1.15	10.75	15.65	5.23	20.23	1.00
1982	23.36	21.97	17.80	14.40	8.91	0.78	1.64	21.54	7.80	5.37	13.37	1.42
1983	12.21	21.83	10.86	11.43	5.72	0.18	0.73	11.30	14.80	3.98	10.52	0.67
1984	14.99	14.57	12.97	13.34	7.17	0.34	0.61	13.62	4.41	1.92	11.97	0.61
1985	15.62	18.10	13.28	15.78	6.69	0.18	0.33	14.44	6.29	2.56	14.56	0.35
1986	21.27	15.49	9.71	21.58	6.53	0.20	1.03	20.01	6.52	9.54	20.26	1.17
1987	34.17	34.45	9.67	10.09	4.93	0.23	0.68	32.50	11.31	3.03	9.49	0.64
1988	11.70	16.08	9.10	11.03	5.00	0.36	0.57	11.08	11.31	2.45	10.45	0.64
1989	16.17	11.65	7.13	9.53	6.07	0.23	0.63	14.93	6.91	2.36	8.73	0.67
1990	18.28	16.85	7.55	9.89	4.75	0.18	1.16	16.95	6.80	2.67	9.18	1.16
1991	20.49	22.50	5.08	7.33	3.49	0.17	0.54	19.40	9.77	2.13	6.99	0.51
1992	7.98	21.58	5.77	7.62	5.83	0.14	0.54	7.75	19.96	2.32	7.38	0.53
1993	6.65	11.43	5.53	8.38	4.44	0.05	0.57	6.48	8.29	2.38	8.15	0.57
1994	10.76	10.38	6.70	8.12	4.50	0.24	0.47	10.33	6.35	2.27	7.77	0.62
1995	6.99	12.65	7.37	9.70	3.94	0.13	0.60	6.67	8.41	1.88	9.11	0.64
1996	13.25	21.06	7.62	9.33	3.89	0.09	0.61	12.63	15.18	2.14	8.87	0.62
1997	21.09	22.13	8.00	10.44	4.10	0.13	0.53	20.01	16.45	2.30	9.91	0.60
1998	27.90	25.76	5.91	7.70	4.63	0.16	0.30	26.69	6.81	4.35	7.24	0.31
1999	15.78	26.31	4.57	5.25	3.45	0.10	0.77	15.02	19.21	1.90	5.00	0.77
2000	16.02	40.42	5.88	6.92	3.43	0.17	0.99	15.14	44.92	4.10	6.58	1.06
2001	18.15	34.55	8.17	9.69	5.00	0.39	1.25	17.52	21.21	6.02	9.31	0.99
2002	16.90	20.14	8.82	12.36	6.77	0.04	0.83	16.64	18.02	4.50	12.15	0.79
2003	14.47	25.04	13.47	14.82	6.22	0.04	1.21	14.33	10.89	2.77	14.66	1.17
2004	8.06	18.81	9.13	9.73	4.88	0.12	1.14	7.90	10.58	1.03	9.61	1.17
2005	8.31	16.11	8.56	9.66	3.76	0.19	1.96	8.03	8.78	1.38	9.39	1.97
2006	6.46	16.09	8.23	8.82	2.46	0.11	1.55	6.18	9.96	2.19	8.38	1.61
2007	10.20	11.57	5.49	7.95	5.33	0.19	1.19	9.70	6.03	4.81	7.64	1.10
2008	14.20	19.83	25.50	22.57	6.94	0.23	3.20	13.96	12.23	11.16	22.44	3.07
2009	28.52	42.42	14.88	14.47	4.85	0.02	1.02	28.48	14.48	16.44	14.44	0.96
2010	22.43	32.44	9.12	13.04	4.20	0.01	0.49	22.40	9.82	7.72	13.02	0.49
2011	16.51	23.35	12.24	15.43	3.41	0.01	1.34	16.51	8.54	9.31	15.42	1.26
2012	12.14	15.55	9.49	10.08	2.10	0.01	1.37	12.14	5.83	7.53	10.08	1.33
2013	11.02	16.57	8.04	8.05	3.28	0.00	0.99	11.02	7.14	3.65	8.05	0.96
2014	9.33	15.73	6.62	8.34	2.50	0.00	1.34	9.33	9.62	2.62	8.34	1.32
2015	14.00	13.96	8.93	11.07	3.29	0.01	1.14	14.00	9.42	3.20	11.06	1.12

Correlation Coefficients: Serial and Cross-Correlations

The behavior of an asset return series over time reveals its predictability. For example, a series may be random or unpredictable, or it may be subject to trends, cycles, or other patterns, making the series predictable to some degree. The serial correlation coefficient of a series determines its predictability given knowledge of the last observation. The cross-correlation coefficient (often shortened to "correlation") between two series determines the predictability of one series, conditional on knowledge of the other.

Serial Correlations

The serial correlation of a return series, also known as the first-order autocorrelation, describes the extent to which the return in one period is related to the return in the next period. A return series with a high (near 1) serial correlation is very predictable from one period to the next, while one with a low (near 0) serial correlation is random and unpredictable.

The serial correlation of a series is closely approximated by the equation for the cross correlation between two series. The data, however, are the series and its "lagged" self. For example, the lagged series is the series of one-period-old returns:

Year	Return Series	Lagged Return Series
1	0.10	*undefined*
2	-0.10	0.10
3	0.15	-0.10
4	0.00	0.15

Cross-Correlations

The cross-correlation between two series measures the extent to which they are linearly related.[6.3] The correlation coefficient measures the sensitivity of return on one asset class or portfolio to the return of another. The correlation equation between return series X and Y is:

$$p_{X,Y} = \left[\frac{Cov(X,Y)}{\sigma_x \sigma_y} \right]$$

Where:

$Cov(X,Y)$	=	The covariance of X and Y, defined below
σ_X	=	The standard deviation of X
σ_y	=	The standard deviation of Y

[6.3] Two series can be related in a nonlinear way and have a correlation coefficient of zero. An example is the function $y = x^2$, for which $p_{x,y} = 0$.

The covariance equation is:

$$Cov(X,Y) = \frac{1}{n-1}\sum_{t=1}^{n}(r_{X,t} - r_{X,A})(r_{Y,t} - r_{Y,A})$$

Where:

$r_{X,t}$	=	The return for series X in period t
$r_{Y,t}$	=	The return for series Y in period t
$r_{X,A}$	=	The arithmetic mean of series X
$r_{Y,A}$	=	The arithmetic mean of series Y
n	=	The number of periods

Correlations of the Basic Series

Exhibit 6.5 presents the annual cross-correlations and serial correlations for the seven basic series. Long-term government bond returns and long-term corporate bond returns are highly correlated with each other, but negatively correlated with inflation. To the degree that inflation is unanticipated, it has a negative effect on fixed-income securities. In addition, U.S. Treasury bills and inflation are reasonably highly correlated, a result of the post-1951 "tracking" described in Chapter 2. Lastly, both the U.S. Treasury bills and inflation series display high serial correlations.

Exhibit 6.5: Basic Series: Serial and Cross-Correlations of Historical Annual Returns 1926–2015

	Large-Cap Stocks	Small-Cap Stocks	Long-term Corp Bonds	Long-term Gov't Bonds	Inter-term Gov't Bonds	U.S. Treasury Bills	Inflation
Large-Cap Stocks	1.00						
Small-Cap Stocks	0.80	1.00					
Long-term Corp Bonds	0.15	0.04	1.00				
Long-term Gov't Bonds	0.00	-0.10	0.90	1.00			
Inter-term Gov't Bonds	-0.03	-0.11	0.86	0.86	1.00		
U.S. Treasury Bills	-0.02	-0.08	0.16	0.18	0.47	1.00	
Inflation	-0.01	0.05	-0.15	-0.14	0.01	0.41	1.00
Serial Correlation	0.02	0.06	0.04	-0.16	0.14	0.91	0.64

Correlations of the Derived Series

The annual cross-correlations and serial correlations for the four risk premium series and inflation are presented in Exhibit 6.6. Notice that inflation is negatively correlated with the horizon premium. Increasing inflation causes long-term bond yields to rise and prices to fall; therefore, a negative horizon premium is observed in times of rising inflation.

Exhibit 6.7 presents annual cross-correlations and serial correlations for the inflation-adjusted asset return series. It is interesting to observe how the relationship between the asset returns are substantially different when these returns are expressed in inflation-adjusted terms (as compared with nominal terms). In general, the cross-correlations between asset classes are higher when one accounts for inflation (i.e., subtracts inflation from the nominal return).

Exhibit 6.6: Risk Premia and Inflation: Serial and Cross-Correlations of Historical Annual Returns 1926–2015

	Equity Risk Premium	Small Stock Premium	Bond Default Premium	Bond Horizon Premium	Inflation
Equity Risk Premium	1.00				
Small Stock Premium	0.28	1.00			
Bond Default Premium	0.29	0.18	1.00		
Bond Horizon Premium	0.01	-0.10	-0.52	1.00	
Inflation	-0.07	0.11	0.00	-0.27	1.00
Serial Correlation	0.02	0.36	-0.30	-0.17	0.64

Exhibit 6.7: Inflation-Adjusted Series: Serial and Cross-Correlations of Historical Annual Returns 1926–2015

Inflation-Adjusted Series	Inflation-Adjusted						
	Large-Cap Stocks	Small-Cap Stocks	Long-term Corp Bonds	Long-term Gov't Bonds	Inter-term Gov't Bonds	U.S. Treasury Bills	Inflation
Large-Cap Stocks	1.00						
Small-Cap Stocks	0.80	1.00					
Long-term Corp Bonds	0.21	0.07	1.00				
Long-term Gov't Bonds	0.08	-0.06	0.92	1.00			
Inter-term Gov't Bonds	0.07	-0.07	0.91	0.90	1.00		
U.S. Treasury Bills	0.09	-0.06	0.53	0.50	0.70	1.00	
Inflation	-0.19	-0.07	-0.54	-0.48	-0.58	-0.71	1.00
Serial Correlation	0.01	0.03	0.15	-0.06	0.21	0.67	0.64

Is Serial Correlation in the Derived Series Random?

The risk/return relationships in the historical data are represented in the equity risk premium, the small-cap premium, the bond horizon premium, and the bond default premium. The real/nominal historical relationships are represented in the inflation rates and the real interest rates. The objective is to uncover whether each series is random or is subject to any trends, cycles, or other patterns.

The one-year serial correlation coefficients measure the degree of correlation between returns from each year and the previous year for the same series, as seen in Exhibit 6.8. Highly positive (near 1) serial correlations indicate trends, while highly negative (near -1) serial correlations indicate cycles. Looking to exhibit 6.8, the analysis suggests that both inflation rates and real riskless rates are follow trends. Serial correlations near zero suggest no patterns (i.e., random behavior), so the analysis suggests that the equity risk premium and the bond horizon premium are random variables.

The small stock premium and the bond default premium, however, fall into a middle range that makes it more difficult to determine whether the small stock premium is a trend (or is random), and whether the bond default premium is a cycle (or is random). In these two cases, one could argue that the small stock premium is a *possible* trend, and the bond default premium is a *possible* cycle.

Exhibit 6.8: Interpretation of the Annual Serial Correlations

Series	Serial Correlation	Interpretation
Equity Risk Premium	0.02	Random
Small Stock Premium	0.36	Possible Trend
Bond Default Premium	-0.30	Possible Cycle
Bond Horizon Premium	-0.17	Random
Inflation	0.64	Trend
Real Interest Rates	0.91	Trend

Basic Series Summary Statistics

Exhibit 6.9 presents summary statistics of annual total return, and where applicable, income and capital appreciation, for each asset class. The summary statistics presented here are arithmetic mean, geometric mean, standard deviation, and serial correlation. Exhibit 6.10 presents summary statistics for the six inflation-adjusted total return series.

Exhibit 6.9: Total Returns, Income Returns, and Capital Appreciation Returns of the SBBI Asset Classes Summary Statistics of Annual Returns (%)
1926–2015

	Geometric Mean (%)	Arithmetic Mean (%)	Standard Deviation (%)	Serial Correlation
Large-Cap Stocks				
Total Return	10.0	12.0	20.0	0.02
Income	4.0	4.0	1.6	0.91
Capital Appreciation	5.8	7.7	19.3	0.01
Small-Cap Stocks (TR)	12.0	16.5	32.0	0.06
Long-term Corp Bonds (TR)	6.0	6.3	8.4	0.04
Long-term Gov't Bonds				
Total Return	5.6	6.0	10.0	-0.16
Income	5.0	5.0	2.6	0.96
Capital Appreciation	0.4	0.7	8.9	-0.26
Inter-term Gov't Bonds				
Total Return	5.2	5.3	5.7	0.14
Income	4.4	4.5	2.9	0.96
Capital Appreciation	0.6	0.7	4.5	-0.17
U.S. Treasury Bills (TR)	3.4	3.5	3.1	0.91
Inflation	2.9	3.0	4.1	0.64

Exhibit 6.9 shows that over 1926–2015 small-cap stocks were the riskiest asset class with a standard deviation of 32.0%, but provided the greatest rewards to long-term investors, with an arithmetic mean annual return of 16.5%. The geometric mean of the small-cap series is 12.0%. Large-cap stocks, long-term government bonds, long-term corporate bonds, and intermediate-term government bonds are progressively less risky, and have lower average returns. Treasury bills were nearly riskless and had the lowest return. In general, risk is rewarded by a higher return over the long term.

Inflation-Adjusted Series Summary Statistics

Inflation-adjusted basic series summary statistics are presented in Exhibit 6.10. Note that the real rate of interest is close to zero (0.5%) on average. For the 90-year period, the geometric and arithmetic means are lower by the amount of inflation than those of the nominal series.

The standard deviations of large-cap and small-cap stock returns remain approximately the same after adjusting for inflation, while inflation-adjusted returns of long-term corporate bonds, long-term government bonds, intermediate-term government bonds, and Treasury bills are more volatile (i.e., have higher standard deviations).

Exhibit 6.10: Inflation-Adjusted Series Summary Statistics of Annual Returns (%) 1926–2015

	Geometric Mean (%)	Arithmetic Mean (%)	Standard Deviation (%)	Serial Correlation
Large-Cap Stocks	6.9	8.8	20.0	0.01
Small-Cap Stocks	8.8	13.2	31.4	0.03
Long-term Corp Bonds	3.0	3.4	9.5	0.15
Long-term Gov't Bonds	2.6	3.1	11.0	-0.06
Inter-term Gov't Bonds	2.2	2.4	6.7	0.21
U.S. Treasury Bills	0.5	0.6	3.8	0.67

Rolling-Period Standard Deviations

Rolling-period standard deviations are obtained by rolling a window of fixed length along each time series and computing the standard deviation for the asset class for each window of time. They are useful for examining the volatility or riskiness of returns for holding periods similar to those actually experienced by investors. Exhibits 6.11 and 6.12 graphically depict the volatility. Monthly data are used to maximize the number of data points included in the standard deviation computation.

Exhibit 6.11 places the 60-month rolling standard deviation for large-cap stocks, small-cap stocks, and long-term government bonds on the same scale. It is interesting to see the relatively high standard deviation for small- and large-cap stocks in the 1930s, with an apparent lessening of volatility for 60-month holding periods during the 1980s. Note also how the standard deviation for long-term government bonds reaches the level of both stock asset classes during part of the 1980s. Exhibit 6.12 places the 60-month rolling standard deviation for long-term and intermediate-term government bonds and Treasury bills on the same scale.

Exhibit 6.11: Rolling 60-month Standard Deviations: Large-cap Stocks, Small-cap Stocks and Long-term Government Bonds (%)

Exhibit 6.12: Rolling 60-month Standard Deviations: Long-term Government Bonds, Intermediate-term Government Bonds, and Treasury Bills (%)

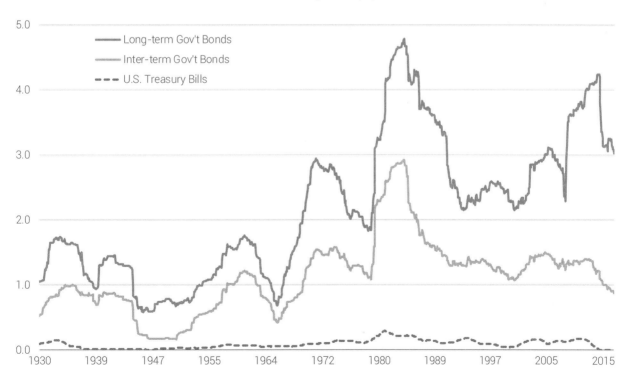

Rolling-Period Correlations

Rolling-period correlations are obtained by moving a window of fixed length along time series for two asset classes and computing the cross-correlation between the two asset classes for each window of time. They are useful for examining how asset class returns vary together for holding periods similar to those actually experienced by investors. Monthly data are used to maximize the number of data points included in the correlation computation.

Exhibits 6.13 and 6.14 show cross-correlations between two asset classes for 60-month holding periods. The first rolling period covered is January 1926 to December 1930, so the graphs begin at December 1930. Exhibit 6.13 shows the volatility of the correlations between large-cap stocks and long-term government bonds. There are wide fluctuations between strong positive and strong negative correlations over the past 90 years. Exhibit 6.14 shows the correlation between Treasury bills and inflation. These asset classes also show wide fluctuations in correlation over the past 90 years.

Exhibit 6.13: Rolling 60-month Correlation: Large-cap Stocks and Long-term Government Bonds 1926–1930 through 2011–2015

Exhibit 6.14: Rolling 60-month Correlation: Treasury Bills and Inflation
1926–1930 through 2011–2015

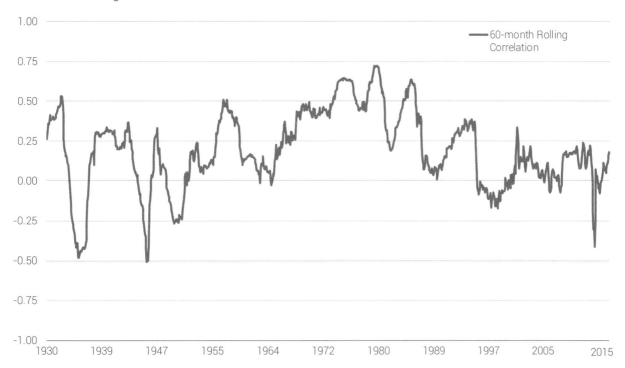

The True Impact of Asset Allocation on Return

The importance of asset allocation has been the subject of considerable debate and misunderstanding for decades. A May 2010 article pinpoints one of the primary sources of confusion surrounding the importance of asset allocation: How much of a portfolio's level of return comes from a fund's asset-allocation policy?[6.4]

Note: This section was written by Thomas Idzorek, head of investment methodology and economic research at Morningstar.

The Debate

The seminal work on the importance of asset allocation, the catalyst of a 25-year debate, and unfortunately the source of what is arguably the most prolific misunderstanding among investment professionals, is the 1986 article, "Determinants of Portfolio Performance," by Gary Brinson, Randolph Hood, and Gilbert Beebower (BHB).[6.5] BHB regressed the time series returns of each fund on a weighted combination of indexes reflecting each fund's asset-allocation policy. In one of the many analyses that BHB carried out (and probably one of the least important ones), they found that the policy mix explained 93.6% of the average fund's return variation over time (as measured by the R-squared of the regression) — the key word being "variation."

[6.4] Idzorek, T. M. "Asset Allocation is King." *Morningstar Advisor*, April/May, 2010, P. 28.

[6.5] Brinson, G.P., Hood, L.R., & Beebower, G.L. 1986. " Determinants of Portfolio Performance." *Financial Analysts Journal*, Vol. 42, No. 4, P. 39.

Unfortunately, this 93.6% has been widely misinterpreted. Many practitioners incorrectly believe the number means that 93.6% of a portfolio's return level (for example, a fund's 10-year annualized return) comes from a fund's asset-allocation policy. This is not true. The truth is that, in aggregate, 100% of portfolio return levels comes from asset allocation policy.

Return 'Levels' Versus Return 'Variations'

It is imperative to distinguish between return levels and return variations. In the big picture, investors care far more about return levels than they do return variation. The often-cited 93.6% says nothing about return levels, even though that is what so many practitioners mistakenly believe. It is possible to have a high R-squared, indicating that the return variations in the asset class factors did a good job of explaining the return variations of the fund in question, yet see the weighted-average composite asset-allocation policy benchmark produce a significantly different return level from the fund in question. This is the case in BHB's study. Despite the high average 93.6% R-squared of their 91 separate time-series regressions, the average geometric annualized return of the 91 funds in their sample was 9.01% versus 10.11% for the corresponding policy portfolios.

So even though 93.6% is the number that seems to be stuck in everyone's mind, 112% (10.11% divided by 9.01%) of return levels in the study's sample came from asset allocation policy. To put it bluntly, when it comes to return levels, asset allocation is king. In aggregate, 100% of return levels come from asset allocation before fees and somewhat more after fees. This is a mathematical truth that stems from the concept of an all-inclusive market portfolio and the fact that active management is a zero-sum game. This fundamental truth is somewhat boring; therefore, it is often lost.

Chapter 7
Company Size and Return[7.1]

One of the most remarkable discoveries of modern finance is the finding of a relationship between company size and return, generally referred to as the "size effect." The size effect is based on the empirical observation that companies of smaller size tend to have higher returns than do larger companies.

In 1981, study by Rolf Banz examined the returns of New York Stock Exchange (NYSE) small-cap companies compared to the returns of NYSE large-cap companies over the period 1926–1975.[7.2] What Banz found was that the returns of small-cap companies were *greater* than the returns for large-cap companies. Banz's 1981 study is often cited as the first comprehensive study of the size effect. There is a significant (negative) relationship between size and historical equity returns as size decreases, returns tend to increase, and vice versa.

The size effect is not without controversy, nor is this controversy something new. Traditionally, small companies are believed to have greater required rates of return than large companies because small companies are inherently riskier.[7.3] It is not clear, however, whether this is due to size itself, or to other factors closely related to or correlated with size, and thus the qualification that Banz noted in his 1981 article remains pertinent today:[7.4, 7.5]

"It is not known whether size [as measured by market capitalization] per se is responsible for the effect or whether size is just a proxy for one or more true unknown factors correlated with size."

[7.1] This chapter is an overview of the relationship between size and return that is limited to analyzing the relative historical performance of "large-cap stocks" and "small-cap stocks," and does *not* include the much expanded analyses of the "size effect" as it relates to the development of cost of equity capital found in the *2016 Valuation Handbook – Guide to Cost of Capital* (also published by John Wiley & Sons). The *2016 Valuation Handbook – Guide to Cost of Capital* includes the data previously published in the Morningstar/Ibbotson® *Stocks, Bonds, Bills, and Inflation®* (SBBI®) *Valuation Yearbook* and the Duff & Phelps *Risk Premium Report*. The *Valuation Handbook – Guide to Cost of Capital* includes the size premia data, the industry risk premia data, the equity risk premia data, and the methodology that can be used to develop cost of equity capital estimates for an individual business, business ownership interest, security, or intangible asset. For more information about the *2016 Valuation Handbook – Guide to Cost of Capital* and other Duff & Phelps valuation data resources published by John Wiley & Sons, please go to: www.wiley.com/go/ValuationHandbooks.

[7.2] Rolf W. Banz, "The Relationship between Return and Market Value of Common Stocks," *Journal of Financial Economics* (March 1981): 3–18. This paper is often cited as the first comprehensive study of the size effect.

[7.3] Typically cited as possible reasons for the greater risks of smaller companies include (not an exhaustive list): Large firms may have greater ability to enter the market of the small firm and take market share. Large companies likely have more resources to "weather the storm" in economic downturns. Large firms can generally spend more on R&D, advertising, and typically even have greater ability to hire the "best and brightest." Larger firms may have greater access to capital, broader management depth, and less dependency on just a few customers. A larger number of analysts typically follow large firms relative to small firms, so there is probably more information available about large firms, etc.

[7.4] Even after controlling for size, research suggests that liquidity is still a systematic factor and a predictor of returns. See Roger G. Ibbotson, Zhiwu Chen, and Wendy Y. Hu, "Liquidity as an Investment Style," Yale Working Paper, updated April 2012. A free download of this paper is available at www.zebracapm.com.

[7.5] "Liquidity" is discussed in detail in Chapter 9, "Liquidity Investing."

Construction of the CRSP Size Decile Portfolios

The portfolios used in this chapter are those created by the Center for Research in Security Prices, or CRSP, at the University of Chicago's Booth School of Business. CRSP has refined the methodology of creating size-based portfolios and has applied this methodology to the entire universe of NYSE/NYSE MKT/NASDAQ-listed securities going back to 1926.[7.6] The universe of companies excludes:

- Closed-end mutual funds

- Preferred stocks

- Real estate investment trusts

- Foreign stocks

- American Depositary Receipts

- Unit investment trusts

- Americus Trusts

All companies on the NYSE are ranked by the combined market capitalization of their eligible equity securities. The companies are then split into 10 equally populated groups, or deciles. Eligible companies traded on the NYSE MKT (the former AMEX) and the Nasdaq National Market (NASDAQ) are then assigned to the appropriate deciles according to their capitalization in relation to the NYSE breakpoints.

The portfolios are rebalanced quarterly, using closing prices for the last trading day of March, June, September, and December. Securities added during the quarter are assigned to the appropriate portfolio when two consecutive month-end prices are available. If the final NYSE price of a security that becomes delisted is a month-end price, then that month's return is included in the quarterly return of the security's portfolio. When a month-end NYSE price is missing, the month-end value of the security is derived from merger terms, quotations on regional exchanges, and other sources. If a month-end value still is not determined, the last available daily price is used. Base security returns are monthly holding period returns. All distributions are added to the month-end prices, and appropriate price adjustments are made to account for stock splits and dividends. The return on a portfolio for one month is calculated as the weighted average of the returns for its individual stocks. Annual portfolio returns are calculated by compounding the monthly portfolio returns.[7.7]

[7.6]   In October, 2008, NYSE Euronext acquired the American Stock Exchange (AMEX). The "NYSE MKT" is the former American Stock Exchange, or AMEX. The CRSP standard market-cap-based NYSE/AMEX/NASDAQ indices are therefore called the NYSE/NYSE MKT/ NASDAQ indices herein.

Size of the Deciles

Exhibit 7.1 provides an overview of the CRSP deciles and size groupings in terms of relative size (by aggregate market capitalization) and number of companies as of December 31, 2015.

Decile 1 has 193 companies in it, and accounts for nearly two-thirds of aggregate market cap (66.21%). Decile 10 has 796 companies in it, and accounts for less than 1% of aggregate market cap (0.36%).

Exhibit 7.1: Aggregate Market Capitalization and Company Counts of the CRSP (NYSE/NYSE MKT/ NASDAQ) Deciles and Size Groupings
December 31, 2015

Decile	Historic Average Percentage of Total Capitalization	Recent Number of Companies	Recent Decile Market Capitalization (in $thousands)	Recent Percentage of Total Capitalization
1-Largest	63.08%	193	14,835,871,930	66.21%
2	13.96%	209	2,942,893,472	13.13%
3	7.56%	208	1,538,888,753	6.87%
4	4.74%	240	998,160,994	4.45%
5	3.26%	240	665,743,390	2.97%
6	2.42%	258	480,964,631	2.15%
7	1.79%	350	419,011,585	1.87%
8	1.33%	392	270,179,790	1.21%
9	1.03%	494	175,122,777	0.78%
10-Smallest	0.83%	796	81,112,944	0.36%
Mid-Cap 3-5	15.56%	688	3,202,793,136	14.29%
Low-Cap 6-8	5.54%	1,000	1,170,156,007	5.22%
Micro-Cap 9-10	1.86%	1,290	256,235,720	1.14%

Source of underlying data: Calculated (or derived) based on data from CRSP ©2016 Center for Research in Security Prices (CRSP®), The University of Chicago Booth School of Business (2016). Calculations by Duff & Phelps LLC.

[7.7] According to CRSP document "Stock & Index RELEASE NOTES, December 2014 Annual UPDATE" (available at: http://crsp.chicagobooth.edu/files/images/release_notes/mdaz_201412_annual.pdf), CRSP reviewed the "shares outstanding" history from 1925–1946 of the CRSP standard market-cap-weighted portfolios as part of a larger pre-1946 shares review project. This review of the database caused small changes in the average annual returns over the 1926–2013 period when compared to the average annual returns over the 1926–2013 period. These changes were not material: the largest/smallest change was 0.11%/-0.11; the average/median change was 0.002%/-0.004%.

In Exhibit 7.2, the largest company in each of the CRSP (NYSE/NYSE MKT/NASDAQ) deciles and size groupings (by market capitalization) are listed as of September 30, 2015.

Exhibit 7.2: Largest Company (by market capitalization) in CRSP (NYSE/NYSE MKT/NASDAQ) Deciles and Size Groupings as of September 30, 2015

Decile	Company Name	Recent Market Capitalization (in $thousands)
1-Largest	Apple Inc.	629,010,254
2	Linkedin Corp.	21,809,433
3	Lennar Corp.	9,611,187
4	Flowers Foods Inc.	5,199,952
5	Verifone Systems Inc.	3,187,480
6	Generac Holdings Inc.	2,083,642
7	Evertec Inc.	1,400,208
8	PHH Corp.	844,475
9	Ennis Inc.	448,079
10-Smallest	Sprague Resources Lp	209,406

Source of underlying data: CRSP databases ©2016 Center for Research in Security Prices (CRSP®), The University of Chicago Booth School of Business (2016).

The CRSP deciles are re-constituted and rebalanced at the end of each calendar quarter (March, June, September, and December). These quarter-end portfolios are then followed for the subsequent three months. For example, the breakpoints in Exhibit 7.2 were a key input in defining the companies placed in each decile at the end of September 2015; these portfolio compositions were then used to calculate the October, November, and December 2015 returns associated with each decile.[7.8]

[7.8] According to the *2016 Valuation Handbook – Guide to Cost of Capital*, large-capitalization companies (those in CRSP deciles 1–2) have equity capitalizations greater than $9,611.187 million; mid-capitalization companies (those in CRSP deciles 3–5) have equity capitalizations between $2,090.566 million and $9,611.187 million (inclusive), low-capitalization companies have equity capitalizations between $448.502 million and $2,083.642 million (inclusive), and micro-capitalization companies (those in CRSP deciles 9–10) have equity capitalizations of equal to or less than $448.079 million.

Presentation of the Decile Data

Exhibit 7.3 is a year-by-year history of the annual returns for the ten CRSP deciles over the 1926–2015 time horizon.

Exhibit 7.4 provides the year-by-year growth of $1.00 over the 1926–2015 time horizon. These are year-end index levels, assuming an investment of $1.00 at year-end 1925.

Exhibit 7.5 is a year-by-year history of the annual *returns*, and the year-by-year *growth* of $1.00 (i.e., year-end index levels; assuming an investment of $1.00 at year-end 1925) over the 1926–2015 time horizon for (i) mid-cap stocks (a portfolio comprised of CRSP deciles 3, 4, and 5), (ii) low-cap stocks (a portfolio comprised of CRSP deciles 6, 7, and 8), (iii) micro-cap stocks (a portfolio comprised of CRSP deciles 9 and 10), and (iv) the "market" (a portfolio comprised of CRSP deciles 1–10).

Exhibit 7.3: Size Decile Portfolios of the NYSE/AMEX/NASDAQ
Annual Returns (decimal format)
1926–2015

Year	Decile 1	Decile 2	Decile 3	Decile 4	Decile 5	Decile 6	Decile 7	Decile 8	Decile 9	Decile 10
1926	0.1415	0.0710	0.0320	0.0080	-0.0216	0.0398	-0.0265	-0.0619	-0.0952	-0.0676
1927	0.3362	0.2925	0.3218	0.3839	0.3657	0.2216	0.3665	0.2548	0.2992	0.2620
1928	0.4011	0.3530	0.3751	0.3383	0.5627	0.3583	0.3341	0.2688	0.3701	0.6634
1929	-0.1083	-0.0677	-0.2471	-0.3206	-0.2577	-0.3892	-0.3790	-0.3925	-0.4924	-0.5131
1930	-0.2481	-0.3648	-0.3737	-0.3590	-0.3417	-0.3799	-0.3690	-0.4762	-0.4616	-0.4473
1931	-0.4195	-0.5032	-0.4748	-0.4655	-0.4521	-0.5218	-0.4784	-0.4980	-0.4994	-0.4750
1932	-0.1048	0.0105	0.0035	-0.1173	-0.1287	-0.0035	-0.0852	0.0109	-0.0149	0.4054
1933	0.4607	0.7273	0.9892	1.1528	1.0142	1.0245	1.0630	1.7050	2.0659	1.9698
1934	0.0052	0.0588	0.0733	0.1596	0.1355	0.2030	0.1897	0.1949	0.3098	0.3214
1935	0.4266	0.5307	0.4033	0.4216	0.5600	0.5756	0.6717	0.5890	0.5750	0.8195
1936	0.3010	0.3410	0.2900	0.3931	0.4980	0.5091	0.5700	0.5231	0.7158	0.8638
1937	-0.3164	-0.3713	-0.3723	-0.4466	-0.4891	-0.4548	-0.5083	-0.5424	-0.5177	-0.5394
1938	0.2509	0.3438	0.3674	0.3536	0.4511	0.4368	0.4021	0.4714	0.2659	0.0912
1939	0.0482	-0.0481	-0.0236	-0.0305	0.0327	0.0637	0.0209	0.0443	-0.0616	0.1829
1940	-0.0703	-0.0986	-0.0594	-0.0561	-0.0231	-0.0494	-0.0575	-0.0512	-0.0727	-0.2836
1941	-0.1119	-0.0818	-0.0726	-0.0734	-0.1164	-0.1039	-0.1134	-0.0801	-0.1512	-0.1117
1942	0.1369	0.2393	0.2085	0.2080	0.2275	0.2137	0.3015	0.3271	0.4377	0.6913
1943	0.2325	0.3475	0.3324	0.3892	0.4910	0.4408	0.7466	0.6446	0.8818	1.4050
1944	0.1680	0.2542	0.2528	0.3066	0.4195	0.4174	0.4011	0.4436	0.5668	0.7905
1945	0.3040	0.4548	0.5459	0.6334	0.5116	0.6112	0.6521	0.7092	0.7956	0.9086
1946	-0.0531	-0.0549	-0.0614	-0.1138	-0.0948	-0.0873	-0.1211	-0.1444	-0.1112	-0.1773
1947	0.0541	0.0098	-0.0040	0.0208	0.0342	-0.0309	-0.0341	-0.0178	-0.0403	-0.0037
1948	0.0337	0.0026	0.0263	-0.0225	-0.0192	-0.0408	-0.0283	-0.0701	-0.0800	-0.0390
1949	0.1852	0.2538	0.2597	0.1983	0.1822	0.2342	0.2189	0.1594	0.1984	0.2509
1950	0.2952	0.2875	0.2685	0.3186	0.3615	0.3406	0.3799	0.4002	0.4034	0.5643
1951	0.2164	0.2263	0.2117	0.1660	0.1483	0.1311	0.1845	0.1517	0.1072	0.0735
1952	0.1433	0.1301	0.1218	0.1190	0.1117	0.0997	0.1031	0.0795	0.0813	0.0259
1953	0.0124	0.0153	0.0030	-0.0137	-0.0288	-0.0096	-0.0253	-0.0772	-0.0434	-0.0825
1954	0.4888	0.4731	0.5887	0.5081	0.5726	0.5956	0.5750	0.5278	0.6148	0.6869
1955	0.2875	0.1806	0.1859	0.1932	0.1771	0.2295	0.1839	0.1976	0.2080	0.2574
1956	0.0811	0.1138	0.0701	0.0885	0.0794	0.0606	0.0724	0.0642	0.0483	-0.0100
1957	-0.0923	-0.0864	-0.1315	-0.1080	-0.1409	-0.1833	-0.1631	-0.1869	-0.1446	-0.1694
1958	0.4070	0.4943	0.5458	0.5893	0.5619	0.5636	0.6832	0.6490	0.7154	0.6834
1959	0.1242	0.1001	0.1305	0.1555	0.1939	0.1537	0.2012	0.1784	0.2041	0.1351
1960	0.0037	0.0612	0.0468	0.0075	-0.0168	-0.0064	-0.0569	-0.0512	-0.0382	-0.0787
1961	0.2627	0.2739	0.2869	0.2914	0.2916	0.2642	0.3104	0.3253	0.3030	0.3235
1962	-0.0878	-0.0959	-0.1190	-0.1272	-0.1681	-0.1771	-0.1629	-0.1489	-0.1701	-0.1498
1963	0.2249	0.2141	0.1647	0.1712	0.1273	0.1853	0.1782	0.1997	0.1280	0.1117
1964	0.1599	0.1428	0.1997	0.1625	0.1623	0.1666	0.1597	0.1714	0.1532	0.2094
1965	0.0893	0.1925	0.2483	0.2425	0.3217	0.3776	0.3374	0.3190	0.3193	0.4315
1966	-0.1027	-0.0574	-0.0507	-0.0623	-0.0721	-0.0452	-0.0955	-0.0864	-0.0589	-0.1008
1967	0.2197	0.2079	0.3169	0.4564	0.5145	0.5343	0.6472	0.8133	0.9064	1.1416
1968	0.0753	0.1654	0.1979	0.1829	0.2759	0.3047	0.2673	0.4047	0.3711	0.6136
1969	-0.0584	-0.1295	-0.1172	-0.1662	-0.1808	-0.1871	-0.2445	-0.2471	-0.3158	-0.3290
1970	0.0231	0.0182	0.0330	-0.0699	-0.0601	-0.0593	-0.0973	-0.1614	-0.1526	-0.1785

Exhibit 7.3: Size Decile Portfolios of the NYSE/AMEX/NASDAQ
Annual Returns (decimal format)
1926–2015

Year	Decile 1	Decile 2	Decile 3	Decile 4	Decile 5	Decile 6	Decile 7	Decile 8	Decile 9	Decile 10
1971	0.1484	0.1328	0.2011	0.2472	0.1890	0.2244	0.2018	0.1735	0.1647	0.1853
1972	0.2212	0.1278	0.0938	0.0881	0.0863	0.0695	0.0632	0.0205	-0.0229	-0.0057
1973	-0.1274	-0.2266	-0.2278	-0.2680	-0.3217	-0.3191	-0.3702	-0.3534	-0.3897	-0.4203
1974	-0.2803	-0.2441	-0.2458	-0.2834	-0.2167	-0.2694	-0.2558	-0.2423	-0.2635	-0.2715
1975	0.3169	0.4573	0.5363	0.6168	0.5966	0.5675	0.6326	0.6579	0.6649	0.7579
1976	0.2073	0.3045	0.3811	0.4008	0.4363	0.4808	0.5018	0.5690	0.5101	0.5516
1977	-0.0884	-0.0367	0.0109	0.0376	0.1126	0.1408	0.1754	0.2261	0.2022	0.2310
1978	0.0637	0.0229	0.1084	0.0974	0.1207	0.1637	0.1705	0.1632	0.1605	0.2815
1979	0.1519	0.2871	0.3061	0.3516	0.3557	0.4889	0.4206	0.4638	0.4594	0.4158
1980	0.3275	0.3442	0.3186	0.3043	0.3193	0.3141	0.3623	0.3233	0.3823	0.3071
1981	-0.0833	0.0059	0.0372	0.0403	0.0484	0.0677	-0.0040	0.0055	0.0802	0.0856
1982	0.1964	0.1749	0.2081	0.2566	0.3076	0.2940	0.2919	0.2955	0.2608	0.2855
1983	0.2057	0.1686	0.2662	0.2633	0.2626	0.2589	0.2727	0.3721	0.3130	0.3690
1984	0.0840	0.0770	0.0253	-0.0458	-0.0269	0.0248	-0.0426	-0.0745	-0.0896	-0.1952
1985	0.3137	0.3770	0.2910	0.3390	0.3115	0.3097	0.3255	0.3651	0.3077	0.2582
1986	0.1801	0.1816	0.1628	0.1732	0.1512	0.0874	0.1248	0.0387	0.0570	0.0041
1987	0.0504	0.0037	0.0393	0.0170	-0.0382	-0.0509	-0.0861	-0.0808	-0.1262	-0.1492
1988	0.1486	0.1982	0.2126	0.2237	0.2138	0.2339	0.2394	0.2854	0.2285	0.2105
1989	0.3295	0.3008	0.2629	0.2308	0.2423	0.2107	0.1785	0.1788	0.1058	0.0550
1990	-0.0088	-0.0853	-0.1015	-0.0875	-0.1409	-0.1849	-0.1532	-0.1979	-0.2460	-0.3128
1991	0.3039	0.3463	0.4140	0.3883	0.4811	0.5326	0.4421	0.4707	0.5066	0.4807
1992	0.0474	0.1577	0.1387	0.1249	0.2613	0.1878	0.1920	0.1287	0.2496	0.3398
1993	0.0732	0.1319	0.1614	0.1562	0.1694	0.1740	0.1900	0.1853	0.1658	0.2558
1994	0.0174	-0.0174	-0.0423	-0.0098	-0.0166	0.0037	-0.0256	-0.0308	-0.0310	-0.0298
1995	0.3940	0.3527	0.3536	0.3271	0.3327	0.2674	0.3303	0.2912	0.3501	0.3047
1996	0.2377	0.1956	0.1714	0.1905	0.1318	0.1756	0.1960	0.1708	0.2073	0.1716
1997	0.3486	0.3004	0.2509	0.2609	0.1574	0.2838	0.2999	0.2560	0.2524	0.2245
1998	0.3515	0.1293	0.0730	0.0723	0.0058	0.0125	-0.0067	0.0063	-0.0490	-0.1159
1999	0.2451	0.2013	0.3312	0.2997	0.2580	0.3526	0.2496	0.3943	0.3414	0.2786
2000	-0.1358	-0.0119	-0.0645	-0.0997	-0.0794	-0.1052	-0.1051	-0.1297	-0.1345	-0.1339
2001	-0.1531	-0.0869	-0.0413	-0.0050	-0.0252	0.0941	0.1170	0.2161	0.3143	0.3641
2002	-0.2238	-0.1767	-0.1938	-0.1794	-0.1750	-0.2144	-0.2283	-0.2001	-0.1867	-0.0555
2003	0.2568	0.3750	0.3990	0.4473	0.4081	0.4769	0.5108	0.5821	0.6859	0.9212
2004	0.0789	0.2033	0.1809	0.1873	0.1752	0.2216	0.1894	0.2186	0.1483	0.1886
2005	0.0370	0.1255	0.1153	0.1101	0.0996	0.0302	0.1054	0.0757	0.0228	0.0576
2006	0.1561	0.1577	0.1453	0.1157	0.1585	0.1496	0.1613	0.1793	0.1676	0.1968
2007	0.0712	0.0733	0.0400	0.0440	0.0765	0.0520	-0.0141	-0.0562	-0.0635	-0.0996
2008	-0.3508	-0.4191	-0.4015	-0.3682	-0.3506	-0.4011	-0.3625	-0.3539	-0.3705	-0.4736
2009	0.2256	0.3827	0.3783	0.4564	0.4420	0.4122	0.4231	0.4904	0.5029	0.8174
2010	0.1312	0.2201	0.3023	0.2121	0.2967	0.2758	0.3147	0.3295	0.2901	0.2930
2011	0.0221	-0.0011	-0.0187	0.0078	-0.0049	-0.0150	-0.0505	-0.0591	-0.0766	-0.1411
2012	0.1591	0.1606	0.1656	0.1637	0.1542	0.1845	0.1834	0.1829	0.1472	0.2145
2013	0.3254	0.3762	0.3662	0.4167	0.4113	0.4309	0.4188	0.4599	0.5030	0.4908
2014	0.1228	0.1600	0.1024	0.0764	0.0536	0.0414	0.0681	0.0174	0.0207	0.0286
2015	0.0174	-0.0369	-0.0280	-0.0477	-0.0735	-0.0733	-0.0587	-0.0781	-0.1134	-0.1161

Source: Morningstar and CRSP. Calculated (or Derived) based on data from CRSP US Stock Database and CRSP US Indices Database ©2016 Center for Research in Security Prices (CRSP®), The University of Chicago Booth School of Business. Used with permission.

Exhibit 7.4: Size Decile Portfolios of the NYSE/AMEX/NASDAQ
Year-end Index Values (Year-end 1925 = $1.00)
1926–2015

Year	Decile 1	Decile 2	Decile 3	Decile 4	Decile 5	Decile 6	Decile 7	Decile 8	Decile 9	Decile 10
1925	1.000	1.000	1.000	1.000	1.000	1.000	1.000	1.000	1.000	1.000
1926	1.142	1.071	1.032	1.008	0.978	1.040	0.974	0.938	0.905	0.932
1927	1.525	1.384	1.364	1.395	1.336	1.270	1.330	1.177	1.175	1.177
1928	2.137	1.873	1.876	1.867	2.088	1.725	1.775	1.494	1.610	1.957
1929	1.906	1.746	1.412	1.268	1.550	1.054	1.102	0.907	0.817	0.953
1930	1.433	1.109	0.884	0.813	1.020	0.653	0.696	0.475	0.440	0.527
1931	0.832	0.551	0.465	0.435	0.559	0.312	0.363	0.239	0.220	0.277
1932	0.745	0.557	0.466	0.384	0.487	0.311	0.332	0.241	0.217	0.389
1933	1.088	0.962	0.927	0.826	0.981	0.630	0.685	0.652	0.665	1.154
1934	1.093	1.018	0.995	0.958	1.114	0.758	0.814	0.780	0.871	1.525
1935	1.559	1.559	1.397	1.361	1.738	1.195	1.362	1.239	1.373	2.775
1936	2.029	2.090	1.802	1.897	2.603	1.803	2.138	1.887	2.355	5.172
1937	1.387	1.314	1.131	1.050	1.330	0.983	1.051	0.863	1.136	2.382
1938	1.735	1.766	1.546	1.421	1.930	1.412	1.474	1.270	1.438	2.600
1939	1.819	1.681	1.510	1.377	1.993	1.502	1.504	1.326	1.349	3.075
1940	1.691	1.516	1.420	1.300	1.947	1.428	1.418	1.258	1.251	2.203
1941	1.502	1.392	1.317	1.205	1.720	1.280	1.257	1.158	1.062	1.957
1942	1.707	1.725	1.591	1.455	2.111	1.553	1.636	1.536	1.527	3.310
1943	2.104	2.324	2.120	2.021	3.148	2.238	2.858	2.527	2.873	7.961
1944	2.458	2.914	2.656	2.641	4.469	3.172	4.004	3.647	4.501	14.254
1945	3.205	4.240	4.107	4.314	6.755	5.111	6.615	6.234	8.083	27.204
1946	3.035	4.007	3.855	3.823	6.115	4.665	5.814	5.334	7.184	22.380
1947	3.199	4.047	3.839	3.903	6.324	4.520	5.616	5.239	6.895	22.297
1948	3.307	4.057	3.940	3.815	6.202	4.336	5.457	4.872	6.343	21.427
1949	3.919	5.087	4.964	4.572	7.332	5.352	6.652	5.648	7.601	26.803
1950	5.076	6.550	6.296	6.028	9.983	7.175	9.178	7.908	10.668	41.928
1951	6.175	8.032	7.629	7.029	11.464	8.116	10.872	9.107	11.811	45.011
1952	7.060	9.077	8.558	7.866	12.745	8.925	11.992	9.831	12.771	46.174
1953	7.148	9.215	8.583	7.758	12.378	8.839	11.689	9.072	12.217	42.366
1954	10.641	13.575	13.637	11.699	19.466	14.104	18.410	13.859	19.728	71.467
1955	13.701	16.027	16.172	13.960	22.914	17.341	21.795	16.599	23.831	89.860
1956	14.812	17.851	17.306	15.196	24.733	18.393	23.373	17.664	24.982	88.963
1957	13.445	16.310	15.029	13.555	21.247	15.021	19.560	14.364	21.369	73.892
1958	18.917	24.372	23.231	21.543	33.186	23.487	32.924	23.686	36.657	124.389
1959	21.267	26.812	26.264	24.893	39.621	27.097	39.548	27.911	44.137	141.200
1960	21.346	28.453	27.492	25.081	38.954	26.923	37.297	26.483	42.451	130.086
1961	26.954	36.245	35.380	32.389	50.315	34.035	48.875	35.098	55.315	172.171
1962	24.587	32.769	31.171	28.270	41.859	28.008	40.914	29.873	45.904	146.373
1963	30.115	39.784	36.306	33.109	47.188	33.198	48.204	35.837	51.777	162.718
1964	34.930	45.465	43.557	38.491	54.849	38.730	55.902	41.978	59.710	196.786
1965	38.048	54.219	54.370	47.825	72.494	53.353	74.761	55.368	78.777	281.695
1966	34.140	51.105	51.611	44.848	67.270	50.942	67.618	50.586	74.134	253.306
1967	41.639	61.731	67.966	65.315	101.882	78.158	111.382	91.730	141.333	542.472
1968	44.775	71.943	81.414	77.258	129.986	101.971	141.159	128.849	193.786	875.330
1969	42.159	62.626	71.873	64.422	106.490	82.896	106.641	97.009	132.594	587.329

Source: Morningstar and CRSP. Calculated (or Derived) based on data from CRSP US Stock Database and CRSP US Indices Database ©2016 Center for Research in Security Prices (CRSP®), The University of Chicago Booth School of Business. Used with permission. All calculations by Duff & Phelps, LLC.

Exhibit 7.4: Size Decile Portfolios of the NYSE/AMEX/NASDAQ
Year-end Index Values (Year-end 1925 = $1.00)
1926–2015

Year	Decile 1	Decile 2	Decile 3	Decile 4	Decile 5	Decile 6	Decile 7	Decile 8	Decile 9	Decile 10
1970	43.134	63.763	74.248	59.919	100.094	77.980	96.265	81.354	112.359	482.513
1971	49.536	72.233	89.180	74.731	119.014	95.482	115.692	95.466	130.859	571.944
1972	60.493	81.466	97.548	81.314	129.283	102.115	123.006	97.425	127.858	568.682
1973	52.789	63.003	75.327	59.518	87.689	69.528	77.473	62.994	78.029	329.654
1974	37.991	47.625	56.810	42.649	68.685	50.799	57.657	47.730	57.472	240.141
1975	50.028	69.403	87.276	68.955	109.662	79.628	94.130	79.130	95.685	422.140
1976	60.401	90.538	120.537	96.593	157.511	117.912	141.366	124.153	144.496	655.008
1977	55.063	87.218	121.847	100.226	175.245	134.515	166.162	152.229	173.714	806.332
1978	58.569	89.216	135.060	109.989	196.400	156.529	194.492	177.073	201.595	1,033.302
1979	67.467	114.834	176.403	148.662	266.258	233.049	276.298	259.193	294.217	1,462.920
1980	89.559	154.358	232.607	193.896	351.286	306.238	376.400	342.979	406.692	1,912.218
1981	82.095	155.272	241.258	201.719	368.291	326.977	374.897	344.860	439.291	2,075.872
1982	98.218	182.435	291.463	253.483	481.587	423.096	484.337	446.771	553.846	2,668.435
1983	118.426	213.192	369.054	320.232	608.059	532.644	616.417	613.019	727.225	3,653.201
1984	128.377	229.615	378.375	305.560	591.726	545.860	590.176	567.330	662.101	2,940.247
1985	168.643	316.171	488.481	409.139	776.057	714.921	782.298	774.468	865.819	3,699.461
1986	199.018	373.577	568.028	480.014	893.409	777.373	879.927	804.416	915.197	3,714.619
1987	209.043	374.954	590.329	488.167	859.267	737.843	804.141	739.410	799.704	3,160.382
1988	240.099	449.270	715.821	597.384	1,042.988	910.444	996.679	950.460	982.429	3,825.601
1989	319.220	584.402	904.026	735.255	1,295.700	1,102.289	1,174.602	1,120.376	1,086.389	4,035.967
1990	316.402	534.544	812.234	670.922	1,113.125	898.424	994.709	898.600	819.158	2,773.393
1991	412.556	719.633	1,148.530	931.409	1,648.701	1,376.962	1,434.424	1,321.599	1,234.118	4,106.516
1992	432.126	833.151	1,307.785	1,047.748	2,079.576	1,635.613	1,709.879	1,491.641	1,542.159	5,502.086
1993	463.770	943.023	1,518.856	1,211.357	2,431.923	1,920.256	2,034.814	1,768.110	1,797.799	6,909.756
1994	471.842	926.645	1,454.677	1,199.433	2,391.563	1,927.444	1,982.809	1,713.650	1,742.022	6,703.985
1995	657.744	1,253.465	1,969.039	1,591.775	3,187.312	2,442.911	2,637.743	2,212.691	2,351.902	8,746.779
1996	814.070	1,498.683	2,306.583	1,894.972	3,607.532	2,871.911	3,154.633	2,590.693	2,839.531	10,247.780
1997	1,097.851	1,948.889	2,885.194	2,389.465	4,175.462	3,686.852	4,100.690	3,253.948	3,556.110	12,548.776
1998	1,483.724	2,200.808	3,095.828	2,562.330	4,199.763	3,733.021	4,073.326	3,274.524	3,381.711	11,094.206
1999	1,847.313	2,643.756	4,121.238	3,330.294	5,283.472	5,049.222	5,089.869	4,565.779	4,536.169	14,184.541
2000	1,596.398	2,612.286	3,855.405	2,998.427	4,863.750	4,517.793	4,555.168	3,973.787	3,926.095	12,284.727
2001	1,352.038	2,385.225	3,696.162	2,983.481	4,741.154	4,942.735	5,088.071	4,832.493	5,159.898	16,757.010
2002	1,049.400	1,963.806	2,979.977	2,448.101	3,911.247	3,882.849	3,926.253	3,865.718	4,196.378	15,827.182
2003	1,318.859	2,700.194	4,168.994	3,543.075	5,507.388	5,734.396	5,931.749	6,116.103	7,074.846	30,406.425
2004	1,422.873	3,249.111	4,923.051	4,206.691	6,472.292	7,005.344	7,054.964	7,452.859	8,123.777	36,140.386
2005	1,475.474	3,656.714	5,490.734	4,669.706	7,116.843	7,216.695	7,798.743	8,016.743	8,309.262	38,220.919
2006	1,705.771	4,233.219	6,288.627	5,210.056	8,245.125	8,296.127	9,056.611	9,454.316	9,701.494	45,741.858
2007	1,827.294	4,543.433	6,539.904	5,439.305	8,875.903	8,727.733	8,928.921	8,923.259	9,085.710	41,186.637
2008	1,186.256	2,639.139	3,914.045	3,436.458	5,763.749	5,226.941	5,692.293	5,765.593	5,719.862	21,679.787
2009	1,453.852	3,649.026	5,394.812	5,004.917	8,311.352	7,381.248	8,100.796	8,592.885	8,596.169	39,401.556
2010	1,644.549	4,452.118	7,025.581	6,066.453	10,776.977	9,417.075	10,649.989	11,424.191	11,089.961	50,947.133
2011	1,680.954	4,447.184	6,894.526	6,114.059	10,723.978	9,275.799	10,112.667	10,748.833	10,240.812	43,757.146
2012	1,948.352	5,161.444	8,036.148	7,114.714	12,378.033	10,987.007	11,967.543	12,714.276	11,748.615	53,141.829
2013	2,582.436	7,103.042	10,979.246	10,079.719	17,469.588	15,720.919	16,979.121	18,561.757	17,657.693	79,222.119
2014	2,899.476	8,239.727	12,103.403	10,849.789	18,406.741	16,371.727	18,134.890	18,884.607	18,022.817	81,490.853
2015	2,949.828	7,935.900	11,764.597	10,331.814	17,054.723	15,171.611	17,069.884	17,410.202	15,978.474	72,026.528

Source: Morningstar and CRSP. Calculated (or Derived) based on data from CRSP US Stock Database and CRSP US Indices Database ©2016 Center for Research in Security Prices (CRSP®), The University of Chicago Booth School of Business. Used with permission. All calculations by Duff & Phelps, LLC.

Exhibit 7.5: Size-Decile Portfolios of the NYSE/AMEX/NASDAQ
Mid-, Low-, Micro-, and Total Capitalization Returns and Index Value
1926–2015

	Total Return (decimal format)				Index Value (Year-end 1925 = $1.00)			
Year	Mid-Cap	Low-Cap	Micro-Cap	The "Market" (Deciles 1-10)	Mid-Cap	Low-Cap	Micro-Cap	The "Market" (Deciles 1-10)
1925	–	–	–	–	1.000	1.000	1.000	1.000
1926	0.0146	-0.0044	-0.0868	0.0965	1.015	0.996	0.913	1.097
1927	0.3483	0.2757	0.2900	0.3281	1.368	1.270	1.178	1.456
1928	0.3996	0.3332	0.4407	0.3898	1.915	1.693	1.697	2.024
1929	-0.2701	-0.3858	-0.4967	-0.1463	1.397	1.040	0.854	1.728
1930	-0.3631	-0.3961	-0.4575	-0.2874	0.890	0.628	0.463	1.231
1931	-0.4678	-0.5041	-0.4939	-0.4391	0.474	0.311	0.235	0.691
1932	-0.0542	-0.0259	0.0854	-0.0825	0.448	0.303	0.255	0.634
1933	1.0388	1.1581	2.0426	0.5698	0.913	0.655	0.774	0.995
1934	0.1095	0.1980	0.3138	0.0318	1.013	0.784	1.018	1.026
1935	0.4375	0.6094	0.6399	0.4486	1.457	1.262	1.669	1.487
1936	0.3616	0.5318	0.7584	0.3249	1.984	1.934	2.934	1.970
1937	-0.4196	-0.4900	-0.5234	-0.3464	1.151	0.986	1.398	1.288
1938	0.3792	0.4322	0.2203	0.2840	1.588	1.412	1.706	1.653
1939	-0.0147	0.0457	0.0005	0.0268	1.564	1.477	1.707	1.697
1940	-0.0511	-0.0522	-0.1296	-0.0714	1.484	1.400	1.486	1.576
1941	-0.0816	-0.1024	-0.1419	-0.1044	1.363	1.256	1.275	1.412
1942	0.2122	0.2644	0.4976	0.1648	1.653	1.589	1.910	1.644
1943	0.3795	0.5815	1.0172	0.2830	2.280	2.512	3.852	2.110
1944	0.3037	0.4177	0.6323	0.2131	2.972	3.562	6.288	2.559
1945	0.5650	0.6474	0.8317	0.3869	4.652	5.868	11.517	3.549
1946	-0.0851	-0.1123	-0.1336	-0.0639	4.256	5.209	9.978	3.323
1947	0.0119	-0.0290	-0.0281	0.0349	4.307	5.058	9.698	3.439
1948	0.0012	-0.0435	-0.0659	0.0190	4.312	4.838	9.059	3.504
1949	0.2245	0.2123	0.2160	0.2023	5.280	5.865	11.016	4.213
1950	0.3030	0.3670	0.4570	0.3007	6.880	8.017	16.050	5.479
1951	0.1839	0.1530	0.0957	0.2080	8.146	9.244	17.586	6.619
1952	0.1189	0.0964	0.0627	0.1346	9.114	10.135	18.689	7.510
1953	-0.0085	-0.0294	-0.0562	0.0071	9.037	9.837	17.639	7.563
1954	0.5612	0.5748	0.6373	0.5022	14.109	15.491	28.880	11.361
1955	0.1862	0.2081	0.2240	0.2533	16.736	18.715	35.348	14.238
1956	0.0776	0.0651	0.0294	0.0837	18.034	19.933	36.387	15.430
1957	-0.1262	-0.1777	-0.1526	-0.1002	15.758	16.390	30.835	13.884
1958	0.5623	0.6187	0.7053	0.4496	24.618	26.531	52.582	20.126
1959	0.1506	0.1740	0.1825	0.1272	28.326	31.147	62.179	22.686
1960	0.0219	-0.0323	-0.0503	0.0121	28.947	30.141	59.053	22.961
1961	0.2891	0.2916	0.3094	0.2696	37.317	38.931	77.324	29.151
1962	-0.1314	-0.1672	-0.1661	-0.1017	32.412	32.424	64.479	26.187
1963	0.1593	0.1867	0.1193	0.2098	37.577	38.475	72.173	31.680
1964	0.1813	0.1652	0.1835	0.1613	44.392	44.833	85.413	36.789
1965	0.2608	0.3499	0.3798	0.1446	55.968	60.521	117.852	42.110
1966	-0.0586	-0.0710	-0.0826	-0.0874	52.689	56.224	108.123	38.429
1967	0.3994	0.6388	1.0344	0.2874	73.731	92.138	219.963	49.473
1968	0.2108	0.3182	0.5015	0.1414	89.273	121.452	330.275	56.469
1969	-0.1469	-0.2216	-0.3236	-0.1091	76.161	94.537	223.386	50.306
1970	-0.0201	-0.0987	-0.1681	0.0000	74.628	85.209	185.829	50.307
1971	0.2123	0.2032	0.1767	0.1615	90.475	102.524	218.660	58.430
1972	0.0906	0.0558	-0.0138	0.1684	98.674	108.248	215.642	68.268
1973	-0.2594	-0.3435	-0.4078	-0.1806	73.079	71.067	127.697	55.935
1974	-0.2513	-0.2587	-0.2676	-0.2704	54.715	52.684	93.523	40.812
1975	0.5709	0.6092	0.7150	0.3875	85.952	84.780	160.389	56.628
1976	0.3979	0.5074	0.5335	0.2676	120.154	127.800	245.965	71.783
1977	0.0385	0.1708	0.2177	-0.0426	124.784	149.624	299.506	68.725

Source: Morningstar and CRSP. Calculated (or Derived) based on data from CRSP US Stock Database and CRSP US Indices Database ©2016 Center for Research in Security Prices (CRSP®), The University of Chicago Booth School of Business. Used with permission. All calculations by Duff & Phelps, LLC.

Exhibit 7.5: Size-Decile Portfolios of the NYSE/AMEX/NASDAQ
Mid-, Low-, Micro-, and Total Capitalization Returns and Index Value
1926–2015

	Total Return (decimal format)				Index Value (Year-end 1925 = $1.00)			
Year	Mid-Cap	Low-Cap	Micro-Cap	The "Market" (Deciles 1-10)	Mid-Cap	Low-Cap	Micro-Cap	The "Market" (Deciles 1-10)
1978	0.1075	0.1663	0.2245	0.0749	138.195	174.501	366.734	73.870
1979	0.3298	0.4626	0.4369	0.2262	183.772	255.225	526.961	90.583
1980	0.3144	0.3310	0.3464	0.3281	241.547	339.694	709.515	120.307
1981	0.0409	0.0305	0.0818	-0.0365	251.427	350.053	767.527	115.917
1982	0.2443	0.2939	0.2723	0.2100	312.848	452.927	976.548	140.260
1983	0.2644	0.2882	0.3410	0.2198	395.563	583.460	1,309.560	171.084
1984	-0.0103	-0.0224	-0.1404	0.0451	391.485	570.415	1,125.754	178.801
1985	0.3115	0.3283	0.2833	0.3217	513.415	757.707	1,444.635	236.318
1986	0.1637	0.0877	0.0320	0.1619	597.446	824.126	1,490.930	274.580
1987	0.0130	-0.0689	-0.1381	0.0167	605.227	767.327	1,284.959	279.166
1988	0.2167	0.2476	0.2192	0.1803	736.377	957.297	1,566.618	329.494
1989	0.2479	0.1923	0.0815	0.2886	918.912	1,141.362	1,694.350	424.596
1990	-0.1053	-0.1779	-0.2745	-0.0596	822.117	938.357	1,229.320	399.297
1991	0.4191	0.4865	0.5005	0.3467	1,166.660	1,394.822	1,844.598	537.722
1992	0.1611	0.1738	0.2814	0.0980	1,354.639	1,637.295	2,363.648	590.406
1993	0.1627	0.1830	0.2010	0.1114	1,574.972	1,936.868	2,838.710	656.186
1994	-0.0263	-0.0152	-0.0314	-0.0006	1,533.621	1,907.397	2,749.571	655.790
1995	0.3405	0.2943	0.3320	0.3679	2,055.816	2,468.814	3,662.451	897.078
1996	0.1683	0.1806	0.1930	0.2136	2,401.850	2,914.621	4,369.285	1,088.652
1997	0.2327	0.2799	0.2402	0.3138	2,960.698	3,730.478	5,418.675	1,430.316
1998	0.0578	0.0052	-0.0812	0.2430	3,131.841	3,749.909	4,978.635	1,777.882
1999	0.3068	0.3291	0.3145	0.2522	4,092.667	4,984.125	6,544.556	2,226.260
2000	-0.0783	-0.1107	-0.1331	-0.1154	3,772.370	4,432.364	5,673.341	1,969.319
2001	-0.0277	0.1313	0.3372	-0.1116	3,667.928	5,014.169	7,586.531	1,749.629
2002	-0.1853	-0.2164	-0.1386	-0.2114	2,988.398	3,929.084	6,535.244	1,379.732
2003	0.4150	0.5155	0.7832	0.3162	4,228.481	5,954.635	11,653.575	1,815.971
2004	0.1817	0.2109	0.1661	0.1197	4,996.638	7,210.407	13,589.695	2,033.280
2005	0.1104	0.0677	0.0366	0.0615	5,548.042	7,698.554	14,087.337	2,158.392
2006	0.1391	0.1619	0.1798	0.1549	6,319.682	8,944.929	16,619.792	2,492.689
2007	0.0489	0.0002	-0.0789	0.0580	6,628.491	8,946.743	15,308.087	2,637.305
2008	-0.3797	-0.3756	-0.4157	-0.3667	4,111.467	5,586.276	8,944.012	1,670.159
2009	0.4181	0.4366	0.6124	0.2880	5,830.339	8,025.128	14,421.284	2,151.160
2010	0.2746	0.3034	0.2901	0.1772	7,431.325	10,460.044	18,604.234	2,532.450
2011	-0.0078	-0.0388	-0.1050	0.0074	7,373.350	10,054.681	16,650.964	2,551.107
2012	0.1627	0.1836	0.1741	0.1615	8,573.345	11,901.071	19,550.705	2,963.109
2013	0.3917	0.4337	0.4971	0.3515	11,931.349	17,062.925	29,269.193	4,004.557
2014	0.0835	0.0433	0.0241	0.1158	12,927.806	17,801.012	29,975.406	4,468.272
2015	-0.0436	-0.0691	-0.1135	-0.0052	12,364.534	16,571.302	26,571.957	4,445.176

Source: Morningstar and CRSP. Calculated (or Derived) based on data from CRSP US Stock Database and CRSP US Indices Database ©2016 Center for Research in Security Prices (CRSP®), The University of Chicago Booth School of Business. Used with permission. All calculations by Duff & Phelps, LLC.

Aspects of the Company Size Effect

The company size phenomenon is remarkable in several ways. First, the greater risk of small-cap does not, in the context of the capital asset pricing model, fully account for their higher returns over the long term. In the CAPM only systematic, or beta risk, is rewarded; small-cap stock returns have exceeded those implied by their betas.

Second, the calendar annual return differences between small- and large-cap companies are serially correlated. This suggests that past annual returns may be of some value in predicting future annual returns. Such serial correlation, or autocorrelation, is practically unknown in the market for large-cap stocks and in most other equity markets but is evident in the size premium series.

Third, the size effect is seasonal. For example, small-cap stocks outperformed large-cap stocks in January in a large majority of the years. Such predictability is surprising and suspicious in light of modern capital market theory. These three aspects of the size effect – long-term returns in excess of systematic risk, serial correlation, and seasonality – will be discussed in the following sections.

The Size Effect: Empirical Evidence

Summary statistics over the 1926–2015 period for CRSP NYSE/NYSE MKT/NASDAQ deciles 1–10 are shown in Exhibit 7.6. As size (in this case, as measured by market cap) *decreases*, return tends to *increase*.[7.9]

For example, the annual arithmetic mean return of decile 1 (the largest-cap companies) was 11.0% over the 1926–2015 period, while the annual arithmetic mean return of decile 10 (the smallest-cap companies) was 20.3%. Note that this increased return comes at a price: risk (as measured by standard deviation) increases from 19.0% for decile 1 to 42.7% for decile 10. The relationship between risk and return is a fundamental principle of finance.

Do Small-Cap Stocks Always Outperform Large-Cap Stocks?

No. For example, large-cap stocks (defined here as deciles 1-2 of NYSE/NYSE MKT/NASDAQ) have outperformed small-cap stocks (defined here as deciles 9-10) in nearly *half* of the years since 1926. More recently, in five of the last 10 years, large-cap stocks have *outperformed* small-cap stocks. While this might lead some market observers to speculate that there is no size premium, statistical evidence suggests that periods of smaller stocks' underperformance should be expected.

[7.9] Traditionally, researchers have used market value of equity (market capitalization, or simply "market cap") as a measure of size in conducting historical rate of return studies. However, market cap is not the only measure of size that can be used to predict return, nor is it necessarily the best measure of size to use. In the *2016 Valuation Handbook – Guide to Cost of Capital*, which includes the data previously published in the Morningstar/Ibbotson® *Stocks, Bonds, Bills, and Inflation® (SBBI®) Valuation Yearbook* and the Duff & Phelps *Risk Premium Report*, the size effect is examined in relation to *eight* measures of company size (including market cap): (i) market capitalization, (ii) book value of equity, (iii) 5-year average net income, (iv) market value of invested capital (MVIC), (v) total assets, (vi) 5-year average EBITDA, (vii) sales, and (viii) number of employees. For more information about the *2016 Valuation Handbook – Guide to Cost of Capital* and other Duff & Phelps valuation data resources published by John Wiley & Sons, please go to: www.wiley.com/go/ValuationHandbooks.

History tells us that small companies are riskier than large companies. Exhibit 7.6 shows the standard deviation (a measure of risk) for each decile of the NYSE/ NYSE AMEX/NASDAQ. As one moves from CRSP decile 1 (comprised of the largest companies) to CRSP decile 10 (comprised of the smallest companies), the standard deviation of return grows. Investors are compensated for taking on this additional risk by the higher returns provided by small companies.

The increased risk faced by investors in small stocks is quite real. It is important to note, however, that the risk/return profile is over the *long-term*. The long-term expected return for any asset class is quite different from short-term expected returns. Investors in small-cap stocks should expect losses and periods of underperformance relative to large-cap stocks, however, the longer small-cap companies are given to "race" against large-cap companies, the greater the chance that small-cap companies outpace their larger counterparts.

Exhibit 7.6: Summary Statistics of Annual Returns (CRSP NYSE/NYSE MKT/NASDAQ Deciles) (%) 1926–2015

Decile	Geometric Mean	Arithmetic Mean	Standard Deviation	Serial Correlation
1 - Largest	9.3	11.0	19.0	0.07
2	10.5	12.8	21.6	0.01
3	11.0	13.5	23.5	-0.03
4	10.8	13.8	25.7	-0.03
5	11.4	14.6	26.3	-0.03
6	11.3	14.8	27.3	0.01
7	11.4	15.3	29.2	0.02
8	11.5	16.1	33.2	0.00
9	11.4	16.8	37.4	0.06
10	13.2	20.3	42.7	0.14
Mid-Cap	11.0	13.8	24.5	-0.03
Low-Cap	11.4	15.2	28.9	0.01
Micro-Cap	12.0	17.9	39.0	0.08
The "Market" (Deciles 1-10)	9.8	11.7	20.1	0.01

Source of underlying data: Morningstar *Direct* and CRSP. Calculated (or derived) based on data from CRSP US Stock Database and CRSP US Indices Database ©2016 Center for Research in Security Prices (CRSP®), The University of Chicago Booth School of Business. Used with permission. All calculations performed by Duff & Phelps LLC.

Exhibit 7.7 is a graphical depiction of the year-end index levels presented in Exhibit 7.5 for mid-cap stocks (a portfolio comprised of CRSP deciles 3, 4, and 5), low-cap stocks (a portfolio comprised of CRSP deciles 6, 7, and 8), micro-cap stocks (a portfolio comprised of CRSP deciles 9 and 10), and the "market" (a portfolio comprised of CRSP deciles 1–10).

Exhibit 7.7: Size-Decile Portfolios: Size Grouping Return Indexes
1926–2015
Index (Year-end 1925 = $1.00)

Long-term Returns in Excess of Systematic Risk

The capital asset pricing model, or CAPM, does not fully account for the higher returns of small-cap stocks. Exhibit 7.8 shows the returns in excess of the riskless rate over the past 90 years for each decile of the NYSE/NYSE MKT/NASDAQ. The CAPM can be expressed as follows:

$$k_e = R_f + \beta \times (RP_m)$$

Where:

k_e	=	Cost of equity capital
R_f	=	Risk-free rate
β	=	Beta
RP_m	=	Equity risk premium (also referred as ERP)

Exhibit 7.8 uses the CAPM to estimate the return in excess of the riskless rate and compares this estimate to historical performance. According to the CAPM, the expected return on a security should consist of the riskless rate plus an additional return to compensate for the systematic risk of the security. The return in excess of the riskless rate is estimated in the context of the CAPM by multiplying the equity risk premium by beta. The equity risk premium is the return that compensates investors for taking on risk equal to the risk of the market as a whole (systematic risk). Beta measures the extent to which a security or portfolio is exposed to systematic risk. The beta of each decile indicates the degree to which the decile's return moves with that of the overall market.

A beta greater than one indicates that the security or portfolio has greater systematic risk than the market; according to the CAPM equation, investors are compensated for taking on this additional risk. Yet, Exhibit 7.8 illustrates that the smaller deciles have had returns that are not fully explained by their higher betas. This return in excess of that predicted by CAPM increases as one moves from the largest companies in decile 1 to the smallest companies in decile 10. This size-related phenomenon prompted a revision to the CAPM, which includes a size premium.

This phenomenon can also be viewed graphically, as depicted in the Exhibit 7.9. The security market line is based on the pure CAPM without adjusting for the size premium. Based on the risk (or beta) of a security, the expected return should fluctuate along the security market line. However, the expected returns for the smaller deciles of the NYSE/NYSE MKT/NASDAQ lie *above* the line, indicating that these deciles have had returns in excess of those appropriate for their systematic risk.

Exhibit 7.8: Size-Decile Portfolios of the NYSE/NYSE MKT/NASDAQ Long-Term Returns in Excess of CAPM

1926–2015

Size Grouping	OLS Beta	Arithmetic Mean	Return in Excess of Risk-free Rate (actual)	Return in Excess of Risk-free Rate (as predicted by CAPM)	Size Premium
Mid-Cap (3–5)	1.12	13.80%	8.75%	7.75%	1.00%
Low-Cap (6–8)	1.22	15.19%	10.14%	8.44%	1.70%
Micro-Cap (9–10)	1.35	17.93%	12.88%	9.31%	3.58%
Breakdown of Deciles 1–10					
1-Largest	0.92	11.05%	6.00%	6.36%	-0.36%
2	1.04	12.78%	7.73%	7.16%	0.57%
3	1.10	13.53%	8.49%	7.63%	0.86%
4	1.12	13.80%	8.75%	7.76%	0.99%
5	1.17	14.59%	9.54%	8.05%	1.49%
6	1.17	14.77%	9.72%	8.09%	1.63%
7	1.25	15.29%	10.25%	8.62%	1.62%
8	1.30	16.08%	11.03%	8.99%	2.04%
9	1.34	16.81%	11.77%	9.23%	2.54%
10-Smallest	1.39	20.26%	15.21%	9.61%	5.60%

Betas are estimated from monthly returns in excess of the 30-day U.S. Treasury bill total return, January 1926–December 2015. Historical riskless rate measured by the 90-year arithmetic mean income return component of 20-year government bonds (5.05%). Calculated in the context of the CAPM by multiplying the equity risk premium by beta. The equity risk premium is estimated by the arithmetic mean total return of the S&P 500 (11.95%) minus the arithmetic mean income return component of 20-year government bonds (5.05%) from 1926–2015. Source: Morningstar *Direct* and CRSP. Calculated based on data from CRSP US Stock Database and CRSP US Indices Database ©2016 Center for Research. Used with permission. All calculations performed by Duff & Phelps LLC.

Exhibit 7.9: Security Market Line Versus Size-Decile Portfolios of the NYSE/NYSE MKT/NADAQ

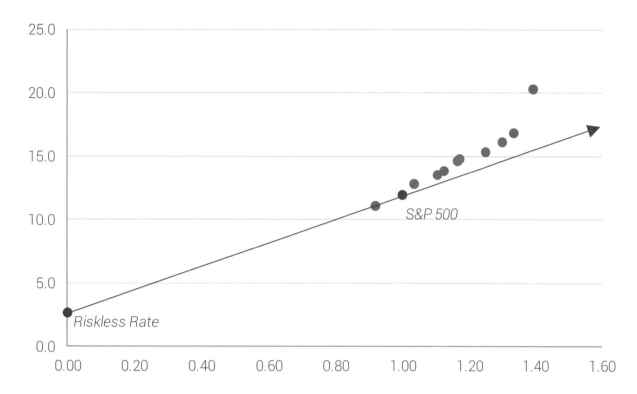

Serial Correlation in Small-Cap Stock Returns

Serial correlation, or first-order autocorrelation, measures the degree to which the return of a given series is related from period to period. Serial correlation, like cross-correlation, ranges from 1.0 to negative 1.0. A positive serial correlation can be an indicator of a trend in a return series. A serial correlation of 1.0 indicates that returns from one period have a perfectly positive relationship to the returns of the next period; returns are therefore perfectly predictable from one period to the next. A negative serial correlation can be an indicator of a cycle in a return series. A serial correlation of negative 1.0 indicates that returns from one period have a perfectly negative relationship to the next period. A serial correlation near zero indicates that returns are random or unpredictable.

If stock returns have a positive or a negative serial correlation, one can gain some information about future performance based on prior period returns. The serial correlation of returns on large-cap stocks is near zero (see Exhibit 7.6). For the smallest deciles of stocks, the serial correlation is above 0.1. This observation bears further examination.

Exhibit 7.10: Size-Decile Portfolios of the NYSE/NYSE MKT/NASDAQ Serial Correlations of Annual Returns in Excess of Decile 1 Returns
1926–2015

Decile	Serial Correlation of Annual Returns in Excess of Decile 1 Returns
Decile 2	0.22
Decile 3	0.31
Decile 4	0.25
Decile 5	0.27
Decile 6	0.33
Decile 7	0.30
Decile 8	0.30
Decile 9	0.32
Decile 10	0.40

Source of underlying data: Morningstar *Direct* and CRSP. Calculated (or Derived) based on data from CRSP US Stock Database and CRSP US Indices Database ©2016 Center for Research in Security Prices (CRSP®), The University of Chicago Booth School of Business. Used with permission. All calculations performed by Duff & Phelps LLC.

To remove the randomizing effect of the market as a whole, the returns for decile 1 are geometrically subtracted from the returns for each other decile, two through 10. The result illustrates that these series in excess of decile 1 exhibit greater serial correlation than the individual decile series themselves.

Exhibit 7.10 presents the serial correlations of the excess returns for deciles 2-10. These serial correlations suggest some predictability of smaller company excess returns; however, caution is necessary. The serial correlation of small company excess returns for non-calendar years (e.g., February through January) do not always confirm the results shown here for calendar years (January through December). Therefore, predicting small-company excess returns may not be easy.

The size premiums developed in this chapter also remove the randomizing effect of the market as a whole and appear to be serially correlated. Exhibit 7.11 shows the size premiums for rolling five-year periods for each of the three size groups: mid-cap, low-cap, and micro-cap (a five-year period is used to calculate the beta for each portfolio, which is then used to calculate the size premium). There are periods in which the size premium is positive and periods in which it is negative. However, none of these periods appears to continue for an extended time. Basing a long-term estimate of the size premium on the most recent periods would therefore be inappropriate.

The logic behind using a long history to estimate the size premium is similar to the argument for using a long history in estimating the equity risk premium (see Chapter 5). Longer historical periods provide more stable estimates of the size premium because unique events are not weighted heavily, and the probability of such events occurring is better represented by an average that covers a long period of time.

Exhibit 7.11: Five-Year Rolling-Period Size Premiums for Portfolios of the NYSE/NYSE MKT/ NASDAQ (%)

1926–2015

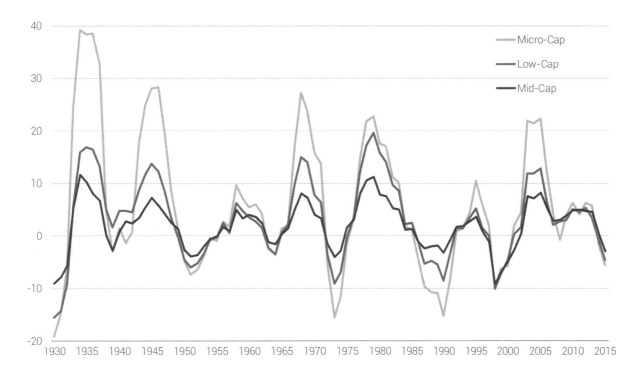

Source of underlying data: Morningstar *Direct* and CRSP. Calculated (or Derived) based on data from CRSP US Stock Database and CRSP US Indices Database ©2016 Center for Research in Security Prices (CRSP®), The University of Chicago Booth School of Business. Used with permission. All calculations performed by Duff & Phelps LLC.

Exhibit 7.12 demonstrates the calculation of the size premium using different starting dates. It shows the realized size premium for a series of periods through 2015. In other words, the left-most values on the graph represents the average realized size premium over the period 1926 to 2015. The next value on the graph represents the average realized size premium over the period 1927 to 2015, and so on, with the last value representing the average over the most recent five years, 2011 to 2015. Concentrating on the left side of Exhibit 7.12, one notices that the realized size premium, when measured over long periods of time, is relatively stable. The increased volatility of the size premium in more recent periods is due to its cyclical nature.

Exhibit 7.12: Size Premiums for Decile Portfolios of NYSE/NYSE MKT/NASDAQ Calculated with Different Starting Dates (%)
1926–2015

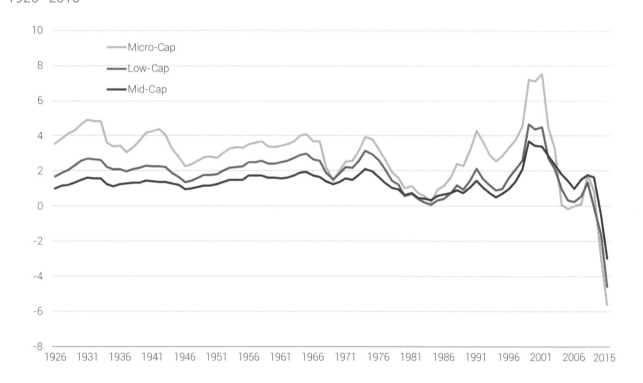

Source of underlying data: Morningstar *Direct* and CRSP. Calculated (or Derived) based on data from CRSP US Stock Database and CRSP US Indices Database ©2016 Center for Research in Security Prices (CRSP®), The University of Chicago Booth School of Business. Used with permission. All calculations performed by Duff & Phelps LLC.

Seasonality

Unlike the returns on large-cap stocks, the returns on small-cap stocks appear to be seasonal. The January effect denotes the empirical regularity with which rates of return for small stocks have historically been higher in January than in the other months of the year. Small-cap stocks' outperformance has been far greater in January far greater than in any other month.

Exhibit 7.13 shows the returns of capitalization deciles 2-10 in excess of the return on decile 1; the excess returns are segregated into months. For each decile and for each month, the exhibit shows both the average excess return and the number of times the excess return was positive. These two statistics measure the seasonality of the excess return in different ways — the average excess return illustrates the size of the seasonality effect, while the number of positive excess returns shows its reliability.

Virtually all of the small-cap effect occurs in January, as the excess outcomes for small-company stocks are mostly negative in the other months of the year. Excess returns in January relate to size in a precisely rank-ordered fashion, and the January effect seems to pervade all size groups. Yet, simply demonstrating that the size effect is largely produced by the January effect does not refute the existence of the size premium.

Exhibit 7.13: Size-Decile Portfolios of the NYSE/NYSE MKT/NASDAQ Returns in Excess of Decile 1 (%)
1926–2015

Decile	Jan	Feb	Mar	Apr	May	Jun	Jul	Aug	Sep	Oct	Nov	Dec	Total (Jan–Dec)
2	0.86	0.49	-0.05	-0.19	0.09	-0.11	-0.18	0.25	-0.01	-0.32	0.11	0.35	1.34
	69	59	43	34	46	43	40	50	43	39	50	50	
3	1.19	0.41	0.09	-0.05	-0.17	-0.15	-0.15	0.43	-0.16	-0.36	0.45	0.32	1.91
	65	60	43	33	40	40	43	56	43	38	50	54	
4	1.39	0.59	0.00	-0.25	0.11	-0.05	-0.22	0.24	-0.01	-0.80	0.33	0.52	1.94
	67	58	45	38	44	45	39	53	43	30	50	52	
5	2.10	0.63	-0.08	-0.12	-0.12	0.06	-0.22	0.38	0.03	-0.71	0.28	0.32	2.65
	67	57	40	41	41	44	43	52	44	37	49	49	
6	2.34	0.50	-0.02	-0.14	0.34	-0.10	-0.30	0.39	0.08	-1.08	0.26	0.29	2.69
	67	57	49	37	44	41	43	52	47	36	46	49	
7	2.99	0.61	0.01	-0.16	0.12	-0.22	-0.19	0.28	0.19	-1.01	0.21	0.15	3.00
	67	58	47	37	39	39	41	44	49	35	47	46	
8	3.92	0.61	-0.17	-0.29	0.30	-0.23	-0.13	0.18	0.01	-0.97	0.16	-0.11	3.55
	67	52	42	34	36	41	44	43	45	35	40	40	
9	5.16	0.82	-0.09	-0.20	0.22	-0.26	-0.19	0.06	-0.09	-1.20	0.06	-0.65	4.00
	66	48	44	34	38	38	40	44	43	36	39	41	
10	8.30	0.95	-0.53	-0.01	0.60	-0.38	0.35	-0.16	0.58	-1.42	-0.66	-1.36	6.92
	78	48	43	38	39	41	42	36	46	33	32	36	

First Row: Average excess return in percent (%)
Second Row: Number of times excess return was positive (in 90 years)

Source of underlying data: Morningstar *Direct* and CRSP. Calculated (or Derived) based on data from CRSP US Stock Database and CRSP US Indices Database ©2016 Center for Research in Security Prices (CRSP®), The University of Chicago Booth School of Business. Used with permission. All calculations performed by Duff & Phelps LLC.

Chapter 8
Growth and Value Investing

Investment style can be defined broadly as an overarching description of groups of stocks or portfolios based on shared characteristics. Probably the first discussion and consideration of style concerned large-company versus small-company investing, and even this distinction was not prominent until the 1960s. Styles of investing are now broken down into more detail and used for performance measurement, asset allocation, and other purposes. Mutual funds and other investment portfolios are often measured against broad growth or value benchmarks. In some cases, investment-manager-specific style benchmarks are constructed to separate pure stock-selection ability from style effects.

Most investors agree on the broad definitions of growth and value, but when it comes to specifics, definitions can vary widely. In general, growth stocks have high relative growth rates in regard to earnings, sales, or return on equity. Growth stocks usually have relatively high price-to-earnings and price-to-book ratios. Value stocks will generally have lower price-to-earnings and price-to-book values and often have higher dividend yields. Value stocks are often turnaround opportunities, companies that have had disappointing news, or companies with low growth prospects. Value investors generally believe that a value stock has been unfairly beaten down by the market, leading the stock to sell below its "intrinsic" value. Therefore, they buy the stock with the hope that the market will realize the stock's full value and eventually bid the price up to its fair value.

Fama-French Growth and Value Series

The following commentary and corresponding data make use of the Fama-French growth and value data series.[8.1,8.2]

Fama-French Index Construction Methodology

Fama-French use all stocks traded on the NYSE to set both growth/value and small/large breakpoints. They then apply these breakpoints to all stocks traded on NYSE, NYSE MKT, and NASDAQ to construct each index.

[8.1] Source of Fama-French growth and value return series data used in this chapter: Morningstar's *Direct* database. To learn more about the Morningstar *Direct* database, visit corporate.morningstar.com. All calculations performed by Duff & Phelps LLC.

[8.2] Eugene Fama, the 2013 Nobel laureate in economic sciences, is the Robert R. McCormick Distinguished Service Professor of Finance and chairman of the Center for Research in Security Prices (CRSP) at the University of Chicago Booth School of Business. Ken French is the Roth Family Distinguished Professor of Finance at the Tuck School of Business at Dartmouth College. Fama and French are prolific researchers and authors who have contributed greatly to the field of modern finance. Fama and French's paper "The Cross-Section of Expected Stock Returns" was the winner of the 1992 Smith Breeden Prize for the best paper in *The Journal of Finance*. See Eugene Fama and Kenneth French, "The Cross-Section of Expected Stock Returns," *Journal of Finance* (June 1992): 427–486. Also see Eugene F. Fama and Kenneth R. French, "A five-factor asset pricing model," *The Journal of Financial Economics* 116 (2015): 1–22.

The market capitalization breakpoint between small-cap and large-cap stocks is set as the median market capitalization of NYSE stocks. This breakpoint is then applied to all stocks traded on NYSE, NYSE MKT, and NASDAQ.

To define value and growth, Fama-French use the book value of equity divided by market capitalization, which is the inverse of how much investors are willing to pay for a dollar of book value. Value companies will have a high book-to-market ratio, while growth companies will have a low book-to-market ratio. Fama-French used *Compustat* as their data source to calculate book value from 1963 forward, and hand-collected data for 1928 to 1962.

Book value was calculated as follows:

$$BV = SE + DT + ITC - PS$$

Where:

BV	=	Fama-French book value
SE	=	Book value of stockholders' equity
DT	=	Balance sheet deferred taxes
ITC	=	Investment tax credit (if available)
PS	=	Book value of preferred stock. Depending on availability, either redemption, liquidation, or par value (in that order) is used to estimate book value of preferred stock

Stocks are put into three groups based on book-to-market: low, medium, or high. The definition of low, medium, and high is based on the breakpoints for the bottom 30%, middle 40%, and top 30% of the value of book-to-market for NYSE stocks. These breakpoints are then applied to all stocks traded on the NYSE, NYSE MKT, and NASDAQ. For the growth/value analysis shown in this chapter, only the low and high portfolios are used. The medium portfolios, which are blends of growth and value, are not shown.

Firms with negative book values are not used when calculating the book-to-market breakpoints or when calculating size-specific book-to-market breakpoints. Also, only firms with ordinary common equity (as classified by the Center for Research in Security Prices at the University of Chicago Booth School of Business) are included in the portfolios. This excludes American Depositary Receipts, real estate investment trusts, and unit trusts.

The four size-specific style indices used in this chapter are small-value, small-growth, large-value, and large-growth. These portfolios are defined as the intersections of the two size groups and the low and high book-to-market groups.

Historical Returns of the Fama-French Series

Using the Fama-French series ("F-F"), Exhibit 8.1 depicts the growth of $1.00 invested in F-F small-growth, F-F small-value, F-F large-growth, and F-F large-value stocks from the end of 1927 to the end of 2015. All results assume reinvestment of dividends and exclude transaction costs. The top two performers during this time period were small-value and large-value stocks, followed by small-growth and large-growth stocks. Over the period from 1928 to 2015, small-value stocks outperformed all other stock series in the graph. One dollar invested in small-value stocks at the end of 1927 grew to $81,430.52 by the end of 2015, decreasing from $94,173.28 at the end of 2014.

Exhibit 8.1: F-F Small-Value Stocks, F-F Small-Growth Stocks, F-F Large-Value Stocks, and F-F Large-Growth Stocks Index (Year-End 1927 = $1.00)
1928–2015

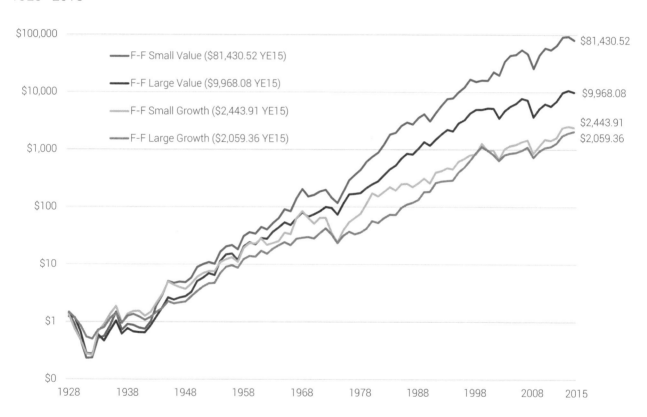

Summary Statistics for the Fama-French Series

Exhibit 8.2 shows summary statistics of annual total returns for the Fama-French growth and value series from 1928 to 2015. The summary statistics presented are geometric mean, arithmetic mean, and standard deviation.

Value significantly outperformed growth across the market capitalization spectrum. In the large-cap arena, the extra return of value over growth was at the expense of increased risk, as the standard deviation of large-value was 27.4 percentage points versus 19.9 percentage points for large-growth. In the small-cap series, small-value significantly outperformed small-growth and did so with lower volatility (32.3 percentage points versus 32.7 percentage points).

Exhibit 8.2: F-F Growth and Value Series Summary Statistics of Annual Returns (%) 1928–2015

	Geometric Mean	Arithmetic Mean	Standard Deviation
F-F Large Growth	9.1	11.0	19.9
F-F Large Value	11.0	14.5	27.4
F-F Small Growth	9.3	13.8	32.7
F-F Small Value	13.7	18.3	32.3

Returns by Decade for Fama-French Series

Exhibit 8.3 shows the compound returns by decade for the Fama-French growth and value series. Small-value stocks beat small-growth stocks in all decades except the 1930s and the 1990s. It is also interesting to note that small-value stocks were never the worst performing among all four stock series in any decade.

Exhibit 8.3: Fama-French Growth and Value Series Compound Annual Rates of Return by Decade (%) 1928–2015

	1920s*	1930s	1940s	1950s	1960s	1970s	1980s	1990s	2000s	2010s**
F-F Large Growth	8.1	1.5	7.3	17.6	7.9	3.4	15.8	19.9	-1.8	14.2
F-F Large Value	9.0	-5.5	17.2	22.2	10.7	12.2	20.2	13.9	0.3	11.6
F-F Small Growth	-13.3	7.4	11.6	17.7	10.7	5.8	10.8	15.0	-1.1	13.3
F-F Small Value	-4.8	-0.3	21.0	20.0	15.4	15.0	21.1	14.5	10.6	10.7

*Based on the period 1928–1929   **Based on the period 2010–2015

Exhibit 8.4: Fama-French Growth and Value Series Compound Annual Rates of Return Over the Most Recent 10 Years (%)
2006–2015

	2006–2015
F-F Large Growth	8.8
F-F Large Value	4.6
F-F Small Growth	7.1
F-F Small Value	6.1

Correlation of Fama-French Series

Exhibit 8.5 presents the annual cross-correlations and serial correlations for the Fama-French growth and value series.

Exhibit 8.5: Fama-French Growth and Value Series Serial and Cross-Correlations of Historical Annual Returns
1928–2015

	F-F Large Growth	**F-F Large Value**	**F-F Small Growth**	**F-F Small Value**	**U.S. Treasury Bills**	**Inflation**
F-F Large Growth	1.00					
F-F Large Value	0.81	1.00				
F-F Small Growth	0.82	0.82	1.00			
F-F Small Value	0.74	0.90	0.87	1.00		
U.S. Treasury Bills	-0.02	-0.04	-0.10	-0.07	1.00	
Inflation	-0.02	0.06	0.00	0.05	0.42	1.00
Serial Correlation	-0.01	-0.07	0.01	0.03	0.91	0.63

Presentation of Annual Fama-French Returns

Exhibit 8.6 shows year-by-year total annual returns for the Fama-French growth and value series from 1928 to 2015. This exhibit compares the performance of large-growth, large-value, small-growth, and small-value.

Conclusion

What can explain this value effect? Readers of Benjamin Graham and David L. Dodd's "Security Analysis,"[8.3] first published in 1934, would say that the outperformance of value stocks is due to the market coming to realize the full value of a company's securities that were once undervalued. The Graham and Dodd approach to security analysis is to do an independent valuation of a company using accounting data and common market multiples, then look at the stock price to see if the stock is under- or overvalued. Several academic studies have shown that the market overreacts to bad news and underreacts to good news. This would lead us to conclude that there is more room for value stocks (which are more likely to have reported bad news) to improve and outperform growth stocks, which already have high expectations built into them.

[8.3] The sixth edition of this book was published in 2008. See also Cottle, S., Murray, R.F., & Block, F.E. 1988. Graham and Dodd's *Security Analysis*, 5th ed. (New York: McGraw-Hill).

Exhibit 8.6: Fama-French Growth and Value Series: Annual Total Returns (decimal format) 1928–2015

Year	F-F Large Growth	F-F Large Value	F-F Small Growth	F-F Small Value
1928	0.4805	0.2363	0.3486	0.4096
1929	-0.2107	-0.0393	-0.4423	-0.3577
1930	-0.2644	-0.4316	-0.3585	-0.4638
1931	-0.3696	-0.5824	-0.4270	-0.5187
1932	-0.0793	-0.0326	-0.0525	0.0135
1933	0.4465	1.1691	1.5941	1.1869
1934	0.1106	-0.2151	0.3589	0.0851
1935	0.4222	0.5114	0.4834	0.5316
1936	0.2646	0.4812	0.3710	0.7319
1937	-0.3412	-0.4107	-0.4864	-0.5147
1938	0.3320	0.2520	0.4381	0.2621
1939	0.0773	-0.1251	0.1072	-0.0355
1940	-0.0981	-0.0262	0.0057	-0.0983
1941	-0.1267	-0.0088	-0.1734	-0.0482
1942	0.1317	0.3371	0.1676	0.3500
1943	0.2204	0.4402	0.4508	0.9182
1944	0.1611	0.4198	0.4123	0.4971
1945	0.3195	0.4906	0.6428	0.7461
1946	-0.0829	-0.0829	-0.1240	-0.0736
1947	0.0410	0.0866	-0.0838	0.0534
1948	0.0335	0.0509	-0.0716	-0.0230
1949	0.2331	0.1871	0.2352	0.2104
1950	0.2311	0.5522	0.3101	0.5216
1951	0.2005	0.1436	0.1626	0.1227
1952	0.1338	0.1954	0.0855	0.0859
1953	0.0229	-0.0704	-0.0068	-0.0692
1954	0.4779	0.7732	0.4320	0.6343
1955	0.2850	0.2978	0.1395	0.2347
1956	0.0652	0.0337	0.0765	0.0598
1957	-0.0914	-0.2272	-0.1699	-0.1590
1958	0.4162	0.7230	0.7522	0.6967
1959	0.1315	0.1882	0.2142	0.1742
1960	-0.0236	-0.0856	-0.0178	-0.0602
1961	0.2643	0.2889	0.2220	0.3085
1962	-0.1089	-0.0309	-0.2233	-0.0947
1963	0.2188	0.3235	0.0798	0.2834
1964	0.1448	0.1916	0.0813	0.2290
1965	0.1336	0.2242	0.3999	0.4250
1966	-0.1077	-0.1021	-0.0532	-0.0776
1967	0.2917	0.3174	0.8842	0.6755
1968	0.0403	0.2708	0.3273	0.4581
1969	0.0288	-0.1639	-0.2368	-0.2584
1970	-0.0565	0.1063	-0.2025	0.0662
1971	0.2394	0.1255	0.2586	0.1447
1972	0.2132	0.1862	0.0039	0.0728

Exhibit 8.6: Fama-French Growth and Value Series: Annual Total Returns (decimal format) 1928–2015

Year	F-F Large Growth	F-F Large Value	F-F Small Growth	F-F Small Value
1973	-0.2179	-0.0367	-0.4507	-0.2723
1974	-0.2924	-0.2340	-0.3190	-0.1902
1975	0.3444	0.5590	0.6132	0.5712
1976	0.1754	0.4462	0.3820	0.5913
1977	-0.0946	0.0164	0.1935	0.2382
1978	0.0700	0.0348	0.1765	0.2212
1979	0.1659	0.2267	0.4884	0.3833
1980	0.3520	0.1645	0.5266	0.2228
1981	-0.0713	0.1280	-0.1153	0.1768
1982	0.2148	0.2767	0.1972	0.3986
1983	0.1467	0.2692	0.2212	0.4758
1984	-0.0072	0.1617	-0.1284	0.0752
1985	0.3264	0.3175	0.2891	0.3212
1986	0.1438	0.2182	0.0195	0.1450
1987	0.0743	-0.0276	-0.1224	-0.0712
1988	0.1253	0.2596	0.1663	0.3076
1989	0.3611	0.2970	0.2058	0.1570
1990	0.0106	-0.1275	-0.1774	-0.2513
1991	0.4333	0.2735	0.5473	0.4056
1992	0.0641	0.2357	0.0582	0.3476
1993	0.0238	0.1951	0.1264	0.2941
1994	0.0195	-0.0578	-0.0436	0.0321
1995	0.3716	0.3768	0.3513	0.2769
1996	0.2125	0.1335	0.1236	0.2071
1997	0.3161	0.3188	0.1529	0.3729
1998	0.3464	0.1623	0.0304	-0.0863
1999	0.2943	-0.0022	0.5475	0.0559
2000	-0.1363	0.0580	-0.2415	-0.0080
2001	-0.1559	-0.0118	0.0016	0.4024
2002	-0.2150	-0.3253	-0.3087	-0.1241
2003	0.2629	0.3507	0.5320	0.7469
2004	0.0653	0.1891	0.1254	0.2659
2005	0.0282	0.1217	0.0545	0.0353
2006	0.0888	0.2261	0.1167	0.2176
2007	0.1408	-0.0645	0.0736	-0.1521
2008	-0.3371	-0.4903	-0.4156	-0.4439
2009	0.2792	0.3915	0.3445	0.7054
2010	0.1587	0.2161	0.3066	0.3354
2011	0.0414	-0.0904	-0.0432	-0.0704
2012	0.1541	0.2299	0.1222	0.2007
2013	0.3428	0.4020	0.4899	0.3940
2014	0.1132	0.0978	0.0572	0.0255
2015	0.0631	-0.0754	-0.0440	-0.1353

Source of data: Morningstar *Direct* database. To learn more about the Morningstar *Direct* database, visit corporate.morningstar.com.

Chapter 9
Liquidity Investing

What Is Liquidity?[9.1]

Liquidity has many different, but similar meanings. In every case it is related to the ease of movement. Even within the context of financial markets, liquidity has several different meanings. In the banking system, liquidity measures the degree to which loans are made. In the securities markets, liquidity is the ease with which transactions can be made. In valuation, this liquidity impacts value, so that the more liquidity an asset has the more value it has, all other things being equal. The absence of liquidity lowers the value of the asset by the amount of a liquidity discount.

In this chapter, we focus on liquidity as the ease of trading securities in general, especially equities. We focus on liquidity's impact on valuation and in particular its impact on security returns. We will demonstrate that less-liquid securities have higher expected returns.

Valuation as Present Value of Cash Flows

In equilibrium, an asset has a value that equals its present value, or the discounted sum of its expected cash flows. These future cash flows are unobservable, except for risk-free assets. For stocks, there is great disagreement as to what these expected cash flows might be. This disagreement is the primary reason that stocks are traded. A secondary reason is that they are bought or sold to meet liquidity needs.

The other component of a present value calculation is the discount rate. Similar to the expected cash flows, these discount rates are unobservable. We can usually observe the riskless discount rates from a term structure of riskless bonds, which we unravel from U.S. government discount bonds. But there are usually other premiums that we would add to the riskless term structure. The most common one is an equity risk premium, which is often modified by a beta in the CAPM framework. We might also add a premium for size and another one for value (or distress). We argue here that another premium should be added for lack of liquidity.

The difference of opinion that investors have about expected cash flows leads to the additional risk of a security. The risk of the security reflects not only the changing economy and company cash-flow expectations, but also the divergence of opinion that changes from moment to moment. This risk reduces the value of a security. Ironically though, this divergence of opinion also leads to most of the trading of a security, thereby making the security more liquid for trades, whether they be active or liquidity traders. The higher liquidity increases the security's value.

[9.1] This chapter was written by Roger G. Ibbotson, chairman and CIO of Zebra Capital Management, Professor in Practice Emeritus at Yale School of Management, and founder and former chairman of Ibbotson Associates, Inc., which was acquired by Morningstar, Inc.; and Daniel Y.-J. Kim, research director of Zebra Capital Management.

We do not mean to imply that most investors actually make these present-value calculations. Instead, investors rely on simple metrics, such as the price/earnings ratio, or PE ratio, trying to buy stocks with relatively high but unspecified cash flow projections, at relatively low PE ratios. Or they may simply feel that a stock's price is too low or high relative to its estimated value, leading them to buy or sell a security.

The Liquidity Premium

Most conventional present-value calculations ignore the liquidity premium. These calculations usually implicitly assume that securities are perfectly liquid. If they are somewhat liquid, a liquidity discount is often made to the present value, at the end of the calculation. Thus, a liquid stock is priced at the present value of the expected cash flows, discounted by the riskless rate and various other risk premiums, such as a beta-adjusted equity risk premium, a size premium, and a value premium. The final present value is then reduced by some percentage due to its lack of liquidity.

The other way to calculate a present value is to add a liquidity premium into the discount rate. Less-liquid securities would then have their cash flows discounted at higher rates. The benefit of this approach is that this liquidity premium can be thought of as causing a higher discount rate. These discount rates are equivalent, under certain conditions, to the expected return that an investor receives for investing in less-liquid securities.

The liquidity premium is the extra return an investor would demand to hold a security that cannot costlessly be traded. This premium is not exactly a risk premium, since it more reflects a transaction cost. We can think of the premium as related to risk, however, because it is the risk of having to buy or sell a security quickly. The less liquid and more hurried the transaction, the higher the cost.

The liquidity premium is potentially interesting to investors who can afford to hold a security over time, instead of continuously trading it. For investors with longer-term horizons, the trading costs become trivial because they happen so infrequently. The liquidity premium is a benefit to the longer-term investor. It means that the less-liquid securities will have higher returns and these higher returns are not likely to be affected by trading costs.

It is sometimes argued that part of the expected return that is demanded from real estate, private equity, or venture capital comes from their relative liquidity.[9.2] In addition to any of their return for other risk characteristics, investors want an extra return for holding an illiquid asset. Thus, investors would want to invest in alternative illiquid assets only if they thought they would receive extra compensation for their lack of liquidity.

The liquidity premium also is substantial within publicly traded securities. There is a difference in the return of the more highly traded securities versus the less traded securities, even though most all public securities can be readily traded. We now examine the relative impact of liquidity across

---

[9.2]   Ibbotson, Roger, Siegel, Laurence B., and Diermeier, Jeffrey "The Demand for Capital Market Returns," *Financial Analysts Journal*, January/February 1984.

publicly traded stocks on the New York Stock Exchange (NYSE), the NYSE MKT (formerly the NYSE Amex), and the NASDAQ Stock Market.

Liquidity and Stock Returns

In the U.S. stock market, liquidity has substantial impact on stock returns. We examine the monthly data for the largest 3,500 U.S. stocks by capitalization over the period 1972 through 2015. These stocks are traded on either the NYSE, the NYSE MKT, or the NASDAQ. All are publicly traded and relatively liquid, but of course some are more liquid than others.

We separate the stocks into four quartiles separated from the prior year by the turnover rate. The turnover rate is the number of shares traded during the year divided by the number of shares outstanding for the stock. The stocks with the highest turnover rates are the most liquid, and the stocks with the lowest turnover rates the least liquid. The return, share volume, and capitalization data are from the Center for Research in Security Prices at the University of Chicago Booth School of Business.

Exhibit 9.1 summarizes the results for the four liquidity quartiles. The exhibit illustrates the historical magnitude of the liquidity premium over the period from 1972–2015. Note that there is a substantial difference in the returns of the least-liquid quartile versus the most-liquid quartile, as well as a continual progression of higher returns as we move to less-liquid quartiles. The less-liquid stocks are not necessarily more risky. Measured by the standard deviation, risk seems to increase with liquidity.

Exhibit 9.1: Liquidity Quartiles of the NYSE/MKT/NASDAQ, Annualized Returns (%) 1972–2015

Quartile	Geometric Mean	Arithmetic Mean	Standard Deviation
1-Less Liquid	14.93	16.74	20.01
2	14.04	16.06	21.29
3	12.20	14.56	22.72
4-More Liquid	7.32	10.94	27.79

Data from 1972–2015. Source: Ibbotson, Roger G., and Daniel Y.-J Kim, "Liquidity as an Investment Style: 2016 Update," available at research.zebracapital.com. Updated version of: Ibbotson, Roger G., Chen, Zhiwu, Kim, Daniel Y.-J., and Hu, Wendy Y. "Liquidity as an Investment Style," *Financial Analysts Journal*, May/June 2013, updated with 2012–2015 data.

Exhibit 9.2 shows the same four quartiles of liquidity, but here presented as indexes of cumulative wealth. The quartiles consist of equally weighted portfolios with all dividends reinvested. The least-liquid quartile of stocks is at the top of the graph, and $1.00 invested at the end of 1971 grows to $456.72 by the end of 2015. One dollar invested in the second-least-liquid quartile grows to $323.47 over the period. One dollar invested in the third-least-liquid quartile (the second-most-liquid-quartile) grows to $158.37 over the period. One dollar invested at year-end 1971 into the most-liquid quartile grows to only $22.43 over the period. These large differences in terminal wealth reflect investments at different share turnover rates, but include most types of companies in each liquidity quartile.

Exhibit 9.2: Wealth Indices of Investments in Low to High Quartiles of Liquidity in NYSE/AMEX/NASDAQ Stocks, Cumulative Total Returns: Index (Year-End 1971 = $1.00) 1972–2015

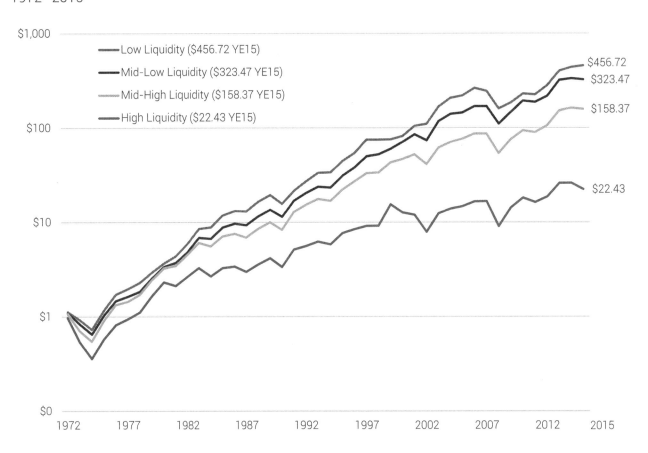

Liquidity as an Investment Style[9.3]

Similar to small-versus-large or value-versus-growth, liquid-versus-illiquid can be viewed as an investment style. Returns are on average higher for small, value, or illiquid stocks. In this way, liquidity can be thought of as another risk factor, with a risk premium. There are some years in which each style outperforms, as well as some years of underperformance. But each style has a *long-run* positive payoff for investing in it.

Returns on stocks typically are greater than the returns on riskless (or default-free) bonds. This extra expected return is called the equity risk premium. The styles of investing can also add or detract from the investor's return. In fact, styles explain about half of the cross-sectional variation in equity mutual funds, with stock selection, market timing, and fees explaining the other half. Styles seem to explain more of the variation in mutual fund portfolio returns than do industry sectors.[9.4]

[9.3] Ibbotson, Roger G., and Daniel Y.-J Kim, "Liquidity as an Investment Style: 2016 Update," available at research.zebracapital.com. Updated version of: Ibbotson, Roger G., Chen, Zhiwu, Kim, Daniel Y.-J., and Hu, Wendy Y. "Liquidity as an Investment Style," *Financial Analysts Journal*, May/June 2013.

[9.4] Xiong, James X., Roger G. Ibbotson, Thomas M. Idzorek, and Peng Chen., "The Equal Importance of Asset Allocation and Active Management," *Financial Analysts Journal*, March/April 2010.

The premiums in the equity market are as follows:

- **Equity Risk Premium:** The excess return of stocks relative to risk-free (default-free) government bonds. This premium can be measured over various bond horizons, and the bonds may themselves contain a horizon premium.

- **Size Premium:** The excess return on small stocks versus the return on larger stocks.

- **Value Premium:** The excess return on value stocks versus growth stocks.

- **Liquidity Premium:** The excess return on less-liquid stocks versus more-liquid stocks.

Liquidity Versus Size

It is natural to think that liquidity and size would be related. The total number of shares of a company that are traded in a given period (say a year) are the number of shares outstanding times the turnover rate. Turnover is a measure of liquidity, adjusted for the number of shares outstanding.

Exhibit 9.3 breaks the universe of stocks into four turnover quartiles and four size-capitalization quartiles, each independently sorted. The numbers in the exhibit are the compound annual (geometric mean) rate of returns for each category. Note that small stocks tend to outperform large stocks in general, but not for the most-liquid stocks. In fact, for the most-liquid stocks shown in column four, the pattern is reversed. The poorest performing category is the highly liquid stocks that are the smallest in size (i.e., that upper-right quartile with a return of -0.19% per year).

The best-performing category is column one, which represents the least-liquid stocks. The worst-performing category is column four, the most-liquid stocks. There is a clear pattern of decreasing returns as the liquidity of the stocks increase. The best-performing category is the small, relatively less liquid stocks, with a 15.92% return.

As shown in the low-minus-high liquidity column, the impact of liquidity is strongest for the smallest companies and weakest for the largest companies. However, the impact of liquidity is strong and consistent across all categories. Liquidity appears to be a much better predictor of returns than does size. Note the mixed results for size shown in the bottom small-minus-large row.

Exhibit 9.3: Size and Liquidity Quartile Portfolios, Independently Sorted Each Year
Compound Annual Returns (%)
1972–2015

	Low Liquidity	Mid-Low Liquidity	Mid-High Liquidity	High Liquidity	Liquidity Effect (%)
Micro-Cap					
Geometric Mean (%)	15.92	15.75	9.48	-0.19	**16.11**
Small-Cap					
Geometric Mean (%)	15.30	14.13	11.98	5.54	**9.76**
Mid-Cap					
Geometric Mean (%)	13.86	13.69	12.58	7.93	**5.93**
Large-Cap					
Geometric Mean (%)	11.16	12.04	11.71	8.77	**2.39**
Size Effect (%)	**4.76**	**3.71**	**-2.23**	**-8.96**	

Compound annual returns (%) from 1972–2015. Source: Ibbotson, Roger G., and Daniel Y.-J Kim, "Liquidity as an Investment Style: 2016 Update," available at research.zebracapital.com. Updated version of: Ibbotson, Roger G., Chen, Zhiwu, Kim, Daniel Y.-J., and Hu, Wendy Y. "Liquidity as an Investment Style," *Financial Analysts Journal*, May/June 2013, updated with 2012–2015 data.

Liquidity Versus Value/Growth

As noted in Chapter 8, value tends to outperform growth over time. In this chapter, less-liquid stocks are shown to outperform more-liquid stocks. In this section, we examine how liquidity and value/growth interact.

The stocks are ranked by turnover rates and separated into quartiles. Similarly, the stocks are ranked by the earnings-to-price ratios and separated into quartiles. The high-earnings-to-price companies are considered value companies, while the low-earnings-to-price companies are growth companies. The inverse, of course is, the PE ratio, with the growth companies having high PE ratios, and the value companies having low PE ratios.

The earnings used are the trailing reported earnings. The earnings data is from *Compustat*, owned by Standard & Poor's. The portfolios are rebalanced once per year with the earnings lagged by two months to reflect delays in compiling the accounting earnings.

Exhibit 9.4 presents the quartile results for the different levels of liquidity and value/growth. Note that both liquidity and value/growth have a strong impact on stock market returns across all categories. The results appear to be additive. There is an excess return for investing in either low-liquidity or value stocks, and the best return of all was earned by investing in the upper-left category: high-value, low-liquidity stocks, which have a realized return of 18.85%. The worst category is the lower-right corner, high-liquidity growth stocks, which have a return of 2.46%.

Exhibit 9.4: Summary Statistics of Value vs. Growth and Liquidity Quartile Portfolios, Independently Sorted Each Year
Compound Annual Returns (%)
1972–2015

	Low Liquidity	Mid-Low Liquidity	Mid-High Liquidity	High Liquidity	Liquidity Effect (%)
High-Value					
Geometric Mean (%)	18.85	16.59	15.85	9.92	**8.93**
Mid-Value					
Geometric Mean (%)	15.15	14.42	12.85	11.84	**3.31**
Mid-Growth					
Geometric Mean (%)	13.05	12.37	10.48	6.74	**6.32***
High-Growth					
Geometric Mean (%)	10.41	12.34	9.04	2.46	**7.95**
Size Effect (%)	**8.44**	**4.25**	**6.81**	**7.46**	

*Difference due to rounding.

Compound annual returns (%) from 1972–2015. Source: Ibbotson, Roger G., and Daniel Y.-J Kim, "Liquidity as an Investment Style: 2016 Update," available at research.zebracapital.com. Updated version of: Ibbotson, Roger G., Chen, Zhiwu, Kim, Daniel Y.-J., and Hu, Wendy Y. "Liquidity as an Investment Style," *Financial Analysts Journal*, May/June 2013, updated with 2012–2015 data.

Conclusion

The results confirm that liquidity impacts returns across styles and locations. Investing in less liquid securities generates higher returns. Liquidity seems to be an investment style that is different from size or value. This result seems to hold up in almost any equity market subset and in any location.

What's Next?

For many years, academics have sought to explain and understand asset prices, with a strong emphasis on market premiums and market anomalies. These premiums and anomalies can be explained by social or behavioral phenomenon in many settings. In a 2014 article, Roger Ibbotson and Tom Idzorek said, "Most of the best-known market premiums and anomalies can be explained by an intuitive and naturally occurring (social or behavioral) phenomenon observed in countless settings: popularity." [9.5]

Popularity

Popularity is often defined as a social phenomenon associated with being admired, sought after, well known, and/or accepted...can we apply the concept of popularity to the relative performance of different asset classes and different securities? Asset pricing theories have long recognized that expected returns should not be the same for the various instruments in the marketplace. The primary explanation for these differences has been differences in risk. Of course, risk is unpopular – investors do not like risk and want to be compensated for it.

[9.5] Ibbotson, R.G., Idzorek, T.H. "Dimensions of Popularity," *Journal of Portfolio Management*, Vol. 40 No. 5, No. 5 (Special 40th Anniversary Issue 2014), P. 68–74.

Stated simply and broadly, if an asset has characteristics that investors really like, its price will be higher. If the asset has characteristics that investors do not like, its price will be lower, all other things being equal. Thus the asset with more desirable characteristics should have lower expected relative returns, whereas the asset with less desirable characteristics should have higher expected relative returns.

From an equilibrium perspective, the expected return is not only for risk but *anything* the investor finds unattractive or unpopular (e.g., less liquid, high taxability, difficult to diversify, bad management, and so on). Therefore, various assets and individual securities will have different returns in equilibrium. From a behavioral finance perspective, mispricing can occur when stocks are highly traded, are "in the news," or there is much excitement about them. In all cases, the movement from the unpopular dimension to the popular dimension corresponds to relative price increases. Mispricing impacts shorter-term returns but not necessarily long-term returns, since the market recognizes the biases and these will eventually get corrected. Popularity is a key concept that helps to explain valuation as well as long- and short-run returns.

Although risk is clearly unpopular, it is only one dimension of popularity. Popularity can include all sorts of other characteristics that do not fit well into the risk and return paradigm. In many ways, the joint awarding of the 2013 Nobel Prize in Economic Sciences to Eugene Fama (an efficient markets advocate) and to Robert Shiller (a behavioral economist) endorses the merit of both approaches. The merit of both approaches and the link to popularity (voting) was recognized more than 80 years ago in *Security Analysis*, when Ben Graham and David Dodd [1934] wrote:

> "...the market is not a weighing machine, in which the value of each issue is registered by an exact and impersonal mechanism, in accordance with its specific qualities. Rather we should say that the market is a voting machine, whereon countless individuals register choices which are partly the product of reason and partly the product of emotion."

Chapter 10
Using Historical Data in Wealth Forecasting and Portfolio Optimization

When forecasting the return on an asset or a portfolio, investors are (or should be) interested in the entire probability distribution of future outcomes, not just the mean or "point estimate." An example of a point estimate forecast is that large-cap stocks will have a return of 13% in 2016. It is more helpful to know the uncertainty surrounding this point estimate than to know the point estimate itself. One measure of uncertainty is standard deviation. The large-cap stock return forecast can be expressed as 13% representing the mean and 20% representing the standard deviation.

If the returns on large-cap stocks are normally distributed, the mean (expected return) and the standard deviation provide enough information to forecast the likelihood of any return. Suppose one wants to ascertain the likelihood that large-cap stocks will have a return of -25% or lower in 2016. Given the above example, a return of -25% is [13 - (-25)] / 20 = 1.9 standard deviations below the mean. The likelihood of an observation 1.9 or more standard deviations below the mean is 2.9%. This can be looked up in any statistics textbook, in the table showing values of the cumulative probability function for a normal distribution. Thus, the likelihood that the stock market will fall by 25% or more in 2016 is 2.9%. This is valuable information, both to the investor who believes that stocks are a sure thing and to the investor who is certain that they will crash tomorrow.

However, historical stock returns are not exactly normally distributed, and a slightly different method needs to be used to make accurate probabilistic forecasts. A description of the model used to forecast the distribution of stock returns appears later in this chapter.

Probabilistic Forecasts

Probabilistic forecasts might seem to be too wide to be useful – the most widely quoted forecasters, after all, make very specific predictions. However, the forecast of a probability distribution actually reveals much more than the point estimate. The point estimate reflects what statisticians call an "expected value," but the actual return will likely be higher or lower than the point estimate. By knowing the extent to which actual returns are likely to deviate from the point estimate, the investor can assess the risk of every asset, and thus compare investment opportunities in terms of their risks as well as their expected returns. As Harry Markowitz showed nearly a half-century ago in his Nobel Prize-winning work on portfolio theory, investors care about avoiding risk as well as seeking return. Probabilistic forecasts enable investors to quantify these concepts.

The Lognormal Distribution

In the lognormal model, the natural logarithms of asset return relatives are assumed to be normally distributed. A return relative is one plus the return. That is, if an asset has a return of 15% in a given period, its return relative is 1.15 (1 + 0.15).

The lognormal distribution is skewed to the right. This means that the expected value, or mean, is greater than the median. Furthermore, if return relatives are lognormally distributed, returns cannot fall below negative 100%. These properties of the lognormal distribution make it a more accurate characterization of the behavior of market returns than does the normal distribution.

In all normal distributions, moreover, the probability of an observation falling one standard deviation below the mean equals the probability of falling one standard deviation above the mean; each has a probability of about 34%. In a lognormal distribution, these probabilities differ and depend on the parameters of the distribution.

Forecasting Wealth Values and Rates of Return

Using the lognormal model, it is fairly simple to form probabilistic forecasts of both compound rates of return and ending period wealth values. Wealth at time n (assuming reinvestment of all income and no taxes) is:

$$W_n = W_0(1+r_1)(1+r_2)...(1+r_n)$$

Where:

W_n	=	The wealth value at time n
W_0	=	The initial investment at time 0
$r_1, r_2,$ etc.	=	The total returns on the portfolio for the rebalancing ending at times 1, 2, and so forth

The compound rate of return or geometric mean return over the same period, r_G, is:

$$r_G = \left(\frac{W_n}{W_0}\right)^{\frac{1}{n}} - 1$$

Where:

r_G	=	The geometric mean return
W_n	=	The ending period wealth value at time n
W_0	=	The initial wealth value at time 0
n	=	The inclusive number of periods

By assuming that all $(1+r_n)$ values are lognormally distributed with the same expected value and standard deviation and are all statistically independent of each other, it follows that W_n and $(1+r_G)$ are lognormally distributed. In fact, even if the $(1+r_n)$ values are not themselves lognormally distributed but are independent and identically distributed, W_n and $(1+r_G)$ are approximately lognormal for large enough values of n. This "central-limit theorem" means that the lognormal model can be useful in long-term forecasting even if short-term returns are not well described by a lognormal distribution.

Calculating Parameters of the Lognormal Model

To use the lognormal model, we must first calculate the expected value and standard deviation of the natural logarithm of the return relative of the portfolio. These parameters, denoted m and s respectively, can be calculated from the expected return (m) and standard deviation (s) of the portfolio as follows:

$$m = \ln(1+\mu) - \left(\frac{s^2}{2}\right)$$

$$s = \sqrt{\ln\left[1+\left(\frac{\sigma}{1+\mu}\right)^2\right]}$$

Where:

    ln   =   The natural logarithm function

To calculate a particular percentile of wealth or return for a given time horizon, the only remaining parameter needed is the z-score of the percentile. The z-score of a percentile ranking is that percentile ranking expressed as the number of standard deviations that it is above or below the mean of a normal distribution. For example, the z-score of the 95th percentile is 1.645 because in a normal distribution, the 95th percentile is 1.645 standard deviations above the 50th percentile or median, which is also the mean. Z-scores can be obtained from a table of cumulative values of the standard normal distribution or from software that produces such values.

Given the logarithmic parameters of a portfolio (m and s), a time horizon (n), and the z-score of a percentile (z), the percentile in question in terms of cumulative wealth at the end of the time horizon (W_n) is:

$$e^{(mn+zs\sqrt{n})}$$

Similarly, the percentile in question in terms of the compound rate of return for the period (r_G) is:

$$e^{\left(m+z\frac{s}{\sqrt{n}}\right)} - 1$$

Mean-Variance Optimization

One important application of the probability forecasts of asset returns is mean-variance optimization. Optimization is the process of identifying portfolios that have the highest possible expected return for a given level of risk, or the lowest possible risk for a given expected return. Such a portfolio is considered "efficient," and the locus of all efficient portfolios is called the efficient frontier. A simple two-asset efficient frontier constructed from large-cap stocks and U.S. Treasury bills is shown in Exhibit 10.1. All investors should hold portfolios that are efficient with respect to the assets in their opportunity set.

Exhibit 10.1: Efficient Frontier; Large-cap Stocks and U.S. Treasury Bills 1926–2015

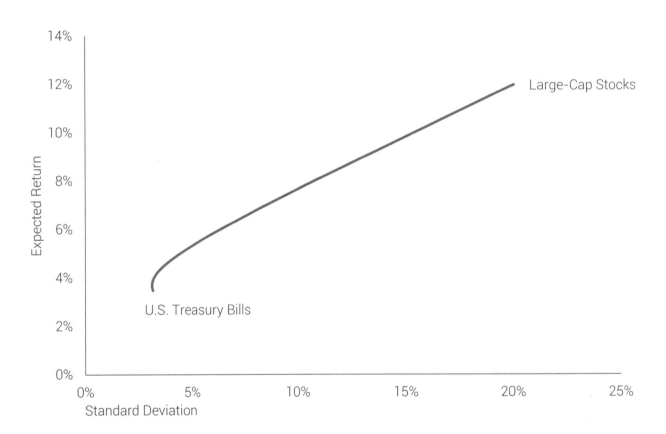

The most widely accepted framework for optimization is Markowitz, or mean-variance, optimization (MVO), which makes the following assumptions: (i) The forecast mean, or expected return, describes the attribute that investors consider to be desirable about an asset; (ii) The risk of the asset is measured by its expected standard deviation of returns; and (iii) The interaction between one asset and another is captured by the expected correlation coefficient of the two assets' returns. MVO thus requires forecasts of the return and standard deviation of each asset, and the correlation of each asset with every other asset.[10.1]

[10.1] The standard deviation is the square root of the variance; hence the term "mean-variance" in describing this form of the optimization problem.

In the 1950s, Harry Markowitz developed both the concept of the efficient frontier and the mathematical means of constructing it (mean-variance optimization).[10.2]

Estimating Returns, Risks, and Correlations

To simulate future probability distributions of asset and portfolio returns, one typically estimates parameters of the historical return data. The parameters that are required to simulate returns on an asset are its mean and standard deviation. To simulate returns on portfolios of assets, one must also estimate the correlation of each asset in the portfolio with every other asset. Thus, the parameters required to conduct a simulation are the same as those required as inputs into a mean-variance optimization.[10.3]

To illustrate how to estimate the parameters of asset class returns relevant to optimization and forecasting, we construct an example using large-cap stocks, long-term government bonds, and Treasury bills. The techniques used to estimate these parameters are described below.

Means, or Expected Returns

The mean return (forecast mean, or expected return) on an asset is the probability-weighted average of all possible returns on the asset over a future period. Estimates of expected returns are based on models of asset returns. While many models of asset returns incorporate estimates of gross national product, the money supply, and other macroeconomic variables, the model employed in this chapter does not. This is because we assume (for the present purpose) that asset markets are informationally efficient, with all relevant and available information fully incorporated in asset prices. If this assumption holds, investor expectations (forecasts) can be discerned from market-observable data. Such forecasts are not attempts to outguess, or beat, the market. They are attempts to discern the market's expectations, i.e., to read what the market itself is forecasting.

For some assets, expected returns can be estimated using current market data alone. For example, the yield on a riskless bond is an estimate of its expected return. For other assets, current data are not sufficient. Stocks, for example, have no exact analogue to the yield on a bond. In such cases, we use the statistical time series properties of historical data in forming the estimates.

To know which data to use when estimating expected returns, we need to know the rebalancing frequency of the portfolios and the investment horizon. In our example, we will assume an annual rebalancing frequency and a 20-year planning horizon. The rebalancing frequency gives the time units in which returns are measured.

[10.2] Markowitz, H.M. 1959. *Portfolio Selection: Efficient Diversification of Investments* (New York: John Wiley & Sons).

[10.3] It is also possible to conduct a simulation using entire data sets, that is, without estimating the statistical parameters of the data sets. Typically, in such a nonparametric simulation, the frequency of an event occurring in the simulated history is equal to the frequency of the event occurring in the actual history used to construct the data set.

With a 20-year horizon, the relevant riskless rate is the yield on a 20-year coupon bond. This riskless rate is the baseline from which the expected return on every other asset class is derived by adding or subtracting risk premiums.

Large-Cap Stocks

The expected return on large-cap stocks is the riskless rate, plus the expected risk premium of large-cap stocks over bonds that are riskless over the investment horizon. With a 20-year horizon, this risk premium is 6.90%, shown as the long-horizon expected equity risk premium in Exhibit 10.2. Hence, the expected return on large-cap stocks is 2.68% (the long-term riskless rate) plus 6.90% (the long-term equity risk premium), or 9.58%.

Bonds and Bills

For default-free bonds with a maturity equal to the planning horizon, the expected return is the yield on the bond; that is, the expected return is the long-term riskless rate of 2.68%. For bonds with other maturities, the expected bond horizon premium should be added to the riskless rate (for longer maturities) or subtracted from the riskless rate (for shorter maturities). Because expected capital gains on a bond are zero, the expected horizon premium is estimated by the historical average difference of the income returns on the bonds.[10.4]

For Treasury bills, the expected return over a given time horizon equals to the expected return on a Treasury bond of a similar horizon, less the expected horizon premium of bonds over bills. The long-term horizon premium is estimated by the historical average of the difference of the income return on bonds and the return on bills. From Exhibit 10.2, this is 1.58%. Subtracting this from the riskless rate (2.68%) gives us an expected return on bills of 1.10%. Of course, this forecast typically differs from the current yield on a Treasury bill because a portfolio of Treasury bills is rolled over (the proceeds of maturing bills are invested in new bills, at yields not yet known) during the time horizon described.

[10.4] The expected capital gain on a par bond is self-evidently zero. For a zero coupon (or other discount) bond, investors expect the price to rise as the bond ages, but the expected portion of this price increase should not be considered a capital gain. It is a form of income return.

Exhibit 10.2: Building Blocks for Expected Return Construction

Yields (Riskless Rates)[*]	Value (%)
Long-term (20-year) U.S. Treasury Coupon Bond Yield	2.68
Intermediate-term (5-year) U.S. Treasury Coupon Note Yield	1.69
Short-term (30-day) U.S. Treasury Bill Yield	0.14

Fixed-Income Risk Premiums [**]	
Expected default premium: long-term corporate bond total returns minus long-term government bond total returns	-0.04
Expected long-term horizon premium: long-term government bond income returns minus U.S. Treasury bill total returns[*]	1.82
Expected intermediate-term horizon premium: intermediate-term government bond income returns minus U.S. Treasury bill total returns[*]	1.11

Equity Risk Premiums [***]	
Long-horizon expected equity risk premium: large-cap stock total returns minus long-term government bond income returns	6.90
Intermediate-horizon expected equity risk premium: large-cap stock total returns minus intermediate-term government bond income returns	7.48
Short-horizon expected equity risk premium: large-cap stock total returns minus U.S. Treasury bill total returns [****]	8.49
Small-cap premium: small-cap stock total return minus large-cap stock total return	4.52

[*] As of December 31, 2015. Maturities are approximate. Source: (i) SBBI Long-term Government Bond series (20-year yield), (ii) SBBI Intermediate-term Government Bond series (5-year yield); Board of Governors of the Federal Reserve website at https://www.federalreserve.gov/releases/h15/data.htm, Treasury constant maturities/1-month/Business day (30-day Treasury Bill).

[**] Expected risk premiums for fixed income are based on the differences of historical arithmetic mean returns from 1970–2015.

[***] Expected risk premiums for equities are based on the differences of historical arithmetic mean returns from 1926–2015.

[****] For U.S. Treasury bills, the income return and total return are the same.

Standard Deviations

Standard deviations are estimated from historical data as described in Chapter 6. There is no evidence of a major change in the variability of returns on large-cap stocks, so we use the entire period 1926 to 2015 to estimate the standard deviation of these asset classes. For long-term government bonds and Treasury bills, we use the period 1970 to 2015 to estimate these inputs (see Exhibit 10.4). This is because the departure from the Bretton Woods fixed-rate currency exchange agreement in the early 1970s caused a structural shift in the U.S. interest-rate environment. Bond volatility spiked as a result, and has remained well above levels experienced before the regime shift, rendering pre-1970 risk comparisons inappropriate.

Correlations

Correlations between the asset classes are estimated from historical data as described in Chapter 6. Correlations between major asset classes change over time. Exhibit 10.3 shows the historical correlation of annual returns on large-cap stocks and long-term bonds over 20-year rolling periods from 1926–1945 through 1996–2015.

Exhibit 10.3: 20-Year Rolling-Period Correlations of Annual Returns of Large-Cap Stocks and Long-term Government Bonds
1926–1945 through 1996–2015

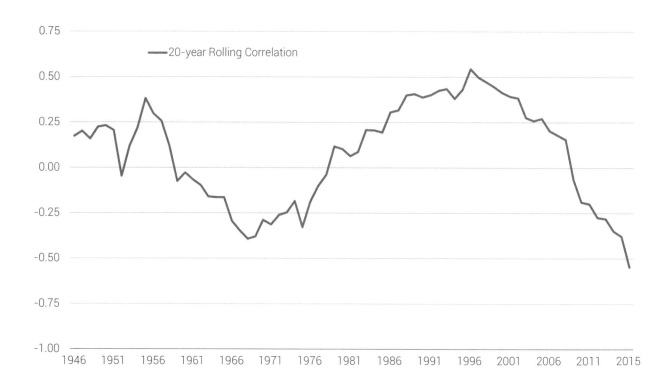

In Exhibit 10.4, a correlation matrix is provided that can be used in conjunction with the information provided in Exhibit 10.2 as inputs in forming portfolios.

Exhibit 10.4: Optimization Inputs: Year-end 2015 Large-Cap Stocks, Long-term Government Bonds, and U.S. Treasury Bills (%)

| | Expected Return (%) | Standard Deviation (%) | Correlation | | |
			Stocks	Bonds	Bills
Stocks	9.6	20.0	1.00		
Bonds	2.7	12.2	0.00	1.00	
Bills	0.1	3.4	-0.02	0.18	1.00

Using Inputs to Form Other Portfolios

Given a complete set of inputs, the expected return and standard deviation of any portfolio (efficient or other) of the asset classes can be calculated. The expected return of a portfolio is the weighted average of the expected returns of the asset classes:

$$r_p = \sum_{i=1}^{n} x_i r_i$$

Where:

r_p = The expected return of the portflio p

n = The number of asset classes

x_i = The portfolio weight of asset class i, scaled such that:

$$\sum_{i=1}^{n} x_i = 1$$

Where:

r_i = The expected return of asset class i

For example, referring to the inputs in Exhibit 10.4 (the expected returns and standard deviations shown in Exhibit 10.4 are the equivalent values from Exhibit 10.2, rounded to one decimal), a portfolio comprised of large-cap stocks only would have an expected return of 9.6% and a standard deviation of 20.0%. If the portfolio mix is changed to, say, 60.0% large cap stocks, 35.0% long-term government bonds, and 5.0% Treasury bills, the expected return of this new portfolio mix can be calculated by applying the above formula (again, using the inputs in Exhibit 10.4):

6.7% = (60.0% x 9.6%) + (35.0% x 2.7%) (5.0% x 0.1%)

The standard deviation of the portfolio depends not only on the standard deviations of the asset classes, but also on all of the correlations. It is given by:

$$\sigma_p = \sqrt{\sum_{i=1}^{n} \sum_{i=1}^{n} x_i x_j \sigma_i \sigma_j p_{ij}}$$

Where:

σ_p	=	The standard deviation of the portfolio
x_i and x_j	=	The portfolio weights of asset classes i and j
σ_i and σ_j	=	The standard deviations of returns on asset classes i and j
p_{ij}	=	The correlation between returns on asset classes i and j
		(note that r_{ii} equals one and that r_{ij} is equal to r_{ji}).

The standard deviation of the new portfolio (60.0% large cap stocks, 35.0% long-term government bonds, and 5.0% Treasury bills) can be calculated using the inputs from Exhibit 10.2 and 10.4 as shown in Exhibit 10.5:

Exhibit 10.5: Calculation of Example Portfolio Comprised of 60.0% Large-cap stocks, 35.0% Long-term Government Bonds, and 5.0% Treasury Bills

Stocks (asset class 1)	Bonds (asset class 2)	Bills (asset class 3)
Stocks & Stocks	Stocks & Bonds	Stocks and Bills
$x_1^2 \sigma_1^2 p_{1,1} =$	$x_1 x_2 \sigma_1 \sigma_2 p_{1,2} =$	$x_1 x_3 \sigma_1 \sigma_3 p_{1,3} =$
$0.60^2 \times 0.20^2 \times 1.00 =$	$0.60 \times 0.35 \times 0.20 \times 0.122 \times -0.002 =$	$0.60 \times 0.05 \times 0.20 \times 0.034 \times -0.017 =$
$=0.014389$	$=-0.000010$	$=-0.000004$
Bonds & Stocks	Bonds & Bonds	Bonds & Bills
$x_1 x_2 \sigma_1 \sigma_2 p_{1,2} =$	$x_2^2 \sigma_2^2 p_{2,2} =$	$x_2 x_3 \sigma_2 \sigma_3 p_{2,3} =$
$0.35 \times 0.60 \times 0.122 \times 0.20 \times -0.002 =$	$0.35^2 \times 0.122^2 \times 1.00 =$	$0.35 \times 0.05 \times 0.122 \times 0.034 \times 0.179 =$
$=-0.000010$	$=0.001817$	$=0.000013$
Bills & Stocks	Bills & Bonds	Bills & Bills
$x_1 x_3 \sigma_1 \sigma_3 p_{1,3} =$	$x_2 x_3 \sigma_2 \sigma_3 p_{2,3} =$	$x_3^2 \sigma_3^2 p_{3,3} =$
$0.05 \times 0.60 \times 0.034 \times 0.20 \times -0.017 =$	$0.05 \times 0.35 \times 0.034 \times 0.122 \times 0.179 =$	$0.05^2 \times 0.034^2 \times 1.00 =$
$=-0.000004$	$=0.000013$	$=0.000003$

By summing these terms and taking the square root of the total, the result is a standard deviation of 12.7%.

$$\sqrt{\begin{array}{l} 0.014389 + -0.000010 + -0.000004 + \\ -0.000010 + 0.001817 + 0.000013 + \\ -0.000004 + 0.000013 + 0.000003 \end{array}} = 12.7\%$$

Enhancements to Mean-Variance Optimization

Ibbotson Associates was an early adopter of mean-variance optimization to develop asset class model guidelines and continues to assist the industry in the development of enhancements to the traditional mean-variance approach as well as the state-of-the-art techniques described later in the chapter. Over the last half century, the Markowitz mean-variance optimization (MVO) framework has become the textbook approach for creating these optimal asset allocations, but the approach has several shortcomings.

Shortcomings of Traditional Optimization Techniques

One notable shortcoming is that the output (optimal asset allocation weights) is very sensitive to the inputs (expected returns, standard deviations, and correlations). Input sensitivity often leads to highly concentrated allocations in only a small number of the available asset classes. For example, if a typical optimization starts with an opportunity set of about 10 asset classes, just a few of these asset choices might end up in the resulting optimal allocation, with the remaining asset choices not even getting a mention.

Mean-variance optimization is a powerful tool, but it needs to be used with caution. For instance, basing mean-variance optimization inputs on shorter periods can contribute to the extreme results. Basing the mean-variance optimization inputs on longer periods, such as those presented elsewhere in this book, can help mitigate the extreme asset allocations mixes. Also, there is usually a more consistent ratio of return to risk amongst the different asset classes when using longer periods.

Placing maximum and minimum allocation constraints on each asset is the most common solution to the problem of highly concentrated asset allocations. For instance, we could specify a minimum allocation of 5% and a maximum allocation of 15% for each of the nine asset choices. This would ensure that each asset gets represented in the final allocation and also that no single asset completely dominates in the final allocation mix. Unfortunately, these artificial minimums and maximums are arbitrary, and usually end up limiting the ability of the optimizer to properly act on the information contained in the inputs.

Black-Litterman and Resampling Techniques

Two popular enhancements to traditional optimization techniques have emerged in recent years that can help overcome these difficulties. While both of these methods can help develop well diversified asset allocations, they approach the problem in very different ways. The first of these, the Black-Litterman model, attempts to create better inputs. The second, resampled mean variance optimization, attempts to build a better optimizer.

The Black-Litterman model was created by Fischer Black and Robert Litterman in the late 1980s. The Black-Litterman model combines investors' views regarding expected returns and the expected returns predicted by the capital asset pricing model to form a single blended estimate of expected returns. When this new combined estimate is used as an input within a traditional mean-variance optimization framework, it produces well-diversified portfolios that include not only market-based asset allocations but also allocations in assets that received favorable views.

The second approach, resampled mean-variance optimization, grew out of the work of a number of authors, but is most closely associated with the work of Richard Michaud. While traditional mean-variance optimization treats the capital market assumptions as if they were known with complete certainty, resampled mean-variance optimization recognizes that the capital market assumptions are forecasts, and are therefore not known with complete certainty.

Conceptually, resampled mean-variance optimization is a combination of Monte Carlo simulation[10.5] and the more traditional Markowitz mean-variance optimization approach. The simulation randomly resamples possible returns from a forecasted return distribution or randomly resamples possible returns from a historical distribution. The simulated returns lead to a simulated set of capital market assumptions that are used in a traditional mean-variance optimizer, and the asset allocations are recorded. After combining the asset allocations from the numerous intermediate optimizations, the resulting asset allocations are those that, on average, are predicted to perform best over the range of potential outcomes implied by the capital market assumptions. Research has shown that asset allocations selected from a resampled efficient frontier may outperform those from a traditional efficient frontier.[10.6]

In addition to the problem of getting results that are highly concentrated in just a few of the assets available, there are two more criticisms of the traditional mean-variance optimization framework.

First, the traditional approach focuses on a subset of the total portfolio. Traditionally, the focus is on finding a mix of asset classes that maximizes the expected return, subject to a risk constraint. However, because the purpose of most asset portfolios is to fund a specified future cash-flow stream – a liability – the true risk for the portfolio is not the standard deviation of the assets or the performance of the assets relative to that of peers, but not being able to fund the future liability.

[10.5] Monte Carlo simulation is a problem-solving technique utilized to approximate the probability of certain outcomes by performing multiple trial runs, called simulations, using random variables. The probability distribution of the results is calculated and analyzed in order to infer which outcomes are most likely to be produced.

[10.6] See Markowitz, H. & Usmen, N. 2003. "Resampled Frontiers vs. Diffuse Bayes: An Experiment." *Journal of Investment Management*, Vo. 1, No. 4.

An asset allocation approach that takes the future liability into account is called liability-relative optimization (or surplus optimization). The usual method employed to accomplish this is to constrain the optimizer to hold short an asset class representing the liability.

Second, the traditional mean-variance optimization framework assumes that the returns of the assets in the optimization are normally distributed. As illustrated in Exhibit 2.3, the return distributions of different asset classes do not always follow a standard, symmetrical bell-shaped curve. Some assets have distributions that are skewed to the left or right, while others have distributions that are skinnier or fatter than others. These more complicated characteristics are called skewness and kurtosis, respectively. The next wave of enhancements to the traditional mean-variance optimization are frameworks that incorporate these additional types of non-normalities into the optimization.

Markowitz 1.0

In 1952, Harry Markowitz, invented portfolio optimization. His genius was based on three principles; risk, reward and the correlation of assets in a portfolio. Over the years, technologies advanced, markets crashed, but the portfolio optimization models used by many investors did not evolve to compensate. This is surprising in light of the fact that Markowitz was a pioneer of technological advancement in the field of computational computer science. Furthermore, he did not stand by idly in the area of portfolio modeling, but continued to make improvements in his own models and to influence the models of others. Few of these improvements, however, were picked up broadly in practice.

Because Markowitz's first effort was so simple and powerful, it attracted a great number of followers. The greater the following became, the fewer questioners debated its merits. Markowitz's original work is synonymous with modern portfolio theory and has been taught in business schools for generations and, not surprisingly, is still widely used today.

Then came the crash of 2008, and people started to ask questions. The confluence of the economic trauma and the technological advances of recent decades made the postcrash environment the perfect moment to upgrade to a new model built around Markowitz's fundamental principles of risk, reward and correlation. We dub our updated model "Markowitz 2.0." This section is an adaptation of a 2009 article, "The New Efficient Frontier," by Paul D. Kaplan, Morningstar Canada's director of research, and Sam L. Savage, consulting professor at Stanford University.

Markowitz 2.0

The Flaw of Averages

The 1952 mean-variance model of Harry Markowitz was the first systematic attempt to cure what Savage (2009) called the "flaw of averages." In general, the flaw of averages is a set of systematic errors that occur when people use single numbers (usually averages) to describe uncertain future quantities. For example, if you plan to rob a bank of $10 million and have one chance in 100 of getting away with it, your average take is $100,000. If you described your activity beforehand as "making $100,000" you would be correct on average. But this is a terrible characterization of a bank heist. Yet as Savage discussed, this very "flaw of averages" is made all the time in business practice, and helps explain why everything is behind schedule, beyond budget, and below projection. This phenomenon was an accessory to the global financial crisis that culminated in 2008.

Markowitz's mean-variance model distinguished between different investments that had the same average (expected) return but different risks, measured as variance or its square root (standard deviation). This breakthrough systematic attempt to cure the flaw of averages ultimately garnered a Nobel Prize for its inventor. However, the use of standard deviation and covariance introduces a higher order version of the flaw of averages in that these concepts are themselves a version of averages.

Making a Great Idea Better

By taking advantage of the very latest in economic thought and computer technology, we can, in effect, add more thrust to the original framework of the Markowitz portfolio optimization model. The result is a dramatically more powerful model that is more aligned with 21st century investor concerns, markets, and financial instruments, such as options.

Our discussion here will focus on five practical enhancements to traditional portfolio optimization that can be made with current technology:

1. First, we use a scenario-based approach to allow for fat-tailed distributions. "Fat-tailed" return distributions are not possible within the context of traditional mean-variance optimization, where return distributions are assumed to be adequately described by mean and variance.

2. Second, we replace the single-period expected return with the long-term forward-looking geometric mean, as this takes into account accumulation of wealth.

3. Third, we substitute conditional value at risk, or CVaR, which focuses on tail risk, for standard deviation, which looks at average variation.

4. Fourth, the original Markowitz model used a covariance matrix to model the distribution of returns on asset classes; we replace this with a scenario-based model that can be generated with Monte Carlo simulation, and can incorporate any number of distributions.

5. Finally, we exploit new statistical technologies pioneered by Savage in the field of probability management. Savage invented an astonishing new technology called the Distribution String, or DIST, which encapsulates thousands of trials as a single data element or spreadsheet cell, thus eliminating the main disadvantage of the scenario-based approach – the need to store and process large amounts of data.

The Scenario Approach vs. Lognormal Distributions

One of the limitations of the traditional mean-variance optimization framework assumes that the distribution of returns of the assets in the optimization can be adequately described simply by mean and variance alone. The most common depiction of this assumption is to draw the distribution of each asset class as a symmetrical bell-shaped curve; but asset class returns do not always fall into normal distributions.

Over the years, various alternatives have been put forth to replace mean-variance optimization with an optimization framework that takes into account the non-normal features of return distributions. Some researchers have proposed using distribution curves that exhibit skewness and kurtosis (i.e., have fat tails) while others have proposed using large numbers of scenarios based on historical data, or Monte Carlo simulation.

The scenario-based approach has two main advantages over a distribution curve approach: (i) It is highly flexible; for example, nonlinear instruments such as options can be modeled in a straightforward manner; and (ii) it is mathematically manageable; for example, portfolio returns under the scenarios are simply weighted averages of asset class returns within the scenarios. In this way, the distribution of a portfolio can be derived from the distributions of the assets classes without working complicated equations that might lack analytical solutions; only straightforward portfolio arithmetic is needed.

In standard scenario analysis, there is no precise graphical representation of return distributions. Histograms serve as approximations, such as those shown in Exhibit 2.3. We augment the scenario approach by employing a smoothing technique so that smooth curves represent return distributions. For example, Exhibit 10.6 shows the distribution curve of annual returns of large-cap stocks under our scenario-based approach. Comparing Exhibit 10.6 with the large-cap stock histogram in Exhibit 2.3, we can see that the smooth distribution curve retains the properties of the historical distribution making it more esthetically pleasing and precise. Further, our model can bring all of the power of continuous mathematics to the scenario approach. This was previously enjoyed only by models based on continuous distributions.

In Exhibit 10.6, the solid gray line represents the distribution of annual returns of large-cap stocks when our smoothed scenario-based approach is used and the red line represents the distribution curve of annual returns of large-cap stocks when traditional mean-variance analysis is used and we assume that returns follow a lognormal distribution.

Exhibit 10.6: Distribution of Annual Returns: Large-cap Stocks (%)
Lognormal Distribution vs. Scenario-Based Model
1926–2015

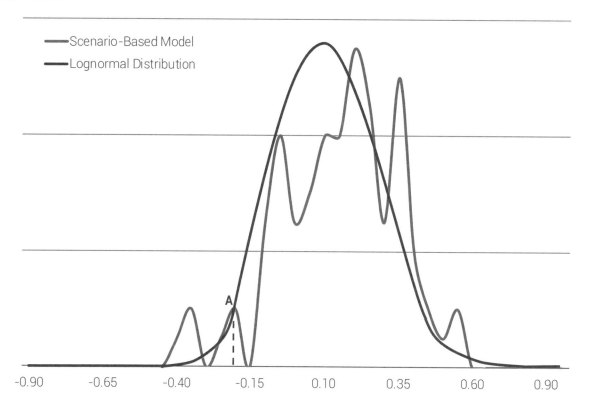

If we extend a vertical line from Point A down to the x-axis, the area to the left (and underneath) each of the curves represents the occurrences of annual returns equal to or less than, in this case, negative 26%. Because these are cumulative distributions, we can calculate the probability that the annual returns of large-cap stocks will be less than or equal to negative 26% by dividing the area underneath each of the smaller curves (to the left of Point A) by the total area underneath each of the entire curves.

For example, looking to the scenario-based model, the area to the left of the vertical line under the scenario-based distribution represents 5% of the total area underneath this entire distribution line. This implies that the probability of large-cap stocks having a loss of 26% or more is 5%. Correspondingly, the area to the left of the vertical line for the lognormal distribution represents 1.6% of the total area under the entire lognormal distribution line. This implies that the probability of large-cap stocks returning negative 26% or less using the traditional mean-variance model is 1.6%.

As Kaplan et al. (2009) discuss, "tail events" have occurred often throughout the history of capital markets all over the world, but the probabilities associated with them may be systematically underestimated within the context of traditional mean-variance analysis, where return distributions are assumed to be lognormal. The scenario-based model proposed by Kaplan and Savage is a real step forward as it better models the nontrivial probabilities associated with tail events. For a more detailed discussion of tail events and their nontriviality, see Chapter 11, where Kaplan introduces a new set of monthly real stock market total returns going back a full 125 years. Using these new returns, we demonstrate that the severity of the financial crisis of 2008 was not unique, but was merely the latest chapter in a long history of market meltdowns.

Geometric Mean vs. Single-Period Expected Return

In mean-variance optimization, reward is measured by expected return, which is a forecast of arithmetic mean. However, over long periods, investors are not concerned with simple averages of return, rather they are concerned with the accumulation of wealth. We use forecasted long-term geometric mean as the measure of reward because investors who plan on repeatedly reinvesting in the same strategy over an indefinite period would seek the highest rate of growth for the portfolios as measured by geometric mean.[10.7]

Conditional Value at Risk vs. Standard Deviation

As for risk, much has been written about how investors are not concerned merely with the degree of dispersion of returns (as measured by standard deviation), but rather with how much wealth they could lose. A number of downside risk measures, including value at risk, conditional value at risk, and maximum drawdown, have been proposed to replace standard deviation as the measure of risk in strategic asset allocation. While any one of these could be used, our preference is to use conditional value at risk.

CVaR is related to value at risk. VaR describes the left tail in terms of how much capital can be lost over a given period of time. For example, a 5% VaR answers a question of the form: Having invested $10,000 there is a 5% chance of losing $X or more in 12 months. (The "or more" implications of VaR are sometimes overlooked by investors with serious implications.) Applying this idea to returns, the 5% VaR is the negative of the 5th percentile of the return distribution. CVaR is the expected or average loss of capital should VaR be breached. Therefore CVaR is always greater than VaR.

Scenarios vs. Correlation

In mean-variance analysis, the covariation of the returns of each pair of asset classes is represented by a single number, the correlation coefficient. This is mathematically equivalent to assuming that a simple linear regression model is an adequate description of how the returns on the two asset classes are related. In fact, the R-squared statistic of a simple linear regression model for two series of returns is equal to the square of the correlation coefficient.

However, for many pairs of asset classes, a linear model misses the most important features of the relationship. For example, during normal times, non-U.S. equities are considered to be good diversifiers for U.S. equity investors. But during global crises, all major equity markets move down together.

[10.7] Ranking investment strategies by forecasted geometric mean is sometimes described as applying the Kelly Criterion, an idea promoted by William Poundstone in his 2005 book, *Fortune's Formula*.

Furthermore, suppose that the returns on two asset class indices were highly correlated, but instead of including direct exposures to both in the model, one was replaced with an option on itself. Instead of having a linear relationship, we now have a nonlinear relationship which cannot be captured by a correlation coefficient.

Fortunately, these sorts of nonlinear relationships between returns on different investments can be handled in a scenario-based model. For example, in scenarios that represent normal times, returns on different equity markets could be modeled as moving somewhat apart from each other; while scenarios that represent global crises could model the markets as moving downward together.

Probability Management Enables Scenario Analysis

Because it may take thousands of scenarios to adequately model return distributions, until recently, a disadvantage of the scenario-based approach has been that it requires large amounts of data to be stored and processed. Even with the advances in computer hardware, the conventional approach of representing scenarios with large tables of explicit numbers remained problematic.

The phenomenal speed of computers has given rise to the field of probability management, an extension of data management to probability distributions, rather than numbers. The key component of probability management is the Distribution String, or DIST, that can encapsulate thousands of trials as a single data element. The use of DISTs greatly saves on storage and speeds up processing time, so that a Monte Carlo simulation consisting of thousands of trials can be performed on a personal computer in an instant. Monte Carlo simulations that use DISTs are also very adaptable, allowing for almost any return distribution or underlying probability model, rather than being contained by parameters. While not all asset management organizations are prepared to create the DISTs needed to drive geometric mean-CVaR optimization, some outside vendors, such as Morningstar/Ibbotson, can fulfill this role.

Another facet of probability management is interactive simulation technology, which can run thousands of scenarios through a model before the sound of your finger leaving the <Enter> key reaches your ear. These supersonic models allow much deeper intuition into the sensitivities of portfolios, and encourage the user to interactively explore different portfolios, distributional assumptions, and potential black swans. A sample of such an interactive model is available for download from http://www.ProbabilityManagement.org.

Finale: The New Efficient Frontier

Putting it all together, we form an efficient frontier of forecasted geometric mean and conditional value at risk as shown in Exhibit 10.7,[10.8] incorporating our scenario approach to covariance and new statistical technology. We believe that this efficient frontier is more relevant to investors than

---

[10.8] Other researchers have also proposed using GM and CVaR as the measures or reward and risk in an efficient frontier. See, for example: Sheikh, A.Z. & Qiao, H. 2009. "Non-Normality of Market Returns: A Framework for Asset allocation Decision Making." Whitepaper, J.P. Morgan Asset Management.

the traditional expected return versus standard deviation frontier of MVO because it shows the trade-off between reward and risk that is meaningful to investors; namely, long-term potential growth versus short-term potential loss.

Exhibit 10.7: Geometric Mean – Conditional Value at Risk Efficient Frontier (%)

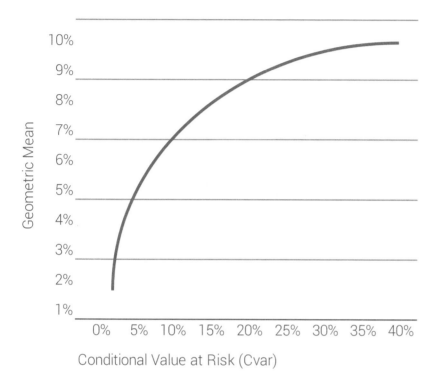

Approaches to Calculating the Equity Risk Premium

Researchers have estimated the expected outperformance of stocks over risk-free bonds – the equity risk premium using many approaches. Such studies can be categorized into four groups based on the approaches they have taken, using:

- Historical returns between stocks and bonds;

- Fundamental information such as earnings, dividends, or overall productivity (supply-side models);

- Payoffs demanded by equity investors for bearing the additional risk (demand-side models); and

- Broad surveys of opinions of financial professionals.

The rest of this chapter will focus on the historical and supply-side methods.

The Historical Equity Risk Premium

The expected equity risk premium can be defined as the additional return an investor expects to receive to compensate for the additional risk associated with investing in equities as opposed to investing in riskless assets.

Unfortunately, the expected equity risk premium is unobservable in the market and therefore must be estimated. Typically, this estimation is arrived at through the use of historical data. The historical equity risk premium can be calculated by subtracting the long-term average of the income return on the riskless asset (Treasuries) from the long-term average stock market return (measured over the same period as that of the riskless asset).

In using a historical measure of the equity risk premium, one assumes that what has happened in the past is representative of what might be expected in the future. In other words, the assumption one makes when using historical data to measure the expected equity risk premium is that the relationship between the returns of the risky asset (equities) and the riskless asset (Treasuries) is stable.

The Stock Market Benchmark

The stock market benchmark chosen should be a broad index that reflects the behavior of the market as a whole. Commonly used indexes include the S&P 500 and the Russell 3000. Although the Dow Jones Industrial Average is a popular index, it would be inappropriate for calculating the equity risk premium because it is too narrow.

We use the total return of our large-cap stock index (currently represented by the S&P 500) as our market benchmark when calculating the equity risk premium. The S&P 500 was selected as the appropriate market benchmark because it is representative of a large sample of companies across a large number of industries. The S&P 500 is also one of the most widely accepted market benchmarks and is a good measure of the equity market as a whole.

Exhibit 10.8 illustrates the equity risk premium calculation using three different market indexes (the S&P 500, a portfolio comprised of CRSP NYSE/NYSE MKT/NASDAQ deciles 1–10, and a portfolio comprised of CRSP NYSE/NYSE MKT/NASDAQ deciles 1–2) and the income return on three government bonds of different horizons.

Exhibit 10.8: Equity Risk Premium with Different Market Indexes (%)
1926–2015

	Long-horizon	Intermediate-horizon	Short-horizon
S&P 500	6.90	7.48	8.49
CRSP NYSE/NYSE MKT/NASDAQ Deciles 1-10	6.70	7.28	8.28
CRSP NYSE/NYSE MKT/NASDAQ Deciles 1-2	6.25	6.83	7.84

The equity risk premium is calculated by subtracting the arithmetic mean of the government bond income return from the arithmetic mean of the stock market total return. Exhibit 10.9 demonstrates this calculation for the long-horizon equity risk premium.

Exhibit 10.9: Long-Horizon Equity Risk Premium Calculation (%)
1926–2015

	Arithmetic Mean		
	Market Total Return	Risk-free Rate	Equity Risk Premium
S&P 500	11.95	5.05 =	6.90
CRSP NYSE/NYSE MKT/NASDAQ Deciles 1-10	11.75	5.05 =	6.70
CRSP NYSE/NYSE MKT/NASDAQ Deciles 1-2	11.30	5.05 =	6.25

Source of underlying data in both Exhibit 10.8 and 10.9: (i) "IA SBBI US Large Stock TR USD Ext" series retrieved from the Morningstar *Direct* database. The "IA SBBI US Large Stock TR USD Ext" return series is essentially the S&P 500 index. The long-term, intermediate-term, and short-term risk-free series used are the "IA SBBI US LT Govt IR USD" series, the "IA SBBI US IT Govt IR USD" series, and the "IA SBBI US 30 Day TBill TR USD" series, respectively. All rights reserved. Used with permission. (ii) CRSP U.S. Stock Database and CRSP U.S. Indices Database © 2016 Center for Research in Security Prices (CRSP®), University of Chicago Booth School of Business. Used with permission. All rights reserved. Calculations performed by Duff & Phelps LLC.

The Market Benchmark and Firm Size

Although not restricted to the 500 largest companies, the S&P 500 is considered a large-cap index. The returns of the S&P 500 are cap-weighted. The larger companies in the index therefore receive the majority of the weight. The use of the "NYSE/NYSE MKT/NASDAQ Deciles 1–2" series results in an even purer large-cap index. However, if using a large-cap index to calculate the equity risk premium, an adjustment is usually needed to account for the different risk and return characteristics of small stocks. This was discussed further in Chapter 7 on the size premium.

The Risk-Free Asset

The equity risk premium can be calculated for a variety of time horizons when given the choice of risk-free asset to be used in the calculation. Chapter 3 provides equity risk premium calculations for short-, intermediate-, and long-term horizons. The short-, intermediate-, and long-horizon equity risk premiums are calculated using the income return from a 30-day Treasury bill, a 5-year Treasury bond, and a 20-year Treasury bond, respectively.

20-Year vs. 30-Year Treasuries

Our methodology for estimating the long-horizon equity risk premium makes use of the income return on a 20-year Treasury bond; however, the Treasury stopped issuing 20-year bonds in 1986. The 30-year bond that the Treasury returned to issuing in 2006 is theoretically more correct when dealing with the long-term nature of business valuation, yet Ibbotson Associates instead creates a series of returns using bonds on the market with approximately 20 years to maturity. The reason for the use of a 20-year maturity bond is that 30-year Treasury securities have only been issued over the relatively recent past, starting in February of 1977, and were suspended from 2002 to 2006.

The same reason applies to why we do not use the 10-year Treasury bond – a long history of market data is not available for 10-year bonds. We have persisted in using a 20-year bond to keep the basis of the time series consistent.

Income Return

Another point to keep in mind when calculating the equity risk premium is that the income return on the appropriate-horizon Treasury security, rather than the total return, is used in the calculation.

The total return comprises three return components: the income return, the capital appreciation return, and the reinvestment return. The income return is defined as the portion of the total return that results from a periodic cash flow or, in this case, the bond coupon payment. The capital appreciation return results from the price change of a bond over a specific period. Bond prices generally change in reaction to unexpected fluctuations in yields. Reinvestment return is the return on a given month's investment income when reinvested into the same asset class in the subsequent months of the year. The income return is thus used in the estimation of the equity risk premium because it represents the truly riskless portion of the return.

Arithmetic vs. Geometric Mean

The equity risk premium data presented in this book are arithmetic average risk premiums as opposed to geometric average risk premiums. The arithmetic average equity risk premium can be demonstrated to be most appropriate when discounting future cash flows. For use as the expected equity risk premium in either the CAPM or the building-block approach, the arithmetic mean or the simple difference of the arithmetic means of stock market returns and riskless rates is the relevant number. This is because both the CAPM and the building-block approach are additive models, in which the cost of capital is the sum of its parts. The geometric average is more appropriate for reporting past performance because it represents the compound average return.

Appropriate Historical Period

The equity risk premium can be estimated using any historical time period. For the U.S., market data exist at least as far back as the late 1800s. Therefore, it is possible to estimate the equity risk premium using data that covers roughly the past 125 years.

Our equity risk premium covers 1926 to the present. The original data source for the time series comprising the equity risk premium is the Center for Research in Security Prices. CRSP chose to begin its analysis of market returns with 1926 for two main reasons. CRSP determined that 1926 was approximately when quality financial data became available. They also made a conscious effort to include the period of extreme market volatility from the late 1920s and early 1930s; 1926 was chosen because it includes one full business cycle of data before the market crash of 1929.

Implicit in using history to forecast the future is the assumption that investors' expectations for future outcomes conform to past results. This method assumes that the price of taking on risk changes only slowly, if at all, over time. This "future equals the past" assumption is most applicable to a random time-series variable. A time-series variable is random if its value in one period is independent of its value in other periods.

Choosing an Appropriate Historical Period

The estimate of the equity risk premium depends on the length of the data series studied. A proper estimate of the equity risk premium requires a data series long enough to give a reliable average without being unduly influenced by very good and very poor short-term returns. When calculated using a long data series, the historical equity risk premium is relatively stable. Furthermore, because an average of the realized equity risk premium is quite volatile when calculated using a short history, using a long series makes it less likely that the analyst can justify any number he or she wants. The magnitude of how shorter periods can affect the result will be explored later in this chapter.

Some analysts estimate the expected equity risk premium using a shorter, more recent period on the basis that recent events are more likely to be repeated in the near future; furthermore, they believe that the 1920s, 1930s, and 1940s contain too many unusual events. This view is suspect because all periods contain unusual events. Some of the most unusual events of the last 100 years took place quite recently, including the inflation of the late 1970s and early 1980s, the October 1987 stock market crash, the collapse of the high-yield bond market, the major contraction and consolidation of the thrift industry, the collapse of the Soviet Union, the development of the European Economic Community, the attacks of Sept. 11, 2001, and the more recent global financial crisis of 2008–2009.

It is even difficult for economists to predict the economic environment of the future. For example, if one were analyzing the stock market in 1987 before the crash, it would be statistically improbable to predict the impending short-term volatility without considering the stock market crash and market volatility of the 1929–1931 period.

Without an appreciation of the 1920s and 1930s, no one would believe that such events could happen. The 90-year period starting with 1926 represents what can happen: It includes high and low returns, volatile and quiet markets, war and peace, inflation and deflation, and prosperity and depression. Restricting attention to a shorter historical period underestimates the amount of change that could occur in a long future period. Finally, because historical event-types (not specific events) tend to repeat themselves, long-run capital market return studies can reveal a great deal about the future. Investors probably expect unusual events to occur from time to time, and their return expectations reflect this.

A Look at the Historical Results

It is interesting to look at the realized returns and realized equity risk premium in the context of the above discussion. Exhibit 10.10 shows the average stock market return and the average (arithmetic mean) realized long-horizon equity risk premium over various historical periods. The exhibit shows that using a longer historical period provides a more stable estimate of the equity risk premium. The reason is that any unique period will not be weighted heavily in an average covering a longer historical period. It better represents the probability of these unique events occurring over a long period of time.

Exhibit 10.10: Stock Market Return and Equity Risk Premium Over Time (%)

Lenth	Period Dates	Large-Cap Arithmetic Average	Long-horizon Equity Risk Premia
90	1926–2015	11.95	6.90
80	1936–2015	12.09	6.83
70	1946–2015	12.24	6.58
60	1956–2015	11.29	5.09
50	1966–2015	11.12	4.44
40	1976–2015	12.66	5.84
30	1986–2015	11.83	6.07
20	1996–2015	9.94	5.28
15	2001–2015	6.79	2.63
10	2006–2015	9.14	5.46
5	2011–2015	13.12	10.11

Looking carefully at Exhibit 10.11 will clarify this point. The graph shows the realized equity risk premium for a series of periods through 2015, starting with 1926. In other words, the first value on the graph represents the average realized equity risk premium over the period 1926–2015. The next value on the graph represents the average realized equity risk premium over the period 1927–2015, and so on, with the last value representing the average over the most recent five years, 2011–2015.

Exhibit 10.11: Equity Risk Premium Using Different Starting Dates
Average Equity Risk Premium Through 2015 (%)

Concentrating on the left side of Exhibit 10.11, one notices that the realized equity risk premium, when measured over long periods, is relatively stable. In viewing the graph from left to right, moving from longer to shorter historical periods, one sees that the value of the realized equity risk premium begins to decline significantly. Why does this occur? The reason is that the severe bear market of 1973–1974 is receiving proportionately more weight in the shorter, more recent average. If you continue to follow the line to the right, however, you will also notice that when 1973 and 1974 fall out of the recent average, the realized equity risk premium jumps up by nearly 1.2 percentage points.

Additionally, use of recent historical periods for estimation purposes can lead to illogical conclusions. As seen in Exhibit 10.10, the bear market in the early 2000s and in 2008 has caused the realized equity risk premium in the shorter historical periods to be lower than the long-term average.

The impact of adding one additional year of data to a historical average is lessened the greater the initial period of measurement. Short-term averages can be affected considerably by one or more unique observations. On the other hand, long-term averages produce more stable results.

Some practitioners argue for a shorter historical period, such as 30 years, as a basis for the equity risk premium estimation. The logic for the use of a shorter period is that historical events and economic scenarios present before this time are unlikely to be repeated. Exhibit 10.12 shows the equity risk premium measured over rolling 30-year periods, and it appears from the graph that the premium has been trending downwards. The 30-year equity risk premium remained close to 4 percentage points for several years in the 1980s and 1990s. However, it has fallen and then risen in the most recent 30-year periods.

Exhibit 10.12: Equity Risk Premium Over Rolling 30-year Periods
Average Equity Risk Premium Through 2015 (%)

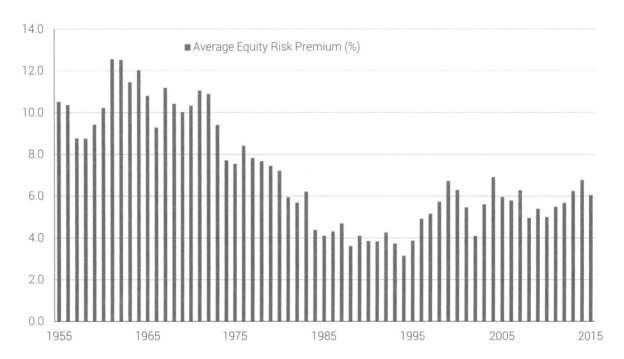

The key to understanding this result lies again in the years 1973 and 1974. The oil embargo during this period had a tremendous effect on the market. The equity risk premium for these years alone was -21% and -34%, respectively. Periods that include the years 1973 and 1974 result in average equity risk premiums as low as 3.2 percentage points. The 2000s have also had an enormous effect on the equity risk premium.

It is difficult to justify such a large divergence in estimates of return over such a short period. This does not suggest, however, that the years 1973 and 1974 should be excluded from any estimate of the equity risk premium; rather, it emphasizes the importance of using a long historical period when measuring the equity risk premium in order to obtain a reliable average that is not overly influenced by short-term returns. The same holds true when analyzing the poor performance of the early 2000s and 2008.

The Supply-Side Model

This section is based on the work by Roger G. Ibbotson and Peng Chen, who combined the first and second approaches to arrive at their forecast of the equity risk premium.[10.9] By proposing a new supply-side methodology, the Ibbotson-Chen study challenges current arguments that future returns on stocks over bonds will be negative or close to zero. The results affirm the relationship between the stock market and the overall economy.

Long-term expected equity returns can be forecasted by the use of supply side models. The supply of stock market returns is generated by the productivity of the corporations in the real economy. Investors should not expect a much higher or lower return than that produced by the companies in the real economy. Thus, over the long run, equity returns should be close to the long-run supply estimate.

Earnings, dividends, and capital gains are supplied by corporate productivity. Exhibit 10.13 illustrates that earnings and dividends have historically grown in tandem with the overall economy (GDP per capita). However, GDP per capita did not outpace the stock market. This is primarily because the P/E ratio increased 2.21 times during the same period. So, assuming that the economy will continue to grow, all three should continue to grow as well.

Exhibit 10.13: Capital Gains, GDP Per Capita, Earnings, and Dividends
Index (Year-end 1925 = $1.00)
1926–2015

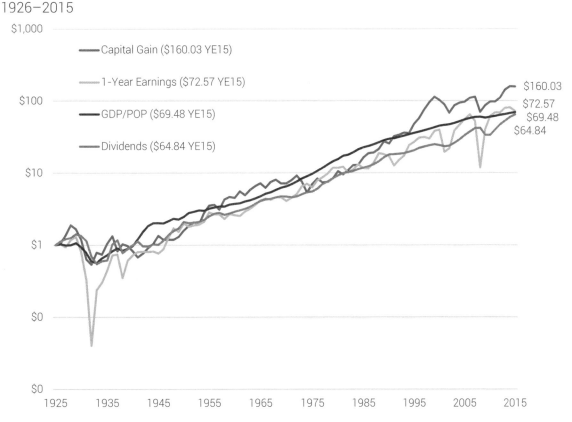

10.9 Ibbotson, R.G., & Chen, P. 2003. "Long-Run Stock Returns: Participating in the Real Economy." *Financial Analysts Journal*, Vol. 59, No. 1, P. 88.

Forward-Looking Earnings Model

Ibbotson and Chen forecast the equity risk premium through a supply-side model using historical data. They used an earnings model as the basis for their supply-side estimate. The earnings model breaks the historical equity return into four pieces, with only three historically being supplied by companies: inflation, income return, and growth in real earnings per share. The growth in the P/E ratio, the fourth piece, is a reflection of investors' changing prediction of future earnings growth. The past supply of corporate growth is forecasted to continue; however, a change in investors' predictions is not. P/E rose dramatically from 1980 through 2001 because people believed that corporate earnings were going to grow faster in the future. This growth in P/E drove a small portion of the rise in equity returns over the same period.

Exhibit 10.14 illustrates the price-to-earnings ratio from 1926 to 2015. The P/E ratio, using one year average earnings, was 10.23 at the beginning of 1926 and ended the year 2015 at 22.57, an average increase of 0.88% per year. The highest P/E was 136.69 recorded in 1932, while the lowest was 7.08 recorded in 1948. Ibbotson Associates revised the calculation of the P/E ratio from a one-year to a three-year average earnings for use in equity forecasting.

Exhibit 10.14: Large-cap Stocks P/E Ratio
1926–2015

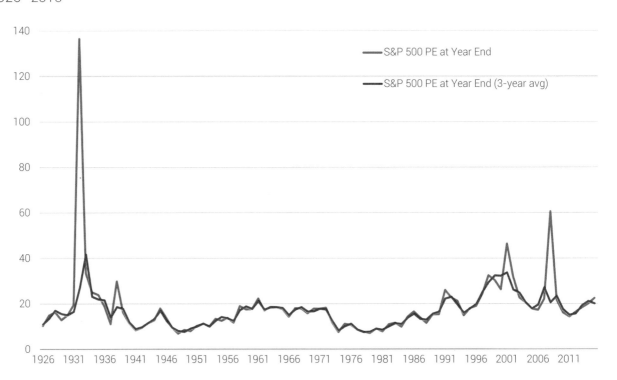

This is because reported earnings are affected not only by the long-term productivity, but also by one-time items that do not necessarily have the same consistent impact year after year. The three year average is more reflective of the long-term trend than the year-by-year numbers. The P/E ratio calculated using the three-year average of earnings had an increase of 0.70% per year.

The historical P/E growth factor, using three-year earnings, of 0.70% per year is subtracted from the equity forecast because it is not believed that P/E will continue to increase in the future. The market serves as the cue. The current P/E ratio is the market's best guess for the future of corporate earnings and there is no reason to believe, at this time, that the market will change its mind. Using this top-down approach, the geometric supply-side equity risk premium is 4.04%, which equates to an arithmetic supply-side equity risk premium of 6.03%.

Another approach in calculating the premium would be to add up the components that constitute the supply of equity return, excluding the P/E component. Thus, the supply of equity return only includes inflation, the growth in real earnings per share, and income return. This forward-looking earnings model calculates the long-term supply of U.S. equity returns to be 9.28%:

$$SR = \left[(1 + CPI) \times (1 + g_{REPS}) - Inc + Rinv \right]$$
$$9.28\%^* = \left[(1 + 2.91\%) \times (1 + 2.09\%) - 1 \right] + 4.00\% + 0.21\%$$

* difference due to rounding

Where:

SR	=	The supply of the equity return
CPI	=	Consumer Price Index (inflation)
g_{REPS}	=	The growth in real earning per share
Inc	=	The income return
$Rinv$	=	The reinvestment return

The equity risk premium, based on the supply-side earnings model, is calculated to be 4.04% on a geometric basis:

$$SERP = \frac{(1 + SR)}{(1 + CPI) \times (1 + RRf)} - 1$$
$$4.04\%^* = \frac{1 + 9.28\%}{(1 + 2.91\%) \times (1 + 2.04\%)} - 1$$

* difference due to rounding

Where:

$SERP$	=	The supply-side equity risk premium
SR	=	The supply of the equity return
CPI	=	Consumer Price Index (inflation)
RRf	=	The real risk-free rate

Converting the geometric average into an arithmetic average results in an equity risk premium of 6.03%:

$$R_A = R_G + \frac{\sigma^2}{2}$$

$$6.03\%^* = 4.04\% + \frac{19.99\%^2}{2}$$

*difference due to rounding

Where:

R_A	=	The arithmetic average
R_G	=	The geometric average
σ	=	The standard deviation of equity returns

As mentioned earlier, one of the key findings of the Ibbotson and Chen study is that P/E increases account for only a small portion of the total return of equity. The reason we present supply-side equity risk premium going back only 25 years in Exhibit 10.15 is because the P/E ratio rose dramatically over this period, which caused the growth rate in the P/E ratio calculated from 1926 to be relatively high. The subtraction of the P/E growth factor from equity returns has been responsible for the downward adjustment in the supply-side equity risk premium compared to the historical estimate. Beyond the last 25 years, the growth factor in the P/E ratio has not been dramatic enough to require an adjustment.

Exhibit 10.15 presents the supply-side equity risk premium, on an arithmetic basis, beginning in 1926 and ending in each of the last 25 years.[10.10]

[10.10] The supply-side equity risk premia values in Exhibit 10.15 have been re-calculated by Duff & Phelps for the *2016 SBBI Yearbook* using (i) the same methodologies and (ii) the same data sources as were used in previous editions of this book. For the calculations presented herein, all data (for each input required in these calculations) was refreshed over the entire 1926–2015 time horizon, thus capturing all prior data revisions. Some of the historical supply-side equity risk premia estimates published herein may therefore differ slightly from the historical supply-side equity risk premia estimates published in previous editions of this book.

Exhibit 10.15: Supply-side Historical Equity Risk Premia over Time

Period Length (Years)	Period Dates	g(P/E)	Supply-Side Equity Risk Premia	Long-horizon Equity Risk Premia
90	1926–2015	0.70	6.03	6.90
89	1926–2014	0.77	6.05	6.99
88	1926–2013	0.67	6.12	6.96
87	1926–2012	0.44	6.11	6.70
86	1926–2011	0.40	6.07	6.62
85	1926–2010	0.59	5.97	6.72
84	1926–2009	0.94	5.57	6.67
83	1926–2008	0.79	5.54	6.47
82	1926–2007	1.14	5.74	7.06
81	1926–2006	0.75	6.22	7.13
80	1926–2005	0.65	6.29	7.08
79	1926–2004	0.83	6.18	7.17
78	1926–2003	1.08	5.94	7.19
77	1926–2002	1.17	5.65	6.97
76	1926–2001	1.52	5.71	7.43
75	1926–2000	1.49	6.06	7.76
74	1926–1999	1.51	6.32	8.07
73	1926–1998	1.40	6.36	7.97
72	1926–1997	1.19	6.38	7.77
71	1926–1996	0.87	6.46	7.50
70	1926–1995	0.74	6.47	7.37
69	1926–1994	0.58	6.33	7.04
68	1926–1993	0.90	6.18	7.22
67	1926–1992	1.15	5.98	7.29
66	1926–1991	1.12	6.12	7.39

Long-Term Market Predictions

The supply-side model estimates that stocks will continue to provide significant returns over the long run, averaging around 9.28% per year, assuming historical inflation rates. The equity risk premium, based on the top-down supply-side earnings model, is calculated to be 4.04% on a geometric basis and 6.03% on an arithmetic basis.

Ibbotson and Chen predict future increased earnings growth that will offset lower dividend yields. The fact that earnings will grow as dividend payouts shrink is in line with the Modigliani-Miller theorem, which here refers to the irrelevance over whether a firm pays a dividend or reinvests its returns.

The forecasts for the market are in line with both the historical supply measures of public corporations (i.e., earnings) and overall economic productivity (GDP per capita).

Chapter 11
Stock Market Returns From 1815–2015

Studies on the long-horizon predictability of stock returns, by necessity, require a database of return information that dates as far back as possible. Since the late 1970s, Ibbotson Associates has produced a broad set of historical returns on asset classes dating back to 1926. Researchers interested in the dynamics of the U.S. capital markets prior to 1926 had to rely on indexes of uneven quality. In 2000, Roger G. Ibbotson and William N. Goetzmann, professors of finance, and Liang Peng, then a Ph.D. candidate in finance, all at Yale School of Management, assembled a New York Stock Exchange database of annual returns for the periods prior to 1926. The first part of this chapter covers the sources and construction of this annual return database extending back to 1815.

The second part of this chapter introduces a new set of monthly real stock market total returns developed by Paul Kaplan, now director of research at Morningstar Canada. Kaplan used these new returns to demonstrate that the severity of the financial crisis of 2008 was not unique, but was merely the latest chapter in a long history of market meltdowns.

While we firmly believe that a 1926 starting date was approximately when quality financial data came into existence, our hope is that the continuing development of these data sets will allow modern researchers of pre-1926 stock returns, along with future researchers, to test a broad range of hypotheses about the U.S. capital markets as well as open up new areas for more accurate analysis.

1815–1925 Data Series Sources and Collection Methods

Share Price Collection

End-of-month equity prices for companies listed on the New York Stock Exchange were hand-collected from three sources published January 1815 to December 1870. For the period 1871 through 1925, end-of-month NYSE stock prices were collected from the major New York newspapers. *The New York Shipping List,* later called *The New York Shipping and Commercial,* served as the "official" source for NYSE share price collection up until the early 1850s. In the mid-1850s, *The New York Shipping List* reported prices for fewer and fewer stocks. This led to the collection of price quotes from *The New York Herald* and *The New York Times.* While neither claimed to be the official list for the NYSE, the number of securities quoted by each far exceeded the number quoted by *The New York Shipping List.*

It is important to note that in instances where no transaction took place in December, the latest bid and ask prices were averaged to obtain a year-end price. In total, at least two prices from 664 companies were collected. From a low number of eight firms in 1815, the number of firms in the index reached a high point in May of 1883 with 114 listed firms.

Share prices for much of the period of analysis remained around $100. Exhibit 11.1 illustrates this point. The graph shows that the most common price of a share of stock was around $100. The distribution of stock prices is significantly skewed to the left with only a few trading above $200. Such a distribution suggests that management maintained a ceiling on stock prices by paying out most earnings as dividends. No reports of stock splits over the period of data were discovered.

Exhibit 11.1: Distribution of Raw Stock Prices 1815–1925

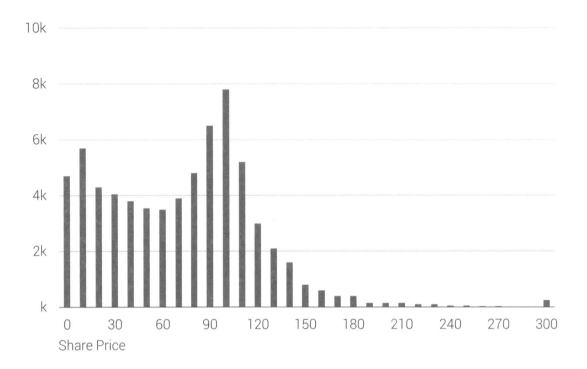

Dividend Collection

Dividend data was collected for the period 1825 to 1870 by identifying the semiannual dividend announcements for equity securities as reported in *The New York Shipping and Commercial*, *The Banker's Magazine*, *The New York Times*, and *The New York Herald*. From 1871 to 1925, aggregate dividend data from the Alfred Cowles[11.1] series was used. Whether the above publications reported dividends for all NYSE stocks is unknown. As a result, there is no way of knowing whether missing dividends meant that they were not paid or possibly not reported. Dividend records were collected for more than 500 stocks in the sample, and most stocks paid dividends semiannually.

Two approaches were used to estimate the income return for each year. The first approach, the low-dividend return estimate, consisted of the summation of all of the dividends paid in a given year by firms whose prices were observed in the preceding year. This number is then divided by the sum of the last available preceding year prices for those firms. The second approach, the high-dividend return estimate, focused solely on firms that paid regular dividends and for which price data was collected. The sample is restricted to firms that have two years of dividend payments (four

---

[11.1]   Cowles, A. 1939. *Common Stock Indices* (Bloomington, Ind.: Principia Press).

semiannual dividends) and for which there was a price observation. Using the second approach, dividend yields tend to be quite high by modern standards.

It is important to note that when both a high- and a low-income return series were present, the average was computed. This holds true for the summary statistics table in this chapter as well as the graphs/tables presented throughout. Also, due to missing income return data for 1868, an average of the previous 43 years was computed.

Price Index Estimation

Index Calculation Concerns

When attempting to construct an index without having market capitalization data readily available, one is left with one of two options: an equal-weighted index or a price-weighted index. One key concern with an equal weighted index is the effect of a bid-ask bounce. Take for example an illiquid stock that trades at either $1.00 or $2.00 per share. When it rises in price from $1.00 to $2.00, it goes up by 100%. When it decreases in price from $2.00 to $1.00, it drops by 50%. Equally weighting these returns can produce a substantial upward bias. This led us to the construction of a price-weighted index.

Calculation of the Price-Weighted Index

The procedure used for calculating the price-weighted index is rather simple. For each month, returns are calculated for all stocks that trade in two consecutive periods. These returns are weighted by the price at the beginning of the two periods.

The return of the price-weighted index closely approximates the return to a "buy-and-hold" portfolio over the period. Buy-and-hold portfolios are not sensitive to bid-ask bounce bias. We believe that the price-weighted index does a fairly good job of avoiding such an upward bias.

Companies were rather concentrated into specific industries. In 1815, the index was about evenly split between banks and insurance companies. Banks, transportation firms (primarily canals and railroads), and insurance companies made up the index by the 1850s. By the end of the sample period, the index was dominated by transport companies and other industrials.

A Look at the Historical Results

It is important to note that there are a few missing months of data that create gaps in the analysis. The NYSE was closed from July 1914 to December 1914 due to World War I. This is obviously an institutional gap. There are additional gaps. We are missing returns for 1822, part of 1848 and 1849, parts of 1866, all of 1867 and January 1868. We do not know whether the records missing from the late 1860s are due to the Civil War, but the NYSE was certainly open at that time — among other things, it was the era of heated speculation and stock price manipulation by legendary financiers Gould, Fisk, and Drew. The number of available security records was quite lower after 1871. A change in the range of coverage by the financial press is the likely culprit for this. Further data collection efforts hopefully will allow these missing records to be filled in.

Exhibit 11.2 illustrates summary statistics of annual returns of large-cap stocks for three periods: (i) the pre-1926 data, (ii) the familiar 1926 to 2015 period, and (iii) a combination of the two.

Price Return

It is interesting to note that the price-weighted index in Exhibit 11.2 has an annual geometric capital appreciation return from 1825 through 1925 of 1.3%. This number is significantly lower when compared to the 5.8% annual capital appreciation return experienced by large-cap stocks from 1926 to 2015. This once again alludes to the suggestion that dividend policies have evolved over the past two centuries, and that managers of old companies most likely paid out earnings to keep their stock prices lower. In today's financial world, capital appreciation is accepted as a substitute for dividend payments.

The rise in capital appreciation returns over the years is more evident when viewing returns on a 20-year rolling period basis, as Exhibit 11.3 demonstrates.

Income Return

Exhibit 11.2 also illustrates the summary statistics for the annual income return series. The higher income return of 5.9% in the earlier period, and the fact the many stocks traded near par, once again suggest that most companies paid out a large share of their profits rather than retaining them.

Exhibit 11.4 shows annual income returns for 1825 to 2015. In fact, when looking at the time distribution of dividend changes over the new period, dividend decreases were only slightly less common than increases, suggesting that managers may have been less averse to cutting dividends than they are today. Perhaps in the pre-income tax environment of the 19th century, investors had a preference for income return as opposed to capital appreciation.

Exhibit 11.2: Large-Cap Stocks: Summary Statistics of Annual Returns (%)

1825–1925	Geometric Mean	Arithmetic Mean	Standard Deviation
Total Return	7.3	8.4	16.3
Income Return	5.9	5.9	1.9
Capital Appreciation	1.3	2.5	16.1
1926–2015			
Total Return	10.0	12.0	20.0
Income Return	4.0	4.0	1.6
Capital Appreciation	5.8	7.7	19.3
1825–2015			
Total Return	8.6	10.1	18.2
Income Return	5.0	5.0	2.0
Capital Appreciation	3.4	5.0	17.8

Exhibit 11.3: Large-Cap Stocks: 20-year Rolling Capital Appreciation Returns (%)
1844–2015

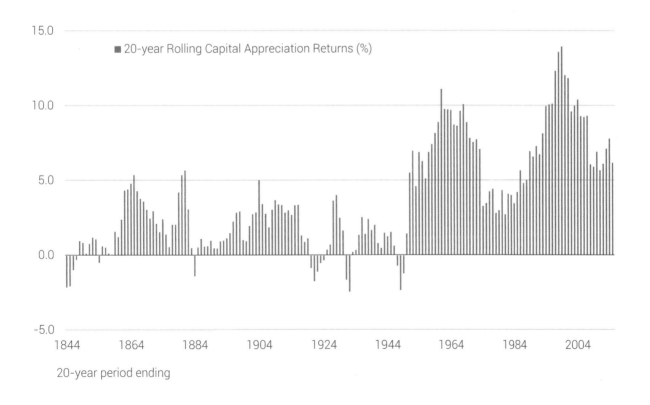

20-year period ending

Exhibit 11.4: Large-Cap Stocks Annual Income Returns (%)
1825–2015

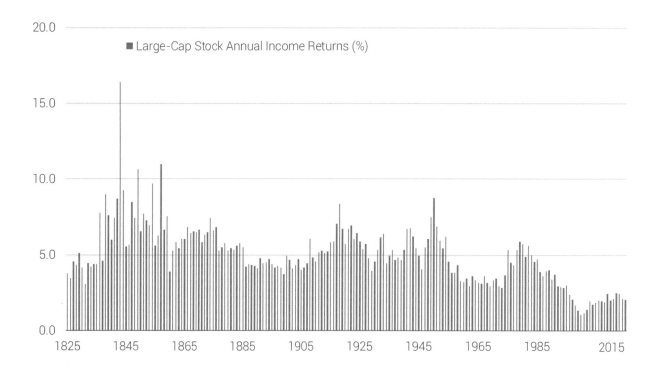

Total Return

Looking once again at the summary statistics in Exhibit 11.2, it is interesting to notice that the annual geometric total return for large-cap stocks from 1825 to 1925 was 7.3%. This is quite low when compared to the 10.0% annual geometric total return of the commonly used 1926 to 2015 period. For the entire period, the total return falls somewhere in between. The standard deviation of total return is also slightly lower for 1825 to 1925 (16.3%) versus 1926 to 2015 (20.0%).

Exhibit 11.5 shows year-by-year capital appreciation, average income, and total return from 1815 to 1925 of large-cap stocks. Exhibit 11.6 shows the growth of a dollar invested in large-cap stocks from the end of 1824 to the end of 2015.

Exhibit 11.5: Large-Cap Stock Annual Capital Appreciation, Income, and Total Returns (%) 1815–1925

Year	Capital App	Avg. Income Return	Total Return	Year	Capital App	Avg. Income Return	Total Return
1815	-6.65	–	–	1871	3.34	5.86	9.2
1816	-1.93	–	–	1872	0.5	6.33	6.83
1817	19.43	–	–	1873	-17.7	6.51	-11.19
1818	-3.76	–	–	1874	-5.77	7.47	1.7
1819	-8.82	–	–	1875	-4.72	6.61	1.89
1820	9.59	–	–	1876	-13.31	6.86	-6.45
1821	3.34	–	–	1877	1.74	5.31	7.05
1822	-12.85	–	–	1878	10.5	5.54	16.04
1823	5.29	–	–	1879	51.31	5.8	57.1
1824	3.7	–	–	1880	19.83	5.28	25.12
1825	-12.99	3.81	-9.18	1881	1.88	5.48	7.36
1826	-1.22	3.48	2.27	1882	-9.54	5.32	-4.22
1827	-6.24	4.57	-1.67	1883	-15.04	5.65	-9.39
1828	-17.95	4.34	-13.61	1884	-24.28	5.81	-18.47
1829	10.33	5.1	15.43	1885	45.32	5.53	50.85
1830	27.31	4.2	31.51	1886	12.46	4.23	16.69
1831	-17.05	3.07	-13.98	1887	-12.13	4.43	-7.7
1832	8.6	4.48	13.08	1888	2.09	4.36	6.45
1833	-6.09	4.24	-1.85	1889	4.49	4.28	8.77
1834	8.84	4.4	13.24	1890	-10.72	4.14	-6.59
1835	-6.74	4.38	-2.36	1891	2.95	4.78	7.74
1836	4.33	7.76	12.09	1892	10.35	4.44	14.79
1837	-18.02	4.6	-13.43	1893	-16.86	4.54	-12.33
1838	12.2	8.99	21.19	1894	-2.82	4.76	1.94
1839	-26.62	7.64	-18.97	1895	2.14	4.42	6.56
1840	3.01	6.03	9.04	1896	0.69	4.17	4.86
1841	-23.52	7.46	-16.06	1897	14.15	4.27	18.41
1842	2.34	8.71	11.05	1898	12.17	4.21	16.38
1843	39.16	16.4	55.56	1899	4.17	3.72	7.89
1844	2.81	9.29	12.11	1900	17.99	4.98	22.97
1845	-11.61	5.56	-6.05	1901	24.6	4.66	29.26
1846	23.21	5.7	28.91	1902	5.29	4.15	9.44
1847	7.65	8.48	16.13	1903	-12.88	4.35	-8.53
1848	5.28	7.45	12.72	1904	14.94	4.72	19.66
1849	7.8	10.64	18.44	1905	6.67	4	10.67
1850	10.48	6.57	17.05	1906	-1.09	4.19	3.1
1851	-5.78	7.74	1.95	1907	-26.26	4.47	-21.79
1852	18.07	7.3	25.38	1908	28.47	6.09	34.56
1853	-8.15	6.94	-1.2	1909	18.12	4.87	22.99
1854	-20.34	9.71	-10.63	1910	-15.5	4.56	-10.94
1855	16.26	5.6	21.86	1911	2.17	5.19	7.37
1856	2.49	6.28	8.77	1912	0.03	5.27	5.3
1857	-24.22	10.99	-13.23	1913	-14.44	5.12	-9.32
1858	10.38	6.68	17.07	1914	-8.47	5.22	-3.25
1859	-0.62	7.56	6.94	1915	15.88	5.85	21.73
1860	-3.93	3.88	-0.06	1916	1.29	5.91	7.19
1861	-3.73	5.27	1.54	1917	-23.48	7.04	-16.44
1862	49.15	5.85	55	1918	2.88	8.38	11.27
1863	40.95	5.46	46.41	1919	9.38	6.71	16.09
1864	10.53	6.07	16.61	1920	-20.74	5.72	-15.02
1865	-1.33	6.08	4.75	1921	4.26	6.75	11.02
1866	0.46	6.85	7.31	1922	19.74	6.98	26.72
1867	-2.61	6.48	3.87	1923	-2.13	6.04	3.9
1868	1.52	6.56	8.08	1924	19.34	6.43	25.77
1869	-2.85	6.53	3.67	1925	23.22	5.91	29.12
1870	-1.44	6.66	5.22				

Exhibit 11.6: Large-Cap Stocks
Annual Capital Appreciation and Total Return Index Values (Year-end 1824 = $1.00)
1825–2015

Year	Capital App	Total Return	Year	Capital App	Total Return	Year	Capital App	Total Return	Year	Capital App	Total Return	Year	Capital App	Total Return
1824	1.00	1.00	1864	1.65	20.48	1904	3.32	322.65	1944	3.98	3,475.00	1984	50.07	253,307.97
1825	0.87	0.91	1865	1.63	21.45	1905	3.54	357.07	1945	5.20	4,741.16	1985	63.25	333,674.52
1826	0.86	0.93	1866	1.64	23.02	1906	3.51	368.14	1946	4.58	4,358.48	1986	72.50	395,955.17
1827	0.81	0.91	1867	1.59	23.91	1907	2.58	287.92	1947	4.58	4,607.26	1987	73.97	416,745.26
1828	0.66	0.79	1868	1.62	25.84	1908	3.32	387.42	1948	4.55	4,860.72	1988	83.14	485,959.49
1829	0.73	0.91	1869	1.57	26.79	1909	3.92	476.49	1949	5.02	5,774.17	1989	105.80	639,941.57
1830	0.93	1.20	1870	1.55	28.19	1910	3.31	424.37	1950	6.11	7,605.32	1990	98.86	620,076.25
1831	0.77	1.03	1871	1.60	30.78	1911	3.39	455.63	1951	7.12	9,431.85	1991	124.87	808,987.42
1832	0.84	1.16	1872	1.61	32.89	1912	3.39	479.76	1952	7.95	11,164.24	1992	130.44	870,627.40
1833	0.79	1.14	1873	1.32	29.21	1913	2.90	435.04	1953	7.43	11,053.81	1993	139.64	958,375.23
1834	0.86	1.29	1874	1.25	29.70	1914	2.65	420.90	1954	10.77	16,870.72	1994	137.49	971,030.23
1835	0.80	1.26	1875	1.19	30.26	1915	3.07	512.38	1955	13.62	22,195.57	1995	184.39	1,335,922.09
1836	0.83	1.42	1876	1.03	28.31	1916	3.11	549.24	1956	13.97	23,650.70	1996	221.76	1,642,651.99
1837	0.68	1.23	1877	1.05	30.31	1917	2.38	458.96	1957	11.97	21,100.58	1997	290.52	2,190,696.19
1838	0.77	1.49	1878	1.16	35.17	1918	2.45	510.66	1958	16.53	30,250.56	1998	368.00	2,816,766.01
1839	0.56	1.20	1879	1.75	55.25	1919	2.68	592.84	1959	17.93	33,867.05	1999	439.86	3,409,456.41
1840	0.58	1.31	1880	2.10	69.13	1920	2.13	503.78	1960	17.40	34,026.09	2000	395.26	3,099,046.19
1841	0.44	1.10	1881	2.14	74.22	1921	2.22	559.27	1961	21.42	43,175.19	2001	343.71	2,730,698.66
1842	0.45	1.22	1882	1.93	71.09	1922	2.65	708.68	1962	18.89	39,406.64	2002	263.40	2,127,200.44
1843	0.63	1.90	1883	1.64	64.41	1923	2.60	736.34	1963	22.46	48,391.83	2003	332.88	2,737,377.48
1844	0.65	2.14	1884	1.24	52.51	1924	3.10	926.09	1964	25.37	56,368.11	2004	362.82	3,035,260.01
1845	0.57	2.01	1885	1.81	79.21	1925	3.82	1,195.79	1965	27.67	63,386.53	2005	373.71	3,184,350.34
1846	0.71	2.59	1886	2.03	92.44	1926	4.04	1,334.79	1966	24.05	57,007.77	2006	424.60	3,687,295.26
1847	0.76	3.00	1887	1.79	85.32	1927	5.29	1,835.18	1967	28.88	70,675.76	2007	439.59	3,889,873.98
1848	0.80	3.39	1888	1.82	90.83	1928	7.29	2,635.47	1968	31.09	78,493.50	2008	270.41	2,450,704.90
1849	0.86	4.01	1889	1.91	98.79	1929	6.42	2,413.69	1969	27.56	71,817.97	2009	333.83	3,099,270.93
1850	0.95	4.69	1890	1.70	92.28	1930	4.59	1,812.75	1970	27.59	74,587.91	2010	376.50	3,566,125.53
1851	0.90	4.78	1891	1.75	99.42	1931	2.43	1,027.17	1971	30.52	85,254.24	2011	376.49	3,641,434.19
1852	1.06	6.00	1892	1.93	114.12	1932	2.06	943.02	1972	35.34	101,448.22	2012	426.96	4,224,190.76
1853	0.97	5.93	1893	1.61	100.06	1933	3.02	1,452.15	1973	29.20	86,546.70	2013	553.34	5,592,327.94
1854	0.78	5.30	1894	1.56	102.00	1934	2.84	1,431.20	1974	20.53	63,640.17	2014	616.37	6,357,834.47
1855	0.90	6.45	1895	1.60	108.69	1935	4.02	2,113.44	1975	27.00	87,332.47	2015	611.89	6,445,816.40
1856	0.92	7.02	1896	1.61	113.97	1936	5.14	2,830.34	1976	32.17	108,228.58			
1857	0.70	6.09	1897	1.83	134.96	1937	3.16	1,838.97	1977	28.47	100,481.60			
1858	0.77	7.13	1898	2.06	157.07	1938	3.95	2,411.29	1978	28.77	107,084.26			
1859	0.77	7.63	1899	2.14	169.45	1939	3.74	2,401.38	1979	32.31	127,012.20			
1860	0.74	7.62	1900	2.53	208.38	1940	3.17	2,166.42	1980	40.64	168,296.17			
1861	0.71	7.74	1901	3.15	269.34	1941	2.60	1,915.29	1981	36.69	160,010.53			
1862	1.06	12.00	1902	3.32	294.77	1942	2.92	2,304.86	1982	42.10	194,486.86			
1863	1.49	17.56	1903	2.89	269.63	1943	3.49	2,901.82	1983	49.38	238,354.20			

144 Years of Stock Market Drawdowns

Those familiar with the history of U.S. capital markets as documented in this book may have found former Federal Reserve Chairman Alan Greenspan's characterization of the financial crisis of 2008 as a "once-in-a century credit tsunami" quite surprising. A more appropriate statement may have been the one made by Leslie Rahl (founder of Capital Market Risk Advisors) more than a year before the crisis when she said, "We seem to have a once-in-a-lifetime crisis every three or four years."[11.2]

The contrast between Mr. Greenspan and Ms. Rahl's perspectives was the inspiration for an article in Morningstar magazine on the history of market meltdowns titled, "Déja Vu All Over Again."[11.3,11.4] In that article, Paul Kaplan illustrated the frequency and severity of the major drawdowns for various countries using time series of stock market total returns. For the U.S., Kaplan naturally used the SBBI large-cap stock index (the SBBI large-cap stock index is essentially the S&P 500 index). The results of the study clearly demonstrate that the severity of the financial crisis of 2008 was not unique, but was merely the latest chapter in a long history of market meltdowns.

In 2009, a team of researchers at Morningstar expanded the analysis into a complete study on global equity market history as a contribution to the CFA Institute's book on the global history of market crashes.[11.5] In this study, the research team used monthly *real* total returns that go back into history as far as was possible with reasonably reliable data.[11.6] The benefit of using real returns is to make meaningful return comparisons, as our study spans such a long period. The benefit of going further back in history is, of course, to give a longer-term and more robust historical perspective on market crashes, in terms of frequency, length, and magnitude.

[11.2] Wright, C. 2007. "Tail Tales." *CFA Institute Magazine,* March/April.

[11.3] Morningstar magazine is a publication for financial advisors and institutional investors. For more information about Morningstar magazine, call 312-384-4000 or visit us online: global.morningstar.com/MorningstarMagazine.

[11.4] Kaplan, P.D. 2009. "Déjà Vu All Over Again." *Morningstar Advisor magazine,* February/March, P. 28.

[11.5] Kaplan, P.D., Idzorek, T., Gambera, M., et al. 2009. "The History and Economics of Stock Market Crashes." In *Insights into the Global Financial Crisis.* Edited by Laurence B. Siegel (Charlottesville, Va.: *CFA Institute*).

[11.6] That is, returns that include the reinvestment of dividends and are adjusted for inflation.

To complete the study, the research team needed to find monthly data from before 1925 on both stock returns and inflation, and calculate real returns. Because there was no such return series in existence, they had to create one out of readable available data.

Robert J. Shiller, 2013 Nobel laureate in economic sciences and the Sterling professor of economics at Yale University, posts monthly U.S. stock market returns and inflation data on his website that go back to 1871. Unfortunately, Shiller's stock data is based on monthly average prices rather than month-end prices. So the research team could use his inflation data, but not his stock market data. Separately, Roger Ibbotson and some colleagues created an annual price and total return series for the NYSE that goes back to 1815 (as previously discussed in this chapter).[11.7] However, annual returns are at too low a frequency to measure the largest drawdowns of the period, such as the large drop in the stock market during the panic of 1907. Fortunately, there is a book that contains daily price data on the Dow Jones Averages going back to 1885.[11.8] The team estimated the monthly price returns in the broader NYSE price index from the monthly price returns on the Dow Jones Averages and then interpolated the total returns by assuming that the dividend levels remained constant during each year.

The Morningstar team produced a time series of U.S. stock market real total returns from 1870 to 2015. The first 15 years of this history (1870–1884) is *annual* real total returns, and the remaining 131 years (1875–2015) is *monthly* total real returns, for a total of 146 years.

Truth in Numbers

The significance of this data is in the lessons that we can learn from it. Over the entire 146-year period, the Real U.S. Stock Market Index grew from $1.00 to $12,011.60 in 1870 dollars. This is a compound annual real total return of 6.7%, almost the same as the post-1925 period. However, as Exhibit 11.7 shows, it was a very bumpy ride with a number of major drawdowns, some of which can be linked with specific economic and political events.

Exhibit 11.7 shows the growth of $1.00 invested in the U.S. stock market at the end of 1869 through December 2015 in real terms, along with a line that shows the highest level that the index had achieved as of that date (shown in gray). Whenever this line is above the cumulative value line (shown in red), the index was below its most recent peak. The bigger the gap, the more severe the decline; the wider the gap, the longer the time until the index returned to its peak. Wherever this line coincides with the index line, the index was climbing to a new peak.

[11.7] Goetzmann, W.N., Ibbotson, R.G., & Peng, L. 2000. "A New Historical Database for the NYSE 1815 to 1925: Performance and Predictability." *Journal of Financial Markets*, Vol. 4, No. 1, P. 1.

[11.8] Pierce, P., ed. 1982. *The Dow Jones Averages 1885-1980* (Homewood, Ill.: Dow Jones-Irwin).

Exhibit 11.7: Large-cap Stocks: Real Return Index
1870–2015

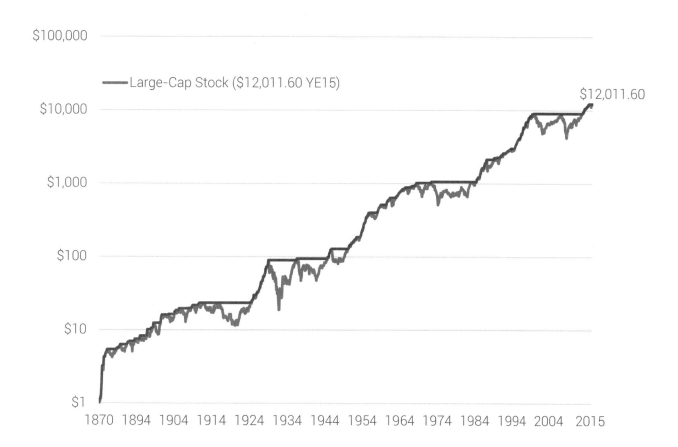

Exhibit 11.8 lists all of the drawdowns that exceeded 20%. There were 17 such declines, including the most recent one that ended in May 2013. Not surprisingly, the largest of all market declines started just before the Crash of 1929 and did not recover until toward the end of 1936. The U.S. stock market lost 79% of its real value in less than three years, and took more than five years to recover. The most recent drawdown, the global financial crisis, was the second greatest decline, and it lasted nearly a decade. The combined effect of the crash of the Internet bubble in 2000 and the global financial crisis of 2008 caused the U.S. stock market to lose 54% of its real value from August of 2000 to February 2009.

The history of stock market drawdowns presented here shows that investing in stocks can be very risky, and that the most recent crisis was hardly a "once-in-a-century" event. We should use this long-run data to better gauge the potential risks and long-term rewards of investing in risky assets such as stocks.

Exhibit 11.8: Largest Declines in U.S. Stock Market History, in Real Total Return Terms 1870–2015

Peak	Trough	Decline (%)	Recovery	Event(s)
Aug. 1929	May 1932	79.00	Nov. 1936	Crash of 1929, 1st part of Great Depression
Aug. 2000	Feb. 2009	54.00	May 2013	Dot-com bubble burst (00-02), Crash 07-09
Dec.1972	Sep. 1974	51.86	Dec, 1984	Inflationary Bear Market, Vietnam, Watergate
Jun.1911	Dec. 1920	50.96	Dec. 1924	WWI, Post-war Auto Bubble Burst
Feb.1937	Mar. 1938	49.93	Feb. 1945	2nd part of Great Depression, WWII
May 1946	Feb. 1948	37.18	Oct. 1950	Post-war Bear Market
Nov.1968	Jun. 1970	35.46	Nov. 1972	Start of Inflationary Bear Market
Jan.1906	Oct. 1907	34.22	Aug. 1908	Panic of 1907
Apr.1899	Jun. 1900	30.41	Mar. 1901	Cornering of Northern Pacific Stock
Aug.1987	Nov. 1987	30.16	Jul. 1989	Black Monday
Oct.1892	Jul. 1893	27.32	Mar. 1894	Silver Agitation
Dec.1961	Jun. 1962	22.80	Apr. 1963	Height of the Cold War, Cuban Missile Crisis
Nov.1886	Mar. 1888	22.04	May 1889	Depression, Railroad Strikes
Apr.1903	Sep. 1903	21.67	Nov. 1904	Rich Man's Panic
Aug.1897	Mar. 1898	21.13	Aug. 1898	Outbreak of Boer War
Sep.1909	Jul. 1910	20.55	Feb. 1911	Enforcement of the Sherman Anti-Trust Act
May1890	Jul. 1891	20.11	Feb. 1892	Baring Brothers Crisis

Traditional measures of risk, such as standard deviation, can underestimate the risk of drawdowns that are many standard deviations away from the mean (i.e., on the left tail of a distribution). We suggest that these traditional measures of risk be supplemented with measures that better capture the "fat-tailed" nature of the historical returns and drawdowns as presented here. A complete discussion of incorporating fat-tailed distributions into risk measures is found in Chapter 10.

Reaching Back Beyond 1926

Collection efforts have yielded a comprehensive database of NYSE security prices for nearly the entire history of the exchange. The goal of these studies is to assemble a NYSE database for the period prior to 1926. The 1926 starting date was approximately when high-quality financial data came into existence. However, with a pre-1926 database assembled, researchers can expand their analyses back to the early 1800s. It is our hope that the long time series outlined in this chapter will lead to a better understanding of how the U.S. stock market evolved from an emerging market at the turn of the 18th century to the largest capital market in the world today.

The Origin of Market Bubbles

As we've seen so far in this chapter, we have witnessed many asset-price bubbles. In each case, the story seems to be the same: Positive feedback and herding among speculative investors produce runaway prices until the deviation from equilibrium is so large that the market becomes unstable, creating a high probability (or an inevitability) of a crash. This raises the question, Do asset-price bubbles typically share the same characteristics and do all bubbles originate in the same manner? If yes, can we identify these factors beforehand and predict when a bubble will burst? James Xiong, head of quantitative research at Morningstar Investment Management, addressed these questions in an article in Morningstar magazine, "The Chinese Art Market and the Origin of Bubbles."[11.9] The rest of this section has been written by Xiong and adapted from his article.

Herd Behavior and Market Bubbles

A number of studies have considered herd behavior as a possible explanation for the excessive volatility observed in financial markets.[11.10] The thinking behind this approach is simple: Interaction of market participants through herding can lead to large fluctuations in aggregate demand, leading to heavy tails in the distribution of returns. In the popular literature, "crowd effects" often have been associated with large fluctuations in market prices of financial assets.

Robert Shiller provides evidence to support his argument that "irrational exuberance" played a role in producing the ups and downs of the stock and real estate markets.[11.11] He listed 12 precipitating factors that gave rise to the booms in the stock markets and housing markets. These factors are amplified via feedback loops and naturally occurring Ponzi schemes, aided by the media, and can ultimately lead to market crashes.

Shiller also demonstrates that psychological factors, such as herd behavior and epidemics, are exerting important effects. For example, the influence of authority over people can be enormous; people are ready to believe authorities even when they plainly contradict matter-of-fact judgment.

[11.9] Xiong, J. 2012. "The Chinese Art Market and the Origin of Bubbles." *Morningstar magazine*, August/September, P. 64.

[11.10] See three references: Bannerjee, A.V. 1992. "A Simple Model of Herd Behavior," *Quarterly Journal of Economics*, Vol. 107, P. 797. Topol, R. 1991. "Bubbles and Volatility of Stock Prices: Effect of Mimetic Contagion," The Economic Journal, Vol. 101, P. 786. Shiller, R.J. 1989. *Market Volatility* (Cambridge, Mass.: MIT Press).

[11.11] Shiller, R.J. 2005. *Irrational Exuberance*, 2nd ed. (Princeton, N.J: Princeton University Press).

He cites many other factors, including that people tend to follow other people and choose not to exercise their own judgment about the market; also, most people purchase stocks based on direct interpersonal communication instead of independent research.

Rama Cont and Jean-Philippe Bouchaud[11.12] provide a mathematical model to link two well-known market phenomena: the heavy tails observed in the distribution of stock market returns on one hand and herding behavior in financial markets on the other hand.

Predicting Crashes

In the 1990s, two groups of researchers[11.13] independently discovered an apparent tendency of stock prices to exhibit log-periodic power laws (LPPL) before a crash. The fundamental hypothesis of the model is that financial crashes are macroscopic examples of critical phenomena. A critical phenomenon indicates a highly correlated unstable market. In other words, as some traders say, "In a market crisis, all correlations jump to one."

Collective behaviors in people emerge through the forces of imitation, which leads to herding. Herding behavior of investors can result in a significant deviation of financial prices from their fundamental values. A speculative bubble, which is caused by a positive feedback investing style, also leads to a faster-than exponential power law growth of prices.[11.14] The competition between such nonlinear positive feedbacks and negative feedbacks contributes to nonlinear oscillations. For example, technical investors who have a positive view of the market bid up prices at the expense of fundamental investors, who view the market as ridiculously overpriced. The result is that a log-periodic modulation of the price accelerates up to the crash point. Exhibit 11.9 shows an example of what smooth log-periodic oscillations look like. Notice how the oscillations and the index value increase at an increasing rate as the date gets closer to the crash date.

Like any other models, the LPPL model has been debated and challenged, and we will not attempt to discuss that here. Major stock market crashes around the world, however, can be quantitatively explained by this model. These crashes include the 1929 crash, the 1987 crash, the crash of the Russian market in 1998, the 1990 Japanese Nikkei Index crash, several Hong Kong crashes in the 1990s, the Internet bubble crash in 2000, the financial crisis of 2008–2009, and more than 20 emerging-markets crashes. All of these market bubbles appeared to show the similar LPPL before they crashed.

[11.12] Cont, R. & Bouchaud, J.-P. 2000. "Herd Behavior and Aggregate Fluctuations in Financial Markets," *Journal of Macroeconomic Dynamics*, Vol. 4, P. 170.

[11.13] See two references: Sornette, D., Johansen, A. & Bouchaud, J.-P. 1996. "Stock Market Crashes, Precursors and Replicas," *J. Phys. I.* (France), Vol. 6, P. 167. Feigenbaum, J. & Freund, P.G.O. 1996. "Discrete Scale Invariance in Stock Markets Before Crashes," *International Journal of Modern Physics B*, Vol. 10, P. 3737.

[11.14] Sornette, D. 2003. *Why Stock Markets Crash: Critical Events in Complex Financial Systems* (Princeton, N.J.: Princeton University Press).

Exhibit 11.9: Example of Log-Periodic Oscillations

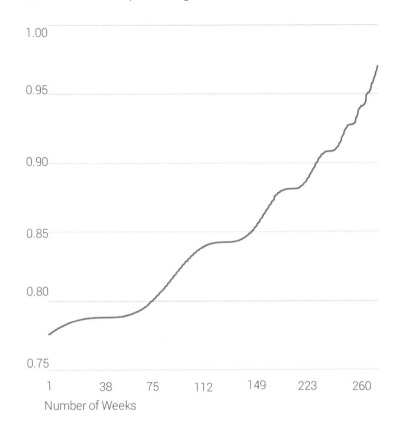

Number of Weeks

Chinese Stock Market Crash of 2007

Greed and fear are rooted in human nature, so it is unlikely that people will change anytime soon. Greediness and fear also drive herding and positive feedbacks, so investors should expect these factors to remain in markets. The latest herding example occurred not too long ago, in 2007. In particular, we'll look at the Chinese stock market crash.

We use the Shanghai Stock Exchange Composite Index to represent the Chinese stock market. The Chinese stock market is dominated by individual investors, unlike equity markets in developed countries where a form of polarization exists between individual and institutional investors. Millions of new Chinese small investors flooded into the booming Chinese stock market from 2005 to 2007, indicating a strong herd behavior. The bubble burst in October 2007. A year after the crash, the Shanghai Composite had lost about 64% of its value, a classic example of herd behavior leading to a market crash in an emerging market.

Using the LPPL model, Exhibit 11.10 shows that the Chinese stock market crash in 2007 was predictable. The red line charts the price of the index. The gray line is the calculated curve based on the LPPL model. The out-of-sample test was made Sept. 25, 2007. The model predicted a crash date of Sept. 5, 2007. The actual crash started Oct. 17, 2007, 42 days later than predicted. The time-series price index is reasonably fitted by the log periodic power law model; we can see the precursors of log-periodic oscillations before the crash occurred.

Exhibit 11.10: Chinese Stock Market Crash Predicted by LPPL Model

NASDAQ Crash of 2000

History provides many examples of bubbles driven by unrealistic expectations of future earnings. These types of bubbles do not just occur in developing markets. An example is the NASDAQ crash of 2000.

The NASDAQ Composite Index consists mainly of technology stocks, such as Internet, e-commerce, software, computer hardware, and telecommunications names. When the NASDAQ closed at a high of 5,049 on March 10, 2000, many stocks were trading at four-digit price/earnings (P/E) ratios.[11.14] Brocade Communications Systems, for example, had a P/E of 6,185; Trend Micro ADR had a P/E of 4,350; and SeaChange International traded at a P/E of 3,765. Investors in these companies seemed to be focusing on high future earnings, and seemingly did not focus on other economic fundamentals.

Exhibit 11.11 shows the bubble phase of the NASDAQ. The red line stands for the price of the index. The gray line is based on the LPPL model. Again, the model clearly picked up the signals of an impending crash and almost perfectly predicted it.

[11.14] The March 10, 2000 closing level (5,049) was an all-time high close for the NASDAQ at the time. The NASDAQ did not close above this price until over 14 years later, April 23, 2014, when the index closed at 5,056.06.

Exhibit 11.11: NASDAQ Market Crash Predicted by LPPL Model

The LPPL Model

The log-periodic power law can be quantified as:[11.15]

$$\ln\big[p(t)\big] = A - B\tau^{m} + C\tau^{m}\cos\big[\omega\ln(\tau) - \varphi\big]$$

Where:

$p(t)$	=	price
A	=	The peak value of $\ln(p(t))$
B	=	Base for the slope of the logarithmic curve
τ	=	$t_c - t$; which is the distance to the end of the bubble
m	=	Growth accelerator; must be $0 < m < 1$
C	=	Base for the oscillations; must be > 0
ω	=	Angular log-frequency
φ	=	Arbitrary phase determining the unit of time

[11.15] Sornette, D. 2003. *Why Stock Markets Crash: Critical Events in Complex Financial Systems* (Princeton, N.J.: Princeton University Press).

A geometric description for LPPL Model is that a log-periodic modulation of the ln(price) accelerates up to the crash point. The combination of B with a value greater than 0 and m with a value between 0 and 1 accelerates the slope so that it is faster than a typical exponential acceleration. The combination of C and the cosine segment determines the amplitude and frequency of the log-periodic oscillations.

We used the Levenberg-Marquardt algorithm to predict the crash for the two bubbles (Exhibits 11.10 and 11.11). The fitted parameters are exhibited in Exhibit 11.12.

Exhibit 11.12: Best Fitted Parameters for the Shanghai Composite Index and the Nasdaq Index

Stock	t_c	m	w	ϕ	A	B	C
Shanghai Index	September 2007	0.64	10.90	4.91	2.17	0.15	-0.01
Nasdaq Index	March 2000	0.45	6.45	5.26	8.61	0.88	0.06

Power of the Model

We showed that two recent market bubbles displayed the same LPPL signature before they crashed. Our analyses indicate that all the bubbles have the same origins and similarly move toward a crash.

Positive feedback and herding produce runaway prices until the deviation from equilibrium is so large that the market is unstable and has a high probability to crash. When the stock price accelerates at a much faster rate than the exponential growth rate, the skyrocketing return will always come with an increased crash hazard rate.

Financial markets are complex systems. In such systems, a speculative bubble can easily be created through positive feedback. What is more challenging is that, as complex systems grow, two things happen.[11.16] These systems require exponentially greater amounts of energy to keep operating, and they become vastly more risky and prone to catastrophic failure.

[11.16] Rickards, J. 2011. *Currency Wars: The Making of the Next Global Crisis* (New York: Portfolio/Penguin).

Chapter 12
International Equity Investing[12.1]

International investment opportunities are growing rapidly, encouraged by open markets and the accelerating economies of many nations. The evidence in favor of taking a global approach to investing is plentiful, as are the possible rewards an investor can reap.

However, significant risks are present as well – risks that apply strictly to the international marketplace. In this chapter, we consider both the rewards and the risks associated with international investments.

Construction of the International Indexes

Our analysis of international investing uses the indexes created by Morgan Stanley Capital International, Inc. The MSCI® indexes are designed to measure the performance of the developed and emerging stock markets, reflecting the performance of the entire range of stocks available to investors in each local market.[12.2]

[12.1]   This chapter is an overview of international equity investing that is limited to analyzing the relative historical performance of international (versus U.S.) equities, and does not include the much-expanded analyses of (i) country-level risks and (ii) industry-level risks (on a global scale) that are the subject of the *International Valuation Handbook – Guide to Cost of Capital* and *International Valuation Handbook – Industry Cost of Capital*, respectively. These two resources are also written by Duff & Phelps, and published by John Wiley & Sons, and are summarized as follows:

International Valuation Handbook – Guide to Cost of Capital: This annual book provides country-level equity risk premia (ERPs), relative volatility (RV) factors, and country risk premia (CRPs) which can be used to estimate country-level cost of equity capital globally, for up to 188 countries, from the perspective of investors based in any one of up to 56 countries (depending on data availability). The *International Valuation Handbook – Guide to of Capital* has been published since 2014 (2014, 2015, and 2016 editions are available with data through (i) December 31, 2013 and March 31, 2014, (ii) December 31, 2014 and March 31, 2015, and (iii) December 31, 2015 and March 31, 2016, respectively). This book includes an optional Semi-annual update, with data through June and September.

International Valuation Handbook – Industry Cost of Capital: This annual book provides the same type of rigorous industry-level analysis published in the U.S.-centric *Valuation Handbook – Industry Cost of Capital*, on a global scale. The inaugural *2015 International Valuation Handbook – Industry Cost of Capital* (with data through March 31, 2015) includes industry-level analyses for four global economic areas: (i) the "World," (ii) the European Union, (iii) the Eurozone, and (iv) the United Kingdom. Industries in the book are identified by their Global Industry Classification Standard (GICS) code. Each of the four global economic area's industry analyses are presented in three currencies: (i) the euro (€ or EUR), (ii) the British pound (£ or GBP), and (iii) the U.S. dollar ($ or USD). The 2016 edition (with data through March 31, 2016) will be available in July 2016. This book includes an optional Semi-annual update, with data through September.

For more information about other Duff & Phelps valuation data resources published by John Wiley & Sons, please go to: www.wiley.com/go/ValuationHandbooks.

[12.2]   The international stock series presented throughout this chapter is represented by the MSCI EAFE® equities index. The MSCI EAFE index is designed to represent the performance of large and mid-cap securities across 21 developed markets, including countries in Europe, Australasia and the Far East, and excluding the U.S. and Canada. The index is available for a number of regions, market segments/sizes and covers approximately 85% of the free-float-adjusted market capitalization in each of the 21 countries MSCI is a leading provider of investment decision support tools to clients worldwide. MSCI provides indexes, portfolio risk and performance analytics, and ESG data and research. To learn more about MSCI, visit www.msci.com.

From January 1970 to October 2001, inclusion in the MSCI indexes was based upon market capitalization. Stocks chosen for the indexes were required to have a target market representation of 60% of total market capitalization.

MSCI has enhanced its index construction methodology by free-float-adjusting constituents' index weights and increasing the target market representation. Target market representation is increased from 60% of total market capitalization to 85% of free-float-adjusted market cap within each industry group, within each country. MSCI defines the free float of a security as the proportion of shares outstanding that is deemed to be available for purchase in the public equity markets by international investors.

Benefits of Investing Internationally

The arguments for investing internationally can be powerful. Examples may include (i) participation in the more than half of the world's investable assets that exist outside the U.S., (ii) growth potential, (iii) diversification, and (iv) potential improvement of the risk/reward trade-off.

Investment Opportunities

An investor who chooses to ignore investment opportunities outside of the U.S. is missing out on over half of the investable developed stock market opportunities in the world. Exhibit 12.1 presents the relative size of international and domestic developed markets as of December 31, 2015. In 2015, the total developed world stock market capitalization was $32.3 trillion, with $13.3 trillion representing international stock market capitalization.[12.3]

Although the domestic (U.S.) stock market continues to account for the largest part of MSCI World Index market capitalization, an investor who chooses to exclude international investments from his or her portfolio is ignoring more than half of the world's investable assets.

Exhibit 12.1: MSCI World Stock Market Capitalization: $32.3 Trillion
December 31, 2015

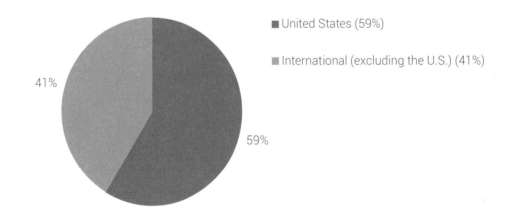

■ United States (59%)

■ International (excluding the U.S.) (41%)

41%

59%

[12.3]   Source: MSCI World Index Equity Fact Sheet. For more information, visit: MSCI.com.

Growth Potential

Exhibit 12.2 depicts the growth of $1.00 invested in international stocks (as represented by the MSCI EAFE index), and U.S. large-cap stocks (i.e., the S&P 500 total return index), long-term government bonds, Treasury bills, and a hypothetical asset returning the inflation rate over the period from the end of 1969 to the end of 2015.[12.4] Of the asset classes shown in Exhibit 12.2, the $1.00 invested at year-end 1969 in U.S. large cap stocks grew the most by year-end 2015 ($89.75), followed by International Stocks ($63.79).

In the time horizon over which this analysis is performed (1970–2015), international stocks generally outperformed U.S. large-cap stocks from 1970 through the late 1990s, but in more recent years U.S. large-cap stocks have generally outperformed international stocks.

To illustrate this seeming reversal of relative performance in more recent years, consider that $1.00 investment at year-end 1969 in U.S. large-cap stocks would have grown to $18.60 by end of 1995, but the same dollar invested in international stocks would have grown to $24.83. However, a $1.00 investment at year-end 1995 in U.S. large-cap stocks would have grown to $4.82 by the end of 2015 (20 years), but the same dollar invested in international stocks would have grown to only $2.57.

Exhibit 12.2: Global Investing
Index (Year-end 1969 = $1.00)
1970–2015

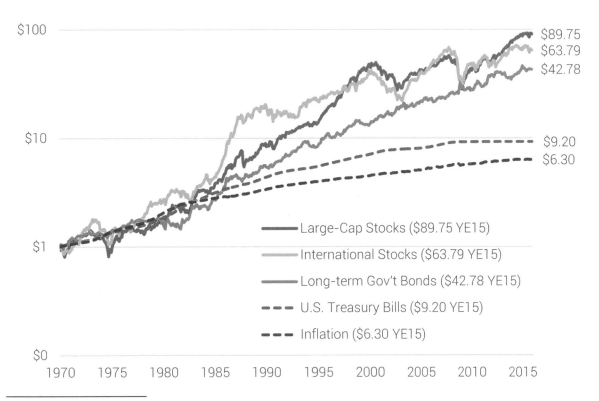

[12.4]   In this chapter, the "U.S." series used are the same "SBBI" series used throughout the rest of this book. "U.S." is added to these series' names in this chapter only to differentiate them from the MSCI EAFE equities index, which is used to represent "international" equities in this chapter.

The effects of the 2008 financial crisis are apparent in Exhibit 12.2. In 2008, U.S. large-cap stocks fell 37.0% and international stocks fell 43.1%. In the seven year period after 2008, both U.S. large-cap stocks and international stocks have recovered, with U.S. large-cap stocks producing a 14.8% annual return, significantly outperforming international stocks, which produced an annual return of 8.3%.

An additional perspective of the relative returns of U.S. large-cap stocks and international stocks is provided in Exhibit 12.3, which shows the performance of international and U.S. large-cap stocks over rolling 10-year holding periods ending 1979 through 2015.

International stocks outperformed in each of the 10-year periods ending 1979 through 1994, but U.S. large-cap stocks outperformed International stocks in 15 out of the 21 10-year periods ending 1995 through 2015, sometimes quite significantly.

Exhibit 12.3: U.S. Large-Cap Stocks and International Stocks, 10-Year Holding Period Annual Total Returns (%)
1970–1979 through 2006–2015

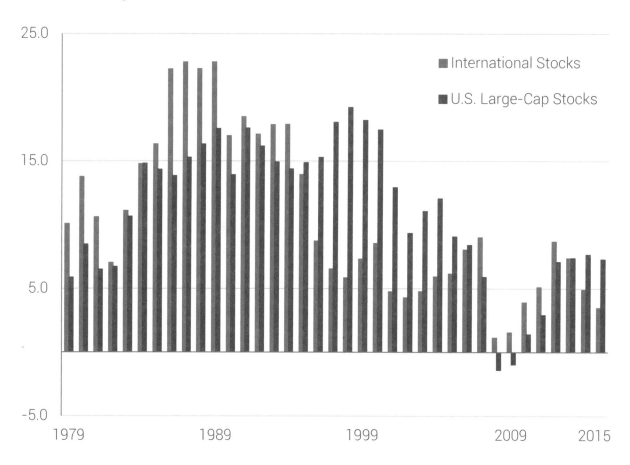

Just as U.S. stock prices fluctuate from one period to the next, prices of international stocks are subject to significant gains and declines. However, past returns from international stocks have fluctuated even more so than the returns of U.S. stocks. Annual ranges of returns provide an indication of the historical volatility (risk) experienced by investments in various markets.

Exhibit 12.4 illustrates the range of annual returns for U.S. large-cap stocks and international stocks, as well as European and Pacific regional equity composites, over the period 1970 through 2015. Although all of the composites have similar compound returns over the period, the three international composites exhibit greater volatility than the U.S. composite. All investments have the potential of dramatic ups and downs; however, a long-term approach to investing may help reduce the pain of volatility.

Exhibit 12.4: Global Stock Market Returns: Annual Ranges of Returns (%) 1970–2015

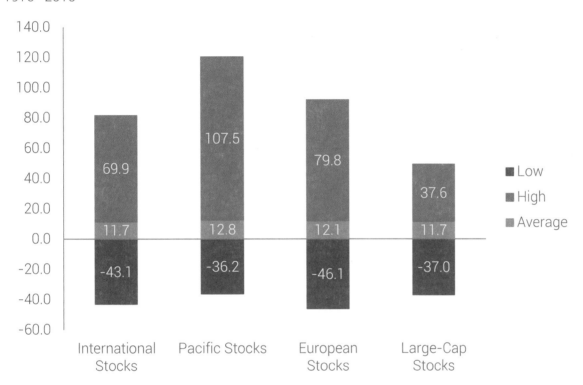

Diversification

Diversification can be another important benefit of international investing. By spreading risks among foreign and U.S. stocks, investors can potentially lower overall investment risk and/or improve investment returns. Fluctuations may occur at different times for different markets, and if growth is slow in one country, global investing provides a means of possibly participating in stronger market returns elsewhere. Investing abroad may help an investor balance such fluctuations. Because it is almost impossible to forecast which markets will be top performers in any given year, it can be very valuable to be invested in a portfolio diversified across several countries.

Exhibit 12.5 depicts the growth of $1.00 invested at year-end 1969 in U.S. large-cap stocks, European, and Pacific stocks as well as a "global portfolio" that is comprised of an equally weighted mix of the U.S., large-cap stocks, European, and Pacific stocks. Notice that the global portfolio was the top performer, followed in order of performance by the U.S., Europe, and Pacific indexes at the end of the 46-year period.

Exhibit 12.5: Benefits of Global Diversification
Index (Year-end 1969 = $1.00)
1970–2015

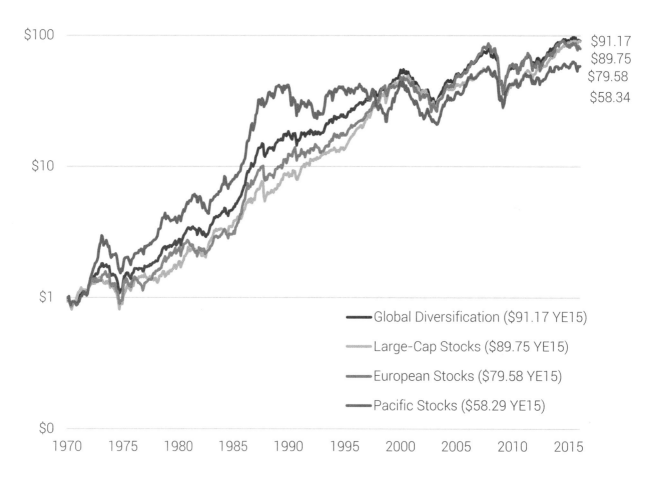

The cross-correlation coefficient between two series, covered in Chapter 6, measures the extent to which they are linearly related. The correlation coefficient measures the sensitivity of returns on one asset class or portfolio to the returns of another.

Exhibit 12.6 examines the 60-month rolling period correlation between international and U.S. large-cap stocks. Exhibit 12.6 illustrates the recent rise in cross-correlation between the two, suggesting that the benefit of diversification has suffered in recent years. The maximum benefit to an investor would have come in the 60-month period ending July 1987, where the cross-correlation was 0.26. The least amount of diversification benefit would have come in the 60-month period ending February 2013, where the cross-correlation was 0.93. The monthly average over the entire period was 0.62.

Exhibit 12.6: Rolling 60-Month Correlations: U.S. Large-Cap Stocks and International Stocks Data from 1970–1974 through 2011–2015.

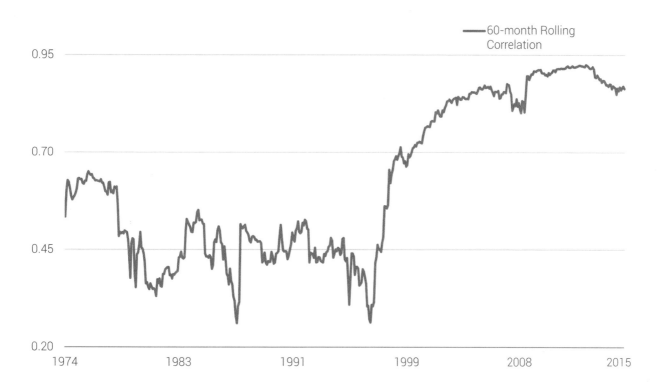

As discussed previously in regard to REITs (see Chapter 2), diversification is "spreading a portfolio over many investments to avoid excessive exposure to any one source of risk".[12.5] Put simply, diversification is "not putting all your eggs in one basket". Diversification offers the potential of higher returns for the same level of risk, or lower risk for the same level of return.

A low correlation between assets in a portfolio allows for the possibility of an increase in returns without a corresponding increase in risk, or alternatively, a reduction in risk without a corresponding decrease in return.

As demonstrated in Exhibit 12.6, the correlation of U.S. equities and international equities has been increasing in more recent years, but still can provide a diversification benefit. For example, from 1970 to 2015, a portfolio (rebalanced monthly) of 100% U.S. large-cap stocks provided an annual return of 10.3%, with an annualized monthly standard deviation of 17.0%. Adding a 5% allocation to international stocks decreases the risk of the portfolio (as measured by standard deviation) to 16.2%, while maintaining approximately the same return (10.3%).

[12.5]   Cara Griffith, "Practical Tax Considerations for Working with REITs," State Tax Notes (October 31, 2011): 315–320, quoting Jennifer Weiss: 316. In 2009, the IRS issued guidance that indicates that the distributions may be in the form of cash or stock in certain instances.

Risks Typically Associated With International Investment

The risks associated with international investing can largely be characterized as *financial, economic,* or *political.* Many of these are the types of risks associated with investing in general – the possibility of loan default, the possibility of delayed payments of suppliers' credits, the possibility of inefficiencies brought about by the work of complying with unfamiliar (or burdensome) regulation, unexpected increases in taxes and transaction fees, differences in information availability, and liquidity issues, to name just a few. Some risks, however, are typically associated more with global investing – currency risk, lack of good accounting information, poorly developed legal systems, and even expropriation, government instability, or war.

Financial Risks

Financial risks typically entail an issue that is specifically money-centric (e.g., loan default, inability to easily repatriate profits to the home country, etc.). Among these types of risks, currency risk is probably the most familiar. Currency risk is the *financial* risk that exchange rates (the value of one currency versus another) will change unexpectedly.

For example, when a French investor invests in Brazil, he or she must first convert Euros into the local currency, in this case the Brazilian Real (BRL). The returns that the French investor experiences in local currency terms are identical to the returns that a Brazilian investor would experience, but the French investor faces an additional risk in the form of currency risk when returns are "brought home" and must be converted back to Euros.[12.6]

Expected changes in exchange rates can often be hedged. However, even when currency hedging is used, exchange rate risk often remains. To the extent the Euro unexpectedly *increases* in value versus the Real (i.e., the Euro appreciates against the Real), the French investor is able to purchase fewer Euros for each Real he realized in the Brazilian investment when returns from the investment are repatriated, and his return is thus *diminished.*[12.7,12.8]

Conversely, to the extent the Euro unexpectedly *decreases* in value versus the Real (i.e., the Euro depreciates against the Real), the French investor is able to purchase more Euros for each Real he realized in the Brazilian investment when returns from the investment are repatriated, and his return is thus *enhanced.*

[12.6] For this example, we assume that the French and local investor are both subject to the same regulations, taxes, and local risks when investing in the same local asset.

[12.7] We say "unexpectedly" for a reason. If the investor had been able to predict (at the time of investing) the precise exchange rate at which he/she would be repatriating his/her returns, these "expected" changes to the exchange rate would have been reflected in the expected cash flows of the investment at inception.

[12.8] For example, say the French investor had achieved a 10% return in local (Brazilian) terms on his investment in a given year, but the Euro had unexpectedly appreciated by 3% in value relative to the Real over the same period. When the returns are repatriated, the French investor's overall return is diminished to approximately 6.7% [(1+10%)*(1-3%)-1] in Euro terms. Conversely, had the Euro depreciated in value versus the Real by 3%, the repatriated returns would be enhanced to approximately 13.3% [(1+10%)*(1+3%)-1] in Euro terms.

For example, in 2007 Brazilian equities returned an astonishing 50% return in local terms (see Exhibit 12.7). Because the Euro *depreciated* against the Real in 2007, French-based investors in Brazilian stocks experienced an even *higher* return (62%) when they repatriated their returns and converted them to Euros. Similarly, in 2009 the Euro *depreciated* relative to the South African Rand (ZAR), and French-based investors realized higher returns in Euros once again versus the local South African investors. In a more recent example, U.S.-based investors investing in U.S. equities realized an approximate return of just 1.0% in 2015, but French investors making a similar investment in the U.S. realized an approximate 13% return when they repatriated their returns and converted them to Euros (the Euro *depreciated* against the U.S. Dollar in 2015, so the French investors could purchase *more* Euros with their Dollars when they repatriated their returns).

It is important to note that currency conversion effects can also work to *diminish* realized returns. For example, in 2015 Brazilian equities returned -12% in local terms. Because the Euro *appreciated* against the Real in 2015, French-based investors in Brazilian stocks experienced an even *lower* return (-34%) when they repatriated their returns and converted them to Euros.

Exhibit 12.7: Currency Conversion Effects

		Return in Local Terms	Return to French Investors (EUR)	Currency Conversion Effect
2007	Brazil (BRL)	50%	62%	12%
2009	South Africa (ZAR)	26%	53%	27%
2015	Japan (JPY)	10%	22%	12%
2015	Switzerland (CHF)	2%	13%	11%
2015	Brazil (BRL)	-12%	-34%	-22%
2015	Argentina (ARS)	52%	11%	-41%
2015	United States (USD)	1%	13%	12%

Source of underlying data: Morgan Stanley Capital International (MSCI) Brazil, South Africa, Japan, Switzerland, Brazil, and Argentina, gross return (GR) equity indices. For more information about MSCI, visit www.msci.com. The S&P 500 Index was used as the proxy for the United States equity market. For more information about S&P indices, visit http://us.spindices.com/indices/equity/sp-500. All data accessed through the Morningstar *Direct* database. For more information about Morningstar *Direct*, visit http://corporate.morningstar.com/.

A common misstep we often encounter is companies constructing forward-looking budgets or projection analyses in local currencies, and then converting these projections to the currency of the parent company using the spot rate.

This mistakenly assumes that the exchange rate will not change in the future. Projections, which are inherently forward-looking, need to embody expected currency conversion rates. We are interested in currency risks over the period of the projected net cash flows, not just in the spot market. Even then, these are merely estimates of future currency exchange rates and the actual exchange rate can vary from these estimates.

Does currency risk affect the cost of capital? One team of researchers found that emerging market exchange risks have a significant impact on risk premiums and are time varying (for countries in the sample). They found that exchange risks affect risk premiums as a separate risk factor and represent more than 50% of total risk premiums for investments in emerging market equities. The exchange risk from investments in emerging markets was found to even affect the risk premiums for investments in developed market equities.[12.9]

While exchange rate volatility appears to be partly systematic, researchers have found that despite not being a constant, the currency risk premium is small and seems to fluctuate around zero.[12.10] A recently published academic paper set out to study whether corporate managers should include foreign exchange risk premia in cost of equity estimations. The authors empirically estimated the differences between the cost of equity estimates of several risk-return models, including some models that have an explicit currency risk premia and others that do not. They found that adjusting for currency risk makes little difference, on average, in the cost of equity estimates, even for small firms and for firms with extreme currency exposure estimates. The authors concluded that, at a minimum, these results applied to U.S. companies, but future research would still have to be conducted for other countries.[12.11]

Rather than attempting to quantify and add a currency risk premium to the discount rate, using expected or forward exchange rates to translate projected cash flows into the home currency will inherently capture the currency risk, if any, priced by market participants.[12.12]

Economic Risks

Global investors may also be exposed to *economic* risks associated with international investing. These risks may include the volatility of a country's economy as reflected in the current (and expected) inflation rate, the current account balance as a percentage of goods and services, burdensome regulation, and labor rules, among others. In the current environment, an economic risk that has come to the forefront is the sovereign debt crisis. The recent economic and financial crisis in Greece, for example, has prompted many governments around the world to re-think their own fiscal policies, as it becomes evident that current debt loads are likely unsustainable in many of these countries.

[12.9] Francesca Carrieri, Vihang Errunza, and Basma Majerbi, "Does Emerging Market Exchange Risk Affect Global Equity Prices?" *Journal of Financial Quantitative Analysis* (September 2006): 511–540.

[12.10] Sercu, Piet (2009), *International Finance: Theory into Practice*, Princeton, NJ: Princeton University Press, Chapter 19.

[12.11] Krapl, A. and O'Brien, T. J. (2016), "Estimating Cost of Equity: Do You Need to Adjust for Foreign Exchange Risk?," *Journal of International Financial Management & Accounting*, 27: 5–25.

[12.12] This assumes that the valuation is being conducted in the home currency, by discounting projected cash flows denominated in the home currency, with a discount rate also denominated in home currency. Alternatively, the analyst can conduct the entire valuation in foreign currency terms (projected cash flows and discount rate are both in foreign currency terms), in which case the estimated value would be translated into the home currency using a spot exchange rate.

In Exhibit 12.8a, the 20 countries with the *overall* highest estimated government debt-to-GDP ratios are shown (regardless of the size of their economies), as of calendar year 2015. For example, the United States has a debt-to-GDP ratio of 106% (i.e., the United States' government debt is 6% *larger* than the United States' annual GDP), and Jordan has a debt-to-GDP ratio of 92% (i.e., Jordan's government debt is 8% *less* than Jordan's annual GDP)

In Exhibit 12.8b, the estimated government debt-to-GDP ratios for the 20 countries with the *largest* economies (as measured by GDP) are shown, also as of calendar year 2015. The rank of GDP size is shown in parentheses after each country's name. Saudi Arabia (with a ranking of "20") is the smallest GDP, and the United States (with a ranking of "1") is the largest GDP.

Exhibit 12.8a: 2015 Government Debt-to-GDP (in percent)

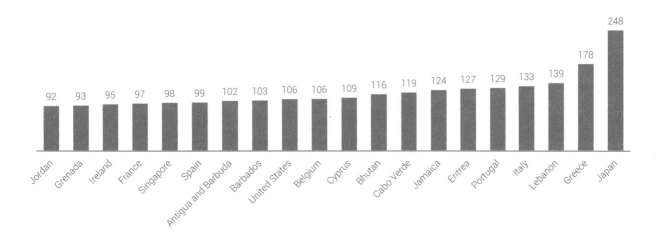

Exhibit 12.8b: 2015 Government Debt-to-GDP (in percent), 20 countries with largest GDP

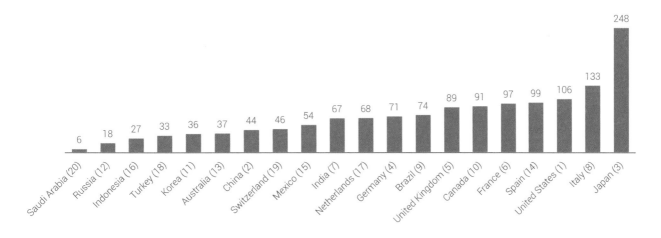

Source of underlying data for Exhibit 12.8a and Exhibit 12.8b: World Economic Outlook Database from the International Monetary Fund (IMF). For additional information, please visit: http://www.imf.org/external/pubs/ft/weo/2016/01/weodata/download.aspx.

There are costs that tend to go hand-in-hand with what might be considered unsustainable debt levels by governments. Lenders may demand a higher expected return to compensate them for additional default risk when investing not only in the country's sovereign debt, but also in businesses operating in those countries.

Governments may decide to increase the money supply in an effort to inflate their way out of debt. Ultimately, some governments may decide on outright currency devaluation or even a repudiation of debt (i.e., defaulting on their debt obligations). These risks are not entirely limited to less developed countries, but less developed countries may be more willing to resort to these extreme measures than developed countries.

Political Risks

Political risks can include government instability, expropriation, bureaucratic inefficiency, corruption, and even war. A relatively recent example of the effects of political risk is Venezuela's expropriation of various foreign-owned oil, gas, and mining interests. These actions tend to reduce Venezuela's attractiveness to foreign investors, who will likely demand a significantly higher expected return in exchange for future investment in the country – in effect raising their cost of capital estimates for projects located in Venezuela.

Exhibit 12.9 summarizes some of the risks that investors may view as unique or country-specific.

Exhibit 12.9: Reasons Typically Cited for Adding a Country Risk Premium Adjustment

Political Risks

- Repudiation of contracts by governments
- Expropriation of private investments in total or part through change in taxation
- Economic planning failures
- Political leadership and frequency of change
- External conflict
- Corruption in government
- Military in politics
- Organized religion in politics
- Lack of law-and-order tradition
- Racial and national tensions
- Civil war
- Poor quality of the bureaucracy
- Poorly developed legal system
- Political terrorism

Financial Risks

- Currency volatility plus the inability to convert, hedge, or repatriate profits
- Loan default or unfavorable loan restructuring
- Delayed payment of suppliers' credits
- Losses from exchange controls
- Foreign trade collection experience

Economic Risks

- Volatility of the economy
- Inflation: current and future expected
- Debt service as a percentage of exports of goods and services
- Current account balance of the country in which the subject company operates as a percentage of goods and services
- Parallel foreign exchange rate market indicators
- Labor issues

International and Domestic Series Summary Data

Exhibit 12.10 shows summary statistics of annual total returns for various international regions and composites. The summary statistics presented are geometric mean, arithmetic mean, and standard deviation. From 1970 to 2015, the Pacific regional composite was the riskiest, with a standard deviation of 29.8 percentage points. The geometric mean of the Pacific regional composite was 9.2%, below that of EAFE and the World composite, which were considerably less risky.

Exhibit 12.10: Summary Statistics of Annual Returns (%)
1970–2015

Series	Geometric Mean	Arithemtic Mean	Standard Deviation
EAFE	9.5	11.7	22.1
Pacific	9.2	12.8	29.8
Europe	10.0	12.1	21.8
World	9.4	11.0	17.8
Canada	8.9	11.2	21.8
U.S.	10.3	11.7	17.3

Exhibit 12.11 shows the compound returns by decade for the various international regions and composites. The Pacific regional composite provided the highest compound annual rate of return in the first two decades but performed rather poorly in the 1990s as well as in the last two periods. The 1990s were a good time to be a domestic investor, with a compound annual rate of return of 18.2%.

Exhibit 12.11: Compound Annual Rates of Return by Decade (%)

Series	1970s	1980s	1990s	2000s	2010s[**]	2006–2015
EAFE	10.1	22.8	7.3	1.6	4.7	3.5
Pacific	14.8	26.4	0.5	-0.3	5.4	2.6
Europe	8.6	18.5	14.5	2.4	4.5	4.0
World	7.0	19.9	12.0	0.2	8.9	5.6
Canada	11.0	11.7	9.8	9.2	-0.5	2.6
U.S.	5.9	17.6	18.2	-0.9	13.0	7.3

[**]Based on the period 2010–2015

Exhibit 12.12 shows the annualized monthly standard deviations by decade for the various international regions and composites. The World composite was the least risky asset in the 1970s, 1980s, and the 1990s. The Canadian index was the riskiest asset in the 2000s as well as the most recent decade. The domestic portfolio was the least risky asset in the most recent decade.

Exhibit 12.12: Annualized Monthly Standard Deviation by Decade (%)

Series	1970s	1980s	1990s	2000s	2010s**	2006–2015
EAFE	17.4	21.6	18.7	18.5	17.4	19.5
Pacific	22.1	26.6	24.8	18.2	15.3	17.2
Europe	18.6	21.5	16.8	20.4	19.8	21.7
World	15.1	17.6	15.7	16.9	15.5	17.5
Canada	20.6	24.8	18.6	25.9	16.9	22.8
U.S.	17.2	19.4	15.9	16.3	14.8	16.3

**Based on the period 2010–2015

Exhibit 12.13 presents annual cross-correlations and serial correlations from 1970 to 2015 for the six basic SBBI series and inflation as well as international stocks, as defined by the MSCI EAFE Index. International stocks, when compared to U.S. large-cap stocks, provided a higher cross-correlation than when compared to U.S. small-cap stocks. The serial correlation of international stocks suggests no pattern, and the return from period to period can best be interpreted as random or unpredictable.

Exhibit 12.13: Basic Series and International Stocks: Serial and Cross-Correlations of Historical Annual Returns
1970–2015

	International Stocks	Large-Cap Stocks	Small-Cap Stocks	Long-term Corp Bonds	Long-term Gov't Bonds	Inter-term Gov't Bonds	U.S. Treasury Bills	Inflation
International Stocks	1.00							
Large-Cap Stocks	0.66	1.00						
Small-Cap Stocks	0.51	0.73	1.00					
Long-term Corp Bonds	0.02	0.23	0.06	1.00				
Long-term Gov't Bonds	-0.14	0.02	-0.14	0.89	1.00			
Inter-term Gov't Bonds	-0.13	0.03	-0.10	0.85	0.85	1.00		
U.S. Treasury Bills	0.02	0.06	0.03	0.05	0.07	0.40	1.00	
Inflation	-0.07	-0.11	0.04	-0.33	-0.28	-0.05	0.68	1.00
Serial Correlation	0.07	0.00	0.01	-0.10	-0.31	0.05	0.88	0.74

Conclusion

Country risk is generally described as financial, economic, or political in nature. These rules may create incremental complexities when developing cost of capital estimates for a business, business ownership interest, security, or an intangible asset based outside of a mature market such as the United States.

International investments are no different from any other investment when it comes to information gathering. Investors interested in or already taking part in the international marketplace should learn as much as possible about the corresponding significant rewards and risks. International investments are not for everyone, and the most appropriate mix for an individual investor depends on his or her risk tolerance, investment goals, time horizon, and financial resources.

Appendix A
Monthly and Annual Returns of Basic Series

Basic Series

Appendix A-1: Large-Capitalization Stocks: Total Return

Appendix A-2: Large-Capitalization Stocks: Income Returns

Appendix A-3: Large-Capitalization Stocks: Capital Appreciation Returns

Appendix A-4: Small-Capitalization Stocks: Total Returns

Appendix A-5: Long-term Corporate Bonds: Total Returns

Appendix A-6: Long-term Government Bonds: Total Returns

Appendix A-7: Long-term Government Bonds: Income Returns

Appendix A-8: Long-term Government Bonds: Capital Appreciation Returns

Appendix A-9: Long-term Government Bonds: Yields

Appendix A-10: Intermediate-term Government Bonds: Total Returns

Appendix A-11: Intermediate-term Government Bonds: Income Returns

Appendix A-12: Intermediate-term Government Bonds: Capital Appreciation Returns

Appendix A-13: Intermediate-term Government Bonds: Yields

Appendix A-14: U.S. Treasury Bills: Total Returns

Appendix A-15: Inflation

Real Riskless Rates of Return

Appendix A-16: U.S. Treasury Bills: Inflation-Adjusted Total Returns

Appendix A-1 (1)

Appendix A-1

Large-Capitalization Stocks: Total Return
From 1926 to 2015

Year	Jan	Feb	Mar	Apr	May	Jun	Jul	Aug	Sep	Oct	Nov	Dec	Year	Jan–Dec*
1926	0.0000	-0.0385	-0.0575	0.0253	0.0179	0.0457	0.0479	0.0248	0.0252	-0.0284	0.0347	0.0196	1926	0.1162
1927	-0.0193	0.0537	0.0087	0.0201	0.0607	-0.0067	0.0670	0.0515	0.0450	-0.0502	0.0721	0.0279	1927	0.3749
1928	-0.0040	-0.0125	0.1101	0.0345	0.0197	-0.0385	0.0141	0.0803	0.0259	0.0168	0.1292	0.0049	1928	0.4361
1929	0.0583	-0.0019	-0.0012	0.0176	-0.0362	0.1140	0.0471	0.1028	-0.0476	-0.1973	-0.1246	0.0282	1929	-0.0842
1930	0.0639	0.0259	0.0812	-0.0080	-0.0096	-0.1625	0.0386	0.0141	-0.1282	-0.0855	-0.0089	-0.0706	1930	-0.2490
1931	0.0502	0.1193	-0.0675	-0.0935	-0.1279	0.1421	-0.0722	0.0182	-0.2973	0.0896	-0.0798	-0.1400	1931	-0.4334
1932	-0.0271	0.0570	-0.1158	-0.1997	-0.2196	-0.0022	0.3815	0.3869	-0.0346	-0.1349	-0.0417	0.0565	1932	-0.0819
1933	0.0087	-0.1772	0.0353	0.4256	0.1683	0.1338	-0.0862	0.1206	-0.1118	-0.0855	0.1127	0.0253	1933	0.5399
1934	0.1069	-0.0322	0.0000	-0.0251	-0.0736	0.0229	-0.1132	0.0611	-0.0033	-0.0286	0.0942	-0.0010	1934	-0.0144
1935	-0.0411	-0.0341	-0.0286	0.0980	0.0409	0.0699	0.0850	0.0280	0.0256	0.0777	0.0474	0.0394	1935	0.4767
1936	0.0670	0.0224	0.0268	-0.0751	0.0545	0.0333	0.0701	0.0151	0.0031	0.0775	0.0134	-0.0029	1936	0.3392
1937	0.0390	0.0191	-0.0077	-0.0809	-0.0024	-0.0504	0.1045	-0.0483	-0.1403	-0.0981	-0.0866	-0.0459	1937	-0.3503
1938	0.0152	0.0674	-0.2487	0.1447	-0.0330	0.2503	0.0744	-0.0226	0.0166	0.0776	-0.0273	0.0401	1938	0.3112
1939	-0.0674	0.0390	-0.1339	-0.0027	0.0733	-0.0612	0.1105	-0.0648	0.1673	-0.0123	-0.0398	0.0270	1939	-0.0041
1940	-0.0336	0.0133	0.0124	-0.0024	-0.2289	0.0809	0.0341	0.0350	0.0123	0.0422	-0.0316	0.0009	1940	-0.0978
1941	-0.0463	-0.0060	0.0071	-0.0612	0.0183	0.0578	0.0579	0.0010	-0.0068	-0.0657	-0.0284	-0.0407	1941	-0.1159
1942	0.0161	-0.0159	-0.0652	-0.0400	0.0796	0.0221	0.0337	0.0164	0.0290	0.0678	-0.0021	0.0549	1942	0.2034
1943	0.0737	0.0583	0.0545	0.0035	0.0552	0.0223	-0.0526	0.0171	0.0263	-0.0108	-0.0654	0.0617	1943	0.2590
1944	0.0171	0.0042	0.0195	-0.0100	0.0505	0.0543	-0.0193	0.0157	-0.0008	0.0023	0.0133	0.0374	1944	0.1975
1945	0.0158	0.0683	-0.0441	0.0902	0.0195	-0.0007	-0.0180	0.0641	0.0438	0.0322	0.0396	0.0116	1945	0.3644
1946	0.0714	-0.0641	0.0480	0.0393	0.0288	-0.0370	-0.0239	-0.0674	-0.0997	-0.0060	-0.0027	0.0457	1946	-0.0807
1947	0.0255	-0.0077	-0.0149	-0.0363	0.0014	0.0554	0.0381	-0.0203	-0.0111	0.0238	-0.0175	0.0233	1947	0.0571
1948	-0.0379	-0.0388	0.0793	0.0292	0.0879	0.0054	-0.0508	0.0158	-0.0276	0.0710	-0.0961	0.0346	1948	0.0550
1949	0.0039	-0.0296	0.0328	-0.0179	-0.0258	0.0014	0.0650	0.0219	0.0263	0.0340	0.0175	0.0486	1949	0.1879
1950	0.0197	0.0199	0.0070	0.0486	0.0509	-0.0548	0.0119	0.0443	0.0592	0.0093	0.0169	0.0513	1950	0.3171
1951	0.0637	0.0157	-0.0156	0.0509	-0.0299	-0.0228	0.0711	0.0478	0.0013	-0.0103	0.0096	0.0424	1951	0.2402
1952	0.0181	-0.0282	0.0503	-0.0402	0.0343	0.0490	0.0196	-0.0071	-0.0176	0.0020	0.0571	0.0382	1952	0.1837
1953	-0.0049	-0.0106	-0.0212	-0.0237	0.0077	-0.0134	0.0273	-0.0501	0.0034	0.0540	0.0204	0.0053	1953	-0.0099
1954	0.0536	0.0111	0.0325	0.0516	0.0418	0.0031	0.0589	-0.0275	0.0851	-0.0167	0.0909	0.0534	1954	0.5262
1955	0.0197	0.0098	-0.0030	0.0396	0.0055	0.0841	0.0622	-0.0025	0.0130	-0.0284	0.0827	0.0015	1955	0.3156

*Compound annual return

Appendix A-1

Large-Capitalization Stocks: Total Return
From 1926 to 2015

Year	Jan	Feb	Mar	Apr	May	Jun	Jul	Aug	Sep	Oct	Nov	Dec	Year	Jan–Dec*
1956	-0.0347	0.0413	0.0710	-0.0004	-0.0593	0.0409	0.0530	-0.0328	-0.0440	0.0066	-0.0050	0.0370	1956	0.0656
1957	-0.0401	-0.0264	0.0215	0.0388	0.0437	0.0004	0.0131	-0.0505	-0.0602	-0.0302	0.0231	-0.0395	1957	-0.1078
1958	0.0445	-0.0141	0.0328	0.0337	0.0212	0.0279	0.0449	0.0176	0.0501	0.0270	0.0284	0.0535	1958	0.4336
1959	0.0053	0.0049	0.0020	0.0402	0.0240	-0.0022	0.0363	-0.0102	-0.0443	0.0128	0.0186	0.0292	1959	0.1196
1960	-0.0700	0.0147	-0.0123	-0.0161	0.0326	0.0211	-0.0234	0.0317	-0.0590	-0.0007	0.0465	0.0479	1960	0.0047
1961	0.0645	0.0319	0.0270	0.0051	0.0239	-0.0275	0.0342	0.0243	-0.0184	0.0298	0.0447	0.0046	1961	0.2689
1962	-0.0366	0.0209	-0.0046	-0.0607	-0.0811	-0.0803	0.0652	0.0208	-0.0465	0.0064	0.1086	0.0153	1962	-0.0873
1963	0.0506	-0.0239	0.0370	0.0500	0.0193	-0.0188	-0.0022	0.0535	-0.0097	0.0339	-0.0046	0.0262	1963	0.2280
1964	0.0283	0.0147	0.0165	0.0075	0.0162	0.0178	0.0195	-0.0118	0.0301	0.0096	0.0005	0.0056	1964	0.1648
1965	0.0345	0.0031	-0.0133	0.0356	-0.0030	-0.0473	0.0147	0.0272	0.0334	0.0289	-0.0031	0.0106	1965	0.1245
1966	0.0062	-0.0131	-0.0205	0.0220	-0.0492	-0.0146	-0.0120	-0.0725	-0.0053	0.0494	0.0095	0.0002	1966	-0.1006
1967	0.0798	0.0072	0.0409	0.0437	-0.0477	0.0190	0.0468	-0.0070	0.0342	-0.0276	0.0065	0.0278	1967	0.2398
1968	-0.0425	-0.0261	0.0110	0.0834	0.0161	0.0105	-0.0172	0.0164	0.0400	0.0087	0.0531	-0.0402	1968	0.1106
1969	-0.0068	-0.0426	0.0359	0.0229	0.0026	-0.0542	-0.0587	0.0454	-0.0236	0.0459	-0.0297	-0.0177	1969	-0.0850
1970	-0.0743	0.0557	0.0044	-0.0875	-0.0578	-0.0466	0.0769	0.0478	0.0362	-0.0083	0.0506	0.0598	1970	0.0386
1971	0.0432	0.0117	0.0394	0.0389	-0.0391	0.0033	-0.0387	0.0388	-0.0044	-0.0391	0.0002	0.0888	1971	0.1430
1972	0.0206	0.0277	0.0083	0.0068	0.0197	-0.0194	0.0048	0.0369	-0.0025	0.0119	0.0481	0.0142	1972	0.1899
1973	-0.0149	-0.0352	0.0008	-0.0383	-0.0163	-0.0040	0.0407	-0.0341	0.0427	0.0017	-0.1109	0.0198	1973	-0.1469
1974	-0.0072	-0.0007	-0.0205	-0.0359	-0.0302	-0.0114	-0.0742	-0.0864	-0.1152	0.1681	-0.0489	-0.0156	1974	-0.2647
1975	0.1272	0.0638	0.0254	0.0510	0.0476	0.0477	-0.0644	-0.0176	-0.0312	0.0653	0.0282	-0.0081	1975	0.3723
1976	0.1217	-0.0084	0.0337	-0.0078	-0.0111	0.0443	-0.0048	-0.0018	0.0258	-0.0186	0.0561	0.0561	1976	0.2393
1977	-0.0473	-0.0182	-0.0105	0.0042	-0.0196	0.0494	-0.0124	-0.0172	0.0015	-0.0389	0.0316	0.0075	1977	-0.0716
1978	-0.0574	-0.0203	0.0294	0.0902	0.0092	-0.0138	0.0583	0.0301	-0.0032	-0.0872	0.0215	0.0196	1978	0.0657
1979	0.0443	-0.0321	0.0596	0.0094	-0.0247	0.0435	0.0134	0.0577	0.0043	-0.0640	0.0475	0.0214	1979	0.1861
1980	0.0622	-0.0001	-0.0972	0.0462	0.0515	0.0316	0.0696	0.0101	0.0294	0.0202	0.1065	-0.0302	1980	0.3250
1981	-0.0418	0.0174	0.0400	-0.0193	0.0026	-0.0063	0.0021	-0.0577	-0.0493	0.0540	0.0413	-0.0256	1981	-0.0492
1982	-0.0131	-0.0559	-0.0052	0.0452	-0.0341	-0.0150	-0.0178	0.1214	0.0125	0.1151	0.0404	0.0193	1982	0.2155
1983	0.0372	0.0229	0.0369	0.0788	-0.0087	0.0389	-0.0295	0.0150	0.0138	-0.0116	0.0211	-0.0052	1983	0.2256
1984	-0.0056	-0.0352	0.0173	0.0095	-0.0554	0.0217	-0.0124	0.1104	0.0002	0.0039	-0.0112	0.0263	1984	0.0627
1985	0.0779	0.0122	0.0007	-0.0009	0.0578	0.0157	-0.0015	-0.0085	-0.0313	0.0462	0.0686	0.0484	1985	0.3173

*Compound annual return

Appendix A-1

Large-Capitalization Stocks: Total Return
From 1926 to 2015

Year	Jan	Feb	Mar	Apr	May	Jun	Jul	Aug	Sep	Oct	Nov	Dec	Year	Jan–Dec*
1986	0.0056	0.0747	0.0558	-0.0113	0.0532	0.0169	-0.0559	0.0742	-0.0827	0.0577	0.0243	-0.0255	1986	0.1867
1987	0.1347	0.0395	0.0289	-0.0089	0.0087	0.0505	0.0507	0.0373	-0.0219	-0.2154	-0.0824	0.0761	1987	0.0525
1988	0.0421	0.0466	-0.0309	0.0111	0.0086	0.0459	-0.0038	-0.0339	0.0426	0.0278	-0.0143	0.0174	1988	0.1661
1989	0.0732	-0.0249	0.0233	0.0519	0.0405	-0.0057	0.0903	0.0195	-0.0041	-0.0232	0.0204	0.0240	1989	0.3169
1990	-0.0671	0.0129	0.0265	-0.0249	0.0975	-0.0067	-0.0032	-0.0904	-0.0487	-0.0043	0.0646	0.0279	1990	-0.0310
1991	0.0436	0.0715	0.0242	0.0024	0.0431	-0.0458	0.0466	0.0237	-0.0167	0.0134	-0.0403	0.1144	1991	0.3047
1992	-0.0186	0.0130	-0.0194	0.0294	0.0049	-0.0149	0.0409	-0.0205	0.0118	0.0035	0.0341	0.0123	1992	0.0762
1993	0.0084	0.0136	0.0211	-0.0242	0.0268	0.0029	-0.0040	0.0379	-0.0077	0.0207	-0.0095	0.0121	1993	0.1008
1994	0.0340	-0.0271	-0.0436	0.0128	0.0164	-0.0245	0.0328	0.0410	-0.0245	0.0225	-0.0364	0.0148	1994	0.0132
1995	0.0259	0.0390	0.0295	0.0294	0.0400	0.0232	0.0332	0.0025	0.0422	-0.0036	0.0439	0.0193	1995	0.3758
1996	0.0340	0.0093	0.0096	0.0147	0.0258	0.0038	-0.0442	0.0211	0.0563	0.0276	0.0756	-0.0198	1996	0.2296
1997	0.0625	0.0078	-0.0411	0.0597	0.0609	0.0448	0.0796	-0.0560	0.0548	-0.0334	0.0463	0.0172	1997	0.3336
1998	0.0111	0.0721	0.0512	0.0101	-0.0172	0.0406	-0.0106	-0.1446	0.0641	0.0813	0.0606	0.0576	1998	0.2858
1999	0.0418	-0.0311	0.0400	0.0387	-0.0236	0.0555	-0.0312	-0.0049	-0.0274	0.0633	0.0203	0.0589	1999	0.2104
2000	-0.0502	-0.0189	0.0978	-0.0301	-0.0205	0.0247	-0.0156	0.0621	-0.0528	-0.0042	-0.0788	0.0049	2000	-0.0910
2001	0.0355	-0.0912	-0.0634	0.0777	0.0067	-0.0243	-0.0098	-0.0626	-0.0808	0.0191	0.0767	0.0088	2001	-0.1189
2002	-0.0146	-0.0193	0.0376	-0.0606	-0.0074	-0.0712	-0.0780	0.0066	-0.1087	0.0880	0.0589	-0.0587	2002	-0.2210
2003	-0.0262	-0.0150	0.0097	0.0824	0.0527	0.0128	0.0176	0.0195	-0.0106	0.0566	0.0088	0.0524	2003	0.2868
2004	0.0184	0.0139	-0.0151	-0.0157	0.0137	0.0194	-0.0331	0.0040	0.0108	0.0153	0.0405	0.0340	2004	0.1088
2005	-0.0244	0.0210	-0.0177	-0.0190	0.0318	0.0014	0.0372	-0.0091	0.0081	-0.0167	0.0378	0.0003	2005	0.0491
2006	0.0265	0.0027	0.0124	0.0134	-0.0288	0.0014	0.0062	0.0238	0.0258	0.0326	0.0190	0.0140	2006	0.1579
2007	0.0151	-0.0196	0.0112	0.0443	0.0349	-0.0166	-0.0310	0.0150	0.0374	0.0159	-0.0418	-0.0069	2007	0.0549
2008	-0.0600	-0.0325	-0.0043	0.0487	0.0130	-0.0843	-0.0084	0.0145	-0.0891	-0.1679	-0.0718	0.0106	2008	-0.3700
2009	-0.0843	-0.1065	0.0876	0.0957	0.0559	0.0020	0.0756	0.0361	0.0373	-0.0186	0.0600	0.0193	2009	0.2646
2010	-0.0360	0.0310	0.0603	0.0158	-0.0799	-0.0523	0.0701	-0.0451	0.0892	0.0380	0.0001	0.0668	2010	0.1506
2011	0.0237	0.0343	0.0004	0.0296	-0.0113	-0.0167	-0.0203	-0.0543	-0.0703	0.1093	-0.0022	0.0102	2011	0.0211
2012	0.0448	0.0432	0.0329	-0.0063	-0.0601	0.0412	0.0139	0.0225	0.0258	-0.0185	0.0058	0.0091	2012	0.1600
2013	0.0518	0.0136	0.0375	0.0193	0.0234	-0.0134	0.0509	-0.0290	0.0314	0.0460	0.0305	0.0253	2013	0.3239
2014	-0.0346	0.0457	0.0084	0.0074	0.0235	0.0207	-0.0138	0.0400	-0.0140	0.0244	0.0269	-0.0025	2014	0.1369
2015	-0.0300	0.0575	-0.0158	0.0096	0.0129	-0.0194	0.0210	-0.0603	-0.0247	0.0844	0.0030	-0.0158	2015	0.0138

*Compound annual return

Appendix A-2

Large-Capitalization Stocks: Income Returns
From 1926 to 2015

Year	Jan	Feb	Mar	Apr	May	Jun	Jul	Aug	Sep	Oct	Nov	Dec	Jan–Dec*
1926	0.0016	0.0055	0.0016	0.0026	0.0102	0.0025	0.0024	0.0078	0.0023	0.0030	0.0123	0.0030	0.0541
1927	0.0015	0.0061	0.0022	0.0029	0.0085	0.0027	0.0020	0.0070	0.0018	0.0029	0.0105	0.0029	0.0571
1928	0.0011	0.0051	0.0017	0.0021	0.0071	0.0020	0.0016	0.0062	0.0019	0.0023	0.0092	0.0021	0.0481
1929	0.0012	0.0039	0.0012	0.0016	0.0066	0.0016	0.0014	0.0048	0.0013	0.0020	0.0091	0.0029	0.0398
1930	0.0014	0.0044	0.0013	0.0016	0.0068	0.0020	0.0020	0.0066	0.0019	0.0032	0.0130	0.0036	0.0457
1931	0.0013	0.0050	0.0017	0.0024	0.0093	0.0031	0.0020	0.0087	0.0022	0.0051	0.0180	0.0053	0.0535
1932	0.0012	0.0063	0.0024	0.0027	0.0137	0.0067	0.0045	0.0115	0.0024	0.0037	0.0172	0.0046	0.0616
1933	0.0015	0.0072	0.0018	0.0034	0.0096	0.0021	0.0018	0.0060	0.0018	0.0031	0.0100	0.0030	0.0639
1934	0.0010	0.0045	0.0009	0.0019	0.0076	0.0021	0.0020	0.0069	0.0022	0.0033	0.0114	0.0031	0.0446
1935	0.0011	0.0055	0.0023	0.0024	0.0086	0.0021	0.0020	0.0063	0.0018	0.0026	0.0080	0.0023	0.0495
1936	0.0015	0.0056	0.0014	0.0020	0.0087	0.0028	0.0020	0.0063	0.0019	0.0025	0.0093	0.0029	0.0536
1937	0.0012	0.0045	0.0017	0.0022	0.0079	0.0025	0.0019	0.0071	0.0019	0.0036	0.0146	0.0045	0.0466
1938	0.0019	0.0065	0.0018	0.0035	0.0113	0.0032	0.0017	0.0048	0.0017	0.0016	0.0061	0.0024	0.0483
1939	0.0015	0.0065	0.0016	0.0027	0.0110	0.0026	0.0018	0.0066	0.0027	0.0023	0.0094	0.0033	0.0469
1940	0.0016	0.0066	0.0025	0.0024	0.0107	0.0043	0.0030	0.0087	0.0028	0.0028	0.0108	0.0038	0.0536
1941	0.0019	0.0089	0.0030	0.0040	0.0140	0.0043	0.0030	0.0096	0.0029	0.0029	0.0137	0.0044	0.0671
1942	0.0023	0.0091	0.0023	0.0037	0.0157	0.0037	0.0024	0.0093	0.0023	0.0034	0.0117	0.0032	0.0679
1943	0.0020	0.0076	0.0018	0.0026	0.0104	0.0025	0.0016	0.0068	0.0025	0.0025	0.0101	0.0027	0.0624
1944	0.0017	0.0068	0.0025	0.0025	0.0101	0.0032	0.0015	0.0071	0.0023	0.0023	0.0094	0.0023	0.0548
1945	0.0015	0.0067	0.0021	0.0022	0.0081	0.0027	0.0020	0.0061	0.0019	0.0019	0.0072	0.0017	0.0497
1946	0.0017	0.0054	0.0017	0.0017	0.0064	0.0021	0.0016	0.0056	0.0018	0.0020	0.0088	0.0027	0.0409
1947	0.0020	0.0070	0.0019	0.0026	0.0103	0.0028	0.0020	0.0076	0.0026	0.0026	0.0110	0.0027	0.0549
1948	0.0020	0.0082	0.0021	0.0027	0.0097	0.0024	0.0024	0.0082	0.0025	0.0032	0.0121	0.0041	0.0608
1949	0.0026	0.0099	0.0027	0.0033	0.0115	0.0035	0.0028	0.0100	0.0026	0.0045	0.0162	0.0050	0.0750
1950	0.0024	0.0100	0.0029	0.0035	0.0116	0.0032	0.0034	0.0118	0.0033	0.0051	0.0179	0.0051	0.0877
1951	0.0024	0.0092	0.0028	0.0028	0.0107	0.0033	0.0024	0.0085	0.0021	0.0034	0.0122	0.0035	0.0691
1952	0.0025	0.0083	0.0026	0.0029	0.0111	0.0029	0.0020	0.0075	0.0020	0.0029	0.0106	0.0027	0.0593
1953	0.0023	0.0076	0.0023	0.0028	0.0110	0.0029	0.0021	0.0077	0.0021	0.0030	0.0114	0.0032	0.0546
1954	0.0024	0.0084	0.0023	0.0026	0.0088	0.0024	0.0017	0.0065	0.0020	0.0028	0.0101	0.0026	0.0621
1955	0.0017	0.0063	0.0019	0.0019	0.0068	0.0018	0.0015	0.0053	0.0016	0.0021	0.0078	0.0022	0.0456

*Compound annual return

Appendix A-2

Large-Capitalization Stocks: Income Returns
From 1926 to 2015

Year	Jan	Feb	Mar	Apr	May	Jun	Jul	Aug	Sep	Oct	Nov	Dec	Year	Jan–Dec*
1956	0.0018	0.0066	0.0018	0.0016	0.0064	0.0018	0.0015	0.0053	0.0015	0.0015	0.0059	0.0018	1956	0.0383
1957	0.0017	0.0063	0.0018	0.0018	0.0068	0.0017	0.0017	0.0056	0.0018	0.0019	0.0071	0.0019	1957	0.0384
1958	0.0018	0.0065	0.0020	0.0019	0.0062	0.0018	0.0018	0.0057	0.0017	0.0016	0.0060	0.0015	1958	0.0438
1959	0.0014	0.0051	0.0014	0.0014	0.0050	0.0014	0.0014	0.0048	0.0013	0.0016	0.0054	0.0015	1959	0.0331
1960	0.0015	0.0056	0.0016	0.0014	0.0057	0.0016	0.0014	0.0056	0.0014	0.0017	0.0062	0.0016	1960	0.0326
1961	0.0014	0.0050	0.0014	0.0012	0.0047	0.0014	0.0014	0.0046	0.0013	0.0015	0.0054	0.0014	1961	0.0348
1962	0.0013	0.0046	0.0013	0.0013	0.0049	0.0015	0.0016	0.0055	0.0017	0.0020	0.0071	0.0018	1962	0.0298
1963	0.0014	0.0050	0.0016	0.0015	0.0050	0.0014	0.0013	0.0048	0.0014	0.0017	0.0059	0.0018	1963	0.0361
1964	0.0013	0.0048	0.0013	0.0014	0.0048	0.0014	0.0012	0.0044	0.0013	0.0015	0.0057	0.0017	1964	0.0333
1965	0.0013	0.0046	0.0013	0.0014	0.0047	0.0014	0.0013	0.0047	0.0014	0.0016	0.0056	0.0016	1965	0.0321
1966	0.0013	0.0047	0.0013	0.0015	0.0049	0.0015	0.0014	0.0053	0.0017	0.0018	0.0064	0.0017	1966	0.0311
1967	0.0016	0.0052	0.0015	0.0014	0.0048	0.0015	0.0014	0.0047	0.0014	0.0014	0.0054	0.0015	1967	0.0364
1968	0.0013	0.0051	0.0016	0.0014	0.0049	0.0014	0.0013	0.0049	0.0014	0.0015	0.0051	0.0014	1968	0.0318
1969	0.0013	0.0048	0.0014	0.0014	0.0048	0.0014	0.0014	0.0053	0.0015	0.0016	0.0056	0.0010	1969	0.0298
1970	0.0021	0.0031	0.0029	0.0030	0.0032	0.0034	0.0036	0.0033	0.0032	0.0031	0.0031	0.0030	1970	0.0333
1971	0.0032	0.0022	0.0026	0.0035	0.0017	0.0026	0.0024	0.0029	0.0025	0.0041	0.0013	0.0041	1971	0.0349
1972	0.0011	0.0024	0.0023	0.0024	0.0041	0.0008	0.0024	0.0024	0.0023	0.0025	0.0025	0.0024	1972	0.0295
1973	0.0022	0.0022	0.0022	0.0025	0.0026	0.0026	0.0027	0.0026	0.0041	0.0015	0.0030	0.0032	1973	0.0286
1974	0.0029	0.0029	0.0028	0.0032	0.0033	0.0033	0.0036	0.0039	0.0042	0.0050	0.0043	0.0046	1974	0.0369
1975	0.0044	0.0039	0.0037	0.0037	0.0035	0.0034	0.0033	0.0035	0.0035	0.0037	0.0035	0.0034	1975	0.0537
1976	0.0034	0.0030	0.0030	0.0032	0.0032	0.0034	0.0033	0.0033	0.0032	0.0036	0.0037	0.0036	1976	0.0449
1977	0.0033	0.0034	0.0035	0.0040	0.0040	0.0034	0.0038	0.0038	0.0040	0.0045	0.0047	0.0046	1977	0.0435
1978	0.0041	0.0045	0.0045	0.0048	0.0044	0.0043	0.0044	0.0042	0.0041	0.0044	0.0048	0.0048	1978	0.0533
1979	0.0046	0.0044	0.0045	0.0077	0.0017	0.0048	0.0047	0.0046	0.0043	0.0046	0.0049	0.0046	1979	0.0589
1980	0.0045	0.0043	0.0046	0.0051	0.0049	0.0047	0.0046	0.0043	0.0043	0.0042	0.0042	0.0037	1980	0.0574
1981	0.0039	0.0041	0.0040	0.0041	0.0042	0.0041	0.0043	0.0044	0.0046	0.0048	0.0047	0.0044	1981	0.0488
1982	0.0045	0.0047	0.0049	0.0055	0.0047	0.0054	0.0051	0.0054	0.0049	0.0047	0.0043	0.0041	1982	0.0561
1983	0.0041	0.0039	0.0038	0.0040	0.0035	0.0037	0.0035	0.0037	0.0041	0.0032	0.0037	0.0036	1983	0.0504
1984	0.0036	0.0037	0.0038	0.0040	0.0040	0.0043	0.0040	0.0041	0.0037	0.0039	0.0039	0.0040	1984	0.0457
1985	0.0038	0.0036	0.0035	0.0037	0.0037	0.0035	0.0034	0.0035	0.0036	0.0036	0.0035	0.0033	1985	0.0472

*Compound annual return

Appendix A-2

Large-Capitalization Stocks: Income Returns
From 1926 to 2015

Year	Jan	Feb	Mar	Apr	May	Jun	Jul	Aug	Sep	Oct	Nov	Dec	Year	Jan–Dec*
1986	0.0032	0.0033	0.0030	0.0029	0.0030	0.0028	0.0028	0.0030	0.0028	0.0030	0.0027	0.0028	1986	0.0392
1987	0.0029	0.0026	0.0025	0.0026	0.0026	0.0026	0.0024	0.0024	0.0022	0.0023	0.0030	0.0032	1987	0.0364
1988	0.0016	0.0048	0.0025	0.0016	0.0055	0.0026	0.0016	0.0047	0.0029	0.0019	0.0046	0.0028	1988	0.0399
1989	0.0021	0.0040	0.0025	0.0018	0.0053	0.0023	0.0019	0.0040	0.0025	0.0020	0.0039	0.0026	1989	0.0403
1990	0.0017	0.0043	0.0022	0.0019	0.0055	0.0021	0.0020	0.0039	0.0025	0.0024	0.0047	0.0030	1990	0.0343
1991	0.0020	0.0042	0.0020	0.0020	0.0046	0.0021	0.0017	0.0040	0.0024	0.0016	0.0036	0.0028	1991	0.0376
1992	0.0013	0.0034	0.0024	0.0015	0.0039	0.0025	0.0015	0.0035	0.0026	0.0013	0.0038	0.0022	1992	0.0298
1993	0.0013	0.0031	0.0024	0.0012	0.0040	0.0022	0.0013	0.0035	0.0023	0.0013	0.0034	0.0020	1993	0.0291
1994	0.0015	0.0029	0.0021	0.0013	0.0040	0.0023	0.0013	0.0034	0.0025	0.0016	0.0031	0.0025	1994	0.0283
1995	0.0017	0.0029	0.0022	0.0015	0.0036	0.0020	0.0014	0.0028	0.0021	0.0014	0.0028	0.0018	1995	0.0304
1996	0.0014	0.0023	0.0017	0.0013	0.0029	0.0016	0.0016	0.0023	0.0021	0.0014	0.0022	0.0017	1996	0.0243
1997	0.0012	0.0019	0.0015	0.0013	0.0023	0.0013	0.0014	0.0014	0.0016	0.0011	0.0017	0.0014	1997	0.0210
1998	0.0009	0.0017	0.0013	0.0010	0.0016	0.0012	0.0010	0.0012	0.0017	0.0010	0.0015	0.0012	1998	0.0167
1999	0.0008	0.0012	0.0012	0.0008	0.0014	0.0011	0.0008	0.0013	0.0011	0.0007	0.0013	0.0011	1999	0.0136
2000	0.0007	0.0012	0.0011	0.0007	0.0014	0.0007	0.0007	0.0014	0.0007	0.0007	0.0012	0.0008	2000	0.0111
2001	0.0008	0.0011	0.0009	0.0009	0.0016	0.0007	0.0009	0.0015	0.0010	0.0010	0.0015	0.0012	2001	0.0118
2002	0.0010	0.0015	0.0009	0.0008	0.0017	0.0012	0.0010	0.0017	0.0013	0.0016	0.0018	0.0016	2002	0.0139
2003	0.0012	0.0020	0.0014	0.0013	0.0018	0.0014	0.0014	0.0016	0.0013	0.0016	0.0017	0.0017	2003	0.0199
2004	0.0011	0.0017	0.0013	0.0011	0.0016	0.0015	0.0012	0.0018	0.0015	0.0013	0.0019	0.0016	2004	0.0176
2005	0.0009	0.0021	0.0014	0.0011	0.0019	0.0016	0.0012	0.0021	0.0012	0.0011	0.0026	0.0013	2005	0.0184
2006	0.0010	0.0023	0.0014	0.0012	0.0021	0.0013	0.0011	0.0025	0.0012	0.0011	0.0025	0.0014	2006	0.0201
2007	0.0011	0.0023	0.0012	0.0010	0.0023	0.0012	0.0010	0.0021	0.0016	0.0011	0.0022	0.0017	2007	0.0196
2008	0.0012	0.0023	0.0016	0.0012	0.0023	0.0017	0.0015	0.0023	0.0017	0.0015	0.0031	0.0028	2008	0.0192
2009	0.0014	0.0035	0.0022	0.0018	0.0028	0.0018	0.0015	0.0025	0.0016	0.0012	0.0026	0.0015	2009	0.0248
2010	0.0010	0.0025	0.0016	0.0010	0.0021	0.0015	0.0013	0.0023	0.0017	0.0012	0.0024	0.0015	2010	0.0202
2011	0.0011	0.0023	0.0015	0.0011	0.0022	0.0016	0.0011	0.0025	0.0015	0.0016	0.0028	0.0017	2011	0.0213
2012	0.0012	0.0027	0.0016	0.0012	0.0026	0.0016	0.0013	0.0028	0.0016	0.0013	0.0030	0.0020	2012	0.0250
2013	0.0014	0.0025	0.0015	0.0012	0.0026	0.0016	0.0014	0.0023	0.0016	0.0014	0.0024	0.0018	2013	0.0248
2014	0.0010	0.0026	0.0015	0.0012	0.0024	0.0016	0.0013	0.0023	0.0015	0.0012	0.0024	0.0017	2014	0.0216
2015	0.0010	0.0026	0.0016	0.0011	0.0024	0.0017	0.0012	0.0022	0.0017	0.0014	0.0025	0.0018	2015	0.0210

*Compound annual return

Appendix A-3

Large-Capitalization Stocks: Capital Appreciation Returns
From 1926 to 2015

Year	Jan	Feb	Mar	Apr	May	Jun	Jul	Aug	Sep	Oct	Nov	Dec	Year	Jan–Dec*
1926	-0.0016	-0.0440	-0.0591	0.0227	0.0077	0.0432	0.0455	0.0171	0.0229	-0.0313	0.0223	0.0166	1926	0.0572
1927	-0.0208	0.0477	0.0065	0.0172	0.0522	-0.0094	0.0650	0.0445	0.0432	-0.0531	0.0616	0.0250	1927	0.3091
1928	-0.0051	-0.0176	0.1083	0.0324	0.0127	-0.0405	0.0125	0.0741	0.0240	0.0145	0.1199	0.0029	1928	0.3788
1929	0.0571	-0.0058	-0.0023	0.0161	-0.0428	0.1124	0.0456	0.0980	-0.0489	-0.1993	-0.1337	0.0253	1929	-0.1191
1930	0.0625	0.0215	0.0799	-0.0095	-0.0165	-0.1646	0.0367	0.0075	-0.1301	-0.0888	-0.0218	-0.0742	1930	-0.2848
1931	0.0489	0.1144	-0.0692	-0.0959	-0.1372	0.1390	-0.0742	0.0095	-0.2994	0.0844	-0.0978	-0.1453	1931	-0.4707
1932	-0.0283	0.0507	-0.1182	-0.2025	-0.2333	-0.0089	0.3770	0.3754	-0.0369	-0.1386	-0.0589	0.0519	1932	-0.1515
1933	0.0073	-0.1844	0.0336	0.4222	0.1587	0.1317	-0.0880	0.1146	-0.1136	-0.0885	0.1027	0.0223	1933	0.4659
1934	0.1059	-0.0367	-0.0009	-0.0270	-0.0813	0.0208	-0.1152	0.0541	-0.0055	-0.0319	0.0829	-0.0042	1934	-0.0594
1935	-0.0421	-0.0396	-0.0309	0.0956	0.0323	0.0678	0.0831	0.0217	0.0239	0.0751	0.0393	0.0371	1935	0.4137
1936	0.0655	0.0168	0.0254	-0.0771	0.0458	0.0306	0.0681	0.0088	0.0013	0.0750	0.0041	-0.0058	1936	0.2792
1937	0.0378	0.0146	-0.0094	-0.0831	-0.0103	-0.0529	0.1026	-0.0554	-0.1421	-0.1017	-0.1011	-0.0504	1937	-0.3859
1938	0.0133	0.0608	-0.2504	0.1412	-0.0443	0.2470	0.0727	-0.0274	0.0149	0.0760	-0.0334	0.0377	1938	0.2521
1939	-0.0689	0.0325	-0.1354	-0.0055	0.0623	-0.0638	0.1087	-0.0714	0.1646	-0.0146	-0.0491	0.0238	1939	-0.0545
1940	-0.0352	0.0066	0.0099	-0.0049	-0.2395	0.0766	0.0311	0.0262	0.0095	0.0394	-0.0424	-0.0028	1940	-0.1529
1941	-0.0482	-0.0149	0.0040	-0.0653	0.0043	0.0535	0.0548	-0.0087	-0.0097	-0.0686	-0.0421	-0.0451	1941	-0.1786
1942	0.0138	-0.0250	-0.0675	-0.0437	0.0640	0.0184	0.0313	0.0070	0.0267	0.0644	-0.0138	0.0517	1942	0.1243
1943	0.0716	0.0506	0.0527	0.0009	0.0449	0.0198	-0.0543	0.0103	0.0237	-0.0132	-0.0755	0.0590	1943	0.1945
1944	0.0154	-0.0025	0.0169	-0.0125	0.0404	0.0510	-0.0208	0.0087	-0.0031	0.0000	0.0039	0.0351	1944	0.1380
1945	0.0143	0.0616	-0.0462	0.0880	0.0115	-0.0033	-0.0201	0.0580	0.0419	0.0303	0.0324	0.0099	1945	0.3072
1946	0.0697	-0.0695	0.0463	0.0376	0.0224	-0.0391	-0.0255	-0.0729	-0.1015	-0.0080	-0.0115	0.0429	1946	-0.1187
1947	0.0235	-0.0147	-0.0169	-0.0389	-0.0089	0.0526	0.0362	-0.0279	-0.0137	0.0212	-0.0285	0.0207	1947	0.0000
1948	-0.0399	-0.0470	0.0771	0.0265	0.0782	0.0030	-0.0532	0.0076	-0.0301	0.0678	-0.1082	0.0305	1948	-0.0065
1949	0.0013	-0.0394	0.0301	-0.0212	-0.0373	-0.0021	0.0621	0.0120	0.0237	0.0295	0.0012	0.0436	1949	0.1026
1950	0.0173	0.0100	0.0041	0.0451	0.0393	-0.0580	0.0085	0.0325	0.0559	0.0041	-0.0010	0.0461	1950	0.2178
1951	0.0612	0.0065	-0.0183	0.0481	-0.0406	-0.0260	0.0687	0.0393	-0.0009	-0.0138	-0.0026	0.0389	1951	0.1646
1952	0.0156	-0.0365	0.0477	-0.0431	0.0232	0.0461	0.0176	-0.0146	-0.0196	-0.0008	0.0465	0.0355	1952	0.1178
1953	-0.0072	-0.0182	-0.0236	-0.0265	-0.0032	-0.0163	0.0253	-0.0578	0.0013	0.0510	0.0090	0.0020	1953	-0.0662
1954	0.0512	0.0027	0.0302	0.0490	0.0329	0.0007	0.0572	-0.0340	0.0831	-0.0195	0.0808	0.0508	1954	0.4502
1955	0.0181	0.0035	-0.0049	0.0377	-0.0013	0.0823	0.0607	-0.0078	0.0113	-0.0305	0.0749	-0.0007	1955	0.2640

*Compound annual return

Appendix A-3

Large-Capitalization Stocks: Capital Appreciation Returns
From 1926 to 2015

Year	Jan	Feb	Mar	Apr	May	Jun	Jul	Aug	Sep	Oct	Nov	Dec	Year	Jan–Dec*
1956	-0.0365	0.0347	0.0693	-0.0021	-0.0657	0.0392	0.0515	-0.0381	-0.0455	0.0051	-0.0110	0.0353	1956	0.0262
1957	-0.0418	-0.0326	0.0196	0.0370	0.0369	-0.0013	0.0114	-0.0561	-0.0619	-0.0321	0.0161	-0.0415	1957	-0.1431
1958	0.0428	-0.0206	0.0309	0.0318	0.0150	0.0261	0.0431	0.0119	0.0484	0.0254	0.0224	0.0520	1958	0.3806
1959	0.0038	-0.0002	0.0005	0.0388	0.0189	-0.0036	0.0349	-0.0150	-0.0456	0.0113	0.0132	0.0276	1959	0.0848
1960	-0.0715	0.0092	-0.0139	-0.0175	0.0269	0.0195	-0.0248	0.0261	-0.0604	-0.0024	0.0403	0.0463	1960	-0.0297
1961	0.0632	0.0269	0.0255	0.0038	0.0191	-0.0288	0.0328	0.0196	-0.0197	0.0283	0.0393	0.0032	1961	0.2313
1962	-0.0379	0.0163	-0.0059	-0.0620	-0.0860	-0.0818	0.0636	0.0153	-0.0482	0.0044	0.1016	0.0135	1962	-0.1181
1963	0.0491	-0.0289	0.0355	0.0485	0.0143	-0.0202	-0.0035	0.0487	-0.0110	0.0322	-0.0105	0.0244	1963	0.1889
1964	0.0269	0.0099	0.0152	0.0061	0.0115	0.0164	0.0182	-0.0162	0.0287	0.0081	-0.0052	0.0039	1964	0.1297
1965	0.0332	-0.0015	-0.0145	0.0342	-0.0077	-0.0486	0.0134	0.0225	0.0320	0.0273	-0.0088	0.0090	1965	0.0906
1966	0.0049	-0.0179	-0.0218	0.0205	-0.0541	-0.0161	-0.0135	-0.0778	-0.0070	0.0475	0.0031	-0.0015	1966	-0.1309
1967	0.0782	0.0020	0.0394	0.0422	-0.0524	0.0175	0.0453	-0.0117	0.0328	-0.0291	0.0011	0.0263	1967	0.2009
1968	-0.0438	-0.0312	0.0094	0.0819	0.0112	0.0091	-0.0185	0.0115	0.0385	0.0072	0.0480	-0.0416	1968	0.0766
1969	-0.0082	-0.0474	0.0344	0.0215	-0.0022	-0.0556	-0.0602	0.0401	-0.0250	0.0442	-0.0353	-0.0187	1969	-0.1136
1970	-0.0765	0.0527	0.0015	-0.0905	-0.0610	-0.0500	0.0733	0.0445	0.0330	-0.0114	0.0474	0.0568	1970	0.0010
1971	0.0400	0.0095	0.0368	0.0354	-0.0407	0.0007	-0.0411	0.0359	-0.0070	-0.0432	-0.0011	0.0847	1971	0.1063
1972	0.0195	0.0253	0.0059	0.0044	0.0156	-0.0202	0.0023	0.0345	-0.0049	0.0093	0.0456	0.0118	1972	0.1579
1973	-0.0171	-0.0375	-0.0014	-0.0408	-0.0189	-0.0066	0.0380	-0.0367	0.0401	-0.0013	-0.1139	0.0166	1973	-0.1737
1974	-0.0100	-0.0036	-0.0233	-0.0391	-0.0336	-0.0147	-0.0778	-0.0903	-0.1193	0.1630	-0.0532	-0.0202	1974	-0.2972
1975	0.1228	0.0599	0.0217	0.0473	0.0441	0.0443	-0.0677	-0.0211	-0.0346	0.0616	0.0247	-0.0115	1975	0.3155
1976	0.1183	-0.0114	0.0307	-0.0110	-0.0144	0.0409	-0.0081	-0.0051	0.0226	-0.0222	-0.0078	0.0525	1976	0.1915
1977	-0.0505	-0.0217	-0.0140	0.0002	-0.0236	0.0454	-0.0162	-0.0210	-0.0025	-0.0434	0.0270	0.0028	1977	-0.1150
1978	-0.0615	-0.0248	0.0249	0.0854	0.0048	-0.0181	0.0539	0.0259	-0.0073	-0.0916	0.0166	0.0149	1978	0.0106
1979	0.0397	-0.0365	0.0552	0.0017	-0.0263	0.0387	0.0087	0.0531	0.0000	-0.0686	0.0426	0.0168	1979	0.1231
1980	0.0576	-0.0044	-0.1018	0.0411	0.0466	0.0270	0.0650	0.0058	0.0252	0.0160	0.1024	-0.0339	1980	0.2577
1981	-0.0457	0.0133	0.0360	-0.0235	-0.0017	-0.0104	-0.0022	-0.0621	-0.0538	0.0491	0.0366	-0.0301	1981	-0.0973
1982	-0.0175	-0.0606	-0.0101	0.0397	-0.0388	-0.0204	-0.0229	0.1160	0.0076	0.1104	0.0361	0.0152	1982	0.1476
1983	0.0331	0.0190	0.0331	0.0748	-0.0122	0.0352	-0.0330	0.0113	0.0097	-0.0148	0.0174	-0.0088	1983	0.1727
1984	-0.0092	-0.0389	0.0135	0.0055	-0.0594	0.0175	-0.0165	0.1063	-0.0035	-0.0001	-0.0151	0.0224	1984	0.0140
1985	0.0741	0.0086	-0.0029	-0.0046	0.0541	0.0121	-0.0048	-0.0120	-0.0348	0.0426	0.0651	0.0451	1985	0.2633

*Compound annual return

Appendix A-3

Large-Capitalization Stocks: Capital Appreciation Returns
From 1926 to 2015

Year	Jan	Feb	Mar	Apr	May	Jun	Jul	Aug	Sep	Oct	Nov	Dec	Year	Jan–Dec*
1986	0.0024	0.0715	0.0528	-0.0141	0.0502	0.0141	-0.0587	0.0712	-0.0854	0.0546	0.0216	-0.0283	1986	0.1462
1987	0.1318	0.0369	0.0264	-0.0115	0.0060	0.0479	0.0482	0.0350	-0.0242	-0.2176	-0.0853	0.0729	1987	0.0203
1988	0.0404	0.0418	-0.0333	0.0094	0.0032	0.0433	-0.0054	-0.0386	0.0397	0.0260	-0.0189	0.0147	1988	0.1240
1989	0.0711	-0.0289	0.0208	0.0501	0.0351	-0.0079	0.0884	0.0155	-0.0065	-0.0252	0.0165	0.0214	1989	0.2725
1990	-0.0688	0.0085	0.0243	-0.0269	0.0920	-0.0089	-0.0052	-0.0943	-0.0512	-0.0067	0.0599	0.0248	1990	-0.0656
1991	0.0415	0.0673	0.0222	0.0003	0.0386	-0.0479	0.0449	0.0196	-0.0191	0.0118	-0.0439	0.1116	1991	0.2631
1992	-0.0199	0.0096	-0.0218	0.0279	0.0010	-0.0174	0.0394	-0.0240	0.0091	0.0021	0.0303	0.0101	1992	0.0446
1993	0.0070	0.0105	0.0187	-0.0254	0.0227	0.0008	-0.0053	0.0344	-0.0100	0.0194	-0.0129	0.0101	1993	0.0706
1994	0.0325	-0.0300	-0.0457	0.0115	0.0124	-0.0268	0.0315	0.0376	-0.0269	0.0209	-0.0395	0.0123	1994	-0.0154
1995	0.0243	0.0361	0.0273	0.0280	0.0363	0.0213	0.0318	-0.0003	0.0401	-0.0050	0.0410	0.0174	1995	0.3411
1996	0.0326	0.0069	0.0079	0.0134	0.0229	0.0023	-0.0457	0.0188	0.0542	0.0261	0.0734	-0.0215	1996	0.2026
1997	0.0613	0.0059	-0.0426	0.0584	0.0586	0.0435	0.0781	-0.0574	0.0532	-0.0345	0.0446	0.0157	1997	0.3101
1998	0.0102	0.0704	0.0499	0.0091	-0.0188	0.0394	-0.0116	-0.1458	0.0624	0.0803	0.0591	0.0564	1998	0.2667
1999	0.0410	-0.0323	0.0388	0.0379	-0.0250	0.0544	-0.0320	-0.0063	-0.0286	0.0625	0.0191	0.0578	1999	0.1953
2000	-0.0509	-0.0201	0.0967	-0.0308	-0.0219	0.0239	-0.0163	0.0607	-0.0535	-0.0049	-0.0801	0.0041	2000	-0.1014
2001	0.0346	-0.0923	-0.0642	0.0768	0.0051	-0.0250	-0.0108	-0.0641	-0.0817	0.0181	0.0752	0.0076	2001	-0.1304
2002	-0.0156	-0.0208	0.0367	-0.0614	-0.0091	-0.0725	-0.0790	0.0049	-0.1100	0.0864	0.0571	-0.0603	2002	-0.2337
2003	-0.0274	-0.0170	0.0084	0.0810	0.0509	0.0113	0.0162	0.0179	-0.0119	0.0550	0.0071	0.0508	2003	0.2638
2004	0.0173	0.0122	-0.0164	-0.0168	0.0121	0.0180	-0.0343	0.0023	0.0094	0.0140	0.0386	0.0325	2004	0.0899
2005	-0.0253	0.0189	-0.0191	-0.0201	0.0300	-0.0001	0.0360	-0.0112	0.0069	-0.0177	0.0352	-0.0009	2005	0.0300
2006	0.0255	0.0005	0.0111	0.0122	-0.0309	0.0001	0.0051	0.0213	0.0246	0.0315	0.0165	0.0126	2006	0.1362
2007	0.0141	-0.0218	0.0100	0.0433	0.0326	-0.0178	-0.0320	0.0129	0.0358	0.0148	-0.0440	-0.0086	2007	0.0353
2008	-0.0612	-0.0348	-0.0060	0.0475	0.0107	-0.0860	-0.0099	0.0122	-0.0908	-0.1694	-0.0749	0.0078	2008	-0.3849
2009	-0.0857	-0.1099	0.0854	0.0939	0.0531	0.0002	0.0741	0.0336	0.0357	-0.0198	0.0574	0.0178	2009	0.2345
2010	-0.0370	0.0285	0.0588	0.0148	-0.0820	-0.0539	0.0688	-0.0475	0.0876	0.0369	-0.0023	0.0653	2010	0.1278
2011	0.0226	0.0320	-0.0011	0.0285	-0.0135	-0.0183	-0.0215	-0.0568	-0.0718	0.1077	-0.0051	0.0085	2011	0.0000
2012	0.0436	0.0406	0.0313	-0.0075	-0.0627	0.0396	0.0126	0.0198	0.0242	-0.0198	0.0028	0.0071	2012	0.1341
2013	0.0504	0.0111	0.0360	0.0181	0.0208	-0.0150	0.0495	-0.0313	0.0297	0.0446	0.0280	0.0236	2013	0.2960
2014	-0.0356	0.0431	0.0069	0.0062	0.0210	0.0191	-0.0151	0.0377	-0.0155	0.0232	0.0245	-0.0042	2014	0.1139
2015	-0.0310	0.0549	-0.0174	0.0085	0.0105	-0.0210	0.0197	-0.0626	-0.0264	0.0830	0.0005	-0.0175	2015	-0.0073

*Compound annual return

Appendix A-4

Small-Capitalization Stocks: Total Returns
From 1926 to 2015

Year	Jan	Feb	Mar	Apr	May	Jun	Jul	Aug	Sep	Oct	Nov	Dec	Year	Jan–Dec*
1926	0.0699	-0.0639	-0.1073	0.0179	-0.0066	0.0378	0.0112	0.0256	-0.0001	-0.0227	0.0207	0.0332	1926	0.0028
1927	0.0296	0.0547	-0.0548	0.0573	0.0734	-0.0303	0.0516	-0.0178	0.0047	-0.0659	0.0808	0.0316	1927	0.2210
1928	0.0482	-0.0236	0.0531	0.0910	0.0438	-0.0842	0.0059	0.0442	0.0890	0.0276	0.1147	-0.0513	1928	0.3969
1929	0.0035	-0.0026	-0.0200	0.0306	-0.1336	0.0533	0.0114	-0.0164	-0.0922	-0.2768	-0.1500	-0.0501	1929	-0.5136
1930	0.1293	0.0643	0.1007	-0.0698	-0.0542	-0.2168	0.0301	-0.0166	-0.1459	-0.1097	-0.0028	-0.1166	1930	-0.3815
1931	0.2103	0.2566	-0.0708	-0.2164	-0.1379	0.1819	-0.0557	-0.0763	-0.3246	0.0770	-0.1008	-0.2195	1931	-0.4975
1932	0.1019	0.0291	-0.1311	-0.2220	-0.1193	0.0033	0.3523	0.7346	-0.1320	-0.1775	-0.1227	-0.0492	1932	-0.0539
1933	-0.0083	-0.1278	0.1118	0.5038	0.6339	0.2617	-0.0550	0.0924	-0.1595	-0.1236	0.0654	0.0055	1933	1.4287
1934	0.3891	0.0166	-0.0012	0.0240	-0.1275	-0.0024	-0.2259	0.1546	-0.0167	0.0097	0.0948	0.0172	1934	0.2422
1935	-0.0328	-0.0592	-0.1189	0.0791	-0.0024	0.0305	0.0855	0.0545	0.0357	0.0994	0.1412	0.0598	1935	0.4019
1936	0.3009	0.0602	0.0066	-0.1795	0.0272	-0.0231	0.0873	0.0210	0.0542	0.0635	0.1400	0.0160	1936	0.6480
1937	0.1267	0.0658	0.0120	-0.1679	-0.0408	-0.1183	0.1235	-0.0736	-0.2539	-0.1093	-0.1453	-0.1694	1937	-0.5801
1938	0.0534	0.0343	-0.3600	0.2776	-0.0849	0.3498	0.1499	-0.1001	-0.0157	0.2136	-0.0689	0.0487	1938	0.3280
1939	-0.0848	0.0107	-0.2466	0.0142	0.1088	-0.1042	0.2535	-0.1590	0.5145	-0.0397	-0.1053	0.0422	1939	0.0035
1940	0.0009	0.0821	0.0632	0.0654	-0.3674	0.1051	0.0231	0.0255	0.0213	0.0545	0.0245	-0.0447	1940	-0.0516
1941	0.0025	-0.0288	0.0319	-0.0669	0.0045	0.0753	0.2165	-0.0060	-0.0469	-0.0672	-0.0495	-0.1204	1941	-0.0900
1942	0.1894	-0.0073	-0.0709	-0.0353	-0.0032	0.0336	0.0737	0.0325	0.0912	0.1087	-0.0511	0.0413	1942	0.4451
1943	0.2132	0.1931	0.1445	0.0933	0.1156	-0.0083	-0.1083	-0.0002	0.0428	0.0123	-0.1113	0.1241	1943	0.8837
1944	0.0641	0.0295	0.0749	-0.0532	0.0740	0.1384	-0.0299	0.0318	-0.0020	-0.0108	0.0499	0.0869	1944	0.5372
1945	0.0482	0.1009	-0.0861	0.1157	0.0500	0.0855	-0.0556	0.0557	0.0679	0.0701	0.1172	0.0171	1945	0.7361
1946	0.1562	-0.0637	0.0273	0.0696	0.0591	-0.0462	-0.0530	-0.0849	-0.1603	-0.0118	-0.0141	0.0373	1946	-0.1163
1947	0.0421	-0.0041	-0.0336	-0.1031	-0.0534	0.0552	0.0789	-0.0037	0.0115	0.0282	-0.0303	0.0359	1947	0.0092
1948	-0.0154	-0.0783	0.0986	0.0368	0.1059	0.0048	-0.0578	0.0006	-0.0526	0.0647	-0.1116	0.0088	1948	-0.0211
1949	0.0182	-0.0481	0.0629	-0.0336	-0.0564	-0.0096	0.0671	0.0256	0.0489	0.0472	0.0016	0.0690	1949	0.1975
1950	0.0492	0.0221	-0.0037	0.0411	0.0255	-0.0777	0.0591	0.0530	0.0521	-0.0059	0.0322	0.0953	1950	0.3875
1951	0.0830	0.0061	-0.0477	0.0367	-0.0331	-0.0529	0.0373	0.0605	0.0215	-0.0222	-0.0083	0.0044	1951	0.0780
1952	0.0191	-0.0300	0.0175	-0.0519	0.0032	0.0272	0.0112	-0.0006	-0.0161	-0.0103	0.0485	0.0160	1952	0.0303
1953	0.0409	0.0269	-0.0067	-0.0287	0.0141	-0.0486	0.0152	-0.0628	-0.0262	0.0292	0.0126	-0.0266	1953	-0.0649
1954	0.0756	0.0094	0.0183	0.0140	0.0451	0.0086	0.0808	0.0014	0.0410	0.0068	0.0779	0.1112	1954	0.6058
1955	0.0201	0.0479	0.0085	0.0150	0.0078	0.0293	0.0064	-0.0028	0.0109	-0.0170	0.0468	0.0163	1955	0.2044

*Compound annual return

Appendix A-4

Small-Capitalization Stocks: Total Returns
From 1926 to 2015

Year	Jan	Feb	Mar	Apr	May	Jun	Jul	Aug	Sep	Oct	Nov	Dec	Year	Jan–Dec*
1956	-0.0047	0.0278	0.0431	0.0047	-0.0398	0.0056	0.0283	-0.0134	-0.0260	0.0104	0.0053	0.0038	1956	0.0428
1957	0.0236	-0.0200	0.0167	0.0248	0.0075	0.0073	-0.0060	-0.0386	-0.0452	-0.0832	0.0113	-0.0481	1957	-0.1457
1958	0.1105	-0.0170	0.0471	0.0376	0.0387	0.0324	0.0492	0.0428	0.0518	0.0407	0.0496	0.0313	1958	0.6489
1959	0.0575	0.0295	0.0027	0.0117	0.0014	-0.0042	0.0327	-0.0088	-0.0431	0.0227	0.0222	0.0322	1959	0.1640
1960	-0.0306	0.0050	-0.0315	-0.0187	0.0205	0.0340	-0.0189	0.0525	-0.0738	-0.0401	0.0437	0.0332	1960	-0.0329
1961	0.0915	0.0589	0.0619	0.0127	0.0427	-0.0543	0.0031	0.0130	-0.0339	0.0262	0.0613	0.0079	1961	0.3209
1962	0.0136	0.0187	0.0057	-0.0777	-0.1009	-0.0785	0.0763	0.0289	-0.0659	-0.0373	0.1248	-0.0089	1962	-0.1190
1963	0.0906	0.0034	0.0149	0.0312	0.0436	-0.0118	0.0033	0.0517	-0.0163	0.0236	-0.0106	-0.0048	1963	0.2357
1964	0.0274	0.0365	0.0219	0.0093	0.0157	0.0163	0.0398	-0.0029	0.0402	0.0205	0.0011	-0.0112	1964	0.2352
1965	0.0529	0.0390	0.0238	0.0509	-0.0078	-0.0901	0.0449	0.0595	0.0347	0.0572	0.0371	0.0622	1965	0.4175
1966	0.0756	0.0311	-0.0192	0.0343	-0.0961	-0.0012	-0.0012	-0.1080	-0.0164	-0.0107	0.0491	0.0065	1966	-0.0701
1967	0.1838	0.0450	0.0615	0.0271	-0.0085	0.1017	0.0951	0.0020	0.0565	-0.0311	0.0117	0.0965	1967	0.8357
1968	0.0154	-0.0709	-0.0109	0.1461	0.0999	0.0030	-0.0345	0.0367	0.0599	0.0030	0.0764	0.0062	1968	0.3597
1969	-0.0166	-0.0990	0.0396	0.0395	0.0173	-0.1165	-0.1070	0.0732	-0.0261	0.0610	-0.0557	-0.0687	1969	-0.2505
1970	-0.0608	0.0387	-0.0285	-0.1728	-0.1031	-0.0929	0.0554	0.0949	0.1086	-0.0706	0.0137	0.0726	1970	-0.1743
1971	0.1592	0.0317	0.0564	0.0247	-0.0605	-0.0319	-0.0563	0.0583	-0.0226	-0.0551	-0.0373	0.1144	1971	0.1650
1972	0.1130	0.0296	-0.0143	0.0129	-0.0191	-0.0305	-0.0413	0.0186	-0.0349	-0.0175	0.0592	-0.0214	1972	0.0443
1973	-0.0432	-0.0799	-0.0208	-0.0621	-0.0811	-0.0290	0.1194	-0.0445	0.1064	0.0084	-0.1962	-0.0014	1973	-0.3090
1974	0.1326	-0.0085	-0.0074	-0.0464	-0.0793	-0.0147	-0.0219	-0.0681	-0.0653	0.1063	-0.0438	-0.0788	1974	-0.1995
1975	0.2767	0.0285	0.0618	0.0531	0.0663	0.0750	-0.0254	-0.0574	-0.0182	-0.0050	0.0320	-0.0197	1975	0.5282
1976	0.2684	0.1390	-0.0015	-0.0359	-0.0361	0.0459	0.0045	-0.0290	0.0104	-0.0209	0.0404	0.1180	1976	0.5738
1977	0.0450	-0.0039	0.0131	0.0228	-0.0028	0.0772	0.0030	-0.0107	0.0092	-0.0330	0.1086	0.0081	1977	0.2538
1978	-0.0189	0.0347	0.1032	0.0788	0.0820	-0.0189	0.0684	0.0939	-0.0032	-0.2427	0.0732	0.0168	1978	0.2346
1979	0.1321	-0.0282	0.1120	0.0387	0.0035	0.0472	0.0171	0.0756	-0.0344	-0.1154	0.0858	0.0588	1979	0.4346
1980	0.0836	-0.0284	-0.1778	0.0694	0.0750	0.0452	0.1323	0.0604	0.0418	0.0333	0.0766	-0.0338	1980	0.3988
1981	0.0207	0.0094	0.0943	0.0657	0.0422	0.0076	-0.0316	-0.0684	-0.0733	0.0742	0.0276	-0.0220	1981	0.1388
1982	-0.0196	-0.0296	-0.0086	0.0383	-0.0248	-0.0159	-0.0015	0.0698	0.0327	0.1305	0.0779	0.0132	1982	0.2801
1983	0.0628	0.0712	0.0525	0.0767	0.0870	0.0348	-0.0088	-0.0197	0.0133	-0.0568	0.0516	-0.0145	1983	0.3967
1984	-0.0008	-0.0645	0.0174	-0.0085	-0.0521	0.0300	-0.0420	0.0998	0.0027	-0.0217	-0.0336	0.0150	1984	-0.0667
1985	0.1059	0.0272	-0.0214	-0.0174	0.0276	0.0106	0.0260	-0.0072	-0.0544	0.0261	0.0620	0.0470	1985	0.2466

*Compound annual return

Appendix A-4

Small-Capitalization Stocks: Total Returns
From 1926 to 2015

Year	Jan	Feb	Mar	Apr	May	Jun	Jul	Aug	Sep	Oct	Nov	Dec	Year	Jan–Dec*
1986	0.0112	0.0719	0.0477	0.0064	0.0360	0.0026	-0.0710	0.0218	-0.0559	0.0346	-0.0031	-0.0262	1986	0.0685
1987	0.0943	0.0809	0.0233	-0.0313	-0.0039	0.0266	0.0364	0.0287	-0.0081	-0.2919	-0.0397	0.0520	1987	-0.0930
1988	0.0556	0.0760	0.0408	0.0209	-0.0179	0.0612	-0.0025	-0.0246	0.0227	-0.0123	-0.0437	0.0394	1988	0.2287
1989	0.0404	0.0083	0.0358	0.0279	0.0362	-0.0201	0.0407	0.0122	0.0000	-0.0604	-0.0051	-0.0134	1989	0.1018
1990	-0.0764	0.0187	0.0368	-0.0266	0.0561	0.0144	-0.0382	-0.1296	-0.0829	-0.0572	0.0450	0.0194	1990	-0.2156
1991	0.0841	0.1113	0.0680	0.0034	0.0334	-0.0485	0.0407	0.0261	0.0032	0.0317	-0.0276	0.0601	1991	0.4463
1992	0.1128	0.0452	-0.0249	-0.0403	-0.0014	-0.0519	0.0370	-0.0228	0.0131	0.0259	0.0885	0.0441	1992	0.2335
1993	0.0543	-0.0180	0.0289	-0.0306	0.0342	-0.0038	0.0166	0.0339	0.0316	0.0471	-0.0175	0.0194	1993	0.2098
1994	0.0618	-0.0023	-0.0446	0.0060	-0.0012	-0.0262	0.0184	0.0337	0.0105	0.0115	-0.0326	0.0002	1994	0.0311
1995	0.0283	0.0252	0.0145	0.0352	0.0298	0.0568	0.0645	0.0358	0.0195	-0.0487	0.0192	0.0239	1995	0.3446
1996	0.0028	0.0369	0.0228	0.0848	0.0749	-0.0582	-0.0943	0.0476	0.0291	-0.0175	0.0288	0.0204	1996	0.1762
1997	0.0420	-0.0206	-0.0490	-0.0276	0.1022	0.0498	0.0605	0.0509	0.0844	-0.0386	-0.0155	-0.0171	1997	0.2278
1998	-0.0059	0.0649	0.0481	0.0168	-0.0497	-0.0206	-0.0671	-0.2010	0.0369	0.0356	0.0758	0.0252	1998	-0.0731
1999	0.0279	-0.0687	-0.0379	0.0949	0.0387	0.1368	0.0092	-0.0191	-0.0221	-0.0087	0.0971	0.1137	1999	0.2979
2000	0.0595	0.2358	-0.0751	-0.1251	-0.0808	0.0359	-0.0322	0.0925	-0.0217	-0.0706	-0.1110	0.0189	2000	-0.0359
2001	0.1380	-0.0702	-0.0480	0.0731	0.0960	0.0359	-0.0254	-0.0295	-0.1278	0.0645	0.0674	0.0672	2001	0.2277
2002	0.0110	-0.0277	0.0884	0.0243	-0.0273	-0.0356	-0.1448	-0.0057	-0.0674	0.0257	0.0836	-0.0429	2002	-0.1328
2003	-0.0223	-0.0288	0.0111	0.0928	0.1162	0.0440	0.0738	0.0473	0.0009	0.0894	0.0430	0.0277	2003	0.6070
2004	0.0578	0.0050	0.0014	-0.0409	0.0000	0.0441	-0.0747	-0.0152	0.0501	0.0184	0.0897	0.0458	2004	0.1839
2005	-0.0410	0.0083	-0.0323	-0.0622	0.0603	0.0452	0.0763	-0.0139	0.0061	-0.0281	0.0453	0.0018	2005	0.0569
2006	0.0914	0.0025	0.0455	-0.0041	-0.0589	-0.0089	-0.0345	0.0278	0.0056	0.0545	0.0225	0.0161	2006	0.1617
2007	0.0115	-0.0050	0.0102	0.0150	0.0315	-0.0033	-0.0651	0.0116	0.0148	0.0170	-0.0842	-0.0006	2007	-0.0522
2008	-0.0765	-0.0314	0.0031	0.0207	0.0398	-0.0905	0.0448	0.0338	-0.0737	-0.2071	-0.1284	0.0566	2008	-0.3672
2009	-0.1191	-0.1311	0.0958	0.1739	0.0343	0.0276	0.0982	0.0273	0.0576	-0.0727	0.0178	0.0869	2009	0.2809
2010	-0.0294	0.0439	0.0808	0.0727	-0.0742	-0.0724	0.0714	-0.0798	0.1216	0.0434	0.0424	0.0819	2010	0.3126
2011	-0.0109	0.0587	0.0325	0.0168	-0.0192	-0.0216	-0.0269	-0.0893	-0.1058	0.1543	-0.0060	0.0086	2011	-0.0326
2012	0.0696	0.0191	0.0298	-0.0142	-0.0697	0.0512	-0.0091	0.0312	0.0419	-0.0205	0.0094	0.0380	2012	0.1824
2013	0.0568	0.0110	0.0487	-0.0079	0.0518	0.0046	0.0741	-0.0348	0.0705	0.0348	0.0555	0.0189	2013	0.4507
2014	-0.0443	0.0421	0.0097	-0.0341	0.0010	0.0434	-0.0584	0.0454	-0.0569	0.0652	-0.0075	0.0337	2014	0.0292
2015	-0.0490	0.0603	0.0229	-0.0195	0.0138	0.0163	-0.0244	-0.0443	-0.0431	0.0603	0.0284	-0.0490	2015	-0.0360

*Compound annual return

Appendix A-5

Long-term Corporate Bonds: Total Returns
From 1926 to 2015

Year	Jan	Feb	Mar	Apr	May	Jun	Jul	Aug	Sep	Oct	Nov	Dec	Year	Jan–Dec*
1926	0.0072	0.0045	0.0084	0.0097	0.0044	0.0004	0.0057	0.0044	0.0057	0.0097	0.0057	0.0056	1926	0.0737
1927	0.0056	0.0069	0.0083	0.0055	-0.0011	0.0043	0.0003	0.0083	0.0149	0.0055	0.0068	0.0068	1927	0.0744
1928	0.0027	0.0068	0.0041	0.0014	-0.0078	-0.0024	-0.0010	0.0083	0.0030	0.0083	-0.0036	0.0084	1928	0.0284
1929	0.0043	0.0030	-0.0087	0.0019	0.0045	-0.0046	0.0020	0.0020	0.0034	0.0073	-0.0018	0.0192	1929	0.0327
1930	0.0059	0.0072	0.0138	0.0084	0.0057	0.0110	0.0056	0.0136	0.0108	0.0054	-0.0012	-0.0090	1930	0.0798
1931	0.0203	0.0068	0.0094	0.0067	0.0134	0.0052	0.0052	0.0012	-0.0014	-0.0363	-0.0189	-0.0286	1931	-0.0185
1932	-0.0052	-0.0238	0.0356	-0.0176	0.0107	-0.0009	0.0043	0.0436	0.0301	0.0074	0.0073	0.0139	1932	0.1082
1933	0.0547	-0.0523	0.0047	-0.0095	0.0588	0.0190	0.0161	0.0093	-0.0014	0.0040	-0.0248	0.0257	1933	0.1038
1934	0.0257	0.0146	0.0187	0.0104	0.0090	0.0158	0.0047	0.0047	-0.0061	0.0102	0.0129	0.0101	1934	0.1384
1935	0.0211	0.0141	0.0043	0.0112	0.0042	0.0112	0.0111	-0.0042	0.0000	0.0042	0.0069	0.0083	1935	0.0961
1936	0.0082	0.0054	0.0082	0.0026	0.0040	0.0082	0.0011	0.0067	0.0067	0.0025	0.0109	0.0010	1936	0.0674
1937	0.0024	-0.0046	-0.0114	0.0068	0.0040	0.0053	0.0039	-0.0017	0.0025	0.0067	0.0067	0.0067	1937	0.0275
1938	0.0038	0.0010	-0.0087	0.0138	0.0010	0.0095	0.0066	-0.0019	0.0109	0.0080	0.0037	0.0122	1938	0.0613
1939	0.0022	0.0064	0.0022	0.0064	0.0049	0.0035	-0.0007	-0.0392	0.0151	0.0237	0.0079	0.0078	1939	0.0397
1940	0.0049	0.0021	0.0049	-0.0092	-0.0021	0.0121	0.0021	0.0007	0.0092	0.0049	0.0063	-0.0023	1940	0.0339
1941	0.0006	0.0006	-0.0022	0.0078	0.0049	0.0063	0.0063	0.0034	0.0048	0.0034	-0.0094	0.0006	1941	0.0273
1942	0.0006	-0.0008	0.0063	0.0006	0.0020	0.0034	0.0020	0.0035	0.0020	0.0006	0.0006	0.0049	1942	0.0260
1943	0.0049	0.0006	0.0020	0.0049	0.0048	0.0048	0.0019	0.0019	0.0005	-0.0009	-0.0023	0.0049	1943	0.0283
1944	0.0020	0.0034	0.0048	0.0034	0.0005	0.0020	0.0034	0.0034	0.0019	0.0019	0.0048	0.0149	1944	0.0473
1945	0.0076	0.0046	0.0018	0.0018	-0.0011	0.0032	-0.0011	0.0004	0.0032	0.0032	0.0032	0.0133	1945	0.0408
1946	0.0128	0.0034	0.0034	-0.0043	0.0019	0.0019	-0.0012	-0.0088	-0.0026	0.0020	-0.0025	0.0113	1946	0.0172
1947	0.0005	0.0005	0.0067	0.0020	0.0020	0.0004	0.0020	-0.0071	-0.0131	-0.0099	-0.0098	0.0024	1947	-0.0234
1948	0.0024	0.0039	0.0115	0.0038	0.0008	-0.0083	-0.0052	0.0055	0.0024	0.0024	0.0085	0.0131	1948	0.0414
1949	0.0038	0.0038	0.0007	0.0023	0.0038	0.0084	0.0099	0.0037	0.0021	0.0067	0.0021	-0.0145	1949	0.0331
1950	0.0037	0.0007	0.0022	-0.0008	-0.0008	0.0023	0.0069	0.0038	-0.0039	-0.0008	0.0054	0.0023	1950	0.0212
1951	0.0019	-0.0044	-0.0237	-0.0009	-0.0015	-0.0093	0.0205	0.0114	-0.0057	-0.0145	-0.0061	0.0058	1951	-0.0269
1952	0.0199	-0.0085	0.0076	-0.0004	0.0031	0.0016	0.0016	0.0063	-0.0018	0.0039	0.0108	-0.0091	1952	0.0352
1953	-0.0080	-0.0040	-0.0033	-0.0248	-0.0030	0.0109	0.0177	-0.0085	0.0253	0.0227	-0.0073	0.0172	1953	0.0341
1954	0.0124	0.0198	0.0039	-0.0034	-0.0042	0.0063	0.0040	0.0018	0.0040	0.0040	0.0025	0.0017	1954	0.0539
1955	-0.0097	-0.0063	0.0092	-0.0001	-0.0018	0.0029	-0.0041	-0.0038	0.0076	0.0078	-0.0030	0.0063	1955	0.0048

*Compound annual return

Appendix A-5

Long-term Corporate Bonds: Total Returns
From 1926 to 2015

Year	Jan	Feb	Mar	Apr	May	Jun	Jul	Aug	Sep	Oct	Nov	Dec	Year	Jan–Dec*
1956	0.0104	0.0026	-0.0146	-0.0115	0.0052	-0.0018	-0.0093	-0.0208	0.0012	-0.0105	-0.0126	-0.0082	1956	-0.0681
1957	0.0197	0.0093	0.0050	-0.0066	-0.0075	-0.0322	-0.0110	-0.0009	0.0095	0.0023	0.0311	0.0685	1957	0.0871
1958	0.0099	-0.0008	-0.0046	0.0163	0.0031	-0.0038	-0.0153	-0.0320	-0.0096	0.0107	0.0105	-0.0058	1958	-0.0222
1959	-0.0028	0.0126	-0.0083	-0.0172	-0.0114	0.0044	0.0089	-0.0068	-0.0088	0.0165	0.0135	-0.0096	1959	-0.0097
1960	0.0107	0.0128	0.0191	-0.0022	-0.0021	0.0141	0.0257	0.0117	-0.0063	0.0008	-0.0070	0.0104	1960	0.0907
1961	0.0148	0.0210	-0.0029	-0.0116	0.0049	-0.0080	0.0040	-0.0018	0.0144	0.0127	0.0028	-0.0026	1961	0.0482
1962	0.0080	0.0052	0.0151	0.0142	0.0000	-0.0026	-0.0015	0.0143	0.0089	0.0068	0.0062	0.0023	1962	0.0795
1963	0.0059	0.0023	0.0026	-0.0051	0.0048	0.0043	0.0028	0.0035	-0.0023	0.0049	0.0015	-0.0034	1963	0.0219
1964	0.0087	0.0054	-0.0062	0.0040	0.0057	0.0048	0.0052	0.0037	0.0021	0.0050	-0.0004	0.0088	1964	0.0477
1965	0.0081	0.0009	0.0012	0.0021	-0.0008	0.0003	0.0019	-0.0006	-0.0015	0.0046	-0.0057	-0.0149	1965	-0.0046
1966	0.0022	-0.0113	-0.0059	0.0013	-0.0026	0.0030	-0.0098	-0.0259	0.0078	0.0261	-0.0020	0.0201	1966	0.0020
1967	0.0450	-0.0201	0.0117	-0.0071	-0.0254	-0.0223	0.0041	-0.0007	0.0094	-0.0281	-0.0272	0.0127	1967	-0.0495
1968	0.0361	0.0037	-0.0197	0.0048	0.0032	0.0122	0.0341	0.0206	-0.0053	-0.0160	-0.0226	-0.0233	1968	0.0257
1969	0.0139	-0.0160	-0.0200	0.0335	-0.0227	0.0035	0.0005	-0.0020	-0.0244	0.0127	-0.0471	-0.0134	1969	-0.0809
1970	0.0141	0.0401	-0.0045	-0.0250	-0.0163	0.0001	0.0556	0.0100	0.0139	-0.0096	0.0584	0.0372	1970	0.1837
1971	0.0532	-0.0366	0.0258	-0.0236	-0.0161	0.0107	-0.0025	0.0554	-0.0102	0.0282	0.0029	0.0223	1971	0.1101
1972	-0.0033	0.0107	0.0024	0.0035	0.0163	-0.0068	0.0030	0.0072	0.0031	0.0101	0.0249	-0.0004	1972	0.0726
1973	-0.0054	0.0023	0.0045	0.0061	-0.0039	-0.0056	-0.0476	0.0356	0.0356	-0.0066	0.0078	-0.0089	1973	0.0114
1974	-0.0053	0.0009	-0.0307	-0.0341	0.0105	-0.0285	-0.0211	-0.0268	0.0174	0.0885	0.0117	-0.0075	1974	-0.0306
1975	0.0596	0.0137	-0.0247	-0.0052	0.0106	0.0304	-0.0030	-0.0175	-0.0126	0.0553	-0.0088	0.0442	1975	0.1464
1976	0.0188	0.0061	0.0167	-0.0015	-0.0103	0.0150	0.0149	0.0231	0.0167	0.0070	0.0319	0.0347	1976	0.1865
1977	-0.0303	-0.0020	0.0094	0.0100	0.0106	0.0175	-0.0005	0.0136	-0.0022	-0.0038	0.0061	-0.0105	1977	0.0171
1978	-0.0089	0.0051	0.0042	-0.0023	-0.0108	0.0023	0.0101	0.0257	-0.0048	-0.0205	0.0134	-0.0133	1978	-0.0007
1979	0.0184	-0.0128	0.0107	-0.0052	0.0228	0.0269	-0.0031	0.0006	-0.0179	-0.0890	0.0222	-0.0108	1979	-0.0418
1980	-0.0645	-0.0665	-0.0062	0.1376	0.0560	0.0341	-0.0429	-0.0445	-0.0237	-0.0159	0.0017	0.0248	1980	-0.0276
1981	-0.0130	-0.0269	0.0311	-0.0769	0.0595	0.0023	-0.0372	-0.0345	-0.0199	0.0521	0.1267	-0.0580	1981	-0.0124
1982	-0.0129	0.0312	0.0306	0.0338	0.0245	-0.0468	0.0540	0.0837	0.0623	0.0759	0.0201	0.0108	1982	0.4256
1983	-0.0094	0.0428	0.0072	0.0548	-0.0324	-0.0046	-0.0455	0.0051	0.0392	-0.0025	0.0142	-0.0033	1983	0.0626
1984	0.0270	-0.0172	-0.0235	-0.0073	-0.0483	0.0199	0.0586	0.0307	0.0314	0.0572	0.0212	0.0128	1984	0.1686
1985	0.0325	-0.0373	0.0179	0.0296	0.0820	0.0083	-0.0121	0.0260	0.0071	0.0329	0.0370	0.0469	1985	0.3009

*Compound annual return

Appendix A-5

Long-term Corporate Bonds: Total Returns
From 1926 to 2015

Year	Jan	Feb	Mar	Apr	May	Jun	Jul	Aug	Sep	Oct	Nov	Dec	Year	Jan–Dec*
1986	0.0045	0.0752	0.0256	0.0016	-0.0164	0.0218	0.0031	0.0275	-0.0114	0.0189	0.0233	0.0117	1986	0.1985
1987	0.0216	0.0058	-0.0087	-0.0502	-0.0052	0.0155	-0.0119	-0.0075	-0.0422	0.0507	0.0125	0.0212	1987	-0.0027
1988	0.0517	0.0138	-0.0188	-0.0149	-0.0057	0.0379	-0.0111	0.0054	0.0326	0.0273	-0.0169	0.0039	1988	0.1070
1989	0.0202	-0.0129	0.0064	0.0213	0.0379	0.0395	0.0178	-0.0163	0.0040	0.0276	0.0070	0.0006	1989	0.1623
1990	-0.0191	-0.0012	-0.0011	-0.0191	0.0385	0.0216	0.0102	-0.0292	0.0091	0.0132	0.0285	0.0167	1990	0.0678
1991	0.0150	0.0121	0.0108	0.0138	0.0039	-0.0018	0.0167	0.0275	0.0271	0.0043	0.0106	0.0436	1991	0.1989
1992	-0.0173	0.0096	-0.0073	0.0016	0.0254	0.0156	0.0308	0.0090	0.0099	-0.0156	0.0069	0.0228	1992	0.0939
1993	0.0250	0.0256	0.0025	0.0052	0.0020	0.0293	0.0100	0.0287	0.0043	0.0051	-0.0188	0.0067	1993	0.1319
1994	0.0202	-0.0286	-0.0383	-0.0097	-0.0062	-0.0081	0.0309	-0.0031	-0.0265	-0.0050	0.0018	0.0157	1994	-0.0576
1995	0.0256	0.0289	0.0095	0.0175	0.0631	0.0079	-0.0101	0.0214	0.0153	0.0185	0.0242	0.0228	1995	0.2720
1996	0.0014	-0.0373	-0.0130	-0.0160	0.0005	0.0172	0.0010	-0.0070	0.0259	0.0361	0.0263	-0.0186	1996	0.0140
1997	-0.0028	0.0028	-0.0221	0.0184	0.0128	0.0187	0.0528	-0.0240	0.0226	0.0191	0.0101	0.0163	1997	0.1295
1998	0.0137	-0.0007	0.0038	0.0053	0.0167	0.0115	-0.0056	0.0089	0.0413	-0.0190	0.0270	0.0010	1998	0.1076
1999	0.0123	-0.0401	0.0002	-0.0024	-0.0176	-0.0160	-0.0113	-0.0026	0.0093	0.0047	-0.0024	-0.0102	1999	-0.0745
2000	-0.0021	0.0092	0.0169	-0.0115	-0.0161	0.0326	0.0179	0.0135	0.0046	0.0045	0.0263	0.0270	2000	0.1287
2001	0.0359	0.0127	-0.0029	-0.0128	0.0132	0.0055	0.0361	0.0157	-0.0152	0.0437	-0.0188	-0.0090	2001	0.1065
2002	0.0175	0.0130	-0.0295	0.0253	0.0113	0.0073	0.0094	0.0452	0.0330	-0.0240	0.0103	0.0361	2002	0.1633
2003	0.0021	0.0264	-0.0080	0.0229	0.0471	-0.0143	-0.0881	0.0219	0.0503	-0.0203	0.0052	0.0139	2003	0.0527
2004	0.0187	0.0178	0.0118	-0.0534	-0.0071	0.0093	0.0184	0.0395	0.0101	0.0164	-0.0200	0.0257	2004	0.0872
2005	0.0277	-0.0112	-0.0125	0.0327	0.0295	0.0141	-0.0244	0.0233	-0.0310	-0.0204	0.0099	0.0225	2005	0.0587
2006	-0.0093	0.0128	-0.0404	-0.0224	-0.0020	0.0039	0.0237	0.0361	0.0183	0.0127	0.0246	-0.0232	2006	0.0324
2007	-0.0051	0.0287	-0.0231	0.0140	-0.0178	-0.0148	-0.0032	0.0152	0.0135	0.0088	0.0079	0.0028	2007	0.0260
2008	0.0017	-0.0071	-0.0059	0.0091	-0.0277	-0.0061	-0.0109	0.0121	-0.0863	-0.0450	0.1174	0.1560	2008	0.0878
2009	-0.0949	-0.0308	-0.0018	-0.0030	0.0489	0.0350	0.0565	0.0235	0.0273	0.0016	0.0044	-0.0275	2009	0.0302
2010	0.0096	0.0039	0.0045	0.0357	-0.0051	0.0519	0.0170	0.0473	-0.0144	-0.0203	-0.0057	-0.0036	2010	0.1244
2011	-0.0198	0.0157	-0.0072	0.0239	0.0257	-0.0210	0.0473	0.0240	0.0575	0.0094	-0.0356	0.0512	2011	0.1795
2012	0.0194	0.0057	-0.0303	0.0251	0.0344	0.0064	0.0612	-0.0093	-0.0126	0.0206	-0.0092	-0.0062	2012	0.1068
2013	-0.0313	0.0093	-0.0018	0.0349	-0.0536	-0.0371	0.0031	-0.0074	0.0014	0.0211	-0.0086	0.0002	2013	-0.0707
2014	0.0331	0.0168	0.0062	0.0160	0.0188	0.0020	0.0024	0.0356	-0.0271	0.0225	0.0173	0.0183	2014	0.1728
2015	0.0599	-0.0320	0.0058	-0.0223	-0.0204	-0.0320	0.0239	-0.0067	0.0133	0.0020	0.0020	0.0000	2015	-0.0102

*Compound annual return

Appendix A-6

Long-term Government Bonds: Total Returns
From 1926 to 2015

Year	Jan	Feb	Mar	Apr	May	Jun	Jul	Aug	Sep	Oct	Nov	Dec	Year	Jan–Dec*
1926	0.0138	0.0063	0.0041	0.0076	0.0014	0.0038	0.0004	0.0000	0.0038	0.0102	0.0160	0.0078	1926	0.0777
1927	0.0075	0.0088	0.0253	-0.0005	0.0109	-0.0069	0.0050	0.0076	0.0018	0.0099	0.0097	0.0072	1927	0.0893
1928	-0.0036	0.0061	0.0045	-0.0004	-0.0077	0.0041	-0.0217	0.0076	-0.0041	0.0158	0.0003	0.0004	1928	0.0010
1929	-0.0090	-0.0157	-0.0144	0.0275	-0.0162	0.0110	0.0000	-0.0034	0.0028	0.0382	0.0236	-0.0089	1929	0.0342
1930	-0.0057	0.0129	0.0083	-0.0016	0.0140	0.0051	0.0034	0.0013	0.0074	0.0035	0.0042	-0.0070	1930	0.0466
1931	-0.0121	0.0085	0.0104	0.0086	0.0145	0.0004	-0.0042	0.0012	-0.0281	-0.0330	0.0027	-0.0220	1931	-0.0531
1932	0.0034	0.0413	-0.0018	0.0604	-0.0188	0.0065	0.0481	0.0003	0.0057	-0.0017	0.0032	0.0131	1932	0.1684
1933	0.0148	-0.0258	0.0097	-0.0032	0.0303	0.0050	-0.0017	0.0044	0.0023	-0.0091	-0.0149	-0.0113	1933	-0.0007
1934	0.0257	0.0081	0.0197	0.0126	0.0131	0.0067	0.0040	-0.0118	-0.0146	0.0182	0.0037	0.0112	1934	0.1003
1935	0.0182	0.0092	0.0041	0.0079	-0.0057	0.0092	0.0046	-0.0133	0.0009	0.0061	0.0010	0.0070	1935	0.0498
1936	0.0055	0.0081	0.0106	0.0035	0.0040	0.0021	0.0060	0.0111	-0.0031	0.0006	0.0205	0.0038	1936	0.0752
1937	-0.0013	0.0086	-0.0412	0.0039	0.0053	-0.0018	0.0138	-0.0104	0.0045	0.0042	0.0096	0.0082	1937	0.0023
1938	0.0057	0.0052	-0.0037	0.0210	0.0044	0.0004	0.0043	0.0000	0.0022	0.0087	-0.0022	0.0080	1938	0.0553
1939	0.0059	0.0080	0.0125	0.0118	0.0171	-0.0027	0.0113	-0.0201	-0.0545	0.0410	0.0162	0.0145	1939	0.0594
1940	-0.0017	0.0027	0.0177	-0.0035	-0.0299	0.0258	0.0052	0.0028	0.0110	0.0031	0.0205	0.0067	1940	0.0609
1941	-0.0201	0.0020	0.0096	0.0129	0.0027	0.0066	0.0022	0.0018	-0.0012	0.0140	-0.0029	-0.0177	1941	0.0093
1942	0.0069	0.0011	0.0092	-0.0029	0.0075	0.0003	0.0018	0.0038	0.0003	0.0024	-0.0035	0.0049	1942	0.0322
1943	0.0033	-0.0006	0.0009	0.0048	0.0050	0.0018	-0.0001	0.0021	0.0011	0.0005	-0.0001	0.0018	1943	0.0208
1944	0.0021	0.0032	0.0021	0.0013	0.0028	0.0008	0.0036	0.0027	0.0014	0.0012	0.0024	0.0042	1944	0.0281
1945	0.0127	0.0077	0.0021	0.0160	0.0056	0.0169	-0.0086	0.0026	0.0054	0.0104	0.0125	0.0194	1945	0.1073
1946	0.0025	0.0032	0.0010	-0.0135	-0.0012	0.0070	-0.0040	-0.0112	-0.0009	0.0074	-0.0054	0.0145	1946	-0.0010
1947	-0.0006	0.0021	0.0020	-0.0037	0.0033	0.0010	0.0063	0.0081	-0.0044	-0.0037	-0.0174	-0.0192	1947	-0.0262
1948	0.0020	0.0046	0.0034	0.0045	0.0141	-0.0084	-0.0021	0.0001	0.0014	0.0007	0.0076	0.0056	1948	0.0340
1949	0.0082	0.0049	0.0074	0.0011	0.0019	0.0167	0.0033	0.0111	-0.0011	0.0019	0.0021	0.0052	1949	0.0645
1950	-0.0061	0.0021	0.0008	0.0030	0.0033	-0.0025	0.0055	0.0014	-0.0072	-0.0048	0.0035	0.0016	1950	0.0006
1951	0.0058	-0.0074	-0.0157	-0.0063	-0.0069	-0.0062	0.0138	0.0099	-0.0080	0.0010	-0.0136	-0.0061	1951	-0.0393
1952	0.0028	0.0014	0.0111	0.0171	-0.0034	0.0003	-0.0020	-0.0070	-0.0130	0.0148	-0.0015	-0.0086	1952	0.0116
1953	0.0012	-0.0087	-0.0088	-0.0105	-0.0148	0.0223	0.0039	-0.0008	0.0299	0.0074	-0.0049	0.0206	1953	0.0364
1954	0.0089	0.0240	0.0058	0.0104	-0.0087	0.0163	0.0134	-0.0036	-0.0010	0.0006	-0.0025	0.0064	1954	0.0719
1955	-0.0241	-0.0078	0.0087	0.0001	0.0073	-0.0076	-0.0102	0.0004	0.0073	0.0144	-0.0045	0.0037	1955	-0.0129

*Compound annual return

Appendix A-6 (16)

Appendix A-6

Long-term Government Bonds: Total Returns
From 1926 to 2015

Year	Jan	Feb	Mar	Apr	May	Jun	Jul	Aug	Sep	Oct	Nov	Dec	Year	Jan–Dec*
1956	0.0083	-0.0002	-0.0149	-0.0113	0.0225	0.0027	-0.0209	-0.0187	0.0050	-0.0054	-0.0057	-0.0179	1956	-0.0559
1957	0.0346	0.0025	-0.0024	-0.0222	-0.0023	-0.0180	-0.0041	0.0002	0.0076	-0.0050	0.0533	0.0307	1957	0.0746
1958	-0.0084	0.0100	0.0102	0.0186	0.0001	-0.0160	-0.0278	-0.0436	-0.0117	0.0139	0.0120	-0.0181	1958	-0.0609
1959	-0.0080	0.0117	0.0017	-0.0117	-0.0006	0.0010	0.0060	-0.0041	-0.0057	0.0150	-0.0119	-0.0159	1959	-0.0226
1960	0.0112	0.0204	0.0282	-0.0170	0.0152	0.0173	0.0368	-0.0067	0.0075	-0.0028	-0.0066	0.0279	1960	0.1378
1961	-0.0107	0.0200	-0.0038	0.0115	-0.0046	-0.0075	0.0035	-0.0038	0.0129	0.0071	-0.0020	-0.0125	1961	0.0097
1962	-0.0014	0.0103	0.0253	0.0082	0.0046	-0.0076	-0.0109	0.0187	0.0061	0.0084	0.0021	0.0035	1962	0.0689
1963	-0.0001	0.0008	0.0009	-0.0012	0.0023	0.0019	0.0031	0.0021	0.0004	-0.0026	0.0051	-0.0006	1963	0.0121
1964	-0.0014	-0.0011	0.0037	0.0047	0.0050	0.0069	0.0008	0.0020	0.0050	0.0043	0.0017	0.0030	1964	0.0351
1965	0.0040	0.0014	0.0054	0.0036	0.0018	0.0047	0.0022	-0.0013	-0.0034	0.0027	-0.0062	-0.0078	1965	0.0071
1966	-0.0104	-0.0250	0.0296	-0.0063	-0.0059	-0.0016	-0.0037	-0.0206	0.0332	0.0228	-0.0149	0.0413	1966	0.0365
1967	0.0154	-0.0221	0.0198	-0.0291	-0.0039	-0.0312	0.0068	-0.0084	-0.0005	-0.0400	-0.0197	0.0192	1967	-0.0918
1968	0.0328	-0.0033	-0.0212	0.0227	0.0043	0.0230	0.0289	-0.0003	-0.0102	-0.0132	-0.0269	-0.0363	1968	-0.0026
1969	-0.0206	0.0042	0.0010	0.0427	-0.0490	0.0214	0.0079	-0.0069	-0.0531	0.0365	-0.0243	-0.0068	1969	-0.0507
1970	-0.0021	0.0587	-0.0068	-0.0413	-0.0468	0.0486	0.0319	-0.0019	0.0228	-0.0109	0.0791	-0.0084	1970	0.1211
1971	0.0506	-0.0163	0.0526	-0.0283	-0.0006	-0.0159	0.0030	0.0471	0.0204	0.0167	-0.0047	0.0044	1971	0.1323
1972	-0.0064	0.0088	-0.0082	0.0027	0.0270	-0.0065	0.0216	0.0029	-0.0083	0.0234	0.0226	-0.0229	1972	0.0569
1973	-0.0321	0.0014	0.0082	0.0046	-0.0105	-0.0021	-0.0433	0.0391	0.0318	0.0215	-0.0183	-0.0082	1973	-0.0111
1974	-0.0083	-0.0024	-0.0292	-0.0253	0.0123	0.0045	-0.0029	-0.0232	0.0247	0.0489	0.0296	0.0171	1974	0.0435
1975	0.0225	0.0131	-0.0267	-0.0182	0.0212	0.0292	-0.0087	-0.0068	-0.0098	0.0475	-0.0109	0.0390	1975	0.0920
1976	0.0090	0.0062	0.0166	0.0018	-0.0158	0.0208	0.0078	0.0211	0.0145	0.0084	0.0339	0.0327	1976	0.1675
1977	-0.0388	-0.0049	0.0091	0.0071	0.0125	0.0164	-0.0070	0.0198	-0.0029	-0.0093	0.0093	-0.0168	1977	-0.0069
1978	-0.0080	0.0004	-0.0021	-0.0005	-0.0058	-0.0062	0.0143	0.0218	-0.0106	-0.0200	0.0189	-0.0130	1978	-0.0118
1979	0.0191	-0.0135	0.0129	-0.0112	0.0261	0.0311	-0.0085	-0.0035	-0.0122	-0.0841	0.0311	0.0057	1979	-0.0123
1980	-0.0741	-0.0467	-0.0315	0.1523	0.0419	0.0359	-0.0476	-0.0432	-0.0262	-0.0263	0.0100	0.0352	1980	-0.0395
1981	-0.0115	-0.0436	0.0384	-0.0518	0.0622	-0.0179	-0.0353	-0.0386	-0.0145	0.0829	0.1410	-0.0713	1981	0.0186
1982	0.0046	0.0182	0.0231	0.0373	0.0034	-0.0223	0.0501	0.0781	0.0618	0.0634	-0.0002	0.0312	1982	0.4036
1983	-0.0309	0.0492	-0.0094	0.0350	-0.0386	0.0039	-0.0486	0.0020	0.0505	-0.0132	0.0183	-0.0059	1983	0.0065
1984	0.0244	-0.0178	-0.0156	-0.0106	-0.0516	0.0150	0.0693	0.0266	0.0343	0.0561	0.0118	0.0091	1984	0.1548
1985	0.0364	-0.0493	0.0307	0.0242	0.0896	0.0142	-0.0180	0.0259	-0.0021	0.0338	0.0401	0.0541	1985	0.3097

*Compound annual return

Appendix A-6

Long-term Government Bonds: Total Returns
From 1926 to 2015

Year	Jan	Feb	Mar	Apr	May	Jun	Jul	Aug	Sep	Oct	Nov	Dec	Year	Jan–Dec*
1986	-0.0025	0.1145	0.0770	-0.0080	-0.0505	0.0613	-0.0108	0.0499	-0.0500	0.0289	0.0267	-0.0018	1986	0.2453
1987	0.0161	0.0202	-0.0223	-0.0473	-0.0105	0.0098	-0.0178	-0.0165	-0.0369	0.0623	0.0037	0.0165	1987	-0.0271
1988	0.0666	0.0052	-0.0307	-0.0160	-0.0102	0.0368	-0.0170	0.0058	0.0345	0.0308	-0.0196	0.0110	1988	0.0967
1989	0.0203	-0.0179	0.0122	0.0159	0.0401	0.0550	0.0238	-0.0259	0.0019	0.0379	0.0078	-0.0006	1989	0.1811
1990	-0.0343	-0.0025	-0.0044	-0.0202	0.0415	0.0230	0.0107	-0.0419	0.0117	0.0215	0.0402	0.0187	1990	0.0618
1991	0.0130	0.0030	0.0038	0.0140	0.0000	-0.0063	0.0157	0.0340	0.0303	0.0054	0.0082	0.0581	1991	0.1930
1992	-0.0324	0.0051	-0.0094	0.0016	0.0243	0.0200	0.0398	0.0067	0.0185	-0.0198	0.0010	0.0246	1992	0.0805
1993	0.0280	0.0354	0.0021	0.0072	0.0047	0.0449	0.0191	0.0434	0.0005	0.0096	-0.0259	0.0020	1993	0.1824
1994	0.0257	-0.0450	-0.0395	-0.0150	-0.0082	-0.0100	0.0363	-0.0086	-0.0331	-0.0025	0.0066	0.0161	1994	-0.0777
1995	0.0273	0.0287	0.0091	0.0169	0.0790	0.0139	-0.0168	0.0236	0.0175	0.0294	0.0249	0.0272	1995	0.3167
1996	-0.0011	-0.0483	-0.0210	-0.0165	-0.0054	0.0203	0.0018	-0.0139	0.0290	0.0404	0.0351	-0.0256	1996	-0.0093
1997	-0.0079	0.0005	-0.0252	0.0255	0.0095	0.0197	0.0626	-0.0317	0.0316	0.0341	0.0148	0.0184	1997	0.1585
1998	0.0200	-0.0072	0.0025	0.0026	0.0182	0.0228	-0.0040	0.0465	0.0395	-0.0218	0.0097	-0.0032	1998	0.1306
1999	0.0121	-0.0520	-0.0008	0.0021	-0.0185	-0.0078	-0.0079	-0.0051	0.0084	-0.0012	-0.0061	-0.0155	1999	-0.0896
2000	0.0228	0.0264	0.0367	-0.0076	-0.0054	0.0244	0.0173	0.0240	-0.0157	0.0187	0.0319	0.0243	2000	0.2148
2001	0.0005	0.0191	-0.0074	-0.0313	0.0037	0.0085	0.0376	0.0206	0.0081	0.0464	-0.0471	-0.0183	2001	0.0370
2002	0.0138	0.0115	-0.0436	0.0410	0.0015	0.0187	0.0303	0.0464	0.0417	-0.0294	-0.0122	0.0507	2002	0.1784
2003	-0.0106	0.0329	-0.0135	0.0102	0.0592	-0.0154	-0.0982	0.0166	0.0546	-0.0283	0.0027	0.0139	2003	0.0145
2004	0.0187	0.0230	0.0141	-0.0588	-0.0051	0.0121	0.0155	0.0395	0.0096	0.0154	-0.0234	0.0250	2004	0.0851
2005	0.0300	-0.0128	-0.0072	0.0373	0.0297	0.0167	-0.0288	0.0333	-0.0338	-0.0196	0.0076	0.0267	2005	0.0781
2006	-0.0118	0.0238	-0.0539	-0.0247	0.0010	0.0092	0.0199	0.0299	0.0170	0.0077	0.0207	-0.0236	2006	0.0119
2007	-0.0102	0.0335	-0.0145	0.0085	-0.0200	-0.0091	0.0284	0.0199	0.0012	0.0155	0.0468	-0.0029	2007	0.0988
2008	0.0213	0.0018	0.0106	-0.0288	-0.0164	0.0220	-0.0025	0.0242	0.0112	-0.0383	0.1443	0.0967	2008	0.2587
2009	-0.1124	-0.0056	0.0641	-0.0649	-0.0248	0.0083	0.0019	0.0231	0.0176	-0.0171	0.0208	-0.0584	2009	-0.1490
2010	0.0264	0.0032	-0.0179	0.0304	0.0437	0.0446	0.0024	0.0702	-0.0153	-0.0317	-0.0137	-0.0388	2010	0.1014
2011	-0.0196	0.0113	-0.0006	0.0199	0.0355	-0.0179	0.0422	0.0862	0.0704	-0.0306	0.0251	0.0270	2011	0.2710
2012	0.0002	-0.0196	-0.0302	0.0409	0.0643	-0.0136	0.0247	-0.0068	-0.0146	-0.0014	0.0144	-0.0202	2012	0.0343
2013	-0.0332	0.0114	-0.0062	0.0378	-0.0629	-0.0285	-0.0173	-0.0079	0.0061	0.0128	-0.0236	-0.0207	2013	-0.1278
2014	0.0548	0.0074	0.0063	0.0181	0.0279	-0.0025	0.0057	0.0369	-0.0170	0.0300	0.0286	0.0290	2014	0.2471
2015	0.0709	-0.0523	0.0137	-0.0250	-0.0159	-0.0298	0.0329	0.0012	0.0174	-0.0053	-0.0065	-0.0022	2015	-0.0065

*Compound annual return

Appendix A-7

Long-term Government Bonds: Income Returns
From 1926 to 2015

Year	Jan	Feb	Mar	Apr	May	Jun	Jul	Aug	Sep	Oct	Nov	Dec	Year	Jan–Dec*
1926	0.0031	0.0028	0.0032	0.0030	0.0028	0.0033	0.0031	0.0031	0.0030	0.0030	0.0031	0.0030	1926	0.0373
1927	0.0030	0.0027	0.0029	0.0027	0.0028	0.0027	0.0027	0.0029	0.0027	0.0028	0.0027	0.0027	1927	0.0341
1928	0.0027	0.0025	0.0027	0.0026	0.0027	0.0027	0.0027	0.0029	0.0027	0.0030	0.0027	0.0029	1928	0.0322
1929	0.0029	0.0027	0.0028	0.0034	0.0030	0.0029	0.0032	0.0030	0.0032	0.0031	0.0026	0.0031	1929	0.0347
1930	0.0029	0.0026	0.0029	0.0027	0.0027	0.0029	0.0028	0.0026	0.0029	0.0027	0.0026	0.0028	1930	0.0332
1931	0.0028	0.0026	0.0029	0.0027	0.0026	0.0028	0.0027	0.0027	0.0027	0.0029	0.0031	0.0032	1931	0.0333
1932	0.0032	0.0032	0.0031	0.0030	0.0028	0.0028	0.0028	0.0028	0.0026	0.0027	0.0026	0.0027	1932	0.0369
1933	0.0027	0.0023	0.0027	0.0025	0.0028	0.0025	0.0026	0.0026	0.0025	0.0026	0.0025	0.0028	1933	0.0312
1934	0.0029	0.0024	0.0027	0.0025	0.0025	0.0024	0.0024	0.0024	0.0023	0.0027	0.0025	0.0025	1934	0.0318
1935	0.0025	0.0021	0.0022	0.0023	0.0023	0.0022	0.0024	0.0023	0.0023	0.0023	0.0024	0.0024	1935	0.0281
1936	0.0024	0.0023	0.0024	0.0022	0.0022	0.0024	0.0023	0.0023	0.0021	0.0023	0.0022	0.0022	1936	0.0277
1937	0.0021	0.0020	0.0022	0.0023	0.0022	0.0025	0.0024	0.0023	0.0023	0.0023	0.0024	0.0023	1937	0.0266
1938	0.0023	0.0021	0.0023	0.0022	0.0022	0.0021	0.0021	0.0022	0.0021	0.0022	0.0021	0.0022	1938	0.0264
1939	0.0021	0.0019	0.0021	0.0019	0.0020	0.0018	0.0019	0.0018	0.0019	0.0023	0.0020	0.0019	1939	0.0240
1940	0.0020	0.0018	0.0019	0.0018	0.0019	0.0019	0.0020	0.0019	0.0018	0.0018	0.0018	0.0017	1940	0.0223
1941	0.0016	0.0016	0.0018	0.0017	0.0017	0.0016	0.0016	0.0016	0.0016	0.0016	0.0014	0.0016	1941	0.0194
1942	0.0021	0.0019	0.0021	0.0020	0.0019	0.0021	0.0021	0.0021	0.0020	0.0021	0.0020	0.0021	1942	0.0246
1943	0.0020	0.0019	0.0021	0.0020	0.0019	0.0021	0.0021	0.0021	0.0020	0.0020	0.0021	0.0021	1943	0.0244
1944	0.0021	0.0020	0.0021	0.0020	0.0022	0.0020	0.0021	0.0021	0.0020	0.0021	0.0020	0.0020	1944	0.0246
1945	0.0021	0.0018	0.0020	0.0019	0.0019	0.0019	0.0018	0.0019	0.0018	0.0019	0.0018	0.0018	1945	0.0234
1946	0.0017	0.0015	0.0016	0.0017	0.0018	0.0016	0.0019	0.0017	0.0018	0.0019	0.0018	0.0019	1946	0.0204
1947	0.0018	0.0016	0.0018	0.0017	0.0017	0.0019	0.0018	0.0017	0.0018	0.0018	0.0017	0.0021	1947	0.0213
1948	0.0020	0.0019	0.0022	0.0020	0.0018	0.0021	0.0019	0.0021	0.0020	0.0019	0.0021	0.0020	1948	0.0240
1949	0.0020	0.0018	0.0019	0.0018	0.0020	0.0019	0.0017	0.0019	0.0017	0.0018	0.0017	0.0017	1949	0.0225
1950	0.0018	0.0016	0.0018	0.0016	0.0019	0.0017	0.0018	0.0018	0.0017	0.0019	0.0018	0.0018	1950	0.0212
1951	0.0020	0.0017	0.0019	0.0020	0.0021	0.0020	0.0023	0.0021	0.0019	0.0023	0.0021	0.0022	1951	0.0238
1952	0.0023	0.0021	0.0023	0.0022	0.0020	0.0022	0.0022	0.0021	0.0023	0.0023	0.0021	0.0024	1952	0.0266
1953	0.0023	0.0021	0.0025	0.0024	0.0024	0.0027	0.0025	0.0025	0.0025	0.0023	0.0024	0.0024	1953	0.0284
1954	0.0023	0.0022	0.0025	0.0022	0.0020	0.0025	0.0022	0.0023	0.0022	0.0021	0.0023	0.0023	1954	0.0279
1955	0.0022	0.0022	0.0024	0.0022	0.0025	0.0023	0.0023	0.0027	0.0024	0.0025	0.0024	0.0024	1955	0.0275

*Compound annual return

Appendix A-7

Long-term Government Bonds: Income Returns
From 1926 to 2015

Year	Jan	Feb	Mar	Apr	May	Jun	Jul	Aug	Sep	Oct	Nov	Dec	Year	Jan–Dec[*]
1956	0.0025	0.0023	0.0023	0.0026	0.0026	0.0023	0.0026	0.0026	0.0025	0.0029	0.0027	0.0028	1956	0.0299
1957	0.0029	0.0025	0.0026	0.0029	0.0029	0.0025	0.0033	0.0030	0.0031	0.0031	0.0029	0.0029	1957	0.0344
1958	0.0027	0.0025	0.0027	0.0026	0.0024	0.0027	0.0027	0.0027	0.0032	0.0032	0.0028	0.0033	1958	0.0327
1959	0.0031	0.0031	0.0035	0.0033	0.0033	0.0036	0.0035	0.0035	0.0034	0.0035	0.0035	0.0036	1959	0.0401
1960	0.0035	0.0037	0.0036	0.0032	0.0037	0.0034	0.0032	0.0034	0.0032	0.0033	0.0032	0.0033	1960	0.0426
1961	0.0033	0.0030	0.0031	0.0031	0.0034	0.0032	0.0033	0.0033	0.0032	0.0034	0.0031	0.0031	1961	0.0383
1962	0.0037	0.0032	0.0033	0.0033	0.0032	0.0030	0.0034	0.0034	0.0030	0.0035	0.0032	0.0032	1962	0.0400
1963	0.0032	0.0029	0.0031	0.0034	0.0033	0.0030	0.0036	0.0033	0.0034	0.0034	0.0032	0.0036	1963	0.0389
1964	0.0035	0.0032	0.0037	0.0035	0.0032	0.0038	0.0035	0.0035	0.0034	0.0034	0.0035	0.0035	1964	0.0415
1965	0.0033	0.0032	0.0038	0.0033	0.0033	0.0038	0.0034	0.0037	0.0035	0.0034	0.0037	0.0037	1965	0.0419
1966	0.0038	0.0034	0.0040	0.0036	0.0041	0.0039	0.0038	0.0043	0.0041	0.0040	0.0038	0.0039	1966	0.0449
1967	0.0040	0.0034	0.0039	0.0035	0.0043	0.0039	0.0043	0.0042	0.0040	0.0045	0.0045	0.0044	1967	0.0459
1968	0.0050	0.0042	0.0043	0.0049	0.0046	0.0042	0.0048	0.0042	0.0044	0.0045	0.0043	0.0049	1968	0.0550
1969	0.0050	0.0046	0.0047	0.0055	0.0047	0.0055	0.0052	0.0048	0.0055	0.0057	0.0049	0.0060	1969	0.0595
1970	0.0056	0.0052	0.0056	0.0054	0.0055	0.0064	0.0059	0.0057	0.0056	0.0055	0.0058	0.0053	1970	0.0674
1971	0.0051	0.0046	0.0056	0.0048	0.0047	0.0056	0.0052	0.0055	0.0050	0.0047	0.0051	0.0050	1971	0.0632
1972	0.0050	0.0047	0.0049	0.0048	0.0055	0.0049	0.0051	0.0049	0.0047	0.0052	0.0048	0.0045	1972	0.0587
1973	0.0054	0.0051	0.0056	0.0057	0.0058	0.0055	0.0061	0.0062	0.0055	0.0063	0.0056	0.0060	1973	0.0651
1974	0.0061	0.0055	0.0059	0.0068	0.0068	0.0061	0.0072	0.0065	0.0071	0.0070	0.0062	0.0067	1974	0.0727
1975	0.0068	0.0060	0.0066	0.0067	0.0067	0.0070	0.0068	0.0065	0.0073	0.0072	0.0061	0.0075	1975	0.0799
1976	0.0065	0.0061	0.0071	0.0064	0.0059	0.0073	0.0065	0.0069	0.0064	0.0061	0.0066	0.0063	1976	0.0789
1977	0.0059	0.0057	0.0065	0.0061	0.0067	0.0062	0.0059	0.0067	0.0061	0.0063	0.0063	0.0062	1977	0.0714
1978	0.0069	0.0060	0.0069	0.0063	0.0075	0.0069	0.0073	0.0070	0.0065	0.0073	0.0071	0.0068	1978	0.0790
1979	0.0079	0.0065	0.0074	0.0076	0.0077	0.0071	0.0076	0.0073	0.0068	0.0082	0.0083	0.0083	1979	0.0886
1980	0.0083	0.0084	0.0099	0.0100	0.0087	0.0086	0.0084	0.0081	0.0097	0.0097	0.0091	0.0108	1980	0.0997
1981	0.0094	0.0088	0.0111	0.0101	0.0104	0.0109	0.0109	0.0110	0.0114	0.0117	0.0113	0.0100	1981	0.1155
1982	0.0108	0.0103	0.0124	0.0112	0.0101	0.0120	0.0114	0.0112	0.0100	0.0091	0.0095	0.0093	1982	0.1350
1983	0.0087	0.0081	0.0089	0.0085	0.0091	0.0090	0.0088	0.0103	0.0096	0.0095	0.0094	0.0094	1983	0.1038
1984	0.0103	0.0092	0.0098	0.0104	0.0103	0.0106	0.0116	0.0106	0.0094	0.0108	0.0091	0.0098	1984	0.1174
1985	0.0096	0.0082	0.0094	0.0102	0.0097	0.0080	0.0094	0.0085	0.0088	0.0089	0.0081	0.0086	1985	0.1125

[*]Compound annual return

Appendix A-7

Long-term Government Bonds: Income Returns
From 1926 to 2015

Year	Jan	Feb	Mar	Apr	May	Jun	Jul	Aug	Sep	Oct	Nov	Dec	Year	Jan–Dec*
1986	0.0079	0.0073	0.0071	0.0063	0.0062	0.0070	0.0066	0.0063	0.0065	0.0069	0.0059	0.0070	1986	0.0898
1987	0.0064	0.0059	0.0066	0.0065	0.0066	0.0075	0.0073	0.0075	0.0075	0.0079	0.0075	0.0078	1987	0.0792
1988	0.0072	0.0071	0.0072	0.0070	0.0078	0.0076	0.0071	0.0083	0.0076	0.0076	0.0070	0.0075	1988	0.0897
1989	0.0080	0.0069	0.0079	0.0070	0.0080	0.0070	0.0068	0.0066	0.0065	0.0072	0.0064	0.0064	1989	0.0881
1990	0.0073	0.0066	0.0071	0.0075	0.0075	0.0068	0.0074	0.0071	0.0069	0.0081	0.0071	0.0072	1990	0.0819
1991	0.0071	0.0064	0.0064	0.0076	0.0068	0.0063	0.0076	0.0068	0.0068	0.0065	0.0060	0.0068	1991	0.0822
1992	0.0061	0.0059	0.0067	0.0065	0.0061	0.0067	0.0063	0.0060	0.0058	0.0057	0.0061	0.0063	1992	0.0726
1993	0.0059	0.0055	0.0063	0.0057	0.0052	0.0062	0.0054	0.0056	0.0050	0.0049	0.0053	0.0055	1993	0.0717
1994	0.0055	0.0049	0.0058	0.0057	0.0063	0.0061	0.0060	0.0066	0.0061	0.0066	0.0064	0.0066	1994	0.0659
1995	0.0070	0.0059	0.0064	0.0058	0.0065	0.0054	0.0056	0.0057	0.0052	0.0057	0.0051	0.0049	1995	0.0760
1996	0.0054	0.0048	0.0052	0.0059	0.0058	0.0054	0.0062	0.0057	0.0060	0.0058	0.0052	0.0056	1996	0.0618
1997	0.0056	0.0051	0.0059	0.0059	0.0058	0.0059	0.0058	0.0049	0.0058	0.0054	0.0047	0.0054	1997	0.0664
1998	0.0048	0.0044	0.0052	0.0049	0.0048	0.0052	0.0049	0.0048	0.0044	0.0042	0.0045	0.0045	1998	0.0583
1999	0.0042	0.0040	0.0053	0.0048	0.0045	0.0055	0.0051	0.0054	0.0052	0.0050	0.0056	0.0055	1999	0.0557
2000	0.0057	0.0051	0.0054	0.0047	0.0056	0.0052	0.0052	0.0050	0.0046	0.0053	0.0048	0.0045	2000	0.0650
2001	0.0049	0.0042	0.0045	0.0047	0.0050	0.0047	0.0052	0.0046	0.0041	0.0048	0.0041	0.0046	2001	0.0553
2002	0.0048	0.0043	0.0043	0.0054	0.0049	0.0044	0.0051	0.0044	0.0042	0.0040	0.0040	0.0045	2002	0.0559
2003	0.0041	0.0038	0.0040	0.0040	0.0039	0.0036	0.0038	0.0042	0.0046	0.0041	0.0039	0.0047	2003	0.0480
2004	0.0042	0.0038	0.0043	0.0039	0.0040	0.0048	0.0043	0.0045	0.0040	0.0038	0.0041	0.0043	2004	0.0502
2005	0.0041	0.0035	0.0041	0.0039	0.0040	0.0036	0.0034	0.0040	0.0035	0.0039	0.0039	0.0039	2005	0.0469
2006	0.0040	0.0036	0.0039	0.0039	0.0048	0.0044	0.0045	0.0043	0.0039	0.0042	0.0039	0.0036	2006	0.0468
2007	0.0043	0.0038	0.0039	0.0042	0.0041	0.0040	0.0046	0.0042	0.0037	0.0043	0.0039	0.0037	2007	0.0486
2008	0.0040	0.0034	0.0037	0.0035	0.0037	0.0040	0.0039	0.0036	0.0039	0.0037	0.0036	0.0033	2008	0.0445
2009	0.0024	0.0030	0.0035	0.0029	0.0033	0.0038	0.0036	0.0036	0.0034	0.0033	0.0035	0.0034	2009	0.0347
2010	0.0036	0.0033	0.0040	0.0038	0.0034	0.0037	0.0031	0.0032	0.0026	0.0027	0.0032	0.0032	2010	0.0425
2011	0.0035	0.0032	0.0036	0.0034	0.0036	0.0032	0.0032	0.0034	0.0026	0.0022	0.0024	0.0022	2011	0.0382
2012	0.0021	0.0020	0.0022	0.0025	0.0023	0.0018	0.0020	0.0018	0.0017	0.0021	0.0019	0.0019	2012	0.0246
2013	0.0022	0.0022	0.0021	0.0026	0.0023	0.0024	0.0030	0.0028	0.0029	0.0029	0.0027	0.0031	2013	0.0288
2014	0.0032	0.0026	0.0029	0.0028	0.0028	0.0025	0.0027	0.0026	0.0023	0.0025	0.0023	0.0022	2014	0.0341
2015	0.0020	0.0015	0.0021	0.0019	0.0020	0.0023	0.0024	0.0022	0.0021	0.0021	0.0022	0.0022	2015	0.0247

*Compound annual return

Appendix A-8

Long-term Government Bonds: Capital Appreciation Returns
From 1926 to 2015

Year	Jan	Feb	Mar	Apr	May	Jun	Jul	Aug	Sep	Oct	Nov	Dec	Year	Jan–Dec*
1926	0.0106	0.0035	0.0009	0.0046	-0.0014	0.0005	-0.0027	-0.0031	0.0007	0.0072	0.0129	0.0048	1926	0.0391
1927	0.0045	0.0061	0.0224	-0.0032	0.0081	-0.0096	0.0022	0.0047	-0.0009	0.0071	0.0071	0.0045	1927	0.0540
1928	-0.0063	0.0036	0.0019	-0.0029	-0.0104	0.0015	-0.0245	0.0047	-0.0067	0.0128	-0.0024	-0.0024	1928	-0.0312
1929	-0.0119	-0.0184	-0.0171	0.0242	-0.0192	0.0081	-0.0032	-0.0064	-0.0004	0.0351	0.0211	-0.0120	1929	-0.0020
1930	-0.0086	0.0102	0.0055	-0.0043	0.0113	0.0022	0.0007	-0.0013	0.0045	0.0008	0.0017	-0.0098	1930	0.0128
1931	-0.0149	0.0059	0.0076	0.0059	0.0119	-0.0024	-0.0069	-0.0015	-0.0307	-0.0360	-0.0004	-0.0252	1931	-0.0846
1932	0.0002	0.0382	-0.0049	0.0574	-0.0216	0.0037	0.0453	-0.0025	0.0031	-0.0044	0.0006	0.0104	1932	0.1294
1933	0.0122	-0.0282	0.0070	-0.0057	0.0274	0.0025	-0.0043	0.0018	-0.0002	-0.0117	-0.0174	-0.0140	1933	-0.0314
1934	0.0228	0.0057	0.0170	0.0101	0.0106	0.0043	0.0016	-0.0143	-0.0169	0.0155	0.0013	0.0087	1934	0.0676
1935	0.0157	0.0070	0.0019	0.0056	-0.0079	0.0070	0.0022	-0.0156	-0.0014	0.0038	-0.0014	0.0047	1935	0.0214
1936	0.0031	0.0059	0.0083	0.0013	0.0019	-0.0003	0.0037	0.0088	-0.0053	-0.0017	0.0183	0.0017	1936	0.0464
1937	-0.0034	0.0067	-0.0434	0.0016	0.0031	-0.0043	0.0114	-0.0128	0.0022	0.0019	0.0072	0.0059	1937	-0.0248
1938	0.0034	0.0031	-0.0059	0.0187	0.0022	-0.0017	0.0022	-0.0022	0.0001	0.0065	-0.0043	0.0059	1938	0.0283
1939	0.0038	0.0061	0.0105	0.0099	0.0151	-0.0045	0.0095	-0.0219	-0.0564	0.0386	0.0142	0.0125	1939	0.0348
1940	-0.0037	0.0009	0.0158	-0.0053	-0.0318	0.0239	0.0032	0.0009	0.0092	0.0013	0.0187	0.0050	1940	0.0377
1941	-0.0217	0.0004	0.0078	0.0112	0.0011	0.0050	0.0005	0.0002	-0.0028	0.0124	-0.0044	-0.0194	1941	-0.0101
1942	0.0048	-0.0008	0.0071	-0.0049	0.0056	-0.0018	-0.0003	0.0017	-0.0017	0.0004	-0.0055	0.0028	1942	0.0074
1943	0.0013	-0.0024	-0.0012	0.0028	0.0031	-0.0003	-0.0021	0.0000	-0.0009	-0.0015	-0.0021	-0.0003	1943	-0.0037
1944	0.0000	0.0012	0.0000	-0.0006	0.0006	-0.0012	0.0015	0.0006	-0.0006	-0.0009	0.0003	0.0022	1944	0.0032
1945	0.0105	0.0058	0.0001	0.0141	0.0037	0.0150	-0.0104	0.0007	0.0037	0.0085	0.0108	0.0177	1945	0.0827
1946	0.0008	0.0017	-0.0006	-0.0152	-0.0030	0.0054	-0.0058	-0.0129	-0.0028	0.0055	-0.0072	0.0126	1946	-0.0215
1947	-0.0024	0.0005	0.0002	-0.0054	0.0016	-0.0009	0.0044	0.0064	-0.0062	-0.0055	-0.0191	-0.0213	1947	-0.0470
1948	0.0000	0.0028	0.0013	0.0025	0.0123	-0.0105	-0.0041	-0.0020	-0.0006	-0.0012	0.0055	0.0036	1948	0.0096
1949	0.0062	0.0031	0.0055	-0.0006	0.0000	0.0148	0.0016	0.0092	-0.0029	0.0001	0.0004	0.0035	1949	0.0415
1950	-0.0080	0.0005	-0.0010	0.0014	0.0014	-0.0042	0.0037	-0.0004	-0.0089	-0.0067	0.0017	-0.0001	1950	-0.0206
1951	0.0038	-0.0091	-0.0176	-0.0083	-0.0090	-0.0082	0.0116	0.0077	-0.0098	-0.0013	-0.0157	-0.0083	1951	-0.0627
1952	0.0005	-0.0007	0.0088	0.0149	-0.0054	-0.0019	-0.0042	-0.0091	-0.0153	0.0124	-0.0036	-0.0110	1952	-0.0148
1953	-0.0011	-0.0108	-0.0113	-0.0129	-0.0171	0.0195	0.0014	-0.0033	0.0275	0.0051	-0.0073	0.0182	1953	0.0067
1954	0.0066	0.0218	0.0034	0.0081	-0.0107	0.0138	0.0113	-0.0059	-0.0031	-0.0015	-0.0048	0.0042	1954	0.0435
1955	-0.0264	-0.0100	0.0063	-0.0022	0.0048	-0.0099	-0.0125	-0.0023	0.0049	0.0119	-0.0069	0.0013	1955	-0.0407

*Compound annual return

Appendix A-8

Long-term Government Bonds: Capital Appreciation Returns
From 1926 to 2015

Year	Jan	Feb	Mar	Apr	May	Jun	Jul	Aug	Sep	Oct	Nov	Dec	Year	Jan–Dec*
1956	0.0058	-0.0025	-0.0172	-0.0139	0.0199	0.0004	-0.0234	-0.0213	0.0025	-0.0084	-0.0084	-0.0207	1956	-0.0846
1957	0.0317	0.0000	-0.0050	-0.0250	-0.0052	-0.0206	-0.0074	-0.0028	0.0045	-0.0081	0.0504	0.0277	1957	0.0382
1958	-0.0112	0.0075	0.0075	0.0160	-0.0024	-0.0187	-0.0306	-0.0463	-0.0149	0.0106	0.0092	-0.0213	1958	-0.0923
1959	-0.0111	0.0087	-0.0018	-0.0150	-0.0038	-0.0026	0.0025	-0.0076	-0.0091	0.0115	-0.0154	-0.0195	1959	-0.0620
1960	0.0077	0.0167	0.0246	-0.0202	0.0115	0.0139	0.0335	-0.0101	0.0043	-0.0061	-0.0098	0.0247	1960	0.0929
1961	-0.0140	0.0170	-0.0069	0.0085	-0.0080	-0.0106	0.0001	-0.0071	0.0097	0.0037	-0.0052	-0.0156	1961	-0.0286
1962	-0.0051	0.0071	0.0220	0.0049	0.0014	-0.0106	-0.0143	0.0153	0.0031	0.0049	-0.0010	0.0003	1962	0.0278
1963	-0.0033	-0.0022	-0.0022	-0.0046	-0.0011	-0.0011	-0.0005	-0.0011	-0.0029	-0.0060	0.0019	-0.0042	1963	-0.0270
1964	-0.0048	-0.0043	0.0000	0.0012	0.0018	0.0031	-0.0028	-0.0015	0.0015	0.0009	-0.0018	-0.0005	1964	-0.0072
1965	0.0007	-0.0018	0.0016	0.0003	-0.0015	0.0009	-0.0012	-0.0050	-0.0069	-0.0007	-0.0100	-0.0115	1965	-0.0345
1966	-0.0142	-0.0284	0.0256	-0.0099	-0.0100	-0.0054	-0.0074	-0.0249	0.0292	0.0188	-0.0187	0.0374	1966	-0.0106
1967	0.0115	-0.0255	0.0159	-0.0326	-0.0082	-0.0351	0.0026	-0.0126	-0.0045	-0.0445	-0.0241	0.0148	1967	-0.1355
1968	0.0278	-0.0075	-0.0254	0.0178	-0.0003	0.0188	0.0241	-0.0045	-0.0146	-0.0177	-0.0312	-0.0412	1968	-0.0551
1969	-0.0256	-0.0005	-0.0036	0.0371	-0.0537	0.0159	0.0027	-0.0117	-0.0586	0.0309	-0.0293	-0.0129	1969	-0.1083
1970	-0.0077	0.0535	-0.0124	-0.0467	-0.0523	0.0422	0.0260	-0.0076	0.0172	-0.0164	0.0733	-0.0137	1970	0.0484
1971	0.0455	-0.0209	0.0470	-0.0331	-0.0053	-0.0214	-0.0022	0.0416	0.0154	0.0120	-0.0098	-0.0006	1971	0.0661
1972	-0.0114	0.0041	-0.0131	-0.0021	0.0215	-0.0113	0.0165	-0.0021	-0.0129	0.0182	0.0178	-0.0275	1972	-0.0035
1973	-0.0375	-0.0037	0.0026	-0.0012	-0.0162	-0.0076	-0.0495	0.0329	0.0263	0.0153	-0.0238	-0.0142	1973	-0.0770
1974	-0.0144	-0.0079	-0.0350	-0.0320	0.0055	-0.0016	-0.0101	-0.0298	0.0176	0.0419	0.0233	0.0105	1974	-0.0345
1975	0.0157	0.0071	-0.0333	-0.0249	0.0145	0.0222	-0.0155	-0.0133	-0.0171	0.0403	-0.0170	0.0316	1975	0.0073
1976	0.0025	0.0001	0.0094	-0.0046	-0.0217	0.0135	0.0013	0.0142	0.0081	0.0023	0.0273	0.0265	1976	0.0807
1977	-0.0447	-0.0106	0.0026	0.0010	0.0058	0.0102	-0.0130	0.0131	-0.0089	-0.0156	0.0031	-0.0230	1977	-0.0786
1978	-0.0149	-0.0056	-0.0090	-0.0068	-0.0133	-0.0132	0.0070	0.0148	-0.0171	-0.0273	0.0117	-0.0198	1978	-0.0905
1979	0.0112	-0.0200	0.0056	-0.0188	0.0184	0.0240	-0.0161	-0.0108	-0.0190	-0.0922	0.0229	-0.0026	1979	-0.0984
1980	-0.0824	-0.0551	-0.0413	0.1424	0.0332	0.0272	-0.0560	-0.0513	-0.0359	-0.0360	0.0009	0.0244	1980	-0.1400
1981	-0.0209	-0.0524	0.0274	-0.0618	0.0518	-0.0288	-0.0462	-0.0496	-0.0259	0.0712	0.1297	-0.0813	1981	-0.1033
1982	-0.0062	0.0079	0.0107	0.0262	-0.0067	-0.0343	0.0387	0.0669	0.0519	0.0543	-0.0097	0.0219	1982	0.2395
1983	-0.0396	0.0410	-0.0183	0.0265	-0.0477	-0.0051	-0.0574	-0.0083	0.0408	-0.0227	0.0089	-0.0152	1983	-0.0982
1984	0.0141	-0.0270	-0.0254	-0.0210	-0.0619	0.0044	0.0577	0.0160	0.0248	0.0453	0.0027	-0.0007	1984	0.0232
1985	0.0268	-0.0575	0.0212	0.0140	0.0798	0.0061	-0.0274	0.0174	-0.0109	0.0248	0.0320	0.0455	1985	0.1784

*Compound annual return

Appendix A-8

Long-term Government Bonds: Capital Appreciation Returns
From 1926 to 2015

Year	Jan	Feb	Mar	Apr	May	Jun	Jul	Aug	Sep	Oct	Nov	Dec	Year	Jan–Dec*
1986	-0.0105	0.1073	0.0699	-0.0142	-0.0567	0.0543	-0.0174	0.0437	-0.0565	0.0220	0.0208	-0.0087	1986	0.1499
1987	0.0096	0.0143	-0.0289	-0.0538	-0.0171	0.0023	-0.0251	-0.0240	-0.0444	0.0544	-0.0038	0.0088	1987	-0.1069
1988	0.0595	-0.0019	-0.0378	-0.0230	-0.0180	0.0292	-0.0241	-0.0025	0.0269	0.0232	-0.0266	0.0035	1988	0.0036
1989	0.0124	-0.0248	0.0044	0.0088	0.0321	0.0480	0.0170	-0.0325	-0.0046	0.0307	0.0014	-0.0070	1989	0.0862
1990	-0.0416	-0.0090	-0.0115	-0.0277	0.0340	0.0162	0.0033	-0.0490	0.0048	0.0135	0.0331	0.0114	1990	-0.0261
1991	0.0059	-0.0033	-0.0026	0.0065	-0.0068	-0.0126	0.0082	0.0272	0.0236	-0.0011	0.0022	0.0513	1991	0.1010
1992	-0.0385	-0.0008	-0.0161	-0.0049	0.0181	0.0133	0.0334	0.0007	0.0127	-0.0255	-0.0051	0.0183	1992	0.0034
1993	0.0222	0.0299	-0.0042	0.0015	-0.0006	0.0387	0.0138	0.0378	-0.0045	0.0048	-0.0312	-0.0035	1993	0.1071
1994	0.0202	-0.0498	-0.0453	-0.0208	-0.0146	-0.0161	0.0303	-0.0152	-0.0392	-0.0091	0.0002	0.0095	1994	-0.1429
1995	0.0203	0.0227	0.0028	0.0112	0.0725	0.0084	-0.0223	0.0179	0.0122	0.0237	0.0198	0.0223	1995	0.2304
1996	-0.0065	-0.0530	-0.0262	-0.0224	-0.0112	0.0149	-0.0045	-0.0196	0.0230	0.0345	0.0299	-0.0312	1996	-0.0737
1997	-0.0135	-0.0046	-0.0311	0.0196	0.0037	0.0138	0.0567	-0.0367	0.0258	0.0287	0.0101	0.0130	1997	0.0851
1998	0.0152	-0.0116	-0.0028	-0.0023	0.0135	0.0176	-0.0088	0.0416	0.0350	-0.0260	0.0052	-0.0077	1998	0.0689
1999	0.0079	-0.0560	-0.0061	-0.0028	-0.0230	-0.0133	-0.0130	-0.0105	0.0032	-0.0062	-0.0117	-0.0210	1999	-0.1435
2000	0.0171	0.0213	0.0312	-0.0123	-0.0111	0.0192	0.0120	0.0190	-0.0203	0.0135	0.0270	0.0198	2000	0.1436
2001	-0.0044	0.0149	-0.0119	-0.0360	-0.0013	0.0038	0.0324	0.0159	0.0040	0.0416	-0.0512	-0.0229	2001	-0.0189
2002	0.0090	0.0072	-0.0479	0.0355	-0.0034	0.0143	0.0252	0.0420	0.0374	-0.0334	-0.0161	0.0462	2002	0.1169
2003	-0.0147	0.0291	-0.0175	0.0062	0.0553	-0.0190	-0.1020	0.0124	0.0501	-0.0324	-0.0012	0.0093	2003	-0.0336
2004	0.0146	0.0192	0.0098	-0.0627	-0.0090	0.0074	0.0113	0.0350	0.0057	0.0115	-0.0275	0.0207	2004	0.0326
2005	0.0260	-0.0163	-0.0112	0.0334	0.0256	0.0131	-0.0322	0.0292	-0.0373	-0.0235	0.0037	0.0228	2005	0.0302
2006	-0.0157	0.0203	-0.0578	-0.0285	-0.0038	0.0048	0.0154	0.0256	0.0132	0.0035	0.0169	-0.0272	2006	-0.0364
2007	-0.0146	0.0297	-0.0184	0.0043	-0.0242	-0.0131	0.0238	0.0157	-0.0025	0.0112	0.0429	-0.0066	2007	0.0469
2008	0.0173	-0.0015	0.0069	-0.0324	-0.0202	0.0180	-0.0064	0.0206	0.0074	-0.0420	0.1407	0.0934	2008	0.2050
2009	-0.1149	-0.0086	0.0606	-0.0679	-0.0281	0.0046	-0.0018	0.0195	0.0142	-0.0203	0.0173	-0.0618	2009	-0.1825
2010	0.0228	-0.0002	-0.0219	0.0266	0.0403	0.0409	-0.0007	0.0670	-0.0180	-0.0344	-0.0169	-0.0420	2010	0.0589
2011	-0.0231	0.0081	-0.0042	0.0165	0.0318	-0.0212	0.0389	0.0829	0.0679	-0.0328	0.0228	0.0248	2011	0.2262
2012	-0.0020	-0.0216	-0.0324	0.0384	0.0620	-0.0153	0.0227	-0.0087	-0.0163	-0.0035	0.0124	-0.0221	2012	0.0095
2013	-0.0354	0.0092	-0.0083	0.0352	-0.0651	-0.0309	-0.0203	-0.0107	0.0032	0.0099	-0.0262	-0.0262	2013	-0.1570
2014	0.0516	0.0048	0.0034	0.0154	0.0251	-0.0051	0.0030	0.0343	-0.0194	0.0274	0.0263	0.0268	2014	0.2093
2015	0.0689	-0.0538	0.0116	-0.0269	-0.0179	-0.0321	0.0305	-0.0010	0.0153	-0.0074	-0.0086	-0.0044	2015	-0.0311

*Compound annual return

Appendix A-9

Long-term Government Bonds: Yields
From 1926 to 2015

Year	Jan	Feb	Mar	Apr	May	Jun	Jul	Aug	Sep	Oct	Nov	Dec	Year	Jan–Dec*
1926	0.0374	0.0372	0.0371	0.0368	0.0369	0.0368	0.0370	0.0373	0.0372	0.0367	0.0358	0.0354	1926	0.0354
1927	0.0351	0.0347	0.0331	0.0333	0.0327	0.0334	0.0333	0.0329	0.0330	0.0325	0.0320	0.0317	1927	0.0317
1928	0.0321	0.0318	0.0317	0.0319	0.0327	0.0326	0.0344	0.0341	0.0346	0.0336	0.0338	0.0340	1928	0.0340
1929	0.0349	0.0363	0.0377	0.0358	0.0373	0.0367	0.0369	0.0375	0.0375	0.0347	0.0331	0.0340	1929	0.0340
1930	0.0347	0.0339	0.0335	0.0338	0.0329	0.0328	0.0327	0.0328	0.0324	0.0324	0.0322	0.0330	1930	0.0330
1931	0.0343	0.0338	0.0332	0.0327	0.0317	0.0319	0.0325	0.0326	0.0353	0.0385	0.0385	0.0407	1931	0.0407
1932	0.0390	0.0367	0.0370	0.0336	0.0349	0.0347	0.0320	0.0321	0.0319	0.0322	0.0322	0.0315	1932	0.0315
1933	0.0308	0.0326	0.0321	0.0325	0.0308	0.0306	0.0309	0.0308	0.0308	0.0315	0.0327	0.0336	1933	0.0336
1934	0.0321	0.0317	0.0307	0.0300	0.0292	0.0289	0.0288	0.0299	0.0310	0.0300	0.0299	0.0293	1934	0.0293
1935	0.0281	0.0275	0.0274	0.0269	0.0276	0.0270	0.0268	0.0281	0.0282	0.0279	0.0280	0.0276	1935	0.0276
1936	0.0285	0.0281	0.0275	0.0274	0.0273	0.0273	0.0271	0.0264	0.0268	0.0269	0.0257	0.0255	1936	0.0255
1937	0.0258	0.0253	0.0285	0.0284	0.0282	0.0285	0.0277	0.0286	0.0284	0.0283	0.0278	0.0273	1937	0.0273
1938	0.0271	0.0268	0.0273	0.0259	0.0257	0.0259	0.0257	0.0259	0.0259	0.0254	0.0257	0.0252	1938	0.0252
1939	0.0249	0.0245	0.0237	0.0229	0.0217	0.0221	0.0213	0.0231	0.0278	0.0247	0.0236	0.0226	1939	0.0226
1940	0.0229	0.0228	0.0215	0.0220	0.0246	0.0227	0.0224	0.0223	0.0215	0.0214	0.0199	0.0194	1940	0.0194
1941	0.0213	0.0213	0.0206	0.0196	0.0195	0.0191	0.0191	0.0190	0.0193	0.0182	0.0186	0.0204	1941	0.0204
1942	0.0247	0.0247	0.0244	0.0246	0.0243	0.0244	0.0244	0.0244	0.0244	0.0244	0.0247	0.0246	1942	0.0246
1943	0.0245	0.0246	0.0247	0.0246	0.0244	0.0244	0.0245	0.0245	0.0246	0.0247	0.0248	0.0248	1943	0.0248
1944	0.0248	0.0247	0.0247	0.0248	0.0247	0.0248	0.0247	0.0247	0.0247	0.0247	0.0247	0.0246	1944	0.0246
1945	0.0240	0.0237	0.0236	0.0228	0.0226	0.0217	0.0224	0.0223	0.0221	0.0216	0.0210	0.0199	1945	0.0199
1946	0.0199	0.0198	0.0198	0.0207	0.0209	0.0206	0.0209	0.0217	0.0219	0.0216	0.0220	0.0212	1946	0.0212
1947	0.0214	0.0214	0.0213	0.0217	0.0216	0.0216	0.0214	0.0210	0.0213	0.0217	0.0229	0.0243	1947	0.0243
1948	0.0243	0.0241	0.0241	0.0239	0.0231	0.0238	0.0241	0.0242	0.0242	0.0243	0.0239	0.0237	1948	0.0237
1949	0.0233	0.0231	0.0227	0.0227	0.0227	0.0217	0.0216	0.0210	0.0212	0.0212	0.0212	0.0209	1949	0.0209
1950	0.0215	0.0214	0.0215	0.0214	0.0213	0.0216	0.0214	0.0214	0.0220	0.0225	0.0224	0.0224	1950	0.0224
1951	0.0221	0.0228	0.0241	0.0248	0.0254	0.0259	0.0252	0.0246	0.0253	0.0254	0.0264	0.0269	1951	0.0269
1952	0.0268	0.0269	0.0263	0.0254	0.0257	0.0259	0.0261	0.0267	0.0277	0.0269	0.0272	0.0279	1952	0.0279
1953	0.0279	0.0287	0.0294	0.0303	0.0314	0.0301	0.0301	0.0303	0.0284	0.0281	0.0286	0.0274	1953	0.0274
1954	0.0291	0.0279	0.0278	0.0273	0.0279	0.0272	0.0266	0.0269	0.0271	0.0272	0.0274	0.0272	1954	0.0272
1955	0.0286	0.0292	0.0288	0.0290	0.0287	0.0293	0.0300	0.0301	0.0298	0.0292	0.0295	0.0295	1955	0.0295

*Compound annual return

Appendix A-9

Long-term Government Bonds: Yields
From 1926 to 2015

Year	Jan	Feb	Mar	Apr	May	Jun	Jul	Aug	Sep	Oct	Nov	Dec	Year	Jan–Dec*
1956	0.0292	0.0293	0.0303	0.0311	0.0299	0.0299	0.0313	0.0325	0.0324	0.0329	0.0333	0.0345	1956	0.0345
1957	0.0328	0.0328	0.0331	0.0345	0.0348	0.0361	0.0365	0.0367	0.0364	0.0369	0.0340	0.0323	1957	0.0323
1958	0.0330	0.0326	0.0321	0.0311	0.0313	0.0324	0.0343	0.0371	0.0380	0.0374	0.0368	0.0382	1958	0.0382
1959	0.0408	0.0402	0.0403	0.0414	0.0417	0.0419	0.0417	0.0423	0.0429	0.0421	0.0432	0.0447	1959	0.0447
1960	0.0441	0.0429	0.0411	0.0426	0.0417	0.0407	0.0382	0.0390	0.0387	0.0391	0.0399	0.0380	1960	0.0380
1961	0.0404	0.0392	0.0397	0.0391	0.0397	0.0404	0.0404	0.0410	0.0403	0.0400	0.0404	0.0415	1961	0.0415
1962	0.0419	0.0414	0.0398	0.0394	0.0393	0.0401	0.0412	0.0401	0.0398	0.0395	0.0396	0.0395	1962	0.0395
1963	0.0398	0.0400	0.0401	0.0405	0.0406	0.0407	0.0407	0.0408	0.0410	0.0415	0.0414	0.0417	1963	0.0417
1964	0.0421	0.0424	0.0424	0.0423	0.0422	0.0419	0.0421	0.0423	0.0421	0.0421	0.0422	0.0423	1964	0.0423
1965	0.0422	0.0424	0.0422	0.0422	0.0423	0.0423	0.0424	0.0428	0.0433	0.0433	0.0441	0.0450	1965	0.0450
1966	0.0458	0.0477	0.0460	0.0467	0.0473	0.0477	0.0482	0.0499	0.0480	0.0467	0.0480	0.0455	1966	0.0455
1967	0.0448	0.0465	0.0455	0.0477	0.0482	0.0507	0.0505	0.0514	0.0517	0.0549	0.0567	0.0556	1967	0.0556
1968	0.0536	0.0542	0.0560	0.0547	0.0548	0.0534	0.0517	0.0520	0.0531	0.0543	0.0566	0.0598	1968	0.0598
1969	0.0617	0.0618	0.0620	0.0593	0.0635	0.0623	0.0621	0.0630	0.0677	0.0653	0.0676	0.0687	1969	0.0687
1970	0.0693	0.0651	0.0661	0.0699	0.0743	0.0709	0.0687	0.0694	0.0680	0.0693	0.0637	0.0648	1970	0.0648
1971	0.0612	0.0629	0.0593	0.0619	0.0624	0.0641	0.0643	0.0610	0.0598	0.0588	0.0596	0.0597	1971	0.0597
1972	0.0606	0.0602	0.0613	0.0615	0.0597	0.0607	0.0593	0.0595	0.0606	0.0591	0.0577	0.0599	1972	0.0599
1973	0.0685	0.0688	0.0686	0.0687	0.0703	0.0710	0.0760	0.0728	0.0703	0.0689	0.0712	0.0726	1973	0.0726
1974	0.0740	0.0748	0.0783	0.0816	0.0810	0.0812	0.0823	0.0855	0.0837	0.0795	0.0771	0.0760	1974	0.0760
1975	0.0796	0.0788	0.0824	0.0852	0.0836	0.0813	0.0829	0.0844	0.0862	0.0819	0.0838	0.0805	1975	0.0805
1976	0.0802	0.0802	0.0792	0.0797	0.0821	0.0807	0.0805	0.0790	0.0781	0.0779	0.0749	0.0721	1976	0.0721
1977	0.0764	0.0775	0.0772	0.0771	0.0765	0.0754	0.0768	0.0754	0.0764	0.0781	0.0777	0.0803	1977	0.0803
1978	0.0816	0.0822	0.0831	0.0838	0.0852	0.0865	0.0858	0.0843	0.0860	0.0889	0.0877	0.0898	1978	0.0898
1979	0.0886	0.0908	0.0902	0.0922	0.0903	0.0877	0.0895	0.0907	0.0927	0.1034	0.1009	0.1012	1979	0.1012
1980	0.1114	0.1186	0.1239	0.1076	0.1037	0.1006	0.1074	0.1140	0.1185	0.1231	0.1230	0.1199	1980	0.1199
1981	0.1211	0.1283	0.1248	0.1332	0.1265	0.1304	0.1370	0.1445	0.1482	0.1384	0.1220	0.1334	1981	0.1334
1982	0.1415	0.1402	0.1387	0.1348	0.1358	0.1412	0.1352	0.1254	0.1183	0.1112	0.1125	0.1095	1982	0.1095
1983	0.1113	0.1060	0.1083	0.1051	0.1112	0.1119	0.1198	0.1210	0.1157	0.1188	0.1176	0.1197	1983	0.1197
1984	0.1180	0.1217	0.1253	0.1284	0.1381	0.1374	0.1293	0.1270	0.1235	0.1173	0.1169	0.1170	1984	0.1170
1985	0.1127	0.1209	0.1181	0.1162	0.1062	0.1055	0.1091	0.1068	0.1082	0.1051	0.1011	0.0956	1985	0.0956

*Compound annual return

Appendix A-9

Long-term Government Bonds: Yields
From 1926 to 2015

Year	Jan	Feb	Mar	Apr	May	Jun	Jul	Aug	Sep	Oct	Nov	Dec	Year	Jan–Dec*
1986	0.0958	0.0841	0.0766	0.0782	0.0848	0.0790	0.0809	0.0763	0.0827	0.0803	0.0779	0.0789	1986	0.0789
1987	0.0778	0.0763	0.0795	0.0859	0.0880	0.0877	0.0907	0.0936	0.0992	0.0926	0.0931	0.0920	1987	0.0920
1988	0.0852	0.0854	0.0901	0.0929	0.0952	0.0917	0.0947	0.0950	0.0917	0.0889	0.0923	0.0919	1988	0.0919
1989	0.0903	0.0935	0.0929	0.0918	0.0878	0.0822	0.0801	0.0841	0.0847	0.0810	0.0808	0.0816	1989	0.0816
1990	0.0865	0.0876	0.0889	0.0924	0.0883	0.0864	0.0860	0.0920	0.0914	0.0898	0.0858	0.0844	1990	0.0844
1991	0.0837	0.0841	0.0844	0.0837	0.0845	0.0860	0.0850	0.0818	0.0790	0.0791	0.0789	0.0730	1991	0.0730
1992	0.0776	0.0777	0.0797	0.0803	0.0781	0.0765	0.0726	0.0725	0.0710	0.0741	0.0748	0.0726	1992	0.0726
1993	0.0725	0.0698	0.0702	0.0701	0.0701	0.0668	0.0656	0.0623	0.0627	0.0623	0.0651	0.0654	1993	0.0654
1994	0.0637	0.0682	0.0725	0.0745	0.0759	0.0774	0.0746	0.0761	0.0800	0.0809	0.0808	0.0799	1994	0.0799
1995	0.0780	0.0758	0.0755	0.0745	0.0677	0.0670	0.0691	0.0674	0.0663	0.0641	0.0623	0.0603	1995	0.0603
1996	0.0609	0.0659	0.0684	0.0706	0.0717	0.0703	0.0707	0.0726	0.0704	0.0671	0.0643	0.0673	1996	0.0673
1997	0.0689	0.0694	0.0723	0.0705	0.0701	0.0688	0.0637	0.0672	0.0649	0.0623	0.0614	0.0602	1997	0.0602
1998	0.0589	0.0599	0.0602	0.0604	0.0592	0.0576	0.0584	0.0547	0.0517	0.0540	0.0535	0.0542	1998	0.0542
1999	0.0536	0.0587	0.0592	0.0594	0.0615	0.0627	0.0639	0.0649	0.0646	0.0651	0.0662	0.0682	1999	0.0682
2000	0.0666	0.0646	0.0618	0.0630	0.0640	0.0622	0.0611	0.0594	0.0612	0.0600	0.0576	0.0558	2000	0.0558
2001	0.0562	0.0549	0.0559	0.0593	0.0594	0.0590	0.0561	0.0546	0.0542	0.0506	0.0553	0.0575	2001	0.0575
2002	0.0569	0.0563	0.0604	0.0575	0.0578	0.0566	0.0544	0.0510	0.0480	0.0508	0.0521	0.0484	2002	0.0484
2003	0.0495	0.0472	0.0486	0.0481	0.0436	0.0452	0.0542	0.0532	0.0490	0.0518	0.0519	0.0511	2003	0.0511
2004	0.0499	0.0483	0.0474	0.0531	0.0539	0.0532	0.0523	0.0493	0.0488	0.0478	0.0502	0.0484	2004	0.0484
2005	0.0465	0.0479	0.0488	0.0461	0.0440	0.0429	0.0456	0.0432	0.0464	0.0484	0.0481	0.0461	2005	0.0461
2006	0.0474	0.0457	0.0507	0.0532	0.0535	0.0531	0.0518	0.0496	0.0484	0.0481	0.0467	0.0491	2006	0.0491
2007	0.0502	0.0477	0.0493	0.0489	0.0510	0.0521	0.0501	0.0487	0.0489	0.0480	0.0445	0.0450	2007	0.0450
2008	0.0436	0.0438	0.0432	0.0458	0.0475	0.0460	0.0465	0.0449	0.0443	0.0478	0.0372	0.0303	2008	0.0303
2009	0.0394	0.0401	0.0355	0.0410	0.0432	0.0429	0.0430	0.0415	0.0403	0.0420	0.0406	0.0458	2009	0.0458
2010	0.0441	0.0441	0.0458	0.0437	0.0407	0.0376	0.0377	0.0327	0.0341	0.0367	0.0380	0.0414	2010	0.0414
2011	0.0432	0.0426	0.0429	0.0416	0.0391	0.0409	0.0378	0.0315	0.0265	0.0291	0.0273	0.0255	2011	0.0255
2012	0.0249	0.0272	0.0297	0.0268	0.0221	0.0233	0.0216	0.0223	0.0235	0.0238	0.0228	0.0246	2012	0.0246
2013	0.0291	0.0285	0.0287	0.0264	0.0309	0.0330	0.0344	0.0351	0.0349	0.0342	0.0361	0.0378	2013	0.0378
2014	0.0342	0.0339	0.0337	0.0326	0.0309	0.0313	0.0310	0.0287	0.0300	0.0282	0.0264	0.0246	2014	0.0246
2015	0.0200	0.0238	0.0230	0.0249	0.0262	0.0285	0.0263	0.0264	0.0253	0.0259	0.0265	0.0268	2015	0.0268

*Compound annual return

Appendix A-10

Intermediate-term Government Bonds: Total Returns
From 1926 to 2015

Year	Jan	Feb	Mar	Apr	May	Jun	Jul	Aug	Sep	Oct	Nov	Dec	Year	Jan–Dec*
1926	0.0068	0.0032	0.0041	0.0090	0.0008	0.0027	0.0013	0.0009	0.0050	0.0054	0.0045	0.0089	1926	0.0538
1927	0.0057	0.0038	0.0038	0.0016	0.0020	0.0029	0.0043	0.0056	0.0060	-0.0035	0.0083	0.0037	1927	0.0452
1928	0.0046	-0.0004	0.0010	-0.0003	-0.0006	0.0017	-0.0090	0.0050	0.0028	0.0032	0.0019	-0.0007	1928	0.0092
1929	-0.0029	-0.0018	0.0005	0.0089	-0.0061	0.0107	0.0066	0.0052	-0.0014	0.0168	0.0180	0.0044	1929	0.0601
1930	-0.0041	0.0094	0.0161	-0.0071	0.0061	0.0142	0.0054	0.0022	0.0063	0.0076	0.0070	0.0024	1930	0.0672
1931	-0.0071	0.0099	0.0052	0.0083	0.0119	-0.0214	0.0016	0.0017	-0.0113	-0.0105	0.0049	-0.0159	1931	-0.0232
1932	-0.0032	0.0128	0.0078	0.0194	-0.0090	0.0108	0.0120	0.0124	0.0027	0.0045	0.0031	0.0118	1932	0.0881
1933	-0.0016	-0.0001	0.0099	0.0057	0.0199	0.0008	-0.0006	0.0073	0.0026	-0.0025	0.0027	-0.0253	1933	0.0183
1934	0.0130	0.0052	0.0189	0.0182	0.0120	0.0091	-0.0024	-0.0092	-0.0138	0.0190	0.0046	0.0125	1934	0.0900
1935	0.0114	0.0105	0.0125	0.0107	-0.0035	0.0113	0.0038	-0.0071	-0.0057	0.0109	0.0014	0.0120	1935	0.0701
1936	-0.0004	0.0069	0.0031	0.0024	0.0038	0.0012	0.0022	0.0050	0.0010	0.0025	0.0081	-0.0057	1936	0.0306
1937	-0.0031	0.0007	-0.0164	0.0047	0.0080	-0.0013	0.0059	-0.0043	0.0081	0.0032	0.0042	0.0062	1937	0.0156
1938	0.0085	0.0052	-0.0013	0.0230	0.0023	0.0075	0.0010	0.0015	-0.0013	0.0093	-0.0001	0.0052	1938	0.0623
1939	0.0029	0.0082	0.0081	0.0038	0.0095	0.0002	0.0040	-0.0147	-0.0263	0.0315	0.0074	0.0108	1939	0.0452
1940	-0.0014	0.0035	0.0088	0.0002	-0.0214	0.0187	0.0003	0.0043	0.0047	0.0036	0.0056	0.0028	1940	0.0296
1941	0.0001	-0.0047	0.0069	0.0033	0.0012	0.0056	0.0000	0.0011	0.0000	0.0023	-0.0092	-0.0016	1941	0.0050
1942	0.0074	0.0015	0.0023	0.0022	0.0016	0.0013	0.0000	0.0017	-0.0023	0.0017	0.0017	0.0000	1942	0.0194
1943	0.0039	0.0013	0.0021	0.0024	0.0057	0.0033	0.0021	0.0002	0.0014	0.0017	0.0015	0.0021	1943	0.0281
1944	0.0011	0.0016	0.0020	0.0028	0.0005	0.0007	0.0029	0.0024	0.0011	0.0011	0.0009	0.0010	1944	0.0180
1945	0.0052	0.0038	0.0004	0.0014	0.0012	0.0019	0.0000	0.0016	0.0017	0.0016	0.0010	0.0021	1945	0.0222
1946	0.0039	0.0048	-0.0038	-0.0020	0.0006	0.0033	-0.0010	0.0004	-0.0011	0.0026	-0.0008	0.0032	1946	0.0100
1947	0.0023	0.0006	0.0024	-0.0013	0.0008	0.0008	0.0006	0.0026	0.0000	-0.0023	0.0006	0.0021	1947	0.0091
1948	0.0015	0.0018	0.0018	0.0019	0.0053	-0.0008	-0.0002	-0.0004	0.0010	0.0013	0.0021	0.0032	1948	0.0185
1949	0.0028	0.0011	0.0025	0.0015	0.0023	0.0050	0.0020	0.0031	0.0008	0.0006	0.0002	0.0012	1949	0.0232
1950	-0.0005	0.0008	0.0000	0.0008	0.0020	0.0003	0.0020	-0.0007	-0.0004	0.0001	0.0018	0.0008	1950	0.0070
1951	0.0022	0.0007	-0.0127	0.0057	-0.0040	0.0050	0.0058	0.0036	-0.0057	0.0016	0.0032	-0.0016	1951	0.0036
1952	0.0038	-0.0020	0.0067	0.0054	0.0019	-0.0035	-0.0034	-0.0024	0.0019	0.0066	-0.0006	0.0019	1952	0.0163
1953	-0.0002	0.0003	-0.0017	-0.0096	-0.0117	0.0155	0.0056	-0.0008	0.0194	0.0038	0.0014	0.0103	1953	0.0323
1954	0.0065	0.0100	0.0027	0.0043	-0.0073	0.0125	-0.0005	0.0011	-0.0020	-0.0009	-0.0001	0.0005	1954	0.0268
1955	-0.0032	-0.0052	0.0024	0.0004	0.0001	-0.0036	-0.0071	0.0007	0.0082	0.0072	-0.0053	-0.0011	1955	-0.0065

*Compound annual return

Appendix A-10

Intermediate-term Government Bonds: Total Returns
From 1926 to 2015

Year	Jan	Feb	Mar	Apr	May	Jun	Jul	Aug	Sep	Oct	Nov	Dec	Year	Jan–Dec*
1956	0.0105	0.0003	-0.0100	-0.0001	0.0112	0.0003	-0.0095	-0.0103	0.0092	-0.0019	-0.0047	0.0011	1956	-0.0042
1957	0.0237	-0.0013	0.0018	-0.0101	-0.0017	-0.0106	-0.0015	0.0109	0.0002	0.0043	0.0396	0.0216	1957	0.0784
1958	0.0034	0.0139	0.0053	0.0052	0.0060	-0.0068	-0.0091	-0.0356	-0.0017	0.0002	0.0132	-0.0061	1958	-0.0129
1959	-0.0013	0.0107	-0.0037	-0.0052	-0.0001	-0.0077	0.0034	-0.0078	0.0020	0.0174	-0.0092	-0.0020	1959	-0.0039
1960	0.0154	0.0072	0.0292	-0.0064	0.0031	0.0217	0.0267	-0.0005	0.0029	0.0016	-0.0094	0.0210	1960	0.1176
1961	-0.0059	0.0090	0.0037	0.0054	-0.0028	-0.0025	0.0007	0.0019	0.0079	0.0014	-0.0019	0.0018	1961	0.0185
1962	-0.0045	0.0155	0.0089	0.0025	0.0049	-0.0028	-0.0012	0.0125	0.0021	0.0051	0.0060	0.0056	1962	0.0556
1963	-0.0029	0.0017	0.0027	0.0030	0.0014	0.0014	0.0003	0.0019	0.0014	0.0011	0.0040	0.0003	1963	0.0164
1964	0.0033	0.0012	0.0016	0.0033	0.0081	0.0036	0.0027	0.0027	0.0045	0.0032	-0.0004	0.0058	1964	0.0404
1965	0.0042	0.0018	0.0043	0.0026	0.0035	0.0049	0.0017	0.0019	-0.0005	0.0000	0.0007	-0.0149	1965	0.0102
1966	0.0003	-0.0084	0.0187	-0.0019	0.0011	-0.0024	-0.0025	-0.0125	0.0216	0.0075	0.0028	0.0223	1966	0.0469
1967	0.0118	-0.0013	0.0183	-0.0089	0.0044	-0.0227	0.0133	-0.0036	0.0007	-0.0049	0.0028	0.0007	1967	0.0101
1968	0.0145	0.0040	-0.0026	-0.0016	0.0064	0.0167	0.0176	0.0021	0.0055	0.0009	-0.0013	-0.0173	1968	0.0454
1969	0.0086	-0.0013	0.0097	0.0079	-0.0082	-0.0084	0.0082	-0.0018	-0.0300	0.0333	-0.0047	-0.0193	1969	-0.0074
1970	0.0030	0.0439	0.0087	-0.0207	0.0110	0.0061	0.0152	0.0116	0.0196	0.0095	0.0451	0.0054	1970	0.1686
1971	0.0168	0.0224	0.0186	-0.0327	0.0011	-0.0187	0.0027	0.0350	0.0026	0.0220	0.0052	0.0110	1971	0.0872
1972	0.0106	0.0014	0.0015	0.0014	0.0016	0.0045	0.0015	0.0015	0.0014	0.0016	0.0045	0.0192	1972	0.0516
1973	-0.0006	-0.0075	0.0046	0.0064	0.0057	-0.0006	-0.0276	0.0254	0.0250	0.0050	0.0064	0.0040	1973	0.0461
1974	0.0009	0.0035	-0.0212	-0.0152	0.0130	-0.0087	0.0007	-0.0012	0.0319	0.0109	0.0236	0.0185	1974	0.0569
1975	0.0053	0.0148	-0.0059	-0.0186	0.0260	0.0027	-0.0030	-0.0009	0.0010	0.0366	-0.0010	0.0198	1975	0.0783
1976	0.0057	0.0084	0.0075	0.0116	-0.0145	0.0159	0.0119	0.0189	0.0076	0.0147	0.0321	0.0026	1976	0.1287
1977	-0.0190	0.0048	0.0055	0.0051	0.0056	0.0102	0.0001	0.0008	0.0015	-0.0060	0.0079	-0.0023	1977	0.0141
1978	0.0013	0.0017	0.0037	0.0024	-0.0002	-0.0021	0.0098	0.0079	0.0057	-0.0112	0.0092	0.0063	1978	0.0349
1979	0.0055	-0.0059	0.0112	0.0033	0.0193	0.0205	-0.0011	-0.0091	0.0006	-0.0468	0.0363	0.0087	1979	0.0409
1980	-0.0135	-0.0641	0.0143	0.1198	0.0490	-0.0077	-0.0106	-0.0387	-0.0038	-0.0152	0.0029	0.0171	1980	0.0391
1981	0.0032	-0.0235	0.0263	-0.0216	0.0245	0.0060	-0.0270	-0.0178	0.0164	0.0611	0.0624	-0.0142	1981	0.0945
1982	0.0050	0.0148	0.0042	0.0299	0.0146	-0.0135	0.0464	0.0469	0.0325	0.0531	0.0080	0.0185	1982	0.2910
1983	0.0007	0.0252	-0.0049	0.0259	-0.0122	0.0016	-0.0198	0.0081	0.0315	0.0019	0.0103	0.0047	1983	0.0741
1984	0.0177	-0.0064	-0.0035	-0.0003	-0.0250	0.0099	0.0393	0.0101	0.0202	0.0383	0.0192	0.0143	1984	0.1402
1985	0.0206	-0.0179	0.0166	0.0264	0.0485	0.0108	-0.0045	0.0148	0.0113	0.0162	0.0195	0.0257	1985	0.2033

*Compound annual return

Appendix A-10

Intermediate-term Government Bonds: Total Returns

From 1926 to 2015

Year	Jan	Feb	Mar	Apr	May	Jun	Jul	Aug	Sep	Oct	Nov	Dec	Year	Jan–Dec*
1986	0.0082	0.0275	0.0338	0.0081	-0.0215	0.0276	0.0157	0.0266	-0.0110	0.0162	0.0113	0.0007	1986	0.1514
1987	0.0107	0.0059	-0.0031	-0.0244	-0.0038	0.0122	0.0025	-0.0038	-0.0141	0.0299	0.0083	0.0093	1987	0.0290
1988	0.0316	0.0123	-0.0086	-0.0044	-0.0049	0.0181	-0.0047	-0.0009	0.0196	0.0148	-0.0115	-0.0010	1988	0.0610
1989	0.0121	-0.0051	0.0049	0.0220	0.0212	0.0324	0.0235	-0.0246	0.0069	0.0237	0.0084	0.0012	1989	0.1329
1990	-0.0105	0.0007	0.0002	-0.0077	0.0261	0.0151	0.0174	-0.0092	0.0094	0.0171	0.0193	0.0161	1990	0.0973
1991	0.0107	0.0048	0.0023	0.0117	0.0059	-0.0023	0.0129	0.0247	0.0216	0.0134	0.0128	0.0265	1991	0.1546
1992	-0.0195	0.0022	-0.0079	0.0098	0.0222	0.0177	0.0242	0.0150	0.0194	-0.0182	-0.0084	0.0146	1992	0.0719
1993	0.0270	0.0243	0.0043	0.0088	-0.0009	0.0201	0.0005	0.0223	0.0056	0.0018	-0.0093	0.0032	1993	0.1124
1994	0.0138	-0.0258	-0.0257	-0.0105	-0.0002	-0.0028	0.0169	0.0026	-0.0158	-0.0023	-0.0070	0.0053	1994	-0.0514
1995	0.0182	0.0234	0.0063	0.0143	0.0369	0.0079	-0.0016	0.0086	0.0064	0.0121	0.0149	0.0095	1995	0.1680
1996	0.0006	-0.0138	-0.0118	-0.0050	-0.0032	0.0117	0.0025	-0.0005	0.0155	0.0183	0.0149	-0.0078	1996	0.0210
1997	0.0025	0.0002	-0.0114	0.0148	0.0077	0.0103	0.0264	-0.0098	0.0151	0.0150	-0.0001	0.0106	1997	0.0838
1998	0.0180	-0.0039	0.0026	0.0061	0.0070	0.0079	0.0027	0.0271	0.0330	0.0041	-0.0098	0.0037	1998	0.1021
1999	0.0055	-0.0262	0.0086	0.0021	-0.0147	0.0032	-0.0005	0.0015	0.0097	-0.0008	-0.0008	-0.0048	1999	-0.0177
2000	-0.0053	0.0078	0.0203	-0.0043	0.0052	0.0191	0.0072	0.0134	0.0096	0.0079	0.0174	0.0214	2000	0.1259
2001	0.0098	0.0105	0.0076	-0.0114	-0.0007	0.0066	0.0247	0.0095	0.0253	0.0180	-0.0171	-0.0082	2001	0.0762
2002	0.0036	0.0108	-0.0242	0.0239	0.0118	0.0169	0.0272	0.0167	0.0288	-0.0024	-0.0169	0.0279	2002	0.1293
2003	-0.0089	0.0179	-0.0007	0.0013	0.0273	-0.0035	-0.0319	-0.0027	0.0307	-0.0136	-0.0014	0.0109	2003	0.0240
2004	0.0052	0.0124	0.0100	-0.0334	-0.0049	0.0049	0.0082	0.0195	0.0012	0.0064	-0.0127	0.0067	2004	0.0225
2005	0.0026	-0.0111	-0.0038	0.0167	0.0103	0.0043	-0.0144	0.0161	-0.0124	-0.0063	0.0059	0.0061	2005	0.0136
2006	-0.0036	-0.0017	-0.0056	-0.0008	-0.0004	0.0022	0.0125	0.0135	0.0079	0.0052	0.0088	-0.0067	2006	0.0314
2007	-0.0020	0.0170	0.0024	0.0047	-0.0102	0.0011	0.0175	0.0185	0.0057	-0.0048	0.0425	0.0048	2007	0.1005
2008	0.0263	0.0234	0.0073	-0.0293	-0.0084	0.0075	0.0064	0.0104	0.0085	0.0146	0.0430	0.0160	2008	0.1311
2009	-0.0163	-0.0082	0.0186	-0.0166	-0.0132	-0.0076	0.0056	0.0097	0.0075	0.0030	0.0184	-0.0241	2009	-0.0240
2010	0.0194	0.0071	-0.0088	0.0094	0.0151	0.0129	0.0158	0.0128	0.0049	0.0064	-0.0082	-0.0171	2010	0.0712
2011	0.0062	-0.0053	-0.0005	0.0154	0.0179	-0.0001	0.0202	0.0210	0.0008	0.0009	0.0036	0.0049	2011	0.0881
2012	0.0008	-0.0052	-0.0070	0.0129	0.0083	-0.0020	0.0077	0.0015	0.0004	-0.0024	0.0048	-0.0031	2012	0.0166
2013	-0.0061	0.0064	-0.0143	0.0060	-0.0165	-0.0139	0.0026	-0.0074	0.0121	0.0051	0.0011	-0.0122	2013	-0.0368
2014	0.0131	0.0024	-0.0068	0.0048	0.0094	-0.0017	-0.0047	0.0075	-0.0049	0.0089	0.0078	-0.0060	2014	0.0300
2015	0.0241	-0.0123	0.0074	-0.0014	0.0005	-0.0053	0.0051	0.0011	0.0099	-0.0052	-0.0040	-0.0017	2015	0.0179

*Compound annual return

Appendix A-11

Intermediate-term Government Bonds: Income Returns
From 1926 to 2015

Year	Jan	Feb	Mar	Apr	May	Jun	Jul	Aug	Sep	Oct	Nov	Dec	Year	Jan–Dec*
1926	0.0032	0.0032	0.0032	0.0031	0.0031	0.0031	0.0032	0.0032	0.0032	0.0031	0.0031	0.0030	1926	0.0378
1927	0.0029	0.0029	0.0029	0.0029	0.0029	0.0029	0.0029	0.0029	0.0028	0.0029	0.0028	0.0028	1927	0.0349
1928	0.0028	0.0028	0.0029	0.0029	0.0030	0.0030	0.0032	0.0032	0.0032	0.0032	0.0032	0.0033	1928	0.0364
1929	0.0034	0.0035	0.0036	0.0035	0.0037	0.0035	0.0035	0.0034	0.0035	0.0033	0.0030	0.0030	1929	0.0407
1930	0.0031	0.0030	0.0028	0.0030	0.0029	0.0027	0.0026	0.0026	0.0026	0.0025	0.0024	0.0024	1930	0.0330
1931	0.0026	0.0025	0.0024	0.0023	0.0021	0.0026	0.0026	0.0026	0.0028	0.0031	0.0031	0.0034	1931	0.0316
1932	0.0035	0.0034	0.0033	0.0030	0.0032	0.0031	0.0029	0.0027	0.0027	0.0027	0.0027	0.0025	1932	0.0363
1933	0.0026	0.0026	0.0025	0.0025	0.0021	0.0022	0.0022	0.0021	0.0021	0.0022	0.0022	0.0027	1933	0.0283
1934	0.0030	0.0024	0.0027	0.0024	0.0023	0.0021	0.0021	0.0021	0.0021	0.0026	0.0022	0.0023	1934	0.0293
1935	0.0021	0.0018	0.0018	0.0017	0.0016	0.0015	0.0015	0.0014	0.0015	0.0016	0.0015	0.0016	1935	0.0202
1936	0.0014	0.0013	0.0013	0.0012	0.0012	0.0013	0.0012	0.0012	0.0011	0.0011	0.0011	0.0010	1936	0.0144
1937	0.0010	0.0010	0.0012	0.0015	0.0013	0.0014	0.0014	0.0013	0.0014	0.0012	0.0012	0.0011	1937	0.0148
1938	0.0018	0.0016	0.0017	0.0017	0.0015	0.0014	0.0013	0.0014	0.0013	0.0014	0.0013	0.0013	1938	0.0182
1939	0.0013	0.0011	0.0012	0.0010	0.0011	0.0009	0.0009	0.0009	0.0011	0.0015	0.0010	0.0009	1939	0.0131
1940	0.0009	0.0008	0.0008	0.0007	0.0007	0.0010	0.0008	0.0008	0.0007	0.0007	0.0006	0.0005	1940	0.0090
1941	0.0006	0.0006	0.0008	0.0006	0.0006	0.0006	0.0005	0.0005	0.0005	0.0005	0.0004	0.0007	1941	0.0067
1942	0.0008	0.0006	0.0007	0.0006	0.0006	0.0006	0.0006	0.0006	0.0006	0.0006	0.0006	0.0006	1942	0.0076
1943	0.0014	0.0013	0.0014	0.0013	0.0013	0.0013	0.0013	0.0012	0.0012	0.0012	0.0012	0.0012	1943	0.0156
1944	0.0013	0.0012	0.0013	0.0012	0.0013	0.0012	0.0012	0.0012	0.0011	0.0012	0.0011	0.0011	1944	0.0144
1945	0.0012	0.0010	0.0010	0.0010	0.0010	0.0010	0.0010	0.0010	0.0009	0.0010	0.0009	0.0009	1945	0.0119
1946	0.0009	0.0008	0.0007	0.0009	0.0009	0.0009	0.0009	0.0009	0.0010	0.0010	0.0009	0.0010	1946	0.0108
1947	0.0010	0.0009	0.0010	0.0009	0.0010	0.0011	0.0010	0.0010	0.0010	0.0010	0.0010	0.0012	1947	0.0121
1948	0.0013	0.0012	0.0014	0.0013	0.0012	0.0013	0.0012	0.0013	0.0013	0.0013	0.0014	0.0013	1948	0.0156
1949	0.0013	0.0012	0.0013	0.0012	0.0013	0.0012	0.0010	0.0011	0.0010	0.0010	0.0010	0.0010	1949	0.0136
1950	0.0011	0.0010	0.0011	0.0010	0.0012	0.0011	0.0012	0.0011	0.0011	0.0013	0.0013	0.0013	1950	0.0139
1951	0.0016	0.0014	0.0015	0.0018	0.0017	0.0017	0.0018	0.0017	0.0015	0.0019	0.0017	0.0018	1951	0.0198
1952	0.0018	0.0017	0.0019	0.0017	0.0016	0.0017	0.0018	0.0018	0.0021	0.0020	0.0017	0.0021	1952	0.0219
1953	0.0019	0.0018	0.0021	0.0021	0.0022	0.0027	0.0024	0.0023	0.0023	0.0020	0.0020	0.0020	1953	0.0255
1954	0.0016	0.0014	0.0014	0.0013	0.0011	0.0016	0.0011	0.0012	0.0011	0.0012	0.0014	0.0014	1954	0.0160
1955	0.0018	0.0017	0.0020	0.0019	0.0021	0.0020	0.0020	0.0025	0.0023	0.0023	0.0021	0.0022	1955	0.0245

*Compound annual return

Appendix A-11

Intermediate-term Government Bonds: Income Returns

From 1926 to 2015

Year	Jan	Feb	Mar	Apr	May	Jun	Jul	Aug	Sep	Oct	Nov	Dec	Year	Jan–Dec*
1956	0.0025	0.0021	0.0022	0.0026	0.0026	0.0023	0.0025	0.0027	0.0026	0.0030	0.0028	0.0030	1956	0.0305
1957	0.0030	0.0025	0.0026	0.0029	0.0030	0.0027	0.0036	0.0032	0.0032	0.0033	0.0031	0.0028	1957	0.0359
1958	0.0024	0.0021	0.0022	0.0021	0.0019	0.0021	0.0021	0.0022	0.0032	0.0032	0.0029	0.0032	1958	0.0293
1959	0.0031	0.0030	0.0033	0.0032	0.0033	0.0037	0.0038	0.0037	0.0039	0.0039	0.0038	0.0041	1959	0.0418
1960	0.0039	0.0039	0.0039	0.0032	0.0037	0.0035	0.0031	0.0030	0.0028	0.0032	0.0028	0.0031	1960	0.0415
1961	0.0030	0.0028	0.0029	0.0027	0.0030	0.0029	0.0031	0.0031	0.0030	0.0032	0.0030	0.0030	1961	0.0354
1962	0.0035	0.0031	0.0031	0.0031	0.0031	0.0029	0.0033	0.0032	0.0028	0.0033	0.0029	0.0030	1962	0.0373
1963	0.0030	0.0028	0.0029	0.0032	0.0031	0.0029	0.0034	0.0031	0.0033	0.0033	0.0031	0.0034	1963	0.0371
1964	0.0034	0.0030	0.0035	0.0033	0.0031	0.0036	0.0034	0.0033	0.0033	0.0033	0.0034	0.0034	1964	0.0400
1965	0.0033	0.0031	0.0037	0.0033	0.0033	0.0037	0.0034	0.0036	0.0034	0.0034	0.0038	0.0037	1965	0.0415
1966	0.0040	0.0036	0.0043	0.0038	0.0042	0.0040	0.0040	0.0047	0.0046	0.0044	0.0042	0.0042	1966	0.0493
1967	0.0041	0.0035	0.0040	0.0033	0.0042	0.0038	0.0045	0.0042	0.0042	0.0047	0.0046	0.0044	1967	0.0488
1968	0.0051	0.0043	0.0043	0.0049	0.0048	0.0043	0.0049	0.0042	0.0044	0.0044	0.0042	0.0047	1968	0.0549
1969	0.0054	0.0048	0.0049	0.0057	0.0050	0.0058	0.0059	0.0054	0.0061	0.0067	0.0056	0.0068	1969	0.0665
1970	0.0066	0.0061	0.0063	0.0059	0.0062	0.0067	0.0065	0.0062	0.0060	0.0057	0.0058	0.0050	1970	0.0749
1971	0.0047	0.0043	0.0047	0.0040	0.0044	0.0053	0.0053	0.0056	0.0048	0.0046	0.0047	0.0046	1971	0.0575
1972	0.0048	0.0044	0.0046	0.0044	0.0052	0.0048	0.0049	0.0050	0.0047	0.0053	0.0051	0.0049	1972	0.0575
1973	0.0056	0.0048	0.0054	0.0056	0.0056	0.0053	0.0059	0.0064	0.0055	0.0060	0.0055	0.0056	1973	0.0658
1974	0.0057	0.0051	0.0054	0.0065	0.0067	0.0059	0.0073	0.0067	0.0072	0.0067	0.0061	0.0064	1974	0.0724
1975	0.0061	0.0055	0.0059	0.0060	0.0063	0.0063	0.0063	0.0061	0.0069	0.0068	0.0055	0.0067	1975	0.0735
1976	0.0060	0.0055	0.0066	0.0059	0.0054	0.0069	0.0060	0.0062	0.0056	0.0054	0.0058	0.0050	1976	0.0710
1977	0.0051	0.0050	0.0056	0.0053	0.0058	0.0055	0.0052	0.0059	0.0056	0.0059	0.0059	0.0059	1977	0.0649
1978	0.0066	0.0057	0.0066	0.0060	0.0071	0.0066	0.0070	0.0068	0.0065	0.0072	0.0072	0.0069	1978	0.0783
1979	0.0079	0.0066	0.0075	0.0077	0.0077	0.0070	0.0074	0.0073	0.0070	0.0084	0.0089	0.0086	1979	0.0904
1980	0.0086	0.0083	0.0107	0.0103	0.0081	0.0075	0.0079	0.0076	0.0097	0.0094	0.0096	0.0111	1980	0.1055
1981	0.0101	0.0095	0.0117	0.0106	0.0110	0.0118	0.0116	0.0120	0.0130	0.0129	0.0121	0.0108	1981	0.1297
1982	0.0107	0.0102	0.0122	0.0112	0.0101	0.0118	0.0113	0.0109	0.0097	0.0089	0.0087	0.0085	1982	0.1281
1983	0.0084	0.0079	0.0084	0.0081	0.0086	0.0085	0.0082	0.0103	0.0094	0.0092	0.0091	0.0091	1983	0.1035
1984	0.0096	0.0088	0.0095	0.0101	0.0104	0.0105	0.0113	0.0105	0.0095	0.0110	0.0093	0.0093	1984	0.1168
1985	0.0090	0.0081	0.0089	0.0097	0.0090	0.0073	0.0083	0.0081	0.0082	0.0081	0.0074	0.0078	1985	0.1029

*Compound annual return

Appendix A-11

Intermediate-term Government Bonds: Income Returns

From 1926 to 2015

Year	Jan	Feb	Mar	Apr	May	Jun	Jul	Aug	Sep	Oct	Nov	Dec	Year	Jan–Dec*
1986	0.0071	0.0066	0.0068	0.0060	0.0060	0.0068	0.0062	0.0057	0.0058	0.0060	0.0052	0.0060	1986	0.0772
1987	0.0055	0.0052	0.0060	0.0058	0.0062	0.0071	0.0066	0.0068	0.0068	0.0073	0.0070	0.0070	1987	0.0747
1988	0.0065	0.0066	0.0064	0.0063	0.0072	0.0070	0.0064	0.0077	0.0072	0.0071	0.0067	0.0071	1988	0.0824
1989	0.0077	0.0066	0.0078	0.0071	0.0080	0.0070	0.0067	0.0061	0.0065	0.0071	0.0063	0.0060	1989	0.0846
1990	0.0071	0.0064	0.0069	0.0071	0.0075	0.0067	0.0072	0.0068	0.0065	0.0074	0.0067	0.0067	1990	0.0815
1991	0.0064	0.0059	0.0059	0.0070	0.0065	0.0059	0.0069	0.0062	0.0061	0.0058	0.0052	0.0056	1991	0.0743
1992	0.0052	0.0052	0.0060	0.0058	0.0056	0.0058	0.0053	0.0050	0.0047	0.0044	0.0050	0.0053	1992	0.0627
1993	0.0049	0.0045	0.0049	0.0045	0.0041	0.0050	0.0041	0.0044	0.0041	0.0038	0.0042	0.0043	1993	0.0553
1994	0.0045	0.0039	0.0048	0.0049	0.0058	0.0055	0.0055	0.0060	0.0055	0.0060	0.0061	0.0063	1994	0.0607
1995	0.0067	0.0056	0.0060	0.0054	0.0062	0.0050	0.0051	0.0051	0.0047	0.0052	0.0047	0.0043	1995	0.0669
1996	0.0046	0.0041	0.0045	0.0053	0.0054	0.0050	0.0058	0.0052	0.0056	0.0053	0.0047	0.0050	1996	0.0582
1997	0.0052	0.0047	0.0054	0.0055	0.0054	0.0055	0.0054	0.0046	0.0054	0.0050	0.0043	0.0052	1997	0.0614
1998	0.0046	0.0041	0.0049	0.0046	0.0045	0.0049	0.0047	0.0046	0.0041	0.0035	0.0036	0.0039	1998	0.0529
1999	0.0037	0.0035	0.0048	0.0043	0.0041	0.0052	0.0048	0.0051	0.0048	0.0046	0.0052	0.0052	1999	0.0530
2000	0.0054	0.0052	0.0056	0.0048	0.0059	0.0054	0.0053	0.0051	0.0047	0.0051	0.0047	0.0043	2000	0.0619
2001	0.0032	0.0026	0.0027	0.0033	0.0042	0.0040	0.0044	0.0039	0.0034	0.0035	0.0030	0.0035	2001	0.0427
2002	0.0038	0.0034	0.0034	0.0045	0.0039	0.0034	0.0037	0.0029	0.0027	0.0022	0.0022	0.0028	2002	0.0398
2003	0.0024	0.0024	0.0024	0.0023	0.0023	0.0019	0.0020	0.0025	0.0029	0.0022	0.0023	0.0029	2003	0.0285
2004	0.0026	0.0024	0.0026	0.0023	0.0027	0.0034	0.0030	0.0031	0.0026	0.0026	0.0027	0.0030	2004	0.0328
2005	0.0031	0.0028	0.0034	0.0033	0.0034	0.0031	0.0030	0.0037	0.0031	0.0035	0.0036	0.0036	2005	0.0392
2006	0.0037	0.0034	0.0039	0.0037	0.0044	0.0041	0.0043	0.0040	0.0036	0.0039	0.0036	0.0034	2006	0.0454
2007	0.0041	0.0036	0.0037	0.0038	0.0038	0.0038	0.0043	0.0038	0.0032	0.0037	0.0035	0.0028	2007	0.0444
2008	0.0031	0.0024	0.0022	0.0020	0.0025	0.0028	0.0028	0.0025	0.0026	0.0024	0.0020	0.0015	2008	0.0296
2009	0.0012	0.0014	0.0013	0.0014	0.0016	0.0021	0.0022	0.0021	0.0019	0.0018	0.0018	0.0015	2009	0.0201
2010	0.0022	0.0019	0.0021	0.0021	0.0018	0.0019	0.0015	0.0013	0.0010	0.0009	0.0009	0.0011	2010	0.0192
2011	0.0019	0.0017	0.0019	0.0019	0.0018	0.0014	0.0014	0.0012	0.0007	0.0008	0.0007	0.0007	2011	0.0164
2012	0.0007	0.0006	0.0008	0.0009	0.0007	0.0005	0.0006	0.0005	0.0004	0.0005	0.0005	0.0004	2012	0.0073
2013	0.0007	0.0007	0.0004	0.0007	0.0006	0.0008	0.0012	0.0011	0.0013	0.0011	0.0009	0.0010	2013	0.0102
2014	0.0016	0.0012	0.0013	0.0014	0.0014	0.0012	0.0013	0.0013	0.0014	0.0014	0.0012	0.0012	2014	0.0163
2015	0.0014	0.0010	0.0014	0.0012	0.0011	0.0013	0.0014	0.0013	0.0013	0.0011	0.0012	0.0014	2015	0.0151

*Compound annual return

Appendix A-12

Intermediate-term Government Bonds: Capital Appreciation Returns
From 1926 to 2015

Year	Jan	Feb	Mar	Apr	May	Jun	Jul	Aug	Sep	Oct	Nov	Dec	Year	Jan–Dec*
1926	0.0036	0.0000	0.0009	0.0059	-0.0023	-0.0005	-0.0018	-0.0023	0.0018	0.0023	0.0014	0.0059	1926	0.0151
1927	0.0027	0.0009	0.0009	-0.0014	-0.0009	0.0000	0.0014	0.0027	0.0032	-0.0064	0.0055	0.0009	1927	0.0096
1928	0.0018	-0.0032	-0.0018	-0.0032	-0.0036	-0.0014	-0.0122	0.0018	-0.0005	0.0000	-0.0014	-0.0041	1928	-0.0273
1929	-0.0063	-0.0054	-0.0031	0.0054	-0.0098	0.0072	0.0031	0.0018	-0.0049	0.0135	0.0150	0.0014	1929	0.0177
1930	-0.0073	0.0064	0.0133	-0.0100	0.0032	0.0115	0.0028	-0.0005	0.0037	0.0051	0.0046	0.0000	1930	0.0330
1931	-0.0097	0.0074	0.0028	0.0060	0.0098	-0.0240	-0.0009	-0.0009	-0.0142	-0.0136	0.0018	-0.0193	1931	-0.0540
1932	-0.0067	0.0094	0.0045	0.0164	-0.0122	0.0077	0.0091	0.0096	0.0000	0.0018	0.0005	0.0092	1932	0.0502
1933	-0.0041	-0.0028	0.0074	0.0032	0.0178	-0.0014	-0.0028	0.0051	0.0005	-0.0047	0.0005	-0.0280	1933	-0.0099
1934	0.0100	0.0028	0.0162	0.0158	0.0097	0.0070	-0.0045	-0.0113	-0.0160	0.0164	0.0024	0.0102	1934	0.0597
1935	0.0093	0.0088	0.0107	0.0090	-0.0050	0.0098	0.0022	-0.0086	-0.0072	0.0093	-0.0002	0.0105	1935	0.0494
1936	-0.0017	0.0056	0.0018	0.0012	0.0026	-0.0001	0.0010	0.0038	-0.0001	0.0014	0.0070	-0.0067	1936	0.0160
1937	-0.0042	-0.0004	-0.0176	0.0032	0.0067	-0.0027	0.0045	-0.0056	0.0068	0.0020	0.0030	0.0051	1937	0.0005
1938	0.0067	0.0036	-0.0030	0.0214	0.0008	0.0061	-0.0003	0.0000	-0.0026	0.0079	-0.0014	0.0039	1938	0.0437
1939	0.0016	0.0071	0.0069	0.0028	0.0084	-0.0007	0.0030	-0.0155	-0.0273	0.0300	0.0063	0.0098	1939	0.0318
1940	-0.0023	0.0027	0.0080	-0.0005	-0.0221	0.0177	-0.0005	0.0035	0.0040	0.0030	0.0050	0.0023	1940	0.0204
1941	-0.0006	-0.0052	0.0061	0.0027	0.0006	0.0051	-0.0004	0.0006	-0.0004	0.0018	-0.0096	-0.0023	1941	-0.0017
1942	0.0066	0.0009	0.0016	0.0016	0.0010	0.0006	-0.0006	0.0011	-0.0029	0.0011	0.0011	-0.0006	1942	0.0117
1943	0.0025	0.0001	0.0007	0.0010	0.0044	0.0020	0.0008	-0.0010	0.0002	0.0005	0.0002	0.0008	1943	0.0123
1944	-0.0002	0.0004	0.0007	0.0016	-0.0008	-0.0005	0.0016	0.0012	0.0000	-0.0001	-0.0003	-0.0001	1944	0.0035
1945	0.0040	0.0028	-0.0006	0.0005	0.0002	0.0009	-0.0010	0.0006	0.0008	0.0006	0.0001	0.0012	1945	0.0102
1946	0.0030	0.0040	-0.0045	-0.0028	-0.0003	0.0024	-0.0019	-0.0005	-0.0020	0.0015	-0.0018	0.0022	1946	-0.0008
1947	0.0012	-0.0003	0.0014	-0.0022	-0.0002	-0.0003	-0.0005	0.0016	-0.0010	-0.0033	-0.0004	0.0008	1947	-0.0030
1948	0.0002	0.0006	0.0003	0.0006	0.0042	-0.0021	-0.0015	-0.0018	-0.0003	0.0000	0.0006	0.0019	1948	0.0027
1949	0.0015	-0.0001	0.0012	0.0003	0.0010	0.0038	0.0010	0.0019	-0.0002	-0.0004	-0.0008	0.0002	1949	0.0095
1950	-0.0016	-0.0002	-0.0011	-0.0003	0.0007	-0.0008	0.0009	-0.0019	-0.0015	-0.0013	0.0005	-0.0004	1950	-0.0069
1951	0.0006	-0.0007	-0.0142	0.0040	-0.0058	0.0033	0.0040	0.0019	-0.0072	-0.0003	0.0015	-0.0034	1951	-0.0163
1952	0.0019	-0.0037	0.0048	0.0037	0.0004	-0.0053	-0.0052	-0.0042	-0.0002	0.0046	-0.0023	-0.0002	1952	-0.0057
1953	-0.0022	-0.0016	-0.0038	-0.0117	-0.0139	0.0129	0.0032	-0.0031	0.0171	0.0018	-0.0006	0.0083	1953	0.0061
1954	0.0049	0.0086	0.0013	0.0031	-0.0084	0.0109	-0.0016	-0.0001	-0.0032	-0.0021	-0.0015	-0.0010	1954	0.0108
1955	-0.0050	-0.0070	0.0004	-0.0015	-0.0020	-0.0057	-0.0091	-0.0018	0.0059	0.0050	-0.0074	-0.0033	1955	-0.0310

*Compound annual return

Appendix A-12

Intermediate-term Government Bonds: Capital Appreciation Returns
From 1926 to 2015

Year	Jan	Feb	Mar	Apr	May	Jun	Jul	Aug	Sep	Oct	Nov	Dec	Year	Jan–Dec*
1956	0.0080	-0.0018	-0.0122	-0.0027	0.0086	-0.0020	-0.0120	-0.0130	0.0066	-0.0049	-0.0075	-0.0019	1956	-0.0345
1957	0.0207	-0.0037	-0.0009	-0.0130	-0.0047	-0.0133	-0.0051	0.0077	-0.0030	0.0010	0.0365	0.0188	1957	0.0405
1958	0.0010	0.0117	0.0031	0.0031	0.0041	-0.0088	-0.0112	-0.0378	-0.0048	-0.0029	0.0103	-0.0093	1958	-0.0417
1959	-0.0045	0.0078	-0.0070	-0.0084	-0.0034	-0.0113	-0.0004	-0.0116	-0.0019	0.0134	-0.0130	-0.0060	1959	-0.0456
1960	0.0115	0.0032	0.0253	-0.0096	-0.0006	0.0182	0.0236	-0.0034	0.0001	-0.0013	-0.0122	0.0180	1960	0.0742
1961	-0.0089	0.0063	0.0008	0.0026	-0.0058	-0.0054	-0.0024	-0.0013	0.0049	-0.0018	-0.0049	-0.0012	1961	-0.0172
1962	-0.0080	0.0124	0.0058	-0.0006	0.0018	-0.0056	-0.0045	0.0092	-0.0007	0.0018	0.0031	0.0026	1962	0.0173
1963	-0.0059	-0.0011	-0.0002	-0.0002	-0.0017	-0.0015	-0.0030	-0.0012	-0.0019	-0.0022	0.0008	-0.0032	1963	-0.0210
1964	-0.0001	-0.0019	-0.0019	-0.0001	0.0049	0.0000	-0.0006	-0.0006	0.0012	0.0000	-0.0037	0.0024	1964	-0.0003
1965	0.0009	-0.0013	0.0006	-0.0007	0.0002	0.0012	-0.0016	-0.0017	-0.0039	-0.0034	-0.0031	-0.0186	1965	-0.0310
1966	-0.0037	-0.0120	0.0145	-0.0056	-0.0032	-0.0064	-0.0065	-0.0171	0.0170	0.0031	-0.0015	0.0180	1966	-0.0041
1967	0.0077	-0.0048	0.0144	-0.0122	0.0002	-0.0265	0.0089	-0.0078	-0.0035	-0.0095	-0.0018	-0.0038	1967	-0.0385
1968	0.0095	-0.0003	-0.0069	-0.0065	0.0015	0.0123	0.0128	-0.0021	0.0011	-0.0035	-0.0054	-0.0220	1968	-0.0099
1969	0.0032	-0.0061	0.0048	0.0021	-0.0131	-0.0142	0.0024	-0.0072	-0.0361	0.0266	-0.0103	-0.0260	1969	-0.0727
1970	-0.0035	0.0378	0.0024	-0.0266	0.0049	-0.0006	0.0087	0.0054	0.0136	0.0037	0.0393	0.0005	1970	0.0871
1971	0.0121	0.0181	0.0139	-0.0367	-0.0034	-0.0240	-0.0027	0.0294	-0.0022	0.0173	0.0005	0.0064	1971	0.0272
1972	0.0058	-0.0030	-0.0031	-0.0030	-0.0035	-0.0003	-0.0034	-0.0035	-0.0033	-0.0037	-0.0006	0.0143	1972	-0.0075
1973	-0.0062	-0.0123	-0.0008	0.0007	0.0001	-0.0059	-0.0336	0.0190	0.0195	-0.0010	0.0009	-0.0016	1973	-0.0219
1974	-0.0048	-0.0016	-0.0266	-0.0217	0.0063	-0.0147	-0.0066	-0.0078	0.0247	0.0043	0.0175	0.0120	1974	-0.0199
1975	-0.0008	0.0092	-0.0119	-0.0246	0.0197	-0.0035	-0.0094	-0.0070	-0.0059	0.0298	-0.0065	0.0131	1975	0.0012
1976	-0.0003	0.0028	0.0010	0.0057	-0.0200	0.0090	0.0059	0.0127	0.0019	0.0093	0.0264	-0.0024	1976	0.0525
1977	-0.0241	-0.0002	-0.0001	-0.0001	-0.0002	0.0048	-0.0051	-0.0052	-0.0041	-0.0118	0.0019	-0.0082	1977	-0.0515
1978	-0.0053	-0.0041	-0.0029	-0.0036	-0.0073	-0.0087	0.0028	0.0010	-0.0008	-0.0184	0.0020	-0.0005	1978	-0.0449
1979	-0.0024	-0.0125	0.0038	-0.0044	0.0116	0.0135	-0.0086	-0.0163	-0.0065	-0.0553	0.0274	0.0001	1979	-0.0507
1980	-0.0221	-0.0724	0.0036	0.1095	0.0409	-0.0152	-0.0185	-0.0463	-0.0135	-0.0246	-0.0067	0.0060	1980	-0.0681
1981	-0.0069	-0.0331	0.0146	-0.0322	0.0135	-0.0059	-0.0386	-0.0298	0.0034	0.0482	0.0502	-0.0250	1981	-0.0455
1982	-0.0057	0.0046	-0.0080	0.0186	0.0045	-0.0253	0.0351	0.0359	0.0228	0.0442	-0.0007	0.0100	1982	0.1423
1983	-0.0076	0.0173	-0.0133	0.0177	-0.0208	-0.0069	-0.0280	-0.0023	0.0220	-0.0073	0.0012	-0.0043	1983	-0.0330
1984	0.0081	-0.0153	-0.0129	-0.0104	-0.0353	-0.0007	0.0280	-0.0005	0.0106	0.0274	0.0099	0.0050	1984	0.0122
1985	0.0116	-0.0261	0.0077	0.0167	0.0395	0.0035	-0.0129	0.0067	0.0031	0.0081	0.0121	0.0178	1985	0.0901

*Compound annual return

Appendix A-12

Intermediate-term Government Bonds: Capital Appreciation Returns

From 1926 to 2015

Year	Jan	Feb	Mar	Apr	May	Jun	Jul	Aug	Sep	Oct	Nov	Dec	Year	Jan–Dec*
1986	0.0011	0.0210	0.0270	0.0021	-0.0274	0.0208	0.0095	0.0209	-0.0168	0.0102	0.0061	-0.0053	1986	0.0699
1987	0.0051	0.0007	-0.0091	-0.0302	-0.0100	0.0051	-0.0040	-0.0106	-0.0209	0.0226	0.0013	0.0023	1987	-0.0475
1988	0.0251	0.0057	-0.0151	-0.0107	-0.0122	0.0111	-0.0111	-0.0086	0.0124	0.0077	-0.0182	-0.0081	1988	-0.0226
1989	0.0044	-0.0117	-0.0029	0.0149	0.0132	0.0254	0.0168	-0.0307	0.0004	0.0166	0.0021	-0.0048	1989	0.0434
1990	-0.0176	-0.0057	-0.0067	-0.0148	0.0186	0.0084	0.0102	-0.0160	0.0030	0.0096	0.0126	0.0095	1990	0.0102
1991	0.0042	-0.0011	-0.0036	0.0046	-0.0006	-0.0081	0.0060	0.0184	0.0155	0.0077	0.0076	0.0209	1991	0.0736
1992	-0.0247	-0.0030	-0.0139	0.0039	0.0166	0.0118	0.0189	0.0100	0.0147	-0.0226	-0.0134	0.0093	1992	0.0064
1993	0.0221	0.0198	-0.0006	0.0043	-0.0051	0.0152	-0.0036	0.0179	0.0015	-0.0020	-0.0135	-0.0011	1993	0.0556
1994	0.0093	-0.0297	-0.0306	-0.0154	-0.0060	-0.0084	0.0115	-0.0034	-0.0213	-0.0084	-0.0131	-0.0010	1994	-0.1114
1995	0.0115	0.0178	0.0003	0.0090	0.0307	0.0030	-0.0066	0.0035	0.0017	0.0069	0.0102	0.0052	1995	0.0966
1996	-0.0040	-0.0178	-0.0164	-0.0103	-0.0086	0.0067	-0.0033	-0.0057	0.0100	0.0129	0.0102	-0.0128	1996	-0.0390
1997	-0.0027	-0.0045	-0.0168	0.0093	0.0024	0.0048	0.0210	-0.0143	0.0098	0.0100	-0.0045	0.0054	1997	0.0195
1998	0.0134	-0.0080	-0.0024	0.0015	0.0025	0.0030	-0.0020	0.0225	0.0289	0.0006	-0.0134	-0.0002	1998	0.0466
1999	0.0018	-0.0297	0.0038	-0.0023	-0.0188	-0.0020	-0.0053	-0.0035	0.0049	-0.0054	-0.0060	-0.0100	1999	-0.0706
2000	-0.0107	0.0026	0.0147	-0.0091	-0.0007	0.0138	0.0019	0.0083	0.0049	0.0028	0.0127	0.0171	2000	0.0594
2001	0.0066	0.0079	0.0049	-0.0146	-0.0049	0.0025	0.0203	0.0056	0.0219	0.0145	-0.0201	-0.0117	2001	0.0323
2002	-0.0003	0.0073	-0.0276	0.0193	0.0079	0.0135	0.0234	0.0138	0.0261	-0.0046	-0.0191	0.0251	2002	0.0865
2003	-0.0113	0.0155	-0.0031	-0.0010	0.0250	-0.0054	-0.0339	-0.0053	0.0279	-0.0158	-0.0038	0.0080	2003	-0.0048
2004	0.0025	0.0100	0.0074	-0.0357	-0.0076	0.0015	0.0051	0.0164	-0.0014	0.0039	-0.0154	0.0036	2004	-0.0107
2005	-0.0005	-0.0139	-0.0073	0.0134	0.0069	0.0012	-0.0173	0.0124	-0.0155	-0.0098	0.0023	0.0026	2005	-0.0258
2006	-0.0073	-0.0051	-0.0095	-0.0045	-0.0049	0.0012	0.0082	0.0095	0.0042	0.0012	0.0052	-0.0102	2006	-0.0151
2007	-0.0061	0.0134	-0.0012	0.0009	-0.0141	-0.0019	0.0132	0.0147	0.0026	-0.0085	0.0390	0.0021	2007	0.0533
2008	0.0231	0.0210	0.0051	-0.0314	-0.0110	0.0047	0.0036	0.0079	0.0058	0.0122	0.0410	0.0145	2008	0.0992
2009	-0.0175	-0.0096	0.0168	-0.0179	-0.0148	-0.0097	0.0034	0.0076	0.0056	0.0012	0.0166	-0.0256	2009	-0.0442
2010	0.0172	0.0052	-0.0109	0.0073	0.0133	0.0111	0.0143	0.0115	0.0039	0.0055	-0.0091	-0.0182	2010	0.0516
2011	0.0044	-0.0070	-0.0024	0.0136	0.0161	-0.0015	0.0188	0.0198	0.0001	0.0002	0.0028	0.0043	2011	0.0709
2012	0.0002	-0.0059	-0.0078	0.0120	0.0075	-0.0025	0.0071	0.0010	0.0000	-0.0029	0.0043	-0.0036	2012	0.0093
2013	-0.0068	0.0057	-0.0146	0.0053	-0.0170	-0.0147	0.0014	-0.0084	0.0108	0.0040	0.0002	-0.0132	2013	-0.0468
2014	0.0115	0.0011	-0.0082	0.0033	0.0080	-0.0030	-0.0060	0.0061	-0.0062	0.0075	0.0066	-0.0072	2014	0.0135
2015	0.0227	-0.0132	0.0061	-0.0025	-0.0007	-0.0065	0.0037	-0.0002	0.0087	-0.0063	-0.0053	-0.0031	2015	0.0029

*Compound annual return

Appendix A-13

Intermediate-term Government Bonds: Yields
From 1926 to 2015

Year	Jan	Feb	Mar	Apr	May	Jun	Jul	Aug	Sep	Oct	Nov	Dec	Year	Jan–Dec*
1926	0.0386	0.0386	0.0384	0.0371	0.0376	0.0377	0.0381	0.0386	0.0382	0.0377	0.0374	0.0361	1926	0.0361
1927	0.0355	0.0353	0.0351	0.0354	0.0356	0.0356	0.0353	0.0347	0.0340	0.0354	0.0342	0.0340	1927	0.0340
1928	0.0336	0.0343	0.0347	0.0354	0.0362	0.0365	0.0392	0.0388	0.0389	0.0389	0.0392	0.0401	1928	0.0401
1929	0.0415	0.0427	0.0434	0.0422	0.0444	0.0428	0.0421	0.0417	0.0428	0.0398	0.0365	0.0362	1929	0.0362
1930	0.0378	0.0364	0.0335	0.0357	0.0350	0.0325	0.0319	0.0320	0.0312	0.0301	0.0291	0.0291	1930	0.0291
1931	0.0312	0.0296	0.0290	0.0277	0.0256	0.0308	0.0310	0.0312	0.0343	0.0373	0.0369	0.0412	1931	0.0412
1932	0.0427	0.0406	0.0396	0.0360	0.0387	0.0370	0.0350	0.0329	0.0329	0.0325	0.0324	0.0304	1932	0.0304
1933	0.0313	0.0319	0.0303	0.0296	0.0258	0.0261	0.0267	0.0256	0.0255	0.0265	0.0264	0.0325	1933	0.0325
1934	0.0325	0.0321	0.0296	0.0272	0.0257	0.0246	0.0253	0.0271	0.0298	0.0271	0.0267	0.0249	1934	0.0249
1935	0.0233	0.0218	0.0199	0.0184	0.0193	0.0175	0.0171	0.0187	0.0201	0.0183	0.0183	0.0163	1935	0.0163
1936	0.0166	0.0155	0.0151	0.0149	0.0143	0.0143	0.0141	0.0133	0.0133	0.0130	0.0114	0.0129	1936	0.0129
1937	0.0134	0.0135	0.0184	0.0175	0.0156	0.0164	0.0151	0.0168	0.0147	0.0141	0.0131	0.0114	1937	0.0114
1938	0.0205	0.0200	0.0204	0.0174	0.0173	0.0164	0.0164	0.0164	0.0168	0.0156	0.0158	0.0152	1938	0.0152
1939	0.0149	0.0138	0.0127	0.0122	0.0108	0.0110	0.0105	0.0131	0.0180	0.0127	0.0116	0.0098	1939	0.0098
1940	0.0103	0.0098	0.0083	0.0084	0.0127	0.0092	0.0093	0.0086	0.0078	0.0072	0.0061	0.0057	1940	0.0057
1941	0.0077	0.0089	0.0075	0.0069	0.0067	0.0055	0.0056	0.0055	0.0056	0.0051	0.0076	0.0082	1941	0.0082
1942	0.0083	0.0081	0.0077	0.0074	0.0071	0.0070	0.0071	0.0069	0.0076	0.0073	0.0070	0.0072	1942	0.0072
1943	0.0166	0.0166	0.0164	0.0162	0.0153	0.0149	0.0147	0.0149	0.0149	0.0147	0.0147	0.0145	1943	0.0145
1944	0.0150	0.0150	0.0148	0.0143	0.0146	0.0147	0.0142	0.0139	0.0139	0.0139	0.0140	0.0140	1944	0.0140
1945	0.0127	0.0118	0.0120	0.0118	0.0117	0.0114	0.0118	0.0115	0.0112	0.0109	0.0109	0.0103	1945	0.0103
1946	0.0099	0.0087	0.0101	0.0111	0.0112	0.0103	0.0110	0.0112	0.0120	0.0114	0.0121	0.0112	1946	0.0112
1947	0.0116	0.0117	0.0112	0.0120	0.0121	0.0122	0.0124	0.0117	0.0121	0.0136	0.0138	0.0134	1947	0.0134
1948	0.0160	0.0158	0.0157	0.0155	0.0142	0.0149	0.0154	0.0160	0.0161	0.0161	0.0158	0.0151	1948	0.0151
1949	0.0153	0.0153	0.0148	0.0147	0.0144	0.0129	0.0125	0.0117	0.0118	0.0120	0.0124	0.0123	1949	0.0123
1950	0.0131	0.0132	0.0137	0.0138	0.0134	0.0139	0.0134	0.0145	0.0154	0.0162	0.0159	0.0162	1950	0.0162
1951	0.0179	0.0180	0.0211	0.0202	0.0215	0.0208	0.0199	0.0194	0.0212	0.0212	0.0209	0.0217	1951	0.0217
1952	0.0212	0.0222	0.0209	0.0199	0.0198	0.0213	0.0228	0.0241	0.0242	0.0227	0.0235	0.0235	1952	0.0235
1953	0.0242	0.0245	0.0253	0.0277	0.0307	0.0279	0.0272	0.0279	0.0241	0.0237	0.0238	0.0218	1953	0.0218
1954	0.0187	0.0157	0.0153	0.0142	0.0173	0.0131	0.0138	0.0138	0.0152	0.0161	0.0168	0.0172	1954	0.0172
1955	0.0227	0.0240	0.0240	0.0242	0.0246	0.0257	0.0276	0.0280	0.0267	0.0257	0.0273	0.0280	1955	0.0280

*Compound annual return

Appendix A-13

Intermediate-term Government Bonds: Yields
From 1926 to 2015

Year	Jan	Feb	Mar	Apr	May	Jun	Jul	Aug	Sep	Oct	Nov	Dec	Year	Jan–Dec*
1956	0.0271	0.0275	0.0300	0.0305	0.0287	0.0292	0.0317	0.0346	0.0331	0.0342	0.0359	0.0363	1956	0.0363
1957	0.0326	0.0333	0.0334	0.0357	0.0366	0.0390	0.0399	0.0385	0.0390	0.0388	0.0320	0.0284	1957	0.0284
1958	0.0282	0.0259	0.0253	0.0246	0.0238	0.0250	0.0281	0.0365	0.0376	0.0382	0.0359	0.0381	1958	0.0381
1959	0.0395	0.0378	0.0393	0.0413	0.0420	0.0447	0.0448	0.0477	0.0482	0.0448	0.0482	0.0498	1959	0.0498
1960	0.0471	0.0464	0.0409	0.0431	0.0432	0.0390	0.0334	0.0343	0.0343	0.0346	0.0377	0.0331	1960	0.0331
1961	0.0363	0.0350	0.0348	0.0342	0.0355	0.0368	0.0373	0.0376	0.0365	0.0369	0.0381	0.0384	1961	0.0384
1962	0.0402	0.0377	0.0366	0.0367	0.0363	0.0375	0.0384	0.0365	0.0366	0.0362	0.0355	0.0350	1962	0.0350
1963	0.0368	0.0370	0.0370	0.0371	0.0374	0.0378	0.0385	0.0388	0.0392	0.0398	0.0396	0.0404	1963	0.0404
1964	0.0402	0.0407	0.0411	0.0411	0.0399	0.0399	0.0401	0.0402	0.0399	0.0399	0.0409	0.0403	1964	0.0403
1965	0.0413	0.0416	0.0414	0.0416	0.0415	0.0413	0.0416	0.0420	0.0429	0.0437	0.0444	0.0490	1965	0.0490
1966	0.0482	0.0507	0.0477	0.0489	0.0496	0.0510	0.0525	0.0565	0.0526	0.0519	0.0522	0.0479	1966	0.0479
1967	0.0459	0.0470	0.0437	0.0466	0.0465	0.0530	0.0508	0.0528	0.0537	0.0562	0.0566	0.0577	1967	0.0577
1968	0.0548	0.0549	0.0563	0.0577	0.0574	0.0547	0.0518	0.0523	0.0520	0.0528	0.0541	0.0596	1968	0.0596
1969	0.0637	0.0651	0.0640	0.0636	0.0666	0.0699	0.0693	0.0711	0.0799	0.0735	0.0761	0.0829	1969	0.0829
1970	0.0820	0.0730	0.0724	0.0790	0.0778	0.0780	0.0757	0.0743	0.0707	0.0697	0.0591	0.0590	1970	0.0590
1971	0.0570	0.0526	0.0493	0.0585	0.0593	0.0656	0.0663	0.0585	0.0591	0.0545	0.0543	0.0525	1971	0.0525
1972	0.0556	0.0563	0.0570	0.0577	0.0586	0.0587	0.0595	0.0604	0.0613	0.0623	0.0625	0.0585	1972	0.0585
1973	0.0641	0.0671	0.0673	0.0671	0.0671	0.0686	0.0776	0.0725	0.0674	0.0677	0.0674	0.0679	1973	0.0679
1974	0.0687	0.0691	0.0751	0.0801	0.0786	0.0822	0.0838	0.0857	0.0797	0.0787	0.0743	0.0712	1974	0.0712
1975	0.0730	0.0709	0.0737	0.0798	0.0749	0.0758	0.0782	0.0800	0.0815	0.0736	0.0754	0.0719	1975	0.0719
1976	0.0743	0.0736	0.0733	0.0719	0.0771	0.0747	0.0732	0.0697	0.0692	0.0667	0.0594	0.0600	1976	0.0600
1977	0.0673	0.0673	0.0673	0.0674	0.0674	0.0662	0.0675	0.0689	0.0700	0.0733	0.0727	0.0751	1977	0.0751
1978	0.0773	0.0784	0.0791	0.0800	0.0820	0.0843	0.0836	0.0833	0.0835	0.0887	0.0882	0.0883	1978	0.0883
1979	0.0895	0.0928	0.0918	0.0929	0.0899	0.0864	0.0887	0.0933	0.0951	0.1112	0.1033	0.1033	1979	0.1033
1980	0.1093	0.1294	0.1285	0.1009	0.0903	0.0944	0.0996	0.1133	0.1171	0.1244	0.1264	0.1245	1980	0.1245
1981	0.1275	0.1371	0.1328	0.1427	0.1385	0.1404	0.1533	0.1636	0.1625	0.1472	0.1311	0.1396	1981	0.1396
1982	0.1397	0.1385	0.1406	0.1355	0.1343	0.1417	0.1315	0.1209	0.1144	0.1018	0.1020	0.0990	1982	0.0990
1983	0.1057	0.1010	0.1048	0.0997	0.1059	0.1080	0.1168	0.1175	0.1108	0.1131	0.1127	0.1141	1983	0.1141
1984	0.1137	0.1181	0.1219	0.1251	0.1363	0.1365	0.1274	0.1276	0.1242	0.1154	0.1121	0.1104	1984	0.1104
1985	0.1081	0.1152	0.1131	0.1084	0.0974	0.0964	0.1002	0.0982	0.0973	0.0949	0.0911	0.0855	1985	0.0855

*Compound annual return

Appendix A-13

Intermediate-term Government Bonds: Yields
From 1926 to 2015

Year	Jan	Feb	Mar	Apr	May	Jun	Jul	Aug	Sep	Oct	Nov	Dec	Year	Jan–Dec*
1986	0.0870	0.0815	0.0743	0.0737	0.0816	0.0756	0.0728	0.0668	0.0718	0.0687	0.0669	0.0685	1986	0.0685
1987	0.0685	0.0683	0.0708	0.0793	0.0821	0.0806	0.0818	0.0849	0.0912	0.0844	0.0840	0.0832	1987	0.0832
1988	0.0782	0.0768	0.0807	0.0836	0.0870	0.0839	0.0871	0.0895	0.0859	0.0837	0.0892	0.0917	1988	0.0917
1989	0.0896	0.0927	0.0934	0.0895	0.0860	0.0791	0.0745	0.0834	0.0833	0.0786	0.0779	0.0794	1989	0.0794
1990	0.0842	0.0855	0.0871	0.0907	0.0864	0.0843	0.0819	0.0859	0.0851	0.0826	0.0795	0.0770	1990	0.0770
1991	0.0772	0.0774	0.0783	0.0772	0.0773	0.0793	0.0778	0.0732	0.0693	0.0673	0.0653	0.0597	1991	0.0597
1992	0.0683	0.0690	0.0720	0.0711	0.0674	0.0647	0.0604	0.0581	0.0547	0.0601	0.0634	0.0611	1992	0.0611
1993	0.0588	0.0547	0.0549	0.0540	0.0551	0.0517	0.0526	0.0486	0.0483	0.0488	0.0519	0.0522	1993	0.0522
1994	0.0515	0.0575	0.0638	0.0670	0.0682	0.0699	0.0675	0.0683	0.0730	0.0749	0.0778	0.0780	1994	0.0780
1995	0.0754	0.0708	0.0707	0.0685	0.0606	0.0598	0.0616	0.0606	0.0601	0.0582	0.0553	0.0538	1995	0.0538
1996	0.0528	0.0573	0.0614	0.0640	0.0663	0.0645	0.0654	0.0670	0.0643	0.0607	0.0578	0.0616	1996	0.0616
1997	0.0629	0.0639	0.0677	0.0656	0.0650	0.0639	0.0589	0.0624	0.0601	0.0576	0.0587	0.0573	1997	0.0573
1998	0.0545	0.0562	0.0567	0.0564	0.0558	0.0551	0.0556	0.0503	0.0435	0.0434	0.0467	0.0468	1998	0.0468
1999	0.0467	0.0535	0.0526	0.0532	0.0576	0.0581	0.0594	0.0602	0.0590	0.0604	0.0619	0.0645	1999	0.0645
2000	0.0675	0.0669	0.0636	0.0657	0.0658	0.0626	0.0621	0.0601	0.0589	0.0582	0.0551	0.0507	2000	0.0507
2001	0.0499	0.0482	0.0471	0.0504	0.0515	0.0510	0.0464	0.0450	0.0399	0.0365	0.0413	0.0442	2001	0.0442
2002	0.0459	0.0442	0.0504	0.0461	0.0443	0.0412	0.0358	0.0325	0.0265	0.0276	0.0323	0.0261	2002	0.0261
2003	0.0310	0.0276	0.0283	0.0285	0.0228	0.0240	0.0322	0.0335	0.0267	0.0307	0.0317	0.0297	2003	0.0297
2004	0.0315	0.0293	0.0276	0.0360	0.0378	0.0374	0.0362	0.0322	0.0326	0.0316	0.0356	0.0347	2004	0.0347
2005	0.0375	0.0405	0.0421	0.0392	0.0377	0.0374	0.0415	0.0385	0.0422	0.0446	0.0440	0.0434	2005	0.0434
2006	0.0449	0.0460	0.0481	0.0491	0.0502	0.0506	0.0487	0.0465	0.0455	0.0452	0.0439	0.0465	2006	0.0465
2007	0.0479	0.0448	0.0451	0.0449	0.0483	0.0490	0.0457	0.0420	0.0413	0.0435	0.0333	0.0328	2007	0.0328
2008	0.0301	0.0256	0.0245	0.0316	0.0340	0.0330	0.0322	0.0303	0.0289	0.0260	0.0161	0.0126	2008	0.0126
2009	0.0180	0.0202	0.0168	0.0206	0.0238	0.0259	0.0251	0.0234	0.0222	0.0219	0.0180	0.0242	2009	0.0242
2010	0.0242	0.0231	0.0254	0.0238	0.0208	0.0184	0.0151	0.0124	0.0115	0.0102	0.0124	0.0170	2010	0.0170
2011	0.0215	0.0229	0.0234	0.0206	0.0172	0.0175	0.0134	0.0091	0.0090	0.0090	0.0084	0.0074	2011	0.0074
2012	0.0078	0.0093	0.0109	0.0084	0.0068	0.0074	0.0058	0.0056	0.0056	0.0062	0.0052	0.0061	2012	0.0061
2013	0.0094	0.0083	0.0079	0.0067	0.0104	0.0136	0.0133	0.0152	0.0127	0.0118	0.0117	0.0149	2013	0.0149
2014	0.0160	0.0158	0.0175	0.0168	0.0150	0.0157	0.0171	0.0157	0.0171	0.0153	0.0137	0.0155	2014	0.0155
2015	0.0125	0.0153	0.0140	0.0146	0.0147	0.0162	0.0154	0.0154	0.0134	0.0149	0.0162	0.0169	2015	0.0169

*Compound annual return

Appendix A-14

U.S. Treasury Bills: Total Returns
From 1926 to 2015

Year	Jan	Feb	Mar	Apr	May	Jun	Jul	Aug	Sep	Oct	Nov	Dec	Jan–Dec*
1926	0.0034	0.0027	0.0030	0.0034	0.0001	0.0035	0.0022	0.0025	0.0023	0.0032	0.0031	0.0028	0.0327
1927	0.0025	0.0026	0.0030	0.0025	0.0030	0.0026	0.0030	0.0028	0.0021	0.0025	0.0021	0.0022	0.0312
1928	0.0025	0.0033	0.0029	0.0022	0.0032	0.0031	0.0032	0.0032	0.0027	0.0041	0.0038	0.0006	0.0356
1929	0.0034	0.0036	0.0034	0.0036	0.0044	0.0052	0.0033	0.0040	0.0035	0.0046	0.0037	0.0037	0.0475
1930	0.0014	0.0030	0.0035	0.0021	0.0026	0.0027	0.0020	0.0009	0.0022	0.0009	0.0013	0.0014	0.0241
1931	0.0015	0.0004	0.0013	0.0008	0.0009	0.0008	0.0006	0.0003	0.0003	0.0010	0.0017	0.0012	0.0107
1932	0.0023	0.0023	0.0016	0.0011	0.0006	0.0002	0.0003	0.0003	0.0003	0.0002	0.0002	0.0001	0.0096
1933	0.0001	-0.0003	0.0004	0.0010	0.0004	0.0002	0.0002	0.0003	0.0002	0.0001	0.0002	0.0002	0.0030
1934	0.0005	0.0002	0.0002	0.0001	0.0001	0.0001	0.0001	0.0001	0.0001	0.0001	0.0001	0.0001	0.0016
1935	0.0001	0.0002	0.0001	0.0001	0.0001	0.0001	0.0001	0.0001	0.0001	0.0001	0.0002	0.0001	0.0017
1936	0.0001	0.0001	0.0002	0.0002	0.0002	0.0003	0.0001	0.0002	0.0001	0.0002	0.0001	0.0000	0.0018
1937	0.0001	0.0002	0.0001	0.0003	0.0006	0.0003	0.0003	0.0002	0.0004	0.0002	0.0002	0.0000	0.0031
1938	0.0000	0.0000	-0.0001	0.0001	0.0000	0.0000	-0.0001	0.0000	0.0002	0.0001	-0.0006	0.0000	-0.0002
1939	-0.0001	0.0001	-0.0001	0.0000	0.0001	0.0001	0.0000	-0.0001	0.0001	0.0000	0.0000	0.0000	0.0002
1940	0.0000	0.0000	0.0000	0.0000	-0.0002	0.0000	0.0001	-0.0001	0.0000	0.0000	0.0000	0.0000	0.0000
1941	-0.0001	-0.0001	0.0001	-0.0001	0.0000	0.0000	0.0003	0.0001	0.0001	0.0000	0.0000	0.0001	0.0006
1942	0.0002	0.0001	0.0001	0.0001	0.0003	0.0002	0.0003	0.0003	0.0003	0.0003	0.0003	0.0003	0.0027
1943	0.0003	0.0003	0.0003	0.0003	0.0003	0.0003	0.0003	0.0003	0.0003	0.0003	0.0003	0.0003	0.0035
1944	0.0003	0.0003	0.0002	0.0003	0.0003	0.0003	0.0003	0.0003	0.0002	0.0003	0.0003	0.0002	0.0033
1945	0.0003	0.0002	0.0002	0.0003	0.0003	0.0002	0.0003	0.0003	0.0003	0.0003	0.0002	0.0003	0.0033
1946	0.0003	0.0003	0.0003	0.0003	0.0003	0.0003	0.0003	0.0003	0.0003	0.0003	0.0003	0.0003	0.0035
1947	0.0003	0.0003	0.0003	0.0003	0.0003	0.0003	0.0003	0.0003	0.0006	0.0006	0.0006	0.0008	0.0050
1948	0.0007	0.0007	0.0009	0.0008	0.0008	0.0009	0.0008	0.0009	0.0004	0.0004	0.0004	0.0004	0.0081
1949	0.0010	0.0009	0.0010	0.0009	0.0010	0.0010	0.0009	0.0009	0.0009	0.0009	0.0008	0.0009	0.0110
1950	0.0009	0.0009	0.0010	0.0009	0.0010	0.0010	0.0010	0.0010	0.0010	0.0012	0.0011	0.0011	0.0120
1951	0.0013	0.0010	0.0011	0.0013	0.0012	0.0012	0.0013	0.0013	0.0012	0.0016	0.0011	0.0012	0.0149
1952	0.0015	0.0012	0.0011	0.0012	0.0013	0.0015	0.0015	0.0015	0.0016	0.0014	0.0010	0.0016	0.0166
1953	0.0016	0.0014	0.0018	0.0016	0.0017	0.0018	0.0015	0.0017	0.0016	0.0013	0.0008	0.0013	0.0182
1954	0.0011	0.0007	0.0008	0.0009	0.0005	0.0006	0.0005	0.0005	0.0009	0.0007	0.0006	0.0008	0.0086
1955	0.0008	0.0009	0.0010	0.0010	0.0014	0.0010	0.0010	0.0016	0.0016	0.0018	0.0017	0.0018	0.0157

*Compound annual return

Appendix A-14

U.S. Treasury Bills: Total Returns
From 1926 to 2015

Year	Jan	Feb	Mar	Apr	May	Jun	Jul	Aug	Sep	Oct	Nov	Dec	Year	Jan–Dec*
1956	0.0022	0.0019	0.0015	0.0019	0.0023	0.0020	0.0022	0.0017	0.0018	0.0025	0.0020	0.0024	1956	0.0246
1957	0.0027	0.0024	0.0023	0.0025	0.0026	0.0024	0.0030	0.0025	0.0026	0.0029	0.0028	0.0024	1957	0.0314
1958	0.0028	0.0012	0.0009	0.0008	0.0011	0.0003	0.0007	0.0004	0.0019	0.0018	0.0011	0.0022	1958	0.0154
1959	0.0021	0.0019	0.0022	0.0020	0.0022	0.0025	0.0025	0.0019	0.0031	0.0030	0.0026	0.0034	1959	0.0295
1960	0.0033	0.0029	0.0035	0.0019	0.0027	0.0024	0.0013	0.0017	0.0016	0.0022	0.0013	0.0016	1960	0.0266
1961	0.0019	0.0014	0.0020	0.0017	0.0018	0.0020	0.0018	0.0014	0.0017	0.0019	0.0015	0.0019	1961	0.0213
1962	0.0024	0.0020	0.0020	0.0022	0.0024	0.0020	0.0027	0.0023	0.0021	0.0026	0.0020	0.0023	1962	0.0273
1963	0.0025	0.0023	0.0023	0.0025	0.0024	0.0023	0.0027	0.0025	0.0027	0.0029	0.0027	0.0029	1963	0.0312
1964	0.0030	0.0026	0.0031	0.0029	0.0026	0.0030	0.0030	0.0028	0.0028	0.0029	0.0029	0.0031	1964	0.0354
1965	0.0028	0.0030	0.0036	0.0031	0.0031	0.0035	0.0031	0.0033	0.0031	0.0031	0.0035	0.0033	1965	0.0393
1966	0.0038	0.0035	0.0038	0.0034	0.0041	0.0038	0.0035	0.0041	0.0040	0.0045	0.0040	0.0040	1966	0.0476
1967	0.0043	0.0036	0.0039	0.0032	0.0033	0.0027	0.0032	0.0031	0.0032	0.0039	0.0036	0.0033	1967	0.0421
1968	0.0040	0.0039	0.0038	0.0043	0.0045	0.0043	0.0048	0.0042	0.0043	0.0044	0.0042	0.0043	1968	0.0521
1969	0.0053	0.0046	0.0046	0.0053	0.0048	0.0051	0.0053	0.0050	0.0062	0.0060	0.0052	0.0064	1969	0.0658
1970	0.0060	0.0062	0.0057	0.0050	0.0053	0.0058	0.0052	0.0053	0.0054	0.0046	0.0046	0.0042	1970	0.0652
1971	0.0038	0.0033	0.0030	0.0028	0.0029	0.0037	0.0040	0.0047	0.0037	0.0037	0.0037	0.0037	1971	0.0439
1972	0.0029	0.0025	0.0027	0.0029	0.0030	0.0029	0.0031	0.0029	0.0034	0.0040	0.0037	0.0037	1972	0.0384
1973	0.0044	0.0042	0.0046	0.0052	0.0051	0.0051	0.0064	0.0070	0.0068	0.0065	0.0056	0.0064	1973	0.0693
1974	0.0063	0.0058	0.0056	0.0075	0.0075	0.0060	0.0070	0.0060	0.0081	0.0051	0.0054	0.0070	1974	0.0800
1975	0.0058	0.0043	0.0041	0.0044	0.0044	0.0041	0.0048	0.0048	0.0053	0.0056	0.0041	0.0048	1975	0.0580
1976	0.0047	0.0034	0.0040	0.0042	0.0037	0.0043	0.0047	0.0042	0.0044	0.0041	0.0040	0.0040	1976	0.0508
1977	0.0036	0.0035	0.0038	0.0038	0.0037	0.0040	0.0042	0.0044	0.0043	0.0049	0.0050	0.0049	1977	0.0512
1978	0.0049	0.0046	0.0053	0.0054	0.0051	0.0054	0.0056	0.0044	0.0062	0.0068	0.0070	0.0078	1978	0.0718
1979	0.0077	0.0073	0.0081	0.0080	0.0082	0.0081	0.0077	0.0077	0.0083	0.0087	0.0099	0.0095	1979	0.1038
1980	0.0080	0.0089	0.0121	0.0126	0.0081	0.0061	0.0053	0.0064	0.0075	0.0095	0.0096	0.0131	1980	0.1124
1981	0.0104	0.0107	0.0121	0.0108	0.0115	0.0135	0.0124	0.0128	0.0124	0.0121	0.0107	0.0087	1981	0.1471
1982	0.0080	0.0092	0.0098	0.0113	0.0106	0.0096	0.0105	0.0076	0.0051	0.0059	0.0063	0.0067	1982	0.1054
1983	0.0069	0.0062	0.0063	0.0071	0.0069	0.0067	0.0074	0.0076	0.0076	0.0076	0.0070	0.0073	1983	0.0880
1984	0.0076	0.0071	0.0073	0.0081	0.0078	0.0075	0.0082	0.0083	0.0086	0.0100	0.0073	0.0064	1984	0.0985
1985	0.0065	0.0058	0.0062	0.0072	0.0066	0.0055	0.0062	0.0055	0.0060	0.0065	0.0061	0.0065	1985	0.0772

*Compound annual return

Appendix A-14

U.S. Treasury Bills: Total Returns
From 1926 to 2015

Year	Jan	Feb	Mar	Apr	May	Jun	Jul	Aug	Sep	Oct	Nov	Dec	Year	Jan–Dec*
1986	0.0056	0.0053	0.0060	0.0052	0.0049	0.0052	0.0052	0.0046	0.0045	0.0046	0.0039	0.0049	1986	0.0616
1987	0.0042	0.0043	0.0047	0.0044	0.0038	0.0048	0.0046	0.0047	0.0045	0.0060	0.0035	0.0039	1987	0.0547
1988	0.0029	0.0046	0.0044	0.0046	0.0051	0.0049	0.0051	0.0059	0.0062	0.0061	0.0057	0.0063	1988	0.0635
1989	0.0055	0.0061	0.0067	0.0067	0.0079	0.0071	0.0070	0.0074	0.0065	0.0068	0.0069	0.0061	1989	0.0837
1990	0.0057	0.0057	0.0064	0.0069	0.0068	0.0063	0.0068	0.0066	0.0060	0.0068	0.0057	0.0060	1990	0.0781
1991	0.0052	0.0048	0.0044	0.0053	0.0047	0.0042	0.0049	0.0046	0.0046	0.0042	0.0039	0.0038	1991	0.0560
1992	0.0034	0.0028	0.0034	0.0032	0.0028	0.0032	0.0031	0.0026	0.0026	0.0023	0.0023	0.0028	1992	0.0351
1993	0.0023	0.0022	0.0025	0.0024	0.0022	0.0025	0.0024	0.0025	0.0026	0.0022	0.0025	0.0023	1993	0.0290
1994	0.0025	0.0021	0.0027	0.0027	0.0032	0.0031	0.0028	0.0037	0.0037	0.0038	0.0037	0.0044	1994	0.0390
1995	0.0042	0.0040	0.0046	0.0045	0.0054	0.0047	0.0045	0.0047	0.0043	0.0047	0.0042	0.0049	1995	0.0560
1996	0.0043	0.0039	0.0039	0.0046	0.0042	0.0040	0.0045	0.0041	0.0044	0.0042	0.0041	0.0046	1996	0.0521
1997	0.0045	0.0039	0.0043	0.0043	0.0049	0.0037	0.0043	0.0041	0.0044	0.0042	0.0039	0.0048	1997	0.0526
1998	0.0043	0.0039	0.0039	0.0043	0.0040	0.0041	0.0040	0.0043	0.0046	0.0032	0.0031	0.0038	1998	0.0486
1999	0.0035	0.0035	0.0043	0.0037	0.0034	0.0040	0.0038	0.0039	0.0039	0.0039	0.0036	0.0044	1999	0.0468
2000	0.0041	0.0043	0.0047	0.0046	0.0050	0.0040	0.0048	0.0050	0.0051	0.0056	0.0051	0.0050	2000	0.0589
2001	0.0054	0.0038	0.0042	0.0039	0.0032	0.0028	0.0030	0.0031	0.0028	0.0022	0.0017	0.0015	2001	0.0383
2002	0.0014	0.0013	0.0013	0.0015	0.0014	0.0013	0.0015	0.0014	0.0014	0.0014	0.0012	0.0011	2002	0.0165
2003	0.0010	0.0009	0.0010	0.0010	0.0009	0.0010	0.0007	0.0007	0.0008	0.0007	0.0007	0.0008	2003	0.0102
2004	0.0007	0.0006	0.0009	0.0008	0.0006	0.0008	0.0010	0.0011	0.0011	0.0011	0.0015	0.0016	2004	0.0120
2005	0.0016	0.0016	0.0021	0.0021	0.0024	0.0023	0.0024	0.0030	0.0029	0.0027	0.0031	0.0032	2005	0.0298
2006	0.0035	0.0034	0.0037	0.0036	0.0043	0.0040	0.0040	0.0042	0.0041	0.0041	0.0042	0.0040	2006	0.0480
2007	0.0044	0.0038	0.0043	0.0044	0.0041	0.0040	0.0040	0.0042	0.0032	0.0032	0.0034	0.0027	2007	0.0466
2008	0.0021	0.0013	0.0017	0.0018	0.0018	0.0017	0.0015	0.0013	0.0015	0.0008	0.0003	0.0000	2008	0.0160
2009	0.0000	0.0001	0.0002	0.0001	0.0000	0.0001	0.0001	0.0001	0.0001	0.0000	0.0000	0.0001	2009	0.0010
2010	0.0000	0.0000	0.0001	0.0001	0.0001	0.0000	0.0001	0.0001	0.0000	0.0001	0.0001	0.0001	2010	0.0012
2011	0.0001	0.0001	0.0001	0.0000	0.0001	0.0000	0.0000	0.0001	0.0001	0.0000	0.0000	0.0000	2011	0.0004
2012	0.0000	0.0000	0.0000	0.0000	0.0000	0.0000	0.0000	0.0000	0.0000	0.0000	0.0000	0.0000	2012	0.0006
2013	0.0000	0.0000	0.0000	0.0000	0.0000	0.0000	0.0000	0.0000	0.0000	0.0000	0.0000	0.0000	2013	0.0002
2014	0.0000	0.0000	0.0000	0.0000	0.0000	0.0000	0.0000	0.0000	0.0000	0.0000	0.0000	0.0000	2014	0.0002
2015	0.0000	0.0000	0.0000	0.0000	0.0000	0.0000	0.0000	0.0000	0.0000	0.0000	0.0000	0.0001	2015	0.0002

*Compound annual return

Appendix A-15

Inflation
From 1926 to 2015

Year	Jan	Feb	Mar	Apr	May	Jun	Jul	Aug	Sep	Oct	Nov	Dec	Year	Jan–Dec*
1926	0.0000	-0.0037	-0.0056	0.0094	-0.0056	-0.0075	-0.0094	-0.0057	0.0057	0.0038	0.0038	0.0000	1926	-0.0149
1927	-0.0076	-0.0076	-0.0058	0.0000	0.0077	0.0096	-0.0190	-0.0058	0.0058	0.0058	-0.0019	-0.0019	1927	-0.0208
1928	-0.0019	-0.0097	0.0000	0.0020	0.0058	-0.0078	0.0000	0.0020	0.0078	-0.0019	-0.0019	-0.0039	1928	-0.0097
1929	-0.0019	-0.0020	-0.0039	-0.0039	0.0059	0.0039	0.0098	0.0039	-0.0019	0.0000	-0.0019	-0.0058	1929	0.0020
1930	-0.0039	-0.0039	-0.0059	0.0059	-0.0059	-0.0059	-0.0139	-0.0060	0.0061	-0.0060	-0.0081	-0.0143	1930	-0.0603
1931	-0.0145	-0.0147	-0.0064	-0.0064	-0.0108	-0.0109	-0.0022	-0.0022	-0.0044	-0.0067	-0.0112	-0.0091	1931	-0.0952
1932	-0.0206	-0.0140	-0.0047	-0.0071	-0.0144	-0.0073	0.0000	-0.0123	-0.0050	-0.0075	-0.0050	-0.0101	1932	-0.1030
1933	-0.0153	-0.0155	-0.0079	-0.0027	0.0027	0.0106	0.0289	0.0102	0.0000	0.0000	0.0000	-0.0051	1933	0.0051
1934	0.0051	0.0076	0.0000	-0.0025	0.0025	0.0025	0.0000	0.0025	0.0150	-0.0074	-0.0025	-0.0025	1934	0.0203
1935	0.0149	0.0074	-0.0024	0.0098	-0.0048	-0.0024	-0.0049	0.0000	0.0049	0.0000	0.0049	0.0024	1935	0.0299
1936	0.0000	-0.0048	-0.0049	0.0000	0.0000	0.0098	0.0048	0.0072	0.0024	-0.0024	0.0000	0.0000	1936	0.0121
1937	0.0072	0.0024	0.0071	0.0047	0.0047	0.0023	0.0046	0.0023	0.0092	-0.0046	-0.0069	-0.0023	1937	0.0310
1938	-0.0139	-0.0094	0.0000	0.0047	-0.0047	0.0000	0.0024	-0.0024	0.0000	-0.0047	-0.0024	0.0024	1938	-0.0278
1939	-0.0048	-0.0048	-0.0024	-0.0024	0.0000	0.0000	0.0000	0.0000	0.0193	-0.0047	0.0000	-0.0048	1939	-0.0048
1940	-0.0024	0.0072	-0.0024	0.0000	0.0024	0.0024	-0.0024	-0.0024	0.0024	0.0000	0.0000	0.0048	1940	0.0096
1941	0.0000	0.0000	0.0047	0.0094	0.0070	0.0186	0.0046	0.0091	0.0180	0.0110	0.0087	0.0022	1941	0.0972
1942	0.0130	0.0085	0.0127	0.0063	0.0104	0.0021	0.0041	0.0061	0.0020	0.0101	0.0060	0.0080	1942	0.0929
1943	0.0000	0.0020	0.0158	0.0117	0.0077	-0.0019	-0.0076	-0.0038	0.0039	0.0038	-0.0019	0.0019	1943	0.0316
1944	-0.0019	-0.0019	0.0000	0.0058	0.0038	0.0019	0.0057	0.0038	0.0000	0.0000	0.0000	0.0038	1944	0.0211
1945	0.0000	-0.0019	0.0000	0.0019	0.0075	0.0093	0.0018	0.0000	-0.0037	0.0000	0.0037	0.0037	1945	0.0225
1946	0.0000	-0.0037	0.0074	0.0055	0.0055	0.0109	0.0590	0.0220	0.0116	0.0196	0.0240	0.0078	1946	0.1816
1947	0.0000	-0.0016	0.0218	0.0000	-0.0030	0.0076	0.0091	0.0105	0.0238	0.0000	0.0058	0.0130	1947	0.0901
1948	0.0114	-0.0085	-0.0028	0.0142	0.0070	0.0070	0.0125	0.0041	0.0000	-0.0041	-0.0068	-0.0069	1948	0.0271
1949	-0.0014	-0.0111	0.0028	0.0014	-0.0014	0.0014	-0.0070	0.0028	0.0042	-0.0056	0.0014	-0.0056	1949	-0.0180
1950	-0.0042	-0.0028	0.0043	0.0014	0.0042	0.0056	0.0098	0.0083	0.0069	0.0055	0.0041	0.0135	1950	0.0579
1951	0.0160	0.0118	0.0039	0.0013	0.0039	-0.0013	0.0013	0.0000	0.0064	0.0051	0.0051	0.0038	1951	0.0587
1952	0.0000	-0.0063	0.0000	0.0038	0.0013	0.0025	0.0076	0.0013	-0.0012	0.0013	0.0000	-0.0012	1952	0.0088
1953	-0.0025	-0.0050	0.0025	0.0013	0.0025	0.0038	0.0025	0.0025	0.0012	0.0025	-0.0037	-0.0012	1953	0.0062
1954	0.0025	-0.0012	-0.0012	-0.0025	0.0037	0.0012	0.0000	-0.0012	-0.0025	-0.0025	0.0012	-0.0025	1954	-0.0050
1955	0.0000	0.0000	0.0000	0.0000	0.0000	0.0000	0.0037	-0.0025	0.0037	0.0000	0.0012	-0.0025	1955	0.0037

*Compound annual return

Appendix A-15

Inflation
From 1926 to 2015

Year	Jan	Feb	Mar	Apr	May	Jun	Jul	Aug	Sep	Oct	Nov	Dec	Year	Jan–Dec*
1956	-0.0012	0.0000	0.0012	0.0012	0.0050	0.0062	0.0074	-0.0012	0.0012	0.0061	0.0000	0.0024	1956	0.0286
1957	0.0012	0.0036	0.0024	0.0036	0.0024	0.0060	0.0047	0.0012	0.0012	0.0000	0.0035	0.0000	1957	0.0302
1958	0.0059	0.0012	0.0070	0.0023	0.0000	0.0012	0.0012	-0.0012	0.0000	0.0000	0.0012	-0.0012	1958	0.0176
1959	0.0012	-0.0012	0.0000	0.0012	0.0012	0.0046	0.0023	-0.0011	0.0034	0.0034	0.0000	0.0000	1959	0.0150
1960	-0.0011	0.0011	0.0000	0.0057	0.0000	0.0023	0.0000	0.0000	0.0011	0.0045	0.0011	0.0000	1960	0.0148
1961	0.0000	0.0000	0.0000	0.0000	0.0000	0.0011	0.0045	-0.0011	0.0022	0.0000	0.0000	0.0000	1961	0.0067
1962	0.0000	0.0022	0.0022	0.0022	0.0000	0.0000	0.0022	0.0000	0.0055	-0.0011	0.0011	0.0022	1962	0.0122
1963	0.0011	0.0011	0.0011	0.0000	0.0000	0.0044	0.0044	0.0000	0.0000	0.0011	0.0011	0.0011	1963	0.0165
1964	0.0011	-0.0011	0.0011	0.0011	0.0000	0.0022	0.0022	-0.0011	0.0022	0.0011	0.0021	0.0011	1964	0.0119
1965	0.0000	0.0000	0.0011	0.0032	0.0021	0.0053	0.0011	-0.0021	0.0021	0.0011	0.0021	0.0032	1965	0.0192
1966	0.0000	0.0063	0.0031	0.0042	0.0010	0.0031	0.0031	0.0051	0.0020	0.0041	0.0000	0.0010	1966	0.0335
1967	0.0000	0.0010	0.0020	0.0020	0.0030	0.0030	0.0050	0.0030	0.0020	0.0030	0.0030	0.0030	1967	0.0304
1968	0.0039	0.0029	0.0049	0.0029	0.0029	0.0058	0.0048	0.0029	0.0029	0.0057	0.0038	0.0028	1968	0.0472
1969	0.0028	0.0037	0.0084	0.0065	0.0028	0.0064	0.0046	0.0045	0.0045	0.0036	0.0054	0.0062	1969	0.0611
1970	0.0035	0.0053	0.0053	0.0061	0.0043	0.0052	0.0034	0.0017	0.0051	0.0051	0.0034	0.0051	1970	0.0549
1971	0.0008	0.0017	0.0034	0.0033	0.0050	0.0058	0.0025	0.0025	0.0008	0.0016	0.0016	0.0041	1971	0.0336
1972	0.0008	0.0049	0.0016	0.0024	0.0032	0.0024	0.0040	0.0016	0.0040	0.0032	0.0024	0.0032	1972	0.0341
1973	0.0031	0.0070	0.0093	0.0069	0.0061	0.0068	0.0023	0.0181	0.0030	0.0081	0.0073	0.0065	1973	0.0880
1974	0.0087	0.0129	0.0113	0.0056	0.0111	0.0096	0.0075	0.0128	0.0120	0.0086	0.0085	0.0071	1974	0.1220
1975	0.0045	0.0070	0.0038	0.0051	0.0044	0.0082	0.0106	0.0031	0.0049	0.0061	0.0061	0.0042	1975	0.0701
1976	0.0024	0.0024	0.0024	0.0042	0.0059	0.0053	0.0059	0.0047	0.0041	0.0041	0.0029	0.0029	1976	0.0481
1977	0.0057	0.0103	0.0062	0.0079	0.0056	0.0066	0.0044	0.0038	0.0038	0.0027	0.0049	0.0038	1977	0.0677
1978	0.0054	0.0069	0.0069	0.0090	0.0099	0.0103	0.0072	0.0051	0.0071	0.0080	0.0055	0.0055	1978	0.0903
1979	0.0089	0.0117	0.0097	0.0115	0.0123	0.0093	0.0130	0.0101	0.0104	0.0090	0.0093	0.0105	1979	0.1331
1980	0.0144	0.0137	0.0144	0.0113	0.0099	0.0110	0.0008	0.0065	0.0092	0.0087	0.0091	0.0086	1980	0.1240
1981	0.0081	0.0104	0.0072	0.0064	0.0082	0.0086	0.0114	0.0077	0.0101	0.0021	0.0029	0.0029	1981	0.0894
1982	0.0036	0.0032	-0.0011	0.0042	0.0098	0.0122	0.0055	0.0021	0.0017	0.0027	-0.0017	-0.0041	1982	0.0387
1983	0.0024	0.0003	0.0007	0.0072	0.0054	0.0034	0.0040	0.0033	0.0050	0.0027	0.0017	0.0013	1983	0.0380
1984	0.0056	0.0046	0.0023	0.0049	0.0029	0.0032	0.0032	0.0042	0.0048	0.0025	0.0000	0.0006	1984	0.0395
1985	0.0019	0.0041	0.0044	0.0041	0.0037	0.0031	0.0016	0.0022	0.0031	0.0031	0.0034	0.0025	1985	0.0377

*Compound annual return

Appendix A-15

Inflation

From 1926 to 2015

Year	Jan	Feb	Mar	Apr	May	Jun	Jul	Aug	Sep	Oct	Nov	Dec	Year	Jan–Dec*
1986	0.0031	-0.0027	-0.0046	-0.0021	0.0031	0.0049	0.0003	0.0018	0.0049	0.0009	0.0009	0.0009	1986	0.0113
1987	0.0060	0.0039	0.0045	0.0054	0.0030	0.0041	0.0021	0.0056	0.0050	0.0026	0.0014	-0.0003	1987	0.0441
1988	0.0026	0.0026	0.0043	0.0052	0.0034	0.0043	0.0042	0.0042	0.0067	0.0033	0.0008	0.0017	1988	0.0442
1989	0.0050	0.0041	0.0058	0.0065	0.0057	0.0024	0.0024	0.0016	0.0032	0.0048	0.0024	0.0016	1989	0.0465
1990	0.0103	0.0047	0.0055	0.0016	0.0023	0.0054	0.0038	0.0092	0.0084	0.0060	0.0022	0.0000	1990	0.0611
1991	0.0060	0.0015	0.0015	0.0015	0.0030	0.0029	0.0015	0.0029	0.0044	0.0015	0.0029	0.0007	1991	0.0306
1992	0.0015	0.0036	0.0051	0.0014	0.0014	0.0036	0.0021	0.0028	0.0028	0.0035	0.0014	-0.0007	1992	0.0290
1993	0.0049	0.0035	0.0035	0.0028	0.0014	0.0014	0.0000	0.0028	0.0021	0.0041	0.0007	0.0000	1993	0.0275
1994	0.0027	0.0034	0.0034	0.0014	0.0007	0.0034	0.0027	0.0040	0.0027	0.0007	0.0013	0.0000	1994	0.0267
1995	0.0040	0.0040	0.0033	0.0033	0.0020	0.0020	0.0000	0.0026	0.0020	0.0033	-0.0007	-0.0007	1995	0.0254
1996	0.0059	0.0032	0.0052	0.0039	0.0019	0.0006	0.0019	0.0019	0.0032	0.0032	0.0019	0.0000	1996	0.0332
1997	0.0032	0.0031	0.0025	0.0013	-0.0006	0.0012	0.0012	0.0019	0.0025	0.0025	-0.0006	-0.0012	1997	0.0170
1998	0.0019	0.0019	0.0019	0.0018	0.0018	0.0012	0.0012	0.0012	0.0012	0.0024	0.0000	-0.0006	1998	0.0161
1999	0.0024	0.0012	0.0030	0.0073	0.0000	0.0000	0.0030	0.0024	0.0048	0.0018	0.0006	0.0000	1999	0.0268
2000	0.0030	0.0059	0.0082	0.0006	0.0012	0.0052	0.0023	0.0000	0.0052	0.0017	0.0006	-0.0006	2000	0.0339
2001	0.0063	0.0040	0.0023	0.0040	0.0045	0.0017	-0.0028	0.0000	0.0045	-0.0034	-0.0017	-0.0039	2001	0.0155
2002	0.0023	0.0040	0.0056	0.0056	0.0000	0.0006	0.0011	0.0033	0.0017	0.0017	0.0000	-0.0022	2002	0.0238
2003	0.0044	0.0077	0.0060	-0.0022	-0.0016	0.0011	0.0011	0.0038	0.0033	-0.0011	-0.0027	-0.0011	2003	0.0188
2004	0.0049	0.0054	0.0064	0.0032	0.0059	0.0032	-0.0016	0.0005	0.0021	0.0053	0.0005	-0.0037	2004	0.0326
2005	0.0021	0.0058	0.0078	0.0067	-0.0010	0.0005	0.0046	0.0051	0.0122	0.0020	-0.0080	-0.0040	2005	0.0342
2006	0.0076	0.0020	0.0055	0.0085	0.0050	0.0020	0.0030	0.0020	-0.0049	-0.0054	-0.0015	0.0015	2006	0.0254
2007	0.0031	0.0054	0.0091	0.0065	0.0061	0.0019	-0.0003	-0.0018	0.0028	0.0021	0.0059	-0.0007	2007	0.0408
2008	0.0050	0.0029	0.0087	0.0061	0.0084	0.0101	0.0053	-0.0040	-0.0014	-0.0101	-0.0192	-0.0103	2008	0.0009
2009	0.0044	0.0050	0.0024	0.0025	0.0029	0.0086	-0.0016	0.0022	0.0006	0.0010	0.0007	-0.0018	2009	0.0272
2010	0.0034	0.0002	0.0041	0.0017	0.0008	-0.0010	0.0002	0.0014	0.0006	0.0012	0.0004	0.0017	2010	0.0150
2011	0.0048	0.0049	0.0098	0.0064	0.0047	-0.0011	0.0009	0.0028	0.0015	-0.0021	-0.0008	-0.0025	2011	0.0296
2012	0.0044	0.0044	0.0076	0.0030	-0.0012	-0.0015	-0.0016	0.0056	0.0045	-0.0004	-0.0047	-0.0027	2012	0.0174
2013	0.0030	0.0082	0.0026	-0.0010	0.0018	0.0024	0.0004	0.0012	0.0012	-0.0026	-0.0020	-0.0001	2013	0.0151
2014	0.0037	0.0037	0.0064	0.0033	0.0035	0.0019	-0.0004	-0.0017	0.0008	-0.0025	-0.0054	-0.0057	2014	0.0076
2015	-0.0047	0.0043	0.0060	0.0020	0.0051	0.0035	0.0001	-0.0014	-0.0016	-0.0004	-0.0021	0.0011	2015	0.0118

*Compound annual return

Appendix A-16

U.S. Treasury Bills: Inflation-Adjusted Total Returns
From 1926 to 2015

Year	Jan	Feb	Mar	Apr	May	Jun	Jul	Aug	Sep	Oct	Nov	Dec	Year	Jan–Dec*
1926	0.0034	0.0064	0.0086	-0.0059	0.0057	0.0110	0.0118	0.0083	-0.0035	-0.0006	-0.0007	0.0028	1926	0.0483
1927	0.0101	0.0103	0.0088	0.0025	-0.0047	-0.0069	0.0224	0.0086	-0.0037	-0.0033	0.0040	0.0042	1927	0.0531
1928	0.0045	0.0131	0.0029	0.0003	-0.0026	0.0110	0.0032	0.0013	-0.0051	0.0060	0.0058	0.0045	1928	0.0457
1929	0.0054	0.0055	0.0074	0.0075	-0.0015	0.0013	-0.0064	0.0002	0.0055	0.0046	0.0057	0.0095	1929	0.0454
1930	0.0053	0.0069	0.0094	-0.0038	0.0085	0.0087	0.0161	0.0070	-0.0039	0.0069	0.0095	0.0159	1930	0.0898
1931	0.0162	0.0153	0.0077	0.0072	0.0118	0.0118	0.0028	0.0026	0.0047	0.0078	0.0130	0.0104	1931	0.1171
1932	0.0234	0.0166	0.0064	0.0083	0.0152	0.0076	0.0003	0.0127	0.0053	0.0077	0.0052	0.0103	1932	0.1255
1933	0.0157	0.0155	0.0084	0.0036	-0.0022	-0.0103	-0.0279	-0.0098	0.0002	0.0001	0.0002	0.0053	1933	-0.0021
1934	-0.0046	-0.0073	0.0002	0.0026	-0.0024	-0.0024	0.0001	-0.0024	-0.0147	0.0075	0.0026	0.0026	1934	-0.0183
1935	-0.0146	-0.0071	0.0026	-0.0095	0.0050	0.0026	0.0050	0.0001	-0.0047	0.0001	-0.0046	-0.0023	1935	-0.0273
1936	0.0001	0.0050	0.0051	0.0002	0.0002	-0.0094	-0.0047	-0.0070	-0.0023	0.0026	0.0001	0.0000	1936	-0.0102
1937	-0.0070	-0.0022	-0.0069	-0.0043	-0.0040	-0.0020	-0.0043	-0.0021	-0.0088	0.0048	0.0071	0.0024	1937	-0.0271
1938	0.0141	0.0095	-0.0001	-0.0046	0.0048	0.0000	-0.0024	0.0024	0.0002	0.0049	0.0018	-0.0024	1938	0.0284
1939	0.0047	0.0049	0.0023	0.0024	0.0001	0.0001	0.0000	-0.0001	-0.0189	0.0048	0.0000	0.0048	1939	0.0050
1940	0.0024	-0.0071	0.0024	0.0000	-0.0025	-0.0023	0.0025	0.0023	-0.0024	0.0000	0.0000	-0.0047	1940	-0.0094
1941	-0.0001	-0.0001	-0.0046	-0.0094	-0.0069	-0.0182	-0.0042	-0.0089	-0.0176	-0.0109	-0.0086	-0.0021	1941	-0.0880
1942	-0.0126	-0.0083	-0.0124	-0.0062	-0.0100	-0.0018	-0.0038	-0.0058	-0.0017	-0.0097	-0.0057	-0.0076	1942	-0.0825
1943	0.0003	-0.0017	-0.0152	-0.0112	-0.0074	0.0022	0.0080	0.0042	-0.0036	-0.0035	0.0022	-0.0016	1943	-0.0273
1944	0.0022	0.0022	0.0002	-0.0055	-0.0036	-0.0016	-0.0054	-0.0035	0.0002	0.0003	0.0003	-0.0035	1944	-0.0174
1945	0.0003	0.0021	0.0002	-0.0016	-0.0072	-0.0090	-0.0015	0.0003	0.0040	0.0003	-0.0034	-0.0034	1945	-0.0188
1946	0.0003	0.0040	-0.0070	-0.0052	-0.0051	-0.0105	-0.0554	-0.0212	-0.0111	-0.0189	-0.0232	-0.0075	1946	-0.1507
1947	0.0003	0.0018	-0.0210	0.0003	0.0033	-0.0073	-0.0087	-0.0101	-0.0226	0.0006	-0.0052	-0.0120	1947	-0.0780
1948	0.0003	0.0093	0.0037	-0.0132	-0.0062	-0.0060	-0.0115	-0.0032	0.0004	0.0045	0.0073	0.0074	1948	-0.0185
1949	0.0023	0.0121	-0.0018	-0.0005	0.0024	-0.0004	0.0079	-0.0019	-0.0033	0.0065	-0.0006	0.0065	1949	0.0296
1950	0.0052	0.0037	-0.0033	-0.0006	-0.0032	-0.0046	-0.0087	-0.0073	-0.0058	-0.0043	-0.0030	-0.0123	1950	-0.0434
1951	-0.0145	-0.0107	-0.0028	0.0000	-0.0026	0.0025	0.0001	0.0013	-0.0052	-0.0035	-0.0040	-0.0026	1951	-0.0414
1952	0.0015	0.0075	0.0011	-0.0026	0.0000	-0.0010	-0.0060	0.0002	0.0029	0.0001	0.0010	0.0029	1952	0.0077
1953	0.0041	0.0064	-0.0007	0.0004	-0.0008	-0.0010	-0.0010	-0.0008	0.0004	-0.0012	0.0045	0.0025	1953	0.0119
1954	-0.0014	0.0019	0.0020	0.0034	-0.0032	-0.0007	0.0005	0.0017	0.0034	0.0032	-0.0006	0.0033	1954	0.0137
1955	0.0008	0.0009	0.0010	0.0010	0.0014	0.0010	-0.0027	0.0041	-0.0021	0.0018	0.0005	0.0043	1955	0.0119

*Compound annual return

Appendix A-16

U.S. Treasury Bills: Inflation-Adjusted Total Returns
From 1926 to 2015

Year	Jan	Feb	Mar	Apr	May	Jun	Jul	Aug	Sep	Oct	Nov	Dec	Year	Jan–Dec*
1956	0.0035	0.0019	0.0003	0.0006	-0.0027	-0.0042	-0.0052	0.0029	0.0006	-0.0036	0.0020	0.0000	1956	-0.0039
1957	0.0015	-0.0012	-0.0001	-0.0011	0.0002	-0.0035	-0.0018	0.0013	0.0014	0.0029	-0.0008	0.0024	1957	0.0011
1958	-0.0031	0.0000	-0.0060	-0.0015	0.0011	-0.0009	-0.0005	0.0016	0.0019	0.0018	-0.0001	0.0034	1958	-0.0022
1959	0.0009	0.0030	0.0022	0.0008	0.0010	-0.0021	0.0002	0.0030	-0.0003	-0.0004	0.0026	0.0034	1959	0.0143
1960	0.0045	0.0017	0.0035	-0.0037	0.0027	0.0001	0.0013	0.0017	0.0005	-0.0023	0.0002	0.0016	1960	0.0117
1961	0.0019	0.0014	0.0020	0.0017	0.0018	0.0009	-0.0026	0.0025	-0.0006	0.0019	0.0015	0.0019	1961	0.0144
1962	0.0024	-0.0002	-0.0002	0.0000	0.0024	0.0020	0.0005	0.0023	-0.0034	0.0037	0.0020	0.0034	1962	0.0149
1963	0.0014	0.0012	0.0012	0.0025	0.0024	-0.0021	-0.0017	0.0025	0.0027	0.0018	0.0016	0.0008	1963	0.0144
1964	0.0019	0.0037	0.0020	0.0018	0.0026	0.0009	0.0008	0.0039	0.0006	0.0019	0.0008	0.0020	1964	0.0232
1965	0.0028	0.0030	0.0025	-0.0001	0.0010	-0.0018	0.0020	0.0054	0.0010	0.0021	0.0014	0.0002	1965	0.0197
1966	0.0038	-0.0028	0.0007	-0.0007	0.0031	0.0007	0.0005	-0.0010	0.0020	0.0005	0.0040	0.0030	1966	0.0136
1967	0.0043	0.0026	0.0019	0.0012	0.0003	-0.0004	-0.0019	0.0001	0.0012	0.0010	0.0006	0.0004	1967	0.0113
1968	0.0001	0.0009	-0.0011	0.0014	0.0015	-0.0015	0.0000	0.0013	0.0014	-0.0013	0.0005	0.0014	1968	0.0046
1969	0.0024	0.0009	-0.0037	-0.0011	0.0021	-0.0013	0.0008	0.0005	0.0017	0.0024	-0.0002	0.0002	1969	0.0045
1970	0.0025	0.0009	0.0004	-0.0011	0.0009	0.0006	0.0018	0.0036	0.0002	-0.0005	0.0012	-0.0008	1970	0.0098
1971	0.0030	0.0016	-0.0004	-0.0006	-0.0020	-0.0020	0.0015	0.0022	0.0029	0.0020	0.0021	-0.0004	1971	0.0099
1972	0.0021	-0.0024	0.0011	0.0005	-0.0002	0.0005	-0.0009	0.0013	-0.0006	0.0008	0.0013	0.0006	1972	0.0041
1973	0.0012	-0.0029	-0.0047	-0.0017	-0.0010	-0.0017	0.0041	-0.0109	0.0038	-0.0016	-0.0017	-0.0002	1973	-0.0172
1974	-0.0024	-0.0070	-0.0057	0.0019	-0.0035	-0.0036	-0.0004	-0.0068	-0.0039	-0.0035	-0.0031	-0.0002	1974	-0.0374
1975	0.0013	-0.0027	0.0003	-0.0007	-0.0001	-0.0040	-0.0057	0.0017	0.0004	-0.0006	-0.0020	0.0006	1975	-0.0113
1976	0.0023	0.0010	0.0016	0.0000	-0.0022	-0.0010	-0.0012	-0.0005	0.0003	0.0000	0.0011	0.0012	1976	0.0026
1977	-0.0021	-0.0067	-0.0024	-0.0041	-0.0018	-0.0026	-0.0002	0.0006	0.0005	0.0022	0.0001	0.0011	1977	-0.0155
1978	-0.0005	-0.0023	-0.0016	-0.0036	-0.0048	-0.0049	-0.0016	0.0005	-0.0009	-0.0012	0.0015	0.0024	1978	-0.0169
1979	-0.0011	-0.0043	-0.0015	-0.0035	-0.0041	-0.0012	-0.0052	-0.0024	-0.0021	-0.0002	0.0005	-0.0010	1979	-0.0259
1980	-0.0063	-0.0048	-0.0023	0.0013	-0.0018	-0.0049	0.0045	-0.0001	-0.0017	0.0008	0.0005	0.0044	1980	-0.0103
1981	0.0022	0.0003	0.0048	0.0043	0.0033	0.0049	0.0010	0.0051	0.0023	0.0099	0.0078	0.0059	1981	0.0530
1982	0.0044	0.0060	0.0109	0.0070	0.0007	-0.0026	0.0050	0.0056	0.0034	0.0032	0.0081	0.0109	1982	0.0642
1983	0.0045	0.0058	0.0056	0.0000	0.0015	0.0033	0.0034	0.0043	0.0026	0.0049	0.0054	0.0059	1983	0.0482
1984	0.0020	0.0025	0.0050	0.0032	0.0049	0.0043	0.0050	0.0041	0.0038	0.0074	0.0073	0.0058	1984	0.0567
1985	0.0046	0.0017	0.0017	0.0031	0.0029	0.0024	0.0047	0.0033	0.0029	0.0034	0.0027	0.0040	1985	0.0381

*Compound annual return

U.S. Treasury Bills: Inflation-Adjusted Total Returns
From 1926 to 2015

Year	Jan	Feb	Mar	Apr	May	Jun	Jul	Aug	Sep	Oct	Nov	Dec	Year	Jan–Dec*
1986	0.0025	0.0081	0.0106	0.0074	0.0019	0.0003	0.0049	0.0028	-0.0004	0.0037	0.0030	0.0040	1986	0.0498
1987	-0.0019	0.0004	0.0002	-0.0009	0.0008	0.0007	0.0025	-0.0009	-0.0004	0.0034	0.0020	0.0042	1987	0.0101
1988	0.0003	0.0020	0.0001	-0.0005	0.0016	0.0006	0.0008	0.0017	-0.0006	0.0028	0.0048	0.0047	1988	0.0185
1989	0.0005	0.0020	0.0009	0.0002	0.0022	0.0047	0.0045	0.0058	0.0033	0.0020	0.0045	0.0045	1989	0.0356
1990	-0.0046	0.0010	0.0010	0.0053	0.0044	0.0008	0.0029	-0.0026	-0.0024	0.0008	0.0034	0.0060	1990	0.0161
1991	-0.0008	0.0033	0.0029	0.0038	0.0018	0.0012	0.0034	0.0017	0.0002	0.0028	0.0010	0.0031	1991	0.0246
1992	0.0019	-0.0008	-0.0017	0.0018	0.0013	-0.0004	0.0009	-0.0002	-0.0003	-0.0012	0.0009	0.0035	1992	0.0059
1993	-0.0026	-0.0013	-0.0010	-0.0004	0.0008	0.0011	0.0024	-0.0003	0.0005	-0.0019	0.0018	0.0023	1993	0.0014
1994	-0.0002	-0.0013	-0.0007	0.0014	0.0025	-0.0003	0.0000	-0.0004	0.0010	0.0032	0.0023	0.0044	1994	0.0120
1995	0.0001	0.0000	0.0013	0.0011	0.0034	0.0027	0.0045	0.0020	0.0023	0.0014	0.0049	0.0055	1995	0.0298
1996	-0.0016	0.0007	-0.0012	0.0007	0.0023	0.0034	0.0026	0.0022	0.0012	0.0011	0.0022	0.0046	1996	0.0182
1997	0.0013	0.0007	0.0018	0.0031	0.0056	0.0024	0.0030	0.0022	0.0019	0.0017	0.0045	0.0060	1997	0.0349
1998	0.0024	0.0020	0.0021	0.0024	0.0022	0.0029	0.0028	0.0031	0.0033	0.0008	0.0031	0.0044	1998	0.0319
1999	0.0011	0.0023	0.0012	-0.0035	0.0034	0.0040	0.0008	0.0015	-0.0009	0.0021	0.0030	0.0044	1999	0.0195
2000	0.0012	-0.0016	-0.0035	0.0040	0.0039	-0.0013	0.0025	0.0050	-0.0001	0.0039	0.0045	0.0056	2000	0.0242
2001	-0.0009	-0.0002	0.0019	0.0000	-0.0013	0.0011	0.0058	0.0031	-0.0017	0.0056	0.0034	0.0054	2001	0.0224
2002	-0.0009	-0.0026	-0.0043	-0.0040	0.0014	0.0007	0.0004	-0.0019	-0.0002	-0.0003	0.0012	0.0033	2002	-0.0071
2003	-0.0034	-0.0068	-0.0050	0.0032	0.0025	-0.0001	-0.0004	-0.0031	-0.0024	0.0018	0.0034	0.0019	2003	-0.0084
2004	-0.0042	-0.0048	-0.0055	-0.0024	-0.0052	-0.0023	0.0026	0.0006	-0.0010	-0.0041	0.0010	0.0053	2004	-0.0199
2005	-0.0005	-0.0041	-0.0057	-0.0046	0.0034	0.0018	-0.0022	-0.0021	-0.0093	0.0007	0.0113	0.0072	2005	-0.0042
2006	-0.0041	0.0013	-0.0019	-0.0049	-0.0006	0.0020	0.0010	0.0023	0.0090	0.0095	0.0057	0.0025	2006	0.0220
2007	0.0014	-0.0015	-0.0048	-0.0021	-0.0020	0.0020	0.0042	0.0060	0.0005	0.0011	-0.0025	0.0034	2007	0.0056
2008	-0.0028	-0.0016	-0.0069	-0.0043	-0.0066	-0.0083	-0.0037	0.0053	0.0029	0.0110	0.0198	0.0105	2008	0.0151
2009	-0.0043	-0.0048	-0.0023	-0.0024	-0.0029	-0.0084	0.0017	-0.0021	-0.0005	-0.0009	-0.0007	0.0018	2009	-0.0256
2010	-0.0034	-0.0002	-0.0040	-0.0016	-0.0007	0.0011	-0.0001	-0.0013	-0.0005	-0.0011	-0.0003	-0.0016	2010	-0.0135
2011	-0.0047	-0.0048	-0.0096	-0.0064	-0.0047	0.0011	-0.0009	-0.0027	-0.0015	0.0021	0.0008	0.0025	2011	-0.0284
2012	-0.0044	-0.0044	-0.0075	-0.0030	0.0012	0.0015	0.0017	-0.0055	-0.0044	0.0005	0.0048	0.0028	2012	-0.0165
2013	-0.0029	-0.0081	-0.0026	0.0011	-0.0018	-0.0024	-0.0004	-0.0012	-0.0012	0.0026	0.0020	0.0001	2013	-0.0146
2014	-0.0037	-0.0036	-0.0064	-0.0033	-0.0035	-0.0018	0.0004	0.0017	-0.0007	0.0025	0.0054	0.0057	2014	-0.0073
2015	0.0047	-0.0043	-0.0059	-0.0020	-0.0051	-0.0035	-0.0001	0.0015	0.0016	0.0004	0.0021	-0.0010	2015	-0.0115

*Compound annual return

Appendix B
Cumulative Wealth Indexes of Basic Series

Basic Series

Appendix B-1: Large-Capitalization Stocks: Total Return Index

Appendix B-2: Large-Capitalization Stocks: Capital Appreciation Index

Appendix B-3: Small-Capitalization Stocks: Total Return Index

Appendix B-4: Long-term Corporate Bonds: Total Return Index

Appendix B-5: Long-term Government Bonds: Total Return Index

Appendix B-6: Long-term Government Bonds: Capital Appreciation Index

Appendix B-7: Intermediate-Term Government Bonds: Total Return Index

Appendix B-8: Intermediate-Term Government Bonds: Capital Appreciation Index

Appendix B-9: U.S. Treasury Bills: Total Return Index

Appendix B-10: Inflation Index

Appendix B-1

Large-Capitalization Stocks: Total Return Index
From 1926 to 2015

Year	Jan	Feb	Mar	Apr	May	Jun	Jul	Aug	Sep	Oct	Nov	Dec	Yr End	Index
1925												1.000	1925	1.000
1926	1.000	0.962	0.906	0.929	0.946	0.989	1.036	1.062	1.089	1.058	1.095	1.116	1926	1.116
1927	1.095	1.154	1.164	1.187	1.259	1.251	1.334	1.403	1.466	1.393	1.493	1.535	1927	1.535
1928	1.529	1.509	1.676	1.733	1.768	1.700	1.724	1.862	1.910	1.942	2.193	2.204	1928	2.204
1929	2.332	2.328	2.325	2.366	2.280	2.540	2.660	2.933	2.794	2.243	1.963	2.018	1929	2.018
1930	2.147	2.203	2.382	2.363	2.340	1.960	2.035	2.064	1.800	1.646	1.631	1.516	1930	1.516
1931	1.592	1.782	1.662	1.506	1.314	1.500	1.392	1.418	0.996	1.085	0.999	0.859	1931	0.859
1932	0.836	0.883	0.781	0.625	0.488	0.487	0.672	0.933	0.900	0.779	0.746	0.789	1932	0.789
1933	0.795	0.654	0.678	0.966	1.129	1.280	1.169	1.310	1.164	1.064	1.184	1.214	1933	1.214
1934	1.344	1.301	1.301	1.268	1.175	1.202	1.066	1.131	1.127	1.095	1.198	1.197	1934	1.197
1935	1.148	1.109	1.077	1.182	1.231	1.317	1.429	1.469	1.507	1.624	1.700	1.767	1935	1.767
1936	1.886	1.928	1.980	1.831	1.931	1.995	2.135	2.167	2.174	2.342	2.374	2.367	1936	2.367
1937	2.459	2.506	2.487	2.286	2.280	2.165	2.391	2.276	1.957	1.765	1.612	1.538	1937	1.538
1938	1.561	1.666	1.252	1.433	1.386	1.733	1.862	1.820	1.850	1.993	1.939	2.016	1938	2.016
1939	1.881	1.954	1.692	1.688	1.811	1.701	1.889	1.766	2.062	2.036	1.955	2.008	1939	2.008
1940	1.941	1.966	1.991	1.986	1.531	1.655	1.712	1.772	1.793	1.869	1.810	1.812	1940	1.812
1941	1.728	1.718	1.730	1.624	1.653	1.749	1.850	1.852	1.839	1.718	1.670	1.602	1941	1.602
1942	1.627	1.602	1.497	1.437	1.552	1.586	1.640	1.666	1.715	1.831	1.827	1.927	1942	1.927
1943	2.070	2.190	2.310	2.318	2.446	2.500	2.368	2.409	2.472	2.446	2.286	2.427	1943	2.427
1944	2.468	2.479	2.527	2.502	2.628	2.771	2.717	2.760	2.758	2.764	2.801	2.906	1944	2.906
1945	2.952	3.154	3.015	3.287	3.351	3.349	3.288	3.499	3.652	3.770	3.919	3.965	1945	3.965
1946	4.248	3.976	4.167	4.330	4.455	4.290	4.188	3.906	3.516	3.495	3.486	3.645	1946	3.645
1947	3.738	3.709	3.654	3.521	3.526	3.721	3.863	3.785	3.743	3.832	3.765	3.853	1947	3.853
1948	3.707	3.563	3.846	3.958	4.305	4.329	4.109	4.174	4.059	4.347	3.929	4.065	1948	4.065
1949	4.081	3.960	4.090	4.017	3.913	3.919	4.174	4.265	4.377	4.526	4.605	4.829	1949	4.829
1950	4.924	5.022	5.057	5.303	5.573	5.267	5.330	5.566	5.895	5.949	6.050	6.360	1950	6.360
1951	6.765	6.871	6.764	7.109	6.896	6.739	7.218	7.563	7.573	7.495	7.567	7.888	1951	7.888
1952	8.030	7.804	8.197	7.867	8.137	8.536	8.703	8.642	8.490	8.507	8.993	9.336	1952	9.336
1953	9.291	9.192	8.997	8.783	8.851	8.732	8.971	8.521	8.551	9.012	9.196	9.244	1953	9.244
1954	9.739	9.848	10.168	10.693	11.139	11.173	11.831	11.506	12.485	12.277	13.393	14.108	1954	14.108
1955	14.387	14.528	14.485	15.059	15.142	16.416	17.437	17.393	17.618	17.118	18.533	18.561	1955	18.561

Appendix B-1

Large-Capitalization Stocks: Total Return Index
From 1926 to 2015

Year	Jan	Feb	Mar	Apr	May	Jun	Jul	Aug	Sep	Oct	Nov	Dec	Yr End	Index
1956	17.917	18.657	19.982	19.973	18.788	19.557	20.594	19.919	19.043	19.169	19.072	19.778	1956	19.778
1957	18.986	18.485	18.882	19.614	20.472	20.481	20.749	19.701	18.516	17.957	18.372	17.646	1957	17.646
1958	18.431	18.170	18.767	19.400	19.810	20.363	21.277	21.651	22.735	23.348	24.012	25.298	1958	25.298
1959	25.430	25.554	25.605	26.635	27.273	27.213	28.199	27.911	26.674	27.017	27.519	28.322	1959	28.322
1960	26.340	26.729	26.400	25.976	26.821	27.388	26.748	27.596	25.968	25.949	27.154	28.455	1960	28.455
1961	30.291	31.257	32.100	32.262	33.033	32.125	33.223	34.029	33.404	34.401	35.940	36.106	1961	36.106
1962	34.784	35.511	35.349	33.204	30.512	28.061	29.891	30.512	29.092	29.279	32.459	32.954	1962	32.954
1963	34.620	33.794	35.045	36.798	37.510	36.805	36.726	38.692	38.318	39.617	39.435	40.469	1963	40.469
1964	41.612	42.222	42.917	43.238	43.940	44.721	45.592	45.055	46.409	46.856	46.878	47.139	1964	47.139
1965	48.763	48.913	48.264	49.984	49.833	47.477	48.177	49.488	51.140	52.618	52.453	53.008	1965	53.008
1966	53.335	52.634	51.555	52.688	50.096	49.363	48.769	45.234	44.993	47.214	47.662	47.674	1966	47.674
1967	51.478	51.846	53.967	56.325	53.641	54.658	57.215	56.817	58.758	57.136	57.507	59.104	1967	59.104
1968	56.592	55.113	55.718	60.363	61.334	61.980	60.916	61.913	64.387	64.945	68.393	65.642	1968	65.642
1969	65.193	62.414	64.653	66.131	66.303	62.708	59.024	61.705	60.251	63.014	61.141	60.059	1969	60.059
1970	55.594	58.693	58.949	53.793	50.685	48.321	52.035	54.522	56.495	56.025	58.858	62.375	1970	62.375
1971	65.070	65.830	68.422	71.082	68.306	68.532	65.879	68.436	68.132	65.465	65.478	71.295	1971	71.295
1972	72.762	74.778	75.396	75.909	77.404	75.898	76.260	79.072	78.872	79.807	83.648	84.838	1972	84.838
1973	83.573	80.627	80.692	77.602	76.340	76.035	79.127	76.429	79.692	79.823	70.971	72.376	1973	72.376
1974	71.857	71.804	70.334	67.812	65.763	65.016	60.193	54.994	48.660	56.840	54.062	53.220	1974	53.220
1975	59.989	63.815	65.435	68.771	72.048	75.486	70.625	69.384	67.220	71.612	73.630	73.033	1975	73.033
1976	81.925	81.234	83.971	83.318	82.391	86.043	85.631	85.473	87.683	86.050	85.698	90.508	1976	90.508
1977	86.229	84.657	83.767	84.116	82.466	86.542	85.465	83.996	84.125	80.849	83.406	84.029	1977	84.029
1978	79.205	77.599	79.881	87.089	87.890	86.679	91.734	94.494	94.193	85.980	87.826	89.551	1978	89.551
1979	93.520	90.517	95.913	96.811	94.421	98.528	99.850	105.611	106.065	99.273	103.993	106.216	1979	106.216
1980	112.819	112.809	101.842	106.550	112.034	115.579	123.622	124.871	128.545	131.147	145.119	140.741	1980	140.741
1981	134.852	137.194	142.681	139.922	140.280	139.402	139.688	131.622	125.137	131.890	137.333	133.812	1981	133.812
1982	132.064	124.682	124.032	129.638	125.218	123.338	121.143	135.849	137.543	153.374	159.568	162.643	1982	162.643
1983	168.691	172.558	178.933	193.029	191.350	198.797	192.931	195.827	198.531	196.236	200.375	199.328	1983	199.328
1984	198.216	191.241	194.553	196.399	185.527	189.557	187.205	207.881	207.932	208.733	206.395	211.833	1984	211.833
1985	228.337	231.134	231.287	231.069	244.420	248.249	247.888	245.771	238.084	249.081	266.165	279.041	1985	279.041

Appendix B-1

Large-Capitalization Stocks: Total Return Index
From 1926 to 2015

Year	Jan	Feb	Mar	Apr	May	Jun	Jul	Aug	Sep	Oct	Nov	Dec	Yr End	Index
1986	280.599	301.573	318.399	314.813	331.562	337.165	318.307	341.911	313.645	331.733	339.795	331.124	1986	331.124
1987	375.712	390.558	401.827	398.259	401.712	421.998	443.376	459.920	449.837	352.959	323.879	348.510	1987	348.510
1988	363.169	380.098	368.356	372.430	375.651	392.890	391.400	378.113	394.222	405.199	399.424	406.392	1988	406.392
1989	436.151	425.282	435.203	457.799	476.321	473.619	516.383	526.478	524.342	512.167	522.612	535.162	1989	535.162
1990	499.233	505.664	519.063	506.113	555.462	551.715	549.946	500.236	475.891	473.865	504.496	518.549	1990	518.549
1991	541.132	579.832	593.873	595.278	620.959	592.510	620.127	634.819	624.195	632.587	607.099	676.530	1991	676.530
1992	663.923	672.521	659.441	678.803	682.131	671.983	699.435	685.120	693.171	695.566	719.250	728.077	1992	728.077
1993	734.164	744.170	759.871	741.505	761.340	763.570	760.498	789.355	783.301	799.504	791.883	801.458	1993	801.458
1994	828.705	806.212	771.064	780.952	793.768	774.311	799.737	832.526	812.168	830.414	800.172	812.041	1994	812.041
1995	833.100	865.567	891.107	917.348	954.012	976.171	1,008.543	1,011.079	1,053.749	1,049.983	1,096.075	1,117.188	1995	1,117.188
1996	1,155.212	1,165.923	1,177.145	1,194.501	1,225.306	1,229.980	1,175.640	1,200.439	1,268.005	1,302.978	1,401.466	1,373.696	1996	1,373.696
1997	1,459.519	1,470.958	1,410.518	1,494.724	1,585.729	1,656.772	1,788.598	1,688.397	1,780.865	1,721.388	1,801.076	1,832.007	1997	1,832.007
1998	1,852.271	1,985.866	2,087.559	2,108.561	2,072.320	2,156.496	2,133.532	1,825.071	1,941.987	2,099.951	2,227.225	2,355.569	1998	2,355.569
1999	2,454.070	2,377.800	2,472.933	2,568.698	2,508.042	2,647.232	2,564.573	2,551.885	2,481.928	2,638.986	2,692.631	2,851.217	1999	2,851.217
2000	2,707.964	2,656.704	2,916.606	2,828.858	2,770.818	2,839.127	2,794.740	2,968.334	2,811.626	2,799.739	2,579.009	2,591.631	2000	2,591.631
2001	2,683.580	2,438.886	2,284.382	2,461.903	2,478.396	2,418.076	2,394.272	2,244.386	2,063.147	2,102.489	2,263.763	2,283.594	2001	2,283.594
2002	2,250.269	2,206.872	2,289.871	2,151.041	2,135.194	1,983.104	1,828.513	1,840.518	1,640.492	1,784.881	1,889.937	1,778.908	2002	1,778.908
2003	1,732.307	1,706.315	1,722.883	1,864.797	1,963.048	1,988.090	2,023.143	2,062.598	2,040.695	2,156.136	2,175.106	2,289.179	2003	2,289.179
2004	2,331.197	2,363.599	2,327.941	2,291.397	2,322.841	2,368.008	2,289.635	2,298.897	2,323.795	2,359.295	2,454.757	2,538.289	2004	2,538.289
2005	2,476.418	2,528.532	2,483.757	2,436.651	2,514.181	2,517.750	2,611.382	2,587.555	2,608.512	2,565.027	2,662.041	2,662.968	2005	2,662.968
2006	2,733.478	2,740.894	2,775.012	2,812.274	2,731.333	2,735.036	2,751.907	2,817.383	2,889.987	2,984.160	3,040.907	3,083.564	2006	3,083.564
2007	3,130.198	3,068.975	3,103.301	3,240.763	3,353.849	3,298.131	3,195.872	3,243.779	3,365.092	3,418.621	3,275.700	3,252.974	2007	3,252.974
2008	3,057.856	2,958.519	2,945.744	3,089.211	3,129.224	2,865.419	2,841.332	2,882.431	2,625.585	2,184.624	2,027.867	2,049.444	2008	2,049.444
2009	1,876.704	1,676.877	1,823.763	1,998.314	2,110.086	2,114.271	2,274.189	2,356.297	2,444.222	2,398.816	2,542.705	2,591.819	2009	2,591.819
2010	2,498.581	2,575.980	2,731.428	2,774.551	2,553.001	2,419.356	2,588.863	2,471.991	2,692.603	2,795.054	2,795.413	2,982.234	2010	2,982.234
2011	3,052.918	3,157.508	3,158.764	3,252.312	3,215.497	3,161.897	3,097.601	2,929.334	2,723.405	3,021.054	3,014.378	3,045.212	2011	3,045.212
2012	3,181.685	3,319.267	3,428.502	3,406.981	3,202.219	3,334.157	3,380.466	3,456.603	3,545.928	3,480.455	3,500.645	3,532.552	2012	3,532.552
2013	3,715.521	3,765.959	3,907.195	3,982.473	4,075.631	4,020.900	4,225.500	4,103.123	4,231.795	4,426.321	4,561.209	4,676.681	2013	4,676.681
2014	4,514.989	4,721.521	4,761.209	4,796.404	4,908.995	5,010.403	4,941.305	5,138.982	5,066.915	5,190.675	5,330.276	5,316.849	2014	5,316.849
2015	5,157.241	5,453.636	5,367.389	5,418.879	5,488.562	5,382.314	5,495.080	5,163.541	5,035.777	5,460.566	5,476.805	5,390.425	2015	5,390.425

Appendix B-2

Large-Capitalization Stocks: Capital Appreciation Index
From 1926 to 2015

Year	Jan	Feb	Mar	Apr	May	Jun	Jul	Aug	Sep	Oct	Nov	Dec	Yr End	Index
1925												1.000	1925	1.000
1926	0.998	0.955	0.898	0.918	0.926	0.966	1.009	1.027	1.050	1.017	1.040	1.057	1926	1.057
1927	1.035	1.085	1.092	1.111	1.168	1.158	1.233	1.288	1.343	1.272	1.350	1.384	1927	1.384
1928	1.377	1.353	1.499	1.548	1.567	1.504	1.523	1.636	1.675	1.699	1.903	1.908	1928	1.908
1929	2.017	2.005	2.001	2.033	1.946	2.165	2.263	2.485	2.364	1.893	1.640	1.681	1929	1.681
1930	1.786	1.824	1.970	1.951	1.919	1.603	1.662	1.675	1.457	1.328	1.299	1.202	1930	1.202
1931	1.261	1.405	1.308	1.183	1.020	1.162	1.076	1.086	0.761	0.825	0.745	0.636	1931	0.636
1932	0.618	0.650	0.573	0.457	0.350	0.347	0.478	0.658	0.633	0.545	0.513	0.540	1932	0.540
1933	0.544	0.444	0.458	0.652	0.755	0.855	0.780	0.869	0.770	0.702	0.774	0.792	1933	0.792
1934	0.875	0.843	0.842	0.820	0.753	0.769	0.680	0.717	0.713	0.690	0.748	0.745	1934	0.745
1935	0.713	0.685	0.664	0.727	0.751	0.802	0.868	0.887	0.908	0.976	1.015	1.053	1935	1.053
1936	1.121	1.140	1.169	1.079	1.129	1.163	1.242	1.253	1.255	1.349	1.354	1.346	1936	1.346
1937	1.397	1.418	1.404	1.288	1.274	1.207	1.331	1.257	1.078	0.969	0.871	0.827	1937	0.827
1938	0.838	0.889	0.666	0.760	0.726	0.906	0.972	0.945	0.959	1.032	0.998	1.035	1938	1.035
1939	0.964	0.995	0.861	0.856	0.909	0.851	0.944	0.876	1.020	1.005	0.956	0.979	1939	0.979
1940	0.944	0.951	0.960	0.955	0.726	0.782	0.806	0.828	0.835	0.868	0.832	0.829	1940	0.829
1941	0.789	0.777	0.781	0.730	0.733	0.772	0.814	0.807	0.799	0.745	0.713	0.681	1941	0.681
1942	0.690	0.673	0.628	0.600	0.639	0.650	0.671	0.676	0.694	0.738	0.728	0.766	1942	0.766
1943	0.821	0.862	0.908	0.908	0.949	0.968	0.915	0.925	0.947	0.934	0.864	0.915	1943	0.915
1944	0.929	0.926	0.942	0.930	0.968	1.017	0.996	1.005	1.002	1.002	1.005	1.041	1944	1.041
1945	1.056	1.121	1.069	1.163	1.176	1.172	1.149	1.216	1.266	1.305	1.347	1.361	1945	1.361
1946	1.455	1.354	1.417	1.470	1.503	1.444	1.408	1.305	1.172	1.163	1.150	1.199	1946	1.199
1947	1.227	1.209	1.189	1.143	1.132	1.192	1.235	1.201	1.184	1.209	1.175	1.199	1947	1.199
1948	1.151	1.097	1.182	1.213	1.308	1.312	1.242	1.252	1.214	1.296	1.156	1.191	1948	1.191
1949	1.193	1.146	1.180	1.155	1.112	1.110	1.179	1.193	1.221	1.257	1.259	1.313	1949	1.313
1950	1.336	1.350	1.355	1.416	1.472	1.386	1.398	1.444	1.524	1.531	1.529	1.600	1950	1.600
1951	1.697	1.708	1.677	1.758	1.687	1.643	1.755	1.824	1.823	1.798	1.793	1.863	1951	1.863
1952	1.892	1.823	1.910	1.828	1.870	1.956	1.991	1.962	1.923	1.922	2.011	2.082	1952	2.082
1953	2.067	2.030	1.982	1.929	1.923	1.892	1.940	1.828	1.830	1.923	1.940	1.944	1953	1.944
1954	2.044	2.049	2.111	2.215	2.288	2.289	2.420	2.338	2.532	2.483	2.683	2.820	1954	2.820
1955	2.871	2.881	2.867	2.975	2.971	3.216	3.411	3.384	3.422	3.318	3.567	3.564	1955	3.564

Appendix B-2

Large-Capitalization Stocks: Capital Appreciation Index
From 1926 to 2015

Year	Jan	Feb	Mar	Apr	May	Jun	Jul	Aug	Sep	Oct	Nov	Dec	Yr End	Index
1956	3.434	3.553	3.799	3.792	3.542	3.681	3.871	3.723	3.554	3.572	3.533	3.658	1956	3.658
1957	3.505	3.390	3.457	3.585	3.717	3.712	3.755	3.544	3.324	3.218	3.270	3.134	1957	3.134
1958	3.268	3.201	3.299	3.404	3.455	3.545	3.698	3.742	3.923	4.023	4.113	4.327	1958	4.327
1959	4.343	4.342	4.345	4.513	4.599	4.582	4.742	4.671	4.458	4.508	4.567	4.694	1959	4.694
1960	4.358	4.398	4.337	4.261	4.375	4.461	4.350	4.464	4.194	4.184	4.353	4.554	1960	4.554
1961	4.842	4.972	5.099	5.118	5.216	5.066	5.232	5.335	5.230	5.378	5.589	5.607	1961	5.607
1962	5.395	5.483	5.451	5.113	4.673	4.291	4.563	4.633	4.410	4.429	4.879	4.945	1962	4.945
1963	5.188	5.038	5.217	5.470	5.549	5.437	5.418	5.682	5.619	5.800	5.739	5.879	1963	5.879
1964	6.038	6.097	6.190	6.227	6.299	6.402	6.519	6.413	6.597	6.650	6.616	6.642	1964	6.642
1965	6.862	6.852	6.752	6.984	6.929	6.592	6.681	6.832	7.050	7.243	7.179	7.244	1965	7.244
1966	7.279	7.149	6.993	7.136	6.750	6.641	6.552	6.042	6.000	6.285	6.305	6.295	1966	6.295
1967	6.788	6.801	7.069	7.368	6.981	7.103	7.426	7.339	7.579	7.359	7.367	7.560	1967	7.560
1968	7.229	7.003	7.069	7.648	7.734	7.804	7.660	7.748	8.046	8.104	8.493	8.140	1968	8.140
1969	8.073	7.690	7.955	8.126	8.108	7.658	7.197	7.485	7.298	7.621	7.352	7.215	1969	7.215
1970	6.663	7.014	7.024	6.389	5.999	5.699	6.117	6.389	6.600	6.524	6.834	7.222	1970	7.222
1971	7.511	7.582	7.861	8.140	7.808	7.814	7.492	7.761	7.707	7.374	7.366	7.990	1971	7.990
1972	8.146	8.352	8.401	8.438	8.570	8.397	8.416	8.706	8.664	8.745	9.143	9.252	1972	9.252
1973	9.093	8.752	8.740	8.383	8.225	8.171	8.481	8.170	8.498	8.487	7.520	7.645	1973	7.645
1974	7.568	7.541	7.365	7.078	6.840	6.740	6.216	5.654	4.980	5.792	5.484	5.373	1974	5.373
1975	6.033	6.394	6.533	6.842	7.143	7.460	6.955	6.809	6.573	6.978	7.150	7.068	1975	7.068
1976	7.904	7.814	8.054	7.966	7.851	8.172	8.107	8.065	8.248	8.064	8.002	8.422	1976	8.422
1977	7.996	7.823	7.713	7.715	7.533	7.875	7.747	7.584	7.565	7.237	7.432	7.453	1977	7.453
1978	6.995	6.821	6.991	7.589	7.625	7.487	7.890	8.095	8.036	7.300	7.422	7.532	1978	7.532
1979	7.832	7.545	7.952	7.975	7.765	8.065	8.136	8.567	8.567	7.980	8.320	8.459	1979	8.459
1980	8.947	8.908	8.001	8.330	8.718	8.953	9.535	9.591	9.832	9.990	11.013	10.640	1980	10.640
1981	10.153	10.288	10.658	10.408	10.391	10.283	10.260	9.623	9.105	9.553	9.902	9.604	1981	9.604
1982	9.436	8.864	8.774	9.122	8.768	8.589	8.393	9.366	9.437	10.479	10.857	11.022	1982	11.022
1983	11.387	11.603	11.988	12.884	12.727	13.175	12.740	12.884	13.009	12.817	13.041	12.926	1983	12.926
1984	12.806	12.309	12.475	12.543	11.799	12.005	11.807	13.063	13.017	13.017	12.820	13.107	1984	13.107
1985	14.078	14.199	14.158	14.093	14.855	15.035	14.962	14.783	14.268	14.876	15.844	16.558	1985	16.558

Appendix B-2

Large-Capitalization Stocks: Capital Appreciation Index
From 1926 to 2015

Year	Jan	Feb	Mar	Apr	May	Jun	Jul	Aug	Sep	Oct	Nov	Dec	Yr End	Index
1986	16.597	17.784	18.723	18.458	19.385	19.658	18.505	19.822	18.129	19.119	19.531	18.979	1986	18.979
1987	21.480	22.273	22.861	22.599	22.735	23.825	24.973	25.846	25.222	19.733	18.049	19.364	1987	19.364
1988	20.147	20.989	20.289	20.480	20.546	21.434	21.318	20.495	21.310	21.863	21.450	21.765	1988	21.765
1989	23.313	22.638	23.109	24.267	25.119	24.920	27.122	27.543	27.363	26.674	27.115	27.696	1989	27.696
1990	25.790	26.010	26.641	25.925	28.310	28.058	27.912	25.279	23.985	23.825	25.252	25.879	1990	25.879
1991	26.954	28.767	29.406	29.416	30.551	29.088	30.393	30.990	30.397	30.756	29.406	32.687	1991	32.687
1992	32.036	32.343	31.637	32.520	32.551	31.986	33.245	32.448	32.743	32.812	33.805	34.147	1992	34.147
1993	34.387	34.748	35.397	34.498	35.281	35.308	35.120	36.329	35.966	36.664	36.191	36.556	1993	36.556
1994	37.744	36.610	34.935	35.338	35.776	34.818	35.914	37.264	36.261	37.018	35.556	35.993	1994	35.993
1995	36.867	38.197	39.241	40.338	41.803	42.692	44.049	44.035	45.800	45.572	47.443	48.271	1995	48.271
1996	49.845	50.191	50.588	51.267	52.439	52.557	50.153	51.097	53.865	55.272	59.328	58.052	1996	58.052
1997	61.611	61.977	59.336	62.801	66.480	69.369	74.788	70.492	74.238	71.679	74.875	76.053	1997	76.053
1998	76.825	82.237	86.344	87.128	85.488	88.859	87.827	75.022	79.703	86.103	91.194	96.335	1998	96.335
1999	100.286	97.048	100.813	104.638	102.025	107.580	104.132	103.481	100.526	106.813	108.849	115.145	1999	115.145
2000	109.284	107.087	117.444	113.827	111.333	113.997	112.134	118.941	112.580	112.022	103.053	103.471	2000	103.471
2001	107.054	97.174	90.935	97.920	98.419	95.958	94.924	88.839	81.579	83.055	89.299	89.975	2001	89.975
2002	88.574	86.735	89.921	84.398	83.632	77.572	71.444	71.793	63.894	69.417	73.379	68.952	2002	68.952
2003	67.061	65.921	66.472	71.859	75.517	76.372	77.611	78.998	78.054	82.344	82.931	87.141	2003	87.141
2004	88.647	89.729	88.261	86.779	87.828	89.408	86.342	86.539	87.350	88.574	91.992	94.978	2004	94.978
2005	92.576	94.326	92.523	90.663	93.378	93.365	96.723	95.638	96.302	94.593	97.922	97.829	2005	97.829
2006	100.320	100.366	101.476	102.713	99.537	99.546	100.052	102.180	104.691	107.990	109.768	111.152	2006	111.152
2007	112.715	110.253	111.353	116.173	119.955	117.818	114.050	115.517	119.651	121.425	116.077	115.076	2007	115.076
2008	108.037	104.282	103.660	108.589	109.748	100.314	99.325	100.535	91.408	75.921	70.238	70.788	2008	70.788
2009	64.724	57.609	62.529	68.402	72.033	72.048	77.389	79.987	82.843	81.206	85.863	87.390	2009	87.390
2010	84.158	86.558	91.647	93.000	85.376	80.776	86.331	82.235	89.435	92.731	92.519	98.560	2010	98.560
2011	100.792	104.013	103.904	106.865	105.422	103.497	101.275	95.524	88.668	98.220	97.723	98.557	2011	98.557
2012	102.852	107.027	110.380	109.553	102.689	106.751	108.096	110.232	112.904	110.670	110.985	111.769	2012	111.769
2013	117.406	118.704	122.976	125.200	127.800	125.883	132.109	127.975	131.781	137.659	141.513	144.853	2013	144.853
2014	139.699	145.722	146.732	147.642	150.747	153.620	151.303	157.001	154.565	158.151	162.031	161.353	2014	161.353
2015	156.344	164.926	162.057	163.438	165.153	161.683	164.874	154.557	150.469	162.956	163.038	160.180	2015	160.180

Appendix B-3

Small-Capitalization Stocks: Total Return Index
From 1926 to 2015

Year	Jan	Feb	Mar	Apr	May	Jun	Jul	Aug	Sep	Oct	Nov	Dec	Yr End	Index
1925												1.000	1925	1.000
1926	1.070	1.001	0.894	0.910	0.904	0.938	0.949	0.973	0.973	0.951	0.971	1.003	1926	1.003
1927	1.032	1.089	1.029	1.088	1.168	1.133	1.191	1.170	1.176	1.098	1.187	1.224	1927	1.224
1928	1.283	1.253	1.319	1.440	1.503	1.376	1.384	1.445	1.574	1.617	1.803	1.710	1928	1.710
1929	1.716	1.712	1.677	1.729	1.498	1.578	1.596	1.569	1.425	1.030	0.876	0.832	1929	0.832
1930	0.939	1.000	1.101	1.024	0.968	0.758	0.781	0.768	0.656	0.584	0.583	0.515	1930	0.515
1931	0.623	0.783	0.727	0.570	0.491	0.581	0.548	0.507	0.342	0.368	0.331	0.259	1931	0.259
1932	0.285	0.293	0.255	0.198	0.175	0.175	0.237	0.411	0.357	0.293	0.257	0.245	1932	0.245
1933	0.243	0.212	0.235	0.354	0.578	0.729	0.689	0.753	0.633	0.555	0.591	0.594	1933	0.594
1934	0.825	0.839	0.838	0.858	0.749	0.747	0.578	0.667	0.656	0.663	0.726	0.738	1934	0.738
1935	0.714	0.672	0.592	0.639	0.637	0.656	0.713	0.751	0.778	0.855	0.976	1.035	1935	1.035
1936	1.346	1.427	1.436	1.179	1.211	1.183	1.286	1.313	1.384	1.472	1.678	1.705	1936	1.705
1937	1.921	2.047	2.072	1.724	1.654	1.458	1.638	1.517	1.132	1.008	0.862	0.716	1937	0.716
1938	0.754	0.780	0.499	0.638	0.584	0.788	0.906	0.815	0.802	0.974	0.907	0.951	1938	0.951
1939	0.870	0.879	0.663	0.672	0.745	0.667	0.837	0.704	1.066	1.023	0.915	0.954	1939	0.954
1940	0.955	1.033	1.099	1.171	0.741	0.818	0.837	0.859	0.877	0.925	0.947	0.905	1940	0.905
1941	0.907	0.881	0.909	0.848	0.852	0.916	1.115	1.108	1.056	0.985	0.936	0.823	1941	0.823
1942	0.979	0.972	0.903	0.872	0.869	0.898	0.964	0.995	1.086	1.204	1.143	1.190	1942	1.190
1943	1.444	1.723	1.971	2.155	2.404	2.384	2.126	2.126	2.217	2.244	1.994	2.242	1943	2.242
1944	2.385	2.456	2.640	2.499	2.684	3.055	2.964	3.059	3.053	3.020	3.170	3.446	1944	3.446
1945	3.612	3.977	3.634	4.055	4.257	4.621	4.364	4.607	4.920	5.265	5.882	5.983	1945	5.983
1946	6.917	6.476	6.653	7.117	7.537	7.189	6.808	6.230	5.232	5.170	5.097	5.287	1946	5.287
1947	5.509	5.487	5.303	4.756	4.502	4.750	5.125	5.106	5.165	5.311	5.150	5.335	1947	5.335
1948	5.254	4.842	5.320	5.515	6.099	6.128	5.774	5.778	5.474	5.828	5.177	5.223	1948	5.223
1949	5.318	5.062	5.380	5.199	4.906	4.859	5.185	5.318	5.578	5.841	5.851	6.254	1949	6.254
1950	6.562	6.706	6.682	6.956	7.134	6.580	6.969	7.338	7.720	7.675	7.922	8.677	1950	8.677
1951	9.398	9.455	9.004	9.334	9.026	8.548	8.867	9.403	9.606	9.392	9.314	9.355	1951	9.355
1952	9.533	9.248	9.410	8.922	8.950	9.193	9.296	9.291	9.142	9.047	9.486	9.638	1952	9.638
1953	10.032	10.302	10.233	9.939	10.079	9.589	9.735	9.123	8.884	9.143	9.258	9.013	1953	9.013
1954	9.694	9.786	9.965	10.104	10.561	10.651	11.512	11.528	12.000	12.082	13.024	14.473	1954	14.473
1955	14.764	15.471	15.602	15.837	15.960	16.428	16.533	16.487	16.667	16.384	17.152	17.431	1955	17.431

Appendix B-3

Small-Capitalization Stocks: Total Return Index
From 1926 to 2015

Year	Jan	Feb	Mar	Apr	May	Jun	Jul	Aug	Sep	Oct	Nov	Dec	Yr End	Index
1956	17.348	17.830	18.598	18.685	17.942	18.042	18.552	18.303	17.827	18.013	18.108	18.177	1956	18.177
1957	18.607	18.234	18.540	19.000	19.143	19.283	19.167	18.427	17.595	16.131	16.314	15.529	1957	15.529
1958	17.245	16.952	17.750	18.418	19.131	19.752	20.722	21.610	22.730	23.655	24.828	25.605	1958	25.605
1959	27.076	27.875	27.951	28.277	28.315	28.196	29.118	28.863	27.619	28.245	28.873	29.804	1959	29.804
1960	28.891	29.034	28.120	27.594	28.158	29.116	28.565	30.064	27.844	26.728	27.896	28.823	1960	28.823
1961	31.460	33.314	35.376	35.825	37.355	35.326	35.436	35.898	34.682	35.590	37.772	38.072	1961	38.072
1962	38.591	39.314	39.537	36.464	32.786	30.213	32.518	33.458	31.254	30.087	33.842	33.540	1962	33.540
1963	36.580	36.705	37.251	38.412	40.088	39.613	39.744	41.799	41.118	42.090	41.642	41.444	1963	41.444
1964	42.581	44.134	45.099	45.520	46.234	46.985	48.857	48.715	50.676	51.716	51.772	51.193	1964	51.193
1965	53.902	56.003	57.335	60.252	59.782	54.397	56.837	60.220	62.310	65.876	68.319	72.567	1965	72.567
1966	78.051	80.479	78.935	81.645	73.797	73.709	73.617	65.669	64.595	63.902	67.041	67.479	1966	67.479
1967	79.884	83.475	88.606	91.003	90.232	99.411	108.862	109.085	115.244	111.662	112.964	123.870	1967	123.870
1968	125.779	116.861	115.586	132.468	145.698	146.137	141.088	146.266	155.034	155.505	167.388	168.429	1968	168.429
1969	165.634	149.238	155.142	161.265	164.063	144.954	129.449	138.925	135.301	143.552	135.552	126.233	1969	126.233
1970	118.554	123.145	119.641	98.970	88.762	80.519	84.975	93.037	103.140	95.856	97.170	104.226	1970	104.226
1971	120.820	124.647	131.675	134.923	126.760	122.710	115.802	122.555	119.780	113.180	108.954	121.423	1971	121.423
1972	135.142	139.141	137.144	138.912	136.257	132.099	126.645	129.005	124.506	122.329	129.576	126.807	1972	126.807
1973	121.329	111.635	109.318	102.527	94.211	91.476	102.398	97.837	108.242	109.155	87.737	87.618	1973	87.618
1974	99.238	98.393	97.661	93.129	85.745	84.485	82.637	77.009	71.978	79.629	76.143	70.142	1974	70.142
1975	89.551	92.105	97.799	102.990	109.821	118.053	115.056	108.456	106.488	105.954	109.341	107.189	1975	107.189
1976	135.960	154.854	154.626	149.081	143.698	150.298	150.976	146.592	148.123	145.028	150.881	168.691	1976	168.691
1977	176.275	175.587	177.880	181.941	181.434	195.445	196.028	193.924	195.715	189.249	209.804	211.500	1977	211.500
1978	207.502	214.707	236.868	255.528	276.484	271.254	289.807	317.010	316.002	239.303	256.811	261.120	1978	261.120
1979	295.623	287.279	319.448	331.805	332.955	348.676	354.642	381.457	368.351	325.827	353.796	374.614	1979	374.614
1980	405.926	394.411	324.303	346.795	372.814	389.666	441.224	467.894	487.473	503.725	542.326	523.992	1980	523.992
1981	534.839	539.866	590.776	629.590	656.158	661.145	640.253	596.460	552.739	593.752	610.140	596.717	1981	596.717
1982	585.021	567.705	562.822	584.378	569.886	560.825	559.983	599.070	618.660	699.395	753.878	763.829	1982	763.829
1983	811.793	869.617	915.267	985.448	1,071.150	1,108.462	1,098.662	1,077.054	1,091.418	1,029.455	1,082.532	1,066.828	1983	1,066.828
1984	1,065.974	997.219	1,014.571	1,005.947	953.537	982.143	940.893	1,034.794	1,037.588	1,015.072	980.966	995.680	1984	995.680
1985	1,101.123	1,131.073	1,106.869	1,087.609	1,117.627	1,129.474	1,158.840	1,150.497	1,087.910	1,116.304	1,185.515	1,241.234	1985	1,241.234

Appendix B-3

Small-Capitalization Stocks: Total Return Index
From 1926 to 2015

Year	Jan	Feb	Mar	Apr	May	Jun	Jul	Aug	Sep	Oct	Nov	Dec	Yr End	Index
1986	1,255.136	1,345.380	1,409.555	1,418.576	1,469.645	1,473.466	1,368.850	1,398.691	1,320.504	1,366.193	1,361.958	1,326.275	1986	1,326.275
1987	1,451.342	1,568.756	1,605.308	1,555.062	1,548.997	1,590.200	1,648.084	1,695.384	1,681.651	1,190.777	1,143.503	1,202.965	1987	1,202.965
1988	1,269.850	1,366.359	1,422.106	1,451.828	1,425.841	1,513.102	1,509.319	1,472.190	1,505.609	1,487.090	1,422.104	1,478.135	1988	1,478.135
1989	1,537.852	1,550.616	1,606.128	1,650.939	1,710.703	1,676.318	1,744.544	1,765.827	1,765.827	1,659.171	1,650.709	1,628.590	1989	1,628.590
1990	1,504.166	1,532.294	1,588.682	1,546.423	1,633.177	1,656.695	1,593.409	1,386.904	1,271.929	1,199.175	1,253.138	1,277.449	1990	1,277.449
1991	1,384.882	1,539.019	1,643.673	1,649.261	1,704.347	1,621.686	1,687.688	1,731.737	1,737.279	1,792.350	1,742.881	1,847.629	1991	1,847.629
1992	2,056.041	2,148.974	2,095.465	2,011.018	2,008.202	1,903.976	1,974.424	1,929.407	1,954.682	2,005.308	2,182.778	2,279.038	1992	2,279.038
1993	2,402.790	2,359.540	2,427.731	2,353.442	2,433.930	2,424.681	2,464.931	2,548.492	2,629.024	2,752.851	2,704.676	2,757.147	1993	2,757.147
1994	2,927.539	2,920.805	2,790.537	2,807.281	2,803.912	2,730.449	2,780.690	2,874.399	2,904.580	2,937.983	2,842.205	2,842.773	1994	2,842.773
1995	2,923.223	2,996.889	3,040.344	3,147.364	3,241.155	3,425.253	3,646.182	3,776.715	3,850.361	3,662.848	3,733.175	3,822.398	1995	3,822.398
1996	3,833.100	3,974.542	4,065.161	4,409.887	4,740.188	4,464.309	4,043.324	4,235.787	4,359.048	4,282.765	4,406.108	4,495.993	1996	4,495.993
1997	4,684.825	4,588.317	4,363.490	4,243.057	4,676.698	4,909.597	5,206.628	5,471.645	5,933.452	5,704.421	5,616.003	5,519.969	1997	5,519.969
1998	5,487.401	5,843.533	6,124.607	6,227.501	5,917.994	5,796.083	5,407.166	4,320.326	4,479.746	4,639.225	4,990.878	5,116.648	1998	5,116.648
1999	5,259.403	4,898.082	4,712.444	5,159.655	5,359.334	5,663.744	5,715.850	5,606.678	5,482.770	5,435.070	5,962.815	6,640.787	1999	6,640.787
2000	7,035.914	8,694.983	8,041.990	7,035.937	6,467.433	7,352.178	7,115.438	7,773.616	7,604.928	7,068.020	6,283.470	6,402.228	2000	6,402.228
2001	7,285.735	6,774.277	6,449.111	6,920.541	7,584.913	7,857.212	7,657.638	7,431.738	6,481.962	6,900.049	7,365.112	7,860.047	2001	7,860.047
2002	7,946.508	7,726.390	8,409.402	8,613.751	8,378.596	8,080.318	6,910.288	6,870.899	6,407.800	6,572.481	7,121.940	6,816.409	2002	6,816.409
2003	6,664.403	6,472.468	6,544.313	7,151.625	7,982.644	8,333.880	8,948.920	9,372.204	9,380.639	10,219.268	10,658.697	10,953.943	2003	10,953.943
2004	11,587.081	11,645.016	11,661.319	11,184.371	11,184.371	11,677.602	10,805.285	10,641.045	11,174.161	11,379.766	12,400.531	12,968.475	2004	12,968.475
2005	12,436.767	12,539.993	12,134.951	11,380.157	12,066.380	12,611.781	13,574.060	13,385.380	13,467.031	13,088.607	13,681.521	13,706.148	2005	13,706.148
2006	14,958.890	14,996.287	15,678.613	15,614.336	14,694.652	14,563.869	14,061.416	14,452.323	14,533.256	15,325.319	15,670.138	15,922.427	2006	15,922.427
2007	16,105.535	16,025.008	16,188.463	16,431.290	16,948.875	16,892.944	15,793.213	15,976.415	16,212.866	16,488.484	15,100.154	15,091.094	2007	15,091.094
2008	13,936.625	13,499.015	13,540.862	13,821.158	14,371.240	13,070.643	13,656.208	14,117.787	13,077.306	10,368.996	9,037.613	9,548.943	2008	9,548.943
2009	8,411.664	7,308.895	8,009.087	9,401.867	9,724.351	9,992.743	10,974.031	11,273.622	11,922.982	11,056.182	11,252.982	12,230.866	2009	12,230.866
2010	11,871.278	12,392.427	13,393.735	14,367.460	13,301.395	12,338.374	13,219.333	12,164.431	13,643.625	14,235.759	14,839.355	16,054.698	2010	16,054.698
2011	15,879.702	16,811.840	17,358.225	17,649.843	17,310.966	16,937.049	16,481.443	15,009.650	13,421.629	15,492.586	15,399.631	15,532.068	2011	15,532.068
2012	16,613.100	16,930.410	17,434.936	17,187.360	15,989.401	16,808.058	16,655.105	17,174.744	17,894.366	17,527.532	17,692.290	18,364.597	2012	18,364.597
2013	19,407.706	19,621.191	20,576.743	20,414.187	21,471.642	21,570.411	23,168.779	22,362.505	23,939.062	24,772.141	26,146.995	26,641.173	2013	26,641.173
2014	25,460.969	26,532.876	26,790.245	25,876.698	25,902.575	27,026.746	25,448.384	26,603.741	25,089.988	26,725.855	26,525.411	27,419.318	2014	27,419.318
2015	26,075.771	27,648.140	28,281.283	27,729.798	28,112.469	28,570.702	27,873.577	26,638.777	25,490.646	27,027.732	27,795.320	26,433.349	2015	26,433.349

Appendix B-4

Long-term Corporate Bonds: Total Return Index
From 1926 to 2015

Year	Jan	Feb	Mar	Apr	May	Jun	Jul	Aug	Sep	Oct	Nov	Dec	Yr End	Index
1925												1.000	1925	1.000
1926	1.007	1.012	1.020	1.030	1.035	1.035	1.041	1.046	1.052	1.062	1.068	1.074	1926	1.074
1927	1.080	1.087	1.096	1.102	1.101	1.106	1.106	1.115	1.132	1.138	1.146	1.154	1927	1.154
1928	1.157	1.165	1.169	1.171	1.162	1.159	1.158	1.168	1.171	1.181	1.177	1.186	1928	1.186
1929	1.192	1.195	1.185	1.187	1.192	1.187	1.189	1.192	1.196	1.204	1.202	1.225	1929	1.225
1930	1.233	1.241	1.259	1.269	1.276	1.290	1.298	1.315	1.329	1.337	1.335	1.323	1930	1.323
1931	1.350	1.359	1.372	1.381	1.400	1.407	1.414	1.416	1.414	1.362	1.337	1.299	1931	1.299
1932	1.292	1.261	1.306	1.283	1.297	1.295	1.301	1.358	1.399	1.409	1.419	1.439	1932	1.439
1933	1.518	1.438	1.445	1.431	1.516	1.544	1.569	1.584	1.582	1.588	1.549	1.588	1933	1.588
1934	1.629	1.653	1.684	1.701	1.717	1.744	1.752	1.760	1.749	1.767	1.790	1.808	1934	1.808
1935	1.846	1.872	1.880	1.901	1.909	1.931	1.952	1.944	1.944	1.952	1.966	1.982	1935	1.982
1936	1.998	2.009	2.026	2.031	2.039	2.056	2.058	2.072	2.086	2.091	2.114	2.116	1936	2.116
1937	2.121	2.111	2.087	2.101	2.110	2.121	2.129	2.125	2.131	2.145	2.159	2.174	1937	2.174
1938	2.182	2.184	2.165	2.195	2.197	2.218	2.233	2.229	2.253	2.271	2.279	2.307	1938	2.307
1939	2.312	2.327	2.332	2.347	2.359	2.367	2.365	2.272	2.307	2.361	2.380	2.399	1939	2.399
1940	2.410	2.415	2.427	2.405	2.400	2.429	2.434	2.436	2.458	2.470	2.486	2.480	1940	2.480
1941	2.482	2.483	2.478	2.497	2.509	2.525	2.541	2.550	2.562	2.570	2.546	2.548	1941	2.548
1942	2.549	2.547	2.563	2.565	2.570	2.579	2.584	2.593	2.598	2.600	2.601	2.614	1942	2.614
1943	2.627	2.628	2.634	2.647	2.659	2.672	2.677	2.682	2.684	2.681	2.675	2.688	1943	2.688
1944	2.693	2.703	2.716	2.725	2.726	2.732	2.741	2.750	2.755	2.761	2.774	2.815	1944	2.815
1945	2.837	2.850	2.855	2.860	2.857	2.866	2.863	2.864	2.873	2.882	2.892	2.930	1945	2.930
1946	2.968	2.978	2.988	2.975	2.981	2.986	2.983	2.956	2.949	2.955	2.947	2.980	1946	2.980
1947	2.982	2.983	3.003	3.009	3.015	3.017	3.023	3.001	2.962	2.933	2.904	2.911	1947	2.911
1948	2.918	2.929	2.963	2.974	2.977	2.952	2.936	2.953	2.960	2.967	2.992	3.031	1948	3.031
1949	3.043	3.054	3.056	3.063	3.075	3.101	3.132	3.143	3.150	3.171	3.178	3.132	1949	3.132
1950	3.143	3.145	3.152	3.150	3.147	3.154	3.176	3.188	3.176	3.173	3.190	3.198	1950	3.198
1951	3.204	3.190	3.114	3.111	3.107	3.078	3.141	3.177	3.159	3.113	3.094	3.112	1951	3.112
1952	3.174	3.147	3.171	3.169	3.179	3.184	3.189	3.209	3.204	3.216	3.251	3.221	1952	3.221
1953	3.196	3.183	3.172	3.094	3.084	3.118	3.173	3.146	3.226	3.299	3.275	3.331	1953	3.331
1954	3.373	3.439	3.453	3.441	3.427	3.448	3.462	3.468	3.482	3.496	3.505	3.511	1954	3.511
1955	3.477	3.455	3.486	3.486	3.480	3.490	3.476	3.462	3.489	3.516	3.505	3.527	1955	3.527

Appendix B-4

Long-term Corporate Bonds: Total Return Index
From 1926 to 2015

Year	Jan	Feb	Mar	Apr	May	Jun	Jul	Aug	Sep	Oct	Nov	Dec	Yr End	Index
1956	3.564	3.573	3.521	3.481	3.499	3.493	3.460	3.388	3.392	3.357	3.314	3.287	1956	3.287
1957	3.352	3.383	3.400	3.377	3.352	3.244	3.209	3.206	3.236	3.244	3.344	3.573	1957	3.573
1958	3.609	3.606	3.589	3.648	3.659	3.645	3.590	3.475	3.441	3.478	3.515	3.494	1958	3.494
1959	3.484	3.528	3.499	3.439	3.400	3.415	3.445	3.422	3.392	3.447	3.494	3.460	1959	3.460
1960	3.498	3.542	3.610	3.602	3.594	3.645	3.739	3.783	3.759	3.762	3.735	3.774	1960	3.774
1961	3.830	3.911	3.899	3.854	3.873	3.842	3.857	3.850	3.906	3.955	3.966	3.956	1961	3.956
1962	3.988	4.008	4.069	4.127	4.127	4.116	4.110	4.169	4.206	4.234	4.261	4.270	1962	4.270
1963	4.296	4.305	4.317	4.295	4.315	4.334	4.346	4.361	4.351	4.372	4.379	4.364	1963	4.364
1964	4.402	4.426	4.398	4.416	4.441	4.463	4.486	4.502	4.512	4.534	4.533	4.572	1964	4.572
1965	4.609	4.614	4.619	4.629	4.625	4.627	4.635	4.633	4.626	4.647	4.620	4.552	1965	4.552
1966	4.562	4.510	4.483	4.489	4.478	4.491	4.447	4.332	4.366	4.480	4.471	4.560	1966	4.560
1967	4.766	4.670	4.724	4.691	4.572	4.470	4.488	4.485	4.527	4.400	4.280	4.335	1967	4.335
1968	4.491	4.508	4.419	4.440	4.454	4.509	4.662	4.758	4.733	4.658	4.552	4.446	1968	4.446
1969	4.508	4.436	4.347	4.493	4.391	4.406	4.408	4.400	4.292	4.347	4.142	4.086	1969	4.086
1970	4.144	4.310	4.291	4.184	4.115	4.116	4.345	4.388	4.449	4.406	4.664	4.837	1970	4.837
1971	5.095	4.908	5.035	4.916	4.837	4.889	4.876	5.146	5.094	5.238	5.253	5.370	1971	5.370
1972	5.352	5.409	5.422	5.441	5.530	5.493	5.509	5.549	5.566	5.622	5.762	5.760	1972	5.760
1973	5.729	5.742	5.768	5.803	5.780	5.748	5.474	5.669	5.871	5.832	5.878	5.825	1973	5.825
1974	5.795	5.800	5.622	5.430	5.487	5.331	5.218	5.078	5.167	5.624	5.690	5.647	1974	5.647
1975	5.984	6.066	5.916	5.885	5.947	6.128	6.110	6.003	5.927	6.255	6.200	6.474	1975	6.474
1976	6.596	6.636	6.747	6.737	6.667	6.767	6.868	7.027	7.144	7.194	7.424	7.681	1976	7.681
1977	7.448	7.434	7.503	7.579	7.659	7.793	7.789	7.895	7.878	7.848	7.895	7.813	1977	7.813
1978	7.743	7.783	7.815	7.797	7.713	7.731	7.809	8.010	7.971	7.808	7.912	7.807	1978	7.807
1979	7.951	7.849	7.932	7.892	8.072	8.289	8.263	8.269	8.121	7.398	7.563	7.481	1979	7.481
1980	6.998	6.533	6.492	7.386	7.799	8.065	7.719	7.376	7.201	7.086	7.098	7.274	1980	7.274
1981	7.180	6.987	7.234	6.650	7.046	7.062	6.799	6.565	6.434	6.769	7.627	7.185	1981	7.185
1982	7.092	7.313	7.537	7.792	7.983	7.609	8.020	8.691	9.233	9.933	10.133	10.242	1982	10.242
1983	10.146	10.580	10.657	11.241	10.876	10.826	10.334	10.386	10.794	10.767	10.920	10.883	1983	10.883
1984	11.177	10.985	10.727	10.649	10.134	10.336	10.942	11.278	11.632	12.297	12.558	12.718	1984	12.718
1985	13.132	12.642	12.868	13.249	14.336	14.455	14.280	14.651	14.755	15.240	15.804	16.546	1985	16.546

Appendix B-4

Long-term Corporate Bonds: Total Return Index
From 1926 to 2015

Year	Jan	Feb	Mar	Apr	May	Jun	Jul	Aug	Sep	Oct	Nov	Dec	Yr End	Index
1986	16.620	17.870	18.327	18.357	18.056	18.449	18.506	19.015	18.799	19.154	19.600	19.829	1986	19.829
1987	20.258	20.375	20.198	19.184	19.084	19.380	19.149	19.006	18.204	19.127	19.366	19.776	1987	19.776
1988	20.799	21.086	20.689	20.381	20.265	21.033	20.800	20.912	21.594	22.183	21.808	21.893	1988	21.893
1989	22.335	22.047	22.188	22.661	23.520	24.449	24.884	24.479	24.576	25.255	25.432	25.447	1989	25.447
1990	24.961	24.931	24.903	24.428	25.368	25.916	26.181	25.416	25.647	25.986	26.726	27.173	1990	27.173
1991	27.580	27.914	28.216	28.605	28.717	28.665	29.144	29.945	30.757	30.889	31.216	32.577	1991	32.577
1992	32.014	32.321	32.085	32.136	32.953	33.467	34.497	34.808	35.153	34.604	34.843	35.637	1992	35.637
1993	36.528	37.463	37.557	37.752	37.828	38.936	39.326	40.454	40.628	40.835	40.068	40.336	1993	40.336
1994	41.151	39.974	38.443	38.070	37.834	37.528	38.687	38.567	37.545	37.358	37.425	38.012	1994	38.012
1995	38.985	40.112	40.493	41.202	43.802	44.148	43.702	44.637	45.320	46.158	47.275	48.353	1995	48.353
1996	48.421	46.615	46.009	45.273	45.295	46.074	46.121	45.798	46.984	48.680	49.960	49.031	1996	49.031
1997	48.894	49.031	47.947	48.829	49.454	50.379	53.039	51.766	52.936	53.947	54.492	55.380	1997	55.380
1998	56.139	56.100	56.313	56.611	57.557	58.219	57.893	58.408	60.820	59.664	61.275	61.339	1998	61.339
1999	62.091	59.603	59.617	59.473	58.427	57.493	56.843	56.693	57.221	57.492	57.356	56.772	1999	56.772
2000	56.652	57.174	58.142	57.476	56.552	58.396	59.442	60.245	60.525	60.797	62.394	64.077	2000	64.077
2001	66.377	67.222	67.026	66.166	67.041	67.412	69.844	70.937	69.858	72.913	71.542	70.900	2001	70.900
2002	72.139	73.080	70.925	72.720	73.542	74.079	74.772	78.152	80.729	78.794	79.605	82.480	2002	82.480
2003	82.651	84.830	84.152	86.083	90.135	88.845	81.016	82.788	86.954	85.192	85.634	86.824	2003	86.824
2004	88.445	90.023	91.081	86.215	85.600	86.400	87.993	91.468	92.391	93.905	92.028	94.396	2004	94.396
2005	97.007	95.924	94.730	97.824	100.711	102.132	99.640	101.959	98.794	96.778	97.734	99.937	2005	99.937
2006	99.012	100.277	96.223	94.068	93.877	94.242	96.478	99.958	101.791	103.085	105.625	103.178	2006	103.178
2007	102.652	105.602	103.167	104.616	102.756	101.231	100.905	102.437	103.825	104.735	105.559	105.858	2007	105.858
2008	106.037	105.284	104.664	105.617	102.688	102.064	100.949	102.173	93.351	89.151	99.616	115.154	2008	115.154
2009	104.231	101.025	100.847	100.543	105.464	109.157	115.322	118.032	121.259	121.450	121.987	118.628	2009	118.628
2010	119.762	120.226	120.768	125.085	124.446	130.911	133.133	139.433	137.426	134.640	133.869	133.384	2010	133.384
2011	130.742	132.801	131.846	134.997	138.468	135.566	141.976	145.378	153.736	155.178	149.657	157.324	2011	157.324
2012	160.381	161.290	156.402	160.328	165.848	166.912	177.119	175.479	173.267	176.836	175.211	174.120	2012	174.120
2013	168.667	170.233	169.933	175.865	166.437	160.269	160.772	159.582	159.806	163.171	161.770	161.802	2013	161.802
2014	167.162	169.977	171.035	173.771	177.034	177.389	177.820	184.154	179.172	183.199	186.359	189.762	2014	189.762
2015	201.120	194.678	195.807	191.443	187.541	181.545	185.882	184.631	187.084	187.455	187.821	187.822	2015	187.822

Appendix B-5

Long-term Government Bonds: Total Return Index
From 1926 to 2015

Year	Jan	Feb	Mar	Apr	May	Jun	Jul	Aug	Sep	Oct	Nov	Dec	Yr End	Index
1925												1.000	1925	1.000
1926	1.014	1.020	1.024	1.032	1.034	1.038	1.038	1.038	1.042	1.053	1.069	1.078	1926	1.078
1927	1.086	1.095	1.123	1.122	1.135	1.127	1.132	1.141	1.143	1.154	1.166	1.174	1927	1.174
1928	1.170	1.177	1.182	1.182	1.173	1.178	1.152	1.161	1.156	1.174	1.175	1.175	1928	1.175
1929	1.165	1.146	1.130	1.161	1.142	1.155	1.155	1.151	1.154	1.198	1.226	1.215	1929	1.215
1930	1.208	1.224	1.234	1.232	1.249	1.256	1.260	1.262	1.271	1.276	1.281	1.272	1930	1.272
1931	1.257	1.267	1.280	1.291	1.310	1.311	1.305	1.307	1.270	1.228	1.231	1.204	1931	1.204
1932	1.208	1.258	1.256	1.332	1.307	1.315	1.379	1.379	1.387	1.385	1.389	1.407	1932	1.407
1933	1.428	1.391	1.405	1.400	1.443	1.450	1.447	1.454	1.457	1.444	1.422	1.406	1933	1.406
1934	1.442	1.454	1.483	1.501	1.521	1.531	1.537	1.519	1.497	1.524	1.530	1.547	1934	1.547
1935	1.575	1.590	1.596	1.609	1.600	1.615	1.622	1.600	1.602	1.611	1.613	1.624	1935	1.624
1936	1.633	1.647	1.664	1.670	1.677	1.680	1.690	1.709	1.704	1.705	1.740	1.746	1936	1.746
1937	1.744	1.759	1.687	1.693	1.702	1.699	1.723	1.705	1.712	1.720	1.736	1.750	1937	1.750
1938	1.760	1.770	1.763	1.800	1.808	1.809	1.817	1.817	1.821	1.837	1.833	1.847	1938	1.847
1939	1.858	1.873	1.896	1.919	1.951	1.946	1.968	1.929	1.824	1.898	1.929	1.957	1939	1.957
1940	1.954	1.959	1.994	1.987	1.927	1.977	1.987	1.993	2.015	2.021	2.062	2.076	1940	2.076
1941	2.034	2.039	2.058	2.085	2.090	2.104	2.109	2.113	2.110	2.140	2.133	2.096	1941	2.096
1942	2.110	2.112	2.132	2.126	2.142	2.142	2.146	2.154	2.155	2.160	2.152	2.163	1942	2.163
1943	2.170	2.169	2.171	2.181	2.192	2.196	2.196	2.201	2.203	2.204	2.204	2.208	1943	2.208
1944	2.213	2.220	2.224	2.227	2.234	2.235	2.243	2.249	2.253	2.255	2.261	2.270	1944	2.270
1945	2.299	2.317	2.321	2.358	2.372	2.412	2.391	2.397	2.410	2.435	2.466	2.514	1945	2.514
1946	2.520	2.528	2.531	2.497	2.493	2.511	2.501	2.473	2.471	2.489	2.475	2.511	1946	2.511
1947	2.510	2.515	2.520	2.511	2.519	2.522	2.537	2.558	2.547	2.537	2.493	2.445	1947	2.445
1948	2.450	2.462	2.470	2.481	2.516	2.495	2.490	2.490	2.494	2.496	2.514	2.529	1948	2.529
1949	2.549	2.562	2.581	2.584	2.589	2.632	2.641	2.670	2.667	2.672	2.678	2.692	1949	2.692
1950	2.675	2.681	2.683	2.691	2.700	2.693	2.708	2.712	2.692	2.679	2.689	2.693	1950	2.693
1951	2.709	2.689	2.646	2.630	2.612	2.596	2.632	2.657	2.636	2.639	2.603	2.587	1951	2.587
1952	2.595	2.598	2.627	2.672	2.663	2.664	2.658	2.640	2.606	2.644	2.640	2.617	1952	2.617
1953	2.620	2.598	2.575	2.548	2.510	2.566	2.576	2.574	2.651	2.671	2.658	2.713	1953	2.713
1954	2.737	2.802	2.819	2.848	2.823	2.869	2.908	2.897	2.894	2.896	2.889	2.907	1954	2.907
1955	2.837	2.815	2.840	2.840	2.861	2.839	2.810	2.811	2.832	2.872	2.859	2.870	1955	2.870

Appendix B-5

Long-term Government Bonds: Total Return Index
From 1926 to 2015

Year	Jan	Feb	Mar	Apr	May	Jun	Jul	Aug	Sep	Oct	Nov	Dec	Yr End	Index
1956	2.894	2.893	2.850	2.818	2.881	2.889	2.829	2.776	2.790	2.775	2.759	2.710	1956	2.710
1957	2.803	2.810	2.804	2.741	2.735	2.686	2.675	2.675	2.696	2.682	2.825	2.912	1957	2.912
1958	2.887	2.916	2.946	3.001	3.001	2.953	2.871	2.746	2.714	2.751	2.785	2.734	1958	2.734
1959	2.712	2.744	2.749	2.717	2.715	2.718	2.734	2.723	2.708	2.748	2.716	2.673	1959	2.673
1960	2.702	2.757	2.835	2.787	2.829	2.878	2.984	2.964	2.986	2.978	2.958	3.041	1960	3.041
1961	3.008	3.068	3.057	3.092	3.078	3.055	3.065	3.054	3.093	3.115	3.109	3.070	1961	3.070
1962	3.066	3.098	3.176	3.202	3.217	3.192	3.158	3.217	3.236	3.263	3.270	3.282	1962	3.282
1963	3.281	3.284	3.287	3.283	3.290	3.297	3.307	3.314	3.315	3.307	3.324	3.322	1963	3.322
1964	3.317	3.313	3.326	3.341	3.358	3.381	3.384	3.390	3.407	3.422	3.428	3.438	1964	3.438
1965	3.452	3.457	3.475	3.488	3.494	3.511	3.518	3.514	3.502	3.511	3.490	3.462	1965	3.462
1966	3.427	3.341	3.440	3.418	3.398	3.393	3.380	3.310	3.420	3.498	3.447	3.589	1966	3.589
1967	3.644	3.564	3.634	3.528	3.515	3.405	3.428	3.399	3.398	3.262	3.198	3.259	1967	3.259
1968	3.366	3.355	3.284	3.359	3.373	3.451	3.550	3.549	3.513	3.466	3.373	3.251	1968	3.251
1969	3.184	3.197	3.201	3.337	3.174	3.242	3.267	3.245	3.073	3.185	3.107	3.086	1969	3.086
1970	3.079	3.260	3.238	3.104	2.959	3.103	3.202	3.196	3.269	3.233	3.489	3.460	1970	3.460
1971	3.634	3.575	3.763	3.657	3.655	3.597	3.607	3.777	3.854	3.918	3.900	3.917	1971	3.917
1972	3.892	3.927	3.895	3.905	4.011	3.985	4.071	4.082	4.049	4.143	4.237	4.140	1972	4.140
1973	4.007	4.013	4.046	4.064	4.021	4.013	3.839	3.989	4.116	4.205	4.128	4.094	1973	4.094
1974	4.060	4.050	3.932	3.833	3.880	3.897	3.886	3.796	3.890	4.080	4.200	4.272	1974	4.272
1975	4.368	4.426	4.308	4.229	4.319	4.445	4.407	4.377	4.334	4.539	4.490	4.665	1975	4.665
1976	4.707	4.736	4.815	4.824	4.747	4.846	4.884	4.987	5.059	5.102	5.274	5.447	1976	5.447
1977	5.236	5.210	5.257	5.295	5.361	5.449	5.411	5.518	5.502	5.451	5.502	5.410	1977	5.410
1978	5.366	5.368	5.357	5.355	5.323	5.290	5.366	5.483	5.425	5.316	5.416	5.346	1978	5.346
1979	5.448	5.375	5.444	5.383	5.524	5.696	5.647	5.627	5.559	5.091	5.250	5.280	1979	5.280
1980	4.889	4.660	4.514	5.201	5.419	5.613	5.346	5.115	4.982	4.851	4.899	5.071	1980	5.071
1981	5.013	4.795	4.979	4.721	5.015	4.925	4.751	4.568	4.502	4.875	5.562	5.166	1981	5.166
1982	5.189	5.284	5.406	5.608	5.627	5.501	5.777	6.228	6.613	7.033	7.031	7.251	1982	7.251
1983	7.027	7.372	7.303	7.558	7.267	7.295	6.940	6.954	7.305	7.209	7.341	7.298	1983	7.298
1984	7.476	7.343	7.228	7.152	6.782	6.884	7.361	7.557	7.816	8.254	8.352	8.427	1984	8.427
1985	8.734	8.304	8.558	8.766	9.551	9.686	9.512	9.759	9.738	10.067	10.471	11.037	1985	11.037

Appendix B-5

Long-term Government Bonds: Total Return Index
From 1926 to 2015

Year	Jan	Feb	Mar	Apr	May	Jun	Jul	Aug	Sep	Oct	Nov	Dec	Yr End	Index
1986	11.009	12.270	13.215	13.109	12.447	13.210	13.068	13.720	13.034	13.410	13.769	13.745	1986	13.745
1987	13.966	14.247	13.930	13.271	13.132	13.260	13.024	12.810	12.337	13.106	13.154	13.372	1987	13.372
1988	14.263	14.337	13.897	13.675	13.536	14.035	13.797	13.876	14.355	14.796	14.506	14.665	1988	14.665
1989	14.963	14.695	14.875	15.111	15.717	16.582	16.977	16.537	16.569	17.198	17.332	17.322	1989	17.322
1990	16.728	16.686	16.613	16.278	16.954	17.344	17.530	16.796	16.992	17.358	18.056	18.392	1990	18.392
1991	18.632	18.689	18.760	19.023	19.024	18.904	19.202	19.855	20.458	20.569	20.738	21.942	1991	21.942
1992	21.231	21.339	21.140	21.173	21.687	22.121	23.001	23.155	23.584	23.117	23.140	23.709	1992	23.709
1993	24.374	25.237	25.290	25.472	25.591	26.739	27.251	28.433	28.448	28.722	27.979	28.034	1993	28.034
1994	28.755	27.462	26.378	25.981	25.767	25.508	26.435	26.209	25.342	25.280	25.447	25.856	1994	25.856
1995	26.561	27.322	27.572	28.039	30.255	30.675	30.161	30.873	31.413	32.337	33.143	34.044	1995	34.044
1996	34.007	32.366	31.687	31.163	30.994	31.622	31.678	31.237	32.142	33.440	34.612	33.727	1996	33.727
1997	33.459	33.476	32.633	33.465	33.783	34.448	36.603	35.441	36.560	37.807	38.366	39.074	1997	39.074
1998	39.856	39.570	39.668	39.771	40.497	41.421	41.256	43.173	44.876	43.896	44.320	44.178	1998	44.178
1999	44.713	42.390	42.355	42.444	41.660	41.337	41.012	40.803	41.147	41.099	40.849	40.218	1999	40.218
2000	41.135	42.220	43.768	43.437	43.200	44.254	45.018	46.100	45.376	46.227	47.699	48.856	2000	48.856
2001	48.882	49.816	49.447	47.899	48.079	48.488	50.309	51.343	51.758	54.160	51.607	50.662	2001	50.662
2002	51.361	51.951	49.686	51.721	51.798	52.769	54.368	56.888	59.258	57.517	56.817	59.699	2002	59.699
2003	59.065	61.011	60.136	60.798	64.397	63.406	57.178	58.129	61.306	59.573	59.732	60.564	2003	60.564
2004	61.699	63.117	64.007	60.244	59.939	60.666	61.609	64.040	64.657	65.649	64.115	65.717	2004	65.717
2005	67.691	66.826	66.348	68.820	70.862	72.047	69.973	72.302	69.860	68.489	69.010	70.852	2005	70.852
2006	70.018	71.687	67.821	66.148	66.213	66.819	68.148	70.186	71.383	71.932	73.425	71.694	2006	71.694
2007	70.961	73.335	72.272	72.887	71.428	70.782	72.790	74.235	74.323	75.476	79.009	78.779	2007	78.779
2008	80.460	80.608	81.460	79.111	77.812	79.526	79.330	81.251	82.164	79.016	90.416	99.161	2008	99.161
2009	88.012	87.518	93.129	87.081	84.921	85.629	85.790	87.769	89.314	87.790	89.620	84.383	2009	84.383
2010	86.608	86.881	85.328	87.921	91.762	95.851	96.085	102.831	101.255	98.041	96.696	92.942	2010	92.942
2011	91.121	92.152	92.095	93.929	97.261	95.516	99.545	108.129	115.743	112.200	115.022	118.130	2011	118.130
2012	118.153	115.832	112.337	116.937	124.452	122.763	125.797	124.936	123.107	122.933	124.699	122.180	2012	122.180
2013	118.128	119.478	118.739	123.222	115.477	112.184	110.242	109.373	110.043	111.454	108.829	106.571	2013	106.571
2014	112.409	113.239	113.951	116.016	119.248	118.944	119.618	124.031	121.919	125.570	129.157	132.900	2014	132.900
2015	142.323	134.875	136.717	133.295	131.172	127.260	131.448	131.603	133.898	133.183	132.321	132.032	2015	132.032

Appendix B-6

Long-term Government Bonds: Capital Appreciation Index
From 1926 to 2015

Year	Jan	Feb	Mar	Apr	May	Jun	Jul	Aug	Sep	Oct	Nov	Dec	Yr End	Index
1925												1.000	1925	1.000
1926	1.011	1.014	1.015	1.020	1.018	1.019	1.016	1.013	1.014	1.021	1.034	1.039	1926	1.039
1927	1.044	1.050	1.074	1.070	1.079	1.069	1.071	1.076	1.075	1.083	1.090	1.095	1927	1.095
1928	1.088	1.092	1.094	1.091	1.080	1.081	1.055	1.060	1.053	1.066	1.064	1.061	1928	1.061
1929	1.048	1.029	1.011	1.036	1.016	1.024	1.021	1.014	1.014	1.050	1.072	1.059	1929	1.059
1930	1.050	1.061	1.066	1.062	1.074	1.076	1.077	1.075	1.080	1.081	1.083	1.072	1930	1.072
1931	1.056	1.063	1.071	1.077	1.090	1.087	1.080	1.078	1.045	1.007	1.007	0.982	1931	0.982
1932	0.982	1.019	1.014	1.072	1.049	1.053	1.101	1.098	1.101	1.097	1.097	1.109	1932	1.109
1933	1.122	1.091	1.098	1.092	1.122	1.124	1.120	1.122	1.122	1.108	1.089	1.074	1933	1.074
1934	1.098	1.105	1.123	1.135	1.147	1.152	1.153	1.137	1.118	1.135	1.137	1.146	1934	1.146
1935	1.164	1.173	1.175	1.181	1.172	1.180	1.183	1.164	1.163	1.167	1.166	1.171	1935	1.171
1936	1.175	1.182	1.191	1.193	1.195	1.195	1.199	1.210	1.203	1.201	1.223	1.225	1936	1.225
1937	1.221	1.229	1.176	1.178	1.182	1.176	1.190	1.175	1.177	1.180	1.188	1.195	1937	1.195
1938	1.199	1.203	1.196	1.218	1.221	1.219	1.222	1.219	1.219	1.227	1.222	1.229	1938	1.229
1939	1.233	1.241	1.254	1.266	1.285	1.280	1.292	1.263	1.192	1.238	1.256	1.272	1939	1.272
1940	1.267	1.268	1.288	1.281	1.241	1.270	1.274	1.275	1.287	1.289	1.313	1.319	1940	1.319
1941	1.291	1.291	1.301	1.316	1.317	1.324	1.325	1.325	1.321	1.338	1.332	1.306	1941	1.306
1942	1.312	1.311	1.321	1.314	1.322	1.319	1.319	1.321	1.319	1.319	1.312	1.316	1942	1.316
1943	1.317	1.314	1.313	1.316	1.320	1.320	1.317	1.317	1.316	1.314	1.311	1.311	1943	1.311
1944	1.311	1.312	1.312	1.312	1.312	1.311	1.313	1.314	1.313	1.312	1.312	1.315	1944	1.315
1945	1.329	1.337	1.337	1.356	1.361	1.381	1.367	1.368	1.373	1.384	1.399	1.424	1945	1.424
1946	1.425	1.427	1.427	1.405	1.401	1.408	1.400	1.382	1.378	1.386	1.376	1.393	1946	1.393
1947	1.390	1.390	1.391	1.383	1.385	1.384	1.390	1.399	1.391	1.383	1.357	1.328	1947	1.328
1948	1.328	1.332	1.333	1.337	1.353	1.339	1.333	1.331	1.330	1.328	1.336	1.341	1948	1.341
1949	1.349	1.353	1.360	1.360	1.360	1.380	1.382	1.395	1.391	1.391	1.391	1.396	1949	1.396
1950	1.385	1.386	1.384	1.386	1.388	1.382	1.387	1.387	1.374	1.365	1.367	1.367	1950	1.367
1951	1.372	1.360	1.336	1.325	1.313	1.302	1.317	1.328	1.315	1.313	1.292	1.282	1951	1.282
1952	1.282	1.281	1.293	1.312	1.305	1.302	1.297	1.285	1.266	1.281	1.277	1.263	1952	1.263
1953	1.261	1.248	1.233	1.218	1.197	1.220	1.222	1.218	1.251	1.258	1.248	1.271	1953	1.271
1954	1.280	1.307	1.312	1.322	1.308	1.326	1.341	1.333	1.329	1.327	1.321	1.326	1954	1.326
1955	1.291	1.279	1.287	1.284	1.290	1.277	1.261	1.258	1.265	1.280	1.271	1.272	1955	1.272

Appendix B-6

Long-term Government Bonds: Capital Appreciation Index
From 1926 to 2015

Year	Jan	Feb	Mar	Apr	May	Jun	Jul	Aug	Sep	Oct	Nov	Dec	Yr End	Index
1956	1.280	1.277	1.255	1.237	1.262	1.262	1.233	1.207	1.210	1.200	1.189	1.165	1956	1.165
1957	1.202	1.202	1.196	1.166	1.160	1.136	1.127	1.124	1.129	1.120	1.177	1.209	1957	1.209
1958	1.196	1.205	1.214	1.233	1.230	1.207	1.170	1.116	1.100	1.111	1.122	1.098	1958	1.098
1959	1.085	1.095	1.093	1.076	1.072	1.070	1.072	1.064	1.054	1.067	1.050	1.030	1959	1.030
1960	1.038	1.055	1.081	1.059	1.071	1.086	1.122	1.111	1.116	1.109	1.098	1.125	1960	1.125
1961	1.109	1.128	1.121	1.130	1.121	1.109	1.109	1.101	1.112	1.116	1.110	1.093	1961	1.093
1962	1.088	1.095	1.119	1.125	1.126	1.115	1.099	1.115	1.119	1.124	1.123	1.124	1962	1.124
1963	1.120	1.117	1.115	1.110	1.109	1.107	1.107	1.106	1.102	1.096	1.098	1.093	1963	1.093
1964	1.088	1.083	1.083	1.085	1.087	1.090	1.087	1.085	1.087	1.088	1.086	1.085	1964	1.085
1965	1.086	1.084	1.086	1.086	1.085	1.086	1.084	1.079	1.072	1.071	1.060	1.048	1965	1.048
1966	1.033	1.004	1.030	1.019	1.009	1.004	0.996	0.971	1.000	1.019	1.000	1.037	1966	1.037
1967	1.049	1.022	1.038	1.005	0.996	0.961	0.964	0.952	0.947	0.905	0.883	0.896	1967	0.896
1968	0.921	0.914	0.891	0.907	0.907	0.924	0.946	0.942	0.928	0.912	0.883	0.847	1968	0.847
1969	0.825	0.825	0.822	0.853	0.807	0.820	0.822	0.812	0.765	0.788	0.765	0.755	1969	0.755
1970	0.750	0.790	0.780	0.743	0.705	0.734	0.753	0.748	0.761	0.748	0.803	0.792	1970	0.792
1971	0.828	0.811	0.849	0.821	0.816	0.799	0.797	0.830	0.843	0.853	0.845	0.844	1971	0.844
1972	0.835	0.838	0.827	0.825	0.843	0.834	0.847	0.846	0.835	0.850	0.865	0.841	1972	0.841
1973	0.810	0.807	0.809	0.808	0.795	0.789	0.750	0.774	0.795	0.807	0.788	0.777	1973	0.777
1974	0.765	0.759	0.733	0.709	0.713	0.712	0.705	0.684	0.696	0.725	0.742	0.750	1974	0.750
1975	0.761	0.767	0.741	0.723	0.733	0.750	0.738	0.728	0.716	0.745	0.732	0.755	1975	0.755
1976	0.757	0.757	0.764	0.761	0.744	0.754	0.755	0.766	0.772	0.774	0.795	0.816	1976	0.816
1977	0.780	0.771	0.773	0.774	0.779	0.787	0.776	0.787	0.780	0.767	0.770	0.752	1977	0.752
1978	0.741	0.737	0.730	0.725	0.715	0.706	0.711	0.721	0.709	0.690	0.698	0.684	1978	0.684
1979	0.692	0.678	0.682	0.669	0.681	0.697	0.686	0.679	0.666	0.604	0.618	0.617	1979	0.617
1980	0.566	0.535	0.512	0.585	0.605	0.621	0.587	0.556	0.537	0.517	0.518	0.530	1980	0.530
1981	0.519	0.492	0.505	0.474	0.499	0.484	0.462	0.439	0.428	0.458	0.518	0.476	1981	0.476
1982	0.473	0.476	0.48`	0.494	0.491	0.474	0.492	0.525	0.552	0.582	0.577	0.589	1982	0.589
1983	0.566	0.589	0.578	0.594	0.565	0.563	0.530	0.526	0.547	0.535	0.540	0.532	1983	0.532
1984	0.539	0.524	0.511	0.500	0.469	0.472	0.499	0.507	0.519	0.543	0.544	0.544	1984	0.544
1985	0.558	0.526	0.538	0.545	0.589	0.592	0.576	0.586	0.580	0.594	0.613	0.641	1985	0.641

Appendix B-6

Long-term Government Bonds: Capital Appreciation Index
From 1926 to 2015

Year	Jan	Feb	Mar	Apr	May	Jun	Jul	Aug	Sep	Oct	Nov	Dec	Yr End	Index
1986	0.634	0.702	0.751	0.741	0.699	0.737	0.724	0.755	0.713	0.728	0.743	0.737	1986	0.737
1987	0.744	0.755	0.733	0.693	0.682	0.683	0.666	0.650	0.621	0.655	0.652	0.658	1987	0.658
1988	0.697	0.696	0.670	0.654	0.642	0.661	0.645	0.644	0.661	0.676	0.658	0.661	1988	0.661
1989	0.669	0.652	0.655	0.661	0.682	0.715	0.727	0.703	0.700	0.722	0.723	0.718	1989	0.718
1990	0.688	0.681	0.674	0.655	0.677	0.688	0.691	0.657	0.660	0.669	0.691	0.699	1990	0.699
1991	0.703	0.701	0.699	0.703	0.699	0.690	0.695	0.714	0.731	0.730	0.732	0.769	1991	0.769
1992	0.740	0.739	0.727	0.724	0.737	0.747	0.772	0.772	0.782	0.762	0.758	0.772	1992	0.772
1993	0.789	0.813	0.809	0.811	0.810	0.841	0.853	0.885	0.881	0.885	0.858	0.855	1993	0.855
1994	0.872	0.829	0.791	0.775	0.763	0.751	0.774	0.762	0.732	0.726	0.726	0.733	1994	0.733
1995	0.748	0.765	0.767	0.775	0.831	0.838	0.820	0.834	0.845	0.865	0.882	0.901	1995	0.901
1996	0.896	0.848	0.826	0.807	0.798	0.810	0.807	0.791	0.809	0.837	0.862	0.835	1996	0.835
1997	0.824	0.820	0.794	0.810	0.813	0.824	0.871	0.839	0.861	0.885	0.894	0.906	1997	0.906
1998	0.920	0.909	0.907	0.904	0.917	0.933	0.925	0.963	0.997	0.971	0.976	0.968	1998	0.968
1999	0.976	0.921	0.916	0.913	0.892	0.880	0.869	0.860	0.863	0.857	0.847	0.829	1999	0.829
2000	0.844	0.862	0.889	0.878	0.868	0.885	0.895	0.912	0.894	0.906	0.930	0.949	2000	0.949
2001	0.944	0.958	0.947	0.913	0.912	0.915	0.945	0.960	0.964	1.004	0.952	0.931	2001	0.931
2002	0.939	0.946	0.900	0.932	0.929	0.943	0.966	1.007	1.045	1.010	0.993	1.039	2002	1.039
2003	1.024	1.054	1.036	1.042	1.100	1.079	0.969	0.981	1.030	0.996	0.995	1.004	2003	1.004
2004	1.019	1.039	1.049	0.983	0.974	0.981	0.992	1.027	1.033	1.045	1.016	1.037	2004	1.037
2005	1.064	1.047	1.035	1.070	1.097	1.111	1.076	1.107	1.066	1.041	1.045	1.069	2005	1.069
2006	1.052	1.073	1.011	0.982	0.978	0.983	0.998	1.024	1.037	1.041	1.058	1.030	2006	1.030
2007	1.015	1.045	1.026	1.030	1.005	0.992	1.016	1.032	1.029	1.040	1.085	1.078	2007	1.078
2008	1.097	1.095	1.102	1.067	1.045	1.064	1.057	1.079	1.087	1.041	1.188	1.299	2008	1.299
2009	1.150	1.140	1.209	1.127	1.095	1.100	1.098	1.120	1.136	1.113	1.132	1.062	2009	1.062
2010	1.086	1.086	1.062	1.090	1.134	1.181	1.180	1.259	1.236	1.194	1.174	1.124	2010	1.124
2011	1.099	1.107	1.103	1.121	1.157	1.132	1.176	1.274	1.360	1.315	1.345	1.379	2011	1.379
2012	1.376	1.346	1.303	1.353	1.437	1.415	1.447	1.434	1.411	1.406	1.423	1.392	2012	1.392
2013	1.343	1.355	1.344	1.391	1.300	1.260	1.235	1.221	1.225	1.237	1.205	1.173	2013	1.173
2014	1.234	1.240	1.244	1.263	1.295	1.288	1.292	1.336	1.311	1.347	1.382	1.419	2014	1.419
2015	1.517	1.435	1.452	1.413	1.387	1.343	1.384	1.382	1.403	1.393	1.381	1.375	2015	1.375

Appendix B-7

Intermediate-term Government Bonds: Total Return Index
From 1926 to 2015

Year	Jan	Feb	Mar	Apr	May	Jun	Jul	Aug	Sep	Oct	Nov	Dec	Yr End	Index
1925												1.000	1925	1.000
1926	1.007	1.010	1.014	1.023	1.024	1.027	1.028	1.029	1.034	1.040	1.044	1.054	1926	1.054
1927	1.060	1.064	1.068	1.070	1.072	1.075	1.079	1.086	1.092	1.088	1.097	1.101	1927	1.101
1928	1.107	1.106	1.107	1.107	1.106	1.108	1.098	1.104	1.107	1.110	1.112	1.112	1928	1.112
1929	1.108	1.106	1.107	1.117	1.110	1.122	1.129	1.135	1.133	1.153	1.173	1.178	1929	1.178
1930	1.174	1.185	1.204	1.195	1.202	1.219	1.226	1.229	1.236	1.246	1.255	1.258	1930	1.258
1931	1.249	1.261	1.267	1.278	1.293	1.266	1.268	1.270	1.255	1.242	1.248	1.228	1931	1.228
1932	1.224	1.240	1.250	1.274	1.263	1.276	1.292	1.307	1.311	1.317	1.321	1.337	1932	1.337
1933	1.335	1.334	1.348	1.355	1.382	1.383	1.382	1.393	1.396	1.393	1.396	1.361	1933	1.361
1934	1.379	1.386	1.412	1.438	1.455	1.468	1.465	1.451	1.431	1.458	1.465	1.483	1934	1.483
1935	1.500	1.516	1.535	1.552	1.546	1.564	1.570	1.558	1.550	1.566	1.569	1.587	1935	1.587
1936	1.587	1.598	1.603	1.607	1.613	1.615	1.618	1.626	1.628	1.632	1.645	1.636	1936	1.636
1937	1.631	1.632	1.605	1.613	1.625	1.623	1.633	1.626	1.639	1.644	1.651	1.661	1937	1.661
1938	1.676	1.684	1.682	1.721	1.725	1.738	1.740	1.742	1.740	1.756	1.756	1.765	1938	1.765
1939	1.770	1.785	1.799	1.806	1.823	1.823	1.831	1.804	1.756	1.812	1.825	1.845	1939	1.845
1940	1.842	1.849	1.865	1.865	1.825	1.860	1.860	1.868	1.877	1.884	1.894	1.899	1940	1.899
1941	1.900	1.891	1.904	1.910	1.912	1.923	1.923	1.925	1.925	1.930	1.912	1.909	1941	1.909
1942	1.923	1.926	1.930	1.935	1.938	1.940	1.940	1.944	1.939	1.943	1.946	1.946	1942	1.946
1943	1.953	1.956	1.960	1.965	1.976	1.983	1.987	1.987	1.990	1.993	1.996	2.000	1943	2.000
1944	2.003	2.006	2.010	2.015	2.016	2.017	2.023	2.028	2.030	2.033	2.034	2.036	1944	2.036
1945	2.047	2.055	2.056	2.059	2.061	2.065	2.065	2.068	2.072	2.075	2.077	2.082	1945	2.082
1946	2.090	2.100	2.092	2.088	2.089	2.096	2.094	2.094	2.092	2.098	2.096	2.102	1946	2.102
1947	2.107	2.109	2.114	2.111	2.112	2.114	2.115	2.121	2.121	2.116	2.117	2.122	1947	2.122
1948	2.125	2.129	2.132	2.136	2.148	2.146	2.146	2.145	2.147	2.149	2.154	2.161	1948	2.161
1949	2.167	2.169	2.175	2.178	2.183	2.194	2.198	2.205	2.207	2.208	2.208	2.211	1949	2.211
1950	2.210	2.212	2.212	2.213	2.218	2.218	2.223	2.221	2.220	2.221	2.225	2.227	1950	2.227
1951	2.231	2.233	2.205	2.217	2.208	2.219	2.232	2.240	2.227	2.231	2.238	2.235	1951	2.235
1952	2.243	2.239	2.253	2.266	2.270	2.262	2.254	2.249	2.253	2.268	2.267	2.271	1952	2.271
1953	2.271	2.271	2.267	2.246	2.219	2.254	2.266	2.265	2.309	2.317	2.321	2.345	1953	2.345
1954	2.360	2.383	2.390	2.400	2.382	2.412	2.411	2.414	2.409	2.406	2.406	2.407	1954	2.407
1955	2.400	2.387	2.393	2.394	2.394	2.386	2.369	2.370	2.390	2.407	2.394	2.392	1955	2.392

Appendix B-7

Intermediate-term Government Bonds: Total Return Index
From 1926 to 2015

Year	Jan	Feb	Mar	Apr	May	Jun	Jul	Aug	Sep	Oct	Nov	Dec	Yr End	Index
1956	2.417	2.418	2.393	2.393	2.420	2.421	2.398	2.373	2.395	2.390	2.379	2.382	1956	2.382
1957	2.438	2.435	2.439	2.415	2.411	2.385	2.382	2.408	2.408	2.418	2.514	2.568	1957	2.568
1958	2.577	2.613	2.627	2.640	2.656	2.638	2.614	2.521	2.517	2.518	2.551	2.535	1958	2.535
1959	2.532	2.559	2.550	2.536	2.536	2.517	2.525	2.505	2.510	2.554	2.530	2.525	1959	2.525
1960	2.564	2.583	2.658	2.641	2.649	2.707	2.779	2.778	2.786	2.790	2.764	2.822	1960	2.822
1961	2.805	2.831	2.841	2.856	2.848	2.841	2.843	2.848	2.871	2.875	2.869	2.874	1961	2.874
1962	2.861	2.906	2.932	2.939	2.953	2.945	2.941	2.978	2.984	3.000	3.018	3.034	1962	3.034
1963	3.026	3.031	3.039	3.048	3.053	3.057	3.058	3.064	3.068	3.071	3.083	3.084	1963	3.084
1964	3.094	3.098	3.103	3.113	3.138	3.150	3.158	3.167	3.181	3.191	3.190	3.209	1964	3.209
1965	3.222	3.228	3.242	3.250	3.262	3.278	3.283	3.290	3.288	3.288	3.290	3.242	1965	3.242
1966	3.242	3.215	3.275	3.269	3.273	3.265	3.257	3.216	3.286	3.311	3.320	3.394	1966	3.394
1967	3.434	3.429	3.492	3.461	3.476	3.397	3.443	3.430	3.433	3.416	3.425	3.428	1967	3.428
1968	3.478	3.491	3.482	3.477	3.499	3.557	3.620	3.628	3.648	3.651	3.646	3.583	1968	3.583
1969	3.614	3.609	3.644	3.673	3.643	3.613	3.642	3.636	3.527	3.644	3.627	3.557	1969	3.557
1970	3.568	3.724	3.757	3.679	3.720	3.742	3.799	3.843	3.919	3.956	4.134	4.156	1970	4.156
1971	4.226	4.321	4.401	4.257	4.262	4.182	4.193	4.340	4.351	4.447	4.470	4.519	1971	4.519
1972	4.567	4.573	4.580	4.586	4.594	4.614	4.621	4.628	4.635	4.642	4.662	4.752	1972	4.752
1973	4.749	4.713	4.735	4.765	4.792	4.790	4.657	4.776	4.895	4.920	4.951	4.971	1973	4.971
1974	4.975	4.993	4.887	4.813	4.876	4.833	4.837	4.831	4.985	5.040	5.159	5.254	1974	5.254
1975	5.282	5.360	5.328	5.229	5.365	5.380	5.363	5.359	5.364	5.561	5.555	5.665	1975	5.665
1976	5.697	5.745	5.788	5.855	5.770	5.862	5.932	6.044	6.089	6.179	6.378	6.394	1976	6.394
1977	6.273	6.303	6.338	6.371	6.407	6.472	6.473	6.478	6.487	6.449	6.499	6.484	1977	6.484
1978	6.492	6.503	6.527	6.543	6.542	6.528	6.592	6.644	6.682	6.608	6.668	6.710	1978	6.710
1979	6.747	6.707	6.783	6.805	6.936	7.079	7.071	7.006	7.010	6.682	6.925	6.985	1979	6.985
1980	6.891	6.449	6.542	7.325	7.684	7.625	7.544	7.252	7.225	7.115	7.136	7.258	1980	7.258
1981	7.281	7.110	7.297	7.140	7.315	7.358	7.160	7.033	7.148	7.585	8.058	7.944	1981	7.944
1982	7.984	8.102	8.137	8.379	8.502	8.387	8.776	9.188	9.486	9.990	10.070	10.256	1982	10.256
1983	10.263	10.522	10.471	10.742	10.611	10.628	10.417	10.501	10.832	10.852	10.964	11.015	1983	11.015
1984	11.211	11.139	11.100	11.097	10.819	10.926	11.355	11.469	11.701	12.149	12.382	12.560	1984	12.560
1985	12.818	12.588	12.798	13.136	13.772	13.922	13.859	14.064	14.222	14.453	14.735	15.113	1985	15.113

Appendix B-7

Intermediate-term Government Bonds: Total Return Index

From 1926 to 2015

Year	Jan	Feb	Mar	Apr	May	Jun	Jul	Aug	Sep	Oct	Nov	Dec	Yr End	Index
1986	15.238	15.657	16.186	16.318	15.968	16.409	16.667	17.109	16.921	17.195	17.389	17.401	1986	17.401
1987	17.587	17.691	17.636	17.205	17.140	17.350	17.394	17.328	17.085	17.596	17.741	17.906	1987	17.906
1988	18.472	18.698	18.537	18.455	18.364	18.698	18.610	18.593	18.957	19.238	19.017	18.999	1988	18.999
1989	19.230	19.133	19.227	19.650	20.067	20.717	21.203	20.682	20.824	21.318	21.497	21.524	1989	21.524
1990	21.299	21.313	21.318	21.154	21.707	22.035	22.418	22.213	22.422	22.804	23.243	23.618	1990	23.618
1991	23.870	23.984	24.039	24.320	24.464	24.409	24.725	25.335	25.881	26.228	26.565	27.270	1991	27.270
1992	26.737	26.796	26.583	26.843	27.438	27.923	28.600	29.029	29.592	29.054	28.810	29.230	1992	29.230
1993	30.021	30.749	30.883	31.156	31.126	31.753	31.769	32.476	32.657	32.714	32.411	32.516	1993	32.516
1994	32.964	32.113	31.286	30.957	30.951	30.863	31.385	31.466	30.968	30.896	30.680	30.843	1994	30.843
1995	31.404	32.140	32.341	32.805	34.014	34.284	34.230	34.525	34.745	35.164	35.687	36.025	1995	36.025
1996	36.048	35.551	35.131	34.955	34.844	35.253	35.340	35.323	35.872	36.527	37.072	36.782	1996	36.782
1997	36.873	36.880	36.460	37.000	37.286	37.671	38.666	38.289	38.867	39.451	39.445	39.864	1997	39.864
1998	40.583	40.426	40.530	40.777	41.062	41.385	41.495	42.619	44.023	44.203	43.772	43.933	1998	43.933
1999	44.175	43.015	43.387	43.476	42.834	42.972	42.950	43.016	43.435	43.401	43.365	43.155	1999	43.155
2000	42.925	43.260	44.140	43.950	44.179	45.024	45.347	45.953	46.394	46.760	47.573	48.589	2000	48.589
2001	49.066	49.583	49.958	49.390	49.356	49.680	50.907	51.391	52.694	53.642	52.725	52.291	2001	52.291
2002	52.477	53.043	51.761	52.997	53.621	54.526	56.007	56.942	58.583	58.442	57.451	59.054	2002	59.054
2003	58.529	59.576	59.534	59.613	61.239	61.027	59.080	58.918	60.730	59.906	59.820	60.469	2003	60.469
2004	60.781	61.533	62.148	60.072	59.777	60.067	60.558	61.740	61.815	62.211	61.422	61.832	2004	61.832
2005	61.995	61.308	61.075	62.095	62.735	63.005	62.099	63.100	62.320	61.930	62.293	62.674	2005	62.674
2006	62.448	62.342	61.992	61.942	61.915	62.054	62.831	63.682	64.183	64.513	65.081	64.643	2006	64.643
2007	64.515	65.615	65.775	66.084	65.407	65.477	66.620	67.852	68.241	67.911	70.799	71.142	2007	71.142
2008	73.011	74.721	75.268	73.059	72.444	72.987	73.452	74.216	74.845	75.936	79.202	80.466	2008	80.466
2009	79.152	78.504	79.966	78.642	77.607	77.014	77.446	78.194	78.778	79.016	80.471	78.532	2009	78.532
2010	80.056	80.621	79.913	80.667	81.883	82.940	84.252	85.331	85.750	86.296	85.586	84.121	2010	84.121
2011	84.645	84.196	84.156	85.453	86.984	86.975	88.735	90.601	90.677	90.760	91.083	91.533	2011	91.533
2012	91.610	91.130	90.488	91.656	92.412	92.231	92.944	93.083	93.122	92.901	93.346	93.054	2012	93.054
2013	92.483	93.076	91.748	92.302	90.782	89.519	89.755	89.095	90.172	90.633	90.737	89.630	2013	89.630
2014	90.804	91.020	90.399	90.833	91.690	91.531	91.101	91.782	91.335	92.150	92.874	92.316	2014	92.316
2015	94.542	93.381	94.076	93.945	93.989	93.493	93.967	94.072	95.005	94.513	94.132	93.970	2015	93.970

Appendix B-8

Intermediate-term Government Bonds: Capital Appreciation Index

From 1926 to 2015

Year	Jan	Feb	Mar	Apr	May	Jun	Jul	Aug	Sep	Oct	Nov	Dec	Yr End	Index
1925												1.000	1925	1.000
1926	1.004	1.004	1.005	1.010	1.008	1.008	1.006	1.004	1.005	1.008	1.009	1.015	1926	1.015
1927	1.018	1.019	1.020	1.018	1.017	1.017	1.019	1.022	1.025	1.018	1.024	1.025	1927	1.025
1928	1.027	1.023	1.022	1.018	1.015	1.013	1.001	1.003	1.002	1.002	1.001	0.997	1928	0.997
1929	0.991	0.985	0.982	0.987	0.978	0.985	0.988	0.990	0.985	0.998	1.013	1.014	1929	1.014
1930	1.007	1.013	1.027	1.017	1.020	1.032	1.034	1.034	1.038	1.043	1.048	1.048	1930	1.048
1931	1.038	1.045	1.048	1.055	1.065	1.040	1.039	1.038	1.023	1.009	1.011	0.991	1931	0.991
1932	0.985	0.994	0.998	1.015	1.002	1.010	1.019	1.029	1.029	1.031	1.032	1.041	1932	1.041
1933	1.037	1.034	1.042	1.045	1.063	1.062	1.059	1.064	1.065	1.060	1.061	1.031	1933	1.031
1934	1.041	1.044	1.061	1.078	1.088	1.096	1.091	1.079	1.061	1.079	1.081	1.092	1934	1.092
1935	1.103	1.112	1.124	1.134	1.129	1.140	1.142	1.132	1.124	1.135	1.134	1.146	1935	1.146
1936	1.144	1.151	1.153	1.154	1.157	1.157	1.158	1.163	1.163	1.164	1.172	1.165	1936	1.165
1937	1.160	1.159	1.139	1.143	1.150	1.147	1.152	1.146	1.154	1.156	1.159	1.165	1937	1.165
1938	1.173	1.177	1.174	1.199	1.200	1.207	1.207	1.207	1.204	1.213	1.211	1.216	1938	1.216
1939	1.218	1.227	1.235	1.239	1.249	1.248	1.252	1.232	1.199	1.235	1.243	1.255	1939	1.255
1940	1.252	1.255	1.265	1.265	1.237	1.259	1.258	1.262	1.267	1.271	1.278	1.280	1940	1.280
1941	1.280	1.273	1.281	1.284	1.285	1.292	1.291	1.292	1.291	1.294	1.281	1.278	1941	1.278
1942	1.287	1.288	1.290	1.292	1.293	1.294	1.293	1.295	1.291	1.293	1.294	1.293	1942	1.293
1943	1.296	1.297	1.297	1.299	1.304	1.307	1.308	1.307	1.307	1.308	1.308	1.309	1943	1.309
1944	1.309	1.309	1.310	1.312	1.311	1.311	1.313	1.314	1.314	1.314	1.314	1.314	1944	1.314
1945	1.319	1.323	1.322	1.323	1.323	1.324	1.323	1.324	1.325	1.325	1.326	1.327	1945	1.327
1946	1.331	1.336	1.330	1.327	1.326	1.329	1.327	1.326	1.324	1.326	1.323	1.326	1946	1.326
1947	1.328	1.327	1.329	1.326	1.326	1.326	1.325	1.327	1.326	1.322	1.321	1.322	1947	1.322
1948	1.322	1.323	1.323	1.324	1.330	1.327	1.325	1.323	1.322	1.322	1.323	1.326	1948	1.326
1949	1.328	1.328	1.329	1.330	1.331	1.336	1.337	1.340	1.340	1.339	1.338	1.338	1949	1.338
1950	1.336	1.336	1.334	1.334	1.335	1.334	1.335	1.333	1.331	1.329	1.330	1.329	1950	1.329
1951	1.330	1.329	1.310	1.315	1.308	1.312	1.317	1.320	1.310	1.310	1.312	1.307	1951	1.307
1952	1.310	1.305	1.311	1.316	1.317	1.310	1.303	1.297	1.297	1.303	1.300	1.300	1952	1.300
1953	1.297	1.295	1.290	1.275	1.257	1.274	1.278	1.274	1.295	1.298	1.297	1.308	1953	1.308
1954	1.314	1.326	1.327	1.331	1.320	1.334	1.332	1.332	1.328	1.325	1.323	1.322	1954	1.322
1955	1.315	1.306	1.307	1.305	1.302	1.295	1.283	1.281	1.288	1.295	1.285	1.281	1955	1.281

Appendix B-8

Intermediate-term Government Bonds: Capital Appreciation Index
From 1926 to 2015

Year	Jan	Feb	Mar	Apr	May	Jun	Jul	Aug	Sep	Oct	Nov	Dec	Yr End	Index
1956	1.291	1.289	1.273	1.270	1.281	1.278	1.263	1.246	1.255	1.248	1.239	1.237	1956	1.237
1957	1.262	1.258	1.257	1.240	1.234	1.218	1.212	1.221	1.217	1.219	1.263	1.287	1957	1.287
1958	1.288	1.303	1.307	1.311	1.317	1.305	1.290	1.242	1.236	1.232	1.245	1.233	1958	1.233
1959	1.228	1.237	1.228	1.218	1.214	1.200	1.200	1.186	1.184	1.200	1.184	1.177	1959	1.177
1960	1.190	1.194	1.224	1.213	1.212	1.234	1.263	1.259	1.259	1.257	1.242	1.264	1960	1.264
1961	1.253	1.261	1.262	1.265	1.258	1.251	1.248	1.246	1.252	1.250	1.244	1.243	1961	1.243
1962	1.233	1.248	1.255	1.254	1.257	1.250	1.244	1.255	1.255	1.257	1.261	1.264	1962	1.264
1963	1.257	1.255	1.255	1.255	1.253	1.251	1.247	1.246	1.243	1.240	1.241	1.237	1963	1.237
1964	1.237	1.235	1.233	1.233	1.239	1.239	1.238	1.237	1.239	1.239	1.234	1.237	1964	1.237
1965	1.238	1.237	1.237	1.236	1.237	1.238	1.236	1.234	1.229	1.225	1.221	1.199	1965	1.199
1966	1.194	1.180	1.197	1.190	1.186	1.179	1.171	1.151	1.171	1.174	1.173	1.194	1966	1.194
1967	1.203	1.197	1.214	1.200	1.200	1.168	1.178	1.169	1.165	1.154	1.152	1.148	1967	1.148
1968	1.159	1.158	1.150	1.143	1.145	1.159	1.173	1.171	1.172	1.168	1.162	1.136	1968	1.136
1969	1.140	1.133	1.139	1.141	1.126	1.110	1.113	1.105	1.065	1.093	1.082	1.054	1969	1.054
1970	1.050	1.090	1.092	1.063	1.068	1.068	1.077	1.083	1.098	1.102	1.145	1.145	1970	1.145
1971	1.159	1.180	1.197	1.153	1.149	1.121	1.118	1.151	1.149	1.169	1.169	1.177	1971	1.177
1972	1.183	1.180	1.176	1.173	1.169	1.168	1.164	1.160	1.156	1.152	1.151	1.168	1972	1.168
1973	1.161	1.146	1.145	1.146	1.146	1.140	1.101	1.122	1.144	1.143	1.144	1.142	1973	1.142
1974	1.137	1.135	1.105	1.081	1.088	1.072	1.065	1.056	1.083	1.087	1.106	1.120	1974	1.120
1975	1.119	1.129	1.116	1.088	1.110	1.106	1.095	1.088	1.081	1.114	1.106	1.121	1975	1.121
1976	1.121	1.124	1.125	1.131	1.109	1.119	1.125	1.139	1.142	1.152	1.183	1.180	1976	1.180
1977	1.151	1.151	1.151	1.151	1.151	1.156	1.150	1.144	1.140	1.126	1.128	1.119	1977	1.119
1978	1.113	1.109	1.105	1.101	1.093	1.084	1.087	1.088	1.087	1.067	1.069	1.069	1978	1.069
1979	1.066	1.053	1.057	1.052	1.064	1.079	1.069	1.052	1.045	0.987	1.015	1.015	1979	1.015
1980	0.992	0.920	0.924	1.025	1.067	1.051	1.031	0.983	0.970	0.946	0.940	0.946	1980	0.946
1981	0.939	0.908	0.921	0.892	0.904	0.898	0.864	0.838	0.841	0.881	0.926	0.903	1981	0.903
1982	0.897	0.902	0.894	0.911	0.915	0.892	0.923	0.956	0.978	1.021	1.021	1.031	1982	1.031
1983	1.023	1.041	1.027	1.045	1.023	1.016	0.988	0.986	1.007	1.000	1.001	0.997	1983	0.997
1984	1.005	0.990	0.977	0.967	0.933	0.932	0.958	0.958	0.968	0.994	1.004	1.009	1984	1.009
1985	1.021	0.994	1.002	1.019	1.059	1.063	1.049	1.056	1.059	1.068	1.081	1.100	1985	1.100

Appendix B-8

Intermediate-term Government Bonds: Capital Appreciation Index
From 1926 to 2015

Year	Jan	Feb	Mar	Apr	May	Jun	Jul	Aug	Sep	Oct	Nov	Dec	Yr End	Index
1986	1.101	1.124	1.155	1.157	1.125	1.149	1.160	1.184	1.164	1.176	1.183	1.177	1986	1.177
1987	1.183	1.184	1.173	1.138	1.126	1.132	1.127	1.116	1.092	1.117	1.118	1.121	1987	1.121
1988	1.149	1.156	1.138	1.126	1.112	1.125	1.112	1.103	1.116	1.125	1.105	1.096	1988	1.096
1989	1.100	1.088	1.085	1.101	1.115	1.144	1.163	1.127	1.128	1.146	1.149	1.143	1989	1.143
1990	1.123	1.117	1.109	1.093	1.113	1.122	1.134	1.116	1.119	1.130	1.144	1.155	1990	1.155
1991	1.160	1.158	1.154	1.160	1.159	1.150	1.156	1.178	1.196	1.205	1.214	1.240	1991	1.240
1992	1.209	1.206	1.189	1.193	1.213	1.228	1.251	1.263	1.282	1.253	1.236	1.248	1992	1.248
1993	1.275	1.301	1.300	1.305	1.299	1.318	1.314	1.337	1.339	1.336	1.318	1.317	1993	1.317
1994	1.329	1.290	1.250	1.231	1.224	1.213	1.227	1.223	1.197	1.187	1.171	1.170	1994	1.170
1995	1.184	1.205	1.205	1.216	1.253	1.257	1.249	1.253	1.255	1.264	1.277	1.283	1995	1.283
1996	1.278	1.255	1.235	1.222	1.212	1.220	1.216	1.209	1.221	1.237	1.249	1.233	1996	1.233
1997	1.230	1.225	1.204	1.215	1.218	1.224	1.250	1.232	1.244	1.256	1.251	1.257	1997	1.257
1998	1.274	1.264	1.261	1.263	1.266	1.270	1.267	1.296	1.333	1.334	1.316	1.316	1998	1.316
1999	1.318	1.279	1.284	1.281	1.257	1.255	1.248	1.244	1.250	1.243	1.235	1.223	1999	1.223
2000	1.210	1.213	1.231	1.220	1.219	1.236	1.238	1.248	1.254	1.258	1.274	1.296	2000	1.296
2001	1.304	1.315	1.321	1.302	1.295	1.298	1.325	1.332	1.361	1.381	1.353	1.338	2001	1.338
2002	1.337	1.347	1.310	1.335	1.346	1.364	1.396	1.415	1.452	1.445	1.418	1.453	2002	1.453
2003	1.437	1.459	1.455	1.453	1.489	1.481	1.431	1.424	1.463	1.440	1.435	1.446	2003	1.446
2004	1.450	1.464	1.475	1.423	1.412	1.414	1.421	1.444	1.442	1.448	1.426	1.431	2004	1.431
2005	1.430	1.410	1.400	1.419	1.429	1.430	1.405	1.423	1.401	1.387	1.390	1.394	2005	1.394
2006	1.384	1.377	1.364	1.357	1.351	1.348	1.359	1.372	1.378	1.380	1.387	1.373	2006	1.373
2007	1.364	1.383	1.381	1.382	1.363	1.359	1.377	1.397	1.401	1.389	1.443	1.446	2007	1.446
2008	1.479	1.511	1.518	1.471	1.455	1.461	1.467	1.478	1.487	1.505	1.567	1.589	2008	1.589
2009	1.562	1.547	1.573	1.545	1.522	1.507	1.512	1.523	1.532	1.534	1.559	1.519	2009	1.519
2010	1.545	1.553	1.537	1.548	1.568	1.586	1.608	1.627	1.633	1.642	1.627	1.598	2010	1.598
2011	1.605	1.593	1.590	1.611	1.637	1.635	1.665	1.698	1.699	1.699	1.704	1.711	2011	1.711
2012	1.711	1.701	1.688	1.708	1.721	1.717	1.729	1.730	1.730	1.726	1.733	1.727	2012	1.727
2013	1.715	1.725	1.699	1.708	1.679	1.655	1.657	1.643	1.661	1.668	1.668	1.646	2013	1.646
2014	1.665	1.667	1.653	1.659	1.672	1.667	1.657	1.667	1.657	1.669	1.680	1.668	2014	1.668
2015	1.706	1.683	1.694	1.689	1.688	1.677	1.683	1.683	1.698	1.687	1.678	1.673	2015	1.673

Appendix B-9

U.S. Treasury Bills: Total Return Index
From 1926 to 2015

Year	Jan	Feb	Mar	Apr	May	Jun	Jul	Aug	Sep	Oct	Nov	Dec	Yr End	Index
1925												1.000	1925	1.000
1926	1.003	1.006	1.009	1.013	1.013	1.016	1.018	1.021	1.023	1.027	1.030	1.033	1926	1.033
1927	1.035	1.038	1.041	1.044	1.047	1.049	1.053	1.055	1.058	1.060	1.063	1.065	1927	1.065
1928	1.068	1.071	1.074	1.077	1.080	1.084	1.087	1.091	1.093	1.098	1.102	1.103	1928	1.103
1929	1.107	1.111	1.114	1.118	1.123	1.129	1.133	1.137	1.141	1.147	1.151	1.155	1929	1.155
1930	1.157	1.160	1.164	1.167	1.170	1.173	1.175	1.176	1.179	1.180	1.181	1.183	1930	1.183
1931	1.185	1.185	1.187	1.188	1.189	1.190	1.190	1.191	1.191	1.192	1.194	1.196	1931	1.196
1932	1.198	1.201	1.203	1.205	1.205	1.206	1.206	1.206	1.207	1.207	1.207	1.207	1932	1.207
1933	1.207	1.207	1.208	1.209	1.209	1.210	1.210	1.210	1.210	1.210	1.211	1.211	1933	1.211
1934	1.211	1.212	1.212	1.212	1.212	1.212	1.212	1.212	1.212	1.213	1.213	1.213	1934	1.213
1935	1.213	1.213	1.213	1.213	1.214	1.214	1.214	1.214	1.214	1.214	1.215	1.215	1935	1.215
1936	1.215	1.215	1.215	1.216	1.216	1.216	1.216	1.216	1.217	1.217	1.217	1.217	1936	1.217
1937	1.217	1.217	1.218	1.218	1.219	1.219	1.219	1.220	1.220	1.220	1.221	1.221	1937	1.221
1938	1.221	1.221	1.221	1.221	1.221	1.221	1.221	1.221	1.221	1.221	1.221	1.221	1938	1.221
1939	1.220	1.221	1.220	1.220	1.220	1.221	1.221	1.221	1.221	1.221	1.221	1.221	1939	1.221
1940	1.221	1.221	1.221	1.221	1.221	1.221	1.221	1.221	1.221	1.221	1.221	1.221	1940	1.221
1941	1.221	1.221	1.221	1.221	1.221	1.221	1.221	1.221	1.221	1.221	1.221	1.222	1941	1.222
1942	1.222	1.222	1.222	1.222	1.222	1.223	1.223	1.223	1.224	1.224	1.225	1.225	1942	1.225
1943	1.225	1.226	1.226	1.226	1.227	1.227	1.227	1.228	1.228	1.228	1.229	1.229	1943	1.229
1944	1.229	1.230	1.230	1.230	1.231	1.231	1.231	1.232	1.232	1.233	1.233	1.233	1944	1.233
1945	1.233	1.234	1.234	1.234	1.235	1.235	1.235	1.236	1.236	1.237	1.237	1.237	1945	1.237
1946	1.238	1.238	1.238	1.239	1.239	1.239	1.240	1.240	1.240	1.241	1.241	1.242	1946	1.242
1947	1.242	1.242	1.243	1.243	1.243	1.244	1.244	1.244	1.245	1.246	1.247	1.248	1947	1.248
1948	1.249	1.250	1.251	1.252	1.253	1.254	1.255	1.256	1.256	1.257	1.257	1.258	1948	1.258
1949	1.259	1.260	1.262	1.263	1.264	1.265	1.266	1.267	1.269	1.270	1.271	1.272	1949	1.272
1950	1.273	1.274	1.275	1.276	1.278	1.279	1.280	1.281	1.283	1.284	1.286	1.287	1950	1.287
1951	1.289	1.290	1.291	1.293	1.295	1.296	1.298	1.300	1.301	1.303	1.305	1.306	1951	1.306
1952	1.308	1.310	1.311	1.313	1.314	1.316	1.318	1.320	1.322	1.324	1.326	1.328	1952	1.328
1953	1.330	1.332	1.334	1.337	1.339	1.341	1.343	1.345	1.348	1.349	1.350	1.352	1953	1.352
1954	1.354	1.355	1.356	1.357	1.357	1.358	1.359	1.360	1.361	1.362	1.363	1.364	1954	1.364
1955	1.365	1.366	1.367	1.369	1.371	1.372	1.373	1.376	1.378	1.380	1.383	1.385	1955	1.385

Appendix B-9

U.S. Treasury Bills: Total Return Index
From 1926 to 2015

Year	Jan	Feb	Mar	Apr	May	Jun	Jul	Aug	Sep	Oct	Nov	Dec	Yr End	Index
1956	1.388	1.391	1.393	1.396	1.399	1.402	1.405	1.407	1.410	1.413	1.416	1.419	1956	1.419
1957	1.423	1.426	1.430	1.433	1.437	1.441	1.445	1.448	1.452	1.456	1.460	1.464	1957	1.464
1958	1.468	1.470	1.471	1.472	1.474	1.474	1.475	1.476	1.479	1.481	1.483	1.486	1958	1.486
1959	1.489	1.492	1.496	1.499	1.502	1.505	1.509	1.512	1.517	1.521	1.525	1.530	1959	1.530
1960	1.535	1.540	1.545	1.548	1.552	1.556	1.558	1.561	1.563	1.567	1.569	1.571	1960	1.571
1961	1.574	1.576	1.579	1.582	1.585	1.588	1.591	1.593	1.596	1.599	1.601	1.604	1961	1.604
1962	1.608	1.612	1.615	1.618	1.622	1.626	1.630	1.634	1.637	1.641	1.645	1.648	1962	1.648
1963	1.652	1.656	1.660	1.664	1.668	1.672	1.677	1.681	1.685	1.690	1.695	1.700	1963	1.700
1964	1.705	1.709	1.715	1.720	1.724	1.729	1.734	1.739	1.744	1.749	1.754	1.760	1964	1.760
1965	1.765	1.770	1.776	1.782	1.787	1.794	1.799	1.805	1.811	1.817	1.823	1.829	1965	1.829
1966	1.836	1.842	1.849	1.856	1.863	1.870	1.877	1.885	1.892	1.901	1.908	1.916	1966	1.916
1967	1.924	1.931	1.939	1.945	1.951	1.957	1.963	1.969	1.975	1.983	1.990	1.997	1967	1.997
1968	2.005	2.012	2.020	2.029	2.038	2.046	2.056	2.065	2.074	2.083	2.092	2.101	1968	2.101
1969	2.112	2.121	2.131	2.143	2.153	2.164	2.175	2.186	2.200	2.213	2.225	2.239	1969	2.239
1970	2.252	2.266	2.279	2.291	2.303	2.316	2.328	2.341	2.353	2.364	2.375	2.385	1970	2.385
1971	2.394	2.402	2.409	2.416	2.423	2.432	2.442	2.453	2.462	2.471	2.480	2.490	1971	2.490
1972	2.497	2.503	2.510	2.517	2.525	2.532	2.540	2.547	2.556	2.566	2.575	2.585	1972	2.585
1973	2.596	2.607	2.619	2.633	2.646	2.660	2.677	2.695	2.714	2.732	2.747	2.764	1973	2.764
1974	2.782	2.798	2.813	2.835	2.856	2.873	2.893	2.911	2.934	2.949	2.965	2.986	1974	2.986
1975	3.003	3.016	3.028	3.042	3.055	3.067	3.082	3.097	3.113	3.131	3.144	3.159	1975	3.159
1976	3.174	3.184	3.197	3.210	3.222	3.237	3.252	3.265	3.280	3.293	3.306	3.319	1976	3.319
1977	3.331	3.343	3.356	3.368	3.381	3.394	3.408	3.423	3.438	3.455	3.472	3.489	1977	3.489
1978	3.506	3.522	3.541	3.560	3.578	3.597	3.618	3.638	3.660	3.685	3.711	3.740	1978	3.740
1979	3.769	3.796	3.827	3.858	3.889	3.921	3.951	3.981	4.014	4.049	4.089	4.128	1979	4.128
1980	4.161	4.198	4.248	4.302	4.336	4.363	4.386	4.414	4.447	4.489	4.532	4.592	1980	4.592
1981	4.639	4.689	4.746	4.797	4.852	4.917	4.978	5.042	5.105	5.166	5.221	5.267	1981	5.267
1982	5.309	5.358	5.411	5.472	5.530	5.583	5.641	5.684	5.713	5.747	5.783	5.822	1982	5.822
1983	5.862	5.899	5.936	5.978	6.020	6.060	6.105	6.151	6.198	6.245	6.289	6.335	1983	6.335
1984	6.383	6.428	6.475	6.528	6.579	6.629	6.683	6.738	6.796	6.864	6.914	6.959	1984	6.959
1985	7.004	7.044	7.088	7.138	7.186	7.225	7.271	7.311	7.355	7.403	7.448	7.496	1985	7.496

Appendix B-9

U.S. Treasury Bills: Total Return Index
From 1926 to 2015

Year	Jan	Feb	Mar	Apr	May	Jun	Jul	Aug	Sep	Oct	Nov	Dec	Yr End	Index
1986	7.538	7.578	7.623	7.663	7.700	7.741	7.781	7.817	7.852	7.889	7.919	7.958	1986	7.958
1987	7.991	8.025	8.063	8.099	8.129	8.169	8.206	8.245	8.282	8.331	8.360	8.393	1987	8.393
1988	8.418	8.456	8.493	8.532	8.576	8.617	8.661	8.712	8.766	8.819	8.869	8.926	1988	8.926
1989	8.975	9.030	9.090	9.152	9.224	9.289	9.354	9.423	9.485	9.549	9.614	9.673	1989	9.673
1990	9.728	9.783	9.846	9.914	9.981	10.043	10.111	10.178	10.238	10.308	10.366	10.429	1990	10.429
1991	10.483	10.533	10.579	10.635	10.685	10.730	10.782	10.832	10.881	10.928	10.970	11.012	1991	11.012
1992	11.049	11.081	11.118	11.154	11.185	11.221	11.255	11.285	11.314	11.340	11.366	11.398	1992	11.398
1993	11.425	11.450	11.479	11.506	11.531	11.561	11.588	11.617	11.647	11.673	11.702	11.728	1993	11.728
1994	11.758	11.783	11.814	11.846	11.884	11.921	11.954	11.998	12.042	12.088	12.132	12.186	1994	12.186
1995	12.237	12.286	12.342	12.397	12.464	12.522	12.579	12.638	12.692	12.752	12.806	12.868	1995	12.868
1996	12.923	12.974	13.025	13.084	13.140	13.192	13.252	13.306	13.365	13.421	13.476	13.538	1996	13.538
1997	13.599	13.652	13.710	13.769	13.837	13.888	13.948	14.005	14.067	14.127	14.182	14.250	1997	14.250
1998	14.311	14.367	14.423	14.485	14.544	14.603	14.662	14.725	14.792	14.840	14.886	14.942	1998	14.942
1999	14.994	15.048	15.112	15.168	15.219	15.280	15.338	15.397	15.457	15.517	15.573	15.641	1999	15.641
2000	15.706	15.774	15.848	15.920	16.001	16.064	16.141	16.223	16.305	16.397	16.480	16.563	2000	16.563
2001	16.652	16.715	16.784	16.850	16.905	16.952	17.004	17.056	17.103	17.142	17.172	17.197	2001	17.197
2002	17.221	17.243	17.266	17.293	17.318	17.340	17.367	17.391	17.416	17.440	17.460	17.480	2002	17.480
2003	17.497	17.512	17.530	17.547	17.563	17.580	17.592	17.604	17.619	17.631	17.644	17.659	2003	17.659
2004	17.671	17.682	17.697	17.711	17.722	17.737	17.754	17.774	17.794	17.814	17.842	17.871	2004	17.871
2005	17.900	17.930	17.968	18.005	18.048	18.089	18.132	18.186	18.238	18.288	18.345	18.403	2005	18.403
2006	18.468	18.530	18.598	18.664	18.745	18.819	18.894	18.974	19.051	19.128	19.209	19.287	2006	19.287
2007	19.372	19.447	19.529	19.615	19.694	19.773	19.851	19.934	19.998	20.063	20.131	20.186	2007	20.186
2008	20.229	20.256	20.291	20.326	20.363	20.398	20.429	20.455	20.486	20.503	20.509	20.509	2008	20.509
2009	20.509	20.512	20.515	20.518	20.518	20.520	20.522	20.525	20.527	20.527	20.527	20.529	2009	20.529
2010	20.529	20.529	20.531	20.533	20.535	20.538	20.541	20.544	20.546	20.549	20.551	20.553	2010	20.553
2011	20.555	20.557	20.559	20.560	20.560	20.561	20.560	20.562	20.562	20.562	20.562	20.562	2011	20.562
2012	20.562	20.563	20.554	20.564	20.565	20.566	20.567	20.568	20.569	20.571	20.572	20.574	2012	20.574
2013	20.575	20.575	20.576	20.577	20.577	20.577	20.577	20.578	20.578	20.578	20.579	20.579	2013	20.579
2014	20.580	20.581	20.581	20.581	20.582	20.582	20.582	20.582	20.582	20.583	20.582	20.583	2014	20.583
2015	20.583	20.583	20.583	20.584	20.584	20.584	20.583	20.584	20.584	20.584	20.584	20.586	2015	20.586

Appendix B-10

Inflation Index
From 1926 to 2015

Year	Jan	Feb	Mar	Apr	May	Jun	Jul	Aug	Sep	Oct	Nov	Dec	Yr End	Index
1925												1.000	1925	1.000
1926	0.978	0.996	0.991	1.000	0.994	0.987	0.978	0.972	0.978	0.981	0.985	0.985	1926	0.985
1927	0.963	0.970	0.965	0.965	0.972	0.981	0.963	0.957	0.963	0.968	0.966	0.965	1927	0.965
1928	0.963	0.953	0.953	0.955	0.961	0.953	0.953	0.955	0.963	0.961	0.959	0.955	1928	0.955
1929	0.953	0.952	0.948	0.944	0.950	0.953	0.963	0.966	0.965	0.965	0.963	0.957	1929	0.957
1930	0.953	0.950	0.944	0.950	0.944	0.939	0.926	0.920	0.926	0.920	0.912	0.899	1930	0.899
1931	0.886	0.873	0.868	0.862	0.853	0.844	0.842	0.840	0.836	0.831	0.821	0.814	1931	0.814
1932	0.797	0.786	0.782	0.777	0.765	0.760	0.760	0.750	0.747	0.741	0.737	0.730	1932	0.730
1933	0.719	0.708	0.702	0.700	0.702	0.709	0.730	0.737	0.737	0.737	0.737	0.734	1933	0.734
1934	0.737	0.743	0.743	0.741	0.743	0.745	0.745	0.747	0.758	0.752	0.750	0.749	1934	0.749
1935	0.760	0.765	0.764	0.771	0.767	0.765	0.762	0.762	0.765	0.765	0.769	0.771	1935	0.771
1936	0.771	0.767	0.764	0.764	0.764	0.771	0.775	0.780	0.782	0.780	0.780	0.780	1936	0.780
1937	0.786	0.788	0.793	0.797	0.801	0.803	0.806	0.808	0.816	0.812	0.806	0.804	1937	0.804
1938	0.793	0.786	0.786	0.790	0.786	0.786	0.788	0.786	0.786	0.782	0.780	0.782	1938	0.782
1939	0.778	0.775	0.773	0.771	0.771	0.771	0.771	0.771	0.782	0.782	0.782	0.778	1939	0.778
1940	0.777	0.782	0.780	0.780	0.782	0.784	0.782	0.780	0.782	0.782	0.782	0.786	1940	0.786
1941	0.786	0.786	0.790	0.797	0.803	0.818	0.821	0.829	0.844	0.853	0.860	0.862	1941	0.862
1942	0.873	0.881	0.892	0.898	0.907	0.909	0.912	0.918	0.920	0.929	0.935	0.942	1942	0.942
1943	0.942	0.944	0.959	0.970	0.978	0.976	0.968	0.965	0.968	0.972	0.970	0.972	1943	0.972
1944	0.970	0.968	0.968	0.974	0.978	0.980	0.985	0.989	0.989	0.989	0.989	0.993	1944	0.993
1945	0.993	0.991	0.991	0.993	1.000	1.009	1.011	1.011	1.007	1.007	1.011	1.015	1945	1.015
1946	1.015	1.011	1.019	1.024	1.030	1.041	1.102	1.127	1.140	1.162	1.190	1.199	1946	1.199
1947	1.199	1.197	1.223	1.223	1.220	1.229	1.240	1.253	1.283	1.283	1.291	1.307	1947	1.307
1948	1.322	1.311	1.307	1.326	1.335	1.345	1.361	1.367	1.367	1.361	1.352	1.343	1948	1.343
1949	1.341	1.326	1.330	1.331	1.330	1.331	1.322	1.326	1.331	1.324	1.326	1.318	1949	1.318
1950	1.313	1.309	1.315	1.317	1.322	1.330	1.343	1.354	1.363	1.371	1.376	1.395	1950	1.395
1951	1.417	1.434	1.439	1.441	1.447	1.445	1.447	1.447	1.456	1.464	1.471	1.477	1951	1.477
1952	1.477	1.467	1.467	1.473	1.475	1.479	1.490	1.492	1.490	1.492	1.492	1.490	1952	1.490
1953	1.486	1.479	1.482	1.484	1.488	1.493	1.497	1.501	1.503	1.507	1.501	1.499	1953	1.499
1954	1.503	1.501	1.499	1.495	1.501	1.503	1.503	1.501	1.497	1.493	1.495	1.492	1954	1.492
1955	1.492	1.492	1.492	1.492	1.492	1.492	1.497	1.493	1.499	1.499	1.501	1.497	1955	1.497

Appendix B-10

Inflation Index
From 1926 to 2015

Year	Jan	Feb	Mar	Apr	May	Jun	Jul	Aug	Sep	Oct	Nov	Dec	Yr End	Index
1956	1.495	1.495	1.497	1.499	1.507	1.516	1.527	1.525	1.527	1.536	1.536	1.540	1956	1.540
1957	1.542	1.547	1.551	1.557	1.561	1.570	1.577	1.579	1.581	1.581	1.587	1.587	1957	1.587
1958	1.596	1.598	1.609	1.613	1.613	1.615	1.616	1.615	1.615	1.615	1.616	1.615	1958	1.615
1959	1.616	1.615	1.615	1.616	1.618	1.626	1.629	1.628	1.633	1.639	1.639	1.639	1959	1.639
1960	1.637	1.639	1.639	1.648	1.648	1.652	1.652	1.652	1.654	1.661	1.663	1.663	1960	1.663
1961	1.663	1.663	1.663	1.663	1.663	1.665	1.672	1.670	1.674	1.674	1.674	1.674	1961	1.674
1962	1.674	1.678	1.682	1.685	1.685	1.685	1.689	1.689	1.698	1.696	1.696	1.695	1962	1.695
1963	1.696	1.698	1.700	1.700	1.700	1.708	1.715	1.715	1.715	1.717	1.719	1.723	1963	1.723
1964	1.724	1.723	1.724	1.726	1.726	1.730	1.734	1.732	1.736	1.737	1.741	1.743	1964	1.743
1965	1.743	1.743	1.745	1.750	1.754	1.764	1.765	1.762	1.765	1.767	1.771	1.777	1965	1.777
1966	1.777	1.788	1.793	1.801	1.803	1.808	1.814	1.823	1.827	1.834	1.834	1.836	1966	1.836
1967	1.836	1.838	1.842	1.845	1.851	1.857	1.866	1.872	1.875	1.881	1.886	1.892	1967	1.892
1968	1.899	1.905	1.914	1.920	1.926	1.937	1.946	1.952	1.957	1.968	1.976	1.981	1968	1.981
1969	1.987	1.994	2.011	2.024	2.030	2.043	2.052	2.061	2.071	2.078	2.089	2.102	1969	2.102
1970	2.110	2.121	2.132	2.145	2.155	2.166	2.173	2.177	2.188	2.199	2.207	2.218	1970	2.218
1971	2.220	2.223	2.231	2.238	2.250	2.263	2.268	2.274	2.276	2.279	2.283	2.292	1971	2.292
1972	2.294	2.305	2.309	2.315	2.322	2.328	2.337	2.341	2.350	2.358	2.363	2.371	1972	2.371
1973	2.378	2.395	2.417	2.434	2.449	2.466	2.471	2.516	2.523	2.544	2.562	2.579	1973	2.579
1974	2.602	2.635	2.665	2.680	2.710	2.736	2.756	2.791	2.825	2.849	2.873	2.894	1974	2.894
1975	2.907	2.927	2.939	2.953	2.967	2.991	3.022	3.032	3.047	3.065	3.084	3.097	1975	3.097
1976	3.104	3.112	3.119	3.132	3.151	3.168	3.186	3.201	3.214	3.227	3.237	3.246	1976	3.246
1977	3.264	3.298	3.318	3.345	3.363	3.386	3.400	3.413	3.426	3.436	3.453	3.466	1977	3.466
1978	3.484	3.508	3.533	3.564	3.600	3.637	3.663	3.682	3.708	3.737	3.758	3.778	1978	3.778
1979	3.812	3.857	3.894	3.939	3.987	4.024	4.076	4.117	4.160	4.197	4.237	4.281	1979	4.281
1980	4.343	4.402	4.466	4.516	4.561	4.611	4.615	4.644	4.687	4.728	4.771	4.812	1980	4.812
1981	4.851	4.901	4.937	4.968	5.009	5.052	5.110	5.149	5.201	5.212	5.227	5.242	1981	5.242
1982	5.261	5.278	5.272	5.294	5.346	5.412	5.441	5.453	5.462	5.477	5.467	5.445	1982	5.445
1983	5.458	5.460	5.464	5.503	5.533	5.551	5.574	5.592	5.620	5.635	5.644	5.652	1983	5.652
1984	5.683	5.710	5.723	5.750	5.767	5.786	5.805	5.829	5.857	5.872	5.872	5.875	1984	5.875
1985	5.886	5.911	5.937	5.961	5.983	6.002	6.011	6.024	6.043	6.061	6.082	6.097	1985	6.097

Appendix B-10

Inflation Index
From 1926 to 2015

Year	Jan	Feb	Mar	Apr	May	Jun	Jul	Aug	Sep	Oct	Nov	Dec	Yr End	Index
1986	6.115	6.099	6.071	6.058	6.076	6.106	6.108	6.119	6.149	6.155	6.160	6.166	1986	6.166
1987	6.203	6.227	6.255	6.289	6.307	6.333	6.346	6.382	6.413	6.430	6.439	6.438	1987	6.438
1988	6.454	6.471	6.499	6.532	6.555	6.583	6.610	6.638	6.683	6.705	6.711	6.722	1988	6.722
1989	6.756	6.783	6.822	6.867	6.906	6.923	6.940	6.951	6.973	7.007	7.023	7.034	1989	7.034
1990	7.107	7.140	7.180	7.191	7.207	7.246	7.274	7.341	7.403	7.447	7.464	7.464	1990	7.464
1991	7.509	7.520	7.531	7.542	7.564	7.587	7.598	7.620	7.654	7.665	7.687	7.693	1991	7.693
1992	7.704	7.732	7.771	7.782	7.793	7.821	7.838	7.860	7.882	7.910	7.921	7.916	1992	7.916
1993	7.955	7.983	8.011	8.033	8.044	8.055	8.055	8.078	8.094	8.128	8.133	8.133	1993	8.133
1994	8.156	8.184	8.212	8.223	8.228	8.256	8.278	8.312	8.334	8.340	8.351	8.351	1994	8.351
1995	8.384	8.418	8.446	8.474	8.490	8.507	8.507	8.530	8.546	8.574	8.569	8.563	1995	8.563
1996	8.613	8.641	8.686	8.719	8.736	8.741	8.758	8.775	8.803	8.831	8.847	8.847	1996	8.847
1997	8.875	8.903	8.926	8.937	8.931	8.942	8.953	8.970	8.993	9.015	9.009	8.998	1997	8.998
1998	9.015	9.032	9.048	9.065	9.082	9.093	9.104	9.115	9.126	9.149	9.149	9.143	1998	9.143
1999	9.165	9.177	9.204	9.271	9.271	9.271	9.299	9.322	9.366	9.383	9.389	9.389	1999	9.389
2000	9.416	9.472	9.550	9.556	9.567	9.617	9.640	9.640	9.690	9.707	9.712	9.707	2000	9.707
2001	9.768	9.807	9.829	9.868	9.913	9.930	9.902	9.902	9.946	9.913	9.896	9.857	2001	9.857
2002	9.879	9.919	9.974	10.030	10.030	10.036	10.047	10.080	10.097	10.114	10.114	10.091	2002	10.091
2003	10.136	10.214	10.276	10.253	10.237	10.248	10.259	10.298	10.331	10.320	10.292	10.281	2003	10.281
2004	10.331	10.387	10.454	10.488	10.549	10.582	10.566	10.571	10.594	10.649	10.655	10.616	2004	10.616
2005	10.638	10.700	10.783	10.856	10.845	10.850	10.900	10.956	11.090	11.112	11.023	10.978	2005	10.978
2006	11.062	11.084	11.146	11.241	11.296	11.319	11.352	11.375	11.319	11.257	11.241	11.257	2006	11.257
2007	11.292	11.352	11.456	11.530	11.600	11.623	11.620	11.599	11.631	11.655	11.725	11.717	2007	11.717
2008	11.775	11.809	11.912	11.984	12.085	12.207	12.271	12.222	12.205	12.081	11.850	11.728	2008	11.728
2009	11.779	11.837	11.866	11.896	11.930	12.032	12.013	12.040	12.048	12.059	12.068	12.047	2009	12.047
2010	12.088	12.091	12.141	12.162	12.171	12.159	12.162	12.178	12.186	12.201	12.206	12.227	2010	12.227
2011	12.285	12.346	12.466	12.546	12.605	12.592	12.603	12.638	12.657	12.631	12.620	12.589	2011	12.589
2012	12.644	12.700	12.797	12.835	12.820	12.801	12.781	12.852	12.909	12.904	12.843	12.808	2012	12.808
2013	12.846	12.951	12.985	12.972	12.995	13.026	13.031	13.047	13.062	13.028	13.002	13.001	2013	13.001
2014	13.050	13.098	13.182	13.226	13.272	13.297	13.291	13.269	13.279	13.246	13.174	13.100	2014	13.100
2015	13.038	13.095	13.173	13.199	13.267	13.313	13.314	13.295	13.274	13.268	13.240	13.254	2015	13.254

Appendix C
Rates of Return for All Yearly Holding Periods
1926–2015

Basic Series: Total Rates of Return for All Holdings Periods

Appendix C-1: Large-Capitalization Stocks

Appendix C-2: Small-Capitalization Stocks

Appendix C-3: Long-term Corporate Bonds

Appendix C-4: Long-term Government Bonds

Appendix C-5: Intermediate-term Government Bonds

Appendix C-6: U.S. Treasury Bills

Appendix C-7: Inflation

Appendix C-1

Large-Capitalization Stocks: Percent per annum total returns for all historical periods

From 1926 to 2015

End Date	1926	1927	1928	1929	1930	1931	1932	1933	1934	1935	1936	1937	1938	1939	1940	1941	1942	1943	1944	1945
1926	11.6																			
1927	23.9	37.5																		
1928	30.1	40.5	43.6																	
1929	19.2	21.8	14.7	-8.4																
1930	8.7	8.0	-0.4	-17.1	-24.9															
1931	-2.5	-5.1	-13.5	-27.0	-34.8	-43.3														
1932	-3.3	-5.6	-12.5	-22.7	-26.9	-27.9	-8.2													
1933	2.5	1.2	-3.8	-11.2	-11.9	-7.1	18.9	54.0												
1934	2.0	0.9	-3.5	-9.7	-9.9	-5.7	11.7	23.2	-1.4											
1935	5.9	5.2	1.8	-3.1	-2.2	3.1	19.8	30.9	20.6	47.7										
1936	8.1	7.8	4.9	0.9	2.3	7.7	22.5	31.6	24.9	40.6	33.9									
1937	3.7	3.0	0.0	-3.9	-3.3	0.2	10.2	14.3	6.1	8.7	-6.7	-35.0								
1938	5.5	5.1	2.5	-0.9	0.0	3.6	13.0	16.9	10.7	13.9	4.5	-7.7	31.1							
1939	5.1	4.6	2.3	-0.8	-0.1	3.2	11.2	14.3	8.7	10.9	3.2	-5.3	14.3	-0.4						
1940	4.0	3.5	1.3	-1.6	-1.0	1.8	8.6	11.0	5.9	7.2	0.5	-6.5	5.6	-5.2	-9.8					
1941	3.0	2.4	0.3	-2.4	-1.9	0.5	6.4	8.2	3.5	4.3	-1.6	-7.5	1.0	-7.4	-10.7	-11.6				
1942	3.9	3.5	1.5	-1.0	-0.4	2.0	7.6	9.3	5.3	6.1	1.2	-3.4	4.6	-1.1	-1.4	3.1	20.3			
1943	5.0	4.7	2.9	0.6	1.3	3.7	9.0	10.8	7.2	8.2	4.0	0.4	7.9	3.8	4.8	10.2	23.1	25.9		
1944	5.8	5.5	3.8	1.7	2.5	4.8	9.8	11.5	8.3	9.3	5.7	2.6	9.5	6.3	7.7	12.5	22.0	22.8	19.8	
1945	7.1	6.9	5.4	3.5	4.3	6.6	11.5	13.2	10.4	11.5	8.4	5.9	12.6	10.1	12.0	17.0	25.4	27.2	27.8	36.4
1946	6.4	6.1	4.7	2.8	3.5	5.6	10.1	11.6	8.8	9.7	6.8	4.4	10.1	7.7	8.9	12.4	17.9	17.3	14.5	12.0
1947	6.3	6.1	4.7	3.0	3.7	5.6	9.8	11.2	8.6	9.4	6.7	4.5	9.6	7.5	8.5	11.4	15.8	14.9	12.3	9.9
1948	6.3	6.1	4.7	3.1	3.8	5.6	9.6	10.8	8.4	9.1	6.6	4.6	9.2	7.3	8.2	10.6	14.2	13.2	10.9	8.8
1949	6.8	6.6	5.3	3.8	4.5	6.3	10.1	11.2	9.0	9.7	7.4	5.6	10.0	8.3	9.2	11.5	14.8	14.0	12.2	10.7
1950	7.7	7.5	6.4	4.9	5.6	7.4	11.1	12.3	10.2	11.0	8.9	7.3	11.5	10.0	11.0	13.4	16.6	16.1	14.8	13.9
1951	8.3	8.1	7.1	5.7	6.4	8.2	11.7	12.9	11.0	11.7	9.8	8.4	12.4	11.1	12.1	14.3	17.3	16.9	15.9	15.3
1952	8.6	8.5	7.5	6.2	6.9	8.6	12.0	13.2	11.3	12.1	10.3	9.0	12.8	11.6	12.5	14.6	17.4	17.1	16.1	15.7
1953	8.3	8.1	7.2	5.9	6.5	8.2	11.4	12.4	10.7	11.4	9.6	8.3	11.9	10.7	11.5	13.4	15.7	15.3	14.3	13.7
1954	9.6	9.5	8.6	7.4	8.1	9.7	12.9	14.0	12.4	13.1	11.6	10.4	13.9	12.9	13.9	15.8	18.2	18.0	17.4	17.1
1955	10.2	10.2	9.3	8.2	8.9	10.5	13.7	14.7	13.2	13.9	12.5	11.4	14.8	13.9	14.9	16.8	19.1	19.0	18.5	18.4
1956	10.1	10.1	9.2	8.2	8.8	10.4	13.4	14.4	12.9	13.6	12.2	11.2	14.4	13.5	14.4	16.1	18.2	18.1	17.5	17.3
1957	9.4	9.3	8.5	7.4	8.1	9.5	12.3	13.2	11.8	12.4	11.0	10.0	13.0	12.1	12.8	14.3	16.2	15.9	15.2	14.9
1958	10.3	10.2	9.5	8.5	9.1	10.6	13.3	14.3	12.9	13.6	12.3	11.4	14.3	13.5	14.3	15.8	17.6	17.5	16.9	16.7
1959	10.3	10.3	9.5	8.6	9.2	10.6	13.3	14.2	12.9	13.5	12.3	11.4	14.2	13.4	14.1	15.6	17.3	17.1	16.6	16.4
1960	10.0	10.0	9.3	8.3	8.9	10.3	12.8	13.7	12.4	13.0	11.8	10.9	13.5	12.8	13.5	14.8	16.4	16.1	15.6	15.3
1961	10.5	10.4	9.7	8.8	9.4	10.8	13.3	14.1	12.9	13.4	12.3	11.5	14.1	13.4	14.0	15.3	16.9	16.7	16.2	16.0
1962	9.9	9.9	9.2	8.3	8.8	10.1	12.5	13.2	12.1	12.6	11.4	10.7	13.0	12.3	12.9	14.1	15.5	15.3	14.7	14.4
1963	10.2	10.2	9.5	8.7	9.2	10.5	12.8	13.5	12.4	12.9	11.8	11.1	13.4	12.7	13.3	14.5	15.8	15.6	15.1	14.9
1964	10.4	10.4	9.7	8.9	9.4	10.6	12.9	13.6	12.5	13.0	12.0	11.3	13.5	12.9	13.5	14.5	15.8	15.6	15.2	14.9
1965	10.4	10.4	9.8	9.0	9.5	10.7	12.9	13.6	12.5	13.0	12.0	11.3	13.5	12.9	13.4	14.5	15.7	15.5	15.0	14.8
1966	9.9	9.8	9.2	8.4	8.9	10.1	12.2	12.8	11.8	12.2	11.2	10.5	12.6	12.0	12.4	13.4	14.5	14.3	13.8	13.6
1967	10.2	10.2	9.6	8.8	9.3	10.4	12.5	13.1	12.1	12.5	11.6	10.9	12.9	12.4	12.8	13.8	14.9	14.7	14.2	14.0
1968	10.2	10.2	9.6	8.9	9.3	10.4	12.4	13.1	12.1	12.5	11.6	10.9	12.9	12.3	12.8	13.7	14.7	14.5	14.1	13.9
1969	9.8	9.7	9.1	8.4	8.9	9.9	11.8	12.4	11.4	11.8	10.9	10.3	12.1	11.6	12.0	12.8	13.8	13.6	13.1	12.9
1970	9.6	9.6	9.0	8.3	8.7	9.7	11.6	12.2	11.2	11.6	10.7	10.1	11.9	11.3	11.7	12.5	13.5	13.2	12.8	12.5

Start Date

Appendix C-1

Large-Capitalization Stocks: Percent per annum total returns for all historical periods

From 1926 to 2015

End Date	Start Date 1926	1927	1928	1929	1930	1931	1932	1933	1934	1935	1936	1937	1938	1939	1940	1941	1942	1943	1944	1945
1971	9.7	9.7	9.1	8.4	8.9	9.8	11.7	12.2	11.3	11.7	10.8	10.2	11.9	11.4	11.8	12.6	13.5	13.3	12.8	12.6
1972	9.9	9.9	9.3	8.7	9.1	10.1	11.9	12.4	11.5	11.9	11.0	10.5	12.1	11.6	12.0	12.8	13.7	13.4	13.0	12.8
1973	9.3	9.3	8.7	8.1	8.5	9.4	11.1	11.7	10.8	11.1	10.3	9.7	11.3	10.8	11.1	11.8	12.6	12.4	12.0	11.7
1974	8.4	8.4	7.8	7.2	7.5	8.4	10.1	10.5	9.7	10.0	9.1	8.5	10.1	9.5	9.8	10.5	11.2	10.9	10.5	10.2
1975	9.0	8.9	8.4	7.7	8.1	9.0	10.6	11.1	10.2	10.5	9.8	9.2	10.7	10.2	10.5	11.1	11.9	11.6	11.2	11.0
1976	9.2	9.2	8.7	8.0	8.4	9.3	10.9	11.4	10.5	10.8	10.1	9.5	11.0	10.5	10.8	11.5	12.2	12.0	11.6	11.3
1977	8.9	8.8	8.3	7.7	8.1	8.9	10.5	10.9	10.1	10.4	9.6	9.1	10.5	10.0	10.3	10.9	11.6	11.4	11.0	10.7
1978	8.9	8.8	8.3	7.7	8.0	8.9	10.4	10.8	10.0	10.3	9.6	9.0	10.4	9.9	10.2	10.8	11.5	11.3	10.9	10.6
1979	9.0	9.0	8.5	7.9	8.2	9.1	10.6	11.0	10.2	10.5	9.8	9.2	10.6	10.2	10.4	11.0	11.7	11.4	11.1	10.8
1980	9.4	9.4	8.9	8.3	8.7	9.5	11.0	11.4	10.6	10.9	10.2	9.7	11.1	10.6	10.9	11.5	12.2	12.0	11.6	11.4
1981	9.1	9.1	8.6	8.1	8.4	9.2	10.6	11.0	10.3	10.6	9.9	9.4	10.7	10.2	10.5	11.1	11.7	11.5	11.1	10.9
1982	9.3	9.3	8.8	8.3	8.6	9.4	10.8	11.2	10.5	10.8	10.1	9.6	10.9	10.5	10.8	11.3	11.9	11.7	11.4	11.2
1983	9.6	9.5	9.1	8.5	8.9	9.6	11.0	11.5	10.7	11.0	10.3	9.9	11.2	10.7	11.0	11.6	12.2	12.0	11.7	11.5
1984	9.5	9.5	9.0	8.5	8.8	9.6	11.0	11.4	10.7	10.9	10.3	9.8	11.0	10.6	10.9	11.4	12.0	11.8	11.5	11.3
1985	9.8	9.8	9.4	8.9	9.2	9.9	11.3	11.7	11.0	11.3	10.7	10.2	11.4	11.1	11.3	11.8	12.4	12.3	12.0	11.8
1986	10.0	10.0	9.5	9.0	9.4	10.1	11.4	11.8	11.2	11.4	10.8	10.4	11.6	11.2	11.5	12.0	12.6	12.4	12.1	11.9
1987	9.9	9.9	9.5	9.0	9.3	10.0	11.3	11.7	11.0	11.3	10.7	10.3	11.5	11.1	11.4	11.8	12.4	12.2	12.0	11.8
1988	10.0	10.0	9.6	9.1	9.4	10.1	11.4	11.8	11.1	11.4	10.8	10.4	11.6	11.2	11.4	11.9	12.5	12.3	12.1	11.9
1989	10.3	10.3	9.9	9.4	9.7	10.5	11.7	12.1	11.5	11.7	11.2	10.8	11.9	11.6	11.8	12.3	12.9	12.7	12.4	12.3
1990	10.1	10.1	9.7	9.2	9.5	10.2	11.5	11.8	11.2	11.5	10.9	10.5	11.6	11.3	11.5	12.0	12.5	12.4	12.1	11.9
1991	10.4	10.4	10.0	9.5	9.8	10.5	11.8	12.1	11.5	11.8	11.2	10.8	11.9	11.6	11.8	12.3	12.9	12.7	12.4	12.3
1992	10.3	10.3	9.9	9.5	9.8	10.5	11.7	12.1	11.5	11.7	11.1	10.8	11.9	11.5	11.8	12.2	12.7	12.6	12.3	12.2
1993	10.3	10.3	9.9	9.5	9.8	10.5	11.7	12.0	11.4	11.7	11.1	10.8	11.8	11.5	11.7	12.2	12.7	12.6	12.3	12.2
1994	10.2	10.2	9.8	9.4	9.7	10.3	11.5	11.8	11.3	11.5	10.9	10.6	11.6	11.3	11.5	12.0	12.5	12.3	12.1	11.9
1995	10.5	10.5	10.2	9.7	10.0	10.7	11.9	12.2	11.6	11.9	11.3	11.0	12.0	11.7	11.9	12.4	12.9	12.8	12.5	12.4
1996	10.7	10.7	10.4	9.9	10.2	10.9	12.0	12.4	11.8	12.0	11.5	11.2	12.2	11.9	12.1	12.6	13.1	12.9	12.7	12.6
1997	11.0	11.0	10.7	10.2	10.5	11.2	12.3	12.7	12.1	12.3	11.9	11.5	12.5	12.2	12.5	12.9	13.4	13.3	13.1	12.9
1998	11.2	11.2	10.9	10.5	10.8	11.4	12.5	12.9	12.4	12.6	12.1	11.8	12.8	12.5	12.7	13.2	13.7	13.5	13.3	13.2
1999	11.3	11.3	11.0	10.6	10.9	11.5	12.7	13.0	12.5	12.7	12.2	11.9	12.9	12.6	12.9	13.3	13.8	13.7	13.5	13.3
2000	11.0	11.0	10.7	10.3	10.6	11.2	12.3	12.6	12.1	12.3	11.9	11.6	12.5	12.2	12.5	12.9	13.3	13.2	13.0	12.9
2001	10.7	10.7	10.4	10.0	10.3	10.9	11.9	12.2	11.7	11.9	11.5	11.2	12.1	11.8	12.0	12.4	12.9	12.7	12.5	12.4
2002	10.2	10.2	9.9	9.5	9.7	10.3	11.4	11.7	11.1	11.3	10.9	10.6	11.5	11.2	11.4	11.8	12.2	12.1	11.8	11.7
2003	10.4	10.4	10.1	9.7	10.0	10.5	11.6	11.9	11.4	11.6	11.1	10.8	11.7	11.4	11.6	12.0	12.4	12.3	12.1	12.0
2004	10.4	10.4	10.1	9.7	10.0	10.6	11.6	11.9	11.4	11.6	11.1	10.8	11.7	11.4	11.6	12.0	12.4	12.3	12.1	11.9
2005	10.4	10.3	10.0	9.7	9.9	10.5	11.5	11.8	11.3	11.5	11.0	10.7	11.6	11.3	11.5	11.9	12.3	12.2	12.0	11.8
2006	10.4	10.4	10.1	9.7	10.0	10.5	11.5	11.8	11.3	11.5	11.1	10.8	11.6	11.4	11.6	11.9	12.3	12.2	12.0	11.9
2007	10.4	10.3	10.0	9.7	9.9	10.5	11.5	11.7	11.3	11.4	11.0	10.7	11.6	11.3	11.5	11.8	12.2	12.1	11.9	11.8
2008	9.6	9.6	9.3	8.9	9.2	9.7	10.6	10.9	10.4	10.6	10.1	9.8	10.7	10.4	10.6	10.9	11.3	11.1	10.9	10.8
2009	9.8	9.8	9.5	9.1	9.4	9.9	10.8	11.1	10.6	10.8	10.4	10.1	10.9	10.6	10.8	11.1	11.5	11.4	11.1	11.0
2010	9.9	9.8	9.6	9.2	9.4	9.9	10.9	11.1	10.7	10.8	10.4	10.1	10.9	10.7	10.7	11.2	11.5	11.4	11.2	11.1
2011	9.8	9.8	9.5	9.1	9.3	9.8	10.8	11.0	10.6	10.7	10.3	10.0	10.8	10.6	10.7	11.0	11.4	11.3	11.1	10.9
2012	9.8	9.8	9.5	9.2	9.4	9.9	10.8	11.1	10.6	10.8	10.4	10.1	10.9	10.6	10.8	11.1	11.5	11.3	11.1	11.0
2013	10.1	10.1	9.8	9.4	9.7	10.2	11.1	11.3	10.9	11.0	10.6	10.4	11.1	10.9	11.0	11.4	11.7	11.6	11.4	11.3
2014	10.1	10.1	9.8	9.5	9.7	10.2	11.1	11.4	10.9	11.1	10.7	10.4	11.2	10.9	11.1	11.4	11.7	11.6	11.4	11.3
2015	10.0	10.0	9.7	9.4	9.6	10.1	11.0	11.2	10.8	10.9	10.5	10.3	11.0	10.8	10.9	11.3	11.6	11.5	11.3	11.2

Appendix C-1

Large-Capitalization Stocks: Percent per annum total returns for all historical periods

From 1926 to 2015

End Date	1946	1947	1948	1949	1950	1951	1952	1953	1954	1955	1956	1957	1958	1959	1960	1961	1962	1963	1964	1965
1926																				
1927																				
1928																				
1929																				
1930																				
1931																				
1932																				
1933																				
1934																				
1935																				
1936																				
1937																				
1938																				
1939																				
1940																				
1941																				
1942																				
1943																				
1944																				
1945																				
1946	-8.1																			
1947	-1.4	5.7																		
1948	0.8	5.6	5.5																	
1949	5.1	9.8	11.9	18.8																
1950	9.9	14.9	18.2	25.1	31.7															
1951	12.1	16.7	19.6	24.7	27.8	24.0														
1952	13.0	17.0	19.4	23.1	24.6	21.2	18.4													
1953	11.2	14.2	15.7	17.9	17.6	13.3	8.3	-1.0												
1954	15.1	18.4	20.4	23.0	23.9	22.0	21.4	22.9	52.6											
1955	16.7	19.8	21.7	24.2	25.2	23.9	23.9	25.7	41.7	31.6										
1956	15.7	18.4	19.9	21.9	22.3	20.8	20.2	20.6	28.9	18.4	6.6									
1957	13.2	15.4	16.4	17.7	17.6	15.7	14.4	13.6	17.5	7.7	-2.5	-10.8								
1958	15.3	17.5	18.7	20.1	20.2	18.8	18.1	18.1	22.3	15.7	10.9	13.1	43.4							
1959	15.1	17.1	18.1	19.3	19.4	18.1	17.3	17.2	20.5	15.0	11.1	12.7	26.7	12.0						
1960	14.0	15.8	16.6	17.6	17.5	16.2	15.3	14.9	17.4	12.4	8.9	9.5	17.3	6.1	0.5					
1961	14.8	16.5	17.3	18.3	18.3	17.1	16.4	16.2	18.6	14.4	11.7	12.8	19.6	12.6	12.9	26.9				
1962	13.3	14.8	15.4	16.1	15.9	14.7	13.9	13.4	15.2	11.2	8.5	8.9	13.3	6.8	5.2	7.6	-8.7			
1963	13.8	15.2	15.8	16.6	16.4	15.3	14.6	14.3	15.9	12.4	10.2	10.8	14.8	9.9	9.3	12.5	5.9	22.8		
1964	13.9	15.3	15.9	16.6	16.4	15.4	14.7	14.4	16.0	12.8	10.9	11.5	15.1	10.9	10.7	13.5	9.3	19.6	16.5	
1965	13.8	15.1	15.7	16.3	16.2	15.2	14.6	14.3	15.7	12.8	11.1	11.6	14.7	11.1	11.0	13.2	10.1	17.2	14.4	12.5
1966	12.6	13.7	14.2	14.7	14.4	13.4	12.7	12.4	13.4	10.7	9.0	9.2	11.7	8.2	7.7	9.0	5.7	9.7	5.6	0.6
1967	13.1	14.2	14.6	15.1	14.9	14.0	13.4	13.1	14.2	11.6	10.1	10.5	12.8	9.9	9.6	11.0	8.6	12.4	9.9	7.8
1968	13.0	14.0	14.5	14.9	14.7	13.8	13.3	13.0	14.0	11.6	10.2	10.5	12.7	10.0	9.8	11.0	8.9	12.2	10.2	8.6
1969	12.0	13.0	13.3	13.7	13.4	12.5	11.9	11.6	12.4	10.1	8.7	8.9	10.7	8.2	7.8	8.7	6.6	9.0	6.8	5.0
1970	11.7	12.6	12.9	13.2	13.0	12.1	11.5	11.1	11.9	9.7	8.4	8.6	10.2	7.8	7.4	8.2	6.3	8.3	6.4	4.8

Appendix C-1

Large-Capitalization Stocks: Percent per annum total returns for all historical periods

From 1926 to 2015

End Date	Start Date 1946	1947	1948	1949	1950	1951	1952	1953	1954	1955	1956	1957	1958	1959	1960	1961	1962	1963	1964	1965
1971	11.8	12.6	12.9	13.3	13.0	12.2	11.6	11.3	12.0	10.0	8.8	8.9	10.5	8.3	8.0	8.7	7.0	9.0	7.3	6.1
1972	12.0	12.9	13.2	13.5	13.3	12.5	12.0	11.7	12.4	10.5	9.4	9.5	11.0	9.0	8.8	9.5	8.1	9.9	8.6	7.6
1973	10.9	11.7	11.9	12.2	11.9	11.2	10.6	10.2	10.8	9.0	7.9	7.9	9.2	7.3	6.9	7.4	6.0	7.4	6.0	4.9
1974	9.4	10.0	10.2	10.4	10.1	9.3	8.7	8.2	8.7	6.9	5.7	5.7	6.7	4.8	4.3	4.6	3.0	4.1	2.5	1.2
1975	10.2	10.9	11.1	11.3	11.0	10.3	9.7	9.4	9.9	8.1	7.1	7.1	8.2	6.4	6.1	6.5	5.2	6.3	5.0	4.1
1976	10.6	11.3	11.5	11.7	11.5	10.8	10.3	9.9	10.4	8.8	7.8	7.9	9.0	7.3	7.1	7.5	6.3	7.5	6.4	5.6
1977	10.0	10.7	10.8	11.0	10.7	10.0	9.5	9.2	9.6	8.1	7.1	7.1	8.1	6.5	6.2	6.6	5.4	6.4	5.4	4.5
1978	9.9	10.5	10.7	10.9	10.6	9.9	9.4	9.1	9.5	8.0	7.1	7.1	8.0	6.5	6.2	6.6	5.5	6.4	5.4	4.7
1979	10.2	10.8	10.9	11.1	10.9	10.2	9.7	9.4	9.8	8.4	7.5	7.6	8.5	7.1	6.8	7.2	6.2	7.1	6.2	5.6
1980	10.7	11.3	11.5	11.7	11.5	10.7	10.4	10.2	10.6	9.2	8.4	8.5	9.4	8.1	7.9	8.3	7.4	8.4	7.6	7.1
1981	10.3	10.8	11.0	11.2	10.9	10.3	9.9	9.6	10.0	8.7	7.9	7.9	8.8	7.5	7.3	7.7	6.8	7.7	6.9	6.3
1982	10.6	11.1	11.3	11.5	11.2	10.7	10.3	10.0	10.4	9.1	8.4	8.4	9.3	8.1	7.9	8.2	7.4	8.3	7.6	7.1
1983	10.9	11.4	11.6	11.8	11.6	11.0	10.6	10.4	10.8	9.6	8.8	8.9	9.8	8.6	8.5	8.8	8.1	8.9	8.3	7.9
1984	10.7	11.3	11.4	11.6	11.4	10.9	10.5	10.2	10.6	9.5	8.8	8.8	9.6	8.5	8.4	8.7	8.0	8.8	8.2	7.8
1985	11.2	11.8	11.9	12.1	11.9	11.4	11.1	10.8	11.2	10.1	9.5	9.6	10.4	9.3	9.2	9.6	8.9	9.7	9.2	8.8
1986	11.4	11.9	12.1	12.3	12.1	11.6	11.3	11.1	11.5	10.4	9.7	9.8	10.6	9.6	9.5	9.9	9.3	10.1	9.6	9.3
1987	11.2	11.8	12.0	12.1	11.9	11.4	11.2	10.9	11.3	10.2	9.6	9.7	10.5	9.5	9.4	9.7	9.1	9.9	9.4	9.1
1988	11.4	11.9	12.0	12.2	12.0	11.6	11.2	11.1	11.4	10.4	9.8	9.9	10.6	9.7	9.6	10.0	9.4	10.1	9.7	9.4
1989	11.8	12.3	12.5	12.6	12.5	12.0	11.7	11.6	11.9	10.9	10.4	10.5	11.3	10.3	10.3	10.6	10.1	10.9	10.4	10.2
1990	11.4	11.9	12.1	12.2	12.1	11.6	11.3	11.2	11.5	10.5	10.0	10.1	10.8	9.9	9.8	10.2	9.6	10.3	9.9	9.7
1991	11.8	12.3	12.5	12.6	12.5	12.1	11.8	11.6	12.0	11.0	10.5	10.6	11.3	10.5	10.4	10.8	10.3	11.0	10.6	10.4
1992	11.7	12.2	12.4	12.5	12.4	11.9	11.7	11.5	11.8	10.9	10.4	10.5	11.2	10.4	10.3	10.7	10.2	10.9	10.5	10.3
1993	11.7	12.2	12.3	12.5	12.3	11.9	11.6	11.5	11.8	10.9	10.6	10.5	11.2	10.4	10.3	10.6	10.2	10.8	10.5	10.3
1994	11.5	11.9	12.1	12.2	12.1	11.7	11.4	11.2	11.5	10.7	10.2	10.3	10.9	10.1	10.1	10.4	9.9	10.5	10.2	10.0
1995	11.9	12.4	12.5	12.7	12.6	12.2	11.9	11.8	12.1	11.3	10.8	10.9	11.5	10.8	10.7	11.1	10.6	11.3	10.9	10.8
1996	12.1	12.6	12.7	12.9	12.8	12.4	12.1	12.0	12.3	11.5	11.1	11.2	11.8	11.1	11.1	11.4	11.0	11.6	11.3	11.1
1997	12.5	13.0	13.1	13.3	13.2	12.8	12.6	12.4	12.8	12.0	11.6	11.7	12.3	11.6	11.6	11.9	11.5	12.2	11.9	11.7
1998	12.8	13.3	13.4	13.6	13.5	13.1	12.9	12.8	13.1	12.3	11.9	12.1	12.7	12.0	12.0	12.3	12.0	12.6	12.3	12.2
1999	13.0	13.4	13.5	13.7	13.5	13.3	13.1	12.9	13.3	12.5	12.1	12.3	12.9	12.2	12.2	12.5	12.2	12.8	12.5	12.4
2000	12.5	12.9	13.1	13.2	13.1	12.8	12.6	12.4	12.7	12.0	11.6	11.7	12.3	11.7	11.6	11.9	11.6	12.2	11.9	11.8
2001	12.0	12.4	12.6	12.7	12.6	12.2	12.0	11.9	12.2	11.4	11.0	11.1	11.7	11.0	11.0	11.3	10.9	11.5	11.2	11.1
2002	11.3	11.7	11.8	11.9	11.8	11.4	11.2	11.1	11.3	10.6	10.2	10.3	10.8	10.1	10.1	10.3	10.0	10.5	10.2	10.0
2003	11.6	12.0	12.1	12.2	12.1	11.7	11.5	11.4	11.7	10.9	10.6	10.6	11.2	10.5	10.5	10.7	10.4	10.9	10.6	10.5
2004	11.6	11.9	12.1	12.2	12.1	11.7	11.5	11.3	11.6	10.9	10.6	10.6	11.2	10.5	10.5	10.7	10.4	10.9	10.6	10.5
2005	11.5	11.8	11.9	12.0	11.9	11.6	11.4	11.3	11.5	10.8	10.4	10.5	11.0	10.4	10.4	10.6	10.3	10.8	10.5	10.3
2006	11.5	11.9	12.0	12.1	12.0	11.7	11.5	11.3	11.6	10.9	10.5	10.6	11.1	10.5	10.5	10.7	10.4	10.9	10.6	10.5
2007	11.4	11.8	11.9	12.0	11.9	11.6	11.4	11.2	11.5	10.8	10.4	10.5	11.0	10.4	10.4	10.6	10.3	10.7	10.5	10.3
2008	10.4	10.8	10.8	10.9	10.8	10.5	10.2	10.1	10.3	9.7	9.3	9.3	9.8	9.2	9.1	9.3	9.0	9.4	9.1	9.0
2009	10.7	11.0	11.1	11.2	11.0	10.7	10.5	10.4	10.6	9.9	9.6	9.6	10.1	9.5	9.5	9.6	9.3	9.7	9.5	9.3
2010	10.7	11.0	11.1	11.2	11.1	10.8	10.6	10.5	10.7	10.0	9.7	9.7	10.2	9.6	9.6	9.8	9.4	9.8	9.6	9.4
2011	10.6	10.9	11.0	11.1	11.0	10.6	10.4	10.3	10.5	9.9	9.5	9.6	10.0	9.5	9.4	9.6	9.3	9.7	9.4	9.3
2012	10.7	11.0	11.1	11.2	11.0	10.7	10.5	10.4	10.6	10.0	9.6	9.7	10.1	9.6	9.5	9.7	9.4	9.8	9.5	9.4
2013	11.0	11.3	11.4	11.5	11.3	11.0	10.8	10.7	10.9	10.3	10.0	10.1	10.5	10.0	9.9	10.1	9.8	10.2	10.0	9.8
2014	11.0	11.3	11.4	11.5	11.4	11.1	10.9	10.8	11.0	10.4	10.1	10.1	10.5	10.0	10.0	10.2	9.9	10.3	10.0	9.9
2015	10.9	11.2	11.2	11.3	11.2	10.9	10.7	10.6	10.8	10.2	9.9	10.0	10.4	9.9	9.8	10.0	9.7	10.1	9.9	9.7

Appendix C-1

Large-Capitalization Stocks: Percent per annum total returns for all historical periods

From 1926 to 2015

	Start Date																			
End Date	1966	1967	1968	1969	1970	1971	1972	1973	1974	1975	1976	1977	1978	1979	1980	1981	1982	1983	1984	1985
1926																				
1927																				
1928																				
1929																				
1930																				
1931																				
1932																				
1933																				
1934																				
1935																				
1936																				
1937																				
1938																				
1939																				
1940																				
1941																				
1942																				
1943																				
1944																				
1945																				
1946																				
1947																				
1948																				
1949																				
1950																				
1951																				
1952																				
1953																				
1954																				
1955																				
1956																				
1957																				
1958																				
1959																				
1960																				
1961																				
1962																				
1963																				
1964																				
1965																				
1966	-10.1																			
1967	5.6	24.0																		
1968	7.4	17.3	11.1																	
1969	3.2	8.0	0.8	-8.5																
1970	3.3	7.0	1.8	-2.5	3.9															

Large-Capitalization Stocks: Percent per annum total returns for all historical periods

From 1926 to 2015

End Date	1966	1967	1968	1969	1970	1971	1972	1973	1974	1975	1976	1977	1978	1979	1980	1981	1982	1983	1984	1985
1971	5.1	8.4	4.8	2.8	9.0	14.3														
1972	6.9	10.1	7.5	6.6	12.2	16.6	19.0													
1973	4.0	6.1	3.4	2.0	4.8	5.1	0.8	-14.7												
1974	0.0	1.4	-1.5	-3.4	-2.4	-3.9	-9.3	-20.8	-26.5											
1975	3.3	4.9	2.7	1.5	3.3	3.2	0.6	-4.9	0.5	37.2										
1976	5.0	6.6	4.8	4.1	6.0	6.4	4.9	1.6	7.7	30.4	23.9									
1977	3.9	5.3	3.6	2.8	4.3	4.3	2.8	-0.2	3.8	16.4	7.3	-7.2								
1978	4.1	5.4	3.8	3.2	4.5	4.6	3.3	0.9	4.4	13.9	7.0	-0.5	6.6							
1979	5.1	6.4	5.0	4.5	5.9	6.1	5.1	3.3	6.6	14.8	9.8	5.5	12.4	18.6						
1980	6.7	8.0	6.9	6.6	8.0	8.5	7.8	6.5	10.0	17.6	14.0	11.7	18.8	25.4	32.5					
1981	6.0	7.1	6.0	5.6	6.9	7.2	6.5	5.2	8.0	14.1	10.6	8.1	12.3	14.3	12.2	-4.9				
1982	6.8	8.0	7.0	6.7	8.0	8.3	7.8	6.7	9.4	15.0	12.1	10.3	14.1	16.1	15.3	7.5	21.5			
1983	7.6	8.8	7.9	7.7	8.9	9.3	8.9	8.1	10.7	15.8	13.4	11.9	15.5	17.4	17.0	12.3	22.0	22.6		
1984	7.6	8.6	7.8	7.6	8.8	9.1	8.7	7.9	10.3	14.8	12.6	11.2	14.1	15.4	14.8	10.8	16.5	14.1	6.3	
1985	8.7	9.7	9.0	8.9	10.1	10.5	10.2	9.6	11.9	16.3	14.3	13.3	16.2	17.6	17.5	14.7	20.2	19.7	18.3	31.7
1986	9.1	10.2	9.5	9.4	10.6	11.0	10.8	10.2	12.4	16.5	14.7	13.8	16.5	17.8	17.6	15.3	19.9	19.5	18.4	25.0
1987	8.9	9.9	9.3	9.2	10.3	10.7	10.4	9.9	11.9	15.6	13.9	13.0	15.3	16.3	16.0	13.8	17.3	16.5	15.0	18.1
1988	9.3	10.2	9.6	9.5	10.6	11.0	10.8	10.3	12.2	15.6	14.1	13.3	15.4	16.3	16.1	14.2	17.2	16.5	15.3	17.7
1989	10.1	11.1	10.5	10.5	11.6	12.0	11.8	11.4	13.3	16.6	15.3	14.6	16.7	17.6	17.6	16.0	18.9	18.5	17.9	20.4
1990	9.6	10.5	9.9	9.9	10.8	11.2	11.0	10.6	12.3	15.3	14.0	13.3	15.0	15.8	15.5	13.9	16.2	15.6	14.6	16.1
1991	10.3	11.2	10.7	10.7	11.6	12.0	11.9	11.5	13.2	16.1	14.9	14.4	16.1	16.8	16.7	15.3	17.6	17.2	16.5	18.0
1992	10.2	11.1	10.6	10.5	11.5	11.8	11.7	11.3	12.9	15.6	14.5	13.9	15.5	16.1	16.0	14.7	16.6	16.2	15.5	16.7
1993	10.2	11.0	10.5	10.5	11.4	11.7	11.6	11.3	12.8	15.3	14.2	13.7	15.1	15.7	15.5	14.3	16.1	15.6	14.9	15.9
1994	9.9	10.7	10.2	10.2	11.0	11.3	11.2	10.8	12.2	14.6	13.5	13.0	14.3	14.8	14.5	13.3	14.9	14.3	13.6	14.4
1995	10.7	11.5	11.1	11.1	11.9	12.2	12.1	11.9	13.2	15.6	14.6	14.1	15.5	16.0	15.8	14.8	16.4	16.0	15.4	16.3
1996	11.1	11.9	11.5	11.5	12.3	12.6	12.6	12.3	13.7	15.9	15.0	14.6	15.8	16.4	16.3	15.3	16.8	16.5	16.0	16.9
1997	11.7	12.5	12.1	12.2	13.0	13.3	13.3	13.1	14.4	16.6	15.8	15.4	16.7	17.2	17.1	16.3	17.8	17.5	17.2	18.1
1998	12.2	13.0	12.6	12.7	13.5	13.8	13.8	13.6	14.9	17.1	16.3	16.0	17.2	17.8	17.7	16.9	18.4	18.2	17.9	18.8
1999	12.4	13.2	12.9	12.9	13.7	14.1	14.1	13.9	15.2	17.3	16.5	16.2	17.4	17.9	17.9	17.2	18.5	18.3	18.1	18.9
2000	11.8	12.5	12.1	12.2	12.9	13.2	13.2	13.0	14.2	16.1	15.3	15.0	16.1	16.5	16.4	15.7	16.9	16.6	16.3	16.9
2001	11.0	11.7	11.3	11.4	12.0	12.3	12.2	12.0	13.1	14.9	14.2	13.8	14.8	15.1	15.0	14.2	15.2	14.9	14.5	15.0
2002	10.0	10.6	10.2	10.2	10.8	11.0	10.9	10.7	11.7	13.4	12.6	12.1	13.0	13.3	13.0	12.2	13.1	12.7	12.2	12.5
2003	10.4	11.0	10.7	10.7	11.3	11.5	11.5	11.2	12.2	13.8	13.1	12.7	13.6	13.8	13.6	12.9	13.8	13.4	13.0	13.3
2004	10.4	11.0	10.7	10.7	11.3	11.5	11.4	11.2	12.2	13.7	13.0	12.6	13.5	13.7	13.5	12.8	13.6	13.3	12.9	13.2
2005	10.3	10.9	10.5	10.5	11.1	11.3	11.2	11.0	11.9	13.5	12.7	12.4	13.1	13.4	13.2	12.5	13.3	12.9	12.5	12.8
2006	10.4	11.0	10.7	10.7	11.2	11.4	11.4	11.1	12.0	13.5	12.8	12.5	13.2	13.5	13.3	12.6	13.4	13.0	12.6	12.9
2007	10.3	10.8	10.5	10.5	11.1	11.3	11.2	11.0	11.8	13.3	12.6	12.2	13.0	13.2	13.0	12.3	13.1	12.7	12.3	12.6
2008	8.9	9.4	9.0	9.0	9.5	9.6	9.5	9.2	10.0	11.3	10.6	10.2	10.9	11.0	10.7	10.0	10.6	10.2	9.8	9.9
2009	9.2	9.7	9.4	9.4	9.9	10.0	9.9	9.7	10.5	11.7	11.1	10.7	11.3	11.5	11.2	10.6	11.2	10.8	10.4	10.5
2010	9.4	9.9	9.5	9.5	10.0	10.2	10.0	9.8	10.6	11.8	11.2	10.8	11.4	11.6	11.4	10.7	11.3	10.9	10.5	10.7
2011	9.2	9.7	9.4	9.3	9.8	9.9	9.8	9.6	10.3	11.6	10.9	10.6	11.1	11.3	11.1	10.4	11.0	10.6	10.2	10.4
2012	9.3	9.8	9.5	9.5	9.9	10.1	10.0	9.8	10.5	11.7	11.1	10.7	11.3	11.4	11.2	10.6	11.1	10.8	10.4	10.6
2013	9.8	10.2	10.0	9.9	10.4	10.6	10.5	10.3	11.0	12.2	11.6	11.3	11.8	12.0	11.8	11.2	11.7	11.4	11.1	11.3
2014	9.9	10.3	10.0	10.0	10.5	10.6	10.5	10.4	11.0	12.2	11.6	11.3	11.9	12.0	11.8	11.3	11.8	11.5	11.2	11.3
2015	9.7	10.1	9.9	9.8	10.3	10.4	10.3	10.1	10.8	11.9	11.4	11.0	11.6	11.7	11.5	11.0	11.5	11.2	10.9	11.0

Start Date

Appendix C-1

Large-Capitalization Stocks: Percent per annum total returns for all historical periods

From 1926 to 2015

End Date	1986	1987	1988	1989	1990	1991	1992	1993	1994	1995	1996	1997	1998	1999	2000	2001	2002	2003	2004	2005
1971																				
1972																				
1973																				
1974																				
1975																				
1976																				
1977																				
1978																				
1979																				
1980																				
1981																				
1982																				
1983																				
1984																				
1985																				
1986	18.7																			
1987	11.8	5.3																		
1988	13.4	10.8	16.6																	
1989	17.7	17.4	23.9	31.7																
1990	13.2	11.9	14.2	13.0	-3.1															
1991	15.9	15.4	18.0	18.5	12.4	30.5														
1992	14.7	14.0	15.9	15.7	10.8	18.5	7.6													
1993	14.1	13.5	14.9	14.5	10.6	15.6	8.8	10.1												
1994	12.6	11.9	12.8	12.2	8.7	11.9	6.3	5.6	1.3											
1995	14.9	14.5	15.7	15.5	13.1	16.6	13.4	15.3	18.1	37.6										
1996	15.6	15.3	16.5	16.4	14.4	17.6	15.2	17.2	19.7	30.1	23.0									
1997	17.0	16.8	18.1	18.2	16.6	19.8	18.1	20.3	23.0	31.2	28.1	33.4								
1998	17.8	17.8	19.0	19.2	17.9	20.8	19.5	21.6	24.1	30.5	28.2	30.9	28.6							
1999	18.1	18.0	19.1	19.4	18.2	20.9	19.7	21.5	23.6	28.6	26.4	27.6	24.8	21.0						
2000	16.0	15.8	16.7	16.7	15.4	17.5	16.1	17.2	18.3	21.3	18.3	17.2	12.3	4.9	-9.1					
2001	14.0	13.7	14.4	14.2	12.9	14.4	12.9	13.5	14.0	15.9	12.7	10.7	5.7	-1.0	-10.5	-11.9				
2002	11.5	11.1	11.5	11.1	9.7	10.8	9.2	9.3	9.3	10.3	6.9	4.4	-0.6	-6.8	-14.6	-17.2	-22.1			
2003	12.4	12.0	12.5	12.2	10.9	12.1	10.7	11.0	11.1	12.2	9.4	7.6	3.8	-0.6	-5.3	-4.1	0.1	28.7		
2004	12.3	12.0	12.4	12.1	10.9	12.0	10.7	11.0	11.0	12.1	9.5	8.0	4.8	1.3	-2.3	-0.5	3.6	19.5	10.9	
2005	11.9	11.6	12.0	11.7	10.5	11.5	10.3	10.5	10.5	11.4	9.1	7.6	4.8	1.8	-1.1	0.5	3.9	14.4	7.9	4.9
2006	12.1	11.8	12.2	11.9	10.9	11.8	10.6	10.9	10.9	11.8	9.7	8.4	6.0	3.4	1.1	2.9	6.2	14.7	10.4	10.2
2007	11.8	11.5	11.8	11.5	10.5	11.4	10.3	10.5	10.5	11.3	9.3	8.2	5.9	3.7	1.7	3.3	6.1	12.8	9.2	8.6
2008	9.1	8.6	8.8	8.4	7.3	7.9	6.7	6.7	6.5	6.8	4.8	3.4	1.0	-1.4	-3.6	-2.9	-1.5	2.4	-2.2	-5.2
2009	9.7	9.4	9.5	9.2	8.2	8.8	7.7	7.8	7.6	8.0	6.2	5.0	2.9	0.9	-0.9	0.0	1.6	5.5	2.1	0.4
2010	9.9	9.6	9.8	9.5	8.5	9.1	8.1	8.1	8.0	8.5	6.8	5.7	3.8	2.0	0.4	1.4	3.0	6.7	3.9	2.7
2011	9.6	9.3	9.5	9.2	8.2	8.8	7.8	7.8	7.7	8.1	6.5	5.5	3.7	2.0	0.6	1.5	2.9	6.2	3.6	2.6
2012	9.9	9.5	9.7	9.4	8.6	9.1	8.2	8.2	8.1	8.5	7.0	6.1	4.5	2.9	1.7	2.6	4.0	7.1	4.9	4.2
2013	10.6	10.3	10.5	10.3	9.5	10.0	9.2	9.3	9.2	9.7	8.3	7.5	6.0	4.7	3.6	4.6	6.2	9.2	7.4	7.0
2014	10.7	10.4	10.6	10.4	9.6	10.2	9.4	9.5	9.4	9.9	8.6	7.8	6.5	5.2	4.2	5.3	6.7	9.6	8.0	7.7
2015	10.4	10.1	10.3	10.0	9.3	9.8	9.0	9.1	9.0	9.4	8.2	7.5	6.2	5.0	4.1	5.0	6.3	8.9	7.4	7.1

Appendix C-1

Large-Capitalization Stocks: Percent per annum total returns for all historical periods

From 1926 to 2015

End Date	Start Date									
	2006	2007	2008	2009	2010	2011	2012	2013	2014	2015
1971										
1972										
1973										
1974										
1975										
1976										
1977										
1978										
1979										
1980										
1981										
1982										
1983										
1984										
1985										
1986										
1987										
1988										
1989										
1990										
1991										
1992										
1993										
1994										
1995										
1996										
1997										
1998										
1999										
2000										
2001										
2002										
2003										
2004										
2005										
2006	15.8									
2007	10.5	5.5								
2008	-8.4	-18.5	-37.0							
2009	-0.7	-5.6	-10.7	26.5						
2010	2.3	-0.8	-2.9	20.6	15.1					
2011	2.3	-0.2	-1.6	14.1	8.4	2.1				
2012	4.1	2.3	1.7	14.6	10.9	8.8	16.0			
2013	7.3	6.1	6.2	17.9	15.9	16.2	23.9	32.4		
2014	8.0	7.0	7.3	17.2	15.5	15.6	20.4	22.7	13.7	
2015	7.3	6.4	6.5	14.8	13.0	12.6	15.3	15.1	7.4	1.4

Appendix C-2

Small-Capitalization Stocks: Percent per annum total returns for all historical periods

From 1926 to 2015

End Date	Start Date 1926	1927	1928	1929	1930	1931	1932	1933	1934	1935	1936	1937	1938	1939	1940	1941	1942	1943	1944	1945
1926	0.3																			
1927	10.7	22.1																		
1928	19.6	30.6	39.7																	
1929	-4.5	-6.0	-17.6	-51.4																
1930	-12.4	-15.4	-25.1	-45.1	-38.1															
1931	-20.2	-23.7	-32.2	-46.7	-44.3	-49.8														
1932	-18.2	-21.0	-27.5	-38.5	-33.5	-31.1	-5.4													
1933	-6.3	-7.2	-11.4	-19.1	-8.1	4.9	51.6	142.9												
1934	-3.3	-3.8	-7.0	-13.1	-2.4	9.4	41.9	73.7	24.2											
1935	0.3	0.3	-2.1	-6.9	3.7	15.0	41.4	61.7	32.0	40.2										
1936	5.0	5.5	3.7	0.0	10.8	22.1	45.8	62.5	42.1	52.0	64.8									
1937	-2.7	-3.0	-5.2	-9.2	-1.9	4.8	18.5	24.0	4.8	-1.0	-16.8	-58.0								
1938	-0.4	-0.4	-2.3	-5.7	1.5	8.0	20.4	25.4	9.9	6.5	-2.8	-25.3	32.8							
1939	-0.3	-0.4	-2.1	-5.2	1.4	7.1	17.7	21.5	8.2	5.3	-2.0	-17.6	15.4	0.3						
1940	-0.7	-0.7	-2.3	-5.2	0.8	5.8	14.9	17.8	6.2	3.5	-2.6	-14.6	8.1	-2.4	-5.2					
1941	-1.2	-1.3	-2.8	-5.5	-0.1	4.4	12.3	14.4	4.2	1.6	-3.7	-13.5	3.6	-4.7	-7.1	-9.0				
1942	1.0	1.1	-0.2	-2.6	2.8	7.2	14.9	17.1	8.0	6.2	2.0	-5.8	10.7	5.8	7.6	14.7	44.5			
1943	4.6	4.8	3.9	1.8	7.3	12.0	19.7	22.3	14.2	13.1	10.1	4.0	21.0	18.7	23.8	35.3	65.0	88.4		
1944	6.7	7.1	6.3	4.5	9.9	14.5	22.0	24.7	17.3	16.7	14.3	9.2	25.2	23.9	29.3	39.7	61.1	70.2	53.7	
1945	9.4	9.9	9.2	7.6	13.1	17.8	25.2	27.9	21.2	21.0	19.2	15.0	30.4	30.1	35.8	45.9	64.2	71.3	63.4	73.6
1946	8.3	8.7	8.0	6.5	11.5	15.7	22.3	24.5	18.3	17.8	16.0	12.0	24.9	23.9	27.7	34.2	45.0	45.2	33.1	23.9
1947	7.9	8.3	7.6	6.2	10.9	14.7	20.8	22.8	17.0	16.4	14.6	10.9	22.2	21.1	24.0	28.8	36.5	35.0	24.2	15.7
1948	7.5	7.8	7.2	5.7	10.2	13.7	19.3	21.1	15.6	15.0	13.3	9.8	19.8	18.6	20.8	24.5	30.2	28.0	18.4	11.0
1949	7.9	8.3	7.7	6.4	10.6	14.0	19.4	21.0	15.8	15.3	13.7	10.5	19.8	18.7	20.7	24.0	28.8	26.7	18.6	12.7
1950	9.0	9.4	8.9	7.7	11.8	15.2	20.3	21.9	17.1	16.7	15.2	12.3	21.2	20.2	22.2	25.4	29.9	28.2	21.3	16.6
1951	9.0	9.3	8.8	7.7	11.6	14.8	19.7	21.1	16.5	16.1	14.8	12.0	20.1	19.2	21.0	23.7	27.5	25.7	19.6	15.3
1952	8.8	9.1	8.6	7.5	11.2	14.2	18.8	20.2	15.8	15.3	14.0	11.4	18.9	18.0	19.5	21.8	25.1	23.3	17.6	13.7
1953	8.2	8.5	8.0	6.9	10.4	13.3	17.5	18.7	14.6	14.1	12.8	10.3	17.2	16.2	17.4	19.3	22.1	20.2	14.9	11.3
1954	9.7	10.0	9.6	8.6	12.1	14.9	19.1	20.4	16.4	16.0	14.9	12.6	19.3	18.6	19.9	21.9	24.7	23.1	18.5	15.4
1955	10.0	10.3	10.0	9.0	12.4	15.1	19.2	20.4	16.6	16.3	15.2	13.0	19.4	18.7	19.9	21.8	24.4	22.9	18.6	15.9
1956	9.8	10.1	9.7	8.8	12.1	14.7	18.5	19.7	16.0	15.7	14.6	12.6	18.6	17.8	18.9	20.6	22.9	21.5	17.5	14.9
1957	8.9	9.2	8.8	7.9	11.0	13.4	17.1	18.1	14.6	14.2	13.1	11.1	16.6	15.8	16.8	18.2	20.1	18.7	14.8	12.3
1958	10.3	10.7	10.3	9.4	12.5	15.0	18.6	19.6	16.2	15.9	15.0	13.1	18.6	17.9	18.9	20.4	22.4	21.1	17.6	15.4
1959	10.5	10.8	10.5	9.7	12.7	15.0	18.5	19.5	16.3	15.9	15.0	13.2	18.5	17.8	18.8	20.2	22.1	20.9	17.6	15.5
1960	10.1	10.4	10.0	9.2	12.1	14.4	17.7	18.6	15.5	15.1	14.2	12.5	17.4	16.8	17.6	18.9	20.6	19.4	16.2	14.2
1961	10.6	10.9	10.6	9.9	12.7	14.9	18.1	19.0	16.0	15.7	14.9	13.2	18.0	17.4	18.2	19.5	21.1	20.0	17.0	15.2
1962	10.0	10.2	9.9	9.1	11.9	13.9	17.0	17.8	14.9	14.6	13.8	12.1	16.6	16.0	16.7	17.8	19.3	18.2	15.3	13.5
1963	10.3	10.6	10.3	9.5	12.2	14.2	17.2	18.0	15.2	14.9	14.1	12.5	16.9	16.3	17.0	18.1	19.5	18.4	15.7	14.0
1964	10.6	10.9	10.6	9.9	12.5	14.5	17.4	18.2	15.5	15.2	14.4	12.9	17.1	16.6	17.3	18.3	19.7	18.6	16.1	14.4
1965	11.3	11.6	11.3	10.7	13.2	15.2	18.0	18.8	16.2	16.0	15.2	13.8	17.9	17.4	18.1	19.2	20.5	19.6	17.1	15.6
1966	10.8	11.1	10.8	10.2	12.6	14.5	17.2	18.0	15.4	15.2	14.4	13.0	17.0	16.4	17.1	18.0	19.3	18.3	16.0	14.5
1967	12.2	12.5	12.2	11.6	14.1	16.0	18.7	19.5	17.0	16.8	16.1	14.8	18.7	18.3	19.0	20.0	21.3	20.4	18.2	16.9
1968	12.7	13.0	12.8	12.2	14.6	16.5	19.1	19.9	17.5	17.3	16.7	15.4	19.3	18.8	19.5	20.5	21.8	21.0	18.9	17.6
1969	11.6	11.9	11.7	11.1	13.4	15.2	17.7	18.4	16.1	15.8	15.2	13.9	17.5	17.1	17.7	18.6	19.7	18.9	16.8	15.5
1970	10.9	11.1	10.9	10.3	12.5	14.2	16.6	17.3	15.0	14.7	14.1	12.9	16.3	15.8	16.3	17.1	18.2	17.3	15.3	14.0

Appendix C-2

Small-Capitalization Stocks: Percent per annum total returns for all historical periods

From 1926 to 2015

End Date	1926	1927	1928	1929	1930	1931	1932	1933	1934	1935	1936	1937	1938	1939	1940	1941	1942	1943	1944	1945
1971	11.0	11.2	11.0	10.4	12.6	14.3	16.6	17.3	15.0	14.8	14.2	13.0	16.3	15.8	16.4	17.1	18.1	17.3	15.3	14.1
1972	10.9	11.1	10.9	10.3	12.4	14.0	16.3	16.9	14.7	14.5	13.9	12.7	15.9	15.5	16.0	16.7	17.6	16.8	14.9	13.7
1973	9.8	10.0	9.7	9.1	11.2	12.7	14.9	15.4	13.3	13.0	12.4	11.2	14.3	13.8	14.2	14.9	15.7	14.9	13.0	11.8
1974	9.1	9.3	9.0	8.4	10.4	11.8	13.9	14.4	12.3	12.1	11.4	10.3	13.2	12.7	13.1	13.7	14.4	13.6	11.7	10.6
1975	9.8	10.0	9.8	9.2	11.1	12.6	14.7	15.2	13.2	12.9	12.3	11.2	14.1	13.6	14.0	14.6	15.4	14.6	12.8	11.7
1976	10.6	10.8	10.6	10.0	12.0	13.4	15.5	16.0	14.0	13.8	13.2	12.2	15.0	14.6	15.0	15.6	16.4	15.7	14.0	12.9
1977	10.8	11.1	10.9	10.3	12.2	13.7	15.7	16.2	14.3	14.1	13.5	12.5	15.3	14.9	15.3	15.9	16.7	16.0	14.3	13.3
1978	11.1	11.3	11.1	10.6	12.4	13.9	15.9	16.4	14.5	14.3	13.7	12.7	15.5	15.1	15.5	16.1	16.8	16.2	14.6	13.6
1979	11.6	11.8	11.6	11.1	13.0	14.4	16.4	16.9	15.0	14.8	14.3	13.4	16.1	15.7	16.1	16.7	17.5	16.8	15.3	14.3
1980	12.1	12.3	12.1	11.6	13.5	14.9	16.8	17.3	15.5	15.3	14.8	13.9	16.6	16.2	16.6	17.2	18.0	17.4	15.9	15.0
1981	12.1	12.3	12.1	11.7	13.5	14.8	16.8	17.3	15.5	15.3	14.8	13.9	16.5	16.2	16.6	17.2	17.9	17.3	15.8	14.9
1982	12.4	12.6	12.4	12.0	13.7	15.1	17.0	17.5	15.7	15.6	15.1	14.2	16.8	16.4	16.8	17.4	18.1	17.5	16.1	15.3
1983	12.8	13.0	12.9	12.4	14.2	15.5	17.4	17.9	16.2	16.0	15.6	14.7	17.2	16.9	17.3	17.9	18.6	18.0	16.7	15.8
1984	12.4	12.6	12.5	12.0	13.8	15.0	16.9	17.3	15.7	15.5	15.0	14.2	16.6	16.3	16.7	17.3	17.9	17.4	16.0	15.2
1985	12.6	12.8	12.7	12.3	13.9	15.2	17.0	17.5	15.8	15.7	15.2	14.4	16.8	16.5	16.9	17.4	18.1	17.5	16.2	15.4
1986	12.5	12.7	12.6	12.2	13.8	15.1	16.8	17.3	15.7	15.5	15.1	14.2	16.6	16.3	16.6	17.2	17.8	17.3	16.0	15.2
1987	12.1	12.3	12.2	11.8	13.4	14.6	16.3	16.7	15.1	15.0	14.5	13.7	16.0	15.7	16.0	16.5	17.2	16.6	15.4	14.6
1988	12.3	12.5	12.3	11.9	13.5	14.7	16.4	16.8	15.3	15.1	14.7	13.9	16.1	15.8	16.2	16.7	17.3	16.8	15.5	14.8
1989	12.2	12.5	12.3	11.9	13.5	14.6	16.3	16.7	15.2	15.0	14.6	13.8	16.0	15.7	16.0	16.5	17.1	16.6	15.4	14.7
1990	11.6	11.8	11.7	11.3	12.8	13.9	15.5	15.9	14.4	14.2	13.8	13.0	15.2	14.9	15.2	15.6	16.2	15.6	14.5	13.7
1991	12.1	12.3	12.1	11.7	13.2	14.4	15.9	16.3	14.9	14.7	14.3	13.5	15.7	15.4	15.7	16.1	16.7	16.2	15.0	14.3
1992	12.2	12.4	12.3	11.9	13.4	14.5	16.1	16.5	15.0	14.9	14.5	13.7	15.8	15.5	15.8	16.3	16.8	16.3	15.2	14.5
1993	12.4	12.5	12.4	12.0	13.5	14.6	16.1	16.5	15.1	15.0	14.6	13.8	15.9	15.6	15.9	16.3	16.9	16.4	15.3	14.6
1994	12.2	12.4	12.3	11.9	13.3	14.4	15.9	16.3	14.9	14.8	14.4	13.6	15.6	15.4	15.7	16.1	16.6	16.1	15.0	14.4
1995	12.5	12.7	12.6	12.2	13.6	14.7	16.2	16.6	15.2	15.1	14.7	14.0	15.9	15.7	16.0	16.4	16.9	16.5	15.4	14.7
1996	12.6	12.8	12.6	12.3	13.7	14.7	16.2	16.6	15.2	15.1	14.7	14.0	16.0	15.7	16.0	16.4	16.9	16.5	15.4	14.8
1997	12.7	12.9	12.8	12.4	13.8	14.9	16.3	16.7	15.3	15.2	14.8	14.2	16.1	15.8	16.1	16.5	17.0	16.6	15.6	14.9
1998	12.4	12.6	12.5	12.1	13.5	14.5	15.9	16.3	15.0	14.8	14.5	13.8	15.7	15.4	15.7	16.1	16.6	16.1	15.1	14.5
1999	12.6	12.8	12.7	12.3	13.7	14.7	16.1	16.5	15.2	15.0	14.7	14.0	15.9	15.6	15.9	16.3	16.8	16.3	15.3	14.7
2000	12.4	12.6	12.4	12.1	13.4	14.4	15.8	16.1	14.9	14.7	14.4	13.7	15.5	15.3	15.5	15.9	16.4	16.0	15.0	14.4
2001	12.5	12.7	12.6	12.2	13.6	14.5	15.9	16.2	15.0	14.8	14.5	13.9	15.6	15.4	15.7	16.0	16.5	16.1	15.1	14.5
2002	12.1	12.3	12.2	11.9	13.1	14.1	15.4	15.7	14.5	14.4	14.0	13.4	15.1	14.9	15.1	15.5	15.9	15.5	14.6	14.0
2003	12.7	12.8	12.7	12.4	13.7	14.6	15.9	16.3	15.1	14.9	14.6	14.0	15.7	15.5	15.7	16.1	16.6	16.1	15.2	14.6
2004	12.7	12.9	12.8	12.5	13.7	14.7	16.0	16.3	15.1	15.0	14.7	14.0	15.8	15.5	15.7	16.1	16.6	16.2	15.3	14.7
2005	12.6	12.8	12.7	12.4	13.6	14.6	15.8	16.2	15.0	14.8	14.5	13.9	15.6	15.4	15.6	16.0	16.4	16.0	15.1	14.6
2006	12.7	12.9	12.7	12.4	13.7	14.6	15.8	16.2	15.0	14.9	14.5	14.0	15.6	15.4	15.6	16.0	16.4	16.0	15.1	14.6
2007	12.5	12.6	12.5	12.2	13.4	14.3	15.5	15.8	14.7	14.6	14.2	13.7	15.3	15.0	15.3	15.6	16.0	15.6	14.8	14.2
2008	11.7	11.8	11.7	11.4	12.6	13.4	14.6	14.9	13.8	13.6	13.3	12.7	14.3	14.1	14.3	14.6	15.0	14.6	13.7	13.2
2009	11.9	12.0	11.9	11.6	12.7	13.6	14.8	15.1	14.0	13.8	13.5	12.9	14.5	14.3	14.5	14.8	15.2	14.8	13.9	13.4
2010	12.1	12.2	12.1	11.8	13.0	13.8	15.0	15.3	14.2	14.0	13.7	13.2	14.7	14.5	14.7	15.0	15.4	15.0	14.2	13.7
2011	11.9	12.0	11.9	11.6	12.7	13.6	14.7	15.0	13.9	13.8	13.5	12.9	14.4	14.2	14.4	14.7	15.1	14.7	13.9	13.4
2012	11.9	12.1	12.0	11.7	12.8	13.6	14.8	15.1	14.0	13.9	13.5	13.0	14.5	14.3	14.5	14.8	15.1	14.8	14.0	13.4
2013	12.3	12.4	12.3	12.0	13.1	14.0	15.1	15.4	14.3	14.2	13.9	13.4	14.9	14.6	14.8	15.1	15.5	15.2	14.3	13.9
2014	12.2	12.3	12.2	11.9	13.0	13.8	15.0	15.2	14.2	14.1	13.8	13.2	14.7	14.5	14.7	15.0	15.3	15.0	14.2	13.7
2015	12.0	12.1	12.0	11.7	12.8	13.6	14.7	15.0	13.9	13.8	13.5	13.0	14.4	14.2	14.4	14.7	15.1	14.7	13.9	13.4

Appendix C-2 (10)

Appendix C-2

Small-Capitalization Stocks: Percent per annum total returns for all historical periods

From 1926 to 2015

End Date	Start Date 1946	1947	1948	1949	1950	1951	1952	1953	1954	1955	1956	1957	1958	1959	1960	1961	1962	1963	1964	1965
1926																				
1927																				
1928																				
1929																				
1930																				
1931																				
1932																				
1933																				
1934																				
1935																				
1936																				
1937																				
1938																				
1939																				
1940																				
1941																				
1942																				
1943																				
1944																				
1945																				
1946	-11.6																			
1947	-5.6	0.9																		
1948	-4.4	-0.6	-2.1																	
1949	1.1	5.8	8.3	19.7																
1950	7.7	13.2	17.6	28.9	38.7															
1951	7.7	12.1	15.1	21.4	22.3	7.8														
1952	7.0	10.5	12.6	16.5	15.5	5.4	3.0													
1953	5.3	7.9	9.1	11.5	9.6	1.3	-1.8	-6.5												
1954	10.3	13.4	15.3	18.5	18.3	13.6	15.7	22.5	60.6											
1955	11.3	14.2	15.9	18.8	18.6	15.0	16.8	21.8	39.1	20.4										
1956	10.6	13.1	14.6	16.9	16.5	13.1	14.2	17.2	26.3	12.1	4.3									
1957	8.3	10.3	11.3	12.9	12.0	8.7	8.8	10.0	14.6	2.4	-5.6	-14.6								
1958	11.8	14.0	15.3	17.2	17.0	14.5	15.5	17.7	23.2	15.3	13.7	18.7	64.9							
1959	12.2	14.2	15.4	17.2	16.9	14.7	15.6	17.5	22.1	15.5	14.4	17.9	38.5	16.4						
1960	11.1	12.9	13.9	15.3	14.9	12.8	13.3	14.7	18.1	12.2	10.6	12.2	22.9	6.1	-3.3					
1961	12.3	14.1	15.1	16.5	16.2	14.4	15.1	16.5	19.7	14.8	13.9	15.9	25.1	14.1	13.0	32.1				
1962	10.7	12.2	13.0	14.2	13.8	11.9	12.3	13.3	15.7	11.1	9.8	10.7	16.6	7.0	4.0	7.9	-11.9			
1963	11.4	12.9	13.7	14.8	14.5	12.8	13.2	14.2	16.5	12.4	11.4	12.5	17.8	10.1	8.6	12.9	4.3	23.6		
1964	12.0	13.4	14.2	15.3	15.0	13.5	14.0	14.9	17.1	13.5	12.7	13.8	18.6	12.2	11.4	15.4	10.4	23.5	23.5	
1965	13.3	14.8	15.6	16.7	16.6	15.2	15.8	16.8	19.0	15.8	15.3	16.6	21.3	16.0	16.0	20.3	17.5	29.3	32.3	41.8
1966	12.2	13.6	14.3	15.3	15.0	13.7	14.1	14.9	16.7	13.7	13.1	14.0	17.7	12.9	12.4	15.2	12.1	19.1	17.6	14.8
1967	14.8	16.2	17.0	18.1	18.0	16.9	17.5	18.6	20.6	18.0	17.8	19.1	23.1	19.1	19.5	23.2	21.7	29.9	31.5	34.3
1968	15.6	17.0	17.9	19.0	18.9	17.9	18.5	19.6	21.6	19.2	19.1	20.4	24.2	20.7	21.2	24.7	23.7	30.9	32.4	34.7
1969	13.5	14.8	15.5	16.4	16.2	15.1	15.6	16.3	17.9	15.5	15.2	16.1	19.1	15.6	15.5	17.8	16.2	20.8	20.4	19.8
1970	12.1	13.2	13.8	14.6	14.3	13.2	13.5	14.1	15.5	13.1	12.7	13.3	15.8	12.4	12.1	13.7	11.8	15.2	14.1	12.6

Small-Capitalization Stocks: Percent per annum total returns for all historical periods

From 1926 to 2015

End Date	Start Date 1946	1947	1948	1949	1950	1951	1952	1953	1954	1955	1956	1957	1958	1959	1960	1961	1962	1963	1964	1965
1971	12.3	13.4	13.9	14.7	14.4	13.4	13.7	14.3	15.5	13.3	12.9	13.5	15.8	12.7	12.4	14.0	12.3	15.4	14.4	13.1
1972	12.0	13.0	13.5	14.2	14.0	13.0	13.2	13.8	14.9	12.8	12.4	12.9	15.0	12.1	11.8	13.1	11.6	14.2	13.2	12.0
1973	10.1	11.0	11.4	11.9	11.6	10.6	10.7	11.1	12.0	9.9	9.4	9.7	11.4	8.5	8.0	8.9	7.2	9.1	7.8	6.2
1974	8.9	9.7	10.0	10.5	10.2	9.1	9.2	9.4	10.3	8.2	7.6	7.8	9.3	6.5	5.9	6.6	4.8	6.3	4.9	3.2
1975	10.1	10.9	11.3	11.8	11.5	10.6	10.7	11.0	11.9	10.0	9.5	9.8	11.3	8.8	8.3	9.2	7.7	9.3	8.2	6.9
1976	11.4	12.2	12.6	13.2	13.0	12.1	12.3	12.7	13.6	11.8	11.4	11.8	13.4	11.0	10.7	11.7	10.4	12.2	11.4	10.4
1977	11.8	12.6	13.1	13.6	13.4	12.6	12.7	13.1	14.1	12.4	12.0	12.4	13.9	11.8	11.5	12.4	11.3	13.1	12.3	11.5
1978	12.1	13.0	13.4	13.9	13.7	12.9	13.1	13.5	14.4	12.8	12.5	12.9	14.4	12.3	12.1	13.0	12.0	13.7	13.1	12.3
1979	12.9	13.8	14.2	14.8	14.6	13.9	14.1	14.5	15.4	13.9	13.6	14.1	15.6	13.6	13.5	14.5	13.5	15.3	14.8	14.2
1980	13.6	14.5	14.9	15.5	15.4	14.6	14.9	15.3	16.2	14.8	14.6	15.0	16.5	14.7	14.6	15.6	14.8	16.5	16.1	15.6
1981	13.6	14.5	14.9	15.4	15.3	14.6	14.9	15.3	16.2	14.8	14.6	15.0	16.4	14.7	14.6	15.5	14.8	16.4	16.0	15.5
1982	14.0	14.8	15.2	15.8	15.7	15.0	15.3	15.7	16.5	15.2	15.0	15.5	16.9	15.2	15.1	16.1	15.4	16.9	16.6	16.2
1983	14.6	15.4	15.9	16.4	16.3	15.7	16.0	16.4	17.2	16.0	15.8	16.3	17.7	16.1	16.1	17.0	16.4	17.9	17.6	17.3
1984	14.0	14.8	15.2	15.7	15.6	15.0	15.2	15.6	16.4	15.1	15.0	15.4	16.7	15.1	15.1	15.9	15.2	16.7	16.3	16.0
1985	14.3	15.0	15.4	15.9	15.8	15.2	15.5	15.9	16.6	15.4	15.3	15.7	16.9	15.5	15.4	16.2	15.6	17.0	16.7	16.4
1986	14.1	14.8	15.2	15.7	15.6	15.0	15.2	15.6	16.3	15.2	15.0	15.4	16.6	15.1	15.1	15.9	15.3	16.6	16.3	15.9
1987	13.5	14.2	14.5	15.0	14.8	14.3	14.4	14.8	15.5	14.3	14.1	14.5	15.6	14.2	14.1	14.8	14.2	15.4	15.1	14.7
1988	13.7	14.4	14.7	15.2	15.0	14.5	14.7	15.0	15.7	14.6	14.4	14.7	15.8	14.5	14.4	15.1	14.5	15.7	15.4	15.0
1989	13.6	14.3	14.6	15.0	15.0	14.4	14.5	14.9	15.5	14.4	14.3	14.6	15.7	14.3	14.3	14.9	14.4	15.5	15.2	14.8
1990	12.7	13.3	13.6	14.0	13.9	13.3	13.4	13.7	14.3	13.3	13.1	13.3	14.3	13.0	12.9	13.5	12.9	13.9	13.5	13.2
1991	13.3	13.9	14.2	14.6	14.5	14.0	14.1	14.4	15.0	14.0	13.8	14.1	15.1	13.8	13.8	14.4	13.8	14.8	14.5	14.2
1992	13.5	14.1	14.4	14.8	14.7	14.2	14.3	14.6	15.2	14.2	14.1	14.4	15.3	14.1	14.0	14.6	14.1	15.1	14.8	14.5
1993	13.6	14.2	14.5	14.9	14.8	14.3	14.5	14.8	15.4	14.4	14.3	14.5	15.5	14.3	14.2	14.8	14.3	15.3	15.0	14.7
1994	13.4	14.0	14.3	14.7	14.6	14.1	14.2	14.5	15.1	14.1	14.0	14.2	15.1	14.0	13.9	14.5	14.0	14.9	14.6	14.3
1995	13.8	14.4	14.7	15.1	15.0	14.5	14.6	14.9	15.5	14.6	14.4	14.7	15.6	14.5	14.4	15.0	14.5	15.4	15.2	14.9
1996	13.9	14.4	14.7	15.1	15.0	14.6	14.7	15.0	15.5	14.6	14.5	14.8	15.6	14.6	14.5	15.1	14.6	15.5	15.3	15.0
1997	14.0	14.6	14.9	15.3	15.2	14.7	14.9	15.2	15.7	14.8	14.7	15.0	15.8	14.8	14.7	15.3	14.8	15.7	15.5	15.2
1998	13.6	14.1	14.4	14.8	14.7	14.2	14.4	14.6	15.1	14.3	14.1	14.4	15.2	14.2	14.1	14.6	14.2	15.0	14.8	14.5
1999	13.9	14.4	14.7	15.0	15.0	14.5	14.7	14.9	15.4	14.6	14.5	14.7	15.5	14.5	14.5	15.0	14.5	15.4	15.1	14.9
2000	13.5	14.0	14.3	14.6	14.6	14.1	14.3	14.5	15.0	14.2	14.0	14.3	15.0	14.1	14.0	14.5	14.0	14.8	14.6	14.4
2001	13.7	14.2	14.5	14.8	14.7	14.3	14.4	14.7	15.1	14.3	14.2	14.4	15.2	14.2	14.2	14.7	14.3	15.0	14.8	14.6
2002	13.1	13.6	13.9	14.2	14.1	13.7	13.8	14.0	14.5	13.7	13.5	13.8	14.5	13.5	13.5	13.9	13.5	14.2	14.0	13.7
2003	13.8	14.3	14.6	14.9	14.8	14.4	14.6	14.8	15.3	14.5	14.4	14.6	15.3	14.4	14.4	14.8	14.4	15.2	15.0	14.8
2004	13.9	14.4	14.7	15.0	14.9	14.5	14.6	14.9	15.4	14.6	14.4	14.7	15.4	14.5	14.5	14.9	14.5	15.2	15.0	14.8
2005	13.8	14.3	14.5	14.8	14.7	14.3	14.5	14.7	15.1	14.4	14.3	14.5	15.2	14.3	14.3	14.7	14.3	15.0	14.8	14.6
2006	13.8	14.3	14.5	14.8	14.7	14.4	14.5	14.7	15.2	14.4	14.3	14.5	15.2	14.3	14.3	14.7	14.4	15.0	14.8	14.6
2007	13.5	13.9	14.2	14.5	14.4	14.0	14.1	14.3	14.7	14.0	13.9	14.1	14.7	13.9	13.9	14.2	13.9	14.5	14.3	14.1
2008	12.4	12.9	13.1	13.3	13.2	12.8	12.9	13.1	13.5	12.8	12.6	12.8	13.4	12.6	12.5	12.9	12.5	13.1	12.8	12.6
2009	12.6	13.1	13.3	13.6	13.5	13.1	13.2	13.4	13.7	13.0	12.9	13.1	13.7	12.9	12.8	13.1	12.8	13.4	13.2	12.9
2010	12.9	13.3	13.6	13.8	13.7	13.4	13.5	13.6	14.0	13.3	13.2	13.4	14.0	13.2	13.1	13.5	13.1	13.7	13.5	13.3
2011	12.7	13.1	13.3	13.5	13.4	13.1	13.2	13.3	13.7	13.0	12.9	13.1	13.6	12.9	12.8	13.1	12.8	13.3	13.1	12.9
2012	12.7	13.1	13.3	13.6	13.5	13.1	13.2	13.4	13.8	13.1	13.0	13.1	13.7	12.9	12.9	13.2	12.9	13.4	13.2	13.0
2013	13.2	13.6	13.8	14.0	13.9	13.6	13.7	13.9	14.2	13.6	13.5	13.6	14.2	13.5	13.4	13.8	13.4	14.0	13.8	13.6
2014	13.0	13.4	13.6	13.9	13.8	13.4	13.5	13.7	14.1	13.4	13.3	13.4	14.0	13.3	13.2	13.5	13.2	13.8	13.6	13.4
2015	12.7	13.1	13.3	13.6	13.5	13.1	13.2	13.4	13.7	13.1	13.0	13.1	13.7	12.9	12.9	13.2	12.9	13.4	13.2	13.0

Appendix C-2

Small-Capitalization Stocks: Percent per annum total returns for all historical periods

From 1926 to 2015

End Date	Start Date 1966	1967	1968	1969	1970	1971	1972	1973	1974	1975	1976	1977	1978	1979	1980	1981	1982	1983	1984	1985
1926																				
1927																				
1928																				
1929																				
1930																				
1931																				
1932																				
1933																				
1934																				
1935																				
1936																				
1937																				
1938																				
1939																				
1940																				
1941																				
1942																				
1943																				
1944																				
1945																				
1946																				
1947																				
1948																				
1949																				
1950																				
1951																				
1952																				
1953																				
1954																				
1955																				
1956																				
1957																				
1958																				
1959																				
1960																				
1961																				
1962																				
1963																				
1964																				
1965																				
1966	-7.0																			
1967	30.7	83.6																		
1968	32.4	58.0	36.0																	
1969	14.8	23.2	0.9	-25.1																
1970	7.5	11.5	-5.6	-21.3	-17.4															

Appendix C-2

Small-Capitalization Stocks: Percent per annum total returns for all historical periods

From 1926 to 2015

End Date	Start Date 1966	1967	1968	1969	1970	1971	1972	1973	1974	1975	1976	1977	1978	1979	1980	1981	1982	1983	1984	1985
1971	9.0	12.5	-0.5	-10.3	-1.9	16.5														
1972	8.3	11.1	0.5	-6.9	0.2	10.3	4.4													
1973	2.4	3.8	-5.6	-12.3	-8.7	-5.6	-15.1	-30.9												
1974	-0.4	0.5	-7.8	-13.6	-11.1	-9.4	-16.7	-25.6	-19.9											
1975	4.0	5.3	-1.8	-6.3	-2.7	0.6	-3.1	-5.4	10.6	52.8										
1976	8.0	9.6	3.5	0.0	4.2	8.4	6.8	7.4	24.4	55.1	57.4									
1977	9.3	10.9	5.5	2.6	6.7	10.6	9.7	10.8	24.6	44.5	40.5	25.4								
1978	10.4	11.9	7.0	4.5	8.4	12.2	11.6	12.8	24.4	38.9	34.6	24.4	23.5							
1979	12.4	14.1	9.7	7.5	11.5	15.3	15.1	16.7	27.4	39.8	36.7	30.5	33.1	43.5						
1980	14.1	15.8	11.7	9.9	13.8	17.5	17.6	19.4	29.1	39.8	37.4	32.8	35.3	41.7	39.9					
1981	14.1	15.6	11.9	10.2	13.8	17.2	17.3	18.8	27.1	35.8	33.1	28.7	29.6	31.7	26.2	13.9				
1982	14.9	16.4	12.9	11.4	14.9	18.1	18.2	19.7	27.2	34.8	32.4	28.6	29.3	30.8	26.8	20.7	28.0			
1983	16.1	17.6	14.4	13.1	16.5	19.6	19.9	21.4	28.4	35.3	33.3	30.1	31.0	32.5	29.9	26.7	33.7	39.7		
1984	14.8	16.1	13.0	11.7	14.8	17.5	17.6	18.7	24.7	30.4	28.1	24.8	24.8	25.0	21.6	17.4	18.6	14.2	-6.7	
1985	15.3	16.6	13.7	12.5	15.4	18.0	18.1	19.2	24.7	29.9	27.8	24.8	24.8	24.9	22.1	18.8	20.1	17.6	7.9	24.7
1986	14.8	16.1	13.3	12.1	14.8	17.2	17.3	18.3	23.2	27.8	25.7	22.9	22.6	22.5	19.8	16.7	17.3	14.8	7.5	15.4
1987	13.6	14.7	12.0	10.9	13.3	15.5	15.4	16.2	20.6	24.4	22.3	19.6	19.0	18.5	15.7	12.6	12.4	9.5	3.0	6.5
1988	14.0	15.1	12.5	11.5	13.8	15.9	15.8	16.6	20.7	24.3	22.4	19.8	19.3	18.9	16.5	13.8	13.8	11.6	6.7	10.4
1989	13.8	14.8	12.4	11.4	13.6	15.6	15.5	16.2	20.0	23.3	21.5	19.1	18.5	18.1	15.8	13.4	13.4	11.4	7.3	10.3
1990	12.2	13.0	10.7	9.6	11.7	13.3	13.2	13.7	17.1	19.9	18.0	15.6	14.8	14.1	11.8	9.3	8.8	6.6	2.6	4.2
1991	13.3	14.2	11.9	11.0	13.0	14.7	14.6	15.1	18.5	21.2	19.5	17.3	16.7	16.2	14.2	12.1	12.0	10.3	7.1	9.2
1992	13.6	14.5	12.4	11.5	13.4	15.1	15.0	15.5	18.7	21.3	19.7	17.7	17.2	16.7	14.9	13.0	13.0	11.6	8.8	10.9
1993	13.9	14.7	12.7	11.8	13.7	15.3	15.3	15.8	18.8	21.3	19.8	17.9	17.4	17.0	15.3	13.6	13.6	12.4	10.0	12.0
1994	13.5	14.3	12.3	11.5	13.3	14.8	14.7	15.2	18.0	20.3	18.8	17.0	16.5	16.1	14.5	12.8	12.8	11.6	9.3	11.1
1995	14.1	14.9	13.0	12.3	14.0	15.5	15.5	16.0	18.7	21.0	19.6	17.8	17.4	17.1	15.6	14.2	14.2	13.2	11.2	13.0
1996	14.2	15.0	13.2	12.4	14.1	15.6	15.5	16.0	18.7	20.8	19.5	17.8	17.5	17.1	15.7	14.4	14.4	13.5	11.7	13.4
1997	14.5	15.3	13.5	12.8	14.4	15.8	15.8	16.3	18.8	20.9	19.6	18.1	17.7	17.4	16.1	14.9	14.9	14.1	12.5	14.1
1998	13.8	14.5	12.8	12.1	13.6	14.9	14.9	15.3	17.7	19.6	18.3	16.8	16.4	16.0	14.8	13.5	13.5	12.6	11.0	12.4
1999	14.2	14.9	13.3	12.6	14.1	15.4	15.4	15.8	18.1	20.0	18.8	17.3	17.0	16.7	15.5	14.3	14.3	13.6	12.1	13.5
2000	13.7	14.3	12.7	12.0	13.5	14.7	14.7	15.0	17.2	19.0	17.8	16.4	16.0	15.7	14.5	13.3	13.3	12.5	11.1	12.3
2001	13.9	14.6	13.0	12.4	13.8	15.0	14.9	15.3	17.4	19.1	18.0	16.6	16.3	16.0	14.8	13.8	13.8	13.1	11.7	12.9
2002	13.1	13.7	12.1	11.5	12.8	14.0	13.9	14.2	16.2	17.8	16.6	15.3	14.9	14.6	13.4	12.4	12.3	11.6	10.3	11.3
2003	14.1	14.7	13.3	12.7	14.0	15.1	15.1	15.5	17.5	19.0	18.0	16.7	16.4	16.1	15.1	14.1	14.1	13.5	12.4	13.5
2004	14.2	14.8	13.4	12.8	14.2	15.2	15.2	15.6	17.5	19.0	18.0	16.8	16.5	16.2	15.2	14.3	14.3	13.7	12.6	13.7
2005	14.0	14.6	13.2	12.6	13.9	15.0	14.9	15.2	17.1	18.5	17.6	16.4	16.1	15.8	14.8	13.9	14.0	13.4	12.3	13.3
2006	14.1	14.6	13.3	12.7	14.0	15.0	14.9	15.3	17.1	18.5	17.5	16.4	16.1	15.8	14.9	14.0	14.0	13.5	12.5	13.4
2007	13.6	14.1	12.8	12.2	13.4	14.4	14.3	14.6	16.4	17.7	16.7	15.6	15.3	15.0	14.1	13.3	13.2	12.7	11.7	12.5
2008	12.0	12.5	11.2	10.6	11.7	12.6	12.5	12.8	14.3	15.5	14.6	13.4	13.1	12.7	11.8	10.9	10.8	10.2	9.2	9.9
2009	12.4	12.9	11.6	11.0	12.1	13.0	12.9	13.1	14.7	15.9	15.0	13.9	13.5	13.2	12.3	11.5	11.4	10.8	9.8	10.6
2010	12.7	13.2	12.0	11.5	12.5	13.4	13.3	13.6	15.1	16.3	15.4	14.3	14.0	13.7	12.9	12.1	12.0	11.5	10.6	11.3
2011	12.4	12.8	11.6	11.1	12.1	13.0	12.9	13.1	14.6	15.7	14.8	13.8	13.5	13.2	12.3	11.6	11.5	10.9	10.0	10.7
2012	12.5	13.0	11.7	11.3	12.3	13.1	13.0	13.2	14.7	15.8	14.9	13.9	13.6	13.3	12.5	11.8	11.7	11.2	10.3	11.0
2013	13.1	13.6	12.4	11.9	12.9	13.8	13.7	13.9	15.4	16.5	15.6	14.7	14.4	14.1	13.4	12.6	12.6	12.1	11.3	12.0
2014	12.9	13.3	12.2	11.7	12.7	13.5	13.4	13.7	15.0	16.1	15.3	14.3	14.1	13.8	13.1	12.3	12.3	11.8	11.0	11.7
2015	12.5	13.0	11.8	11.4	12.3	13.1	13.0	13.2	14.6	15.6	14.8	13.8	13.5	13.3	12.6	11.9	11.8	11.3	10.6	11.2

Appendix C-2

Small-Capitalization Stocks: Percent per annum total returns for all historical periods

From 1926 to 2015

End Date	Start Date 1986	1987	1988	1989	1990	1991	1992	1993	1994	1995	1996	1997	1998	1999	2000	2001	2002	2003	2004	2005
1971																				
1972																				
1973																				
1974																				
1975																				
1976																				
1977																				
1978																				
1979																				
1980																				
1981																				
1982																				
1983																				
1984																				
1985																				
1986	6.9																			
1987	-1.6	-9.3																		
1988	6.0	5.6	22.9																	
1989	7.0	7.1	16.4	10.2																
1990	0.6	-0.9	2.0	-7.0	-21.6															
1991	6.9	6.9	11.3	7.7	6.5	44.6														
1992	9.1	9.4	13.6	11.4	11.9	33.6	23.3													
1993	10.5	11.0	14.8	13.3	14.1	29.2	22.2	21.0												
1994	9.6	10.0	13.1	11.5	11.8	22.1	15.4	11.7	3.1											
1995	11.9	12.5	15.5	14.5	15.3	24.5	19.9	18.8	17.7	34.5										
1996	12.4	13.0	15.8	14.9	15.6	23.3	19.5	18.5	17.7	25.8	17.6									
1997	13.2	13.8	16.5	15.8	16.5	23.3	20.0	19.4	19.0	24.8	20.2	22.8								
1998	11.5	11.9	14.1	13.2	13.6	18.9	15.7	14.4	13.2	15.8	10.2	6.7	-7.3							
1999	12.7	13.2	15.3	14.6	15.1	20.1	17.3	16.5	15.8	18.5	14.8	13.9	9.7	29.8						
2000	11.6	11.9	13.7	13.0	13.3	17.5	14.8	13.8	12.8	14.5	10.9	9.2	5.1	11.9	-3.6					
2001	12.2	12.6	14.3	13.7	14.0	18.0	15.6	14.7	14.0	15.6	12.8	11.8	9.2	15.4	8.8	22.8				
2002	10.5	10.8	12.3	11.5	11.6	15.0	12.6	11.6	10.6	11.6	8.6	7.2	4.3	7.4	0.9	3.2	-13.3			
2003	12.9	13.2	14.8	14.3	14.6	18.0	16.0	15.3	14.8	16.2	14.1	13.6	12.1	16.4	13.3	19.6	18.1	60.7		
2004	13.1	13.5	15.0	14.5	14.8	18.0	16.2	15.6	15.1	16.4	14.5	14.2	13.0	16.8	14.3	19.3	18.2	37.9	18.4	
2005	12.8	13.1	14.5	14.0	14.2	17.1	15.4	14.8	14.3	15.4	13.6	13.2	12.0	15.1	12.8	16.4	14.9	26.2	11.9	5.7
2006	12.9	13.2	14.6	14.1	14.4	17.1	15.4	14.9	14.4	15.4	13.9	13.5	12.5	15.2	13.3	16.4	15.2	23.6	13.3	10.8
2007	12.0	12.3	13.5	13.0	13.2	15.6	14.0	13.4	12.9	13.7	12.1	11.6	10.6	12.8	10.8	13.0	11.5	17.2	8.3	5.2
2008	9.3	9.4	10.4	9.8	9.8	11.8	10.1	9.4	8.6	9.0	7.3	6.5	5.1	6.4	4.1	5.1	2.8	5.8	-2.7	-7.4
2009	10.0	10.1	11.1	10.6	10.6	12.6	11.1	10.4	9.8	10.2	8.7	8.0	6.9	8.2	6.3	7.5	5.7	8.7	1.9	-1.2
2010	10.8	10.9	11.9	11.5	11.5	13.5	12.1	11.5	10.9	11.4	10.0	9.5	8.6	10.0	8.4	9.6	8.3	11.3	5.6	3.6
2011	10.2	10.3	11.2	10.8	10.8	12.6	11.2	10.6	10.1	10.5	9.2	8.6	7.7	8.9	7.3	8.4	7.0	9.6	4.5	2.6
2012	10.5	10.6	11.5	11.1	11.1	12.9	11.6	11.0	10.5	10.9	9.7	9.2	8.3	9.6	8.1	9.2	8.0	10.4	5.9	4.4
2013	11.6	11.8	12.7	12.3	12.3	14.1	12.9	12.4	12.0	12.5	11.4	11.0	10.3	11.6	10.4	11.6	10.7	13.2	9.3	8.3
2014	11.3	11.4	12.3	11.9	12.0	13.6	12.4	12.0	11.6	12.0	10.9	10.6	9.9	11.1	9.9	10.9	10.1	12.3	8.7	7.8
2015	10.7	10.9	11.7	11.3	11.3	12.9	11.7	11.2	10.8	11.2	10.2	9.8	9.1	10.1	9.0	9.9	9.0	11.0	7.6	6.7

Appendix C-2

Small-Capitalization Stocks: Percent per annum total returns for all historical periods

From 1926 to 2015

End Date	Start Date									
	2006	2007	2008	2009	2010	2011	2012	2013	2014	2015
1971										
1972										
1973										
1974										
1975										
1976										
1977										
1978										
1979										
1980										
1981										
1982										
1983										
1984										
1985										
1986										
1987										
1988										
1989										
1990										
1991										
1992										
1993										
1994										
1995										
1996										
1997										
1998										
1999										
2000										
2001										
2002										
2003										
2004										
2005										
2006	16.2									
2007	4.9	-5.2								
2008	-11.3	-22.6	-36.7							
2009	-2.8	-8.4	-10.0	28.1						
2010	3.2	0.2	2.1	29.7	31.3					
2011	2.1	-0.5	0.7	17.6	12.7	-3.3				
2012	4.3	2.4	4.0	17.8	14.5	7.0	18.2			
2013	8.7	7.6	9.9	22.8	21.5	18.4	31.0	45.1		
2014	8.0	7.0	8.9	19.2	17.5	14.3	20.9	22.2	2.9	
2015	6.8	5.8	7.3	15.7	13.7	10.5	14.2	12.9	-0.4	-3.6

Appendix C-3

Long-term Corporate Bonds: Percent per annum total returns for all historical periods

From 1926 to 2015

End Date	1926	1927	1928	1929	1930	1931	1932	1933	1934	1935	1936	1937	1938	1939	1940	1941	1942	1943	1944	1945
1926	7.4																			
1927	7.4	7.4																		
1928	5.9	5.1	2.8																	
1929	5.2	4.5	3.1	3.3																
1930	5.8	5.4	4.7	5.6	8.0															
1931	4.4	3.9	3.0	3.1	2.9	-1.9														
1932	5.3	5.0	4.5	4.9	5.5	4.3	10.8													
1933	6.0	5.8	5.5	6.0	6.7	6.3	10.6	10.4												
1934	6.8	6.7	6.6	7.3	8.1	8.1	11.7	12.1	13.8											
1935	7.1	7.0	7.0	7.6	8.3	8.4	11.2	11.3	11.7	9.6										
1936	7.1	7.0	7.0	7.5	8.1	8.1	10.3	10.1	10.0	8.2	6.7									
1937	6.7	6.6	6.5	7.0	7.4	7.4	9.0	8.6	8.2	6.3	4.7	2.7								
1938	6.6	6.6	6.5	6.9	7.3	7.2	8.6	8.2	7.8	6.3	5.2	4.4	6.1							
1939	6.4	6.4	6.3	6.6	6.9	6.8	8.0	7.6	7.1	5.8	4.9	4.3	5.0	4.0						
1940	6.2	6.2	6.1	6.3	6.6	6.5	7.5	7.0	6.6	5.4	4.6	4.1	4.5	3.7	3.4					
1941	6.0	5.9	5.8	6.1	6.3	6.1	7.0	6.6	6.1	5.0	4.3	3.8	4.0	3.4	3.1	2.7				
1942	5.8	5.7	5.6	5.8	6.0	5.8	6.6	6.2	5.7	4.7	4.0	3.6	3.8	3.2	3.1	2.7	2.6			
1943	5.6	5.5	5.4	5.6	5.8	5.6	6.3	5.8	5.4	4.5	3.9	3.5	3.6	3.1	2.9	2.7	2.7	2.8		
1944	5.6	5.5	5.4	5.5	5.7	5.5	6.1	5.8	5.3	4.5	4.0	3.6	3.8	3.4	3.3	3.2	3.4	3.8	4.7	
1945	5.5	5.4	5.3	5.5	5.6	5.4	6.0	5.6	5.2	4.5	4.0	3.7	3.8	3.5	3.4	3.4	3.6	3.9	4.4	4.1
1946	5.3	5.2	5.1	5.3	5.4	5.2	5.7	5.3	5.0	4.3	3.8	3.5	3.6	3.3	3.2	3.1	3.2	3.3	3.5	2.9
1947	5.0	4.9	4.7	4.8	4.9	4.7	5.2	4.8	4.4	3.7	3.3	2.9	3.0	2.6	2.4	2.3	2.2	2.2	2.0	1.1
1948	4.9	4.8	4.7	4.8	4.9	4.7	5.1	4.8	4.4	3.8	3.3	3.0	3.1	2.8	2.6	2.5	2.5	2.5	2.4	1.9
1949	4.9	4.8	4.6	4.7	4.8	4.6	5.0	4.7	4.3	3.7	3.3	3.1	3.1	2.8	2.7	2.5	2.6	2.6	2.6	2.2
1950	4.8	4.7	4.5	4.6	4.7	4.5	4.9	4.5	4.2	3.6	3.2	3.0	3.0	2.8	2.6	2.6	2.6	2.6	2.5	2.1
1951	4.5	4.3	4.2	4.3	4.3	4.2	4.5	4.1	3.8	3.2	2.9	2.6	2.6	2.3	2.2	2.1	2.0	2.0	1.8	1.4
1952	4.4	4.3	4.2	4.2	4.3	4.1	4.4	4.1	3.8	3.3	2.9	2.7	2.7	2.4	2.3	2.2	2.2	2.1	2.0	1.7
1953	4.4	4.3	4.2	4.2	4.3	4.1	4.4	4.1	3.8	3.3	2.9	2.7	2.7	2.5	2.4	2.3	2.3	2.2	2.2	1.9
1954	4.4	4.3	4.2	4.3	4.3	4.2	4.4	4.1	3.8	3.4	3.1	2.9	2.9	2.7	2.6	2.5	2.5	2.5	2.5	2.2
1955	4.3	4.2	4.1	4.1	4.2	4.0	4.3	4.0	3.7	3.2	2.9	2.7	2.7	2.5	2.4	2.4	2.4	2.3	2.3	2.1
1956	3.9	3.8	3.7	3.7	3.7	3.6	3.8	3.5	3.2	2.8	2.4	2.2	2.2	2.0	1.9	1.8	1.7	1.6	1.6	1.3
1957	4.1	4.0	3.8	3.9	3.9	3.7	4.0	3.7	3.4	3.0	2.7	2.5	2.5	2.3	2.2	2.2	2.1	2.1	2.1	1.9
1958	3.9	3.8	3.6	3.7	3.7	3.5	3.7	3.5	3.2	2.8	2.5	2.3	2.3	2.1	2.0	1.9	1.9	1.8	1.8	1.6
1959	3.7	3.6	3.5	3.5	3.5	3.4	3.6	3.3	3.0	2.6	2.3	2.2	2.1	1.9	1.8	1.8	1.7	1.7	1.6	1.4
1960	3.9	3.8	3.7	3.7	3.7	3.6	3.7	3.5	3.3	2.9	2.6	2.4	2.4	2.3	2.2	2.1	2.1	2.1	2.0	1.8
1961	3.9	3.8	3.7	3.7	3.7	3.6	3.8	3.5	3.3	2.9	2.7	2.5	2.5	2.4	2.3	2.2	2.2	2.2	2.2	2.0
1962	4.0	3.9	3.8	3.8	3.9	3.7	3.9	3.7	3.5	3.1	2.9	2.7	2.7	2.6	2.5	2.5	2.5	2.5	2.5	2.3
1963	4.0	3.9	3.8	3.8	3.8	3.7	3.9	3.6	3.4	3.1	2.9	2.7	2.7	2.6	2.5	2.5	2.5	2.5	2.5	2.3
1964	4.0	3.9	3.8	3.8	3.8	3.7	3.9	3.7	3.5	3.1	2.9	2.8	2.8	2.7	2.6	2.6	2.6	2.6	2.6	2.5
1965	3.9	3.8	3.7	3.7	3.7	3.6	3.8	3.6	3.3	3.0	2.8	2.7	2.7	2.5	2.5	2.5	2.4	2.4	2.4	2.3
1966	3.8	3.7	3.6	3.6	3.6	3.5	3.7	3.5	3.2	2.9	2.7	2.6	2.6	2.5	2.4	2.4	2.4	2.3	2.3	2.2
1967	3.6	3.5	3.4	3.4	3.5	3.3	3.4	3.2	3.0	2.7	2.5	2.3	2.3	2.2	2.1	2.1	2.1	2.0	2.0	1.9
1968	3.5	3.4	3.3	3.4	3.4	3.2	3.4	3.2	3.0	2.7	2.5	2.3	2.3	2.2	2.2	2.1	2.1	2.1	2.0	1.9
1969	3.3	3.2	3.1	3.1	3.1	2.9	3.1	2.9	2.7	2.4	2.2	2.0	2.0	1.9	1.8	1.7	1.7	1.7	1.6	1.5
1970	3.6	3.5	3.4	3.4	3.4	3.3	3.4	3.2	3.1	2.8	2.6	2.5	2.5	2.3	2.3	2.3	2.2	2.2	2.2	2.1

Appendix C-3

Long-term Corporate Bonds: Percent per annum total returns for all historical periods

From 1926 to 2015

End Date	Start Date 1926	1927	1928	1929	1930	1931	1932	1933	1934	1935	1936	1937	1938	1939	1940	1941	1942	1943	1944	1945
1971	3.7	3.6	3.6	3.6	3.6	3.5	3.6	3.4	3.3	3.0	2.8	2.7	2.7	2.6	2.6	2.5	2.5	2.5	2.5	2.4
1972	3.8	3.7	3.6	3.7	3.7	3.6	3.7	3.5	3.4	3.1	2.9	2.8	2.8	2.7	2.7	2.7	2.7	2.7	2.7	2.6
1973	3.7	3.7	3.6	3.6	3.6	3.5	3.6	3.5	3.3	3.0	2.9	2.8	2.8	2.7	2.6	2.6	2.6	2.6	2.6	2.5
1974	3.6	3.5	3.4	3.4	3.5	3.4	3.5	3.3	3.1	2.9	2.7	2.6	2.6	2.5	2.5	2.4	2.4	2.4	2.4	2.3
1975	3.8	3.7	3.7	3.7	3.7	3.6	3.7	3.6	3.4	3.2	3.0	2.9	2.9	2.8	2.8	2.8	2.8	2.8	2.8	2.7
1976	4.1	4.0	3.9	4.0	4.0	3.9	4.0	3.9	3.7	3.5	3.4	3.3	3.3	3.2	3.2	3.2	3.2	3.2	3.2	3.2
1977	4.0	4.0	3.9	3.9	3.9	3.9	4.0	3.8	3.7	3.5	3.3	3.2	3.2	3.2	3.2	3.1	3.2	3.2	3.2	3.1
1978	4.0	3.9	3.8	3.8	3.9	3.8	3.9	3.7	3.6	3.4	3.2	3.2	3.2	3.1	3.1	3.1	3.1	3.1	3.1	3.0
1979	3.8	3.7	3.7	3.7	3.7	3.6	3.7	3.6	3.4	3.2	3.1	3.0	3.0	2.9	2.9	2.9	2.9	2.9	2.9	2.8
1980	3.7	3.6	3.5	3.5	3.6	3.5	3.6	3.4	3.3	3.1	2.9	2.8	2.8	2.8	2.7	2.7	2.7	2.7	2.7	2.7
1981	3.6	3.5	3.4	3.5	3.5	3.4	3.5	3.3	3.2	3.0	2.8	2.8	2.8	2.7	2.6	2.6	2.6	2.6	2.6	2.6
1982	4.2	4.1	4.1	4.1	4.1	4.0	4.1	4.0	3.9	3.7	3.6	3.5	3.5	3.4	3.4	3.4	3.5	3.5	3.5	3.5
1983	4.2	4.1	4.1	4.1	4.1	4.1	4.2	4.0	3.9	3.7	3.6	3.5	3.6	3.5	3.5	3.5	3.5	3.5	3.6	3.5
1984	4.4	4.4	4.3	4.3	4.3	4.3	4.4	4.3	4.2	4.0	3.9	3.8	3.8	3.8	3.8	3.8	3.8	3.8	3.9	3.8
1985	4.8	4.7	4.7	4.7	4.8	4.7	4.8	4.7	4.6	4.4	4.3	4.3	4.3	4.3	4.3	4.3	4.3	4.4	4.4	4.4
1986	5.0	5.0	4.9	5.0	5.0	5.0	5.1	5.0	4.9	4.7	4.6	4.6	4.6	4.6	4.6	4.6	4.7	4.7	4.8	4.8
1987	4.9	4.9	4.8	4.9	4.9	4.9	5.0	4.9	4.8	4.6	4.5	4.5	4.5	4.5	4.5	4.5	4.6	4.6	4.6	4.6
1988	5.0	5.0	4.9	5.0	5.0	5.0	5.1	5.0	4.9	4.7	4.6	4.6	4.6	4.6	4.6	4.6	4.7	4.7	4.8	4.8
1989	5.2	5.2	5.1	5.2	5.2	5.1	5.3	5.2	5.1	4.9	4.8	4.8	4.8	4.8	4.8	4.9	4.9	5.0	5.0	5.0
1990	5.2	5.2	5.1	5.2	5.2	5.2	5.3	5.2	5.1	5.0	4.9	4.8	4.9	4.9	4.9	4.9	4.9	5.0	5.0	5.1
1991	5.4	5.4	5.4	5.4	5.4	5.4	5.5	5.4	5.3	5.2	5.1	5.1	5.1	5.1	5.1	5.2	5.2	5.3	5.3	5.3
1992	5.5	5.4	5.4	5.5	5.5	5.5	5.6	5.5	5.4	5.3	5.2	5.2	5.2	5.2	5.2	5.3	5.3	5.4	5.4	5.4
1993	5.6	5.6	5.5	5.6	5.6	5.6	5.7	5.6	5.5	5.4	5.3	5.3	5.4	5.3	5.4	5.4	5.5	5.5	5.6	5.6
1994	5.4	5.4	5.4	5.4	5.4	5.4	5.5	5.4	5.3	5.2	5.1	5.1	5.1	5.1	5.2	5.2	5.2	5.3	5.3	5.3
1995	5.7	5.7	5.6	5.7	5.7	5.7	5.8	5.7	5.7	5.5	5.5	5.4	5.5	5.5	5.5	5.5	5.6	5.7	5.7	5.7
1996	5.6	5.6	5.6	5.6	5.7	5.6	5.7	5.7	5.6	5.5	5.4	5.4	5.4	5.4	5.4	5.5	5.5	5.6	5.6	5.6
1997	5.7	5.7	5.7	5.7	5.8	5.7	5.9	5.8	5.7	5.6	5.5	5.5	5.5	5.5	5.6	5.6	5.7	5.7	5.8	5.8
1998	5.8	5.8	5.8	5.8	5.8	5.8	5.9	5.9	5.8	5.7	5.6	5.6	5.6	5.6	5.6	5.7	5.7	5.8	5.9	5.9
1999	5.6	5.6	5.6	5.6	5.6	5.6	5.7	5.6	5.6	5.4	5.4	5.4	5.4	5.4	5.4	5.4	5.5	5.5	5.6	5.6
2000	5.7	5.7	5.7	5.7	5.7	5.7	5.8	5.7	5.7	5.6	5.5	5.5	5.5	5.5	5.5	5.6	5.6	5.7	5.7	5.7
2001	5.8	5.7	5.7	5.8	5.8	5.8	5.9	5.8	5.7	5.6	5.6	5.6	5.6	5.6	5.6	5.7	5.8	5.8	5.8	5.8
2002	5.9	5.9	5.9	5.9	5.9	5.9	6.0	6.0	5.9	5.8	5.7	5.7	5.8	5.7	5.8	5.8	5.9	5.9	6.0	6.0
2003	5.9	5.9	5.9	5.9	5.9	5.9	6.0	6.0	5.9	5.8	5.7	5.7	5.7	5.7	5.8	5.8	5.9	5.9	6.0	6.0
2004	5.9	5.9	5.9	5.9	6.0	5.9	6.0	5.9	5.9	5.8	5.8	5.7	5.8	5.8	5.9	5.9	5.9	6.0	6.0	6.0
2005	5.9	5.9	5.9	5.9	6.0	5.9	6.0	5.9	5.9	5.8	5.8	5.8	5.8	5.8	5.8	5.9	5.9	6.0	6.0	6.0
2006	5.9	5.9	5.9	5.9	5.9	5.9	6.0	5.9	5.9	5.8	5.7	5.7	5.8	5.7	5.8	5.8	5.9	5.9	5.9	6.0
2007	5.9	5.8	5.8	5.8	5.8	5.7	6.0	5.9	5.8	5.7	5.7	5.7	5.7	5.7	5.7	5.8	5.8	5.9	5.9	5.9
2008	5.9	5.9	5.8	5.9	5.9	5.9	6.0	5.9	5.9	5.8	5.7	5.8	5.8	5.7	5.8	5.8	5.9	5.9	6.0	6.0
2009	5.9	5.8	5.8	5.8	5.9	5.9	6.0	5.9	5.8	5.7	5.7	5.7	5.7	5.7	5.7	5.8	5.8	5.9	5.9	5.9
2010	5.9	5.9	5.9	5.9	6.0	5.9	6.0	6.0	5.9	5.8	5.8	5.8	5.8	5.8	5.8	5.9	6.0	6.0	6.0	6.0
2011	6.1	6.0	6.0	6.1	6.1	6.1	6.2	6.1	6.1	6.0	5.9	5.9	6.0	6.0	6.0	6.0	6.1	6.1	6.2	6.2
2012	6.1	6.1	6.1	6.1	6.1	6.1	6.2	6.2	6.1	6.0	6.0	6.0	6.0	6.0	6.0	6.1	6.1	6.2	6.2	6.3
2013	6.0	5.9	5.9	6.0	6.0	6.0	6.1	6.0	5.9	5.9	5.8	5.8	5.8	5.8	5.9	5.9	5.9	6.0	6.0	6.0
2014	6.1	6.1	6.0	6.1	6.1	6.1	6.2	6.1	6.1	6.0	5.9	6.0	6.0	6.0	6.0	6.0	6.1	6.1	6.2	6.2
2015	6.0	6.0	6.0	6.0	6.0	6.0	6.1	6.0	6.0	5.9	5.9	5.9	5.9	5.9	5.9	5.9	6.0	6.0	6.0	6.1

Appendix C-3 (18)

Appendix C-3

Long-term Corporate Bonds: Percent per annum total returns for all historical periods

From 1926 to 2015

End Date	Start Date 1946	1947	1948	1949	1950	1951	1952	1953	1954	1955	1956	1957	1958	1959	1960	1961	1962	1963	1964	1965
1926																				
1927																				
1928																				
1929																				
1930																				
1931																				
1932																				
1933																				
1934																				
1935																				
1936																				
1937																				
1938																				
1939																				
1940																				
1941																				
1942																				
1943																				
1944																				
1945																				
1946	1.7																			
1947	-0.3	-2.3																		
1948	1.1	0.8	4.1																	
1949	1.7	1.7	3.7	3.3																
1950	1.8	1.8	3.2	2.7	2.1															
1951	1.0	0.9	1.7	0.9	-0.3	-2.7														
1952	1.4	1.3	2.0	1.5	0.9	0.4	3.5													
1953	1.6	1.6	2.3	1.9	1.6	1.4	3.5	3.4												
1954	2.0	2.1	2.7	2.5	2.3	2.4	4.1	4.4	5.4											
1955	1.9	1.9	2.4	2.2	2.0	2.0	3.2	3.1	2.9	0.5										
1956	1.1	1.0	1.4	1.0	0.7	0.5	1.1	0.5	-0.4	-3.2	-6.8									
1957	1.7	1.7	2.1	1.8	1.7	1.6	2.3	2.1	1.8	0.6	0.7	8.7								
1958	1.4	1.3	1.7	1.4	1.2	1.1	1.7	1.4	1.0	-0.1	-0.3	3.1	-2.2							
1959	1.2	1.2	1.5	1.2	1.0	0.9	1.3	1.0	0.6	-0.3	-0.5	1.7	-1.6	-1.0						
1960	1.7	1.7	2.0	1.8	1.7	1.7	2.2	2.0	1.8	1.2	1.4	3.5	1.8	3.9	9.1					
1961	1.9	1.9	2.2	2.1	2.0	2.0	2.4	2.3	2.2	1.7	1.9	3.8	2.6	4.2	6.9	4.8				
1962	2.2	2.3	2.6	2.5	2.4	2.4	2.9	2.9	2.8	2.5	2.8	4.5	3.6	5.1	7.3	6.4	7.9			
1963	2.2	2.3	2.6	2.5	2.4	2.4	2.9	2.8	2.7	2.4	2.7	4.1	3.4	4.5	6.0	5.0	5.0	2.2		
1964	2.4	2.4	2.7	2.6	2.6	2.6	3.0	3.0	2.9	2.7	2.9	4.2	3.6	4.6	5.7	4.9	4.9	3.5	4.8	
1965	2.2	2.3	2.5	2.4	2.4	2.4	2.8	2.7	2.6	2.4	2.6	3.7	3.1	3.8	4.7	3.8	3.6	2.1	2.1	-0.5
1966	2.1	2.1	2.4	2.3	2.2	2.2	2.6	2.5	2.4	2.2	2.4	3.3	2.7	3.4	4.0	3.2	2.9	1.7	1.5	-0.1
1967	1.8	1.8	2.0	1.9	1.8	1.8	2.1	2.0	1.9	1.6	1.7	2.5	1.9	2.4	2.9	2.0	1.5	0.3	-0.2	-1.8
1968	1.8	1.8	2.0	1.9	1.9	1.8	2.1	2.0	1.9	1.7	1.8	2.5	2.0	2.4	2.8	2.1	1.7	0.7	0.4	-0.7
1969	1.4	1.4	1.6	1.4	1.3	1.3	1.5	1.4	1.3	1.0	1.1	1.7	1.1	1.4	1.7	0.9	0.4	-0.6	-1.1	-2.2
1970	2.0	2.0	2.2	2.1	2.1	2.1	2.3	2.3	2.2	2.0	2.1	2.8	2.4	2.7	3.1	2.5	2.3	1.6	1.5	0.9

Long-term Corporate Bonds: Percent per annum total returns for all historical periods

From 1926 to 2015

End Date	1946	1947	1948	1949	1950	1951	1952	1953	1954	1955	1956	1957	1958	1959	1960	1961	1962	1963	1964	1965
1971	2.4	2.4	2.6	2.5	2.5	2.5	2.8	2.7	2.7	2.5	2.7	3.3	3.0	3.4	3.7	3.3	3.1	2.6	2.6	2.3
1972	2.5	2.6	2.8	2.7	2.7	2.7	3.0	2.9	2.9	2.8	2.9	3.6	3.2	3.6	4.0	3.6	3.5	3.0	3.1	2.9
1973	2.5	2.5	2.7	2.7	2.6	2.6	2.9	2.9	2.8	2.7	2.8	3.4	3.1	3.5	3.8	3.4	3.3	2.9	2.9	2.7
1974	2.3	2.3	2.5	2.4	2.4	2.4	2.6	2.6	2.5	2.4	2.5	3.1	2.7	3.0	3.3	2.9	2.8	2.4	2.4	2.1
1975	2.7	2.7	2.9	2.9	2.8	2.9	3.1	3.1	3.1	3.0	3.1	3.6	3.4	3.7	4.0	3.7	3.6	3.3	3.3	3.2
1976	3.2	3.2	3.4	3.4	3.4	3.4	3.7	3.7	3.7	3.6	3.8	4.3	4.1	4.5	4.8	4.5	4.5	4.3	4.4	4.4
1977	3.1	3.2	3.3	3.3	3.3	3.4	3.6	3.6	3.6	3.5	3.7	4.2	4.0	4.3	4.6	4.4	4.3	4.1	4.2	4.2
1978	3.0	3.1	3.2	3.2	3.2	3.2	3.5	3.5	3.5	3.4	3.5	4.0	3.8	4.1	4.4	4.1	4.1	3.8	4.0	3.9
1979	2.8	2.8	3.0	3.0	2.9	3.0	3.2	3.2	3.2	3.1	3.2	3.6	3.4	3.7	3.9	3.7	3.6	3.4	3.4	3.3
1980	2.6	2.7	2.8	2.8	2.8	2.8	3.0	3.0	2.9	2.8	2.9	3.4	3.1	3.4	3.6	3.3	3.3	3.0	3.1	2.9
1981	2.5	2.5	2.7	2.6	2.6	2.6	2.8	2.8	2.8	2.7	2.8	3.2	3.0	3.2	3.4	3.1	3.0	2.8	2.8	2.7
1982	3.4	3.5	3.7	3.6	3.7	3.7	3.9	3.9	3.9	3.9	4.0	4.5	4.3	4.6	4.8	4.6	4.6	4.5	4.6	4.6
1983	3.5	3.6	3.7	3.7	3.7	3.8	4.0	4.0	4.0	4.0	4.1	4.5	4.4	4.6	4.9	4.7	4.7	4.6	4.7	4.7
1984	3.8	3.9	4.1	4.1	4.1	4.1	4.4	4.4	4.4	4.4	4.5	5.0	4.8	5.1	5.3	5.2	5.2	5.1	5.2	5.2
1985	4.4	4.5	4.7	4.7	4.7	4.8	5.0	5.1	5.1	5.1	5.3	5.7	5.6	5.9	6.2	6.1	6.1	6.1	6.2	6.3
1986	4.8	4.9	5.0	5.1	5.1	5.2	5.4	5.5	5.6	5.6	5.7	6.2	6.1	6.4	6.7	6.6	6.7	6.6	6.8	6.9
1987	4.7	4.7	4.9	4.9	5.0	5.0	5.3	5.3	5.4	5.4	5.5	6.0	5.9	6.2	6.4	6.3	6.4	6.3	6.5	6.6
1988	4.8	4.9	5.0	5.1	5.1	5.2	5.4	5.5	5.5	5.5	5.7	6.1	6.0	6.3	6.6	6.5	6.5	6.5	6.7	6.7
1989	5.0	5.1	5.3	5.3	5.4	5.5	5.7	5.7	5.8	5.8	6.0	6.4	6.3	6.6	6.9	6.8	6.9	6.8	7.0	7.1
1990	5.1	5.2	5.3	5.4	5.4	5.5	5.7	5.8	5.8	5.8	6.0	6.4	6.3	6.6	6.9	6.8	6.9	6.8	7.0	7.1
1991	5.4	5.5	5.6	5.7	5.7	5.8	6.0	6.1	6.2	6.2	6.4	6.8	6.7	7.0	7.3	7.2	7.3	7.3	7.4	7.5
1992	5.5	5.5	5.7	5.8	5.8	5.9	6.1	6.2	6.3	6.3	6.5	6.8	6.8	7.1	7.3	7.3	7.3	7.3	7.5	7.6
1993	5.6	5.7	5.9	5.9	6.0	6.1	6.3	6.4	6.4	6.5	6.6	7.0	7.0	7.2	7.5	7.4	7.5	7.5	7.8	7.8
1994	5.4	5.4	5.6	5.7	5.7	5.8	6.0	6.1	6.1	6.1	6.3	6.7	6.6	6.9	7.1	7.0	7.1	7.1	7.2	7.3
1995	5.8	5.9	6.0	6.1	6.1	6.2	6.4	6.5	6.6	6.6	6.8	7.1	7.1	7.4	7.6	7.6	7.6	7.6	7.8	7.9
1996	5.7	5.8	5.9	6.0	6.0	6.1	6.3	6.4	6.5	6.5	6.6	7.0	6.9	7.2	7.4	7.4	7.5	7.4	7.6	7.7
1997	5.8	5.9	6.1	6.1	6.2	6.3	6.5	6.5	6.6	6.6	6.8	7.1	7.1	7.3	7.6	7.5	7.6	7.6	7.8	7.9
1998	5.9	6.0	6.2	6.2	6.3	6.3	6.5	6.6	6.7	6.7	6.9	7.2	7.2	7.4	7.7	7.6	7.7	7.7	7.8	7.9
1999	5.6	5.7	5.9	5.9	6.0	6.0	6.2	6.3	6.4	6.4	6.5	6.9	6.8	7.0	7.2	7.2	7.3	7.2	7.4	7.5
2000	5.8	5.8	6.0	6.0	6.1	6.2	6.4	6.4	6.5	6.5	6.7	7.0	6.9	7.2	7.4	7.3	7.4	7.4	7.5	7.6
2001	5.9	5.9	6.1	6.1	6.2	6.3	6.5	6.5	6.6	6.6	6.7	7.1	7.0	7.3	7.5	7.4	7.5	7.5	7.6	7.7
2002	6.0	6.1	6.3	6.3	6.4	6.4	6.6	6.7	6.7	6.8	6.9	7.3	7.2	7.4	7.7	7.6	7.7	7.7	7.8	7.9
2003	6.0	6.1	6.3	6.3	6.4	6.4	6.6	6.7	6.7	6.8	6.9	7.2	7.2	7.4	7.6	7.6	7.6	7.6	7.8	7.8
2004	6.1	6.1	6.3	6.3	6.4	6.5	6.7	6.7	6.8	6.8	6.9	7.2	7.2	7.4	7.6	7.6	7.7	7.6	7.8	7.9
2005	6.1	6.1	6.3	6.3	6.4	6.5	6.6	6.7	6.8	6.8	6.9	7.2	7.2	7.4	7.6	7.6	7.6	7.6	7.7	7.8
2006	6.0	6.1	6.2	6.3	6.3	6.4	6.6	6.6	6.7	6.7	6.8	7.1	7.1	7.3	7.5	7.5	7.5	7.5	7.6	7.7
2007	6.0	6.0	6.2	6.2	6.3	6.3	6.5	6.6	6.6	6.6	6.8	7.0	7.0	7.2	7.4	7.4	7.4	7.4	7.5	7.6
2008	6.0	6.1	6.2	6.2	6.3	6.4	6.5	6.6	6.7	6.7	6.8	7.1	7.0	7.2	7.4	7.4	7.4	7.4	7.5	7.6
2009	6.0	6.0	6.2	6.2	6.2	6.3	6.5	6.5	6.6	6.6	6.7	7.0	7.0	7.2	7.3	7.3	7.3	7.3	7.4	7.5
2010	6.1	6.1	6.3	6.3	6.3	6.4	6.6	6.6	6.7	6.7	6.8	7.1	7.1	7.3	7.4	7.4	7.4	7.4	7.5	7.6
2011	6.2	6.3	6.4	6.5	6.5	6.6	6.8	6.8	6.9	6.9	7.0	7.3	7.3	7.4	7.6	7.6	7.6	7.6	7.8	7.8
2012	6.3	6.4	6.5	6.5	6.6	6.7	6.8	6.9	6.9	7.0	7.1	7.3	7.3	7.5	7.7	7.6	7.7	7.7	7.8	7.9
2013	6.1	6.1	6.3	6.3	6.4	6.4	6.6	6.6	6.7	6.7	6.8	7.1	7.0	7.2	7.4	7.3	7.4	7.4	7.5	7.5
2014	6.2	6.3	6.4	6.5	6.5	6.6	6.7	6.8	6.9	6.9	7.0	7.2	7.2	7.4	7.6	7.5	7.6	7.6	7.7	7.7
2015	6.1	6.2	6.3	6.4	6.4	6.5	6.6	6.7	6.7	6.7	6.8	7.1	7.1	7.2	7.4	7.4	7.4	7.4	7.5	7.6

Start Date

Appendix C-3

Long-term Corporate Bonds: Percent per annum total returns for all historical periods
From 1926 to 2015

Start Date	1966	1967	1968	1969	1970	1971	1972	1973	1974	1975	1976	1977	1978	1979	1980	1981	1982	1983	1984	1985
End Date																				
1926																				
1927																				
1928																				
1929																				
1930																				
1931																				
1932																				
1933																				
1934																				
1935																				
1936																				
1937																				
1938																				
1939																				
1940																				
1941																				
1942																				
1943																				
1944																				
1945																				
1946																				
1947																				
1948																				
1949																				
1950																				
1951																				
1952																				
1953																				
1954																				
1955																				
1956																				
1957																				
1958																				
1959																				
1960																				
1961																				
1962																				
1963																				
1964																				
1965																				
1966	0.2																			
1967	-2.4	-5.0																		
1968	-0.8	-1.3	2.6																	
1969	-2.7	-3.6	-2.9	-8.1																
1970	1.2	1.5	3.7	4.3	18.4															

Long-term Corporate Bonds: Percent per annum total returns for all historical periods

From 1926 to 2015

End Date	Start Date 1966	1967	1968	1969	1970	1971	1972	1973	1974	1975	1976	1977	1978	1979	1980	1981	1982	1983	1984	1985
1971	2.8	3.3	5.5	6.5	14.6	11.0														
1972	3.4	4.0	5.8	6.7	12.1	9.1	7.3													
1973	3.1	3.6	5.0	5.6	9.3	6.4	4.2	1.1												
1974	2.4	2.7	3.9	4.1	6.7	3.9	1.7	-1.0	-3.1											
1975	3.6	4.0	5.1	5.5	8.0	6.0	4.8	4.0	5.4	14.6										
1976	4.9	5.4	6.6	7.1	9.4	8.0	7.4	7.5	9.7	16.6	18.6									
1977	4.6	5.0	6.1	6.5	8.4	7.1	6.4	6.3	7.6	11.4	9.9	1.7								
1978	4.2	4.6	5.5	5.8	7.5	6.2	5.5	5.2	6.0	8.4	6.4	0.8	-0.1							
1979	3.6	3.9	4.7	4.8	6.2	5.0	4.2	3.8	4.3	5.8	3.7	-0.9	-2.1	-4.2						
1980	3.2	3.4	4.1	4.2	5.4	4.2	3.4	3.0	3.2	4.3	2.4	-1.4	-2.4	-3.5	-2.8					
1981	2.9	3.1	3.7	3.8	4.8	3.7	3.0	2.5	2.7	3.5	1.8	-1.3	-2.1	-2.7	-2.0	-1.2				
1982	4.9	5.2	5.9	6.1	7.3	6.5	6.0	5.9	6.5	7.7	6.8	4.9	5.6	7.0	11.0	18.7	42.6			
1983	5.0	5.2	5.9	6.1	7.2	6.4	6.1	6.0	6.4	7.6	6.7	5.1	5.7	6.9	9.8	14.4	23.1	6.3		
1984	5.6	5.9	6.5	6.8	7.9	7.1	6.9	6.8	7.4	8.5	7.8	6.5	7.2	8.5	11.2	15.0	21.0	11.4	16.9	
1985	6.7	7.0	7.7	8.0	9.1	8.5	8.4	8.5	9.1	10.3	9.8	8.9	9.8	11.3	14.1	17.9	23.2	17.3	23.3	30.1
1986	7.3	7.6	8.3	8.7	9.7	9.2	9.1	9.2	9.9	11.0	10.7	9.9	10.9	12.4	14.9	18.2	22.5	18.0	22.1	24.9
1987	6.9	7.2	7.9	8.2	9.2	8.6	8.5	8.6	9.1	10.1	9.8	9.0	9.7	10.9	12.9	15.4	18.4	14.1	16.1	15.9
1988	7.1	7.4	8.0	8.3	9.2	8.7	8.6	8.7	9.2	10.2	9.8	9.1	9.8	10.9	12.7	14.8	17.3	13.5	15.0	14.5
1989	7.4	7.8	8.4	8.7	9.6	9.1	9.0	9.1	9.7	10.6	10.3	9.7	10.3	11.3	13.0	14.9	17.1	13.9	15.2	14.9
1990	7.4	7.7	8.3	8.6	9.4	9.0	8.9	9.0	9.5	10.3	10.0	9.4	10.1	11.0	12.4	14.1	15.9	13.0	14.0	13.5
1991	7.9	8.2	8.8	9.0	9.7	9.5	9.4	9.5	10.0	10.9	10.6	10.1	10.7	11.6	13.0	14.6	16.3	13.7	14.7	14.4
1992	7.9	8.2	8.8	9.1	9.9	9.5	9.4	9.5	10.0	10.8	10.6	10.1	10.6	11.5	12.8	14.2	15.7	13.3	14.1	13.7
1993	8.1	8.4	9.0	9.2	10.0	9.7	9.6	9.7	10.2	10.9	10.7	10.2	10.8	11.6	12.8	14.1	15.5	13.3	14.0	13.7
1994	7.6	7.9	8.4	8.6	9.3	9.0	8.9	9.0	9.3	10.0	9.8	9.3	9.8	10.4	11.4	12.5	13.7	11.5	12.0	11.6
1995	8.2	8.5	9.0	9.2	10.0	9.6	9.6	9.7	10.1	10.8	10.6	10.2	10.7	11.3	12.4	13.5	14.6	12.7	13.2	12.9
1996	8.0	8.2	8.7	9.0	9.6	9.3	9.2	9.3	9.7	10.3	10.1	9.7	10.1	10.7	11.7	12.7	13.7	11.8	12.3	11.9
1997	8.1	8.4	8.9	9.1	9.8	9.4	9.4	9.5	9.8	10.4	10.2	9.9	10.3	10.9	11.8	12.7	13.6	11.9	12.3	12.0
1998	8.2	8.5	8.9	9.1	9.8	9.5	9.4	9.5	9.9	10.4	10.3	9.9	10.3	10.9	11.7	12.6	13.4	11.8	12.2	11.9
1999	7.7	7.9	8.4	8.6	9.2	8.9	8.8	8.8	9.2	9.7	9.5	9.1	9.4	9.9	10.7	11.4	12.2	10.6	10.9	10.5
2000	7.8	8.1	8.5	8.7	9.3	9.0	8.9	9.0	9.3	9.8	9.6	9.2	9.6	10.0	10.8	11.5	12.2	10.7	11.0	10.6
2001	7.9	8.2	8.6	8.8	9.3	9.0	9.0	9.0	9.3	9.8	9.6	9.3	9.6	10.1	10.8	11.5	12.1	10.7	11.0	10.6
2002	8.1	8.4	8.8	9.0	9.5	9.3	9.2	9.3	9.6	10.1	9.9	9.6	9.9	10.3	11.0	11.7	12.3	11.0	11.2	10.9
2003	8.1	8.3	8.7	8.9	9.4	9.3	9.1	9.1	9.4	9.9	9.7	9.4	9.7	10.1	10.8	11.4	12.0	10.7	10.9	10.6
2004	8.1	8.3	8.7	8.9	9.4	9.1	9.1	9.1	9.4	9.8	9.7	9.4	9.7	10.1	10.7	11.3	12.0	10.7	10.9	10.6
2005	8.0	8.2	8.6	8.8	9.3	9.0	9.0	9.0	9.3	9.7	9.6	9.3	9.5	9.9	10.5	11.0	11.6	10.4	10.6	10.3
2006	7.9	8.1	8.5	8.6	9.1	8.9	8.8	8.9	9.1	9.5	9.3	9.0	9.3	9.7	10.2	10.7	11.2	10.1	10.3	10.0
2007	7.8	8.0	8.3	8.5	8.9	8.7	8.6	8.7	8.9	9.3	9.1	8.8	9.1	9.4	9.9	10.4	10.9	9.8	9.9	9.7
2008	7.8	8.0	8.3	8.5	8.9	8.7	8.6	8.7	8.9	9.3	9.1	8.8	9.1	9.4	9.9	10.4	10.8	9.8	9.9	9.6
2009	7.7	7.9	8.2	8.3	8.8	8.6	8.5	8.5	8.7	9.1	8.9	8.6	8.9	9.2	9.6	10.1	10.5	9.5	9.6	9.3
2010	7.8	8.0	8.3	8.4	8.9	8.6	8.6	8.6	8.8	9.2	9.0	8.8	9.0	9.3	9.7	10.2	10.6	9.6	9.7	9.5
2011	8.0	8.2	8.5	8.6	9.1	8.9	8.8	8.9	9.1	9.4	9.3	9.0	9.3	9.5	10.0	10.4	10.8	9.9	10.0	9.8
2012	8.1	8.2	8.6	8.7	9.1	8.9	8.9	8.9	9.1	9.4	9.3	9.1	9.3	9.6	10.0	10.4	10.8	9.9	10.0	9.8
2013	7.7	7.9	8.2	8.3	8.7	8.5	8.4	8.5	8.7	9.0	8.8	8.6	8.8	9.0	9.5	9.9	10.2	9.3	9.4	9.2
2014	7.9	8.1	8.4	8.5	8.9	8.7	8.6	8.7	8.9	9.2	9.0	8.8	9.0	9.3	9.7	10.1	10.4	9.6	9.7	9.4
2015	7.7	7.9	8.2	8.3	8.7	8.5	8.4	8.4	8.6	8.9	8.8	8.5	8.7	9.0	9.4	9.7	10.1	9.2	9.3	9.1

Appendix C-3

Long-term Corporate Bonds: Percent per annum total returns for all historical periods
From 1926 to 2015

End Date	Start Date 1986	1987	1988	1989	1990	1991	1992	1993	1994	1995	1996	1997	1998	1999	2000	2001	2002	2003	2004	2005
1971																				
1972																				
1973																				
1974																				
1975																				
1976																				
1977																				
1978																				
1979																				
1980																				
1981																				
1982																				
1983																				
1984																				
1985																				
1986	19.8																			
1987	9.3	-0.3																		
1988	9.8	5.1	10.7																	
1989	11.4	8.7	13.4	16.2																
1990	10.4	8.2	11.2	11.4	6.8															
1991	12.0	10.4	13.3	14.2	13.1	19.9														
1992	11.6	10.3	12.5	13.0	11.9	14.5	9.4													
1993	11.8	10.7	12.6	13.0	12.2	14.1	11.3	13.2												
1994	9.7	8.5	9.8	9.6	8.4	8.8	5.3	3.3	-5.8											
1995	11.3	10.4	11.8	12.0	11.3	12.2	10.4	10.7	9.5	27.2										
1996	10.4	9.5	10.6	10.6	9.8	10.3	8.5	8.3	6.7	13.6	1.4									
1997	10.6	9.8	10.8	10.9	10.2	10.7	9.2	9.2	8.2	13.4	7.0	12.9								
1998	10.6	9.9	10.8	10.9	10.3	10.7	9.5	9.5	8.7	12.7	8.3	11.8	10.8							
1999	9.2	8.4	9.2	9.0	8.4	8.5	7.2	6.9	5.9	8.4	4.1	5.0	1.2	-7.4						
2000	9.4	8.7	9.5	9.4	8.8	9.0	7.8	7.6	6.8	9.1	5.8	6.9	5.0	2.2	12.9					
2001	9.5	8.9	9.5	9.5	8.9	9.1	8.1	7.9	7.3	9.3	6.6	7.7	6.4	4.9	11.8	10.6				
2002	9.9	9.3	10.0	9.9	9.5	9.7	8.8	8.8	8.3	10.2	7.9	9.1	8.3	7.7	13.3	13.5	16.3			
2003	9.6	9.1	9.7	9.6	9.2	9.3	8.5	8.4	8.0	9.6	7.6	8.5	7.8	7.2	11.2	10.7	10.7	5.3		
2004	9.6	9.1	9.6	9.6	9.1	9.3	8.5	8.5	8.0	9.5	7.7	8.5	7.9	7.4	10.7	10.2	10.0	7.0	8.7	
2005	9.4	8.9	9.3	9.3	8.9	9.1	8.3	8.3	7.9	9.2	7.5	8.2	7.7	7.2	9.9	9.3	9.0	6.6	7.3	5.9
2006	9.1	8.6	9.0	9.0	8.6	8.7	8.0	7.9	7.5	8.7	7.1	7.7	7.2	6.7	8.9	8.3	7.8	5.8	5.9	4.5
2007	8.8	8.3	8.7	8.6	8.2	8.3	7.6	7.5	7.1	8.2	6.7	7.2	6.7	6.3	8.1	7.4	6.9	5.1	5.1	3.9
2008	8.8	8.3	8.8	8.7	8.3	8.4	7.7	7.6	7.2	8.2	6.9	7.4	6.9	6.5	8.2	7.6	7.2	5.7	5.8	5.1
2009	8.6	8.1	8.5	8.4	8.0	8.1	7.4	7.3	7.0	7.9	6.6	7.0	6.6	6.2	7.6	7.1	6.6	5.3	5.3	4.7
2010	8.7	8.3	8.7	8.6	8.2	8.3	7.7	7.6	7.3	8.2	7.0	7.4	7.0	6.7	8.1	7.6	7.3	6.2	6.3	5.9
2011	9.0	8.6	9.0	9.0	8.6	8.7	8.2	8.1	7.9	8.7	7.7	8.1	7.7	7.5	8.9	8.5	8.3	7.4	7.7	7.6
2012	9.1	8.7	9.1	9.0	8.7	8.8	8.3	8.3	8.0	8.8	7.8	8.2	7.9	7.7	9.0	8.7	8.5	7.8	8.0	8.0
2013	8.5	8.1	8.4	8.3	8.0	8.1	7.6	7.5	7.2	7.9	6.9	7.3	6.9	6.7	7.8	7.4	7.1	6.3	6.4	6.2
2014	8.8	8.4	8.7	8.7	8.4	8.4	8.0	7.9	7.7	8.4	7.5	7.8	7.5	7.3	8.4	8.1	7.9	7.2	7.4	7.2
2015	8.4	8.1	8.4	8.3	8.0	8.0	7.6	7.5	7.2	7.9	7.0	7.3	7.0	6.8	7.8	7.4	7.2	6.5	6.6	6.5

Appendix C-3

Long-term Corporate Bonds: Percent per annum total returns for all historical periods

From 1926 to 2015

End Date	Start Date 2006	2007	2008	2009	2010	2011	2012	2013	2014	2015
1971										
1972										
1973										
1974										
1975										
1976										
1977										
1978										
1979										
1980										
1981										
1982										
1983										
1984										
1985										
1986										
1987										
1988										
1989										
1990										
1991										
1992										
1993										
1994										
1995										
1996										
1997										
1998										
1999										
2000										
2001										
2002										
2003										
2004										
2005										
2006	3.2									
2007	2.9	2.6								
2008	4.8	5.6	8.8							
2009	4.4	4.8	5.9	3.0						
2010	5.9	6.6	8.0	7.6	12.4					
2011	7.9	8.8	10.4	11.0	15.2	17.9				
2012	8.3	9.1	10.5	10.9	13.6	14.3	10.7			
2013	6.2	6.6	7.3	7.0	8.1	6.6	1.4	-7.1		
2014	7.4	7.9	8.7	8.7	9.9	9.2	6.4	4.4	17.3	
2015	6.5	6.9	7.4	7.2	8.0	7.1	4.5	2.6	7.7	-1.0

Appendix C-4

Long-term Government Bonds: Percent per annum total returns for all historical periods

From 1926 to 2015

End Date	Start Date 1926	1927	1928	1929	1930	1931	1932	1933	1934	1935	1936	1937	1938	1939	1940	1941	1942	1943	1944	1945
1926	7.8																			
1927	8.3	8.9																		
1928	5.5	4.4	0.1																	
1929	5.0	4.1	3.4	3.4																
1930	4.9	4.2	2.7	4.0	4.7															
1931	3.1	2.2	0.6	0.8	-0.5	-5.3														
1932	5.0	4.5	3.7	4.6	5.0	5.2	16.8													
1933	4.4	3.9	3.1	3.7	3.4	3.4	8.1	-0.1												
1934	5.0	4.6	4.0	4.7	4.9	5.0	8.7	4.9	10.0											
1935	5.0	4.7	4.1	4.7	5.0	5.4	7.8	4.9	7.5	5.0										
1936	5.2	4.9	4.5	5.1	5.3	5.4	7.7	5.5	7.5	6.2	7.5									
1937	4.8	4.5	4.1	4.5	4.7	4.7	6.4	4.5	5.6	4.2	3.8	0.2								
1938	4.8	4.6	4.2	4.6	4.8	4.8	6.3	4.6	5.6	4.5	4.4	2.8	5.5							
1939	4.9	4.7	4.4	4.7	4.9	4.9	6.3	4.8	5.7	4.8	4.8	3.9	5.7	5.9						
1940	5.0	4.8	4.5	4.9	5.0	5.0	6.2	5.0	5.7	5.0	5.0	4.4	5.9	6.0	6.1					
1941	4.7	4.5	4.2	4.5	4.6	4.6	5.7	4.5	5.1	4.4	4.3	3.7	4.6	4.3	3.5	0.9				
1942	4.6	4.5	4.2	4.5	4.5	4.5	5.5	4.4	4.9	4.3	4.2	3.6	4.3	4.0	3.4	2.1	3.2			
1943	4.5	4.3	4.0	4.3	4.4	4.3	5.2	4.2	4.6	4.0	3.9	3.4	3.9	3.6	3.1	2.1	2.6	2.1		
1944	4.4	4.2	4.0	4.2	4.3	4.2	5.0	4.1	4.5	3.9	3.8	3.3	3.8	3.5	3.0	2.3	2.7	2.4	2.8	
1945	4.7	4.6	4.3	4.6	4.6	4.6	5.4	4.6	5.0	4.5	4.5	4.1	4.6	4.5	4.3	3.9	4.7	5.1	6.7	10.7
1946	4.5	4.3	4.1	4.3	4.4	4.3	5.0	4.2	4.6	4.1	4.0	3.7	4.1	3.9	3.6	3.2	3.7	3.8	4.4	5.2
1947	4.1	4.0	3.7	3.9	4.0	3.9	4.5	3.8	4.0	3.6	3.5	3.1	3.4	3.2	2.8	2.4	2.6	2.5	2.6	2.5
1948	4.1	4.0	3.7	3.9	3.9	3.9	4.5	3.7	4.0	3.6	3.5	3.1	3.4	3.2	2.9	2.5	2.7	2.6	2.7	2.7
1949	4.2	4.1	3.8	4.0	4.1	4.0	4.6	3.9	4.1	3.8	3.7	3.4	3.7	3.5	3.2	2.9	3.2	3.2	3.4	3.5
1950	4.0	3.9	3.7	3.8	3.9	3.8	4.3	3.7	3.9	3.5	3.4	3.1	3.4	3.2	2.9	2.6	2.8	2.8	2.9	2.9
1951	3.7	3.6	3.3	3.5	3.5	3.4	3.9	3.3	3.4	3.1	3.0	2.7	2.8	2.6	2.4	2.0	2.1	2.0	2.0	1.9
1952	3.6	3.5	3.3	3.4	3.4	3.3	3.8	3.2	3.3	3.0	2.8	2.6	2.7	2.5	2.3	1.9	2.0	1.9	1.9	1.8
1953	3.6	3.5	3.3	3.4	3.4	3.3	3.8	3.2	3.3	3.0	2.9	2.6	2.8	2.6	2.4	2.1	2.2	2.1	2.1	2.0
1954	3.7	3.6	3.4	3.5	3.6	3.5	3.9	3.4	3.5	3.2	3.1	2.9	3.0	2.9	2.7	2.4	2.6	2.5	2.5	2.5
1955	3.6	3.4	3.2	3.4	3.4	3.3	3.7	3.1	3.3	3.0	2.9	2.6	2.8	2.6	2.4	2.2	2.3	2.2	2.2	2.2
1956	3.3	3.1	2.9	3.0	3.0	3.0	3.3	2.8	2.9	2.6	2.5	2.2	2.3	2.2	1.9	1.7	1.7	1.6	1.6	1.5
1957	3.4	3.3	3.1	3.2	3.2	3.1	3.5	3.0	3.1	2.8	2.7	2.5	2.6	2.4	2.2	2.0	2.1	2.0	2.0	1.9
1958	3.1	3.0	2.8	2.9	2.8	2.8	3.1	2.6	2.7	2.4	2.3	2.1	2.1	2.0	1.8	1.5	1.6	1.5	1.4	1.3
1959	2.9	2.8	2.6	2.7	2.7	2.6	2.9	2.4	2.5	2.2	2.1	1.9	1.9	1.8	1.6	1.3	1.4	1.3	1.2	1.1
1960	3.2	3.1	2.9	3.0	3.0	2.9	3.2	2.8	2.9	2.6	2.5	2.3	2.4	2.3	2.1	1.9	2.0	1.9	1.9	1.8
1961	3.3	3.1	2.9	3.0	3.0	2.9	3.2	2.7	2.8	2.6	2.5	2.3	2.4	2.2	2.1	1.9	1.9	1.8	1.8	1.8
1962	3.2	3.1	3.0	3.1	3.0	3.0	3.3	2.9	3.0	2.7	2.6	2.5	2.5	2.4	2.3	2.1	2.2	2.1	2.1	2.1
1963	3.2	3.1	2.9	3.0	3.1	3.0	3.2	2.8	2.9	2.7	2.6	2.4	2.5	2.4	2.2	2.1	2.1	2.1	2.1	2.0
1964	3.2	3.1	2.9	3.0	3.0	3.0	3.2	2.8	2.9	2.6	2.6	2.4	2.5	2.4	2.3	2.2	2.2	2.1	2.1	2.1
1965	3.2	3.0	2.9	3.0	3.0	2.9	3.2	2.8	2.9	2.7	2.6	2.4	2.5	2.4	2.2	2.1	2.1	2.1	2.1	2.0
1966	3.2	3.1	2.9	3.0	2.9	2.9	3.2	2.8	2.9	2.7	2.6	2.4	2.5	2.4	2.3	2.1	2.2	2.1	2.1	2.1
1967	2.9	2.7	2.6	2.7	2.6	2.6	2.8	2.4	2.5	2.3	2.2	2.0	2.1	2.0	1.8	1.7	1.7	1.6	1.6	1.6
1968	2.8	2.7	2.5	2.6	2.6	2.5	2.7	2.4	2.4	2.2	2.1	2.0	2.0	1.9	1.8	1.6	1.6	1.6	1.6	1.5
1969	2.6	2.5	2.3	2.4	2.4	2.3	2.5	2.1	2.2	2.0	1.9	1.7	1.8	1.7	1.5	1.4	1.4	1.3	1.3	1.2
1970	2.8	2.7	2.5	2.6	2.6	2.5	2.7	2.4	2.5	2.3	2.2	2.0	2.1	2.0	1.9	1.7	1.7	1.7	1.7	1.6

Appendix C-4

Long-term Government Bonds: Percent per annum total returns for all historical periods

From 1926 to 2015

End Date	Start Date 1926	1927	1928	1929	1930	1931	1932	1933	1934	1935	1936	1937	1938	1939	1940	1941	1942	1943	1944	1945
1971	3.0	2.9	2.8	2.8	2.8	2.8	3.0	2.7	2.7	2.5	2.5	2.3	2.4	2.3	2.2	2.1	2.1	2.1	2.1	2.0
1972	3.1	3.0	2.8	2.9	2.9	2.8	3.1	2.7	2.8	2.6	2.6	2.4	2.5	2.4	2.3	2.2	2.2	2.2	2.2	2.2
1973	3.0	2.9	2.8	2.8	2.8	2.8	3.0	2.6	2.7	2.5	2.5	2.3	2.4	2.3	2.2	2.1	2.1	2.1	2.1	2.1
1974	3.0	2.9	2.8	2.8	2.8	2.8	3.0	2.7	2.7	2.6	2.5	2.4	2.4	2.4	2.3	2.1	2.2	2.2	2.2	2.1
1975	3.1	3.0	2.9	3.0	3.0	2.9	3.1	2.8	2.9	2.7	2.7	2.6	2.6	2.5	2.4	2.3	2.4	2.4	2.4	2.4
1976	3.4	3.3	3.2	3.2	3.2	3.2	3.4	3.1	3.2	3.0	3.0	2.9	3.0	2.9	2.8	2.7	2.8	2.8	2.8	2.8
1977	3.3	3.2	3.1	3.2	3.2	3.1	3.3	3.0	3.1	3.0	2.9	2.8	2.9	2.8	2.7	2.6	2.7	2.7	2.7	2.7
1978	3.2	3.1	3.0	3.1	3.1	3.0	3.2	2.9	3.0	2.9	2.8	2.7	2.8	2.7	2.6	2.5	2.6	2.5	2.6	2.6
1979	3.1	3.0	2.9	3.0	3.0	2.9	3.1	2.9	2.9	2.8	2.7	2.6	2.7	2.6	2.5	2.4	2.5	2.5	2.5	2.4
1980	3.0	2.9	2.8	2.9	2.8	2.8	3.0	2.7	2.8	2.6	2.6	2.5	2.5	2.4	2.3	2.3	2.3	2.3	2.3	2.3
1981	3.0	2.9	2.8	2.8	2.8	2.8	3.0	2.7	2.7	2.6	2.5	2.4	2.5	2.4	2.2	2.2	2.3	2.3	2.3	2.2
1982	3.5	3.5	3.4	3.4	3.4	3.4	3.6	3.3	3.4	3.3	3.2	3.1	3.2	3.2	3.0	3.0	3.1	3.1	3.1	3.1
1983	3.5	3.4	3.3	3.4	3.4	3.4	3.5	3.3	3.3	3.2	3.2	3.1	3.2	3.1	3.0	3.0	3.0	3.0	3.0	3.0
1984	3.7	3.6	3.5	3.6	3.6	3.6	3.7	3.5	3.6	3.4	3.4	3.3	3.4	3.4	3.3	3.2	3.3	3.3	3.3	3.3
1985	4.1	4.0	3.9	4.0	4.0	4.0	4.2	4.0	4.0	3.9	3.9	3.8	3.9	3.9	3.8	3.8	3.8	3.9	3.9	3.9
1986	4.4	4.3	4.3	4.3	4.3	4.3	4.5	4.3	4.4	4.3	4.3	4.2	4.3	4.3	4.2	4.2	4.3	4.3	4.3	4.4
1987	4.3	4.2	4.1	4.2	4.2	4.2	4.4	4.2	4.3	4.2	4.1	4.1	4.2	4.1	4.1	4.0	4.1	4.1	4.2	4.2
1988	4.4	4.3	4.2	4.3	4.3	4.3	4.5	4.3	4.4	4.3	4.2	4.2	4.3	4.2	4.2	4.2	4.2	4.2	4.3	4.3
1989	4.6	4.5	4.4	4.5	4.5	4.5	4.7	4.5	4.6	4.5	4.5	4.4	4.5	4.5	4.5	4.4	4.5	4.5	4.6	4.6
1990	4.6	4.5	4.5	4.5	4.6	4.6	4.7	4.5	4.6	4.5	4.5	4.5	4.5	4.5	4.5	4.5	4.5	4.6	4.6	4.7
1991	4.8	4.7	4.7	4.8	4.8	4.8	5.0	4.8	4.9	4.8	4.8	4.7	4.8	4.8	4.8	4.7	4.8	4.8	4.9	4.9
1992	4.8	4.8	4.7	4.8	4.8	4.8	5.0	4.8	4.9	4.8	4.8	4.8	4.9	4.8	4.8	4.8	4.9	4.9	5.0	5.0
1993	5.0	5.0	4.9	5.0	5.0	5.0	5.2	5.0	5.1	5.0	5.0	5.0	5.1	5.1	5.1	5.0	5.1	5.2	5.2	5.3
1994	4.8	4.8	4.7	4.8	4.8	4.8	5.0	4.8	4.9	4.8	4.8	4.8	4.8	4.8	4.8	4.8	4.9	4.9	4.9	5.0
1995	5.2	5.1	5.1	5.2	5.2	5.2	5.4	5.2	5.3	5.2	5.2	5.2	5.3	5.2	5.2	5.2	5.3	5.3	5.4	5.5
1996	5.1	5.0	5.0	5.1	5.1	5.1	5.3	5.1	5.2	5.1	5.1	5.1	5.1	5.1	5.1	5.1	5.2	5.2	5.3	5.3
1997	5.2	5.2	5.1	5.2	5.2	5.2	5.4	5.2	5.3	5.3	5.3	5.2	5.3	5.3	5.3	5.3	5.4	5.4	5.5	5.5
1998	5.3	5.3	5.2	5.3	5.3	5.4	5.5	5.4	5.4	5.4	5.4	5.3	5.4	5.4	5.4	5.4	5.5	5.5	5.6	5.7
1999	5.1	5.1	5.0	5.1	5.1	5.1	5.3	5.1	5.2	5.1	5.1	5.1	5.2	5.2	5.2	5.2	5.2	5.3	5.3	5.4
2000	5.3	5.3	5.2	5.3	5.3	5.4	5.5	5.4	5.4	5.4	5.4	5.3	5.4	5.4	5.4	5.4	5.5	5.5	5.6	5.6
2001	5.3	5.3	5.2	5.3	5.3	5.3	5.5	5.3	5.4	5.3	5.4	5.3	5.4	5.4	5.4	5.4	5.5	5.5	5.6	5.6
2002	5.5	5.4	5.4	5.5	5.5	5.5	5.7	5.5	5.6	5.5	5.5	5.5	5.6	5.6	5.6	5.6	5.6	5.7	5.7	5.8
2003	5.4	5.4	5.3	5.4	5.4	5.4	5.6	5.4	5.5	5.5	5.5	5.5	5.5	5.5	5.5	5.5	5.6	5.6	5.7	5.7
2004	5.4	5.4	5.4	5.4	5.4	5.4	5.6	5.5	5.6	5.5	5.5	5.5	5.6	5.6	5.6	5.5	5.6	5.7	5.7	5.8
2005	5.5	5.4	5.4	5.5	5.5	5.5	5.7	5.5	5.6	5.5	5.5	5.5	5.6	5.6	5.6	5.6	5.7	5.7	5.7	5.8
2006	5.4	5.4	5.3	5.4	5.4	5.4	5.6	5.5	5.5	5.5	5.5	5.5	5.5	5.5	5.5	5.5	5.6	5.6	5.7	5.7
2007	5.5	5.4	5.4	5.5	5.5	5.5	5.7	5.5	5.6	5.5	5.5	5.5	5.6	5.6	5.6	5.6	5.6	5.7	5.7	5.8
2008	5.7	5.7	5.6	5.7	5.7	5.7	5.9	5.8	5.8	5.8	5.8	5.8	5.9	5.9	5.9	5.9	5.9	6.0	6.0	6.1
2009	5.4	5.4	5.4	5.4	5.4	5.5	5.6	5.5	5.5	5.5	5.5	5.5	5.5	5.5	5.5	5.5	5.6	5.6	5.7	5.7
2010	5.5	5.4	5.5	5.5	5.5	5.5	5.7	5.6	5.6	5.5	5.5	5.5	5.6	5.6	5.6	5.6	5.6	5.7	5.7	5.8
2011	5.7	5.7	5.6	5.7	5.8	5.8	5.9	5.8	5.8	5.8	5.8	5.8	5.9	5.9	5.9	5.9	5.9	6.0	6.0	6.1
2012	5.7	5.7	5.6	5.7	5.7	5.7	5.9	5.7	5.8	5.8	5.8	5.7	5.8	5.8	5.8	5.8	5.9	5.9	6.0	6.0
2013	5.4	5.4	5.4	5.4	5.5	5.5	5.6	5.5	5.6	5.5	5.5	5.5	5.6	5.6	5.6	5.5	5.6	5.6	5.7	5.7
2014	5.6	5.6	5.6	5.7	5.7	5.7	5.8	5.7	5.8	5.7	5.7	5.7	5.8	5.8	5.8	5.8	5.8	5.9	5.9	6.0
2015	5.6	5.6	5.5	5.6	5.6	5.6	5.8	5.6	5.7	5.6	5.7	5.6	5.7	5.7	5.7	5.7	5.8	5.8	5.8	5.9

Appendix C-4

Long-term Government Bonds: Percent per annum total returns for all historical periods

From 1926 to 2015

End Date	Start Date 1946	1947	1948	1949	1950	1951	1952	1953	1954	1955	1956	1957	1958	1959	1960	1961	1962	1963	1964	1965
1926																				
1927																				
1928																				
1929																				
1930																				
1931																				
1932																				
1933																				
1934																				
1935																				
1936																				
1937																				
1938																				
1939																				
1940																				
1941																				
1942																				
1943																				
1944																				
1945																				
1946	-0.1																			
1947	-1.4	-2.6																		
1948	0.2	0.3	3.4																	
1949	1.7	2.3	4.9	6.4																
1950	1.4	1.8	3.3	3.2	0.1															
1951	0.5	0.6	1.4	0.8	-2.0	-3.9														
1952	0.6	0.7	1.4	0.9	-0.9	-1.4	1.2													
1953	1.0	1.1	1.7	1.4	0.2	0.2	2.4	3.6												
1954	1.6	1.8	2.5	2.4	1.6	1.9	4.0	5.4	7.2											
1955	1.3	1.5	2.0	1.8	1.1	1.3	2.6	3.1	2.9	-1.3										
1956	0.7	0.8	1.1	0.9	0.1	0.1	0.9	0.9	0.0	-3.5	-5.6									
1957	1.2	1.4	1.8	1.6	1.0	1.1	2.0	2.2	1.8	0.0	0.7	7.5								
1958	0.6	0.7	1.0	0.8	0.2	0.2	0.8	0.7	0.2	-1.5	-1.6	0.5	-6.1							
1959	0.4	0.5	0.7	0.5	-0.1	-0.1	0.4	0.3	-0.2	-1.7	-1.8	-0.5	-4.2	-2.3						
1960	1.3	1.4	1.7	1.5	1.1	1.2	1.8	1.9	1.6	0.7	1.2	2.9	1.5	5.5	13.8					
1961	1.3	1.3	1.6	1.5	1.1	1.2	1.7	1.8	1.6	0.8	1.1	2.5	1.3	3.9	7.2	1.0				
1962	1.6	1.7	2.0	1.9	1.5	1.7	2.2	2.3	2.1	1.5	1.9	3.2	2.4	4.7	7.1	3.9	6.9			
1963	1.6	1.7	1.9	1.8	1.5	1.6	2.1	2.2	2.0	1.5	1.8	3.0	2.2	4.0	5.6	3.0	4.0	1.2		
1964	1.7	1.8	2.0	1.9	1.6	1.8	2.2	2.3	2.2	1.7	2.0	3.0	2.4	3.9	5.2	3.1	3.8	2.4	3.5	
1965	1.6	1.7	2.0	1.9	1.6	1.7	2.1	2.2	2.1	1.6	1.9	2.8	2.2	3.4	4.4	2.6	3.1	1.8	2.1	0.7
1966	1.7	1.8	2.0	2.0	1.7	1.8	2.2	2.3	2.2	1.8	2.1	2.9	2.4	3.5	4.3	2.8	3.2	2.3	2.6	2.2
1967	1.2	1.2	1.4	1.3	1.1	1.1	1.5	1.5	1.3	0.9	1.1	1.7	1.1	2.0	2.5	1.0	1.0	-0.1	-0.5	-1.8
1968	1.1	1.2	1.4	1.3	1.0	1.1	1.4	1.4	1.2	0.8	1.0	1.5	1.0	1.7	2.2	0.8	0.8	-0.2	-0.4	-1.4
1969	0.9	0.9	1.1	1.0	0.7	0.7	1.0	1.0	0.8	0.4	0.5	1.0	0.5	1.1	1.4	0.2	0.1	-0.9	-1.2	-2.1
1970	1.3	1.3	1.5	1.4	1.2	1.3	1.5	1.6	1.4	1.1	1.3	1.8	1.3	2.0	2.4	1.3	1.3	0.7	0.6	0.1

Appendix C-4

Long-term Government Bonds: Percent per annum total returns for all historical periods

From 1926 to 2015

End Date	Start Date 1946	1947	1948	1949	1950	1951	1952	1953	1954	1955	1956	1957	1958	1959	1960	1961	1962	1963	1964	1965
1971	1.7	1.8	2.0	1.9	1.7	1.8	2.1	2.1	2.1	1.8	2.0	2.5	2.1	2.8	3.2	2.3	2.5	2.0	2.1	1.9
1972	1.9	1.9	2.1	2.1	1.9	2.0	2.3	2.3	2.3	2.0	2.2	2.7	2.4	3.0	3.4	2.6	2.8	2.4	2.5	2.3
1973	1.8	1.8	1.9	1.9	1.9	1.8	2.1	2.2	2.1	1.8	2.0	2.5	2.2	2.7	3.1	2.3	2.4	2.0	2.1	2.0
1974	1.8	1.9	2.1	2.0	1.9	1.9	2.2	2.3	2.2	1.9	2.1	2.6	2.3	2.8	3.2	2.5	2.6	2.2	2.3	2.2
1975	2.1	2.2	2.3	2.3	2.1	2.2	2.5	2.5	2.5	2.3	2.5	2.9	2.7	3.2	3.5	2.9	3.0	2.7	2.9	2.8
1976	2.5	2.6	2.8	2.8	2.6	2.7	3.0	3.1	3.1	2.9	3.1	3.6	3.4	3.9	4.3	3.7	3.9	3.7	3.9	3.9
1977	2.4	2.5	2.7	2.7	2.5	2.6	2.9	2.9	2.9	2.7	2.9	3.3	3.1	3.7	4.0	3.4	3.6	3.4	3.5	3.5
1978	2.3	2.4	2.6	2.5	2.4	2.5	2.7	2.8	2.8	2.6	2.7	3.1	2.9	3.4	3.7	3.2	3.3	3.1	3.2	3.2
1979	2.2	2.3	2.4	2.4	2.3	2.3	2.6	2.6	2.6	2.4	2.6	2.9	2.7	3.2	3.5	2.9	3.1	2.8	2.9	2.9
1980	2.0	2.1	2.2	2.2	2.1	2.1	2.3	2.4	2.3	2.2	2.3	2.6	2.4	2.8	3.1	2.6	2.7	2.4	2.5	2.5
1981	2.0	2.1	2.2	2.2	2.1	2.1	2.3	2.4	2.3	2.2	2.3	2.6	2.4	2.8	3.0	2.6	2.6	2.4	2.5	2.4
1982	2.9	3.0	3.2	3.1	3.0	3.1	3.4	3.5	3.4	3.3	3.5	3.9	3.7	4.1	4.4	4.0	4.2	4.0	4.2	4.2
1983	2.8	2.9	3.1	3.1	3.0	3.1	3.3	3.4	3.4	3.2	3.4	3.7	3.6	4.0	4.3	3.9	4.0	3.9	4.0	4.0
1984	3.2	3.2	3.4	3.4	3.3	3.4	3.6	3.7	3.7	3.6	3.8	4.1	4.0	4.4	4.7	4.3	4.5	4.4	4.5	4.6
1985	3.8	3.9	4.0	4.1	4.0	4.1	4.4	4.5	4.5	4.4	4.6	5.0	4.9	5.3	5.6	5.3	5.5	5.4	5.6	5.7
1986	4.2	4.3	4.5	4.6	4.5	4.6	4.9	5.0	5.0	5.0	5.2	5.6	5.5	5.9	6.3	6.0	6.2	6.1	6.4	6.5
1987	4.1	4.2	4.3	4.4	4.3	4.4	4.7	4.8	4.8	4.7	4.9	5.3	5.2	5.6	5.9	5.6	5.8	5.8	6.0	6.1
1988	4.2	4.3	4.5	4.5	4.4	4.6	4.8	4.9	4.9	4.9	5.1	5.4	5.4	5.8	6.0	5.8	6.0	5.9	6.1	6.2
1989	4.5	4.6	4.8	4.8	4.8	4.9	5.1	5.2	5.3	5.2	5.4	5.8	5.7	6.1	6.4	6.2	6.4	6.4	6.6	6.7
1990	4.5	4.6	4.8	4.8	4.8	4.9	5.2	5.3	5.3	5.3	5.5	5.8	5.7	6.1	6.4	6.2	6.4	6.3	6.5	6.7
1991	4.8	4.9	5.1	5.2	5.1	5.2	5.5	5.6	5.7	5.6	5.8	6.2	6.1	6.5	6.8	6.6	6.8	6.8	7.0	7.1
1992	4.9	5.0	5.2	5.2	5.2	5.3	5.6	5.7	5.7	5.7	5.9	6.2	6.2	6.6	6.8	6.6	6.8	6.8	7.0	7.1
1993	5.2	5.3	5.4	5.5	5.5	5.6	5.8	6.0	6.0	6.0	6.2	6.5	6.5	6.9	7.2	7.0	7.2	7.2	7.4	7.5
1994	4.9	5.0	5.1	5.2	5.2	5.3	5.5	5.6	5.7	5.6	5.8	6.1	6.1	6.4	6.7	6.5	6.7	6.7	6.8	7.0
1995	5.3	5.5	5.6	5.7	5.7	5.8	6.0	6.1	6.2	6.2	6.4	6.7	6.7	7.1	7.3	7.1	7.3	7.3	7.5	7.7
1996	5.2	5.3	5.5	5.5	5.5	5.6	5.9	6.0	6.0	6.0	6.2	6.5	6.5	6.8	7.1	6.9	7.1	7.1	7.3	7.4
1997	5.4	5.5	5.7	5.7	5.7	5.9	6.1	6.2	6.3	6.2	6.4	6.7	6.7	7.1	7.3	7.1	7.3	7.3	7.5	7.6
1998	5.6	5.7	5.8	5.9	5.9	6.0	6.2	6.3	6.4	6.4	6.6	6.9	6.9	7.2	7.5	7.3	7.5	7.5	7.7	7.8
1999	5.3	5.4	5.5	5.6	5.6	5.7	5.9	6.0	6.0	6.0	6.2	6.5	6.5	6.8	7.0	6.8	7.0	7.0	7.2	7.3
2000	5.5	5.7	5.8	5.9	5.8	6.0	6.2	6.3	6.3	6.3	6.5	6.8	6.8	7.1	7.3	7.2	7.4	7.4	7.5	7.7
2001	5.5	5.6	5.8	5.8	5.8	5.9	6.1	6.2	6.3	6.3	6.4	6.7	6.7	7.0	7.3	7.1	7.3	7.3	7.4	7.5
2002	5.7	5.8	6.0	6.0	6.0	6.1	6.3	6.5	6.5	6.5	6.7	7.0	6.9	7.3	7.5	7.3	7.5	7.5	7.7	7.8
2003	5.6	5.7	5.9	5.9	5.9	6.0	6.3	6.4	6.4	6.4	6.6	6.8	6.8	7.1	7.4	7.2	7.4	7.4	7.5	7.6
2004	5.7	5.8	5.9	6.0	6.0	6.1	6.3	6.4	6.4	6.4	6.6	6.9	6.9	7.2	7.4	7.2	7.4	7.4	7.6	7.7
2005	5.7	5.8	6.0	6.0	6.0	6.1	6.3	6.4	6.5	6.5	6.6	6.9	6.9	7.2	7.4	7.2	7.4	7.4	7.6	7.7
2006	5.6	5.7	5.9	5.9	5.9	6.0	6.2	6.3	6.4	6.4	6.5	6.8	6.8	7.0	7.2	7.1	7.3	7.3	7.4	7.5
2007	5.7	5.8	6.0	6.0	6.0	6.1	6.3	6.4	6.4	6.4	6.6	6.8	6.8	7.1	7.3	7.2	7.3	7.3	7.5	7.6
2008	6.0	6.1	6.3	6.3	6.3	6.4	6.6	6.7	6.8	6.8	6.9	7.2	7.2	7.4	7.7	7.5	7.7	7.7	7.8	7.9
2009	5.6	5.7	5.9	5.9	5.9	6.0	6.2	6.3	6.3	6.3	6.5	6.7	6.7	7.0	7.1	7.0	7.1	7.2	7.3	7.4
2010	5.7	5.8	5.9	6.0	6.0	6.1	6.3	6.3	6.4	6.4	6.5	6.8	6.8	7.0	7.2	7.1	7.2	7.2	7.3	7.4
2011	6.0	6.1	6.2	6.3	6.3	6.4	6.6	6.7	6.7	6.7	6.9	7.1	7.1	7.4	7.6	7.4	7.6	7.6	7.7	7.8
2012	6.0	6.1	6.2	6.2	6.2	6.3	6.5	6.6	6.7	6.7	6.8	7.0	7.0	7.3	7.5	7.4	7.5	7.5	7.6	7.7
2013	5.7	5.8	5.9	5.9	5.9	6.0	6.2	6.3	6.3	6.3	6.4	6.7	6.6	6.9	7.1	6.9	7.1	7.1	7.2	7.3
2014	5.9	6.0	6.1	6.2	6.2	6.3	6.5	6.5	6.6	6.6	6.7	6.9	6.9	7.2	7.4	7.2	7.4	7.4	7.5	7.6
2015	5.8	5.9	6.0	6.1	6.1	6.2	6.3	6.4	6.5	6.5	6.6	6.8	6.8	7.0	7.2	7.1	7.2	7.2	7.3	7.4

Appendix C-4

Long-term Government Bonds: Percent per annum total returns for all historical periods

From 1926 to 2015

End Date	Start Date 1966	1967	1968	1969	1970	1971	1972	1973	1974	1975	1976	1977	1978	1979	1980	1981	1982	1983	1984	1985
1926																				
1927																				
1928																				
1929																				
1930																				
1931																				
1932																				
1933																				
1934																				
1935																				
1936																				
1937																				
1938																				
1939																				
1940																				
1941																				
1942																				
1943																				
1944																				
1945																				
1946																				
1947																				
1948																				
1949																				
1950																				
1951																				
1952																				
1953																				
1954																				
1955																				
1956																				
1957																				
1958																				
1959																				
1960																				
1961																				
1962																				
1963																				
1964																				
1965																				
1966	3.7																			
1967	-3.0	-9.2																		
1968	-2.1	-4.8	-0.3																	
1969	-2.8	-4.9	-2.7	-5.1																
1970	0.0	-0.9	2.0	3.2	12.1															

Appendix C-4

Long-term Government Bonds: Percent per annum total returns for all historical periods

From 1926 to 2015

End Date	1966	1967	1968	1969	1970	1971	1972	1973	1974	1975	1976	1977	1978	1979	1980	1981	1982	1983	1984	1985
1971	2.1	1.8	4.7	6.4	12.7	13.2														
1972	2.6	2.4	4.9	6.2	10.3	9.4	5.7													
1973	2.1	1.9	3.9	4.7	7.3	5.8	2.2	-1.1												
1974	2.4	2.2	3.9	4.7	6.7	5.4	2.9	1.6	4.4											
1975	3.0	3.0	4.6	5.3	7.1	6.2	4.5	4.1	6.7	9.2										
1976	4.2	4.3	5.9	6.7	8.5	7.9	6.8	7.1	10.0	12.9	16.8									
1977	3.8	3.8	5.2	5.8	7.3	6.6	5.5	5.5	7.2	8.2	7.7	-0.7								
1978	3.4	3.4	4.6	5.1	6.3	5.6	4.5	4.4	5.5	5.8	4.6	-0.9	-1.2							
1979	3.1	3.0	4.1	4.5	5.5	4.8	3.8	3.5	4.3	4.3	3.1	-1.0	-1.2	-1.2						
1980	2.6	2.5	3.5	3.8	4.6	3.9	2.9	2.6	3.1	2.9	1.7	-1.8	-2.1	-2.6	-3.9					
1981	2.5	2.5	3.3	3.6	4.4	3.7	2.8	2.5	2.9	2.7	1.7	-1.1	-1.1	-1.1	-1.1	1.9				
1982	4.4	4.5	5.5	5.9	6.8	6.4	5.8	5.8	6.6	6.8	6.5	4.9	6.0	7.9	11.2	19.6	40.4			
1983	4.2	4.3	5.2	5.5	6.3	5.9	5.3	5.3	6.0	6.1	5.8	4.3	5.1	6.4	8.4	12.9	18.9	0.7		
1984	4.8	4.9	5.7	6.1	6.9	6.6	6.1	6.1	6.8	7.0	6.8	5.6	6.5	7.9	9.8	13.5	17.7	7.8	15.5	
1985	6.0	6.1	7.0	7.5	8.3	8.0	7.7	7.8	8.6	9.0	9.0	8.2	9.3	10.9	13.1	16.8	20.9	15.0	23.0	31.0
1986	6.8	6.9	7.9	8.3	9.2	9.0	8.7	8.9	9.8	10.2	10.3	9.7	10.9	12.5	14.6	18.1	21.6	17.3	23.5	27.7
1987	6.3	6.5	7.3	7.7	8.5	8.3	8.0	8.1	8.8	9.2	9.2	8.5	9.5	10.7	12.3	14.9	17.2	13.0	16.3	16.6
1988	6.5	6.6	7.4	7.8	8.5	8.4	8.1	8.2	8.9	9.2	9.2	8.6	9.5	10.6	12.0	14.2	16.1	12.5	15.0	14.9
1989	6.9	7.1	7.9	8.3	9.0	8.8	8.6	8.8	9.4	9.8	9.8	9.3	10.2	11.3	12.6	14.6	16.3	13.2	15.5	15.5
1990	6.9	7.0	7.8	8.2	8.9	8.7	8.5	8.6	9.2	9.6	9.6	9.1	9.9	10.8	12.0	13.7	15.2	12.3	14.1	13.9
1991	7.4	7.5	8.3	8.7	9.3	9.2	9.0	9.2	9.8	10.1	10.2	9.7	10.5	11.5	12.6	14.2	15.6	13.1	14.8	14.6
1992	7.4	7.5	8.3	8.6	9.3	9.1	9.0	9.1	9.7	10.0	10.0	9.6	10.4	11.2	12.2	13.7	14.9	12.6	14.0	13.8
1993	7.8	7.9	8.6	9.0	9.6	9.5	9.4	9.5	10.1	10.4	10.5	10.1	10.8	11.7	12.7	14.1	15.1	13.1	14.4	14.3
1994	7.2	7.3	8.0	8.3	8.9	8.7	8.6	8.7	9.2	9.4	9.4	9.0	9.6	10.4	11.2	12.3	13.2	11.2	12.2	11.9
1995	7.9	8.1	8.7	9.1	9.7	9.6	9.4	9.6	10.1	10.4	10.4	10.1	10.8	11.5	12.4	13.5	14.4	12.6	13.7	13.5
1996	7.6	7.8	8.4	8.7	9.3	9.2	9.0	9.1	9.6	9.8	9.9	9.5	10.1	10.8	11.5	12.6	13.3	11.6	12.5	12.3
1997	7.9	8.0	8.6	9.0	9.5	9.4	9.2	9.4	9.9	10.1	10.1	9.8	10.4	11.0	11.8	12.8	13.5	11.9	12.7	12.5
1998	8.0	8.2	8.8	9.1	9.6	9.5	9.4	9.5	10.0	10.2	10.3	10.0	10.5	11.1	11.8	12.8	13.5	12.0	12.8	12.6
1999	7.5	7.6	8.2	8.5	8.9	8.8	8.7	8.8	9.2	9.4	9.4	9.1	9.5	10.1	10.7	11.5	12.1	10.6	11.3	11.0
2000	7.9	8.0	8.5	8.8	9.3	9.2	9.1	9.2	9.6	9.8	9.9	9.6	10.0	10.6	11.2	12.0	12.6	11.2	11.8	11.6
2001	7.7	7.9	8.4	8.7	9.1	9.0	8.9	9.0	9.4	9.6	9.6	9.3	9.8	10.3	10.8	11.6	12.1	10.8	11.4	11.1
2002	8.0	8.1	8.7	8.9	9.4	9.3	9.2	9.3	9.7	9.9	9.9	9.6	10.1	10.6	11.1	11.9	12.4	11.1	11.7	11.5
2003	7.8	7.9	8.5	8.7	9.2	9.1	8.9	9.0	9.4	9.6	9.6	9.3	9.7	10.2	10.7	11.4	11.8	10.6	11.2	10.9
2004	7.8	8.0	8.5	8.7	9.1	9.0	8.9	9.0	9.4	9.5	9.6	9.3	9.7	10.1	10.6	11.3	11.8	10.5	11.0	10.8
2005	7.8	7.9	8.4	8.7	9.1	9.0	8.9	9.0	9.3	9.5	9.5	9.2	9.6	10.0	10.5	11.1	11.5	10.4	10.9	10.7
2006	7.7	7.8	8.2	8.5	8.9	8.8	8.7	8.7	9.1	9.2	9.2	9.0	9.3	9.7	10.1	10.7	11.1	10.0	10.4	10.2
2007	7.7	7.8	8.3	8.5	8.9	8.8	8.7	8.8	9.1	9.2	9.2	9.0	9.3	9.7	10.1	10.7	11.0	10.0	10.4	10.2
2008	8.1	8.2	8.7	8.9	9.3	9.2	9.1	9.2	9.5	9.7	9.7	9.5	9.8	10.2	10.6	11.2	11.6	10.6	11.0	10.8
2009	7.5	7.6	8.1	8.3	8.6	8.5	8.4	8.5	8.8	8.9	8.9	8.7	9.0	9.3	9.7	10.2	10.5	9.5	9.9	9.7
2010	7.6	7.7	8.1	8.3	8.7	8.6	8.5	8.5	8.8	8.9	8.9	8.7	9.0	9.3	9.7	10.2	10.5	9.5	9.9	9.7
2011	8.0	8.1	8.5	8.7	9.1	9.0	8.9	9.0	9.3	9.4	9.4	9.2	9.5	9.8	10.2	10.7	11.0	10.1	10.5	10.3
2012	7.9	8.0	8.4	8.6	8.9	8.9	8.8	8.8	9.1	9.2	9.2	9.0	9.3	9.6	10.0	10.5	10.7	9.9	10.2	10.0
2013	7.4	7.5	7.9	8.1	8.4	8.3	8.2	8.2	8.5	8.6	8.6	8.4	8.6	8.9	9.2	9.7	9.9	9.1	9.3	9.1
2014	7.7	7.8	8.2	8.4	8.7	8.6	8.5	8.6	8.9	9.0	9.0	8.8	9.0	9.3	9.7	10.1	10.3	9.5	9.8	9.6
2015	7.6	7.6	8.0	8.2	8.5	8.4	8.3	8.4	8.6	8.7	8.7	8.5	8.8	9.1	9.4	9.8	10.0	9.2	9.5	9.3

Start Date

Appendix C-4

Long-term Government Bonds: Percent per annum total returns for all historical periods
From 1926 to 2015

End Date	Start Date 1986	1987	1988	1989	1990	1991	1992	1993	1994	1995	1996	1997	1998	1999	2000	2001	2002	2003	2004	2005
1971																				
1972																				
1973																				
1974																				
1975																				
1976																				
1977																				
1978																				
1979																				
1980																				
1981																				
1982																				
1983																				
1984																				
1985																				
1986	24.5																			
1987	10.1	-2.7																		
1988	9.9	3.3	9.7																	
1989	11.9	8.0	13.8	18.1																
1990	10.8	7.6	11.2	12.0	6.2															
1991	12.1	9.8	13.2	14.4	12.6	19.3														
1992	11.5	9.5	12.1	12.8	11.0	13.5	8.1													
1993	12.4	10.7	13.1	13.8	12.8	15.1	13.0	18.2												
1994	9.9	8.2	9.9	9.9	8.3	8.9	5.6	4.4	-7.8											
1995	11.9	10.6	12.4	12.8	11.9	13.1	11.6	12.8	10.2	31.7										
1996	10.7	9.4	10.8	11.0	10.0	10.6	9.0	9.2	6.4	14.2	-0.9									
1997	11.1	10.0	11.3	11.5	10.7	11.4	10.1	10.5	8.7	14.8	7.1	15.9								
1998	11.3	10.2	11.5	11.7	11.0	11.6	10.5	10.9	9.5	14.3	9.1	14.4	13.1							
1999	9.7	8.6	9.6	9.6	8.8	9.1	7.9	7.8	6.2	9.2	4.3	6.0	1.5	-9.0						
2000	10.4	9.5	10.5	10.5	9.9	10.3	9.3	9.5	8.3	11.2	7.5	9.7	7.7	5.2	21.5					
2001	10.0	9.1	10.0	10.0	9.4	9.6	8.7	8.8	7.7	10.1	6.8	8.5	6.7	4.7	12.2	3.7				
2002	10.4	9.6	10.5	10.5	10.0	10.3	9.5	9.7	8.8	11.0	8.4	10.0	8.8	7.8	14.1	10.5	17.8			
2003	9.9	9.1	9.9	9.9	9.4	9.6	8.8	8.9	8.0	9.9	7.5	8.7	7.6	6.5	10.8	7.4	9.3	1.4		
2004	9.8	9.1	9.8	9.8	9.3	9.5	8.8	8.9	8.1	9.8	7.6	8.7	7.7	6.8	10.3	7.7	9.1	4.9	8.5	
2005	9.7	9.0	9.7	9.7	9.2	9.4	8.7	8.8	8.0	9.6	7.6	8.6	7.7	7.0	9.9	7.7	8.7	5.9	8.2	7.8
2006	9.3	8.6	9.2	9.2	8.7	8.9	8.2	8.2	7.5	8.9	7.0	7.8	7.0	6.2	8.6	6.6	7.2	4.7	5.8	4.4
2007	9.3	8.7	9.3	9.3	8.8	8.9	8.3	8.3	7.7	8.9	7.2	8.0	7.3	6.6	8.8	7.1	7.6	5.7	6.8	6.2
2008	10.0	9.4	10.0	10.0	9.6	9.8	9.3	9.4	8.8	10.1	8.6	9.4	8.8	8.4	10.5	9.3	10.1	8.8	10.4	10.8
2009	8.8	8.2	8.7	8.7	8.2	8.3	7.8	7.8	7.1	8.2	6.7	7.3	6.6	6.1	7.7	6.3	6.6	5.1	5.7	5.1
2010	8.9	8.3	8.8	8.8	8.3	8.4	7.9	7.9	7.3	8.3	6.9	7.5	6.9	6.4	7.9	6.6	7.0	5.7	6.3	5.9
2011	9.5	9.0	9.5	9.5	9.1	9.3	8.8	8.8	8.3	9.3	8.1	8.7	8.2	7.9	9.4	8.4	8.8	7.9	8.7	8.7
2012	9.3	8.8	9.3	9.2	8.9	9.0	8.5	8.5	8.1	9.0	7.8	8.4	7.9	7.5	8.9	7.9	8.3	7.4	8.1	8.1
2013	8.4	7.9	8.3	8.3	7.9	7.9	7.4	7.4	6.9	7.7	6.5	7.0	6.5	6.0	7.2	6.2	6.4	5.4	5.8	5.5
2014	9.0	8.4	8.9	8.8	8.5	8.6	8.1	8.2	7.7	8.5	7.4	7.9	7.5	7.1	8.3	7.4	7.7	6.9	7.4	7.3
2015	8.6	8.1	8.5	8.5	8.1	8.2	7.8	7.8	7.3	8.1	7.0	7.4	7.0	6.7	7.7	6.9	7.1	6.3	6.7	6.5

Appendix C-4

Long-term Government Bonds: Percent per annum total returns for all historical periods

From 1926 to 2015

| | Start Date | | | | | | | | | |
	2006	2007	2008	2009	2010	2011	2012	2013	2014	2015
End Date										
1971										
1972										
1973										
1974										
1975										
1976										
1977										
1978										
1979										
1980										
1981										
1982										
1983										
1984										
1985										
1986										
1987										
1988										
1989										
1990										
1991										
1992										
1993										
1994										
1995										
1996										
1997										
1998										
1999										
2000										
2001										
2002										
2003										
2004										
2005										
2006	1.2									
2007	5.4	9.9								
2008	11.9	17.6	25.9							
2009	4.5	5.6	3.5	-14.9						
2010	5.6	6.7	5.7	-3.2	10.1					
2011	8.9	10.5	10.7	6.0	18.3	27.1				
2012	8.1	9.3	9.2	5.4	13.1	14.7	3.4			
2013	5.2	5.8	5.2	1.5	6.0	4.7	-5.0	-12.8		
2014	7.2	8.0	7.8	5.0	9.5	9.4	4.0	4.3	24.7	
2015	6.4	7.0	6.7	4.2	7.7	7.3	2.8	2.6	11.3	-0.7

Appendix C-5

Intermediate-term Government Bonds: Percent per annum total returns for all historical periods

From 1926 to 2015

End Date	1926	1927	1928	1929	1930	1931	1932	1933	1934	1935	1936	1937	1938	1939	1940	1941	1942	1943	1944	1945
1926	5.4																			
1927	4.9	4.5																		
1928	3.6	2.7	0.9																	
1929	4.2	3.8	3.4	6.0																
1930	4.7	4.5	4.5	6.4	6.7															
1931	3.5	3.1	2.8	3.4	2.1	-2.3														
1932	4.2	4.0	3.9	4.7	4.3	3.1	8.8													
1933	3.9	3.7	3.6	4.1	3.7	2.7	5.3	1.8												
1934	4.5	4.4	4.3	4.9	4.7	4.2	6.5	5.4	9.0											
1935	4.7	4.7	4.7	5.2	5.1	4.8	6.6	5.9	8.0	7.0										
1936	4.6	4.5	4.5	4.9	4.8	4.5	5.9	5.2	6.3	5.0	3.1									
1937	4.3	4.2	4.2	4.6	4.4	4.1	5.2	4.4	5.1	3.8	2.3	1.6								
1938	4.5	4.4	4.4	4.7	4.6	4.3	5.3	4.7	5.3	4.4	3.6	3.9	6.2							
1939	4.5	4.4	4.4	4.7	4.6	4.3	5.2	4.7	5.2	4.5	3.8	4.1	5.4	4.5						
1940	4.4	4.3	4.3	4.6	4.4	4.2	5.0	4.5	4.9	4.2	3.7	3.8	4.6	3.7	3.0					
1941	4.1	4.0	4.0	4.2	4.1	3.9	4.5	4.0	4.3	3.7	3.1	3.1	3.5	2.6	1.7	0.5				
1942	4.0	3.9	3.9	4.2	4.1	3.7	4.3	3.8	4.1	3.4	3.0	3.1	3.2	2.5	1.8	1.2	1.9			
1943	3.9	3.8	3.8	4.1	3.9	3.6	4.1	3.7	3.9	3.4	2.9	2.9	3.1	2.5	2.0	1.7	2.4	2.8		
1944	3.8	3.7	3.7	4.0	3.7	3.5	4.0	3.6	3.7	3.2	2.8	2.8	2.9	2.4	2.0	1.8	2.2	2.3	1.8	
1945	3.7	3.6	3.6	3.9	3.6	3.4	3.8	3.5	3.6	3.1	2.7	2.7	2.9	2.4	2.0	1.8	2.2	2.3	2.0	2.2
1946	3.6	3.5	3.5	3.8	3.5	3.3	3.6	3.3	3.4	2.9	2.6	2.5	2.7	2.2	1.9	1.7	2.0	2.0	1.7	1.6
1947	3.5	3.4	3.5	3.6	3.5	3.1	3.5	3.1	3.2	2.8	2.4	2.4	2.5	2.1	1.8	1.6	1.8	1.7	1.5	1.4
1948	3.4	3.3	3.3	3.4	3.2	3.1	3.4	3.0	3.1	2.7	2.4	2.3	2.4	2.0	1.8	1.6	1.8	1.8	1.6	1.5
1949	3.4	3.3	3.2	3.3	3.2	3.0	3.3	3.0	3.1	2.7	2.4	2.3	2.4	2.1	1.8	1.7	1.9	1.8	1.7	1.7
1950	3.3	3.2	3.1	3.2	3.1	2.9	3.2	2.9	2.9	2.6	2.3	2.2	2.3	2.0	1.7	1.6	1.7	1.7	1.5	1.5
1951	3.1	3.1	3.0	3.1	3.0	2.8	3.0	2.7	2.8	2.4	2.2	2.1	2.1	1.8	1.6	1.5	1.6	1.5	1.4	1.3
1952	3.1	3.0	2.9	3.0	2.9	2.7	3.0	2.7	2.7	2.4	2.1	2.1	2.1	1.8	1.6	1.5	1.6	1.6	1.4	1.4
1953	3.1	3.0	2.9	3.0	2.9	2.7	3.0	2.7	2.8	2.4	2.2	2.1	2.2	1.9	1.7	1.6	1.7	1.7	1.6	1.6
1954	3.1	3.0	2.9	3.0	2.9	2.7	3.0	2.7	2.8	2.5	2.2	2.2	2.2	2.0	1.8	1.7	1.8	1.8	1.7	1.7
1955	2.9	2.9	2.8	2.9	2.8	2.6	2.8	2.6	2.6	2.3	2.1	2.0	2.0	1.8	1.6	1.5	1.6	1.6	1.5	1.5
1956	2.8	2.8	2.7	2.6	2.6	2.5	2.7	2.4	2.5	2.2	2.0	1.9	1.9	1.7	1.5	1.4	1.5	1.5	1.4	1.3
1957	3.0	2.9	2.9	2.9	2.8	2.7	2.9	2.6	2.7	2.4	2.2	2.2	2.2	2.0	1.9	1.8	1.9	1.9	1.8	1.8
1958	2.9	2.8	2.7	2.8	2.7	2.5	2.7	2.5	2.5	2.3	2.1	2.0	2.0	1.8	1.7	1.6	1.7	1.7	1.6	1.6
1959	2.8	2.7	2.6	2.7	2.6	2.4	2.6	2.4	2.4	2.2	2.0	1.9	1.9	1.7	1.6	1.5	1.6	1.5	1.5	1.4
1960	3.0	2.9	2.9	3.0	2.9	2.7	2.9	2.7	2.7	2.5	2.3	2.3	2.3	2.2	2.0	2.0	2.1	2.1	2.0	2.1
1961	3.0	3.0	2.9	2.9	2.8	2.7	2.9	2.7	2.7	2.5	2.3	2.3	2.3	2.1	2.0	2.0	2.1	2.1	2.0	2.0
1962	3.0	3.0	2.9	3.0	2.9	2.8	3.0	2.8	2.8	2.6	2.4	2.4	2.4	2.3	2.2	2.2	2.2	2.2	2.2	2.2
1963	3.0	2.9	2.9	3.0	2.9	2.8	2.9	2.7	2.8	2.6	2.4	2.4	2.4	2.3	2.2	2.1	2.2	2.2	2.3	2.2
1964	3.0	3.0	2.9	3.0	2.9	2.8	3.0	2.8	2.8	2.6	2.5	2.4	2.5	2.3	2.2	2.2	2.3	2.3	2.3	2.3
1965	3.0	2.9	2.9	3.0	2.9	2.7	2.9	2.7	2.7	2.6	2.4	2.4	2.4	2.3	2.2	2.2	2.2	2.2	2.2	2.2
1966	3.0	3.0	2.9	3.0	2.9	2.8	2.9	2.8	2.8	2.6	2.5	2.5	2.5	2.4	2.3	2.3	2.3	2.3	2.3	2.3
1967	3.0	2.9	2.9	2.9	2.8	2.7	2.9	2.7	2.8	2.6	2.4	2.4	2.4	2.3	2.2	2.2	2.3	2.3	2.3	2.3
1968	3.0	3.0	2.9	3.0	2.9	2.8	2.9	2.8	2.8	2.6	2.5	2.5	2.5	2.4	2.3	2.3	2.4	2.4	2.4	2.4
1969	2.9	2.9	2.8	2.9	2.8	2.7	2.8	2.7	2.7	2.5	2.4	2.4	2.4	2.3	2.2	2.2	2.3	2.3	2.2	2.3
1970	3.2	3.2	3.1	3.2	3.1	3.0	3.2	3.0	3.1	2.9	2.8	2.8	2.8	2.7	2.7	2.6	2.7	2.7	2.7	2.8

Appendix C-5

Intermediate-term Government Bonds: Percent per annum total returns for all historical periods

From 1926 to 2015

End Date	Start Date 1926	1927	1928	1929	1930	1931	1932	1933	1934	1935	1936	1937	1938	1939	1940	1941	1942	1943	1944	1945
1971	3.3	3.3	3.3	3.3	3.3	3.2	3.3	3.2	3.2	3.1	2.9	2.9	3.0	2.9	2.8	2.8	2.9	2.9	3.0	3.0
1972	3.4	3.3	3.3	3.4	3.3	3.2	3.4	3.2	3.3	3.1	3.0	3.0	3.0	3.0	2.9	2.9	3.0	3.0	3.0	3.1
1973	3.4	3.4	3.3	3.4	3.3	3.2	3.4	3.3	3.3	3.1	3.0	3.0	3.1	3.0	3.0	3.0	3.0	3.1	3.1	3.1
1974	3.4	3.4	3.4	3.4	3.3	3.3	3.4	3.3	3.3	3.2	3.1	3.1	3.2	3.1	3.1	3.0	3.1	3.2	3.2	3.2
1975	3.5	3.5	3.5	3.5	3.5	3.4	3.5	3.4	3.5	3.3	3.2	3.2	3.3	3.2	3.2	3.2	3.3	3.3	3.3	3.4
1976	3.7	3.7	3.7	3.7	3.7	3.6	3.7	3.6	3.7	3.5	3.5	3.5	3.5	3.4	3.4	3.4	3.5	3.6	3.6	3.6
1977	3.7	3.6	3.6	3.7	3.6	3.6	3.7	3.6	3.6	3.5	3.4	3.4	3.5	3.4	3.4	3.4	3.5	3.5	3.5	3.6
1978	3.7	3.6	3.6	3.7	3.6	3.6	3.7	3.6	3.6	3.5	3.4	3.4	3.5	3.4	3.4	3.4	3.5	3.5	3.5	3.6
1979	3.7	3.6	3.6	3.7	3.6	3.6	3.7	3.6	3.6	3.5	3.4	3.4	3.5	3.4	3.4	3.4	3.5	3.5	3.5	3.6
1980	3.7	3.6	3.6	3.7	3.6	3.6	3.7	3.6	3.6	3.5	3.4	3.4	3.5	3.4	3.4	3.4	3.5	3.5	3.5	3.6
1981	3.8	3.7	3.7	3.8	3.7	3.7	3.8	3.7	3.7	3.6	3.6	3.6	3.6	3.6	3.5	3.6	3.6	3.7	3.7	3.7
1982	4.2	4.1	4.1	4.2	4.2	4.1	4.2	4.2	4.2	4.1	4.0	4.1	4.1	4.1	4.1	4.1	4.2	4.2	4.3	4.3
1983	4.2	4.2	4.2	4.3	4.2	4.2	4.3	4.2	4.3	4.2	4.1	4.1	4.2	4.2	4.1	4.2	4.3	4.3	4.4	4.4
1984	4.4	4.4	4.4	4.4	4.4	4.4	4.5	4.4	4.5	4.4	4.3	4.3	4.4	4.4	4.4	4.4	4.5	4.5	4.6	4.7
1985	4.6	4.6	4.6	4.7	4.7	4.6	4.8	4.7	4.7	4.7	4.6	4.6	4.7	4.7	4.7	4.7	4.8	4.9	4.9	5.0
1986	4.8	4.8	4.8	4.9	4.8	4.8	4.9	4.9	4.9	4.8	4.8	4.8	4.9	4.9	4.9	4.9	5.0	5.1	5.2	5.2
1987	4.8	4.8	4.8	4.8	4.8	4.8	4.9	4.8	4.9	4.8	4.8	4.8	4.9	4.8	4.8	4.9	5.0	5.1	5.1	5.2
1988	4.8	4.8	4.8	4.8	4.8	4.8	4.9	4.9	4.9	4.8	4.8	4.8	4.9	4.9	4.9	4.9	5.0	5.1	5.1	5.2
1989	4.9	4.9	4.9	5.0	5.0	4.9	5.1	5.0	5.1	5.0	4.9	5.0	5.0	5.0	5.0	5.1	5.2	5.2	5.3	5.4
1990	5.0	5.0	5.0	5.1	5.0	5.0	5.1	5.1	5.1	5.1	5.0	5.1	5.1	5.1	5.1	5.2	5.3	5.3	5.4	5.5
1991	5.1	5.1	5.1	5.2	5.2	5.2	5.3	5.2	5.3	5.2	5.2	5.2	5.3	5.3	5.3	5.4	5.5	5.5	5.6	5.7
1992	5.2	5.2	5.2	5.2	5.2	5.2	5.3	5.3	5.3	5.3	5.2	5.3	5.4	5.4	5.3	5.4	5.5	5.6	5.6	5.7
1993	5.3	5.3	5.3	5.3	5.3	5.3	5.4	5.4	5.4	5.4	5.3	5.4	5.5	5.4	5.5	5.5	5.6	5.7	5.7	5.8
1994	5.1	5.1	5.1	5.2	5.2	5.1	5.2	5.2	5.2	5.2	5.2	5.2	5.3	5.2	5.3	5.3	5.4	5.5	5.5	5.6
1995	5.3	5.3	5.3	5.3	5.3	5.3	5.4	5.4	5.4	5.4	5.3	5.4	5.4	5.4	5.5	5.5	5.6	5.7	5.7	5.8
1996	5.2	5.2	5.2	5.3	5.3	5.2	5.4	5.3	5.4	5.3	5.3	5.3	5.4	5.4	5.4	5.4	5.5	5.6	5.6	5.7
1997	5.3	5.3	5.3	5.4	5.3	5.3	5.4	5.4	5.4	5.4	5.3	5.4	5.4	5.4	5.4	5.5	5.6	5.6	5.7	5.8
1998	5.4	5.4	5.4	5.5	5.5	5.5	5.5	5.5	5.5	5.5	5.4	5.5	5.6	5.5	5.6	5.6	5.7	5.7	5.8	5.9
1999	5.3	5.3	5.3	5.4	5.4	5.4	5.4	5.3	5.4	5.3	5.3	5.3	5.4	5.4	5.4	5.4	5.5	5.6	5.6	5.7
2000	5.3	5.4	5.3	5.4	5.4	5.4	5.5	5.4	5.5	5.4	5.4	5.4	5.5	5.5	5.5	5.6	5.6	5.7	5.8	5.8
2001	5.3	5.3	5.4	5.5	5.5	5.4	5.5	5.5	5.5	5.5	5.4	5.5	5.5	5.5	5.5	5.6	5.7	5.7	5.8	5.9
2002	5.4	5.4	5.5	5.5	5.5	5.5	5.6	5.6	5.6	5.6	5.5	5.6	5.6	5.6	5.7	5.7	5.8	5.9	5.9	6.0
2003	5.4	5.4	5.4	5.5	5.5	5.4	5.6	5.5	5.6	5.5	5.5	5.5	5.6	5.6	5.6	5.6	5.7	5.8	5.8	5.9
2004	5.4	5.4	5.4	5.4	5.4	5.4	5.5	5.5	5.5	5.5	5.5	5.4	5.5	5.5	5.6	5.6	5.7	5.7	5.8	5.9
2005	5.3	5.3	5.3	5.4	5.4	5.3	5.5	5.4	5.5	5.4	5.4	5.4	5.5	5.5	5.5	5.5	5.6	5.7	5.7	5.8
2006	5.3	5.3	5.3	5.3	5.3	5.3	5.4	5.4	5.4	5.4	5.4	5.4	5.4	5.4	5.4	5.4	5.5	5.6	5.6	5.7
2007	5.3	5.3	5.3	5.4	5.4	5.4	5.5	5.4	5.5	5.4	5.4	5.5	5.5	5.5	5.5	5.5	5.6	5.6	5.7	5.8
2008	5.4	5.4	5.4	5.5	5.5	5.5	5.6	5.5	5.6	5.5	5.5	5.6	5.6	5.6	5.6	5.7	5.7	5.8	5.8	5.9
2009	5.3	5.3	5.3	5.4	5.4	5.4	5.5	5.4	5.5	5.4	5.4	5.4	5.5	5.5	5.5	5.5	5.6	5.7	5.7	5.8
2010	5.4	5.4	5.4	5.4	5.4	5.4	5.5	5.5	5.5	5.5	5.4	5.5	5.5	5.5	5.5	5.6	5.6	5.7	5.7	5.8
2011	5.4	5.4	5.4	5.5	5.5	5.4	5.5	5.5	5.5	5.5	5.5	5.5	5.6	5.6	5.6	5.6	5.7	5.7	5.8	5.8
2012	5.3	5.3	5.4	5.4	5.4	5.4	5.5	5.4	5.5	5.4	5.4	5.5	5.5	5.5	5.5	5.6	5.6	5.7	5.7	5.8
2013	5.2	5.2	5.2	5.3	5.3	5.3	5.4	5.3	5.4	5.3	5.3	5.3	5.4	5.4	5.4	5.4	5.5	5.5	5.6	5.6
2014	5.2	5.2	5.2	5.3	5.3	5.2	5.3	5.3	5.3	5.3	5.3	5.3	5.4	5.3	5.4	5.4	5.5	5.5	5.5	5.6
2015	5.2	5.2	5.2	5.2	5.2	5.2	5.3	5.3	5.3	5.3	5.2	5.3	5.3	5.3	5.3	5.3	5.4	5.5	5.5	5.5

Appendix C-5

Intermediate-term Government Bonds: Percent per annum total returns for all historical periods

From 1926 to 2015

End Date	Start Date 1946	1947	1948	1949	1950	1951	1952	1953	1954	1955	1956	1957	1958	1959	1960	1961	1962	1963	1964	1965
1926																				
1927																				
1928																				
1929																				
1930																				
1931																				
1932																				
1933																				
1934																				
1935																				
1936																				
1937																				
1938																				
1939																				
1940																				
1941																				
1942																				
1943																				
1944																				
1945																				
1946	1.0																			
1947	1.0	0.9																		
1948	1.3	1.4	1.8																	
1949	1.5	1.7	2.1	2.3																
1950	1.4	1.4	1.6	1.5	0.7															
1951	1.2	1.2	1.3	1.1	0.5	0.4														
1952	1.3	1.3	1.4	1.3	0.9	1.0	1.6													
1953	1.5	1.6	1.7	1.6	1.5	1.7	2.4	3.2												
1954	1.6	1.7	1.8	1.8	1.7	2.0	2.5	3.0	2.7											
1955	1.4	1.4	1.5	1.5	1.3	1.4	1.7	1.7	1.0	-0.7										
1956	1.2	1.3	1.3	1.2	1.1	1.1	1.3	1.2	0.5	-0.5	-0.4									
1957	1.8	1.8	1.9	1.9	1.9	2.1	2.3	2.5	2.3	2.2	3.6	7.8								
1958	1.5	1.6	1.6	1.6	1.5	1.6	1.8	1.9	1.6	1.3	2.0	3.2	-1.3							
1959	1.4	1.4	1.5	1.4	1.3	1.4	1.5	1.5	1.2	1.0	1.4	2.0	-0.8	-0.4						
1960	2.1	2.1	2.2	2.3	2.2	2.4	2.6	2.8	2.7	2.7	3.4	4.3	3.2	5.5	11.8					
1961	2.0	2.1	2.2	2.2	2.2	2.3	2.5	2.7	2.6	2.6	3.1	3.8	2.9	4.3	6.7	1.8				
1962	2.2	2.3	2.4	2.5	2.5	2.6	2.8	2.9	2.9	2.9	3.5	4.1	3.4	4.6	6.3	3.7	5.6			
1963	2.2	2.3	2.4	2.4	2.4	2.5	2.7	2.8	2.8	2.8	3.2	3.8	3.1	4.0	5.1	3.0	3.6	1.6		
1964	2.3	2.4	2.5	2.5	2.5	2.6	2.8	2.9	2.9	2.9	3.3	3.8	3.2	4.0	4.9	3.3	3.7	2.8	4.0	
1965	2.2	2.3	2.4	2.5	2.4	2.5	2.7	2.8	2.7	2.7	3.1	3.5	3.0	3.6	4.2	2.8	3.1	2.2	2.5	1.0
1966	2.4	2.4	2.5	2.6	2.6	2.7	2.8	2.9	2.9	2.9	3.2	3.6	3.1	3.7	4.3	3.1	3.4	2.8	3.2	2.8
1967	2.3	2.4	2.4	2.5	2.5	2.6	2.7	2.8	2.8	2.8	3.0	3.4	2.9	3.4	3.9	2.8	3.0	2.5	2.7	2.2
1968	2.4	2.5	2.6	2.6	2.6	2.7	2.8	2.9	2.9	2.9	3.2	3.5	3.1	3.5	4.0	3.0	3.2	2.8	3.0	2.8
1969	2.3	2.3	2.4	2.4	2.4	2.5	2.6	2.7	2.6	2.6	2.9	3.1	2.8	3.1	3.5	2.6	2.7	2.3	2.4	2.1
1970	2.8	2.9	3.0	3.0	3.1	3.2	3.3	3.4	3.4	3.5	3.8	4.1	3.8	4.2	4.6	3.9	4.2	4.0	4.4	4.4

Appendix C-5

Intermediate-term Government Bonds: Percent per annum total returns for all historical periods

From 1926 to 2015

End Date	Start Date 1946	1947	1948	1949	1950	1951	1952	1953	1954	1955	1956	1957	1958	1959	1960	1961	1962	1963	1964	1965
1971	3.0	3.1	3.2	3.3	3.3	3.4	3.6	3.7	3.7	3.8	4.1	4.4	4.1	4.5	5.0	4.4	4.6	4.5	4.9	5.0
1972	3.1	3.2	3.3	3.3	3.4	3.5	3.7	3.8	3.8	3.9	4.1	4.4	4.2	4.6	5.0	4.4	4.7	4.6	4.9	5.0
1973	3.2	3.2	3.3	3.4	3.4	3.6	3.7	3.8	3.8	3.9	4.1	4.4	4.2	4.6	5.0	4.5	4.7	4.6	4.9	5.0
1974	3.2	3.3	3.4	3.5	3.5	3.6	3.8	3.9	3.9	4.0	4.2	4.5	4.3	4.7	5.0	4.5	4.7	4.7	5.0	5.1
1975	3.4	3.5	3.6	3.6	3.7	3.8	4.0	4.1	4.1	4.2	4.4	4.7	4.5	4.8	5.2	4.8	5.0	4.9	5.2	5.3
1976	3.7	3.8	3.9	4.0	4.0	4.1	4.3	4.4	4.5	4.5	4.8	5.1	4.9	5.3	5.6	5.2	5.5	5.5	5.8	5.9
1977	3.6	3.7	3.8	3.9	3.9	4.0	4.2	4.3	4.3	4.4	4.6	4.9	4.7	5.1	5.4	5.0	5.2	5.2	5.5	5.6
1978	3.6	3.7	3.8	3.8	3.9	4.0	4.2	4.3	4.3	4.4	4.6	4.8	4.7	5.0	5.3	4.9	5.1	5.1	5.3	5.4
1979	3.6	3.7	3.8	3.9	3.9	4.0	4.2	4.2	4.3	4.4	4.6	4.8	4.7	4.9	5.2	4.9	5.1	5.0	5.2	5.3
1980	3.6	3.7	3.8	3.9	3.9	4.0	4.1	4.2	4.3	4.3	4.5	4.8	4.6	4.9	5.2	4.8	5.0	5.0	5.2	5.2
1981	3.8	3.9	4.0	4.0	4.1	4.2	4.3	4.4	4.5	4.5	4.7	4.9	4.8	5.1	5.3	5.1	5.2	5.2	5.4	5.5
1982	4.4	4.5	4.6	4.7	4.8	4.9	5.0	5.2	5.2	5.3	5.5	5.8	5.7	6.0	6.3	6.0	6.2	6.3	6.5	6.7
1983	4.5	4.6	4.7	4.8	4.8	5.0	5.1	5.2	5.3	5.4	5.6	5.8	5.8	6.1	6.3	6.1	6.3	6.3	6.6	6.7
1984	4.7	4.8	4.9	5.0	5.1	5.2	5.4	5.5	5.6	5.7	5.9	6.1	6.1	6.3	6.6	6.4	6.6	6.7	6.9	7.1
1985	5.1	5.2	5.3	5.4	5.5	5.6	5.8	5.9	6.0	6.1	6.3	6.6	6.5	6.8	7.1	6.9	7.2	7.2	7.5	7.7
1986	5.3	5.4	5.5	5.6	5.7	5.9	6.0	6.2	6.3	6.4	6.6	6.9	6.8	7.1	7.4	7.2	7.5	7.5	7.8	8.0
1987	5.3	5.4	5.5	5.6	5.7	5.8	6.0	6.1	6.2	6.3	6.5	6.7	6.7	7.0	7.2	7.1	7.3	7.4	7.6	7.8
1988	5.3	5.4	5.5	5.6	5.7	5.8	6.0	6.1	6.2	6.3	6.5	6.7	6.7	6.9	7.2	7.0	7.2	7.3	7.5	7.7
1989	5.5	5.6	5.7	5.8	5.9	6.0	6.1	6.3	6.4	6.5	6.7	6.9	6.9	7.1	7.4	7.3	7.5	7.5	7.8	7.9
1990	5.5	5.7	5.8	5.9	5.9	6.1	6.2	6.4	6.4	6.5	6.8	7.0	7.0	7.2	7.5	7.3	7.5	7.6	7.8	8.0
1991	5.8	5.9	6.0	6.1	6.2	6.3	6.5	6.6	6.7	6.8	7.0	7.2	7.2	7.5	7.7	7.6	7.8	7.9	8.1	8.2
1992	5.8	5.9	6.0	6.1	6.2	6.3	6.5	6.6	6.7	6.8	7.0	7.2	7.2	7.5	7.7	7.6	7.8	7.8	8.1	8.2
1993	5.9	6.0	6.1	6.2	6.3	6.4	6.6	6.7	6.8	6.9	7.1	7.3	7.3	7.6	7.8	7.7	7.9	8.0	8.2	8.3
1994	5.7	5.8	5.9	5.9	6.0	6.2	6.3	6.4	6.5	6.6	6.8	7.0	6.9	7.2	7.4	7.3	7.5	7.5	7.7	7.8
1995	5.9	6.0	6.1	6.2	6.3	6.4	6.5	6.6	6.7	6.8	7.0	7.2	7.2	7.4	7.7	7.5	7.7	7.8	8.0	8.1
1996	5.8	5.9	6.0	6.1	6.2	6.3	6.4	6.5	6.6	6.7	6.9	7.1	7.1	7.3	7.5	7.4	7.6	7.6	7.8	7.9
1997	5.8	5.9	6.0	6.1	6.2	6.3	6.5	6.6	6.7	6.7	6.9	7.1	7.1	7.3	7.5	7.4	7.6	7.6	7.8	7.9
1998	5.9	6.0	6.1	6.2	6.3	6.4	6.5	6.7	6.7	6.8	7.0	7.2	7.2	7.4	7.6	7.5	7.6	7.7	7.9	8.0
1999	5.8	5.9	6.0	6.0	6.1	6.2	6.4	6.5	6.5	6.6	6.8	7.0	6.9	7.2	7.4	7.2	7.4	7.4	7.6	7.7
2000	5.9	6.0	6.1	6.2	6.2	6.4	6.5	6.6	6.7	6.8	6.9	7.1	7.1	7.3	7.5	7.4	7.5	7.6	7.7	7.8
2001	5.9	6.0	6.1	6.2	6.3	6.4	6.5	6.6	6.7	6.8	6.9	7.1	7.1	7.3	7.5	7.4	7.5	7.6	7.7	7.8
2002	6.0	6.1	6.2	6.3	6.4	6.5	6.6	6.7	6.8	6.9	7.1	7.2	7.2	7.4	7.6	7.5	7.7	7.7	7.9	8.0
2003	6.0	6.1	6.2	6.2	6.3	6.4	6.5	6.6	6.7	6.8	7.0	7.1	7.1	7.3	7.5	7.4	7.5	7.6	7.7	7.8
2004	5.9	6.0	6.1	6.2	6.2	6.3	6.5	6.6	6.6	6.7	6.9	7.0	7.0	7.2	7.4	7.3	7.4	7.4	7.6	7.7
2005	5.8	5.9	6.0	6.1	6.2	6.3	6.4	6.5	6.5	6.6	6.7	6.9	6.9	7.1	7.2	7.1	7.3	7.3	7.4	7.5
2006	5.8	5.9	6.0	6.0	6.1	6.2	6.3	6.4	6.5	6.5	6.7	6.8	6.8	7.0	7.1	7.0	7.2	7.2	7.3	7.4
2007	5.9	5.9	6.0	6.1	6.2	6.3	6.4	6.5	6.5	6.6	6.7	6.9	6.9	7.0	7.2	7.1	7.2	7.3	7.4	7.5
2008	6.0	6.1	6.1	6.2	6.3	6.4	6.5	6.6	6.6	6.7	6.9	7.0	7.0	7.2	7.3	7.2	7.3	7.4	7.5	7.6
2009	5.8	5.9	6.0	6.1	6.1	6.2	6.3	6.4	6.5	6.5	6.7	6.8	6.8	7.0	7.1	7.0	7.1	7.2	7.3	7.4
2010	5.9	5.9	6.0	6.1	6.1	6.2	6.3	6.4	6.5	6.6	6.7	6.8	6.8	7.0	7.1	7.0	7.1	7.2	7.3	7.4
2011	5.9	6.0	6.1	6.1	6.2	6.3	6.4	6.5	6.5	6.6	6.7	6.9	6.8	7.0	7.1	7.1	7.2	7.2	7.3	7.4
2012	5.8	5.9	6.0	6.1	6.1	6.2	6.3	6.4	6.4	6.5	6.6	6.8	6.7	6.9	7.0	7.0	7.1	7.1	7.2	7.3
2013	5.7	5.8	5.8	5.9	6.0	6.0	6.1	6.2	6.3	6.3	6.4	6.6	6.5	6.7	6.8	6.7	6.8	6.9	7.0	7.0
2014	5.6	5.7	5.8	5.9	5.9	6.0	6.1	6.2	6.2	6.3	6.4	6.5	6.5	6.6	6.8	6.7	6.8	6.8	6.9	6.9
2015	5.6	5.7	5.7	5.8	5.8	5.9	6.0	6.1	6.1	6.2	6.3	6.4	6.4	6.5	6.7	6.6	6.7	6.7	6.8	6.8

Appendix C-5 (36)

Appendix C-5

Intermediate-term Government Bonds: Percent per annum total returns for all historical periods

From 1926 to 2015

End Date	Start Date 1966	1967	1968	1969	1970	1971	1972	1973	1974	1975	1976	1977	1978	1979	1980	1981	1982	1983	1984	1985
1926																				
1927																				
1928																				
1929																				
1930																				
1931																				
1932																				
1933																				
1934																				
1935																				
1936																				
1937																				
1938																				
1939																				
1940																				
1941																				
1942																				
1943																				
1944																				
1945																				
1946																				
1947																				
1948																				
1949																				
1950																				
1951																				
1952																				
1953																				
1954																				
1955																				
1956																				
1957																				
1958																				
1959																				
1960																				
1961																				
1962																				
1963																				
1964																				
1965																				
1966	4.7																			
1967	2.8	1.0																		
1968	3.4	2.8	4.5																	
1969	2.3	1.6	1.9	-0.7																
1970	5.1	5.2	6.6	7.7	16.9															

Appendix C-5

Intermediate-term Government Bonds: Percent per annum total returns for all historical periods

From 1926 to 2015

End Date	1966	1967	1968	1969	1970	1971	1972	1973	1974	1975	1976	1977	1978	1979	1980	1981	1982	1983	1984	1985
1971	5.7	5.9	7.2	8.0	12.7	8.7														
1972	5.6	5.8	6.8	7.3	10.1	6.9	5.2													
1973	5.5	5.6	6.4	6.8	8.7	6.1	4.9	4.6												
1974	5.5	5.6	6.3	6.6	8.1	6.0	5.2	5.1	5.7											
1975	5.7	5.9	6.5	6.8	8.1	6.4	5.8	6.0	6.8	7.8										
1976	6.4	6.5	7.2	7.5	8.7	7.4	7.2	7.7	8.8	10.3	12.9									
1977	5.9	6.1	6.6	6.8	7.8	6.6	6.2	6.4	6.9	7.3	7.0	1.4								
1978	5.8	5.8	6.3	6.5	7.3	6.2	5.8	5.9	6.2	6.3	5.8	2.4	3.5							
1979	5.6	5.7	6.1	6.3	7.0	5.9	5.6	5.7	5.8	5.9	5.4	3.0	3.8	4.1						
1980	5.5	5.6	5.9	6.1	6.7	5.7	5.4	5.4	5.6	5.5	5.1	3.2	3.8	4.0	3.9					
1981	5.8	5.8	6.2	6.3	6.9	6.1	5.8	5.9	6.0	6.1	5.8	4.4	5.2	5.8	6.6	9.5				
1982	7.0	7.2	7.6	7.8	8.5	7.8	7.7	8.0	8.4	8.7	8.8	8.2	9.6	11.2	13.7	18.9	29.1			
1983	7.0	7.2	7.6	7.8	8.4	7.8	7.7	7.9	8.3	8.6	8.7	8.1	9.2	10.4	12.1	14.9	17.8	7.4		
1984	7.4	7.5	7.9	8.2	8.8	8.2	8.2	8.4	8.8	9.1	9.2	8.8	9.9	11.0	12.5	14.7	16.5	10.7	14.0	
1985	8.0	8.2	8.6	8.8	9.5	9.0	9.0	9.3	9.7	10.1	10.3	10.0	11.2	12.3	13.7	15.8	17.4	13.8	17.1	20.3
1986	8.3	8.5	8.9	9.2	9.8	9.4	9.4	9.7	10.1	10.5	10.7	10.5	11.6	12.6	13.9	15.7	17.0	14.1	16.5	17.7
1987	8.1	8.2	8.6	8.8	9.4	9.0	9.0	9.2	9.6	9.9	10.1	9.8	10.7	11.5	12.5	13.8	14.5	11.8	12.9	12.5
1988	8.0	8.1	8.5	8.7	9.2	8.8	8.8	9.0	9.4	9.6	9.8	9.5	10.3	11.0	11.8	12.8	13.3	10.8	11.5	10.9
1989	8.2	8.4	8.7	8.9	9.4	9.0	9.1	9.3	9.6	9.9	10.0	9.8	10.5	11.2	11.9	12.8	13.3	11.2	11.8	11.4
1990	8.3	8.4	8.8	8.9	9.4	9.1	9.1	9.3	9.6	9.8	10.0	9.8	10.5	11.1	11.7	12.5	12.9	11.0	11.5	11.1
1991	8.5	8.7	9.0	9.2	9.7	9.4	9.4	9.6	9.9	10.2	10.3	10.2	10.8	11.4	12.0	12.8	13.1	11.5	12.0	11.7
1992	8.5	8.6	9.0	9.1	9.6	9.3	9.3	9.5	9.8	10.0	10.1	10.0	10.6	11.1	11.6	12.3	12.6	11.0	11.5	11.1
1993	8.6	8.7	9.0	9.2	9.7	9.4	9.4	9.6	9.8	10.1	10.2	10.0	10.6	11.1	11.6	12.2	12.5	11.1	11.4	11.1
1994	8.1	8.2	8.5	8.6	9.0	8.7	8.7	8.9	9.1	9.3	9.3	9.1	9.6	10.0	10.4	10.9	11.0	9.6	9.8	9.4
1995	8.4	8.5	8.8	8.9	9.3	9.0	9.0	9.2	9.4	9.6	9.7	9.5	10.0	10.4	10.8	11.3	11.4	10.1	10.4	10.1
1996	8.2	8.3	8.5	8.7	9.0	8.7	8.7	8.9	9.1	9.2	9.3	9.1	9.6	9.9	10.3	10.7	10.8	9.6	9.7	9.4
1997	8.2	8.3	8.5	8.7	9.0	8.7	8.7	8.9	9.1	9.2	9.3	9.1	9.5	9.8	10.2	10.5	10.6	9.5	9.6	9.3
1998	8.2	8.3	8.6	8.7	9.1	8.8	8.8	8.9	9.1	9.3	9.3	9.2	9.5	9.9	10.2	10.5	10.6	9.5	9.7	9.4
1999	7.9	8.0	8.2	8.4	8.7	8.4	8.4	8.5	8.7	8.8	8.8	8.7	9.0	9.3	9.5	9.8	9.9	8.8	8.9	8.6
2000	8.0	8.1	8.4	8.5	8.8	8.5	8.5	8.7	8.8	8.9	9.0	8.8	9.2	9.4	9.7	10.0	10.0	9.0	9.1	8.8
2001	8.0	8.1	8.3	8.5	8.8	8.5	8.5	8.6	8.8	8.9	8.9	8.8	9.1	9.3	9.6	9.9	9.9	9.0	9.0	8.8
2002	8.2	8.3	8.5	8.6	8.9	8.6	8.6	8.8	8.9	9.0	9.1	8.9	9.2	9.5	9.7	10.0	10.0	9.1	9.2	9.0
2003	8.0	8.1	8.3	8.4	8.7	8.5	8.4	8.6	8.7	8.8	8.8	8.7	9.0	9.2	9.4	9.7	9.7	8.8	8.9	8.6
2004	7.9	7.9	8.1	8.2	8.5	8.3	8.3	8.4	8.5	8.6	8.6	8.4	8.7	8.9	9.1	9.3	9.3	8.5	8.6	8.3
2005	7.7	7.8	7.9	8.0	8.3	8.1	8.0	8.1	8.2	8.3	8.3	8.2	8.4	8.6	8.8	9.0	9.0	8.2	8.2	8.0
2006	7.6	7.6	7.8	7.9	8.2	7.9	7.9	8.0	8.1	8.2	8.2	8.0	8.3	8.4	8.6	8.8	8.7	8.0	8.0	7.7
2007	7.6	7.7	7.9	8.0	8.2	8.0	8.0	8.0	8.1	8.2	8.2	8.1	8.3	8.5	8.6	8.8	8.8	8.1	8.1	7.8
2008	7.8	7.8	8.0	8.1	8.3	8.1	8.1	8.2	8.3	8.4	8.4	8.2	8.5	8.6	8.8	9.0	9.0	8.2	8.3	8.0
2009	7.5	7.6	7.7	7.8	8.0	7.8	7.8	7.9	8.0	8.0	8.0	7.9	8.1	8.3	8.4	8.6	8.5	7.8	7.8	7.6
2010	7.5	7.6	7.7	7.8	8.0	7.8	7.8	7.9	7.9	8.0	8.0	7.9	8.1	8.2	8.4	8.6	8.5	7.8	7.8	7.6
2011	7.5	7.6	7.8	7.8	8.0	7.8	7.8	7.9	8.0	8.0	8.0	7.9	8.1	8.2	8.4	8.5	8.5	7.8	7.9	7.6
2012	7.4	7.5	7.6	7.7	7.9	7.7	7.7	7.7	7.8	7.9	7.9	7.7	7.9	8.0	8.2	8.3	8.3	7.6	7.6	7.4
2013	7.2	7.2	7.4	7.4	7.6	7.4	7.4	7.4	7.5	7.5	7.5	7.4	7.6	7.7	7.8	7.9	7.9	7.2	7.2	7.0
2014	7.1	7.1	7.3	7.3	7.5	7.3	7.3	7.3	7.4	7.4	7.4	7.3	7.4	7.6	7.7	7.8	7.7	7.1	7.1	6.9
2015	7.0	7.0	7.1	7.2	7.4	7.2	7.1	7.2	7.2	7.3	7.3	7.1	7.3	7.4	7.5	7.6	7.5	6.9	6.9	6.7

(Start Date across top; End Date down the side)

Appendix C-5

Intermediate-term Government Bonds: Percent per annum total returns for all historical periods

From 1926 to 2015

End Date	Start Date 1986	1987	1988	1989	1990	1991	1992	1993	1994	1995	1996	1997	1998	1999	2000	2001	2002	2003	2004	2005
1971																				
1972																				
1973																				
1974																				
1975																				
1976																				
1977																				
1978																				
1979																				
1980																				
1981																				
1982																				
1983																				
1984																				
1985	15.1																			
1986	8.8	2.9																		
1987	7.9	4.5	6.1																	
1988	9.2	7.3	9.6	13.3																
1989	9.3	7.9	9.7	11.5	9.7															
1990	10.3	9.4	11.1	12.8	12.6	15.5														
1991	9.9	9.0	10.3	11.4	10.7	11.2	7.2													
1992	10.1	9.3	10.5	11.3	10.9	11.2	9.2	11.2												
1993	8.2	7.4	8.1	8.4	7.5	6.9	4.2	2.7	-5.1											
1994	9.1	8.4	9.1	9.6	9.0	8.8	7.2	7.2	5.3	16.8										
1995	8.4	7.8	8.3	8.6	8.0	7.7	6.2	5.9	4.2	9.2	2.1									
1996	8.4	7.8	8.3	8.6	8.0	7.8	6.5	6.4	5.2	8.9	5.2	8.4								
1997	8.6	8.0	8.5	8.7	8.3	8.1	7.1	7.0	6.2	9.2	6.8	9.3	10.2							
1998	7.8	7.2	7.6	7.7	7.2	6.9	5.9	5.7	4.8	6.9	4.6	5.5	4.0	-1.8						
1999	8.1	7.6	8.0	8.1	7.7	7.5	6.6	6.6	5.9	7.9	6.2	7.2	6.8	5.2	12.6					
2000	8.1	7.6	8.0	8.1	7.7	7.5	6.7	6.7	6.1	7.8	6.4	7.3	7.0	6.0	10.1	7.6				
2001	8.3	7.9	8.3	8.4	8.1	7.9	7.3	7.3	6.9	8.5	7.3	8.2	8.2	7.7	11.0	10.2	12.9			
2002	8.0	7.6	7.9	8.0	7.7	7.5	6.9	6.8	6.4	7.8	6.7	7.4	7.2	6.6	8.8	7.6	7.5	2.4		
2003	7.7	7.3	7.6	7.7	7.3	7.1	6.5	6.4	6.0	7.2	6.2	6.7	6.5	5.9	7.5	6.2	5.7	2.3	2.3	
2004	7.4	7.0	7.2	7.3	6.9	6.7	6.1	6.0	5.6	6.7	5.7	6.1	5.8	5.2	6.4	5.2	4.6	2.0	1.8	1.4
2005	7.2	6.8	7.0	7.0	6.7	6.5	5.9	5.8	5.4	6.4	5.5	5.8	5.5	4.9	5.9	4.9	4.3	2.3	2.3	2.2
2006	7.3	6.9	7.1	7.2	6.9	6.7	6.2	6.1	5.8	6.6	5.8	6.2	6.0	5.5	6.4	5.6	5.3	3.8	4.1	4.8
2007	7.5	7.2	7.4	7.5	7.2	7.0	6.6	6.5	6.2	7.1	6.4	6.7	6.6	6.2	7.2	6.5	6.4	5.3	5.9	6.8
2008	7.1	6.8	7.0	7.0	6.7	6.5	6.1	6.0	5.7	6.4	5.7	6.0	5.8	5.4	6.2	5.5	5.2	4.2	4.5	4.9
2009	7.1	6.8	7.0	7.0	6.7	6.6	6.1	6.0	5.8	6.5	5.8	6.1	5.9	5.6	6.3	5.6	5.4	4.5	4.8	5.3
2010	7.2	6.9	7.0	7.1	6.8	6.7	6.2	6.2	5.9	6.6	6.0	6.3	6.1	5.8	6.5	5.9	5.8	5.0	5.3	5.8
2011	7.0	6.7	6.8	6.8	6.6	6.4	6.0	6.0	5.7	6.3	5.7	6.0	5.8	5.5	6.1	5.6	5.4	4.7	4.9	5.2
2012	6.6	6.3	6.4	6.4	6.1	6.0	5.6	5.5	5.2	5.8	5.2	5.4	5.2	4.9	5.4	4.8	4.6	3.9	4.0	4.2
2013	6.4	6.1	6.3	6.3	6.0	5.8	5.4	5.4	5.1	5.6	5.1	5.2	5.1	4.8	5.2	4.7	4.5	3.8	3.9	4.1
2014	6.3	6.0	6.1	6.1	5.8	5.7	5.3	5.2	4.9	5.4	4.9	5.1	4.9	4.6	5.0	4.5	4.3	3.6	3.7	3.9

Appendix C-5

Intermediate-term Government Bonds: Percent per annum total returns for all historical periods

From 1926 to 2015

End Date	Start Date 2006	2007	2008	2009	2010	2011	2012	2013	2014	2015
1971										
1972										
1973										
1974										
1975										
1976										
1977										
1978										
1979										
1980										
1981										
1982										
1983										
1984										
1985										
1986										
1987										
1988										
1989										
1990										
1991										
1992										
1993										
1994										
1995										
1996										
1997										
1998										
1999										
2000										
2001										
2002										
2003										
2004										
2005										
2006	3.1									
2007	6.5	10.1								
2008	8.7	11.6	13.1							
2009	5.8	6.7	5.1	-2.4						
2010	6.1	6.8	5.7	2.2	7.1					
2011	6.5	7.2	6.5	4.4	8.0	8.8				
2012	5.8	6.3	5.5	3.7	5.8	5.2	1.7			
2013	4.6	4.8	3.9	2.2	3.4	2.1	-1.0	-3.7		
2014	4.4	4.6	3.8	2.3	3.3	2.4	0.3	-0.4	3.0	
2015	4.1	4.2	3.5	2.2	3.0	2.2	0.7	0.3	2.4	1.8

Appendix C-6

U.S. Treasury Bills: Percent per annum total returns for all historical periods

From 1926 to 2015

End Date	Start Date 1926	1927	1928	1929	1930	1931	1932	1933	1934	1935	1936	1937	1938	1939	1940	1941	1942	1943	1944	1945
1926	3.3																			
1927	3.2	3.1																		
1928	3.3	3.3	3.6																	
1929	3.7	3.8	4.2	4.7																
1930	3.4	3.5	3.6	3.6	2.4															
1931	3.0	3.0	2.9	2.7	1.7	1.1														
1932	2.7	2.6	2.5	2.3	1.5	1.0	1.0													
1933	2.4	2.3	2.2	1.9	1.2	0.8	0.6	0.3												
1934	2.2	2.0	1.9	1.6	1.0	0.6	0.5	0.2	0.2											
1935	2.0	1.8	1.7	1.4	0.8	0.5	0.4	0.2	0.2	0.2										
1936	1.8	1.7	1.5	1.2	0.7	0.5	0.4	0.2	0.2	0.2	0.2									
1937	1.7	1.5	1.4	1.1	0.7	0.4	0.3	0.2	0.2	0.2	0.2	0.3								
1938	1.5	1.4	1.2	1.0	0.6	0.4	0.3	0.2	0.2	0.2	0.2	0.1	0.0							
1939	1.4	1.3	1.1	0.9	0.6	0.3	0.3	0.2	0.2	0.1	0.1	0.1	0.0	0.0						
1940	1.3	1.2	1.1	0.9	0.5	0.3	0.2	0.1	0.1	0.1	0.1	0.1	0.0	0.0	0.0					
1941	1.3	1.1	1.0	0.8	0.5	0.3	0.2	0.1	0.1	0.1	0.1	0.1	0.0	0.0	0.0	0.1				
1942	1.2	1.1	0.9	0.8	0.5	0.3	0.2	0.1	0.1	0.1	0.1	0.1	0.1	0.1	0.0	0.2	0.3			
1943	1.2	1.0	0.9	0.7	0.4	0.3	0.2	0.1	0.2	0.1	0.1	0.1	0.1	0.1	0.1	0.2	0.3	0.3		
1944	1.1	1.0	0.9	0.7	0.4	0.3	0.2	0.2	0.2	0.1	0.1	0.1	0.1	0.1	0.2	0.2	0.3	0.3	0.3	
1945	1.1	1.0	0.8	0.7	0.4	0.3	0.2	0.2	0.2	0.2	0.2	0.2	0.2	0.2	0.2	0.3	0.3	0.3	0.3	0.3
1946	1.0	0.9	0.8	0.7	0.4	0.3	0.3	0.2	0.2	0.2	0.2	0.2	0.2	0.2	0.2	0.3	0.3	0.3	0.3	0.3
1947	1.0	0.9	0.8	0.7	0.4	0.3	0.3	0.2	0.2	0.2	0.2	0.2	0.2	0.2	0.3	0.3	0.4	0.4	0.4	0.4
1948	1.0	0.9	0.8	0.7	0.4	0.3	0.3	0.3	0.3	0.3	0.3	0.3	0.3	0.3	0.3	0.4	0.4	0.4	0.4	0.4
1949	1.0	0.9	0.8	0.7	0.5	0.4	0.3	0.3	0.3	0.3	0.3	0.3	0.3	0.4	0.4	0.5	0.5	0.5	0.5	0.5
1950	1.0	0.9	0.8	0.7	0.5	0.4	0.4	0.4	0.4	0.4	0.4	0.4	0.4	0.4	0.5	0.5	0.6	0.6	0.6	0.6
1951	1.0	0.9	0.9	0.7	0.6	0.5	0.4	0.4	0.4	0.4	0.5	0.5	0.5	0.5	0.6	0.6	0.7	0.7	0.7	0.8
1952	1.1	1.0	0.9	0.8	0.6	0.5	0.5	0.5	0.5	0.5	0.5	0.5	0.6	0.6	0.6	0.7	0.8	0.8	0.8	0.9
1953	1.1	1.0	0.9	0.8	0.7	0.6	0.6	0.5	0.6	0.6	0.6	0.6	0.7	0.7	0.7	0.8	0.9	0.9	0.9	1.0
1954	1.1	1.0	0.9	0.8	0.7	0.6	0.6	0.6	0.6	0.6	0.6	0.7	0.7	0.7	0.7	0.8	0.9	0.9	0.9	1.0
1955	1.1	1.0	0.9	0.8	0.7	0.6	0.6	0.6	0.6	0.6	0.7	0.7	0.7	0.7	0.8	0.9	0.9	1.0	1.0	1.0
1956	1.1	1.1	1.0	0.9	0.8	0.7	0.7	0.7	0.7	0.7	0.7	0.8	0.8	0.8	0.9	0.9	1.0	1.1	1.1	1.2
1957	1.2	1.1	1.1	1.0	0.8	0.8	0.8	0.8	0.8	0.8	0.9	0.9	1.0	1.0	1.0	1.1	1.1	1.3	1.3	1.3
1958	1.2	1.1	1.1	1.0	0.9	0.8	0.8	0.8	0.8	0.9	0.9	0.9	1.0	1.0	1.0	1.1	1.2	1.2	1.3	1.3
1959	1.3	1.2	1.1	1.1	0.9	0.9	0.9	0.9	0.9	0.9	1.0	1.0	1.0	1.1	1.1	1.2	1.3	1.3	1.4	1.4
1960	1.3	1.2	1.2	1.1	1.0	1.0	0.9	0.9	1.0	1.0	1.0	1.1	1.1	1.2	1.2	1.3	1.3	1.4	1.5	1.5
1961	1.3	1.3	1.2	1.1	1.0	1.0	1.0	1.0	1.0	1.0	1.1	1.1	1.2	1.2	1.3	1.3	1.4	1.4	1.5	1.6
1962	1.4	1.3	1.3	1.2	1.1	1.1	1.0	1.0	1.1	1.1	1.1	1.2	1.2	1.3	1.3	1.4	1.4	1.5	1.6	1.6
1963	1.4	1.4	1.3	1.2	1.1	1.1	1.1	1.1	1.1	1.2	1.2	1.2	1.3	1.3	1.4	1.4	1.5	1.6	1.6	1.7
1964	1.5	1.4	1.4	1.3	1.2	1.2	1.2	1.2	1.2	1.2	1.3	1.3	1.4	1.4	1.5	1.5	1.6	1.6	1.7	1.7
1965	1.5	1.5	1.4	1.4	1.3	1.3	1.3	1.3	1.3	1.3	1.4	1.4	1.5	1.5	1.6	1.6	1.7	1.8	1.8	1.9
1966	1.6	1.6	1.5	1.5	1.4	1.3	1.4	1.4	1.4	1.4	1.5	1.5	1.6	1.6	1.7	1.7	1.8	1.9	1.9	2.0
1967	1.7	1.6	1.6	1.5	1.5	1.4	1.4	1.4	1.5	1.5	1.6	1.6	1.7	1.7	1.8	1.8	1.9	2.0	2.0	2.1
1968	1.7	1.7	1.7	1.6	1.5	1.5	1.5	1.6	1.6	1.6	1.7	1.7	1.8	1.8	1.9	2.0	2.0	2.1	2.2	2.2
1969	1.8	1.8	1.8	1.7	1.7	1.6	1.7	1.7	1.7	1.8	1.8	1.9	1.9	2.0	2.0	2.1	2.2	2.3	2.3	2.4
1970	2.0	1.9	1.9	1.9	1.8	1.8	1.8	1.8	1.8	1.9	1.9	2.0	2.1	2.1	2.2	2.3	2.3	2.4	2.5	2.6

Appendix C-6

U.S. Treasury Bills: Percent per annum total returns for all historical periods

From 1926 to 2015

End Date	Start Date 1926	1927	1928	1929	1930	1931	1932	1933	1934	1935	1936	1937	1938	1939	1940	1941	1942	1943	1944	1945
1971	2.0	2.0	1.9	1.9	1.8	1.8	1.9	1.9	1.9	2.0	2.0	2.1	2.1	2.2	2.3	2.3	2.4	2.5	2.6	2.6
1972	2.0	2.0	2.0	2.0	1.9	1.9	1.9	1.9	2.0	2.0	2.1	2.1	2.2	2.2	2.3	2.4	2.4	2.5	2.6	2.7
1973	2.1	2.1	2.1	2.1	2.0	2.0	2.0	2.0	2.1	2.1	2.2	2.2	2.3	2.4	2.4	2.5	2.6	2.7	2.7	2.8
1974	2.3	2.2	2.2	2.2	2.1	2.1	2.2	2.2	2.2	2.3	2.3	2.4	2.4	2.5	2.6	2.7	2.7	2.8	2.9	3.0
1975	2.3	2.3	2.3	2.3	2.2	2.2	2.2	2.3	2.3	2.4	2.4	2.5	2.5	2.6	2.7	2.8	2.8	2.9	3.0	3.1
1976	2.4	2.4	2.3	2.3	2.3	2.3	2.3	2.3	2.4	2.4	2.5	2.5	2.6	2.7	2.7	2.8	2.9	3.0	3.1	3.1
1977	2.4	2.4	2.4	2.4	2.3	2.3	2.4	2.4	2.4	2.5	2.5	2.6	2.7	2.7	2.8	2.9	3.0	3.0	3.1	3.2
1978	2.5	2.5	2.5	2.5	2.4	2.4	2.5	2.5	2.5	2.6	2.6	2.7	2.8	2.8	2.9	3.0	3.1	3.1	3.2	3.3
1979	2.7	2.6	2.6	2.6	2.6	2.6	2.6	2.7	2.7	2.8	2.8	2.9	2.9	3.0	3.1	3.2	3.3	3.3	3.4	3.5
1980	2.8	2.8	2.8	2.8	2.7	2.7	2.8	2.8	2.9	2.9	3.0	3.1	3.1	3.2	3.3	3.4	3.5	3.5	3.6	3.7
1981	3.0	3.0	3.0	3.0	3.0	3.0	3.0	3.1	3.1	3.2	3.2	3.3	3.4	3.5	3.5	3.6	3.7	3.8	3.9	4.0
1982	3.1	3.1	3.1	3.1	3.1	3.1	3.2	3.2	3.3	3.3	3.4	3.5	3.5	3.6	3.7	3.8	3.9	4.0	4.1	4.2
1983	3.2	3.2	3.2	3.2	3.2	3.2	3.3	3.3	3.4	3.4	3.5	3.6	3.6	3.7	3.8	3.9	4.0	4.1	4.2	4.3
1984	3.3	3.3	3.3	3.3	3.3	3.3	3.4	3.4	3.5	3.6	3.6	3.7	3.8	3.9	3.9	4.0	4.1	4.2	4.3	4.4
1985	3.4	3.4	3.4	3.4	3.4	3.4	3.5	3.5	3.6	3.6	3.7	3.8	3.9	3.9	4.0	4.1	4.2	4.3	4.4	4.5
1986	3.5	3.5	3.5	3.5	3.4	3.5	3.5	3.6	3.6	3.7	3.8	3.8	3.9	4.0	4.1	4.2	4.3	4.3	4.4	4.5
1987	3.5	3.5	3.5	3.5	3.5	3.5	3.5	3.6	3.7	3.7	3.8	3.9	3.9	4.0	4.1	4.2	4.3	4.4	4.5	4.6
1988	3.5	3.5	3.5	3.5	3.5	3.5	3.6	3.6	3.7	3.8	3.8	3.9	4.0	4.1	4.1	4.2	4.3	4.4	4.5	4.6
1989	3.6	3.6	3.6	3.6	3.6	3.6	3.7	3.7	3.8	3.8	3.9	4.0	4.1	4.1	4.2	4.3	4.4	4.5	4.6	4.7
1990	3.7	3.7	3.7	3.7	3.7	3.7	3.7	3.8	3.8	3.9	4.0	4.0	4.1	4.2	4.3	4.4	4.5	4.6	4.7	4.8
1991	3.7	3.7	3.7	3.7	3.7	3.7	3.8	3.8	3.9	3.9	4.0	4.1	4.2	4.2	4.3	4.4	4.5	4.6	4.7	4.8
1992	3.7	3.7	3.7	3.7	3.7	3.7	3.8	3.8	3.9	3.9	4.0	4.1	4.1	4.2	4.3	4.4	4.4	4.5	4.6	4.7
1993	3.7	3.7	3.7	3.7	3.7	3.7	3.8	3.8	3.9	3.9	4.0	4.1	4.1	4.2	4.3	4.4	4.4	4.5	4.6	4.7
1994	3.7	3.7	3.7	3.7	3.7	3.7	3.8	3.8	3.9	3.9	4.0	4.1	4.1	4.2	4.3	4.4	4.4	4.5	4.6	4.7
1995	3.7	3.7	3.7	3.7	3.7	3.7	3.8	3.8	3.9	3.9	4.0	4.1	4.1	4.2	4.3	4.4	4.5	4.5	4.6	4.7
1996	3.7	3.7	3.7	3.7	3.7	3.8	3.8	3.8	3.9	4.0	4.0	4.1	4.2	4.2	4.3	4.4	4.5	4.5	4.6	4.7
1997	3.8	3.8	3.8	3.8	3.8	3.8	3.8	3.9	3.9	4.0	4.0	4.1	4.2	4.3	4.3	4.4	4.5	4.6	4.6	4.7
1998	3.8	3.8	3.8	3.8	3.8	3.8	3.8	3.9	3.9	4.0	4.1	4.1	4.2	4.3	4.3	4.4	4.5	4.6	4.6	4.7
1999	3.8	3.8	3.8	3.8	3.8	3.8	3.9	3.9	4.0	4.0	4.1	4.1	4.2	4.3	4.3	4.4	4.5	4.6	4.7	4.7
2000	3.8	3.8	3.8	3.8	3.8	3.8	3.9	3.9	4.0	4.0	4.1	4.2	4.2	4.3	4.4	4.4	4.5	4.6	4.7	4.7
2001	3.8	3.8	3.8	3.8	3.8	3.8	3.9	3.9	4.0	4.0	4.1	4.2	4.2	4.3	4.4	4.4	4.5	4.6	4.7	4.8
2002	3.8	3.8	3.8	3.8	3.8	3.8	3.9	3.9	3.9	4.0	4.0	4.1	4.1	4.2	4.3	4.4	4.5	4.5	4.6	4.7
2003	3.7	3.8	3.8	3.7	3.8	3.8	3.9	3.9	3.9	4.0	4.0	4.1	4.1	4.2	4.3	4.3	4.4	4.5	4.5	4.6
2004	3.7	3.7	3.7	3.7	3.7	3.7	3.8	3.9	3.9	3.9	4.0	4.0	4.1	4.2	4.2	4.3	4.4	4.5	4.5	4.6
2005	3.7	3.7	3.7	3.7	3.7	3.7	3.8	3.8	3.9	3.9	4.0	4.0	4.1	4.1	4.2	4.3	4.3	4.4	4.5	4.5
2006	3.7	3.7	3.7	3.7	3.7	3.8	3.8	3.8	3.9	3.9	4.0	4.0	4.1	4.1	4.2	4.3	4.3	4.4	4.5	4.5
2007	3.7	3.7	3.7	3.7	3.7	3.8	3.8	3.9	3.9	3.9	4.0	4.0	4.1	4.2	4.2	4.3	4.3	4.4	4.5	4.5
2008	3.7	3.7	3.7	3.7	3.7	3.7	3.8	3.8	3.8	3.9	3.9	4.0	4.1	4.1	4.2	4.2	4.3	4.4	4.4	4.5
2009	3.7	3.7	3.6	3.7	3.7	3.7	3.7	3.8	3.8	3.8	3.9	3.9	4.0	4.1	4.1	4.2	4.2	4.3	4.4	4.4
2010	3.6	3.6	3.6	3.6	3.6	3.6	3.7	3.7	3.7	3.8	3.8	3.9	3.9	4.0	4.1	4.1	4.2	4.2	4.3	4.4
2011	3.6	3.6	3.6	3.6	3.6	3.6	3.6	3.7	3.7	3.7	3.8	3.8	3.9	3.9	4.0	4.1	4.1	4.2	4.2	4.3
2012	3.5	3.5	3.6	3.6	3.5	3.5	3.6	3.6	3.7	3.7	3.7	3.8	3.8	3.9	3.9	4.0	4.1	4.1	4.2	4.2
2013	3.5	3.5	3.5	3.5	3.5	3.5	3.6	3.6	3.6	3.6	3.7	3.7	3.8	3.8	3.9	3.9	4.0	4.1	4.1	4.2
2014	3.5	3.5	3.5	3.5	3.4	3.5	3.5	3.5	3.6	3.6	3.6	3.7	3.7	3.8	3.9	3.9	3.9	4.0	4.0	4.1
2015	3.4	3.4	3.4	3.4	3.4	3.4	3.5	3.5	3.5	3.6	3.6	3.6	3.7	3.7	3.8	3.8	3.9	3.9	4.0	4.0

Appendix C-6

U.S. Treasury Bills: Percent per annum total returns for all historical periods

From 1926 to 2015

End Date	Start Date 1946	1947	1948	1949	1950	1951	1952	1953	1954	1955	1956	1957	1958	1959	1960	1961	1962	1963	1964	1965
1926																				
1927																				
1928																				
1929																				
1930																				
1931																				
1932																				
1933																				
1934																				
1935																				
1936																				
1937																				
1938																				
1939																				
1940																				
1941																				
1942																				
1943																				
1944																				
1945																				
1946	0.4																			
1947	0.4	0.5																		
1948	0.6	0.7	0.8																	
1949	0.7	0.8	1.0	1.1																
1950	0.8	0.9	1.0	1.1	1.2															
1951	0.9	1.0	1.2	1.3	1.3	1.5														
1952	1.0	1.1	1.3	1.4	1.4	1.6	1.7													
1953	1.1	1.2	1.3	1.5	1.5	1.7	1.7	1.8												
1954	1.1	1.2	1.3	1.4	1.4	1.5	1.4	1.3	0.9											
1955	1.1	1.2	1.3	1.4	1.4	1.5	1.5	1.4	1.2	1.6										
1956	1.3	1.3	1.4	1.5	1.6	1.6	1.7	1.7	1.6	2.0	2.5									
1957	1.4	1.5	1.6	1.7	1.8	1.9	1.9	2.0	2.0	2.4	2.8	3.1								
1958	1.4	1.5	1.6	1.7	1.7	1.8	1.9	1.9	1.9	2.2	2.4	2.3	1.5							
1959	1.5	1.6	1.7	1.8	1.9	1.9	2.0	2.0	2.1	2.3	2.5	2.5	2.2	3.0						
1960	1.6	1.7	1.8	1.9	1.9	2.0	2.1	2.1	2.2	2.4	2.5	2.6	2.4	2.8	2.7					
1961	1.6	1.7	1.8	1.9	2.0	2.0	2.1	2.1	2.2	2.3	2.5	2.5	2.3	2.6	2.4	2.1				
1962	1.7	1.8	1.9	1.9	2.0	2.1	2.1	2.2	2.2	2.4	2.5	2.5	2.4	2.6	2.5	2.4	2.7			
1963	1.8	1.9	2.0	2.0	2.1	2.2	2.2	2.3	2.3	2.5	2.6	2.6	2.5	2.7	2.7	2.7	2.9	3.1		
1964	1.9	2.0	2.0	2.1	2.2	2.3	2.3	2.4	2.4	2.6	2.7	2.7	2.7	2.9	2.8	2.9	3.1	3.3	3.5	
1965	2.0	2.1	2.1	2.2	2.3	2.4	2.4	2.5	2.5	2.7	2.8	2.9	2.8	3.0	3.0	3.1	3.3	3.5	3.7	3.9
1966	2.1	2.2	2.3	2.4	2.4	2.5	2.6	2.7	2.7	2.9	3.0	3.0	3.0	3.2	3.3	3.4	3.6	3.8	4.1	4.3
1967	2.2	2.3	2.4	2.5	2.5	2.6	2.7	2.8	2.8	3.0	3.1	3.2	3.2	3.3	3.4	3.5	3.7	3.9	4.1	4.3
1968	2.3	2.4	2.5	2.6	2.7	2.8	2.8	2.9	3.0	3.1	3.3	3.3	3.3	3.5	3.6	3.7	3.9	4.1	4.3	4.5
1969	2.5	2.6	2.7	2.8	2.9	3.0	3.0	3.1	3.2	3.4	3.5	3.6	3.6	3.8	3.9	4.0	4.3	4.5	4.7	4.9
1970	2.7	2.8	2.9	3.0	3.0	3.1	3.2	3.3	3.4	3.6	3.7	3.8	3.8	4.0	4.1	4.3	4.5	4.7	5.0	5.2

Appendix C-6

U.S. Treasury Bills: Percent per annum total returns for all historical periods

From 1926 to 2015

End Date	Start Date 1946	1947	1948	1949	1950	1951	1952	1953	1954	1955	1956	1957	1958	1959	1960	1961	1962	1963	1964	1965
1971	2.7	2.8	2.9	3.0	3.1	3.2	3.3	3.4	3.4	3.6	3.7	3.8	3.9	4.0	4.1	4.3	4.5	4.7	4.9	5.1
1972	2.8	2.9	3.0	3.0	3.1	3.2	3.3	3.4	3.5	3.6	3.7	3.8	3.9	4.0	4.1	4.2	4.4	4.6	4.8	4.9
1973	2.9	3.0	3.1	3.2	3.3	3.4	3.5	3.6	3.6	3.8	3.9	4.0	4.1	4.2	4.3	4.4	4.6	4.8	5.0	5.1
1974	3.1	3.2	3.3	3.4	3.5	3.6	3.7	3.8	3.8	4.0	4.1	4.2	4.3	4.5	4.6	4.7	4.9	5.1	5.3	5.4
1975	3.2	3.3	3.4	3.5	3.6	3.7	3.7	3.8	3.9	4.1	4.2	4.3	4.4	4.5	4.6	4.8	5.0	5.1	5.3	5.5
1976	3.2	3.3	3.4	3.5	3.6	3.7	3.8	3.9	4.0	4.1	4.2	4.3	4.4	4.6	4.7	4.8	5.0	5.1	5.3	5.4
1977	3.3	3.4	3.5	3.6	3.7	3.8	3.9	3.9	4.0	4.2	4.3	4.4	4.4	4.6	4.7	4.8	5.0	5.1	5.3	5.4
1978	3.4	3.5	3.6	3.7	3.8	3.9	4.0	4.1	4.2	4.3	4.4	4.5	4.6	4.7	4.8	4.9	5.1	5.3	5.4	5.5
1979	3.6	3.7	3.8	3.9	4.0	4.1	4.2	4.3	4.4	4.5	4.7	4.8	4.8	5.0	5.1	5.2	5.4	5.5	5.7	5.8
1980	3.8	3.9	4.0	4.1	4.2	4.3	4.4	4.5	4.6	4.8	4.9	5.0	5.1	5.3	5.4	5.5	5.7	5.9	6.0	6.2
1981	4.1	4.2	4.3	4.4	4.5	4.7	4.8	4.9	5.0	5.1	5.3	5.4	5.5	5.7	5.8	5.9	6.1	6.3	6.5	6.7
1982	4.3	4.4	4.5	4.6	4.7	4.8	4.9	5.1	5.2	5.3	5.5	5.6	5.7	5.9	6.0	6.1	6.3	6.5	6.7	6.9
1983	4.4	4.5	4.6	4.7	4.8	4.9	5.1	5.2	5.3	5.4	5.6	5.7	5.8	6.0	6.1	6.2	6.4	6.6	6.8	7.0
1984	4.5	4.6	4.8	4.9	5.0	5.1	5.2	5.3	5.4	5.6	5.7	5.8	5.9	6.1	6.2	6.4	6.6	6.8	6.9	7.1
1985	4.6	4.7	4.8	4.9	5.1	5.2	5.3	5.4	5.5	5.7	5.8	5.9	6.0	6.2	6.3	6.4	6.6	6.8	7.0	7.1
1986	4.6	4.8	4.9	5.0	5.1	5.2	5.3	5.4	5.5	5.7	5.8	5.9	6.0	6.2	6.3	6.4	6.6	6.8	6.9	7.1
1987	4.7	4.8	4.9	5.0	5.1	5.2	5.3	5.4	5.5	5.7	5.8	5.9	6.0	6.2	6.3	6.4	6.6	6.7	6.9	7.0
1988	4.7	4.8	4.9	5.0	5.1	5.2	5.3	5.4	5.5	5.7	5.8	5.9	6.0	6.2	6.3	6.4	6.6	6.7	6.9	7.0
1989	4.8	4.9	5.0	5.1	5.2	5.3	5.4	5.5	5.6	5.8	5.9	6.0	6.1	6.2	6.3	6.5	6.6	6.8	6.9	7.1
1990	4.9	5.0	5.1	5.2	5.3	5.4	5.5	5.6	5.7	5.8	5.9	6.0	6.1	6.3	6.4	6.5	6.7	6.8	6.9	7.1
1991	4.9	5.0	5.1	5.2	5.3	5.4	5.5	5.6	5.7	5.8	5.9	6.0	6.1	6.3	6.4	6.5	6.6	6.8	6.9	7.0
1992	4.8	4.9	5.0	5.1	5.2	5.3	5.4	5.5	5.6	5.7	5.9	6.0	6.0	6.2	6.3	6.4	6.5	6.7	6.8	6.9
1993	4.8	4.9	5.0	5.1	5.2	5.3	5.4	5.5	5.5	5.7	5.8	5.9	6.0	6.1	6.2	6.3	6.4	6.5	6.7	6.8
1994	4.8	4.9	4.9	5.0	5.1	5.2	5.3	5.4	5.5	5.6	5.7	5.8	5.9	6.0	6.1	6.2	6.3	6.5	6.6	6.7
1995	4.8	4.9	5.0	5.1	5.2	5.2	5.3	5.4	5.5	5.6	5.7	5.8	5.9	6.0	6.1	6.2	6.3	6.4	6.5	6.6
1996	4.8	4.9	5.0	5.1	5.2	5.2	5.3	5.4	5.5	5.6	5.7	5.8	5.9	6.0	6.1	6.2	6.3	6.4	6.5	6.6
1997	4.8	4.9	5.0	5.1	5.2	5.2	5.3	5.4	5.5	5.6	5.7	5.8	5.9	6.0	6.1	6.1	6.3	6.4	6.5	6.5
1998	4.8	4.9	5.0	5.1	5.2	5.2	5.3	5.4	5.5	5.6	5.7	5.8	5.8	5.9	6.0	6.1	6.2	6.3	6.4	6.5
1999	4.8	4.9	5.0	5.1	5.2	5.2	5.3	5.4	5.5	5.6	5.7	5.7	5.8	5.9	6.0	6.1	6.2	6.3	6.4	6.4
2000	4.8	4.9	5.0	5.1	5.2	5.2	5.3	5.4	5.5	5.6	5.7	5.7	5.8	5.9	6.0	6.1	6.2	6.3	6.3	6.4
2001	4.8	4.9	5.0	5.1	5.1	5.2	5.3	5.4	5.4	5.5	5.6	5.7	5.8	5.9	5.9	6.0	6.1	6.2	6.3	6.4
2002	4.7	4.8	4.9	5.0	5.1	5.1	5.2	5.3	5.4	5.5	5.5	5.6	5.7	5.8	5.8	5.9	6.0	6.1	6.2	6.2
2003	4.7	4.8	4.9	4.9	5.0	5.1	5.1	5.2	5.3	5.4	5.4	5.5	5.6	5.7	5.7	5.8	5.9	6.0	6.0	6.1
2004	4.6	4.7	4.8	4.9	5.0	5.0	5.1	5.1	5.2	5.3	5.4	5.4	5.5	5.6	5.6	5.7	5.8	5.8	5.9	6.0
2005	4.6	4.7	4.8	4.8	4.9	5.0	5.0	5.1	5.1	5.2	5.3	5.4	5.4	5.5	5.6	5.6	5.7	5.8	5.8	5.9
2006	4.6	4.7	4.8	4.8	4.9	5.0	5.0	5.1	5.1	5.2	5.3	5.4	5.4	5.5	5.5	5.6	5.7	5.7	5.8	5.9
2007	4.6	4.7	4.7	4.8	4.9	4.9	5.0	5.1	5.1	5.2	5.3	5.3	5.4	5.5	5.5	5.6	5.7	5.7	5.8	5.8
2008	4.6	4.6	4.7	4.8	4.8	4.9	4.9	5.0	5.1	5.1	5.2	5.3	5.3	5.4	5.4	5.5	5.6	5.6	5.7	5.7
2009	4.5	4.6	4.6	4.7	4.7	4.8	4.9	4.9	5.0	5.1	5.1	5.2	5.3	5.3	5.4	5.4	5.5	5.6	5.6	5.6
2010	4.4	4.5	4.5	4.6	4.6	4.7	4.8	4.8	4.9	5.0	5.0	5.1	5.2	5.2	5.3	5.4	5.5	5.4	5.6	5.5
2011	4.4	4.4	4.5	4.5	4.6	4.6	4.7	4.8	4.8	4.9	4.9	5.0	5.0	5.1	5.1	5.2	5.2	5.3	5.3	5.4
2012	4.3	4.3	4.4	4.5	4.5	4.6	4.6	4.7	4.7	4.8	4.8	4.9	4.9	5.0	5.0	5.1	5.1	5.2	5.2	5.3
2013	4.2	4.3	4.3	4.4	4.4	4.5	4.5	4.6	4.6	4.7	4.8	4.8	4.8	4.9	4.9	5.0	5.0	5.1	5.1	5.1
2014	4.2	4.2	4.3	4.3	4.4	4.4	4.5	4.5	4.6	4.6	4.7	4.7	4.7	4.8	4.8	4.9	4.9	5.0	5.0	5.0
2015	4.1	4.2	4.2	4.3	4.3	4.4	4.4	4.4	4.5	4.6	4.6	4.6	4.7	4.7	4.8	4.8	4.8	4.9	4.9	4.9

Appendix C-6

U.S. Treasury Bills: Percent per annum total returns for all historical periods

From 1926 to 2015

End Date	Start Date 1966	1967	1968	1969	1970	1971	1972	1973	1974	1975	1976	1977	1978	1979	1980	1981	1982	1983	1984	1985
1926																				
1927																				
1928																				
1929																				
1930																				
1931																				
1932																				
1933																				
1934																				
1935																				
1936																				
1937																				
1938																				
1939																				
1940																				
1941																				
1942																				
1943																				
1944																				
1945																				
1946																				
1947																				
1948																				
1949																				
1950																				
1951																				
1952																				
1953																				
1954																				
1955																				
1956																				
1957																				
1958																				
1959																				
1960																				
1961																				
1962																				
1963																				
1964																				
1965																				
1966	4.8																			
1967	4.5	4.2																		
1968	4.7	4.7	5.2																	
1969	5.2	5.3	5.9	6.6																
1970	5.5	5.6	6.1	6.6	6.5															

Appendix C-6

U.S. Treasury Bills: Percent per annum total returns for all historical periods

From 1926 to 2015

End Date	Start Date 1966	1967	1968	1969	1970	1971	1972	1973	1974	1975	1976	1977	1978	1979	1980	1981	1982	1983	1984	1985
1971	5.3	5.4	5.7	5.8	5.5	4.4														
1972	5.1	5.1	5.3	5.3	4.9	4.1	3.8													
1973	5.3	5.4	5.3	5.6	5.4	5.0	5.4	6.9												
1974	5.6	5.7	5.9	5.6	5.9	5.8	6.2	7.5	8.0											
1975	5.6	5.7	5.9	6.0	5.9	5.8	6.1	6.9	6.9	5.8										
1976	5.6	5.6	5.8	5.9	5.8	5.7	5.9	6.4	6.3	5.4	5.1									
1977	5.5	5.6	5.7	5.8	5.7	5.6	5.8	6.2	6.0	5.3	5.1	5.1								
1978	5.7	5.7	5.9	5.9	5.9	5.8	6.0	6.3	6.2	5.8	5.8	6.1	7.2							
1979	6.0	6.1	6.2	6.3	6.3	6.3	6.5	6.9	6.9	6.7	6.9	7.5	8.8	10.4						
1980	6.3	6.4	6.6	6.7	6.7	6.8	7.0	7.4	7.5	7.4	7.8	8.5	9.6	10.8	11.2					
1981	6.8	7.0	7.2	7.3	7.4	7.5	7.8	8.2	8.4	8.4	8.9	9.7	10.8	12.1	13.0	14.7				
1982	7.0	7.2	7.4	7.6	7.6	7.7	8.0	8.5	8.6	8.7	9.1	9.8	10.8	11.7	12.1	12.6	10.5			
1983	7.1	7.3	7.5	7.6	7.7	7.8	8.1	8.5	8.6	8.7	9.1	9.7	10.4	11.1	11.3	11.3	9.7	8.8		
1984	7.3	7.4	7.6	7.8	7.9	7.9	8.2	8.6	8.8	8.8	9.2	9.7	10.4	10.9	11.0	11.0	9.7	9.3	9.8	
1985	7.3	7.4	7.6	7.8	7.8	7.9	8.2	8.5	8.7	8.7	9.0	9.5	10.0	10.4	10.5	10.3	9.2	8.8	8.8	7.7
1986	7.3	7.4	7.5	7.7	7.7	7.8	8.1	8.4	8.5	8.5	8.8	9.1	9.6	9.9	9.8	9.6	8.6	8.1	7.9	6.9
1987	7.2	7.3	7.4	7.6	7.6	7.7	7.9	8.2	8.3	8.3	8.5	8.8	9.2	9.4	9.3	9.0	8.1	7.6	7.3	6.4
1988	7.1	7.2	7.4	7.5	7.6	7.6	7.8	8.1	8.1	8.1	8.3	8.6	8.9	9.1	8.9	8.7	7.8	7.4	7.1	6.4
1989	7.2	7.3	7.4	7.5	7.6	7.7	7.8	8.1	8.1	8.2	8.3	8.6	8.9	9.0	8.9	8.6	7.9	7.5	7.3	6.8
1990	7.2	7.3	7.5	7.6	7.6	7.7	7.8	8.1	8.1	8.1	8.3	8.5	8.8	8.9	8.8	8.5	7.9	7.6	7.4	7.0
1991	7.1	7.2	7.4	7.5	7.5	7.6	7.7	7.9	8.0	8.0	8.1	8.3	8.6	8.7	8.5	8.3	7.7	7.3	7.2	6.8
1992	7.0	7.1	7.2	7.3	7.3	7.4	7.5	7.7	7.7	7.7	7.8	8.0	8.2	8.3	8.1	7.9	7.3	6.9	6.7	6.4
1993	6.9	6.9	7.0	7.1	7.1	7.2	7.3	7.5	7.7	7.5	7.6	7.7	7.9	7.9	7.8	7.5	6.9	6.6	6.4	6.0
1994	6.8	6.8	7.0	7.0	7.0	7.0	7.1	7.3	7.5	7.3	7.4	7.5	7.6	7.7	7.6	7.2	6.7	6.3	6.1	5.8
1995	6.7	6.8	6.9	6.9	7.0	7.0	7.1	7.3	7.3	7.2	7.3	7.4	7.5	7.5	7.4	7.1	6.6	6.3	6.1	5.7
1996	6.7	6.7	6.8	6.8	6.9	6.9	7.0	7.2	7.2	7.1	7.2	7.3	7.4	7.4	7.3	7.0	6.5	6.2	6.0	5.7
1997	6.6	6.7	6.8	6.8	6.8	6.8	6.9	7.1	7.1	7.0	7.1	7.2	7.3	7.3	7.2	6.9	6.4	6.1	6.0	5.7
1998	6.6	6.6	6.7	6.7	6.8	6.8	6.9	7.1	7.0	6.9	7.0	7.1	7.2	7.2	7.1	6.8	6.3	6.1	5.9	5.6
1999	6.5	6.6	6.6	6.7	6.7	6.7	6.8	7.0	6.9	6.9	6.9	7.0	7.1	7.1	7.0	6.7	6.2	6.0	5.8	5.6
2000	6.5	6.5	6.6	6.6	6.7	6.7	6.8	6.9	6.9	6.8	6.9	6.9	7.0	7.0	6.9	6.6	6.2	6.0	5.8	5.6
2001	6.4	6.5	6.5	6.6	6.6	6.6	6.7	6.8	6.7	6.7	6.7	6.8	6.9	6.9	6.7	6.5	6.1	5.9	5.7	5.5
2002	6.3	6.3	6.4	6.4	6.4	6.4	6.5	6.6	6.6	6.5	6.5	6.6	6.7	6.6	6.5	6.3	5.9	5.7	5.5	5.3
2003	6.1	6.2	6.2	6.3	6.3	6.3	6.4	6.4	6.4	6.3	6.3	6.4	6.4	6.4	6.2	6.0	5.7	5.4	5.3	5.0
2004	6.0	6.1	6.1	6.1	6.2	6.1	6.2	6.2	6.2	6.2	6.2	6.2	6.2	6.2	6.0	5.8	5.5	5.2	5.1	4.8
2005	5.9	6.0	6.0	6.0	6.1	6.0	6.1	6.1	6.1	6.1	6.1	6.1	6.1	6.1	5.9	5.7	5.4	5.1	5.0	4.7
2006	5.9	5.9	6.0	6.0	6.0	5.9	6.0	6.1	6.1	6.0	6.0	6.0	6.1	6.0	5.9	5.7	5.3	5.1	5.0	4.7
2007	5.9	5.9	6.0	6.0	6.0	5.9	6.0	6.0	6.0	6.0	6.0	6.0	6.0	6.0	5.8	5.6	5.3	5.1	4.9	4.7
2008	5.8	5.8	5.8	5.9	5.8	5.8	5.9	5.9	5.9	5.8	5.8	5.9	5.9	5.8	5.7	5.5	5.2	5.0	4.8	4.6
2009	5.6	5.7	5.7	5.7	5.7	5.7	5.7	5.8	5.7	5.7	5.7	5.7	5.7	5.6	5.5	5.3	5.0	4.8	4.6	4.4
2010	5.5	5.5	5.6	5.6	5.6	5.5	5.7	5.6	5.6	5.5	5.5	5.5	5.5	5.5	5.3	5.1	4.8	4.6	4.5	4.3
2011	5.4	5.4	5.4	5.4	5.4	5.4	5.4	5.5	5.4	5.4	5.3	5.3	5.4	5.3	5.1	5.0	4.6	4.4	4.3	4.1
2012	5.3	5.3	5.3	5.3	5.3	5.3	5.3	5.3	5.3	5.2	5.2	5.2	5.2	5.1	5.0	4.8	4.5	4.3	4.1	3.9
2013	5.2	5.2	5.2	5.2	5.2	5.1	5.2	5.2	5.1	5.1	5.1	5.1	5.1	5.0	4.8	4.7	4.4	4.2	4.0	3.8
2014	5.1	5.1	5.1	5.1	5.1	5.0	5.0	5.1	5.0	4.9	4.9	4.9	4.9	4.9	4.7	4.5	4.2	4.0	3.9	3.7
2015	5.0	5.0	5.0	5.0	4.9	4.9	4.9	4.9	4.9	4.8	4.8	4.8	4.8	4.7	4.6	4.4	4.1	3.9	3.8	3.6

Appendix C-6

U.S. Treasury Bills: Percent per annum total returns for all historical periods
From 1926 to 2015

End Date	Start Date 1986	1987	1988	1989	1990	1991	1992	1993	1994	1995	1996	1997	1998	1999	2000	2001	2002	2003	2004	2005
1971																				
1972																				
1973																				
1974																				
1975																				
1976																				
1977																				
1978																				
1979																				
1980																				
1981																				
1982																				
1983																				
1984																				
1985																				
1986	6.2																			
1987	5.8	5.5																		
1988	6.0	5.9	6.3																	
1989	6.6	6.7	7.4	8.4																
1990	6.8	7.0	7.5	8.1	7.8															
1991	6.6	6.7	7.0	7.3	6.7	5.6														
1992	6.2	6.2	6.3	6.3	5.6	4.5	3.5													
1993	5.8	5.7	5.7	5.6	4.9	4.0	3.2	2.9												
1994	5.5	5.5	5.5	5.3	4.7	4.0	3.4	3.4	3.9											
1995	5.6	5.5	5.5	5.4	4.9	4.3	4.0	4.1	4.7	5.6										
1996	5.5	5.5	5.5	5.3	4.9	4.4	4.2	4.4	4.9	5.4	5.2									
1997	5.5	5.4	5.4	5.3	5.0	4.6	4.4	4.6	5.0	5.4	5.2	5.3								
1998	5.4	5.4	5.4	5.3	5.0	4.6	4.5	4.6	5.0	5.2	5.1	5.1	4.9							
1999	5.4	5.3	5.3	5.2	4.9	4.6	4.5	4.6	4.9	5.1	5.0	4.9	4.8	4.7						
2000	5.4	5.4	5.4	5.3	5.0	4.7	4.6	4.8	5.1	5.2	5.2	5.2	5.1	5.3	5.9					
2001	5.3	5.3	5.3	5.2	4.9	4.7	4.6	4.7	4.9	5.0	5.0	4.9	4.8	4.8	4.9	3.8				
2002	5.1	5.0	5.0	4.9	4.7	4.4	4.3	4.4	4.5	4.6	4.5	4.4	4.2	4.0	3.8	2.7	1.6			
2003	4.9	4.8	4.8	4.7	4.4	4.1	4.0	4.1	4.2	4.2	4.0	3.9	3.6	3.4	3.1	2.2	1.3	1.0		
2004	4.7	4.6	4.5	4.4	4.2	3.9	3.8	3.8	3.9	3.9	3.7	3.5	3.3	3.0	2.7	1.9	1.3	1.1	1.2	
2005	4.6	4.5	4.5	4.3	4.1	3.9	3.7	3.8	3.8	3.8	3.6	3.5	3.2	3.0	2.7	2.1	1.7	1.7	2.1	3.0
2006	4.6	4.5	4.5	4.4	4.1	3.9	3.8	3.8	3.9	3.9	3.7	3.6	3.4	3.2	3.0	2.6	2.3	2.5	3.0	3.9
2007	4.6	4.5	4.5	4.4	4.2	4.0	3.9	3.9	4.0	4.0	3.8	3.7	3.5	3.4	3.2	2.9	2.7	2.9	3.4	4.1
2008	4.5	4.4	4.3	4.2	4.0	3.8	3.7	3.7	3.8	3.8	3.7	3.5	3.4	3.2	3.1	2.7	2.5	2.7	3.0	3.5
2009	4.3	4.2	4.1	4.0	3.8	3.6	3.5	3.5	3.6	3.5	3.4	3.3	3.1	2.9	2.8	2.4	2.2	2.3	2.5	2.8
2010	4.1	4.0	4.0	3.9	3.7	3.5	3.3	3.3	3.4	3.3	3.2	3.0	2.9	2.7	2.5	2.2	2.0	2.0	2.2	2.4
2011	4.0	3.9	3.8	3.7	3.5	3.3	3.2	3.2	3.2	3.1	3.0	2.8	2.7	2.5	2.3	2.0	1.8	1.8	1.9	2.0
2012	3.8	3.7	3.7	3.5	3.3	3.1	3.0	3.0	3.0	3.0	2.8	2.7	2.5	2.3	2.1	1.8	1.6	1.6	1.7	1.8
2013	3.7	3.6	3.5	3.4	3.2	3.0	2.9	2.9	2.9	2.8	2.6	2.5	2.3	2.2	2.0	1.7	1.5	1.5	1.5	1.6
2014	3.5	3.5	3.4	3.3	3.1	2.9	2.8	2.7	2.7	2.7	2.5	2.4	2.2	2.0	1.8	1.6	1.4	1.4	1.4	1.4
2015	3.4	3.3	3.3	3.1	2.9	2.8	2.6	2.6	2.6	2.5	2.4	2.2	2.1	1.9	1.7	1.5	1.3	1.3	1.3	1.3

Appendix C-6

U.S. Treasury Bills: Percent per annum total returns for all historical periods

From 1926 to 2015

End Date	Start Date 2006	2007	2008	2009	2010	2011	2012	2013	2014	2015
1971										
1972										
1973										
1974										
1975										
1976										
1977										
1978										
1979										
1980										
1981										
1982										
1983										
1984										
1985										
1986										
1987										
1988										
1989										
1990										
1991										
1992										
1993										
1994										
1995										
1996										
1997										
1998										
1999										
2000										
2001										
2002										
2003										
2004										
2005										
2006	4.8									
2007	4.7	4.7								
2008	3.7	3.1	1.6							
2009	2.8	2.1	0.8	0.1						
2010	2.2	1.6	0.6	0.1	0.1					
2011	1.9	1.3	0.5	0.1	0.1	0.0				
2012	1.6	1.1	0.4	0.1	0.1	0.1	0.1			
2013	1.4	0.9	0.3	0.1	0.1	0.0	0.0	0.0		
2014	1.3	0.8	0.3	0.1	0.1	0.0	0.0	0.0	0.0	
2015	1.1	0.7	0.2	0.1	0.0	0.0	0.0	0.0	0.0	0.0

2016 SBBI Yearbook

Appendix C-6 (48)

Appendix C-7

Inflation: Percent per annum total returns for all historical periods

From 1926 to 2015

End Date	Start Date 1926	1927	1928	1929	1930	1931	1932	1933	1934	1935	1936	1937	1938	1939	1940	1941	1942	1943	1944	1945
1926	-1.5																			
1927	-1.8	-2.1																		
1928	-1.5	-1.5	-1.0																	
1929	-1.1	-1.0	-0.4	0.2																
1930	-2.1	-2.2	-2.3	-3.0	-6.0															
1931	-3.4	-3.7	-4.2	-5.2	-7.8	-9.5														
1932	-4.4	-4.9	-5.4	-6.5	-8.6	-9.9	-10.3													
1933	-3.8	-4.1	-4.5	-5.1	-6.4	-6.6	-5.0	0.5												
1934	-3.2	-3.4	-3.6	-4.0	-4.8	-4.5	-2.7	1.3	2.0											
1935	-2.6	-2.7	-2.8	-3.0	-3.5	-3.0	-1.3	1.8	2.5	3.0										
1936	-2.2	-2.3	-2.3	-2.5	-2.9	-2.3	-0.8	1.7	2.1	2.1	1.2									
1937	-1.8	-1.8	-1.8	-1.9	-2.1	-1.6	-0.2	2.0	2.3	2.4	2.2	3.1								
1938	-1.9	-1.9	-1.9	-2.0	-2.2	-1.7	-0.6	1.2	1.3	1.1	0.5	0.1	-2.8							
1939	-1.8	-1.8	-1.8	-1.8	-2.0	-1.6	-0.6	0.9	1.0	0.8	0.2	-0.1	-1.6	-0.5						
1940	-1.6	-1.6	-1.6	-1.6	-1.8	-1.3	-0.4	0.9	1.0	0.8	0.4	0.2	-0.8	0.2	1.0					
1941	-0.9	-0.9	-0.8	-0.8	-0.9	-0.4	0.6	1.9	2.0	2.0	1.9	2.0	1.7	3.3	5.2	9.7				
1942	-0.3	-0.3	-0.2	-0.1	-0.1	0.4	1.3	2.6	2.8	2.9	2.9	3.2	3.2	4.8	6.6	9.5	9.3			
1943	-0.2	-0.1	0.0	0.1	0.1	0.6	1.5	2.6	2.9	2.9	2.9	3.2	3.2	4.4	5.7	7.3	6.2	3.2		
1944	0.0	0.0	0.2	0.2	0.2	0.7	1.5	2.6	2.8	2.9	2.8	3.1	3.0	4.1	5.0	6.0	4.8	2.6	2.1	
1945	0.1	0.2	0.3	0.4	0.4	0.8	1.6	2.6	2.7	2.8	2.8	3.0	2.9	3.8	4.5	5.2	4.2	2.5	2.2	2.3
1946	0.9	1.0	1.2	1.3	1.3	1.8	2.6	3.6	3.9	4.0	4.1	4.4	4.5	5.5	6.4	7.3	6.8	6.2	7.3	9.9
1947	1.2	1.4	1.5	1.7	1.7	2.2	3.0	4.0	4.2	4.4	4.5	4.8	5.0	5.9	6.7	7.5	7.2	6.8	7.7	9.6
1948	1.3	1.4	1.6	1.7	1.8	2.3	3.0	3.9	4.1	4.3	4.4	4.6	4.8	5.6	6.2	6.9	6.5	6.1	6.7	7.8
1949	1.2	1.3	1.4	1.5	1.6	2.0	2.7	3.5	3.7	3.8	3.9	4.1	4.2	4.9	5.4	5.9	5.5	4.9	5.2	5.8
1950	1.3	1.5	1.6	1.7	1.8	2.2	2.9	3.7	3.9	4.0	4.0	4.2	4.3	4.9	5.4	5.9	5.5	5.0	5.3	5.8
1951	1.5	1.6	1.8	1.9	2.0	2.4	3.0	3.8	4.0	4.1	4.1	4.3	4.4	5.0	5.5	5.9	5.5	5.1	5.4	5.8
1952	1.5	1.6	1.8	1.9	1.9	2.3	2.9	3.6	3.8	3.9	4.0	4.1	4.2	4.7	5.1	5.5	5.1	4.7	4.9	5.2
1953	1.5	1.6	1.7	1.8	1.9	2.2	2.8	3.5	3.6	3.7	3.8	3.9	4.0	4.4	4.8	5.1	4.7	4.3	4.4	4.7
1954	1.4	1.5	1.6	1.7	1.8	2.1	2.7	3.3	3.4	3.5	3.5	3.7	3.7	4.1	4.4	4.7	4.3	3.9	4.0	4.2
1955	1.4	1.5	1.6	1.7	1.7	2.1	2.6	3.2	3.3	3.4	3.4	3.5	3.5	3.9	4.2	4.4	4.0	3.6	3.7	3.8
1956	1.4	1.5	1.6	1.7	1.8	2.1	2.6	3.2	3.3	3.3	3.3	3.5	3.5	3.8	4.1	4.3	3.9	3.6	3.6	3.7
1957	1.5	1.5	1.7	1.8	1.8	2.1	2.6	3.2	3.3	3.3	3.3	3.4	3.5	3.8	4.0	4.2	3.9	3.5	3.6	3.7
1958	1.5	1.6	1.7	1.8	1.8	2.1	2.6	3.1	3.2	3.3	3.3	3.4	3.4	3.7	3.9	4.1	3.8	3.4	3.4	3.5
1959	1.5	1.6	1.7	1.8	1.8	2.1	2.5	3.0	3.1	3.2	3.2	3.3	3.3	3.6	3.8	3.9	3.6	3.3	3.3	3.4
1960	1.5	1.6	1.7	1.7	1.8	2.1	2.5	3.0	3.1	3.1	3.1	3.2	3.2	3.5	3.7	3.8	3.5	3.2	3.2	3.3
1961	1.4	1.5	1.6	1.7	1.8	2.0	2.4	2.9	3.0	3.0	3.0	3.1	3.1	3.4	3.5	3.7	3.4	3.1	3.1	3.1
1962	1.4	1.5	1.6	1.7	1.7	2.0	2.4	2.8	2.9	3.0	3.0	3.0	3.0	3.3	3.4	3.6	3.3	3.0	3.0	3.0
1963	1.4	1.5	1.6	1.7	1.7	2.0	2.4	2.8	2.9	2.9	2.9	3.0	3.0	3.2	3.4	3.5	3.2	2.9	2.9	2.9
1964	1.4	1.5	1.6	1.7	1.7	2.0	2.3	2.8	2.8	2.9	2.9	2.9	2.9	3.1	3.3	3.4	3.1	2.8	2.8	2.9
1965	1.4	1.5	1.6	1.7	1.7	2.0	2.3	2.7	2.8	2.8	2.8	2.9	2.9	3.1	3.2	3.3	3.1	2.8	2.8	2.8
1966	1.5	1.6	1.7	1.7	1.8	2.0	2.4	2.8	2.8	2.8	2.8	2.9	2.9	3.1	3.2	3.3	3.1	2.8	2.8	2.8
1967	1.5	1.6	1.7	1.8	1.8	2.0	2.4	2.8	2.8	2.8	2.8	2.9	2.9	3.1	3.2	3.3	3.1	2.8	2.8	2.8
1968	1.6	1.7	1.8	1.8	1.9	2.1	2.4	2.8	2.8	2.9	2.9	3.0	3.0	3.1	3.3	3.4	3.1	2.9	2.9	2.9
1969	1.7	1.8	1.9	1.9	2.0	2.2	2.5	2.9	3.0	3.0	3.0	3.0	3.0	3.2	3.4	3.5	3.2	3.0	3.0	3.0
1970	1.8	1.9	2.0	2.0	2.1	2.3	2.6	3.0	3.0	3.1	3.1	3.1	3.1	3.3	3.4	3.5	3.3	3.1	3.1	3.1

Appendix C-7

Inflation: Percent per annum total returns for all historical periods

From 1926 to 2015

End Date	Start Date 1926	1927	1928	1929	1930	1931	1932	1933	1934	1935	1936	1937	1938	1939	1940	1941	1942	1943	1944	1945
1971	1.8	1.9	2.0	2.1	2.1	2.3	2.6	3.0	3.0	3.1	3.1	3.1	3.1	3.3	3.4	3.5	3.3	3.1	3.1	3.1
1972	1.9	1.9	2.0	2.1	2.1	2.3	2.6	3.0	3.1	3.1	3.1	3.1	3.1	3.3	3.4	3.5	3.3	3.1	3.1	3.2
1973	2.0	2.1	2.2	2.2	2.3	2.5	2.8	3.1	3.2	3.2	3.2	3.3	3.3	3.5	3.6	3.7	3.5	3.3	3.3	3.3
1974	2.2	2.3	2.4	2.4	2.5	2.7	3.0	3.3	3.4	3.4	3.4	3.5	3.5	3.7	3.8	3.9	3.7	3.6	3.6	3.6
1975	2.3	2.4	2.5	2.5	2.6	2.8	3.1	3.4	3.5	3.5	3.5	3.6	3.6	3.8	3.9	4.0	3.8	3.7	3.7	3.7
1976	2.3	2.4	2.5	2.6	2.6	2.8	3.1	3.4	3.5	3.6	3.6	3.6	3.6	3.8	3.9	4.0	3.9	3.7	3.7	3.8
1977	2.4	2.5	2.6	2.7	2.7	2.9	3.2	3.5	3.6	3.6	3.6	3.7	3.7	3.9	4.0	4.1	3.9	3.8	3.8	3.9
1978	2.5	2.6	2.7	2.8	2.8	3.0	3.3	3.6	3.7	3.7	3.8	3.8	3.8	4.0	4.1	4.2	4.1	3.9	4.0	4.0
1979	2.7	2.8	2.9	3.0	3.0	3.2	3.5	3.8	3.9	4.0	4.0	4.0	4.1	4.2	4.4	4.4	4.3	4.2	4.2	4.3
1980	2.9	3.0	3.1	3.2	3.2	3.4	3.7	4.0	4.1	4.1	4.2	4.2	4.2	4.4	4.5	4.6	4.5	4.4	4.4	4.5
1981	3.0	3.1	3.2	3.3	3.3	3.5	3.8	4.1	4.2	4.2	4.3	4.3	4.4	4.5	4.6	4.7	4.6	4.5	4.5	4.6
1982	3.0	3.1	3.2	3.3	3.3	3.5	3.8	4.1	4.2	4.2	4.2	4.3	4.3	4.5	4.6	4.7	4.6	4.5	4.5	4.6
1983	3.0	3.1	3.2	3.3	3.3	3.5	3.8	4.1	4.2	4.2	4.2	4.3	4.3	4.5	4.6	4.7	4.6	4.5	4.5	4.6
1984	3.0	3.1	3.2	3.3	3.4	3.5	3.8	4.1	4.2	4.2	4.2	4.3	4.3	4.5	4.6	4.7	4.6	4.5	4.5	4.5
1985	3.1	3.1	3.2	3.3	3.4	3.5	3.8	4.1	4.2	4.2	4.2	4.3	4.3	4.5	4.6	4.7	4.5	4.4	4.5	4.5
1986	3.0	3.1	3.2	3.3	3.3	3.5	3.8	4.0	4.1	4.1	4.2	4.2	4.2	4.4	4.5	4.6	4.5	4.4	4.4	4.4
1987	3.0	3.1	3.2	3.3	3.3	3.5	3.8	4.0	4.1	4.1	4.2	4.2	4.2	4.4	4.5	4.6	4.5	4.4	4.4	4.4
1988	3.1	3.1	3.2	3.3	3.4	3.5	3.8	4.0	4.1	4.1	4.1	4.2	4.3	4.4	4.5	4.6	4.5	4.4	4.4	4.4
1989	3.1	3.2	3.3	3.3	3.4	3.5	3.8	4.1	4.1	4.2	4.1	4.2	4.3	4.4	4.5	4.6	4.5	4.4	4.4	4.4
1990	3.1	3.2	3.3	3.4	3.4	3.6	3.8	4.1	4.2	4.2	4.1	4.3	4.3	4.4	4.5	4.6	4.5	4.4	4.4	4.5
1991	3.1	3.2	3.3	3.4	3.4	3.6	3.8	4.1	4.1	4.2	4.1	4.2	4.3	4.4	4.5	4.6	4.5	4.4	4.4	4.5
1992	3.1	3.2	3.3	3.4	3.4	3.6	3.8	4.1	4.1	4.2	4.0	4.2	4.2	4.4	4.5	4.5	4.4	4.3	4.4	4.4
1993	3.1	3.2	3.3	3.3	3.4	3.6	3.8	4.0	4.1	4.1	4.0	4.2	4.2	4.3	4.4	4.5	4.4	4.3	4.3	4.4
1994	3.1	3.2	3.3	3.3	3.4	3.5	3.7	4.0	4.1	4.1	4.0	4.2	4.2	4.3	4.4	4.5	4.4	4.3	4.3	4.4
1995	3.1	3.1	3.3	3.3	3.4	3.5	3.7	4.0	4.0	4.1	4.0	4.1	4.2	4.3	4.4	4.4	4.3	4.3	4.3	4.3
1996	3.1	3.2	3.3	3.3	3.4	3.5	3.7	4.0	4.0	4.1	4.0	4.1	4.1	4.3	4.4	4.4	4.3	4.2	4.3	4.3
1997	3.1	3.2	3.2	3.3	3.4	3.5	3.7	3.9	4.0	4.0	4.0	4.1	4.1	4.2	4.3	4.4	4.3	4.2	4.2	4.2
1998	3.1	3.1	3.2	3.3	3.3	3.5	3.7	3.9	4.0	4.0	4.0	4.0	4.1	4.2	4.3	4.3	4.2	4.1	4.2	4.2
1999	3.1	3.1	3.1	3.3	3.3	3.3	3.7	3.9	3.9	4.0	4.0	4.0	4.0	4.2	4.2	4.3	4.2	4.1	4.1	4.2
2000	3.1	3.1	3.2	3.3	3.3	3.5	3.7	3.9	3.9	4.0	4.0	4.0	4.0	4.1	4.2	4.2	4.2	4.1	4.1	4.2
2001	3.1	3.1	3.1	3.2	3.3	3.4	3.6	3.8	3.9	3.9	3.9	4.0	4.0	4.1	4.2	4.2	4.1	4.1	4.1	4.1
2002	3.0	3.0	3.1	3.2	3.3	3.4	3.6	3.8	3.9	3.9	3.9	4.0	4.0	4.1	4.2	4.2	4.1	4.0	4.0	4.1
2003	3.0	3.0	3.1	3.2	3.3	3.4	3.6	3.8	3.8	3.9	3.9	3.9	3.9	4.0	4.1	4.2	4.1	4.0	4.0	4.0
2004	3.0	3.0	3.1	3.2	3.3	3.4	3.6	3.8	3.8	3.9	3.9	3.9	3.9	4.0	4.1	4.2	4.1	4.0	4.0	4.0
2005	3.0	3.1	3.2	3.2	3.3	3.4	3.6	3.8	3.8	3.9	3.9	3.9	3.9	4.0	4.1	4.1	4.1	4.0	4.0	4.0
2006	3.0	3.1	3.2	3.2	3.3	3.4	3.6	3.8	3.8	3.8	3.8	3.9	3.9	4.0	4.1	4.1	4.0	4.0	4.0	4.0
2007	3.0	3.1	3.2	3.2	3.3	3.4	3.5	3.8	3.8	3.8	3.9	3.9	3.9	4.0	4.1	4.1	4.0	4.0	4.0	4.0
2008	3.0	3.0	3.1	3.2	3.2	3.3	3.5	3.7	3.8	3.8	3.8	3.8	3.8	3.9	4.0	4.1	4.0	3.9	4.0	4.0
2009	3.0	3.0	3.1	3.2	3.2	3.3	3.5	3.7	3.7	3.8	3.8	3.8	3.8	3.9	4.0	4.0	4.0	3.9	3.9	3.9
2010	3.0	3.0	3.1	3.1	3.2	3.3	3.5	3.7	3.7	3.8	3.8	3.8	3.8	3.9	4.0	4.0	4.0	3.8	3.9	3.9
2011	3.0	3.0	3.1	3.2	3.2	3.3	3.5	3.7	3.7	3.7	3.7	3.8	3.8	3.9	4.0	4.0	3.9	3.8	3.9	3.9
2012	3.0	3.0	3.1	3.1	3.2	3.3	3.5	3.6	3.7	3.7	3.7	3.8	3.8	3.9	3.9	4.0	3.9	3.8	3.8	3.8
2013	3.0	3.0	3.1	3.1	3.2	3.3	3.4	3.6	3.7	3.7	3.7	3.7	3.7	3.8	3.9	3.9	3.8	3.8	3.8	3.8
2014	2.9	3.0	3.0	3.1	3.1	3.2	3.4	3.6	3.6	3.6	3.7	3.7	3.7	3.8	3.8	3.9	3.8	3.7	3.7	3.8
2015	2.9	3.0	3.0	3.1	3.1	3.2	3.4	3.6	3.6	3.6	3.6	3.7	3.7	3.7	3.8	3.8	3.8	3.7	3.7	3.7

Appendix C-7

Inflation: Percent per annum total returns for all historical periods

From 1926 to 2015

End Date	Start Date 1946	1947	1948	1949	1950	1951	1952	1953	1954	1955	1956	1957	1958	1959	1960	1961	1962	1963	1964	1965
1926																				
1927																				
1928																				
1929																				
1930																				
1931																				
1932																				
1933																				
1934																				
1935																				
1936																				
1937																				
1938																				
1939																				
1940																				
1941																				
1942																				
1943																				
1944																				
1945																				
1946	18.2																			
1947	13.5	9.0																		
1948	9.8	5.8	2.7																	
1949	6.8	3.2	0.4	-1.8																
1950	6.6	3.8	2.2	1.9	5.8															
1951	6.5	4.3	3.1	3.2	5.8	5.9														
1952	5.6	3.7	2.6	2.6	4.2	3.3	0.9													
1953	5.0	3.2	2.3	2.2	3.3	2.4	0.8	0.6												
1954	4.4	2.8	1.9	1.8	2.5	1.7	0.3	0.1	-0.5											
1955	4.0	2.5	1.7	1.6	2.1	1.4	0.3	0.2	-0.1	0.4										
1956	3.9	2.5	1.8	1.7	2.2	1.7	0.8	0.8	0.9	1.6	2.9									
1957	3.8	2.6	2.0	1.9	2.3	1.9	1.2	1.3	1.4	2.1	2.9	3.0								
1958	3.6	2.5	1.9	1.9	2.3	1.8	1.3	1.3	1.5	2.0	2.5	2.4	1.8							
1959	3.5	2.4	1.9	1.8	2.2	1.8	1.3	1.4	1.5	1.9	2.3	2.1	1.6	1.5						
1960	3.3	2.4	1.9	1.8	2.1	1.8	1.3	1.4	1.5	1.8	2.1	1.9	1.6	1.5	1.5					
1961	3.2	2.2	1.8	1.7	2.0	1.7	1.3	1.3	1.4	1.7	1.9	1.7	1.4	1.2	1.1	0.7				
1962	3.1	2.2	1.7	1.7	1.9	1.6	1.3	1.3	1.4	1.6	1.8	1.6	1.3	1.2	1.1	0.9	1.2			
1963	3.0	2.2	1.7	1.7	1.9	1.6	1.3	1.3	1.4	1.6	1.8	1.6	1.4	1.3	1.3	1.2	1.4	1.6		
1964	2.9	2.1	1.7	1.6	1.9	1.6	1.3	1.3	1.4	1.6	1.7	1.6	1.4	1.3	1.2	1.2	1.4	1.4	1.2	
1965	2.8	2.1	1.7	1.7	1.9	1.6	1.3	1.4	1.4	1.6	1.7	1.6	1.4	1.4	1.4	1.3	1.5	1.6	1.6	1.9
1966	2.9	2.2	1.8	1.8	2.0	1.7	1.5	1.5	1.6	1.7	1.9	1.8	1.6	1.6	1.6	1.7	1.9	2.0	2.2	2.6
1967	2.9	2.2	1.9	1.8	2.0	1.8	1.6	1.6	1.7	1.8	2.0	1.9	1.8	1.8	1.8	1.9	2.1	2.2	2.4	2.8
1968	3.0	2.3	2.0	2.0	2.2	2.0	1.7	1.8	1.9	2.0	2.2	2.1	2.0	2.1	2.1	2.2	2.4	2.6	2.8	3.3
1969	3.1	2.5	2.2	2.2	2.4	2.2	2.0	2.0	2.1	2.3	2.5	2.4	2.4	2.4	2.5	2.6	2.9	3.1	3.4	3.8
1970	3.2	2.6	2.3	2.3	2.5	2.3	2.2	2.2	2.3	2.5	2.7	2.6	2.6	2.7	2.8	2.9	3.2	3.4	3.7	4.1

Appendix C-7

Inflation: Percent per annum total returns for all historical periods

From 1926 to 2015

End Date	Start Date 1946	1947	1948	1949	1950	1951	1952	1953	1954	1955	1956	1957	1958	1959	1960	1961	1962	1963	1964	1965
1971	3.2	2.6	2.4	2.4	2.5	2.4	2.2	2.3	2.4	2.6	2.7	2.7	2.7	2.7	2.8	3.0	3.2	3.4	3.6	4.0
1972	3.2	2.7	2.4	2.4	2.6	2.4	2.3	2.3	2.4	2.6	2.7	2.7	2.7	2.8	2.9	3.0	3.2	3.4	3.6	3.9
1973	3.4	2.9	2.6	2.6	2.8	2.7	2.6	2.6	2.8	2.9	3.1	3.1	3.1	3.2	3.3	3.4	3.7	3.9	4.1	4.4
1974	3.7	3.2	3.0	3.0	3.2	3.1	3.0	3.1	3.2	3.4	3.5	3.6	3.6	3.7	3.9	4.0	4.3	4.6	4.8	5.2
1975	3.8	3.3	3.1	3.1	3.3	3.2	3.1	3.2	3.4	3.5	3.7	3.7	3.8	3.9	4.1	4.2	4.5	4.7	5.0	5.4
1976	3.8	3.4	3.2	3.2	3.4	3.3	3.2	3.3	3.4	3.6	3.8	3.8	3.8	4.0	4.1	4.3	4.5	4.8	5.0	5.3
1977	3.9	3.5	3.3	3.3	3.5	3.4	3.3	3.4	3.6	3.7	3.9	3.9	4.0	4.1	4.2	4.4	4.7	4.9	5.1	5.4
1978	4.1	3.7	3.5	3.5	3.7	3.6	3.5	3.6	3.8	3.9	4.1	4.2	4.2	4.3	4.5	4.7	4.9	5.1	5.4	5.7
1979	4.3	3.9	3.8	3.8	4.0	3.9	3.9	4.0	4.1	4.3	4.5	4.5	4.6	4.8	4.9	5.1	5.4	5.6	5.9	6.2
1980	4.5	4.2	4.0	4.1	4.3	4.2	4.2	4.3	4.4	4.6	4.8	4.9	4.9	5.1	5.3	5.5	5.7	6.0	6.2	6.6
1981	4.7	4.3	4.2	4.2	4.4	4.4	4.3	4.4	4.6	4.8	4.9	5.0	5.1	5.3	5.4	5.6	5.9	6.1	6.4	6.7
1982	4.6	4.3	4.2	4.2	4.4	4.3	4.3	4.4	4.5	4.7	4.9	5.0	5.1	5.2	5.4	5.5	5.8	6.0	6.2	6.5
1983	4.6	4.3	4.2	4.2	4.4	4.3	4.3	4.4	4.5	4.7	4.9	4.9	5.0	5.1	5.3	5.5	5.7	5.9	6.1	6.4
1984	4.6	4.3	4.1	4.2	4.4	4.3	4.3	4.4	4.5	4.7	4.8	4.9	5.0	5.1	5.2	5.4	5.6	5.8	6.0	6.3
1985	4.6	4.3	4.1	4.2	4.3	4.3	4.3	4.4	4.5	4.6	4.8	4.9	4.9	5.0	5.2	5.3	5.5	5.7	5.9	6.1
1986	4.5	4.2	4.1	4.1	4.3	4.2	4.2	4.3	4.4	4.5	4.7	4.7	4.8	4.9	5.0	5.2	5.4	5.5	5.7	5.9
1987	4.5	4.2	4.1	4.1	4.3	4.2	4.2	4.3	4.4	4.5	4.7	4.7	4.8	4.9	5.0	5.1	5.3	5.5	5.6	5.8
1988	4.5	4.2	4.1	4.1	4.3	4.2	4.2	4.3	4.4	4.5	4.7	4.7	4.8	4.9	5.0	5.1	5.3	5.4	5.6	5.8
1989	4.5	4.2	4.1	4.1	4.3	4.2	4.2	4.3	4.4	4.5	4.7	4.7	4.8	4.9	5.0	5.1	5.3	5.4	5.6	5.7
1990	4.5	4.2	4.1	4.2	4.3	4.3	4.2	4.3	4.4	4.6	4.7	4.8	4.8	4.9	5.0	5.1	5.3	5.4	5.6	5.8
1991	4.5	4.2	4.1	4.1	4.3	4.3	4.2	4.3	4.4	4.5	4.7	4.7	4.8	4.8	5.0	5.1	5.2	5.4	5.5	5.7
1992	4.5	4.2	4.1	4.1	4.3	4.2	4.2	4.3	4.4	4.5	4.6	4.6	4.7	4.8	4.9	5.0	5.1	5.3	5.4	5.6
1993	4.4	4.2	4.1	4.1	4.2	4.2	4.1	4.2	4.3	4.4	4.6	4.6	4.6	4.7	4.8	4.9	5.1	5.2	5.3	5.5
1994	4.4	4.1	4.0	4.1	4.2	4.2	4.1	4.2	4.3	4.4	4.5	4.5	4.6	4.7	4.8	4.9	5.0	5.1	5.2	5.4
1995	4.4	4.1	4.0	4.0	4.2	4.1	4.1	4.2	4.2	4.4	4.5	4.5	4.5	4.6	4.7	4.8	4.9	5.0	5.1	5.3
1996	4.3	4.1	4.0	4.0	4.1	4.1	4.1	4.1	4.2	4.3	4.4	4.5	4.5	4.6	4.7	4.8	4.9	5.0	5.1	5.2
1997	4.3	4.0	3.9	4.0	4.1	4.0	4.0	4.1	4.2	4.3	4.4	4.4	4.4	4.5	4.6	4.7	4.8	4.9	5.0	5.1
1998	4.2	4.0	3.9	3.9	4.0	4.0	4.0	4.0	4.1	4.2	4.3	4.3	4.4	4.4	4.5	4.6	4.7	4.8	4.9	5.0
1999	4.2	4.0	3.9	3.9	4.0	4.0	3.9	4.0	4.1	4.2	4.3	4.3	4.3	4.4	4.5	4.5	4.6	4.7	4.8	4.9
2000	4.2	3.9	3.9	3.9	4.0	4.0	3.9	4.0	4.1	4.2	4.2	4.3	4.3	4.4	4.4	4.5	4.6	4.7	4.8	4.9
2001	4.1	3.9	3.8	3.8	3.9	3.9	3.9	3.9	4.0	4.1	4.2	4.2	4.2	4.3	4.4	4.4	4.5	4.6	4.7	4.8
2002	4.1	3.9	3.8	3.8	3.9	3.9	3.8	3.9	4.0	4.1	4.1	4.2	4.2	4.3	4.3	4.4	4.5	4.6	4.6	4.7
2003	4.1	3.8	3.8	3.8	3.9	3.8	3.8	3.9	3.9	4.0	4.1	4.1	4.1	4.2	4.3	4.3	4.4	4.5	4.6	4.7
2004	4.1	3.8	3.7	3.8	3.9	3.8	3.8	3.8	3.9	4.0	4.1	4.1	4.1	4.2	4.3	4.3	4.4	4.5	4.5	4.7
2005	4.0	3.8	3.7	3.8	3.9	3.8	3.8	3.8	3.9	4.0	4.1	4.1	4.1	4.2	4.2	4.3	4.4	4.4	4.5	4.6
2006	4.0	3.8	3.7	3.7	3.8	3.8	3.8	3.8	3.9	4.0	4.0	4.1	4.1	4.1	4.2	4.2	4.3	4.4	4.5	4.5
2007	4.0	3.8	3.7	3.7	3.8	3.8	3.8	3.8	3.9	4.0	4.0	4.1	4.1	4.1	4.2	4.2	4.3	4.4	4.5	4.5
2008	4.0	3.7	3.7	3.7	3.8	3.7	3.7	3.8	3.8	3.9	4.0	4.0	4.0	4.0	4.1	4.2	4.2	4.3	4.4	4.4
2009	3.9	3.7	3.6	3.7	3.7	3.7	3.7	3.7	3.8	3.9	3.9	4.0	4.0	4.0	4.1	4.1	4.2	4.3	4.3	4.4
2010	3.9	3.7	3.6	3.6	3.7	3.7	3.6	3.7	3.8	3.8	3.9	3.9	3.9	4.0	4.0	4.1	4.2	4.3	4.3	4.3
2011	3.9	3.7	3.6	3.6	3.7	3.7	3.6	3.7	3.7	3.8	3.9	3.9	3.9	4.0	4.0	4.0	4.1	4.2	4.2	4.3
2012	3.9	3.7	3.6	3.6	3.7	3.6	3.6	3.7	3.7	3.8	3.8	3.9	3.9	3.9	4.0	4.0	4.1	4.1	4.2	4.2
2013	3.8	3.6	3.5	3.6	3.6	3.6	3.6	3.6	3.7	3.7	3.8	3.8	3.8	3.9	3.9	4.0	4.0	4.1	4.1	4.2
2014	3.8	3.6	3.5	3.5	3.6	3.6	3.5	3.6	3.6	3.7	3.7	3.8	3.8	3.8	3.9	3.9	4.0	4.0	4.1	4.1
2015	3.7	3.5	3.5	3.5	3.6	3.5	3.5	3.5	3.6	3.6	3.7	3.7	3.7	3.8	3.8	3.8	3.9	4.0	4.0	4.1

Appendix C-7

Inflation: Percent per annum total returns for all historical periods

From 1926 to 2015

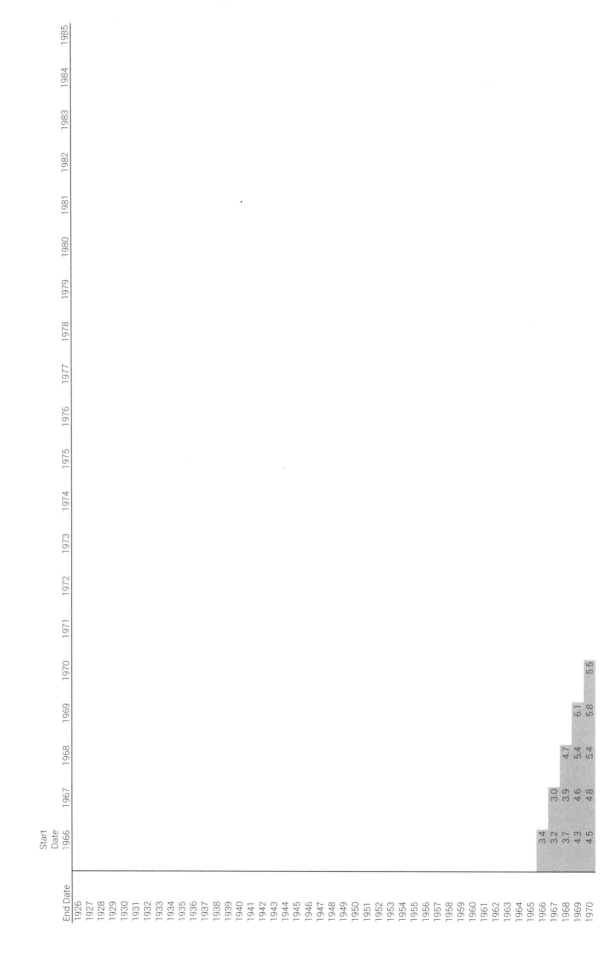

Start Date																			
End Date	1966	1967	1968	1969	1970	1971	1972	1973	1974	1975	1976	1977	1978	1979	1980	1981	1982	1983	1984	1985
1966	3.4																			
1967	3.2	3.0																		
1968	3.7	3.9	4.7																	
1969	4.3	4.6	5.4	6.1																
1970	4.5	4.8	5.4	5.8	5.5															

Appendix C-7

Inflation: Percent per annum total returns for all historical periods

From 1926 to 2015

End Date	Start Date 1966	1967	1968	1969	1970	1971	1972	1973	1974	1975	1976	1977	1978	1979	1980	1981	1982	1983	1984	1985
1971	4.3	4.5	4.9	5.0	4.4	3.4														
1972	4.2	4.3	4.6	4.6	4.1	3.4	3.4													
1973	4.8	5.0	5.3	5.4	5.2	5.2	6.1	8.8												
1974	5.6	5.9	6.3	6.5	6.6	6.9	8.1	10.5	12.2											
1975	5.7	6.0	6.4	6.6	6.7	6.9	7.8	9.3	9.6	7.0										
1976	5.6	5.9	6.2	6.4	6.4	6.6	7.2	8.2	8.0	5.9	4.8									
1977	5.7	5.9	6.2	6.4	6.4	6.6	7.1	7.9	7.7	6.2	5.8	6.8								
1978	6.0	6.2	6.5	6.7	6.7	6.9	7.4	8.1	7.9	6.9	6.9	7.9	9.0							
1979	6.5	6.7	7.0	7.3	7.4	7.6	8.1	8.8	8.8	8.1	8.4	9.7	11.1	13.3						
1980	6.9	7.1	7.4	7.7	7.8	8.1	8.6	9.3	9.3	8.8	9.2	10.3	11.6	12.9	12.4					
1981	7.0	7.2	7.6	7.8	7.9	8.1	8.6	9.2	9.3	8.9	9.2	10.1	10.9	11.5	10.7	8.9				
1982	6.8	7.0	7.3	7.5	7.6	7.8	8.2	8.7	8.7	8.2	8.4	9.0	9.5	9.6	8.3	6.4	3.9			
1983	6.6	6.8	7.1	7.2	7.3	7.5	7.8	8.2	8.2	7.7	7.8	8.2	8.5	8.4	7.2	5.5	3.8	3.8		
1984	6.5	6.7	6.9	7.0	7.1	7.2	7.5	7.9	7.8	7.3	7.4	7.7	7.8	7.6	6.5	5.1	3.9	3.9	4.0	
1985	6.4	6.5	6.7	6.8	6.9	7.0	7.2	7.5	7.4	7.0	7.0	7.3	7.3	7.1	6.1	4.8	3.8	3.8	3.9	3.8
1986	6.1	6.2	6.4	6.5	6.5	6.6	6.8	7.1	6.9	6.5	6.5	6.6	6.6	6.3	5.3	4.2	3.3	3.2	2.9	2.4
1987	6.0	6.2	6.3	6.4	6.4	6.5	6.7	6.9	6.8	6.3	6.3	6.4	6.4	6.1	5.2	4.2	3.5	3.4	3.3	3.1
1988	6.0	6.1	6.2	6.3	6.3	6.4	6.5	6.7	6.6	6.2	6.1	6.3	6.2	5.9	5.1	4.3	3.6	3.6	3.5	3.4
1989	5.9	6.0	6.2	6.2	6.2	6.3	6.4	6.6	6.5	6.1	6.0	6.1	6.1	5.8	5.1	4.3	3.7	3.7	3.7	3.7
1990	5.9	6.0	6.1	6.2	6.2	6.3	6.4	6.6	6.5	6.1	6.0	6.1	6.1	5.8	5.2	4.5	4.0	4.0	4.1	4.1
1991	5.8	5.9	6.0	6.1	6.1	6.1	6.2	6.4	6.3	5.9	5.9	5.9	5.9	5.6	5.0	4.4	3.9	3.9	3.9	3.9
1992	5.7	5.8	5.9	5.9	5.9	6.0	6.1	6.2	6.1	5.7	5.7	5.7	5.7	5.4	4.8	4.2	3.8	3.8	3.8	3.8
1993	5.6	5.7	5.8	5.8	5.8	5.8	5.9	6.0	5.9	5.6	5.5	5.6	5.5	5.2	4.7	4.1	3.7	3.7	3.7	3.7
1994	5.5	5.6	5.7	5.7	5.7	5.7	5.8	5.9	5.8	5.4	5.4	5.4	5.3	5.1	4.6	4.0	3.6	3.6	3.6	3.6
1995	5.4	5.5	5.5	5.6	5.5	5.6	5.6	5.7	5.6	5.3	5.2	5.2	5.2	4.9	4.4	3.9	3.6	3.5	3.5	3.5
1996	5.3	5.4	5.5	5.5	5.5	5.5	5.6	5.6	5.5	5.2	5.1	5.1	5.1	4.8	4.4	3.9	3.6	3.5	3.5	3.5
1997	5.2	5.3	5.3	5.4	5.3	5.3	5.4	5.5	5.3	5.1	5.0	5.0	4.9	4.7	4.2	3.8	3.4	3.4	3.4	3.3
1998	5.1	5.1	5.2	5.2	5.2	5.2	5.3	5.3	5.2	4.9	4.8	4.8	4.7	4.5	4.1	3.6	3.3	3.3	3.3	3.2
1999	5.0	5.1	5.1	5.1	5.1	5.1	5.2	5.2	5.1	4.8	4.7	4.7	4.6	4.4	4.0	3.6	3.3	3.3	3.2	3.2
2000	5.0	5.0	5.1	5.1	5.1	5.0	5.1	5.2	5.0	4.8	4.7	4.7	4.6	4.4	4.0	3.6	3.3	3.3	3.2	3.2
2001	4.9	4.9	5.0	5.0	4.9	4.9	5.0	5.0	4.9	4.6	4.6	4.5	4.5	4.3	3.9	3.5	3.2	3.2	3.1	3.1
2002	4.8	4.8	4.9	4.9	4.9	4.8	4.9	4.9	4.8	4.5	4.5	4.5	4.4	4.2	3.8	3.4	3.2	3.1	3.1	3.1
2003	4.7	4.8	4.8	4.8	4.8	4.8	4.8	4.8	4.7	4.5	4.4	4.4	4.3	4.1	3.7	3.4	3.1	3.1	3.0	3.0
2004	4.7	4.7	4.8	4.8	4.7	4.7	4.8	4.8	4.7	4.4	4.3	4.3	4.2	4.1	3.7	3.4	3.1	3.1	3.0	3.0
2005	4.7	4.7	4.7	4.7	4.7	4.7	4.7	4.8	4.6	4.4	4.3	4.3	4.2	4.0	3.7	3.4	3.1	3.1	3.1	3.0
2006	4.6	4.6	4.7	4.7	4.6	4.6	4.7	4.7	4.6	4.3	4.3	4.2	4.1	4.0	3.6	3.3	3.1	3.1	3.0	3.0
2007	4.5	4.6	4.7	4.7	4.6	4.6	4.6	4.7	4.6	4.3	4.2	4.2	4.1	4.0	3.7	3.4	3.1	3.1	3.1	3.0
2008	4.5	4.6	4.5	4.5	4.5	4.5	4.5	4.5	4.4	4.2	4.1	4.1	4.0	3.8	3.5	3.2	3.0	3.0	3.0	2.9
2009	4.4	4.5	4.5	4.5	4.5	4.5	4.5	4.5	4.4	4.2	4.1	4.1	4.0	3.8	3.5	3.2	3.0	3.0	3.0	2.9
2010	4.4	4.4	4.4	4.4	4.4	4.4	4.4	4.4	4.3	4.1	4.0	4.0	3.9	3.7	3.4	3.2	3.0	2.9	2.9	2.9
2011	4.3	4.4	4.4	4.4	4.4	4.3	4.4	4.4	4.3	4.1	4.0	3.9	3.9	3.7	3.4	3.2	3.0	2.9	2.9	2.9
2012	4.3	4.3	4.3	4.3	4.3	4.3	4.3	4.3	4.2	4.0	3.9	3.9	3.8	3.7	3.4	3.1	2.9	2.9	2.9	2.8
2013	4.2	4.3	4.3	4.3	4.2	4.2	4.2	4.2	4.1	3.9	3.8	3.8	3.7	3.6	3.3	3.1	2.9	2.8	2.8	2.8
2014	4.2	4.2	4.2	4.2	4.1	4.1	4.1	4.2	4.0	3.8	3.8	3.7	3.7	3.5	3.2	3.0	2.8	2.8	2.7	2.7
2015	4.1	4.2	4.1	4.1	4.1	4.1	4.1	4.1	4.0	3.8	3.7	3.7	3.6	3.5	3.2	2.9	2.8	2.7	2.7	2.7

Appendix C-7

Inflation: Percent per annum total returns for all historical periods

From 1926 to 2015

End Date	Start Date 1986	1987	1988	1989	1990	1991	1992	1993	1994	1995	1996	1997	1998	1999	2000	2001	2002	2003	2004	2005
1971																				
1972																				
1973																				
1974																				
1975																				
1976																				
1977																				
1978																				
1979																				
1980																				
1981																				
1982																				
1983																				
1984																				
1985																				
1986	1.1																			
1987	2.8	4.4																		
1988	3.3	4.4	4.4																	
1989	3.6	4.5	4.5	4.6																
1990	4.1	4.9	5.1	5.4	6.1															
1991	4.0	4.5	4.6	4.6	4.6	3.1														
1992	3.8	4.3	4.2	4.2	4.0	3.0	2.9													
1993	3.7	4.0	4.0	3.9	3.7	2.9	2.8	2.7												
1994	3.6	3.9	3.8	3.7	3.5	2.8	2.8	2.7	2.7											
1995	3.5	3.7	3.6	3.5	3.3	2.8	2.7	2.7	2.6	2.5										
1996	3.4	3.7	3.6	3.5	3.3	2.9	2.8	2.8	2.8	2.9	3.3									
1997	3.3	3.5	3.4	3.3	3.1	2.7	2.6	2.6	2.6	2.9	2.5	1.7								
1998	3.2	3.3	3.2	3.1	3.0	2.6	2.5	2.4	2.4	2.3	2.2	1.7	1.6							
1999	3.1	3.3	3.2	3.1	2.9	2.6	2.5	2.5	2.4	2.4	2.3	2.0	2.1	2.7						
2000	3.1	3.3	3.2	3.1	3.0	2.7	2.6	2.6	2.6	2.5	2.5	2.3	2.6	3.0	3.4					
2001	3.0	3.2	3.1	3.0	2.9	2.6	2.5	2.5	2.4	2.4	2.4	2.2	2.3	2.5	2.5	1.6				
2002	3.0	3.1	3.0	2.9	2.8	2.5	2.5	2.5	2.4	2.4	2.4	2.2	2.3	2.5	2.4	2.0	2.4			
2003	2.9	3.1	3.0	2.9	2.7	2.5	2.4	2.4	2.4	2.3	2.3	2.2	2.2	2.4	2.3	1.9	2.1	1.9		
2004	3.0	3.1	3.0	2.9	2.8	2.5	2.5	2.5	2.5	2.4	2.4	2.3	2.4	2.5	2.5	2.3	2.5	2.6	3.3	
2005	3.0	3.1	3.0	2.9	2.8	2.6	2.6	2.5	2.5	2.5	2.5	2.4	2.5	2.6	2.6	2.5	2.7	2.8	3.3	3.4
2006	3.0	3.1	3.0	2.9	2.8	2.6	2.6	2.5	2.5	2.5	2.5	2.4	2.5	2.6	2.6	2.5	2.7	2.8	3.1	3.0
2007	3.0	3.1	3.0	3.0	2.9	2.7	2.7	2.6	2.6	2.6	2.6	2.6	2.7	2.8	2.8	2.7	2.9	3.0	3.3	3.3
2008	2.9	3.0	2.9	2.8	2.7	2.5	2.5	2.5	2.5	2.5	2.4	2.4	2.4	2.5	2.5	2.4	2.5	2.5	2.7	2.5
2009	2.9	3.0	2.9	2.8	2.7	2.6	2.5	2.5	2.5	2.5	2.5	2.4	2.5	2.5	2.5	2.4	2.5	2.6	2.7	2.6
2010	2.8	2.9	2.8	2.8	2.7	2.5	2.5	2.4	2.4	2.4	2.4	2.3	2.4	2.5	2.4	2.3	2.4	2.4	2.5	2.4
2011	2.8	2.9	2.8	2.8	2.7	2.5	2.5	2.5	2.5	2.4	2.4	2.4	2.4	2.5	2.5	2.4	2.5	2.5	2.6	2.5
2012	2.8	2.9	2.8	2.7	2.6	2.5	2.5	2.4	2.4	2.4	2.4	2.3	2.4	2.4	2.4	2.3	2.4	2.4	2.5	2.4
2013	2.7	2.8	2.7	2.7	2.6	2.4	2.4	2.4	2.4	2.4	2.3	2.3	2.3	2.4	2.4	2.3	2.3	2.3	2.4	2.3
2014	2.7	2.7	2.7	2.6	2.5	2.4	2.3	2.3	2.3	2.3	2.3	2.2	2.2	2.3	2.2	2.2	2.2	2.2	2.2	2.1
2015	2.6	2.7	2.6	2.5	2.5	2.3	2.3	2.3	2.2	2.2	2.2	2.2	2.2	2.2	2.2	2.1	2.1	2.1	2.1	2.0

Inflation: Percent per annum total returns for all historical periods

From 1926 to 2015

End Date	Start Date									
	2006	2007	2008	2009	2010	2011	2012	2013	2014	2015
1971										
1972										
1973										
1974										
1975										
1976										
1977										
1978										
1979										
1980										
1981										
1982										
1983										
1984										
1985										
1986										
1987										
1988										
1989										
1990										
1991										
1992										
1993										
1994										
1995										
1996										
1997										
1998										
1999										
2000										
2001										
2002										
2003										
2004										
2005										
2006	2.5									
2007	3.3	4.1								
2008	2.2	2.1	0.1							
2009	2.3	2.3	1.4	2.7						
2010	2.2	2.1	1.4	2.1	1.5					
2011	2.3	2.3	1.8	2.4	2.2	3.0				
2012	2.2	2.2	1.8	2.2	2.1	2.3	1.7			
2013	2.1	2.1	1.7	2.1	1.9	2.1	1.6	1.5		
2014	2.0	1.9	1.6	1.9	1.7	1.7	1.3	1.1	0.8	
2015	1.9	1.8	1.6	1.8	1.6	1.6	1.3	1.1	1.0	1.2

2016 SBBI Yearbook

Appendix C-7 (56)